Greater Los Angeles

ARTS Resource Directory

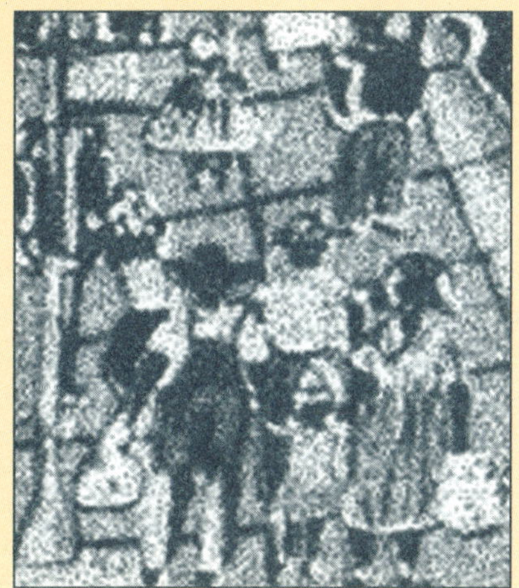

and

Arts & Education Guide

Fourth Edition

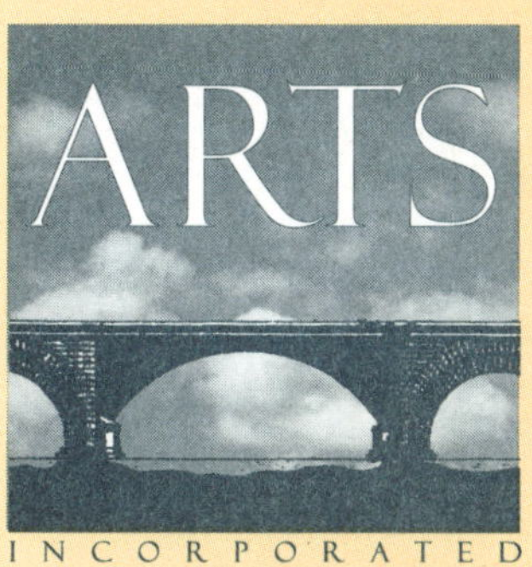

sponsored by
The Getty Grant Program
The Boeing Company

with generous support from
ARCO Foundation
California Community Foundation
Los Angeles County Arts Commission

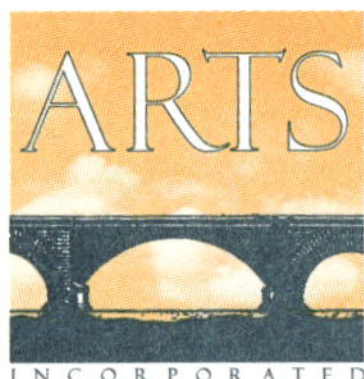

Cover artwork: "Avenida Cesar Chavez" Serigraph by Roberto Gutierrez printed at Self-Help Graphics and Art, Inc. in Atelier XXII. Courtesy Self-Help Graphics and Art, Inc.

Executive Director: Beth Fox
Directory Project Coordinator: Ricardo Soliz
Directory Project Associate: Lauren Derrington
Art Direction, Cover/Text Design, Ad Design Assistance: Andrea Miles & Patty Arnold of Menagerie Design & Publishing
Program Coordinator: Jennifer Wong

4th edition *Greater Los Angeles Arts Resource Directory and Arts & Education Guide*
Printed and bound in the United States of America.

Library of Congress Card Number: 99-72384
ISBN 0-9664318-0-4

Individual/bulk mail orders may be directed to:

ARTS, Inc.
315 W. Ninth Street, Suite 201
Los Angeles, CA 90015
(213) 627-9276

Sales to the trade should be addressed to:

SCB Distributors
15608 S. New Century Drive
Gardena, CA 90248
(310) 532-9400
(800) 729-6423

Acknowledgements:

Cindy Casama, Liz Pruyn, Bill Fox, Mark Slavkin, Dick Orend, Tim Whalen, Gwen Walden, Aaron Paley, Robert Barrett, Ann Stone & Joy Moini from the RAND Corporation in partnership with Catherine Rice and Al Nodal of the City of Los Angeles Cultural Affairs Department through the Arts & Public Impact Study, Alice Espy, James Burkes, Laurie Schell, David Tokofsky, Earl Sherburn, Jacki Breger, Amanda Parsons, Cameron Taylor-Brown, Lauren Derrington, Stan Holt, Aaron Silverman, Don Dustin, Don Doyle, Regan Hardman, Lucia Aguayo-Huerta, Elisa Crystal, Barbara Becker, Stephanie Kimmel, Laura Stickney, Joanne Michiuye, Roberta Romero, Christine Yazzie, Iva Milson, Jeanette Cole, Madeleine Pfeiffer, Tomás Benitez, Pat Gomez, Roberto Gutierrez, Pam Anderson, Josephine Ramirez, Andrea Miles, Patty Arnold, Shana Levy, Stacey Hong, Darius Adle, Barbara Golding, Miyoko Oshima, Lisa Citron, Pam Kaizer, Claire Peeps, Sandra Gibson, Kevin Higa, Peter Sellars and ARTS, Inc's charter Arts & Business Council members, Edison International, Academy of Television Arts & Sciences Foundation, ARCO, and The Boeing Company.

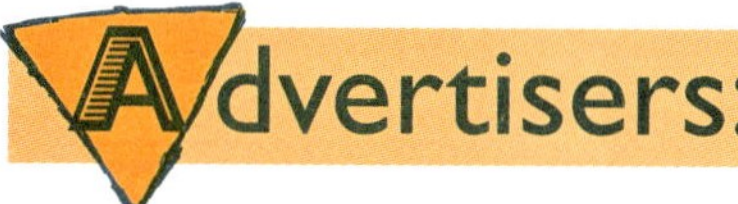

Advertisers:

18th Street Arts Complex
Academy of Television Arts & Sciences Foundation
Access Cultural Liaison Services
Alicia Millikan Consulting
Americans for the Arts
Animaction
Architours
ARCO Foundation
Armory Center for the Arts
Art Pic
Arts Consulting Group
ArtScene
BEEM Foundation for the Advancement of Music
Bilingual Foundation of the Arts
Brazilian Nites Productions
California Assembly of Local Arts Agencies (CALAA)
California Arts Council
California Design College
CalArts
Campbell Communications
Center for Nonprofit Management
Center for the Study of Political Graphics
City of Los Angeles Cultural Affairs Department
Colburn School for the Performing Arts
Collage Digital Video
Creative PR
Culture-Call
Dance & Fitness Magazine
Dance Resource Center
David Pankratz
The Durfee Foundation
The Getty Center
Grand Performances
Grey Advertising
Harbour Entertainment Insurance
Hollywood Arts Council
LA Foto
Lee Draper Consulting
Lloyd E. Rigler/Lawrence E. Deutsch Foundation
Los Angeles Convention & Visitors Bureau
Los Angeles County Arts Commission
Los Angeles Educational Partnership
Los Angeles Philharmonic Association
Los Angeles Times Calendar Live!
Harriet & Charles Luckman Fine Arts Complex
Mission Renaissance
Mural Conservancy of Los Angeles
Music Center Education Division
Nonprofit Incorporators
Paul, Hastings, Janofsky & Walker LLP
Performing Arts Books
Performing Tree
Ryman Program for Young Artists
Skirball Cultural Center
Tani and Friends
Theatre LA
University of California, Los Angeles (UCLA)
University of Southern California (USC)
Western States Arts Federation (WESTAF)

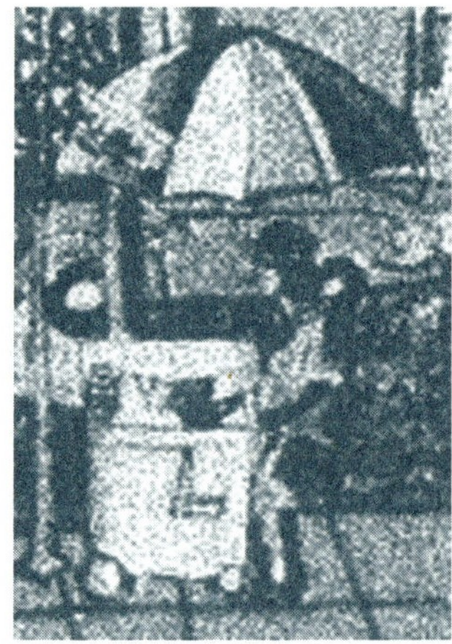

Good Morning and welcome to greater Los Angeles!

The book you hold is not the Los Angeles that meets the eye, but the hope and guide for the inner life, the deep structure and the hidden threads that gently hold this astonishing, strange, violent and sunny part of the world together. In a landscape that reinforces dispersion, anomaly and sometimes just plain indifference, ARTS, Inc. has gathered the forces of commitment, focus, and the folks who understand and flourish within contradiction.

The arts are coming through a period of being under attack, consistently ignored, undersupported and in some cases erased all together. The recovery and forward motion that the coming century invites us to create will require all the solidarity we can muster; all the networking and coalition building that we can offer. The political and economic impasses of this nation and this region, the hopes for civil rights, the necessity of serious communication across deep divisions, and the profound necessity in a democracy where a wide representation of voices are actually represented — these are all cultural questions. And our work is in front of us.

You hold in your hand the first steps and the first links for a new era that insists that we move forward together. As we reimagine and reconfigure democracy at the grassroots, this book is the first and foremost grassroots guide.

It's awfully hard to stay in touch in Los Angeles, much less get together. The artistic synergy that is a daily fact of life in most regions is almost entirely missing here. If you want to see people, it requires effort and special attention. But then I suppose that means that we really have to mean it.

Let's start dialing, faxing and e-mailing. And seeing each other.

Peter Sellars

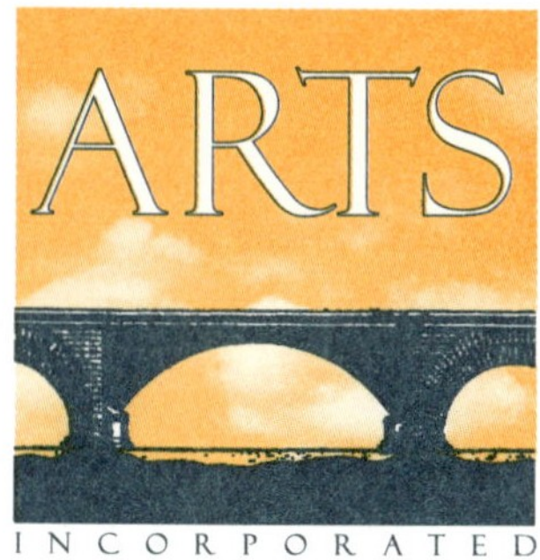

As the local affiliate in the nation–wide Arts & Business Council network, making connections for the arts of greater Los Angeles is what ARTS, Inc. is all about. Specifics on our free and low–cost services are in the "Service Providers" section of this publication. It is this *Arts Resource Directory and Arts & Education Guide*—with its unparalleled scope of information, opportunities, and resources—that is the greatest manifestation of ARTS, Inc.'s core connector role.

When we first conceived of this fourth edition, we thought it would simply be a matter of updating the third edition's existing entries and adding some new ones. However, as we queried past and potential readers as part of our market research, we came to realize that their needs and interests had grown exponentially beyond what a simple update could address.

Teachers tell us that they want a user–friendly guide to locate arts programs and providers that will help them implement the exciting but challenging new arts standards in their classrooms. Parents are similarly looking for after–school and weekend programs close to home. Arts groups repeatedly ask for a basic listing of area arts funders. Arts–savvy consultants are seeking more ways to promote their much–needed services. Further, when we honed our research and data collection techniques, we discovered that there are hundreds of wonderful community–based arts organizations and cultural programs that had never before reached our radar screen.

We are pleased to present this next generation of ARTS, Inc.'s *Directory*—updated and greatly expanded. Its a fast–forward version of a beloved publication that will now reach a vast readership well beyond its loyal following of arts administrators. For the first time, print distribution is nationwide in independent, chain, and museum bookstores. In fact, the 4th edition pre–sales exceed total sales for all previous editions, telling us we're hitting the mark by listening to the needs of our growing readership. Also, before year–end 1999, look for the *Directory* online—thanks to an innovative partnership ARTS, Inc. initiated with the *LA Times* through their "Calendar Live" website. What unprecedented marketing and audience development opportunities for all those listed!

ARTS, Inc. envisions a future for greater Los Angeles in which the arts thrive and are valued for their excellence, diversity, and integral relationship to the quality of civic life. We know that this *Directory and Arts & Education Guide* takes an important step in this direction. Moreover, we hope this book will inspire other arts service groups to produce similar resource guides in their municipalities, thus sharing the wealth of arts and culture that enlivens communities throughout our great nation.

Beverly Ryder
Board President

Beth Fox
Executive Director

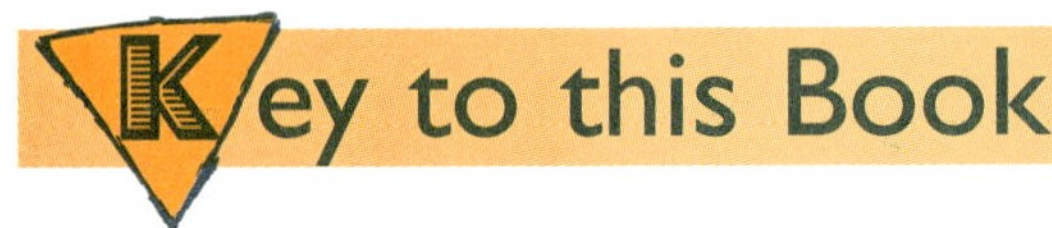

Key to this Book

Label	Sample listing
	VERY BEST SCHOOL OF PERFORMING ARTS, THE
site location	200 S. West Avenue — 501 (c) 3 **DSC** (geographical keys, see below)
	Los Angeles, CA 90012
general phone	Ph: 213-000-2200
administrative phone	Admin: 213-000-0000
education phone	Educ: 213-000-0000
fax	Fax: 213-000-0000
website address	www.talented.com
organization contact	Martha Graham — Community Liaison/x 100 — martha@talented.com
artistic head	Edward Hopper — Artistic Director/x 101 — eddie_h@talented.com
administrative head	Igor Stravinsky — Executive Director/x 102 — igorlives!@talented.com
education contact	Greta Garbo — Public Education/x 103 — gg@talented.com
other contact	Sam Peckinpah — Roustabout/x 104 — bangbang@talented.com

The Very Best School is a community arts center that engages broad participation through innovative approaches to creating, exploring and presenting the visual and performing arts.

- exhibitions of traditional visual art
- contemporary and chamber music presentations
- rotating performances of contemporary musical theater
- movement and dance classes for adults and children

education programs description:

The school provides a unique environment in which adults and children of all ages can experience, understand, appreciate and create within a broad spectrum of media and disciplines. All teachers are professional practitioners of their art.

(free programs indicator — some or all programs are free)

Pre/K-12, Youth or Family Programs indicator: PRE/K-12 (program disciplines, see below)

PROGRAMS: PERFORMANCES, WORKSHOPS, STUDIO CLASSES RESIDENCIES, SELF-GUIDED TOURS, GUIDED TOURS

SCHEDULE: YEAR-ROUND, WEEKDAYS, EVENINGS, WEEKENDS (season(s) & time(s) of operation)

DETAILS: HISTORY/SOC. SCIENCES, MATH/SCIENCES, VISUAL/PERFORMING ARTS, LANGUAGE ARTS, MULTICULTURAL, AESTHETIC VALUING, CREATIVE EXPRESSION, HISTORICAL/CULTURAL CONTEXTS, CONNECTIONS/RELATIONS/APPLICATIONS COST FOR SOME PROGRAMS, TEACHER-TRAINING PROGRAMS (SALARY POINTS), TRAVEL TO SCHOOLS, PROGRAMS ON SITE, INDIVIDUALLY TAILORED PROGRAMS, EDUCATIONAL MATERIALS, BILINGUAL: SPANISH

For Pre/K-12 Programs
- applicable grade levels
- primary curriculum focus
- visual/performing arts focus
- other programs, features, emphases

geographical keys (see below)

AV: Antelope Valley
DSC: Downtown/South Central –includes Exposition Park, Baldwin Hills, Inglewood, Watts, Leimert Park and Crenshaw
ELA: East Los Angeles County—includes Southeast Los Angeles County, Highland Park, Boyle Heights, Downey, Whittier, and La Puente
HSM: Hollywood/Silverlake/Mid-City—includes Koreatown
LB: Long Beach—includes Lakewood, Compton, and Cerritos
PO: Pomona—includes Claremont, LaVerne and Inland Empire
PSG: Pasadena/San Gabriel Valley—includes cities north of the 10 Freeway
SB: South Bay—includes Torrance, Gardena, San Pedro, Palos Verdes Penninsula, Wilmington and Catalina Island
VEN: Includes some organizations within Ventura County
SFV: San Fernando Valley—includes Burbank, Glendale, Valencia Úand Santa Clarita Valley
WS: Westside–includes Beverly Hills, West Hollywood, West Los Angeles, Santa Monica, Culver City and Venice

free programs indicator (some or all programs are free)

program disciplines (see below)

- Dance
- Music
- Theater
- Visual Arts

This 4th edition Directory contains close to 1,100 listings, providing a broad overview of artistic and cultural activities that regularly occur throughout the region as well as support services for the arts. The term "Greater Los Angeles" indicates that Directory listings reach beyond Los Angeles City borders to the edges of Los Angeles County and, sometimes, beyond—to those organizations that include Los Angeles County in their overall service area. Geographical keys indicate the region in which each organization exists. These keys provide yet another way for you to better navigate toward those organizations in which you have an interest as well as a means of mapping the amount of arts activity within each specific area.

As part of the Local Arts & Cultural Organizations section, the Arts & Education Guide refers to the golden boxes in the listing for organizations that offer programs for Pre/K-12 schools and teachers, extracurricular youth activities or family programming. The Service Providers section includes individual consultants as well as groups that provide services to artists and arts organizations. The Local Funding Resources section lists funders that are based locally and whose giving includes the arts. It lists only the most basic information; more complete listings can be found in other resources.

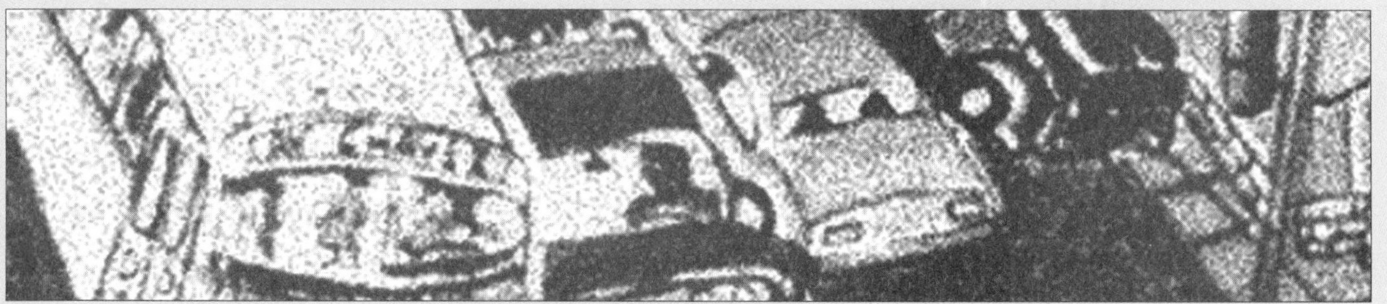

FOURTH EDITION
GREATER
LOS ANGELES

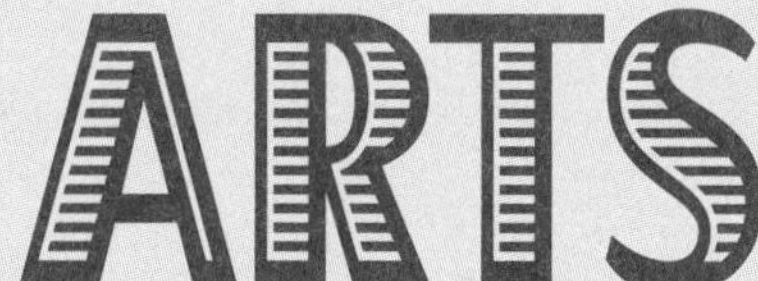

RESOURCE DIRECTORY
AND
ARTS & EDUCATION GUIDE

Table of Contents

Local Arts and Cultural Organizations and Educational Programs

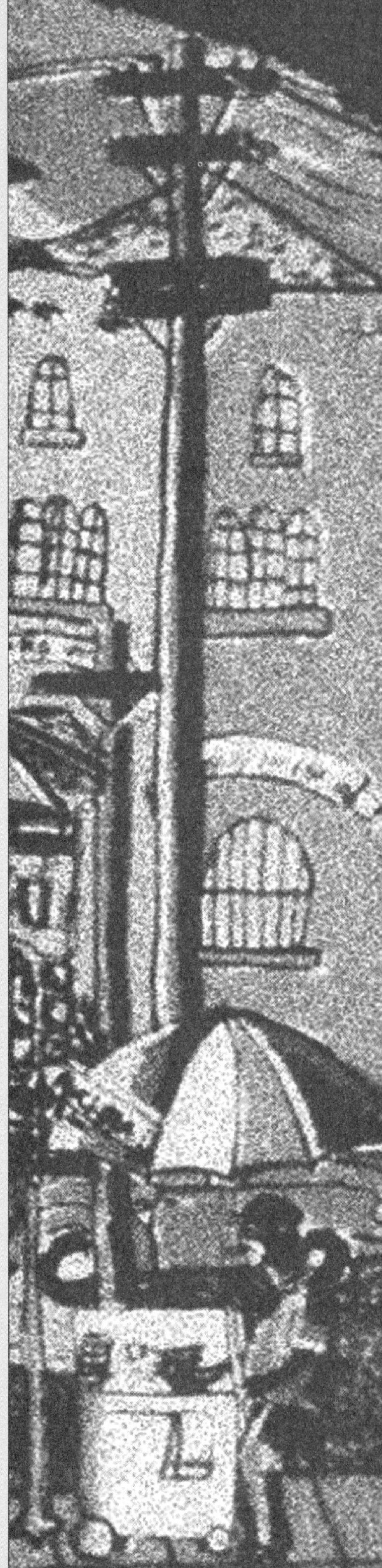

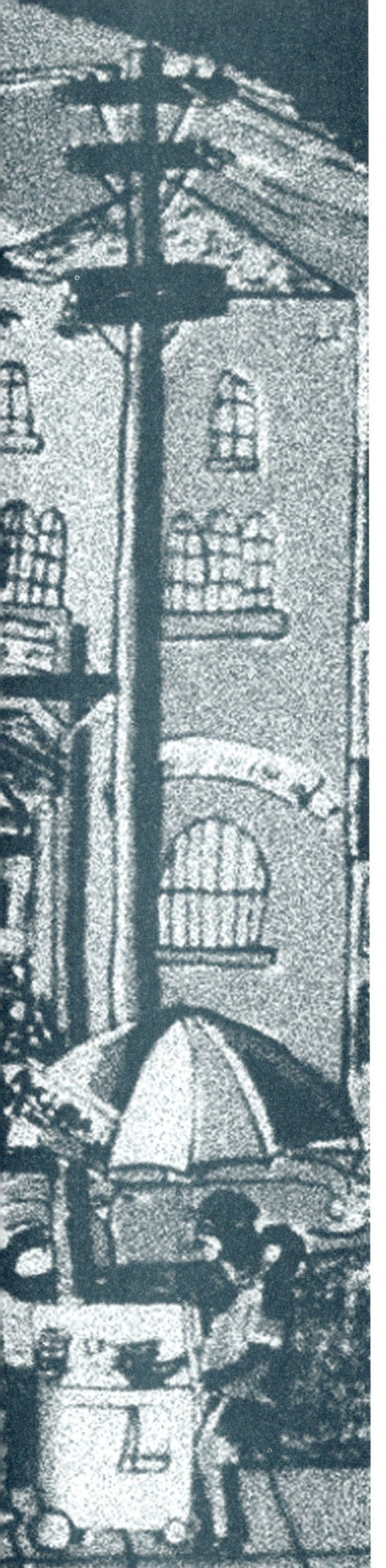

Introduction: Local Arts and Cultural Organizations and Educational Programs

One special Sunday afternoon in the early Sixties, my mother took me on a journey—four buses, three hours, and a very long walk up the hill—to see the Salvador Dali exhibit at the Barnsdall Art Gallery. I knew then that art had to be important because we took so much effort to enjoy it and because she told me so—"Art is good."

Art and culture are still good, in all their manifestations, forms and mediums. Some experiences are yet a long bus ride away, but in these times, creativity thrives in every local neighborhood and takes only the effort of the willing conscript to enjoy it.

The range of arts experiences and cultural opportunities extends from the grandeur of The Getty Center to the finite wisdom of the Museum of Jurassic Technology. We enjoy the preservation of ancient cultures at places such as the Pacific Asia Museum, as well as the presentation of modern variants at local treasures like St. Elmo's Village. A plethora of venues, theaters and alternative spaces, such as Grand Performances, the John Anson Ford Amphitheater, and Highways Performance Space present the artistry of performers and other artists whose work reflects the best of human creativity, from the classics and folk traditions, to challenging innovation and new emerging forms.

We are surrounded by a cluster of outstanding major regional institutions in all disciplines, and they are surrounded by a legion of equally outstanding community-based organizations in all paradigms. Thus, it is these separate parts that works together, fueled by the endeavors of both artists and audiences, to forge our remarkable, diverse cultural profile.

The matrix of arts and cultural institutions and organizations, local arts centers, educational programs, alternative and other spaces that serve Southern California is as vast and far reaching as the very landscape itself. The volume of resources at our disposal, as evidenced in the following chapter, draws a complex picture of the leadership and momentum that exists as we become the new world center for arts and culture in the coming century.

Tomás Benitez, Director
Self-Help Graphics & Art, Inc

How to Use this Section: For Teachers, Youth, and Families:

There is increased understanding these days of the important role that the arts play in a student's success, whether one continues his/her life as a practicing artist or not. Skills learned through the creative process encourage self-discipline and critical thinking. Participation in the arts also nourishes self–esteem while emphasizing excellence. As an educator, I know first hand how art can excite a child's imagination. This *Directory* provides a comprehensive overview for teachers, students and parents of the tremendous opportunities available throughout metropolitan Los Angeles to learn about, explore or participate in the arts at a multitude of venues.

The new *Arts & Education Guide*, highlighted in yellow boxes, is an addendum to the listing for each organization that offers programs for Pre/K-12 schools, extracurricular activities for youth, or family programs. Used together with the geographical markers, and discipline symbols, this book reveals the enormous wealth of activity and creativity that currently exists in communities across Southern California. It's the resource parents and teachers have been waiting for!

Unless otherwise noted, all of the programs listed herein are ongoing, and are offered free or at low-cost. (To find the free programs, simply look for the piggy bank symbol.) As you'll find, there is much to be discovered. There's something out there for everyone and I urge you to take advantage of the creative opportunities that await. These programs are planned expressly for you. Enjoy!

Don Dustin, Director
Visual and Performing Arts
Los Angeles Unified School District

A special note to teachers:
Not all arts activities have to be field trips. Many arts groups travel directly to your school, and tailor programs to your curriculum and classroom needs. Performing Tree and Music Center Education Division are two of our metro area's largest resources, and you'll see from this Directory that there are many other groups that you can turn to right in your own backyard. Also, be aware that many programs offer teacher training institutes on the weekends and several have arrangements with LAUSD to offer salary points. These features are all highlighted in the Arts & Education Guide. There are also support networks for educators to share experiences with each other. The Galef Institute, Los Angeles Educational Partnership and Getty Education Institute web sites (each of which are listed in this Directory) are some of the excellent springboards available for research and peer networking.

18TH STREET ARTS COMPLEX

1639 18th Street
Santa Monica, CA 90404-3807
Ph: 310-453-3711
Fax: 310-453-4347
www.artswire.org/arts18st

501(c)3 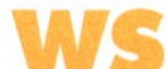

Cindy De Santis	Office Manager	Arts18thSt@aol.com
Clayton Campbell	Co-Director/ x18	
Jan Williamson	Co-Director	

18th Street is an arts community in Santa Monica for emerging and mid-career artists dedicated to issues of community and diversity in contemporary society.

- changing exhibitions featuring local/international artists
- Traffic Report—a Los Angeles journal of literature and visual arts
- Arts Fest in October
- workshops
- theater Performances

Artists work with teachers to jointly create a project resulting in a clearly defined product (puppet, play, etc..) so students are given an opportunity to think about their studies through a different medium.

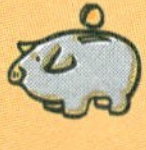

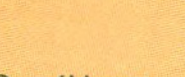

Pre/K-12

PROGRAMS: **PERFORMANCES, WORKSHOPS, RESIDENCIES, SELF-GUIDED TOURS**
SCHEDULE: YEAR-ROUND, WEEKDAYS
DETAILS: PRE/K-8, HISTORY/SOCIAL SCIENCES, VISUAL & PERFORMING ARTS, LANGUAGE ARTS, MULTICULTURAL AESTHETIC VALUING, CREATIVE EXPRESSION, HISTORICAL/ CULTURAL CONTEXT, CONNECTIONS/RELATIONS/APPLICATIONS
TRAVEL TO SCHOOLS
INDIVIDUALLY TAILORED PROGRAMS

24TH STREET THEATER

1117 W. 24th Street
Los Angeles, CA 90007
Ph: 213-745-6516
Admin: 323-667-0417
Fax: 323-667-2961

501(c)3 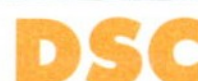

Jon White-Spunner	Executive Director	spunner@mizar.usc.edu
Stephanie Shroyer	Artistic Director	
Debbie Devine	Family Programming Director	

The 24th Street Theater is a nonprofit arts center offering performances, workshops, and educational opportunities in theater and music to the residents and youth of North University Park and the city of Los Angeles.

- annual series of three to five professional productions drawn from classic and new work
- "The Dr. Endesha Mae Holland Theatre Salon", a series of new play readings designed to develop and nurture playwrights
- "Faultlines," a monthly concert series for contemporary music
- exhibition space for photographers and artists to show their work
- access for community groups to use the theatre

24TH STREET THEATER (CONTINUED)

24th Street Theater is one of L. A.'s leaders in Arts Education and youth programming, with a resident Family Theater Company, Glorious Repertory. In addition to creating innovative professional theater, we offer teacher training, drama classes and workshops for at-risk youth.

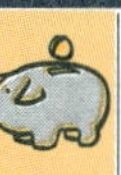

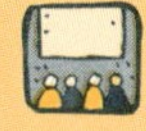

Pre/K-12

PROGRAMS: **PERFORMANCES, WORKSHOPS, RESIDENCIES**
SCHEDULE: YEAR-ROUND, EVENINGS, WEEKENDS
DETAILS: PRE/K-12, HISTORY/SOCIAL SCIENCES, VISUAL & PERFORMING ARTS, AESTHETIC VALUING, CREATIVE EXPRESSION, HISTORICAL/ CULTURAL CONTEXT, CONNECTIONS/RELATIONS/APPLICATIONS
TEACHER TRAINING PROGRAMS, PROGRAMS ON-SITE, INDIVIDUALLY TAILORED PROGRAMS, EDUCATIONAL MATERIALS

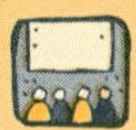

Youth

PROGRAMS: **PERFORMANCES, WORKSHOPS**
SCHEDULE: YEAR-ROUND, WEEKDAYS, EVENINGS, WEEKENDS

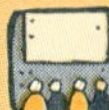

Families

PROGRAMS: **WORKSHOPS**
SCHEDULE: YEAR-ROUND, WEEKDAYS, EVENINGS, WEEKENDS

341 GALLERY

341 W. 7th Street
San Pedro, CA 90731
Ph: 310-831-0013

SB

Ron Stanford	Co-Director
Jerome Block	Co-Director

Contemporary original art and design.

A NIGHT ON BROADWAY

P.O. Box 68
Woodland Hills, CA 91365
Ph: 818-716-7372
Fax: 818-884-9795

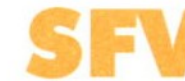

Rene Dictor LeBlanc Founder/President

A Night on Broadway offers unique parties for single music lovers featuring professional singers and pianists performing top hits from Broadway shows once a month in private homes and other locations.

- monthly parties including great live Broadway musical entertainment

A NOISE WITHIN

234 S. Brand Boulevard 501 (c) 3 **SFV**
Glendale, CA 91204
Ph: 818-546-1924
Admin: 818-546-1449
Educ: 818-546-1449
Fax: 818-240-3004

Julia Rodriguez-Elliott	Artistic Director
Geoff Elliott	Artistic Director
Art Manke	Artistic Director
Emily Heebner	Student Outreach Director
Jennifer Moss	Production Manager/ 818-240-1540

Located in Glendale, A Noise Within is Southern California's critically acclaimed classical theatre company that has, in just eight years, established a highly respected reputation for producing first-rate classic productions and is one of only a handful of theatres in the country with a resident acting company.

- regular season of plays
- conservatory classes for adults and teenagers
- "Summer with Shakespeare," a seven-week actor training program for teens
- professional intern program
- student outreach program

Artists-in-Residence: Actors from our resident company are available to come into the classroom for scheduled workshops and lecture/demonstrations. Symposia Within: Noted scholars join artists in a lively discussion series. Teachers may attend free-of-charge with a reservation.

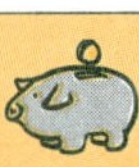

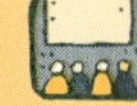

Pre/K-12

Programs: **Performances, Workshops, Studio Classes, Residencies**
Schedule: Year-round, Evenings, Weekends
Details: Grades 5-12, Visual & Performing Arts, Creative Expression, Historical/Cultural Context Teacher training programs , Travel to schools Facility for school visits, Individually tailored pro grams, Educational materials available

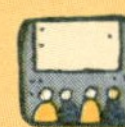

Families

Programs: **Performances**
Schedule: Year-round, Weekends

A.S.K. THEATER PROJECTS

11845 W. Olympic Boulevard, Suite 1250 501 (c) 3 **WS**
West Los Angeles, CA 90064
Ph: 310-478-3200
Fax: 310-478-5300
www.askplay.org

Sydney Young	Office Manager
Mead Hunter	Director of Literary Programs
Kym Eisner	Executive Director
Bryan Davidson	Playwright Education and Outreach

A.S.K. Theater Projects, a local and national resource for the theater and its artists, offers an energetic year-round schedule of forums for exploring issues vital to the theater. All of A.S.K.'s programs, services and publications are offered free of charge.

- writer's retreat
- rehearsed reading series
- community affinity groups
- Common Ground Festival
- workshop productions
- Stage One Readings
- National Playwright Exchanges
- playwright practical labs
- play commissioning
- playwright composer studio
- ASK Interchange Online
- Playwrights-in-the-Schools
- workshop playscripts
- ASK newsletter

Since 1996, the Playwrights-in-the-Schools program has created successful partnerships between professional playwrights and educators in Los Angeles high schools. Beginning fall 1998, professional playwrights will work with students from four high schools, teaching dramatic and playwriting skills. This program is offered as a grant to eligible high schools.

Pre/K-12

Programs: **Workshops, Residencies**
Schedule: Year-round, Weekdays
Details: Grades 9-12, Visual & performing arts, Language arts Creative Expression, Travel to schools Individually tailored programs

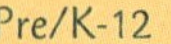

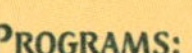

A. SHENERE VELT GALLERY

1525 S. Robertson Boulevard 501 (c) 10 **WS**
Los Angeles, CA 90035-4231
Ph: 310-552-2007
Fax: 310-552-3417
www.circle.org

Mary Koukhab	Assistant Director
Eric Gordon	Director

A. Shenere Velt Gallery exhibits the work of artists whose themes, broadly conceived, are consistent with Workmen's Circle concerns for Jewish culture and education, universal fraternalism, and social justice.

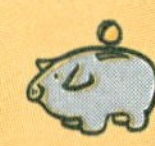

Families

Programs: **Self-Guided Tours**
Schedule: Year-round, Weekdays

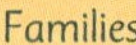

A WINDOW BETWEEN WORLDS

710 4th Avenue, #4 501(c)3 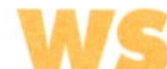
Venice, CA 90291
Ph: 310-396-0317
Fax: 310-396-9698
www.awbw.org

Dolores Sanico	Executive Director	dsanico@primenet.com

A Window Between Worlds is a non-profit organization dedicated to using art to help end domestic violence. Through creative expression, battered women and children recover a sense of renewal and power.

- volunteer opportunites
- art as healing tool for women and children surviving domestic violence
- hands-on art workshops using art as a healing tool
- exhibitions of art by survivors of domestic violence

ABOUT PRODUCTIONS

1724 N. Whitley Avenue 501(c)3 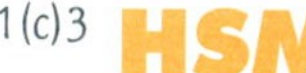
Hollywood, CA 90028
Ph: 323-462-3166
Fax: 323-962-6710

Pamela Harris	Administrative Director	phalta@aol.com
Theresa Chavez	Co-Artistic Director	
Alan Pulner	Co-Artistic Director	

About Productions creates original interdisciplinary theater work that provokes new perspectives on history and humanity which challenges traditional assumptions about cultural and gender identity.

- original theater productions and readings
- panel discussions
- collaborative education programs

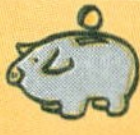

About Productions seeks to incorporate educational programs such as panel discussions and workshops for youth and adults into each production. Our focus is community-based, collaborative initiatives with secondary schools.

Pre/K-12

Programs:	**Performances**
Schedule:	Spring, Fall, Weekdays, Evenings
Details:	Grades 9-12, Fees for some programs, History/Soc. Sciences, Visual & Performing Arts, Multicultural, Historical/Cultural Context, Connections/Relations/Applications

ACADEMY OF DANCE ON FILM

P.O Box 750 501(c)3 HSM
Hollywood, CA 90028
Ph: 323-463-7009
Fax: 323-463-7906

Saadia Billman	Office Manager	adof_adm@pacbell.net
Larry Billman	Executive Director	adof@pacbell.net

The Academy of Dance on Film is a research center which collects and shares information on dancers and choreographers who contributed to motion pictures, television and music video.

- discussions with choreographers and dancers about their lives and careers
- lectures on the art and history of film choreography
- research service
- archival service

ACADEMY OF ENTERTAINMENT & TECHNOLOGY

Santa Monica College 501(c)3 WS
1900 Pico Boulevard
Santa Monica, CA 90405
Ph: 310-434-3700
Admin: 310-434-9703
Educ: 310-434-3711
Fax: 310-434-3709

Andrea (Andi) Hyman	Administrative Assistant/ x3703	academy@smc.edu
Jim Keeshen	Computer Animation Faculty/ x3722	
Katharine Muller	Dean/ x3701	
Linda Sinclair	Assistant Dean/ x4702	
Judith Penchansky	Student Services/ x4711	

A satellite campus of Santa Monica College, the Academy has programs for creative adult students in preparation for jobs in media and entertainment related fields.

- computer animation
- new media (internet/multimedia applications)
- entertainment industry business (accounting focus)
- themed entertainment operations and management (theme park management/product merchandising)

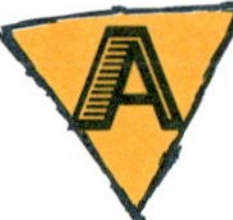

ACADEMY OF MOTION PICTURE ARTS & SCIENCES (AMPAS)

8949 Wilshire Boulevard 501(c)3 WS
Beverly Hills, CA 90211-1972
Ph: 310-247-3000
Fax: 310-859-9351
www.oscars.org

Bruce Davis Executive Director

Organized in 1927, the purposes of the Academy are to advance the arts and sciences of motion pictures; foster cooperation among creative leaders for cultural, educational and technological progress; recognize outstanding achievements; cooperate on technical research and improvement of methods and equipment; provide a common forum and meeting ground for various branches and crafts; represent the viewpoint of actual creators of the motion picture; and foster educational activities between the professional community and the public-at-large.

- Academy Awards
- Academy Film Archive
- lectures and seminars
- exhibits
- Margaret Herrick Library
- National Film Information Service
- annual index to motion picture credits
- scholarships and grants
- Visiting Artists Program
- Student Film Awards
- Samuel Goldwyn Theater
- Academy Players Directory
- Fellowships in Screenwriting

ACADEMY OF MOTION PICTURE ARTS & SCIENCES (AMPAS) CENTER FOR MOTION PICTURE STUDY

333 S. La Cienega Boulevard 501(c)3 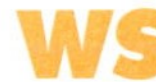
Beverly Hills, CA 90211
Ph: 310-247-3020
Fax: 310-657-5193
www.oscars.org

Located in La Cienega Park in Beverly Hills, the Center houses the Margaret Herrick Library and the Academy Film Archive. Both are the keystone activities of the Academy Foundation, the eductional, cultural, and preservation arm of the Academy of Motion Picture Arts and Sciences.

ACADEMY OF TELEVISION ARTS & SCIENCES (ATAS) FOUNDATION

5220 Lankershim Boulevard 501(c)3 SFV
North Hollywood, CA 91601-3109
Ph: 818-754-2800
Fax: 818-761-2827
www.emmys.org

The ATAS Foundation utilizes the resources and membership of the Television Academy and the Foundation to help guide those who will be responsible for the future of the telecommunications industry and viewing audiences of all ages.

- Archive of American Television

Community & Institutional Partnerships

- S.T.A.R.T. Initiative (schoolchildren grades 5&6)
- Family Screenings

Education Programs & Services

- College Faculty Seminar (annual)
- College Television Awards
- student internship programs
- Visiting Artist Program

ACTION SPACE

734 E. 3rd Street DSC
Los Angeles, CA 90013
Ph: 213 680-4237
Fax: 213 680-3422
www.actionspace.com

An independent studio for film, art, and architecture.

ACTORS ALLEY AT THE EL PORTAL

5269 Lankershim Boulevard 501(c)3 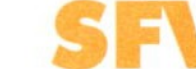
North Hollywood, CA 91601
Ph: 818-508-4200
Admin: 818-508-4234
Fax: 818-508-5113
www.actorsalley.com

Jill Jones Administration Director
Jeremiah Morris Artistic Director
Robert Caine Managing Director/818-908-2121

Actors Alley is currently in their 28th year. We produce a variety of programs including subscription production seasons, free public theatre, a new works reading series, and aftershow musical cabaret as well as offer classes for the Youth Academy and other outreach programs.

- subscription production seasons in the 90 and 40 seat performance venues
- free Public Theatre season and New Works Reading series
- special performance series for music, dance and holidays
- playwrights workshops
- outreach partnerships with social service and schools for service to at-risk youth, seniors, and students
- adult c lasses for both the community and professionals
- partnerships with the Center for Government, Society and the Arts (Federal Theater Projects and ANTA) for theater history archiving (one of four national sites)

Actors Alley provides Youth Theatre, children's classes and workshops.

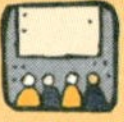

Youth

PROGRAMS: **PERFORMANCES, WORKSHOPS**
SCHEDULE: SPRING, FALL, WINTER, WEEKENDS

ACTORS CO-OP/ CROSSLEY THEATRE

1760 N. Gower Street 501(c)3 HSM
Hollywood, CA 90028
Ph: 323-462-8460
Fax: 323-462-3199

Deborah Scott Box Office Manager DeborahS@fpch.org
Mark Henderson Artistic Director
Bonnie Hellman Producing Director BonnieH@fpch.org

The Crossley Theatre on the grounds of First Presbyterian Church of Hollywood is home to the award-winning acting company Actors Co-op, presenting classic, contemporary, and children's theatre.

- four mainstage productions per year
- Co-op Too! experimental and original shows
- Actors Academy—acting training for adults and children
- volunteer opportunities

ACTORS CO-OP/ CROSSLEY THEATRE (CONTINUED)

Actors Co-op sponsors Actors Academy and Young Actors Academy, an acting training program for adults and youth taught by members of the award- winning Actors Co-op.

Pre/K-12 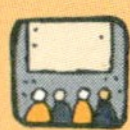

PROGRAMS: PERFORMANCES, WORKSHOPS, STUDIO CLASSES, GUIDED TOURS
SCHEDULE: YEAR-ROUND, WEEKDAYS, EVENINGS, WEEKENDS
DETAILS: GRADES PRE/K-12, VISUAL & PERFORMING ARTS CREATIVE EXPRESSION, TRAVEL TO SCHOOLS, PROGRAMS ON-SITE , INDIVIDUALLY TAILORED PROGRAMS

Youth

PROGRAMS: PERFORMANCES, WORKSHOPS, CLASSES, GUIDED TOURS
SCHEDULE: YEAR-ROUND, EVENINGS, WEEKENDS

Families 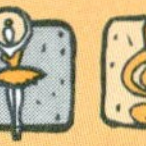 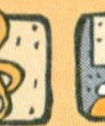 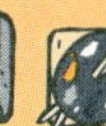 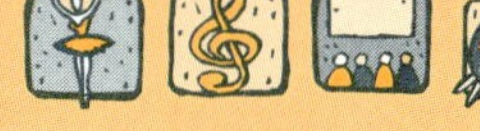

PROGRAMS: PERFORMANCES, WORKSHOPS, CLASSES
SCHEDULE: YEAR-ROUND

ACTORS FORUM THEATRE

10655 Magnolia Boulevard 501(c)3 **SFV**
North Hollywood, CA 91601
Ph: 818-506-0600
Fax: 323-465-6002

Audrey Singer President audsin@aol.com

We are dedicated to the principle that life without art is no life at all. As long as we can breathe it will be our goal to bring theater to the community, and to give talent of all ages and in all the creative arts an opportunity to be seen and heard.

- senior outreach program
- give away over 100 tickets yearly

ACTORS' GANG, THE

6209 Santa Monica Boulevard 501(c)3 **HSM** 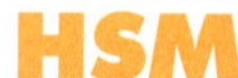
Hollywood, CA 90038
Ph: 323-465-0566
Fax: 323-467-1246

Don Luce Production Manager actorsgng1@aol.com
Ned Bellamy Chair, Artistic Committee
Mark Seldis Managing Director

The Actors' Gang is Los Angeles' most enduring theatre ensemble. Founded in 1981 by a group of renegade theater artists, the Gang's mission is to create bold original works for the stage and daring reinterpretations of classics.

- year-round theater performances
- readings
- teen theater workshops
- intensive style workshops/ mime
- performance/rehearsal space rentals
- youth mentorship program
- group discounts
- volunteer opportunities

ACTORS' GANG, THE (CONTINUED)

Youth 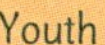

PROGRAMS: PERFORMANCES
SCHEDULE: YEAR-ROUND, EVENINGS, WEEKENDS

ACTORS' PLAYHOUSE, THE

1409 E. Fourth Street **LB**
Long Beach, CA 90802
Ph: 562-590-9396

J. Albertella Artistic Director

ADAMM'S STAINED GLASS AND AMERICAN CRAFT

1426 4th Street **WS**
Santa Monica, CA 90401
Ph: 310-451-9390
Fax: 310-451-9386

Adamm Gritlefeld Owner

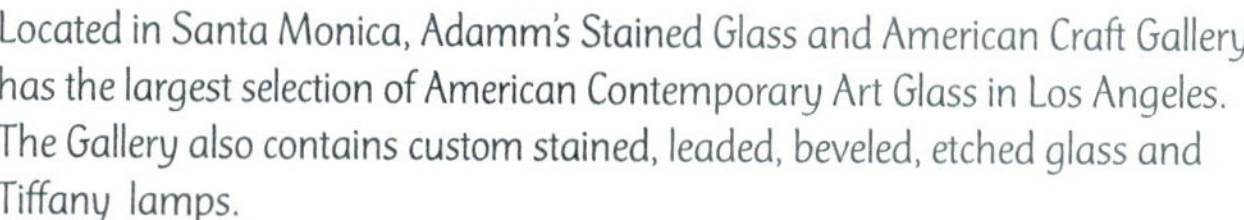

Located in Santa Monica, Adamm's Stained Glass and American Craft Gallery has the largest selection of American Contemporary Art Glass in Los Angeles. The Gallery also contains custom stained, leaded, beveled, etched glass and Tiffany lamps.

- open gallery of fine American crafts
- stained glass classes
- supplies for the stained glass artist
- expert repairs and restoration

ADAMSON-DUVANNES GALLERIES

484 S. San Vicente Boulevard **WS**
Los Angeles, CA 90048
Ph: 323-653-1015
Fax: 323-653-3875

Jerome Adamson Executive Director

Located on the edge of Beverly Hills and near the Los Angeles County Museum of Art, the Adamson-Duvannes Gallery exhibits period, traditional and contemporary fine art.

- one annual, major exhibition accompanied by a catalogue
- talks with artists
- monthly changing exhibitions focusing on individual artists, periods of art, subjects and media.

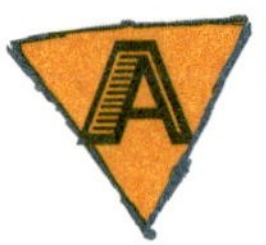

AFRICAN AMERICAN UNITY CENTER

5300 S. Vermont Avenue 501(c)3 DSC
Los Angeles, CA 90037
Ph: 323-789-7300
Fax: 323-791-4188

Albert Gill Facility Manager

The Center for the Performing Arts represents the "Heart and Soul" of the African America Unity Center complex. Where creative expression is the focal point for an affordable venue for performances and job training. It's also a gathering place for cultural and ethnic exchange through music, dance, theater and the media arts.

AFRICAN HERITAGE FOUNDATION, THE

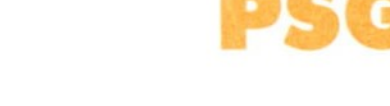

P.O. Box 40971
Pasadena, CA 91114
Ph: 626-398-1781
Fax: 626-240-0269

The African Heritage Foundation was established to share the traditional values of African art, wisdom and culture with children and adults through dance workshops and performances, documentaries, arts and crafts exhibitions and other media.

AFRICAN MARKETPLACE, INC.

2520 S. West View Street 501(c)3 HSM
Los Angeles, CA 90016
Ph: 213-237-1540
Fax: 213-485-1610

James Burks Executive Director African-Marketplace@Juno.com

The AMP seeks to promote the construction of a permanent cultural anchor in the African American community which fosters cultural sharing, knowledge and entrepeneurial ventures.

- African Marketplace boutique in Baldwin Hills/Crenshaw Plaza
- African Marketplace and Cultural Faire in August

AFTER SCHOOL MUSIC CONSERVATORY

1570 E. Colorado Boulevard, K308 PSG
Pasadena, CA 91106-2003
Ph: 626-585-7102

Mark Wallace Director, Public Relations/626-585-7315
Paul Kilian Division Dean, Music/626-585-7208

Located in the Music Building of Pasadena City College, the After School Music Conservatory provides an opportunity for low-cost music study to students in local schools at all levels as well as adults

- individually taught music lessons on a variety of instruments, including voice
- professional musicians and music educators
- quality instruction at various levels of proficiency

AFTER SCHOOL MUSIC CONSERVATORY (CONTINUED)

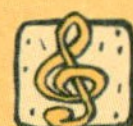

Youth

PROGRAMS: **PERFORMANCES, CLASSES**
SCHEDULE: YEAR-ROUND, WEEKDAYS, WEEKENDS

AGUALUNA DANCE THEATER

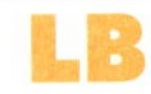

4915 San Luis Street
East Rancho Dominguez, CA 90221
Ph/Fax: 562-537-0969

Gustavo Gonzalez Director

AHMANSON THEATRE/CENTER THEATRE GROUP

135 N. Grand Avenue 501(c)3 DSC
Los Angeles, CA 90012
Ph: 213-628-2772
Educ: 213-977-7231
Fax: 213-972-3000
www.TaperAhmanson.com

Trevor O'Donnell Director of Group Sales/213-972-7231
Gordon Davidson Artistic Director
Charles Dillingham Managing Director
Dolores Chavez Director PLAY/213-972-0720

The newly-renovated, state-of-the-art Ahmanson Theatre is one of the most exciting theaters in America, appealing to a broad base of theatrical tastes by presenting a wide variety of musicals, comedies (including the world premieres of five Neil Simon plays), dramas and classical revivals.

- year-round presentation of plays and musicals

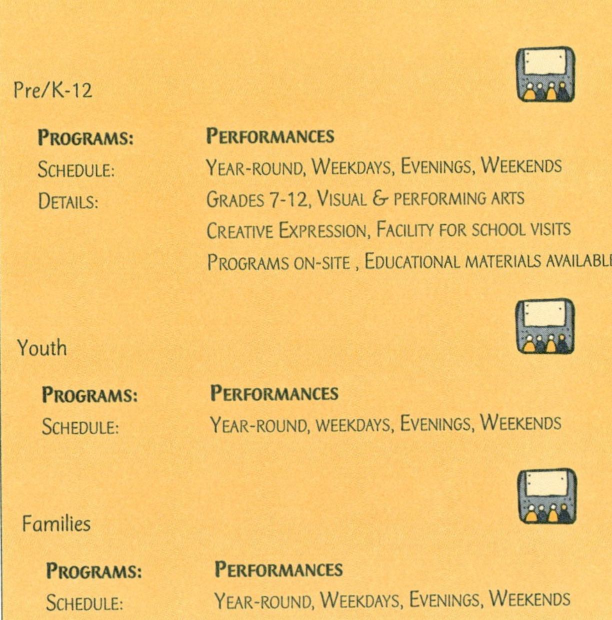

Pre/K-12

PROGRAMS: **PERFORMANCES**
SCHEDULE: YEAR-ROUND, WEEKDAYS, EVENINGS, WEEKENDS
DETAILS: GRADES 7-12, VISUAL & PERFORMING ARTS
CREATIVE EXPRESSION, FACILITY FOR SCHOOL VISITS
PROGRAMS ON-SITE, EDUCATIONAL MATERIALS AVAILABLE

Youth

PROGRAMS: **PERFORMANCES**
SCHEDULE: YEAR-ROUND, WEEKDAYS, EVENINGS, WEEKENDS

Families

PROGRAMS: **PERFORMANCES**
SCHEDULE: YEAR-ROUND, WEEKDAYS, EVENINGS, WEEKENDS

AINAHAU O KALEPONI HAWAIIAN CIVIC CLUB

8855 Atlanta Avenue, Suite 147 — 501 (c)4
Huntington Beach, CA 92646-7119
Ph: 562-401-7202

Ka'ala (Jane) Pang — Na Mea Hawai'i Chair — kaiwipang@earthlink.net
Ku'ulei Fahilga — President/714-536-0206

Ainahau o Kaleponi is a civic organization committed to the promotion of cultural arts, traditional practices, beliefs, and native language of the indigenous people of Hawaii and other Pacific Island communities.

- monthly newsletter for members
- festivals and cultural programs at local museums, theaters, libraries, schools, colleges, and universities
- 'Ohana Retreat: a three day weekend immersion in Hawaiian experience: Hawaiian protocol, practices, traditional arts, and native language program for multi-generational families
- scholarship funds
- cultural arts projects
- community service programs
- hula/dance, music, and choral workshops for members
- health education and advocacy programs for native Hawaiians and other Pacific Islanders

Presentation of traditional Hawaiian and Pacific Island arts, cultural practices, beliefs, stories, and "hands on projects" for children and adults to experience including music and dance, sports and games, and arts and crafts of native resource materials.

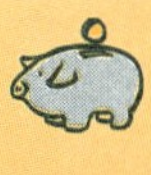

Pre/K-12

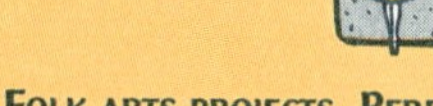

PROGRAMS: FOLK ARTS PROJECTS, PERFORMANCES
SCHEDULE: YEAR-ROUND, EVENINGS, WEEKENDS
DETAILS: PRE/K-12, HISTORICAL/CULTURAL CONTEXT,
CONNECTIONS/RELATIONS/APPLICATIONS
TEACHER TRAINING PROGRAMS
TRAVEL TO SCHOOLS
EDUCATIONAL MATERIALS AVAILABLE
BILINGUAL: PACIFIC ISLANDER

Youth

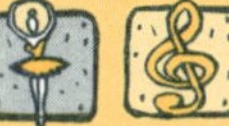
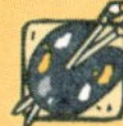

PROGRAMS: FOLK ARTS PROJECTS, PERFORMANCES
SCHEDULE: YEAR-ROUND, EVENINGS, WEEKENDS

Families

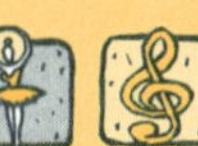
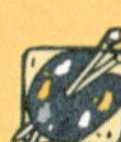

PROGRAM: FOLK ARTS PROJECTS, PERFORMANCES
SCHEDULE: YEAR-ROUND, EVENINGS, WEEKENDS

ALIBI 13

4470 Sunset Boulevard, #736
Los Angeles, CA 90027
Ph: 323-644-0031

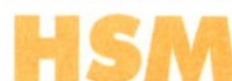

Jeffrey McDaniel — Director

ALKEBU-LAN CULTURAL CENTER

1435 N. Raymond Avenue — 501 (c)3 — PSG
Pasadena, CA 91104-2229
Ph: 626-794-9570
Fax: 626-794-4460

Versie Mae Richardson — Executive Director

Located in North West Pasadena, we are dedicated to teaching the African and African-American culture of fine arts.

- quarterly exhibits featuring local artists
- summer jazz concerts
- lectures on early African history
- African attire shows
- drumming lessons

We provide excellent coaching and instruction in an encouraging environment for children to learn the arts.

Pre/K-12

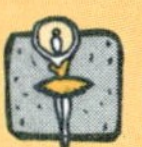
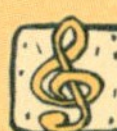
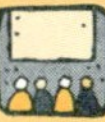

PROGRAMS: PERFORMANCES, WORKSHOPS
SCHEDULE: YEAR-ROUND, WEEKDAYS, EVENINGS, WEEKENDS
DETAILS: GRADES 5-12, VISUAL & PERFORMING ARTS,
AESTHETIC VALUING, CREATIVE EXPRESSION,
HISTORICAL/CULTURAL CONTEXT
CONNECTIONS/RELATIONS/APPLICATIONS,
TRAVEL TO SCHOOLS, PROGRAMS ON-SITE

Youth

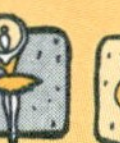
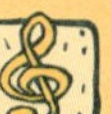
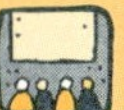

PROGRAMS: PERFORMANCES, WORKSHOPS
SCHEDULE: YEAR-ROUND

ALLELUIA DANCE THEATRE

P.O. Box 641 — 501 (c)3 — VEN
Moorpark, CA 93021
Ph: 805-529-4873

Stella Matsuda — Executive/Administrative Director — smatsuda@gte.net
Julia Felker — Co-artistic Director
Catherine Foley — Board Member/Teacher/Dancer

Established in 1997, Alleluia Dance Theatre presents dance in their work as an affirmation of life that glorifies God.

- concerts
- workshops
- retreats

ALLIANCE REPERTORY COMPANY

3204 West Magnolia Boulevard — 501 (c)3
Burbank, CA 91505
Ph: 818-566-7935

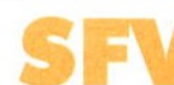

Peter Fox — Board President
Dyanne DiRosario — Artistic Director
Joel Stoffer — Vice President and Treasurer

ALTADENA HERITAGE

P.O. Box 218 501(c)3 **PSG**
Altadena, CA 91003
Ph: 626-683-1785

Steve Haussler	Chairman/626-844-2245
Tim Gregory	Archivist/626-792-7465

Altadena Heritage is a historic preservation organization which identifies, preserves and protects significant architecture and cultural landmarks.

- newsletter and publications
- historic home tours
- seminars, workshops on restoration and rehabilitation
- home histories researched
- works with other regional community organizations
- architectural and restoration consulting
- landmark and walking tour maps
- nominates structures/landmarks to the Nat'l Registry of Historic Places
- developing inventories of cultural and landscapes for California State

AMERICAN ACADEMY FOR DANCE AND KINDRED ARTS

1245 Fifth Street 501(c)3 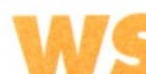
Santa Monica, CA 90401
Ph: 310-656-8899
Fax: 310-656-8897

Margot Bush	Registrar
Frank Bourman	Artistic Director
Cecilia Soriano	Executive Director

Located in Santa Monica, the American Academy for Dance and Kindred Arts is dedicated to the development of the individual through experiencing the basics of dance and the related arts- music, visual arts, and theater. The AADKA provides professional training in dance and these related arts.

- monthly "informances" for the community which provide entertaining insights into different aspects of the arts and how they relate to each other.

Training in classical dance builds basic developmental skills such as focus, improved listening, non-verbal communication, cooperation, following directions, and working with a group to build an ensemble. 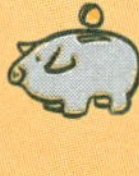

Pre/K-12 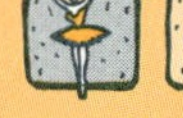 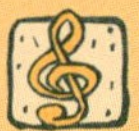 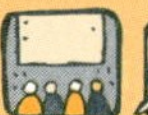 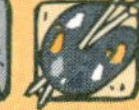

PROGRAMS:	**WORKSHOPS, STUDIO CLASSES**
SCHEDULE:	YEAR-ROUND, WEEKDAYS, EVENINGS, WEEKENDS
DETAILS:	GRADES 3-12, VISUAL & PERFORMING ARTS AESTHETIC VALUING, CREATIVE EXPRESSION, CONNECTIONS/RELATIONS/APPLICATIONS TEACHER TRAINING PROGRAMS (SALARY POINTS) TRAVEL TO SCHOOLS, PROGRAMS ON-SITE INDIVIDUALLY TAILORED PROGRAMS, BILINGUAL: SPANISH

Youth 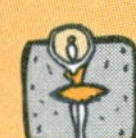 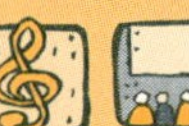 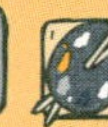

PROGRAMS:	**CLASSES**
SCHEDULE:	YEAR-ROUND, EVENINGS, WEEKDAYS, WEEKENDS

Families 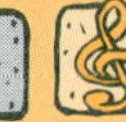 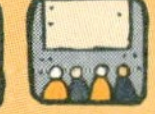 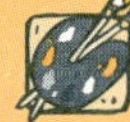

PROGRAMS:	**CLASSES**
SCHEDULE:	YEAR-ROUND, WEEKDAYS, EVENINGS, WEEKENDS

AMERICAN CHOREOGRAPHY AWARDS

627 N. Palm Drive 501(c)3 **WS**
Beverly Hills, CA 90210
Ph: 310-271-7766
Fax: 310-271-1288

Cecilie Stuart	Board of Governors
Julie Arenal	Board of Governors
Grover Dale	Board of Governors
PeggyHolmes	Board of Governors

The American Choreography Awards offers recognition for the craft of choreography and dance education. Proceeds have benefitted support and health organizations.

- volunteer opportunities

AMERICAN CINEMATHEQUE EGYPTIAN THEATRE

1800 N. Highland Avenue, #717 501(c)3 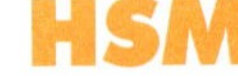
Hollywood, CA 90028
Ph: 323-466-3456
Fax: 323-461-9737
www.americancinematheque.com

Margot Gerber	Public Information/ x115
Barbara Smith	Director/ x111

The American Cinematheque, established in 1984, is a non-profit, viewer-supported film exhibition and cultural organization dedicated to the celebration of the Moving Picture in all of its forms.

- weekly film and video programs which range from the classics and world cinemas to the outer frontiers of the art form
- exhibitions of rare works and special prints
- post-screening discussions with filmmakers

AMERICAN FILM INSTITUTE, THE (AFI)

2021 N.Western Avenue 501(c)3 **HSM**
Los Angeles, CA 90027
Ph: 323-856-7600
Fax: 323-467-4578
www.afionline.org

Lynn Mazzucchi	Registrar/323-856-7698
Jean Firstenberg	Director/CEO
Jackie Stefanko	Assistant Director, Education and Training/323-856-7710

The American Film Institute is dedicated to advancing and preserving the art of the moving image. AFI's programs promote innovation and excellence through teaching, presenting, preserving, and redefining the moving image.

- AFI Los Angeles International Film Festival
- Center for Advanced Film and Television Studies—graduate programs
- professional training
- Directing Workshop for Women
- Television Writers Workshop
- California Digital Arts Workshop
- Intel Enhanced T.V. Workshop

AMERICAN INSTITUTE OF ARCHITECTS/LOS ANGELES (AIA/LA)

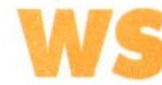

Pacific Design Center
8687 Melrose Avenue, Suite M3
Los Angeles, CA 90069
Ph: 310-785-1809
Fax: 310-785-1814

AMERICAN MUSEUM OF STRAW ART

2324 Snowden Avenue
Long Beach, CA 90815
Ph: 562-431-3540
Fax: 562-598-0457
www.strawartmuseum.org

501 (c) 3

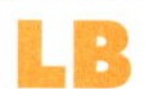

Morgyn Owens-Celli Director/Curator strawworkz@aol.com
Frank Fox, IV Education Director
Christine Gilbreath Internet Access Manager

The American Museum of Straw Arts is a facility dedicated to the education, preservation and exhibition of cultural and folk arts in straw.

- exhibitions
- hands-on activities connected with straw arts and crafts
- docent tours
- "Straw Museum without Walls" offers programs in the community

School and children's programs about the history of folk and cultural arts in straw.

Pre/K-12

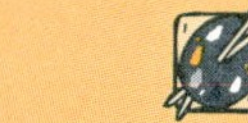

Programs: Workshops
Schedule: Year-round
Details: Grades Pre/K-12, History/soc. sciences, Visual & performing arts, Aesthetic valuing Creative Expression, Historical/Cultural Context Travel to schools, Educational materials available

Youth

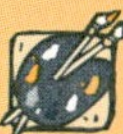

Programs: Workshops
Schedule: Year-round

Families

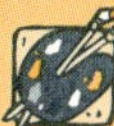

Programs: Workshops
Schedule: Year-round

AMERICAN RENEGADE THEATRE COMPANY

11136 Magnolia Boulevard
North Hollywood, CA 91601
Ph: 818-763-4430
Admin: 818-763-1834
Fax: 818-763-8082

501 (c) 3

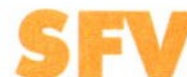

David Cox Artistic Director
Barry Thompson Dramaturg

- volunteer opportunities

AMERICAN REPERTORY DANCE COMPANY

4848 Bonvue Avenue
Los Angeles, CA 90027
Ph: 323-664-0553

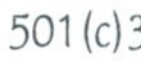

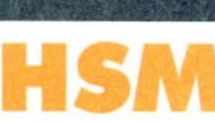

Bonnie Homsey Co-Director bhomsey@earthlink.net

ARDC's mission is to sustain the legacy of American modern dance through reconstruction, performance, and education of timeless issues and classical style.

AMERICAN SOCIETY OF BOOKPLATE COLLECTORS AND DESIGNERS

605 N. Stoneman Avenue, #F
Alhambra, CA 91801
Ph: 626-570-9404

501 (c) 3

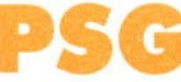

Audrey Spencer Arellanes Director

ASBC&D, formed in 1922, is of interest to those who design bookplates, who use bookplates (owners) and who collect them.

- exhibitions of bookplate prints
- literature in libraries
- two publications: "Yearbook" and the quarterly "Bookplates in the News" featuring articles on contemporary and historical bookplates, news of exhibitions, competitions, and bookplate literature

AMERICAN YOUTH SYMPHONY, INC.

P.O. Box 492493
Los Angeles, CA 90049
Ph: 310-476-2825
Fax: 310-476-2807
www.aysymphony.org

501 (c) 3 WS

James Forward Executive Manager/Director of Outreach
Alexander Treger Conductor/Musical Director
Elise Rips President

For 33 years the American Youth Symphony has been providing symphonic orchestral training and performance opportunities for 110 talented young instrumentalists between the ages of 16 and 25.

- 6 free concerts at Royce Hall on the UCLA campus

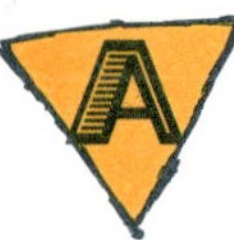

AMERICAN YOUTH SYMPHONY, INC. (CONTINUED)

Our ensemble-in-residence program will offer on-going chamber music performances at four LAUSD elementary schools throughout the school year. Teachers are given the opportunity to use music and still teach from their particular discipline.

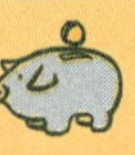

Pre/K-12

PROGRAMS:	**PERFORMANCES, RESIDENCIES**
SCHEDULE:	SPRING, FALL, WINTER, WEEKDAYS
DETAILS:	GRADES 3-6, VISUAL & PERFORMING ARTS
	CURRICULUM-INTEGRATED MUSIC EDUCATION
	AESTHETIC VALUING, HISTORICAL/CULTURAL CONTEXT
	TRAVEL TO SCHOOLS, INDIVIDUALLY TAILORED PROGRAMS
	EDUCATIONAL MATERIALS AVAILABLE

Youth

PROGRAMS:	**PERFORMANCES**
SCHEDULE:	SPRING, FALL, WINTER

Families

PROGRAM:	**PERFORMANCES**
SCHEDULE:	SPRING, FALL, WINTER

ANGELES CHORALE

P.O. Box 8347 501(c)3 **SFV**
Northridge, CA 91327
Ph: 818-888-6293
Fax: 818-888-6225
www.chorale.net

Sharon Mountford	Administrator	smtford@aol.com
Donald Neven	Artistic Director/310- 206-1094	

This outstanding chorale of 100 voices is under direction of Donald Neuen, reknowned Professor of Conducting and Director of Choral Activites at UCLA. Our repertoire consists primarily of oratorio and other classic music for mixed chorus.

- three-concert season
- opportunity for community members to sing
- available for contracted performances
- small groups available for programs at local organizations, homes, etc.

ANGELES CHORALE (CONTINUED)

We offer a three-level children/youth chorus. They rehearse weekly and perform several times a year. We also offer a summer one-week music day camp.

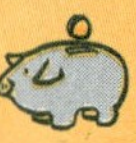

Pre/K-12

PROGRAMS:	**PERFORMANCES**
SCHEDULE:	SPRING, FALL, WINTER
DETAILS:	GRADES 3-12, VISUAL & PERFORMING ARTS
	CREATIVE EXPRESSION
	TRAVEL TO SCHOOLS

Youth

PROGRAMS:	**CLASSES**
SCHEDULE:	SPRING, FALL, WINTER, WEEKDAYS, EVENINGS
DETAILS:	COST FOR SOME PROGRAMS

Families

PROGRAMS:	**PERFORMANCES**
SCHEDULE:	SPRING, FALL, WINTER
DETAILS:	COST FOR SOME PROGRAMS

ANGELS GATE CULTURAL CENTER

3601 S. Gaffey Street 501(c)3 **SB**
San Pedro, CA 90731
Ph: 310-519-0936
Fax: 310-519-8698

Andrea Lien	Administrative Coordinator	artatgate@aol.com
Robin Hinchliffe	Executive Director	
Liat Yossifor	Education Director	

Angels Gate Cultural Center is a non-profit, community center which houses over forty artists. The center offers a year-round education program for children and adults, an annual exhibition schedule, lively performances, concerts and collaborative programming with other arts organizations.

- studio rentals
- classes and workshops for children and adults
- classes include Mudworks, Clay en Francais, Arttalk and Strings at the Gate
- free art programs to San Pedro schools

ANGELS GATE CULTURAL CENTER (CONTINUED)

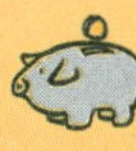

Angels Gate Cultural Center provides year-round education programs for children and adults. Last year the center provided the Arts in Schools Partnership program, a free program to schools in San Pedro.

 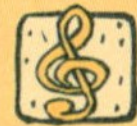 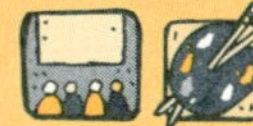

Pre/K-12

PROGRAMS: **PERFORMANCES, WORKSHOPS, STUDIO CLASSES, RESIDENCIES, SELF-GUIDED TOURS, GUIDED TOURS**

SCHEDULE: YEAR-ROUND, WEEKDAYS, EVENINGS, WEEKENDS

GRADES 5-12, VISUAL & PERFORMING ARTS
CREATIVE EXPRESSION, COST FOR SOME PROGRAMS
TRAVEL TO SCHOOLS, PROGRAMS ON-SITE
EDUCATIONAL MATERIALS AVAILABLE, BILINGUAL: FRENCH

 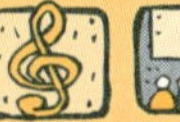 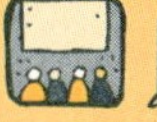

Youth

PROGRAMS: **PERFORMANCES, WORKSHOPS, CLASSES, RESIDENCIES SELF-GUIDED TOURS, GUIDED TOURS**

SCHEDULE: YEAR-ROUND, WEEKDAYS, EVENINGS, WEEKENDS

DETAILS: COST FOR SOME PROGRAMS

 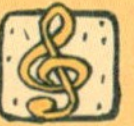 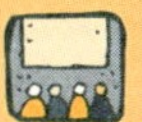

Families

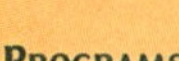

PROGRAMS: **PERFORMANCES, WORKSHOPS, CLASSES, RESIDENCIES SELF-GUIDED TOURS, GUIDED TOURS**

SCHEDULE: YEAR-ROUND, WEEKDAYS, EVENINGS, WEEKENDS

DETAILS: COST FOR SOME PROGRAMS

ANGELUS AWARDS STUDENT FILM FESTIVAL

7201 Sunset Boulevard
Hollywood, CA 90046
Ph: 800-874-0999
Fax: 323-874-1168
www.angelus.org

501(c)3 **HSM**

Monike-Moreno Associate Director angaward@aol.com
Emily Patton Festival Coordinator

Angelus Awards Student Film Festival is a student film competition and festival that awards works which explore the complexity of the human condition with compassion, respect and creativity. The event is held each year at the Directors Guild in Hollywood.

- screenings of award winning films are open to the public in October

ANIMACTION, INC.

SFV

415 S. Topanga Boulevard, #193
Topanga, CA 90290
Ph: 310-455-9912
Fax: 310-455-9942
www.animaction.com

Nigel Zeid Producer workshops@animaction.com
Clifford Cohen Executive Producer

AnimAction gives young people the opportunity to experience the joys of collaboration and creativity through animation production. Student produced and animated PSA's have been shown all over the world on T.V.

- one and two day animation workshops
- after school programs
- screenings and community screenings
- animation award ceremonies
- animation marathons

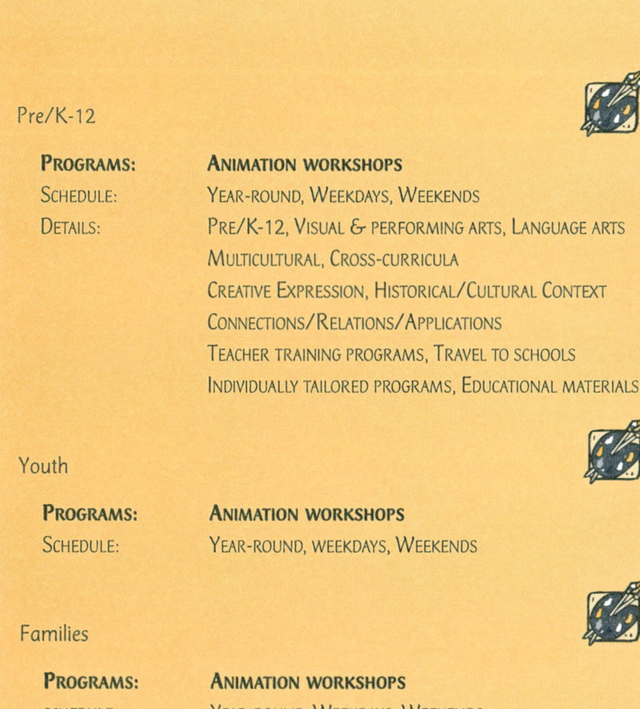

Pre/K-12

PROGRAMS: **ANIMATION WORKSHOPS**

SCHEDULE: YEAR-ROUND, WEEKDAYS, WEEKENDS

DETAILS: PRE/K-12, VISUAL & PERFORMING ARTS, LANGUAGE ARTS
MULTICULTURAL, CROSS-CURRICULA
CREATIVE EXPRESSION, HISTORICAL/CULTURAL CONTEXT
CONNECTIONS/RELATIONS/APPLICATIONS
TEACHER TRAINING PROGRAMS, TRAVEL TO SCHOOLS
INDIVIDUALLY TAILORED PROGRAMS, EDUCATIONAL MATERIALS

Youth

PROGRAMS: **ANIMATION WORKSHOPS**

SCHEDULE: YEAR-ROUND, WEEKDAYS, WEEKENDS

Families

PROGRAMS: **ANIMATION WORKSHOPS**

SCHEDULE: YEAR-ROUND, WEEKDAYS, WEEKENDS

ANTAEUS COMPANY, THE

4916 Vineland Avenue
North Hollywood, CA 91601
Ph: 818-506-5436
Fax: 818-506-6505

501(c)3 **SFV**

Dakin Matthews Manager/ 818-506-3137 Dakinm@aol.com
John Apicella Associate Manager

The Antaeus Company is an ensemble of professional theater artists committed to resident classical repertory theater.

- productions of the classics in workshops and full productions
- demonstrations of classical theater technique
- readings of contemporary and classical scripts, including new translations

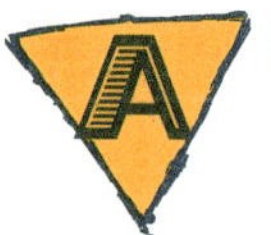

ANTELOPE VALLEY ALLIED ARTS ASSOCIATION

P.O. Box 51 — 501 (c) 3 — **AV**
Lancaster, CA 93584
Ph: 805-726-0655

Judith Burnett	President
Walt Carrier	Building Director

A.V. Allied Arts Cedar Centre is a community center for all the arts. Located in downtown Lancaster, the buildings are listed in the National Registry of Historical Sites.

- monthly meetings featuring demonstrations by well-known artists
- annual fine arts festivals
- fine art gallery
- auditorium with stage
- scholarship awards
- supports many community events
- workshops, classes
- showcase of artists, members display their work in local businesses

ANTELOPE VALLEY COLLEGE ART GALLERY

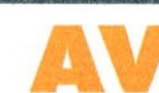

3041 W. Avenue K
Lancaster, CA 93536
Ph: 805-722-6395
Fax: 805-722-6390

Patricia Crosby-Hinds — Director

ANTIOCH UNIVERSITY OF LOS ANGELES

13274 Fiji Way — 501 (c) 3 — **WS**
Marina del Rey, CA 90292
Ph: 310-578-1080

Eloise Klein Healy	Chair/x 227
Courtney McNeal	Program Coordinator/x 231

The MFA in creative program is a low-residency graduate writing program offering degrees in fiction, poetry, creative nonfiction, and in a dual concentration. A Certificate in the Pedagogy of Creative Writing is also available.

APEX FINE ART

332 1/2 N. La Brea Avenue — **HSM**
Los Angeles, CA 90036
Ph: 323-634-7887
Fax: 323-634-7885

David Barenholtz — Director — apexart@earthlink.net

Modern and contemporary photography, specializing in photojournalism, fashion and glamour fine art photography.

ARBORETUM OF LOS ANGELES COUNTY, THE

333 N. Baldwin Avenue — 501 (c) 3 — **PSG**
Arcadia, CA 91007
Ph: 626-821-3222
Educ: 626-447-8207
Fax: 626-447-3763

Joan Murphine	Communications/949-650-4846
Judith Morse	Executive Director
Phyllis Wilburn	Program/Education Director

Located on 127 acres in Arcadia, the Arboretum is a horticultural and botanical museum with early California historical buildings and up-to-date research, programs, and classes provided on-site.

- garden shop
- Peacock Cafe
- children's gardening programs and events year-round
- tram tours
- docent tours
- volunteer opportunities

The Arboretum's educational programs are unique because the subejct matter is horticultural, botanical, and environmental based. The programs are popular because gardening is high on the list of past-times and because we provide high caliber instructional demonstrations.

Pre/K-12

Programs:	**Gardening programs**
Schedule:	Year-round, Weekdays, Weekends
Details:	Grades 3-12, Horticultural and botanical Facility for school visits, Programs on-site Educational materials available

Youth

Programs:	**Gardening programs**
Schedule:	Year-round, weekdays, Weekends

Families

Programs:	**Gardening programs**
Schedule:	Year-round, Weekdays, Weekends

ARCADIA RECREATION DEPARTMENT, CITY OF

375 Campus Drive
Arcadia, CA 91007
Ph: 626-574-5113
Admin: 626-821-4369
Educ: 626-821-4367
Fax: 626-821-4370

PSG

Roberta White	Assistant Director of Recreation
Jerome Collins	Director of Recreation

The City of Arcadia Recreation Department offers a variety of recreational classes to persons of all ages in oil painting, watercolors, crafts, ballet, tap, jazz, ballroom, line dancing, drama and guitar.

- craft shop open at Arcadia Community Center (365 Campus Drive, Arcadia)
- free six-week summer concert series on the lawn behind the Arcadia Community Center in July and August

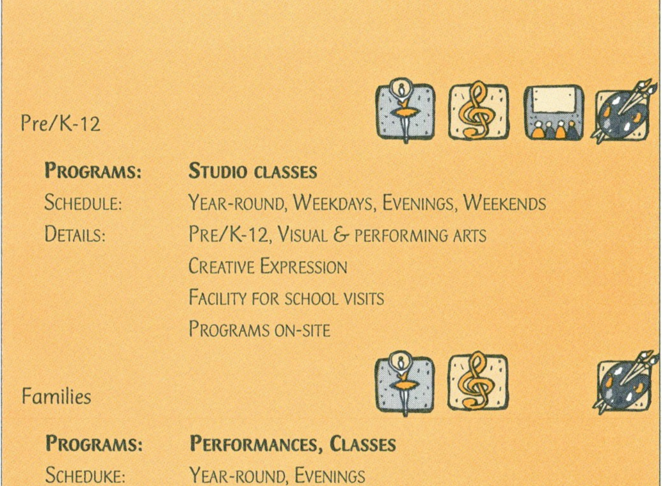

Pre/K-12

PROGRAMS: **STUDIO CLASSES**
SCHEDULE: YEAR-ROUND, WEEKDAYS, EVENINGS, WEEKENDS
DETAILS: PRE/K-12, VISUAL & PERFORMING ARTS
CREATIVE EXPRESSION
FACILITY FOR SCHOOL VISITS
PROGRAMS ON-SITE

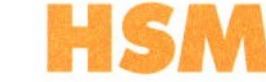

Families

PROGRAMS: **PERFORMANCES, CLASSES**
SCHEDUKE: YEAR-ROUND, EVENINGS

ARCHITOURS

P.O. Box 8057
Los Angeles, CA 90008-0057
Ph/Fax: 323-294-5825
www.architours.org

HSM

Rochelle Mills	Director	architours@aol.com

Architours organizes, researches and conducts tours, symposia, programs, and events that cultivate the awareness, appreciation, and discussion of architecture, art, landscapes, and designs.

- tours, lectures, symposia, special events, and receptions of architecture, art, design, landscapes, and restaurants
- cultural tours on individuals, groups, communities that may not fit into mainstream programming

ARCHITOURS (CONTINUED)

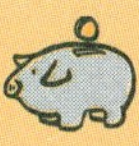
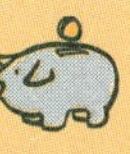

Pre/K-12

PROGRAMS: **WORKSHOPS, SELF-GUIDED TOURS, GUIDED TOURS**
SCHEDULE: YEAR-ROUND, WEEKDAYS, EVENINGS, WEEKENDS
DETAILS: PRE/K-12, VISUAL & PERFORMING ARTS
AESTHETIC VALUING, CREATIVE EXPRESSION
HISTORICAL/CULTURAL CONTEXT, CONNECTIONS/RELATIONS/ APPLICATIONS, COST FOR SOME PROGRAMS
TEACHER TRAINING PROGRAMS, TRAVEL TO SCHOOLS, INDIVIDUALLY TAILORED PROGRAMS, EDUCATIONAL MATERIALS

Youth

PROGRAMS: **WORKSHOPS, SELF-GUIDED TOURS, GUIDED TOURS**
SCHEDULE: YEAR-ROUND, WEEKDAYS, EVENINGS, WEEKENDS
DETAILS: COST FOR SOME PROGRAMS

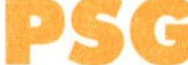

Families

PROGRAMS: **WORKSHOPS, SELF-GUIDED TOURS, GUIDED TOURS**
SCHEDULES: YEAR-ROUND, WEEKDAYS, EVENINGS, Weekends
DETAILS: COST FOR SOME PROGRAMS

ARMORY CENTER FOR THE ARTS

145 N. Raymond Avenue
Pasadena, CA 91103
Ph: 626-792-5101
Fax: 626-449-0139
www.armoryarts.org

501(c)3 **PSG**

Miriam Gonzalez	Community Liaison/ x120	mimi_gonzalez@yahoo.com
Elisa Greben Crystal	Executive Director/ x114	ecrystal@armoryarts.org
Doris Hausmann	New & Developing Pgms/ x113	d_hausmann@yahoo.com
Jay Belloli	Director, Gallery Programs/ x117	jaybelloli@yahoo.com

The Armory Center is a community arts center that engages broad participation through innovative approaches to creating, exploring and presenting the visual and performing arts.

- exhibitions of contemporary visual art
- gallery education includes free tours and the "Projects Room," an educational and particpatory installation
- Breaking the Code of Contemporary Music and Soliloquy Series, presents innovative contemporary music with Southwest Chamber Music
- Friday Nights at the Armory— readings, performances, conversations with exhibition artists and curators, lectures by experts on contemporary art and discussions on art issues.
- art classes for adults

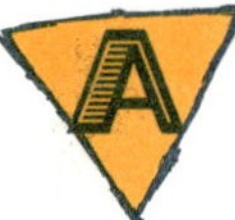

ARMORY CENTER FOR THE ARTS(CONTINUED)

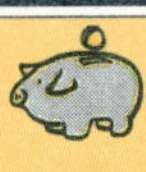

The Armory's unique education and exhibition programs encourage children and adults to experience, understand and appreciate contemporary art while being involved in the creative process of art making. All teachers are professional artists.

Pre/K-12

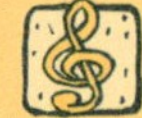
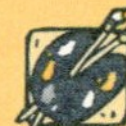

PROGRAMS:	**PERFORMANCES, WORKSHOPS, STUDIO CLASSES, RESIDENCIES, SELF-GUIDED TOURS, GUIDED TOURS**
SCHEDULE:	YEAR-ROUND, WEEKDAYS
DETAILS:	HISTORY/SOC. SCIENCES, MATH/SCIENCES, VISUAL & PERFORMING ARTS, LANGUAGE ARTS, MULTICULTURAL, AESTHETIC VALUING, CREATIVE EXPRESSION, HISTORICAL/CULTURAL CONTEXT, CONNECTIONS/RELATIONS/APPLICATIONS COST FOR SOME PROGRAMS, TEACHER TRAINING PROGRAMS (SALARY POINTS), TRAVEL TO SCHOOLS, PROGRAMS ON-SITE INDIVIDUALLY TAILORED PROGRAMS, EDUCATIONAL MATERIALS BILINGUAL: SPANISH

Youth

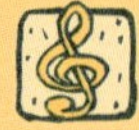
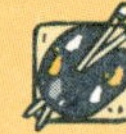

PROGRAMS:	**PERFORMANCES, WORKSHOPS, CLASSES, RESIDENCIES, SELF-GUIDED TOURS, GUIDED TOURS**
SCHEDULE:	YEAR-ROUND, WEEKDAYS, WEEKENDS

Families

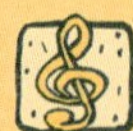
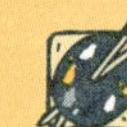

PROGRAMS:	**PERFORMANCES, WORKSHOPS, CLASSES RESIDENCIES, SELF-GUIDED TOURS, GUIDED TOURS**
SCHEDULES:	YEAR-ROUND, WEEKDAYS, WEEKENDS
DETAILS:	COST FOR SOME PROGRAMS

ARROYO ARTS COLLECTIVE

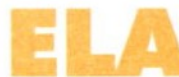

P.O. Box 50835 — 501(c)3
Highland Park, CA 90050
Ph/Fax: 323-221-3225
www.oversight.com/Arroyo.html

Laurie Arroyo — President/ 323-258-5292

The Arroyo Arts Collective is a non-profit grass roots organization presenting contemporary art with a focus on the community of the Northeast Highlands.

- bi-monthly newsletter
- annual juried art show
- varied community exhibition opportunities
- volunteer opportunities
- community-centered art events

ART CENTER COLLEGE OF DESIGN

1700 Lida Street — 501(c)3 — PSG
Pasadena, CA 91103
Ph: 626-396-2200
Admin: 626-396-2394
Educ: 626-396-2319
Fax: 626-795-0578
www.artcenter.edu

Jan Kingaard — Director of Public Relations/Communications
David Walker — Director of Special Programs/ 626-396-2319

Art Center, an independent, nonprofit four-year college with an enrollment of approximately 1,300 full-time students, specializes in educating visual artists and designers. Art Center's areas of specialty include Advertising, Animation, Communication and New Media Design, Entertainment Design, Film, Fine Art, Graphic Design, Illustration, Photography, Product Design, and Transportation Design.

- Bachelors degrees offered in nine majors and Masters degrees in six majors; admission tours and counseling; scholarships and financial aid available
- Art Center at Night: part-time, non-degree courses for the general public for career exploration, personal achievement, or portfolio preparation for application to the degree program; scholarships available
- Alyce de Roulet Williamson Gallery and Student Gallery: professional changing exhibitions and examples for Art Center's degree programs

Pre/K-12

PROGRAMS:	**STUDIO CLASSES, GUIDED TOURS**
SCHEDULE:	YEAR-ROUND, WEEKDAYS, WEEKENDS
DETAILS:	GRADES 9-12, VISUAL & PERFORMING ARTS CREATIVE EXPRESSION

Youth

PROGRAMS:	**STUDIO CLASSES, GUIDED TOURS**
SCHEDULE:	YEAR-ROUND, WEEKDAYS, WEEKENDS

Families

PROGRAMS:	**WORKSHOPS, STUDIO CLASSES, GUIDED TOURS**
SCHEDULE:	YEAR-ROUND, WEEKDAYS, EVENINGS, WEEKENDS

ART DEALERS ASSOCIATION OF SOUTHERN CALIFORNIA

718 N. La Cienega Boulevard 501(c)3 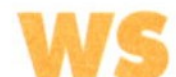

Los Angeles, CA 90069
Ph: 310-652-7465
Fax: 310-454-0313

Charlotte Sherman Public Information
Ronald Dammann President

Art Dealers Association of Southern California is a non-profit organization which serves as a means of communication and source of information among those in every aspect of the art community including art dealers, artists, collectors, educators, and museum professionals.

- two annual newsletters
- two sponsored lectures by noted art experts in many different fields

ART DECO SOCIETY OF LOS ANGELES

P.O. Box 972 501(c)3 HSM
Hollywood, CA 90078
Ph: 310-659-3326

Mitzi Mogul President

The Art Deco Society of L.A. is a non-profit organization dedicated to the preservation and awareness of Art Deco as a major influence on the twentieth century.

- walking tours
- lectures
- vintage fashion shows
- social events in unusual or private spaces
- preservation campaigns
- other special events and educational opportunities

ART EXPERIENCE STUDIO GALLERY

11830 Ventura Boulevard 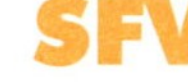

Studio City, CA 91604
Ph: 818-506-7804
Admin: 818-995-0009
Fax: 818-995-0020

Susan Manders Director skmanders@aol.com

ART IN THE PARK

5568 Via Marisol, Arroyo Seco Park 501(c)3 ELA
Los Angeles, CA 90042
Ph: 323-259-0861
Fax: 323-259-0550

Berta Sosa Director

We provide art programs for children of all ages. Our festivals draw thousands each year and have been acknowledged by La Opinon as the more significant cultural events in the city.

- Lalo Guerrero School of Music for children and adults
- community events/festivals (i.e.: the Corn Festival and Dia de los Muertos)
- art classes satellite program which takes art classes to children who cannot come to the park

ART IN THE PARK (CONTINUED)

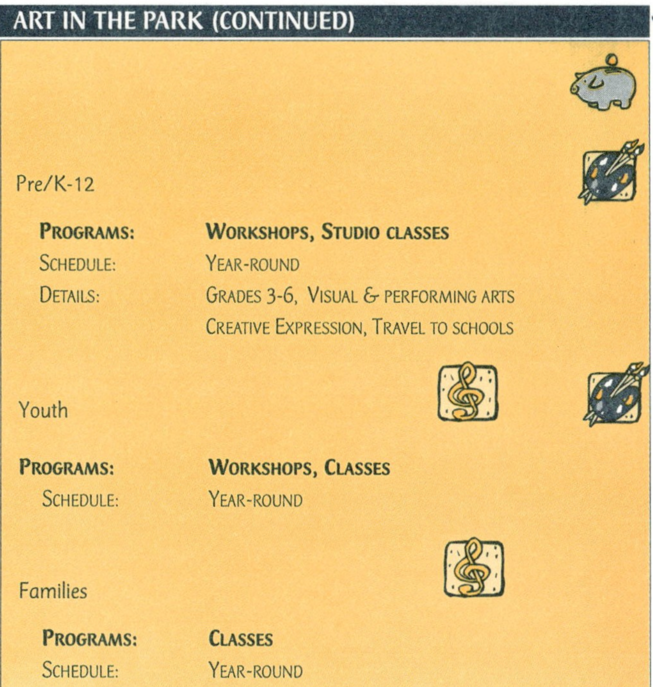

Pre/K-12

PROGRAMS: **WORKSHOPS, STUDIO CLASSES**
SCHEDULE: YEAR-ROUND
DETAILS: GRADES 3-6, VISUAL & PERFORMING ARTS
CREATIVE EXPRESSION, TRAVEL TO SCHOOLS

Youth

PROGRAMS: **WORKSHOPS, CLASSES**
SCHEDULE: YEAR-ROUND

Families

PROGRAMS: **CLASSES**
SCHEDULE: YEAR-ROUND

ART INSTITUTE OF LOS ANGELES,THE

2900 31st Street WS
Santa Monica, CA 90405
Ph: 310-752-4700
Admin: 888-646-4610
Fax: 310-752-4708
www.aila.edu

Mary Jo Placka Director of Admissions
Greg Strick President

The Art Institute of Los Angeles is a leading institution for career preparation in the visual and practical arts. Programs are offered year-round, with an impressive faculty of working professionals striving to strengthen students' skills and talents through well-designed curricula.

- guided tours for potential students and their families
- on-going gallery showings
- student and teacher summer workshops
- Associate of Science degree programs in Computer Animation, Culinary Arts, Graphic Design, Multimedia, Video Production, and Web Site Administration.

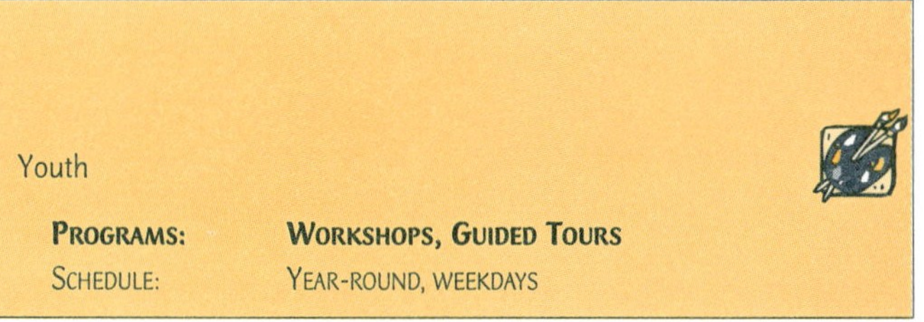

Youth

PROGRAMS: **WORKSHOPS, GUIDED TOURS**
SCHEDULE: YEAR-ROUND, WEEKDAYS

ART ISSUES PRESS

6764 Milner Road
Los Angeles, CA 90068
Ph: 323-876-4508
Fax: 323-876-5061

501(c)3 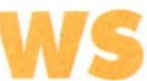

Gary Kornblau — President

Art Issues Press publishes magazines and books of contemporary art and cultural criticism.

ART SHARE LOS ANGELES

801 E. 4th Place
Los Angeles, CA 90013
Ph: 213-687-4ART
Fax: 213-687-7FAX

501(c)3 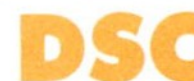

Alena Barrios	Office Manager	artshare@aol.com
Chip Hunter	Executive DIrector	

Art Share Los Angeles is a community arts incubator whose mission is to shape lives through art, education and community action.

- monthly exhibitions featuring local artists
- volunteer opportunities
- theater
- small group shows
- one-man shows
- dance
- work in conjunction with other organizations to provide art classes for chidren and adults.

Programs for public schools include scheduled classes, workshops, and special events. Programs in cooperation with community-based organizations such as Para Los Niños serve neighborhood children, youth-at-risk, and persons with special needs.

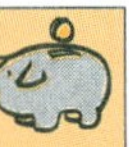

Pre/K-12

PROGRAMS:	**WORKSHOPS**
SCHEDULE:	YEAR-ROUND, WEEKDAYS, EVENINGS, WEEKENDS
DETAILS:	PRE/K-12, VISUAL & PERFORMING ARTS CREATIVE EXPRESSION, CONNECTIONS/RELATIONS/APPLICATIONS TEACHER TRAINING PROGRAMS (SALARY POINTS) TRAVEL TO SCHOOLS, PROGRAMS ON-SITE INDIVIDUALLY TAILORED PROGRAMS

ART & SOUL FESTIVAL

184 N. Cañon Drive
Beverly Hills, CA 90210
Ph: 310-385-0297
Fax: 310-385-0867
www.vsa.org

501(c)3 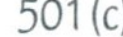

Lisa Insana	Community Relations Manager	lisai@vsarts.org
Rod Lathim	Director	rodl@vsarts.org
Kay Hullings	Executive Producer	

Each spring, the Art & Soul Festival, produced by Very Special Arts (VSA) will feature international visual and performing artists with disabilities in celebration of the arts and disability culture.

- exhibitions
- performances in all disciplines of the arts including dance, music, theater, writing and the visual arts
- volunteer opportunities
- arts career expo
- workshops
- cultural exchange program with the Los Angeles Unified School District

As part of the Art & Soul Festival, the Global Unity Project is a nine-month cultural exchange program that matches Los Angeles Unified School District students with international visual and performing artists with disabilities.

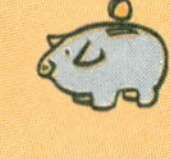

Pre/K-12

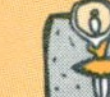  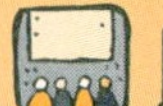 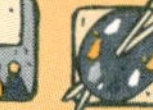

PROGRAMS:	**PERFORMANCES, WORKSHOPS**
SCHEDULE:	SPRING, WEEKDAYS, EVENINGS, WEEKENDS
DETAILS:	GRADES 3-6, HISTORY/SOC. SCIENCES, VISUAL & PERFORMING ARTS LANGUAGE ARTS, MULTICULTURAL CREATIVE EXPRESSION, HISTORICAL/CULTURAL CONTEXT CONNECTIONS/RELATIONS/APPLICATIONS TRAVEL TO SCHOOLS, PROGRAMS ON-SITE EDUCATIONAL MATERIALS AVAILABLE

Youth

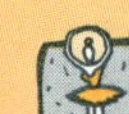 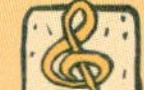 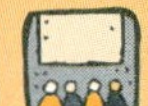 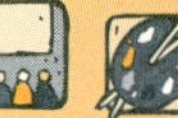

PROGRAMS:	**PERFORMANCES, WORKSHOPS**
SCHEDULE:	SPRING, WEEKDAYS, EVENINGS, WEEKENDS

Families

PROGRAMS:	**PERFORMANCES, WORKSHOPS**
SCHEDULE:	SPRING, WEEKDAYS, EVENINGS, WEEKENDS

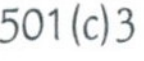
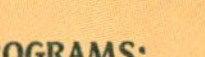

ART SOURCE L.A., INC.

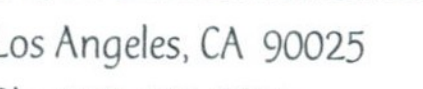

11901 Santa Monica Boulevard, #555
Los Angeles, CA 90025
Ph: 310-479-6649
Fax: 310-479-3400
www.artsourcela.com

Francine Ellman ellmanART@aol.com

Modern & Contemporary art in all media by emerging and established artists, master prints, commissions. Professional art consulting, private/corporate acquisitions, public art programs, curatorial services, studio tours, educational programs for new collectors, traveling exhibitions, exhibitions in alternative spaces, exhibition design.

ARTISTS' (FLOATING, INVISIBLE) MUSEUM OF ACTUAL ART, THE

672 S. Avenue 21, Studio 4 501(c)3
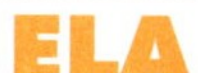
Los Angeles, CA 90031
Ph/Fax: 323-227-6771
www.floatingmuseum.com

Eugenia Butler	Organizing Artist	eugeniap@aol.com
Joy Decena	Educational Assistant	

The Artists' (Floating, Invisible) Museum of Actual Art organizes and produces large-scale international projects which address the nature, form and function of contempory art at the end of the twentieth century.

- "The Book of Lies Project", a collaborative dialogue about truth and lies in contemporary culture held through the mediums of art and poetry with artists and poets world-wide
- publish books
- create and produce exhibitions
- create artist networks
- "The Fire in the Library/Fires in the Mind Conversation Series", ongoing series of public cross-fertilizing conversations among articulate deep thinkers in literature, arts, science and philosophy

ARTISTS' (FLOATING, INVISIBLE) MUSEUM OF ACTUAL ART, THE (CONTINUED)

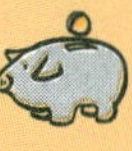

The Website, www.floatingmuseum.com is based on "The Book of Lies", an international project. Each of the twenty artworks has discussion questions, art and writing exercises. Information about the artists and project background can be printed from the site.

Pre/K-12

PROGRAMS: SELF-GUIDED TOURS ON THE INTERNET
SCHEDULE: YEAR-ROUND, WEEKDAYS, EVENINGS, WEEKENDS
DETAILS: GRADES 9-12, VISUAL & PERFORMING ARTS
AESTHETIC VALUING, CREATIVE EXPRESSION
HISTORICAL/CULTURAL CONTEXT
CONNECTIONS/RELATIONS/APPLICATIONS
TRAVEL TO SCHOOLS, EDUCATIONAL MATERIALS AVAILABLE

Youth

PROGRAMS: SELF-GUIDED TOURS ON THE INTERNET
SCHEDULE: YEAR-ROUND, WEEKDAYS, EVENINGS, WEEKENDS

Families

PROGRAMS: SELF-GUIDED TOURS ON THE INTERNET
SCHEDULE: YEAR-ROUND, WEEKDAYS, EVENINGS, WEEKENDS

ARTISTS RIGHTS FOUNDATION

7920 Sunset Boulevard, Suite 260 501(c)3
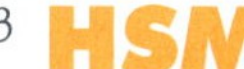
Los Angeles, CA 90046
Ph: 323-436-5060
Fax: 323-436-5061
www.artistsrights.org

Jennifer Ahn	Special Programs
Kathy Garmezy	Executive Director

Founded in 1991 by the Directors Guild of America and bringing together some of the industry's foremost creative leaders, the Artists Rights Foundation seeks to safeguard the rights of film artists, protect their works from alteration, and ensure that the artist's vision remains intact for future generations to enjoy.

- annual John Huston Award for distinguished efforts toward promoting artists rights and protecting artists' works
- quarterly newsletter
- Technology and Artists Rights College Campus Tour
- Consumer Awareness Campaign
- Kids Creativity Campaign

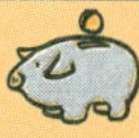

Still in development, the Kids Creativity Campaign reaches young people with an interactive approach to understanding creativity--what it means to create and how the creative process works in filmmaking.

Pre/K-12

PROGRAMS: WORKSHOPS
DETAILS: GRADES 7-12
AESTHETIC VALUING, CREATIVE EXPRESSION
EDUCATIONAL MATERIALS AVAILABLE

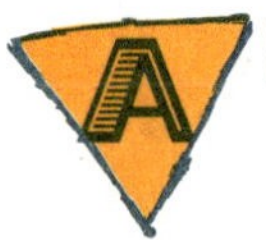

ARTLUXE

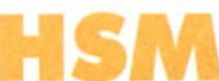

7005 Melrose Avenue
Los Angeles, CA 90046
Ph/Fax: 323-930-2407
artluxe@aol.com

ARTS EXPAND

P.O. Box 3462 501 (c) 3 **WS**
Los Angeles, CA 90078
Ph: 323-464-5398
Fax: 323-464-3957

Thom Vernon	Managing Director	ArtsExpand@aol.com
Rana Hauger	Co-Artistic Director	
Ann Cusach	President	

Arts Expand is a unique collective of professional artists who design workshops that service each group in a way unique to them. The program is free of charge. Arts Expand facilitates theatre, storytelling,performance, and creative writing for young people growing up in poverty, abuse, and homelessness.

- creative workshops
- storytelling
- volunteer opportunities
- performance

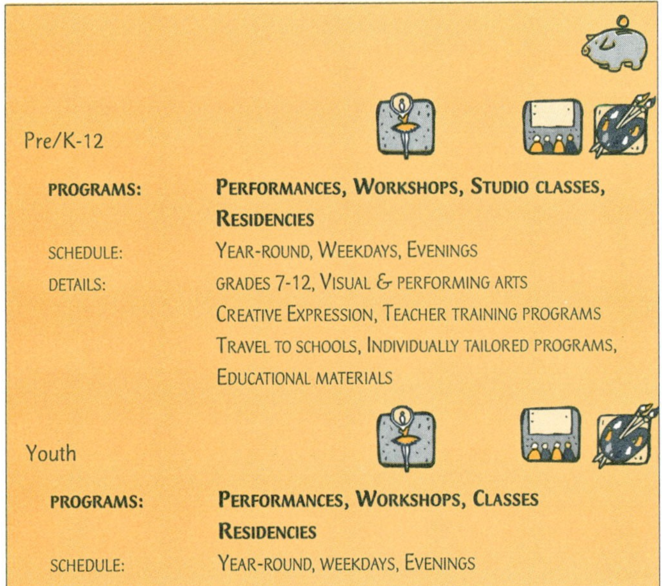

Pre/K-12

PROGRAMS: PERFORMANCES, WORKSHOPS, STUDIO CLASSES, RESIDENCIES
SCHEDULE: YEAR-ROUND, WEEKDAYS, EVENINGS
DETAILS: GRADES 7-12, VISUAL & PERFORMING ARTS
CREATIVE EXPRESSION, TEACHER TRAINING PROGRAMS
TRAVEL TO SCHOOLS, INDIVIDUALLY TAILORED PROGRAMS,
EDUCATIONAL MATERIALS

Youth

PROGRAMS: PERFORMANCES, WORKSHOPS, CLASSES RESIDENCIES
SCHEDULE: YEAR-ROUND, WEEKDAYS, EVENINGS

ARTS IN CORRECTIONS

P.O. Box 1841
Norco, CA 91760
909-737-2683 x2370
909-736-1488

Mr. Zoot	Institution Artist Facilitator

Arts In Corrections is a comprehensive mulit-disciplinary arts program bringing professional arts classes, workshops, and community projects to felon and drug treatment inmates of the California Rehabilitation Center.

- Classes are not open to the public, however, artists are hired from the community through our contractor
- Community programs for area schools, treatment programs, etc.

ARTS & SERVICES FOR THE DISABLED

3962 Studebaker Road, Suite 206 501 (c) 3 **LB**
Long Beach, CA 90808
Ph: 562-982-0247
Fax: 562-982-0254

Helen Dolas	Program Admin./562-982-0249	artsnservices@telis.org
Katie Stubblefield	Exhibits Coordinator/562-982-0248	
Maria Rubino	Executive Director/562-982-0250	
Carol Balogh	Gallery Coordinator	

Our programs focus on our belief that an individual provided with a loving, receptive environment where creative expression is focused into a viable artistic channel can have unlimited potential to learn and grow.

- Therapeutic Arts Program
- Creative Arts Program
- Encore Program
- Encouraging Personal Independence
- George V. Deneff Art Gallery
- community workshops
- volunteer opportunities

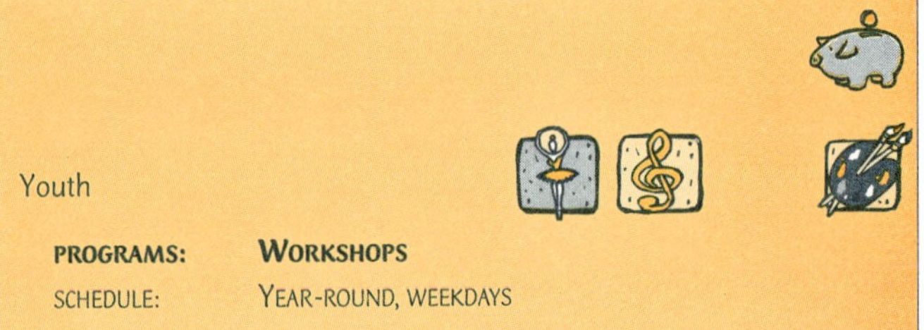

Youth

PROGRAMS: WORKSHOPS
SCHEDULE: YEAR-ROUND, WEEKDAYS

ARTSCAPE

2226 E. 4th Street **LB**
Long Beach, CA 90814
Ph: 562-434-2486
Admin: 562-434-3224
www.artscape-gallery.com

Jeannie McWhorter	Director	bcr8f@aol.com

ARTSCORPS LA

P.O. Box 421133 — 501(c)3 — 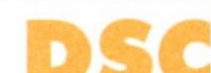

Los Angeles, CA 90042
Ph: 213-617-3877
Admin: 213-617-3876
Fax: 213-617-3878
www.LACN.org/LACN//artscorpsla/index.html

Julie Bach	Public Relations	aclaacla@earthlink.net
Tricia Ward	Artistic Director	

ARTScorps LA works with low-income communities in Los Angeles on neighborhood revitalization and public art projects that integrate community building and the development of life skills with the study of arts and culture. Two model community artparks "La Tierra de la Culebra" in Highland Park and "Spiraling Orchard" in Temple-Beaudry neighborhoods have emerged from abandoned land through the collaborative effort of local youth participants.

- citywide mural program
- volunteer opportunities
- exhibition space
- community celebration (summer & winter solstice)
- site construction/making place
- site tours

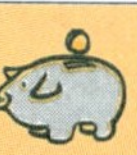

ARTSCorpsLA encourages experiential, active and cooperative learning in its unique outdoors setting. Youth are encouraged to share their vision, becoming effective mobilizers for each other, en masse functioning as powerful agents of community revitalization. The artparks offer a platform for self-expression and endless explorations to the community.

Pre/K-12

PROGRAMS: **Performances, Workshops, Studio classes**
Self-guided tours, Guided tours
SCHEDULE; Year-round, Weekdays, Evenings, Weekends
DETAILS: Grades Pre/K-12, Visual & performing arts
Creative Expression, Historical/Cultural Context
Connections/Relations/Applications
Travel to schools, Programs on-site
Individually tailored programs, Bilingual: Spanish

Youth

PROGRAMS: **Performances, Workshops, Classes**
Self-Guided Tours, Guided Tours
SCHEDULE: Year-round, weekdays, Evenings, Weekends

Families

PROGRAMS: **Performances, Workshops, Classes**
Residencies, Guided Tours
SCHEDULE: Year-round, Weekdays, Evenings, Weekends

ARTSREACH

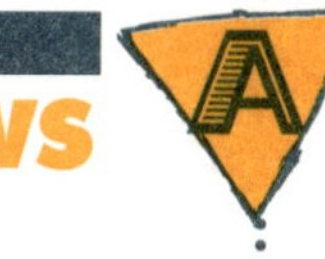

10995 Le Conte Avenue, Room 413 — 501(c)3 — WS

Los Angeles, CA 90024
Ph: 310-825-9493
Fax: 310-206-7382

Susan Hill	Director	shill@unex.ucla.edu

Artsreach is a non-profit community service organization founded by UCLA Extension; we create fine arts programs in places where they would not otherwise exist such as prisons, hospitals, etc.

- multidisciplinary art workshops
- performances

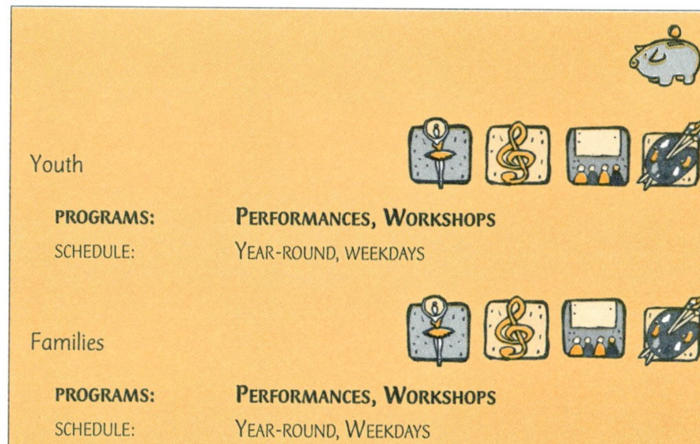

Youth

PROGRAMS: **Performances, Workshops**
SCHEDULE: Year-round, weekdays

Families

PROGRAMS: **Performances, Workshops**
SCHEDULE: Year-round, Weekdays

ARTWORKS - BOOK ARTS

WS

2525 Michigan Avenue
Bergamot Station- Building T2
Santa Monica, CA 90404
Ph: 310-828-4749

Barbara Pascal — Director

Unique and small edition books made by international artists.

ASHKENAZY GALLERY

HSM

5858 Wilshire Boulevard
Los Angeles, CA 90036
Ph: 323-938-1999
Fax: 323-938-3758

Arnold Askhenazy — Executive Director

19th and 20th Century art.

ASIA A+ ARTIST GROUP, INC.

PSG

5339 N. Rosemead Boulevard, #16
San Gabriel, CA 91776
Ph/Fax: 626-309-6080
Admin: 818-903-1646

Karen Han	Artistic Director	Karen_han@yahoo.com

Established in 1992, we are a group of more than 50 professional musicians, artists and dancers from Asia and China .

- concerts
- events

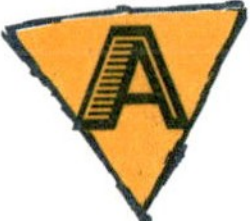

ASSEMBLAGE GROUP OF LOS ANGELES, THE

SB

29214 Trotwood Avenue
Rancho Palos Verdes, CA 90275
Ph: 310-832-9767
Fax: 310-832-0847

Annemarie Rawlinson Chairperson edkubis@earthlink.net

The Assemblage Group grew out of a desire of a few artists who work primarily in the medium of assemblage to improve their work and success and share their individual experiences in the world of art with others.

- networking/sharing of work strategies, technique, and materials
- members critique work, discuss recent shows and set new goals and challenges for membership
- collaborative projects and works with shared themes
- pursue opportunities to exhibit work individually or as a group
- present two or three exhibits per year
- group meets 3rd Saturday of each month

ASSISTANCE LEAGUE OF SOUTHERN CALIFORNIA

1370 N. Saint Andrews Place 501(c)3 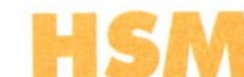
Hollywood, CA 90028
Ph: 323-469-1973
Fax: 323-469-3533

Janet Harrison Public Relations Director/x 239
Sandy Doerschlag Chief Executive Director/x218

Assistance League of Southern California, a non-profit philanthropic organization established in 1919, provides essential human services to families, children, seniors and individuals where needs are the greatest.

- theater for children

Children's Club, one of nine services of Assistance League of Southern California, has a strong performing arts program that helps at-risk youth develop self-esteem and self-discipline, while achieving a sense of accomplishment. 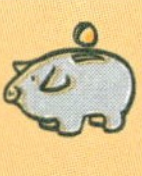

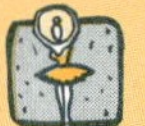 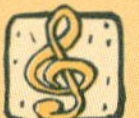 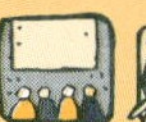

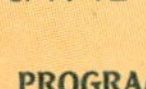

Pre/K-12

PROGRAMS:	**PERFORMANCES, WORKSHOPS, GUIDED TOURS**
SCHEDULE:	SPRING, WINTER, WEEKDAYS
DETAILS:	PRE/K-12, ACADEMIC ENRICHMENT TEACHER TRAINING PROGRAMS (SALARY POINTS) COST FOR SOME PROGRAMS, PROGRAMS ON-SITE

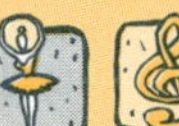 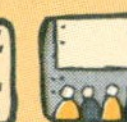 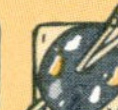

Youth

PROGRAMS:	**PERFORMANCES, WORKSHOPS, GUIDED TOURS**
SCHEDULE:	SPRING, WINTER, WEEKDAYS
DETAILS:	COST FOR SOME PROGRAMS

AT THE BREWERY PROJECT

HSM

650 S. Avenue 21, #33 East
Los Angeles, CA 90031
Ph: 323-222-3007

John O'Brien Director jobrien@artcenter.edu

AVAZ INTERNATIONAL DANCE THEATRE

3756 Aloha Street 501(c)3 HSM
Los Angeles, CA 90027-3302
Ph/Fax: 323-663-2829

Anthony Shay Artistic Director
Jamal Co-Artistic Director and Executive Director

AVAZ International Dance Theater performs the vivid and exciting dances of the Middle East, Central Asia and Eastern Europe.

- concerts
- lectures, demonstrations and classes
- concerts
- master classes
- K-12 classes
- lectures in Islamic art, history, dance and ethnology

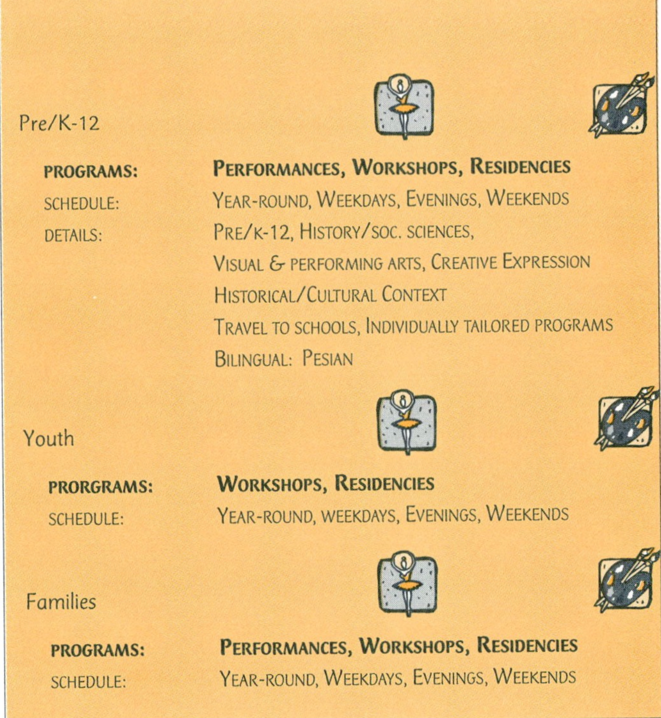

Pre/K-12

PROGRAMS:	**PERFORMANCES, WORKSHOPS, RESIDENCIES**
SCHEDULE:	YEAR-ROUND, WEEKDAYS, EVENINGS, WEEKENDS
DETAILS:	PRE/K-12, HISTORY/SOC. SCIENCES, VISUAL & PERFORMING ARTS, CREATIVE EXPRESSION HISTORICAL/CULTURAL CONTEXT TRAVEL TO SCHOOLS, INDIVIDUALLY TAILORED PROGRAMS BILINGUAL: PESIAN

Youth

PRORGRAMS:	**WORKSHOPS, RESIDENCIES**
SCHEDULE:	YEAR-ROUND, WEEKDAYS, EVENINGS, WEEKENDS

Families

PROGRAMS:	**PERFORMANCES, WORKSHOPS, RESIDENCIES**
SCHEDULE:	YEAR-ROUND, WEEKDAYS, EVENINGS, WEEKENDS

AZTLAN CULTURAL ARTS FOUNDATION

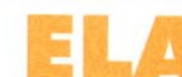

401 N. Avenue 19
Los Angeles, CA 90031
Ph: 323-227-1519

AZUSA PACIFIC UNIVERSITY

501(c)3 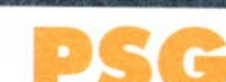

901 E. Alosta Avenue
Azusa, CA 91702-7000
Ph: 626-969-3434
Educ: 800-825-5278
Fax: 626-815-3880
www.apu.edu

Maureen Reigert-Foley	Assistant Director of Creative Media/ 626-815-5344
Jerry Lund	Art Director/ 626-815-5433
Richard Felix	President
Alice Watkins	Dean of Education

Azusa Pacific University, a Christian, evangelical, coeducational, liberal arts university accredited by WASC, offers more than 40 undergraduate fields of study, 18 master's degree programs and 3 doctorates.

- weekly musical performances
- gallery openings
- art therapy with City of Hope
- community outreach

"BACK TO THE SHTETL" YIDDISH MUSIC PARTIES

SFV

P.O. Box 68
Woodland Hills, CA 91364
Ph: 818-887-6053
Fax: 818-884-9795

Rena Dictor LeBlanc Producer

Yiddish Music Parties features professional singers and musicians performing Yiddish folk music, socializing, refreshments and sing-alongs. Music parties are held several times a year in private homes or meeting halls.

BALI AND BEYOND

SFV

9119 Remick Avenue
Arleta, CA 91331
Ph/Fax: 818-768-7696
www.balibeyond.com/gamelan

Maria Bodmann	Artist/Manager	shadow@balibeyond.com
Cliff DeArment	Artistl/Director	

Bali & Beyond is a company of Los Angeles performing artists inspired by the cultures of Indonesia. The ensemble offers Gamelan music and Indonesian arts presentations as well as original music and theater.

- concerts, workshops, and residencies for universities and civic venues; music, visual effects, and consultations for the film and recording industry; educational programs for arts organizations, museums, and schools
- traditional Gamelan and creative world music programs in a variety of styles and settings from small touring ensembles to large student groups
- traditional Balinese Wayang Kulit (shadow theater) as well as renditions of Lewis Carroll's classic literary tales in shadow

Bali & Beyond offers the following assemblies: The Music & Culture of Bali, The Shadow Theater of Bali, and Alice in the Shadows. The following workshops for students are offered: Gamelan Music from Indonesia, Chant (up to one hundred may participate), Shadow Theater, and Making Shadow Characters.

Pre/K-12 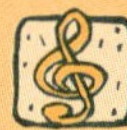 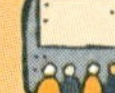 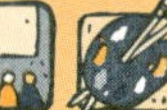

PROGRAMS: **PERFORMANCES, WORKSHOPS, RESIDENCIES**
SCHEDULE: YEAR-ROUND, WEEKDAYS, EVENINGS, WEEKENDS
DETAILS: PRE/K-12, VISUAL & PERFORMING ARTS
HISTORICAL/CULTURAL CONTEXT
TEACHER TRAINING PROGRAMS, TRAVEL TO SCHOOLS
INDIVIDUALLY TAILORED PROGRAMS, EDUCATIONAL MATERIALS

Youth 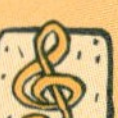 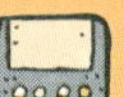 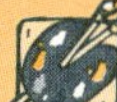

PROGRAMS: **PERFORMANCES, WORKSHOPS, RESIDENCIES**
SCHEDULE: YEAR-ROUND, WEEKDAYS, EVENINGS, WEEKENDS
DETAILS: SOME FREE PROGRAMS

Families 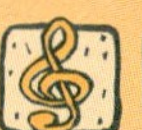 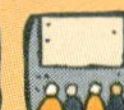 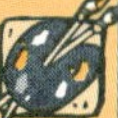

PROGRAMS: **PERFORMANCES, WORKSHOPS, RESIDENCIES**

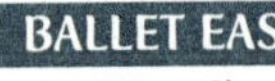

BALLET EAST

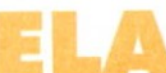

701 West Cleveland — 501(c)3 — ELA
Montebello, CA 90640
Ph: 323-725-1088

Melinda Reyes	Artistic Director
Angel Rodriguez	Assistant Director/562-943-2433
Joyce Garza	Assistant to Director/562-801-9107
Lisa Volkou	Assistant to Director/562-862-8107

Located in the San Gabriel Valley, Ballet East is a multi-ethnic ballet company dedicated to bringing the arts to their local community . The company offers a unique, original theatrical dance experience.

- several preformances year-round
- dance classes
- parent volunteer involvement
- choreographic opportunities
- classes for children

BALLET FOLKLORICO VIVA PANAMA

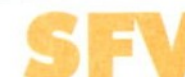

P.O. Box 207 — 501(c)3 — SFV
Canoga Park, CA 91305
Ph: 818-410-1236

Victor Grimaldo — Director — vivapanama@earthlink.net

Located in the San Fernando Valley, the Ballet Folklorico Viva Panama provides a sample of the different faces of the Panamaniam culture through its music, dance, arts and crafts, literature, and painting.

- participates in local and international events organized by government institutions, universities, community organizations, and private institutions

This is the only educational organization that performs dances linked with different periods of history of Panama. This program can be performed in English or Spanish by people well documented about history and dance.

Pre/K-12

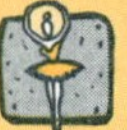
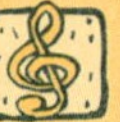
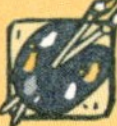

PROGRAMS: **PERFORMANCES, WORKSHOPS, STUDIO CLASSES**
SCHEDULE: YEAR-ROUND, EVENINGS, WEEKENDS
GRADES PRE/K-12, HISTORY/SOC. SCIENCES
VISUAL & PERFORMING ARTS, HISTORICAL/CULTURAL CONTEXT
TEACHER TRAINING PROGRAMS (SALARY POINTS)
TRAVEL TO SCHOOLS, EDUCATIONAL MATERIALS
BILINGUAL: SPANISH

Youth

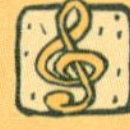
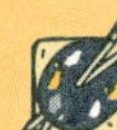

PROGRAMS: **PERFORMANCES, WORKSHOPS, CLASSES**
SCHEDULE: YEAR-ROUND, EVENINGS, WEEKENDS

Families

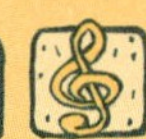
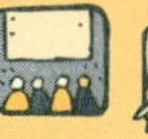

PROGRAMS: **PERFORMANCES, WORKSHOPS, CLASSES**
SCHEDUE: YEAR-ROUND, EVENINGS, WEEKENDS

BAMN-BAMN YOUTH ENSEMBLE

3616 Cardiff Avenue, Suite 201 — WS
Los Angeles, CA 90034-4086
Ph: 310-836-0997
Fax: 310-815-0141

Deborah Kellar — Artistic/Executive Director — BamnBamn@yahoo.com
Nora Buron — Associate Artistic Director

BAMN-BAMN Youth Ensemble, a professional theatrical ensemble for youth ages 8-21, provides performing opportunities year-round.

- year-round stage productions
- workshops and classes
- agent workshops
- casting director workshops
- apprenticeships
- mentorships
- commercial and voiceover training
- volunteer opportunities

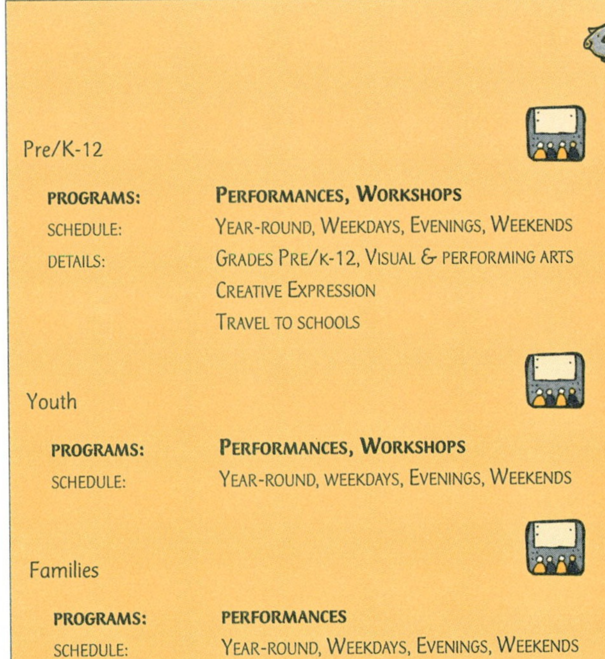

Pre/K-12

PROGRAMS: **PERFORMANCES, WORKSHOPS**
SCHEDULE: YEAR-ROUND, WEEKDAYS, EVENINGS, WEEKENDS
DETAILS: GRADES PRE/K-12, VISUAL & PERFORMING ARTS
CREATIVE EXPRESSION
TRAVEL TO SCHOOLS

Youth

PROGRAMS: **PERFORMANCES, WORKSHOPS**
SCHEDULE: YEAR-ROUND, WEEKDAYS, EVENINGS, WEEKENDS

Families

PROGRAMS: **PERFORMANCES**
SCHEDULE: YEAR-ROUND, WEEKDAYS, EVENINGS, WEEKENDS

BANNING RESIDENCE MUSEUM

401 E. M Street
Wilmington, CA 90744
Ph: 310-548-7777
Fax: 310-548-2644
www.banning.org

SB

Linda Annala	Secretary
Jeffrey Herr	Director

The Banning Museum, a national, state, and city historical site houses a collection of Victorian decorative arts, textiles, and furnishings. The museum also features a barn, schoolhouse, garden, and gift shop.

- gift shop
- lecture series
- docent tours
- volunteer opportunities
- special public events

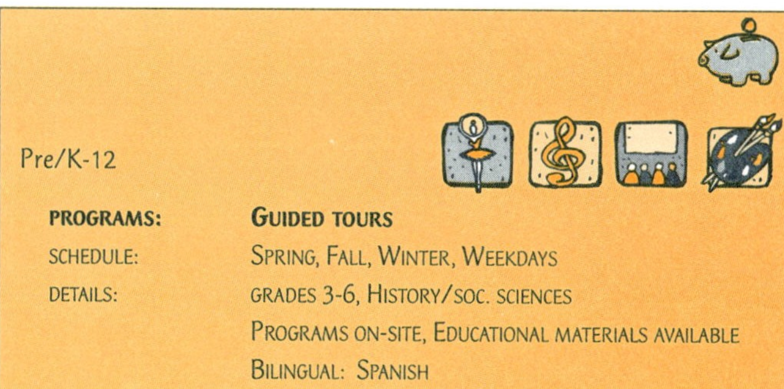

Pre/K-12

PROGRAMS:	**GUIDED TOURS**
SCHEDULE:	SPRING, FALL, WINTER, WEEKDAYS
DETAILS:	GRADES 3-6, HISTORY/SOC. SCIENCES
	PROGRAMS ON-SITE, EDUCATIONAL MATERIALS AVAILABLE
	BILINGUAL: SPANISH

BARD IN THE YARD

6443 Los Arcos
Long Beach, CA 90815
Ph: 562-598-8942
Educ: 562-597-1310
www.bard in the yard.com

501(c)3 **LB**

Bianca Sovich	President
Helen Borgers	Artistic Director

Bard in the Yard, a non-profit theater arts organization, uses live performances in public venues to captivate attention of audiences towards classic literature, a world beyond television and cinema.

- free public performances presented in Long Beach parks
- summer program consists of three shortend Shakespearean plays
- seasonal programs in summer, fall and winter
- participate in local community events
- tour Renaissance fairs
- actor training offered through the apprentice training program
- choral director provides musical training

BARD IN THE YARD (CONTINUED)

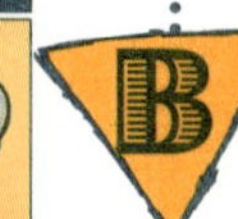

Interactive workshops in public schools

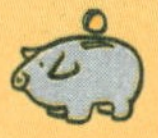

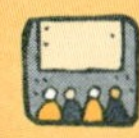

Pre/K-12

PROGRAMS:	**PERFORMANCES**
SCHEDULE:	YEAR-ROUND, WEEKDAYS, EVENINGS, WEEKENDS
DETAILS:	PRE/K-12, VISUAL & PERFORMING ARTS, AESTHETIC VALUING
	HISTORICAL/CULTURAL CONTEXT
	TRAVEL TO SCHOOLS
	INDIVIDUALLY TAILORED PROGRAMS, EDUCATIONAL MATERIALS

Youth

PROGRAMS:	**PERFORMANCES**
SCHEDULE:	YEAR-ROUND, WEEKDAYS, EVENINGS, WEEKENDS

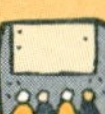

Familes

PROGRAMS:	**PERFORMANCES**
SCHEDULE:	WEEKDAYS, EVENINGS, WEEKENDS

BARNSDALL ART PARK
BARNSDALL ARTS CENTER

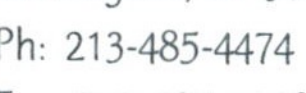

4814 Hollywood Boulevard
Los Angeles, CA 90027
Ph: 213-485-4474
Fax: 213-485-7456

HSM

Richard Ellis	Junior Arts Center Director
Patty Sue Jones	Program Director
Rosie Lee Hooks	Director of Festivals/Gallery Theatre/213-485-0709

The art centers in Barnsdall Art Park provide instruction in a unique and beautiful park site. The Barnsdall Art Center is for adults and the Junior Arts Center is for children.

- daytime, evening, and Saturday classes for adults
- exhibition schedules for adults and children
- special events for all ages

BARNSDALL ART PARK
BARNSDALL ARTS CENTER (CONTINUED)

The Junior Arts Center offers after school, Saturday and summer classes for children and youth. The Cultural Affairs Department funding allows low-cost, high-quality instruction in fine facilities and in a beautiful park.

Pre/K-12 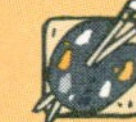

PROGRAMS: **STUDIO CLASSES**
SCHEDULE: YEAR-ROUND, WEEKDAYS, WEEKENDS
DETAILS: PRE/K-12, VISUAL & PERFORMING ARTS
CREATIVE EXPRESSION
TEACHER TRAINING PROGRAMS (SALARY POINTS)
PROGRAMS ON-SITE

Youth 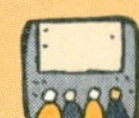 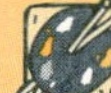

PROGRAMS: **CLASSES**
SCHEDULE: YEAR-ROUND, WEEKDAYS, WEEKENDS

Families 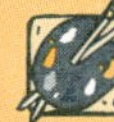

PROGRAMS: **CLASSES**
SCHEDULE: YEAR-ROUND, WEEKDAYS, EVENINGS, WEEKENDS

BEACH CITIES' SYMPHONY ASSOCIATION

P.O. Box 248 501 (c) 3 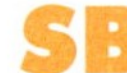
Redondo Beach, CA 90277-0248
Ph: 310-379-9725
Fax: 310-378-2834

Margaret McWilliams Public Information
Ruth MacFarlane Development/Fund Raiser/310-378-7873

The Beach Cities' Symphony Association presents four free symphonic concerts annually at El Camino College. The Association serves South Bay audiences while providing performance opportunities for community musicians. One concert showcases prize-winning young musicians.

- four free symphonic concerts annually
- volunteer opportunities
- performance opportunities for advanced local players, by audition
- classical masterworks and premieres of new compositions
- prize-winning young players perform with the orchestra
- advertisements for business and music instructors featured in four concert program books, reaching 800+ audience members per concert
- pre-concert informational lecture introduces programs

BEEM FOUNDATION FOR THE ADVANCEMENT OF MUSIC, THE

3864 Grayburn Avenue 501 (c) 3 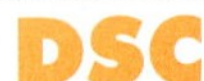
Los Angeles, CA 90008
Ph: 323-291-7252
Fax: 323-291-7752
www.primenet.com/~beem.la

Bette Cox Founder/President beem_la@primenet.com
John Herod Artistic Director/323-731-7145
Marion Maddox Secretary/Educational Programs/213-737-2236
Marilyn Barlow Administrative Assistant

The BEEM Foundation is a group of professional educators organized to stimulate awareness and understanding of music derived from African-American heritage. We create/perform in free concerts, present videos and offer scholarships to the general public.

- exhibitions, videos, and classical and jazz concerts in the summer and Black History Month

BENCH MOVIES

2505 W. Silverlake Drive 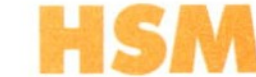
Los Angeles, CA 90039
Ph: 323-662-5353

Edward Landler Writer/Director/Storyteller

Bench Movies is the name under which Edward Landler does business as a teller of stories through various disciplines, producing films, and teaching the oral, written and visual arts of narrative.

- school and youth facility programs including storytelling and workshops
- story research and script consultation services for documentary and fiction video and film projects

Using many hats and voices, a multicultural wealth of stories, and original exercises to stimulate the imagination, I lead my students through the tradition of storytelling from the cave paintings to the present and into their own experiments with story writing and experimentation.

Pre/K-12 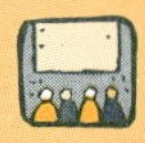

PROGRAMS: **PERFORMANCE, WORKSHOPS, RESIDENCIES**
SCHEDULE: YEAR-ROUND, WEEKDAYS
DETAILS: GRADES PRE/K-12
STORY IN FILM, LITERATURE, AND PERFORMANCE
VISUAL & PERFORMING ARTS, LANGUAGE ARTS
MULTICULTURAL, AESTHETIC VALUING, CREATIVE EXPRESSION
HISTORICAL/CULTURAL CONTEXT,
CONNECTIONS/RELATIONS/APPLICATIONS
TEACHER TRAINING PROGRAMS, TRAVEL TO SCHOOLS
INDIVIDUALLY TAILORED PROGRAMS

Youth 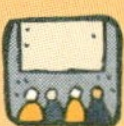

PROGRAMS: **PERFORMANCES, WORKSHOPS, RESIDENCIES**
SCHEDULE: YEAR-ROUND, WEEKDAYS, EVENINGS, WEEKENDS

BENITA BIKE'S DANCEART COMPANY

10211 Sunland Boulevard
Sunland, CA 91040
Ph: 818-353-5734
Fax: 818-353-8215
www.danceart.org

501(c)3 **SFV**

Benita Bike — Director — benita@danceart.org

Benita Bike's DanceArt is a chamber modern dance company which performs throughout the greater Los Angeles area and beyond both in concerts programs and in educational dance programs.

- Concert dance performances
- "Double Take" educational dance programs for adults

A "Double Take" program is a great introduction to dance. It begins with a lecture on modern dance and includes performances of two dances, a discussion period for audience and artists, and a second performance of one of the dances.

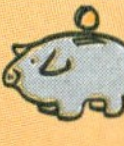

Familes

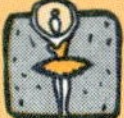

PROGRAMS: PERFORMANCES
SCHEDULE: YEAR-ROUND

BERNIE PEARL BLUES BAND

2256 Magnolia Avenue
Long Beach, CA 90806
Ph: 562-426-0761

LB

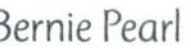

Bernie Pearl — Leader

The Bernie Pearl Blues Band performs contemporary and traditional blues music in solo, duo, and full band (6 piece) formats with acoustic and electric instruments.

- performances of blues music at festivals, clubs, concerts, and workshops
- "Blues in Schools" services for K-12
- lectures and courses on blues music and history
- full music festival services including booking, production, publicity, and promotion

The Bernie Pearl Blues Band offers first hand knowledge of the history and cultural significance of the Blues. The program includes personal recollections of many important artists and their works.

Pre/K-12

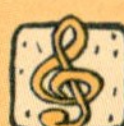

PROGRAMS: PERFORMANCES, WORKSHOPS
SCHEDULE: YEAR-ROUND, WEEKDAYS, EVENINGS, WEEKENDS
DETAILS: GRADES PRE/K-12, VISUAL & PERFORMING ARTS
CREATIVE EXPRESSION, HISTORICAL/CULTURAL CONTEXT
CONNECTIONS/RELATIONS/APPLICATIONS
TRAVEL TO SCHOOLS

BEVERLY HILLS PRESBYTERIAN CHURCH

505 N. Rodeo Drive
Beverly Hills, CA 90210-3206
Ph: 310-271-5194
Fax: 310-271-3985
www.bhpc.org

WS

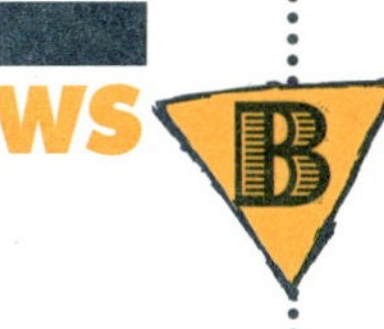

Catherine Cummings — Administrative Assistant
Nick Strimple — Minister of Music
James Morrison — Pastor

Located in the heart of Beverly Hills, Beverly Hills Presbyterian Church offers a variety of muscial programs and occasionally original stage productions.

- worship services
- special music programs including solo, choral, orchestral, and instrumental

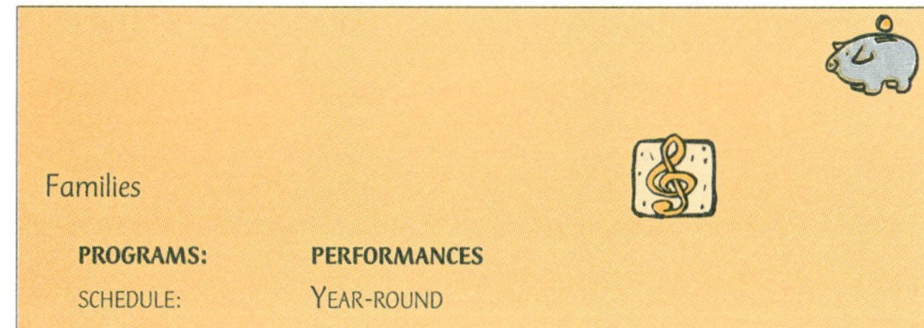

Families

PROGRAMS: PERFORMANCES
SCHEDULE: YEAR-ROUND

BEYOND BAROQUE LITERARY/ARTS CENTER

681 Venice Boulevard
Venice, CA 90291
Ph: 310-822-3006
Fax: 310-827-7432

501(c)3 **WS**

Fred Dewey — Executive Director

A nationally recognized literary arts center for 27 years providing a forum for readings, performance art, films and visual art.

- readings
- performances
- poetry and fiction workshops
- archive
- bookstore
- special events

BIBAK DANCE ENSEMBLE

3335 Appleton Street
Los Angeles, CA 90039-1701
Ph: 323-665-9771
Fax: 323-663-2112

501(C)3 **HSM**

Marshall Wandag — Public Information Coordinator — adelmars@earthlink.net
Michael Wandag — Executive Director — mikewandag@hotmail.com

BIBAK Dance Ensemble covers traditional music and dance of the Igorot Hill Tribes of the Northern Philippines.

- live music and dance performances
- workshops on traditional Igorot Tribal music and dance
- workshops on Igorot native crafts

BIG TIME BLUES PRODUCTIONS

LB

323 Main Street, 2nd floor
Seal Beach, CA 90740
Ph: 562-493-8300
Admin/Educ: 562-426-0761
Fax: 562-596-3661

Tim Lashlee	Secretary/562 426-6860
Bernie Pearl	President
Gene Kinsey	Treasurer/562 596-8177

Big Time Blues Productions presents Blues and related music in Festival and concert format, featuring several artists on each program. Performances are open to the public.

- Big Time Blues Festival held in Long Beach, usually mid-July
- annual Blues Harmonica Blowdown, presented in early March at several

BILINGUAL FOUNDATION OF THE ARTS

501 (c) 3 ELA

421 N. Avenue 19
Los Angeles, CA 90031
Ph: 323-225-4044
Fax: 323-225-1250

Elena Minor	Managing Director
Margarita Galban	Artistic Director
Carmen Zapata	Producing Director
Natalie Skelton	Education Coordinator

The Bilingual Foundation of the Arts (BFA) is a bilingual theater company presenting classic and contemporary Hispanic plays, as well as touring a theater-in-education program to local schools.

- "Theatre/Teatro"- four mainstage productions, alternating in Spanish and English
- "Teatro Leido" - a series of nine staged readings of new work
- translations of contemporary and classic plays by Hispanic writers

The Bilingual Foundation for the Arts programs include "Teatro Para Los Niños/Theatre for Children", a theater-in-education program that presents bilingual plays to elementary schools. Programs also include "Teatro Para Los Jóvenes/Theatre for Young People", presentations to secondary school audiences that deal with social issues confronting at-risk students.

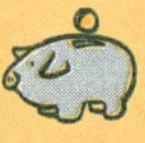

Pre/K-12

PROGRAMS:	**PERFORMANCES**
SCHEDULE:	YEAR-ROUND, WEEKDAYS
DETAILS:	PRE/K-12, VISUAL & PERFORMING ARTS
	CONNECTIONS/RELATIONS/APPLICATIONS
	TRAVEL TO SCHOOLS, PROGRAMS ON-SITE
	EDUCATIONAL MATERIALS AVAILABLE
	BILINGUAL: SPANISH

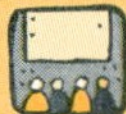

Families

PROGRAMS:	**PERFORMANCES**
SCHEDULE:	WINTER, EVENINGS, WEEKENDS
DETAILS:	COST FOR SOME PROGRAMS

BIOLA UNIVERSITY ART GALLERY

ELA

13800 Biola Avenue
La Mirada, CA 90639
Ph: 562-903-4807
Fax: 562-903-4748

Eric Pleschner	Director
Barry Krammes	Director

BLACK INVENTIONS MUSEUM, INC., THE

501 (c) 3

P.O. Box 76122
Los Angeles, CA 90076
Ph: 310-859-4602
Fax: 323-935-3761

Valerie Robinson	Director
Janie Chavers	Educational Director

The Black Inventions Museum is a traveling mobile display highlighting scientific and industrial contributions by people of African heritage throughout the world.

The display contains information constantly not contained in history books or publicized periodicals and magazines other, than the prescribed time known as Black History Month, informing society of significant innovations that make life easy.

Pre/K-12

PROGRAMS:	**PERFORMANCES, WORKSHOPS, GUIDED TOURS**
SCHEDULE:	YEAR-ROUND, WEEKDAYS, EVENINGS, WEEKENDS
DETAILS:	PRE/K-12, HISTORY/SOC. SCIENCES

Youth

PROGRAMS:	**PERFORMANCES, WORKSHOPS, GUIDED TOURS**
SCHEDULE:	YEAR-ROUND, WEEKDAYS, EVENINGS, WEEKENDS

Families

PROGRAMS:	**PERFORMANCES, WORKSHOPS, GUIDED TOURS**
SCHEDULE:	YEAR-ROUND, WEEKDAYS, EVENINGS, WEEKENDS

BLACK PHOTOGRAPHERS OF CALIFORNIA, INC.

P.O. Box 8778 501(c)3 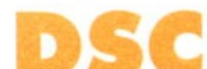
Los Angeles, CA 90008-2508
Ph: 323-294-9024
www.labridge.com/blackphotographers

Roland Charles Executive Director

Black Photographers of California, (BPC), is a non-profit arts organization dedicated to presenting and preserving African American art and culture through photography. Our mission is to increase awareness of photography as art and a profession.

- organize and present exhibitions, audio/visual programs, and seminars
- produce monthly program titled "The Photographers Roundtable"
- offer summer workshop for amateur and professional photographers
- traveling exhibitions

Our educational programming is unique to the community it serves by featuring topics and issues relevant to interested people of diverse backgrounds. 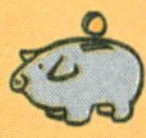

Youth 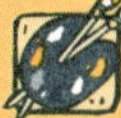

PROGRAMS: **PHOTOGRAPHY WORKSHOPS, RESIDENCIES**
SCHEDULE: SUMMER, WEEKDAYS

BLANK THEATRE COMPANY, THE

1301 Lucille Avenue 501(c)3 HSM
Los Angeles, CA 90026
Ph: 323-882-8065
Admin: 323-662-7734
Fax: 323-661-3903
www.primenet.com/~portal/

Daniel Henning Artistic Director/Producer

The Blank Theatre Company is an arts producing organization.

- mainstage productions
- workshops
- annual Young Playwrights Festival

BLUE PALM

3418 Winslow Drive 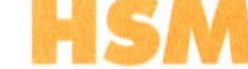
Los Angeles, CA 90026
Ph: 323-663-2683
Fax: 323-663-2903

Tom Crocker Company Manage bluepalm@prodigy.net
Jackie Planeix Artistic Director

Blue Palm updates the classic comedy couples of the past with intelligent, contemporary humor and hilarious dances.

- Regular live performances in English and French

BLUE PALM (CONTINUED)

Blue Palm's education programs focus on each individual's relationship to the arts and to themselves. Guided exercises in theater and movement assist participants in finding their own voice, while deepening their appreciation for the arts as a whole.

Pre/K-12 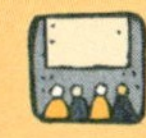

PROGRAMS: **PERFORMANCES, WORKSHOPS, STUDIO CLASSES, RESIDENCIES**
SCHEDULE: YEAR-ROUND, WEEKDAYS
DETAILS: GRADES PRE/K-8, VISUAL & PERFORMING ARTS
PHYSICAL EDUCATION, AESTHETIC VALUING
CREATIVE EXPRESSION, CONNECTIONS/RELATIONS/APPLICATIONS
TEACHER TRAINING PROGRAMS, TRAVEL TO SCHOOLS
INDIVIDUALLY TAILORED PROGRAMS, EDUCATIONAL MATERIALS
BILINGUAL: SPANISH

Youth 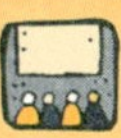

PROGRAMS: **PERFORMANCES, WORKSHOPS, CLASSES RESIDENCIES**
SCHEDULE: YEAR-ROUND, WEEKDAYS

Families 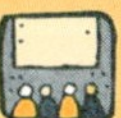

PROGRAMS: **PERFORMANCES, WORKSHOPS, CLASSES RESIDENCIES**
SCHEDULE: YEAR-ROUND, WEEKDAYS

BOB BAKER MARIONETTE THEATRE

1345 W. First Street 501(c)3 HSM
Los Angeles, CA 90026
Ph: 213-250-9995
Admin: 323 663-6688
Fax: 213-250-1120

Bob Baker Founder/213-250-9996
Alton Wood Founder
Tom Ray Business and Road Show Manager

Located in Downtown Los Angeles with free parking, the Bob Baker Marionette Theater is a non-profit organization promoting, perpetuating and furthering the art of puppetry for all ages to enjoy.

- school/organization discounts
- birthday celebrations and birthday cake parties
- marionette puppet rental and sales
- night-time theater rental
- gift shop

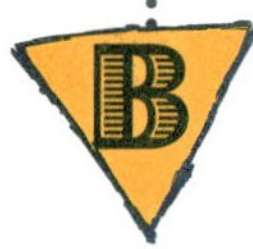

BOB BAKER MARIONETTE THEATRE (CONTINUED)

Founded in 1963, the Bob Baker Marionette Theater established the longest running children's theater in Los Angeles. They have delighted not only families, but thousands of young school children on sponsored weekday programs.

Pre/K-12 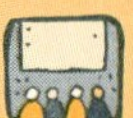

PROGRAMS: PERFORMANCES
SCHEDULE: YEAR-ROUND, WEEKDAYS, WEEKENDS
DETAILS: PRE/K-12, VISUAL & PERFORMING ARTS
CREATIVE EXPRESSION
TRAVEL TO SCHOOLS
PROGRAMS ON-SITE

Youth 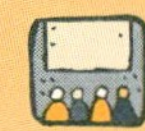

PROGRAMS: PERFORMANCES
SCHEDULE: YEAR-ROUND, WEEKENDS

Families 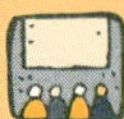

PROGRAMS: PERFORMANCES
SCHEDULE: YEAR-ROUND, WEEKDAYS, WEEKENDS

BOBBIE GREENFIELD GALLERY

2525 Michigan Avenue
Bergamot Station, B6
Santa Monica, CA 90404
Ph: 310-264-0640
Fax: 310-264-0740

WS

Rachel Benoff Assistant Director
Bobbie Greenfield Director

Contemporary masters, prints, drawings, and multiples.

BOOK GRINDERS, THE

13321 Burbank Boulevard
Valley Glen, CA 91401
Ph: 818-998-4503
Fax: 818-998-4590

SFV

Gary Kean Owner
Kadimah Elson Event Coordinator

Located near L.A. Valley College, the Book Grinders offers a variety of musical and literary events at no charge to the public.

- stand-up comedy every Wednesday
- classical guitar ensembles
- jazz
- shakespeare readings
- monthly meeting place for Humanist Society of San Fernando Valley

BOOK GRINDERS,THE (CONTINUED)

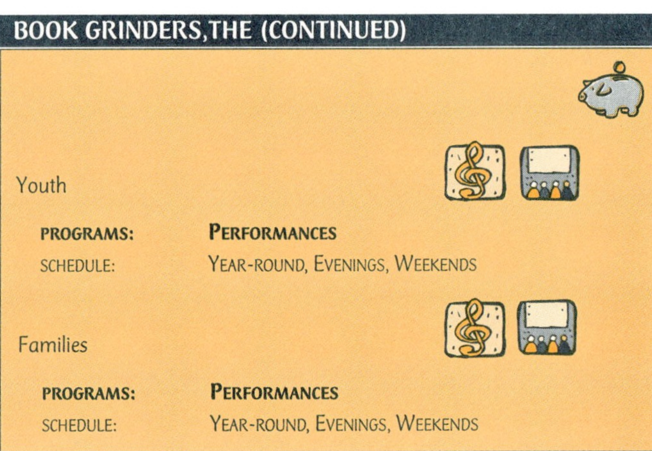

Youth

PROGRAMS: PERFORMANCES
SCHEDULE: YEAR-ROUND, EVENINGS, WEEKENDS

Families

PROGRAMS: PERFORMANCES
SCHEDULE: YEAR-ROUND, EVENINGS, WEEKENDS

BORDER PRODUCTIONS

11718 Barrington Court, #111
Los Angeles, CA 90049
Ph: 818-509-7880

WS

Carolyn Cumming Executive Producer

Border Productions produces youth television programming, providing opportunities for youths/adults to learn more about film by volunteering on the set. One of our most recent projects spotlights Latino teens.

- youth television prgramming
- youth home videos
- film production volunteer opportunities
- volunteer actor opportunities

BRAILLE INSTITUTE

741 N.Vermont Avenue
Los Angeles, CA 90029-4512
Ph: 323-663-1111
Fax: 323-663-0867

501(c)3 

Rosalie Copeland Creative Arts Program Coordinator/ x 325

The Braille Institute provides programs for legally blind adults Monday thru Friday from 10am to 12pm and 1-3pm. Classes include fine arts, crafts, music, exercise, dance and writing and theater arts. Other programs include choral groups, bands and performing groups.

- three yearly exhibitions featuring blind artists
- volunteer opportunities
- docent tours

BRAND LIBRARY AND ART CENTER

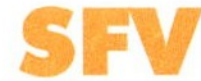

1601 W. Mountain Street
Glendale, CA 91201
Ph: 818-548-2051
www.library.ci.glendale.ca.us/brand/

Joe Fuchs — Manager/818-548-2026

Brand Library, a division of the Glendale Public Library, offers art and music books, magazines, scores, LPs, and compact discs for the public, as well as a gallery and recital hall.

- eight exhibitions a year featuring emerging California artists
- modern dance series
- chamber music series
- series of artists' talks by gallery artists

BRASIL BRASIL CULTURAL CENTER

3021 Airport Avenue, 104B — 501(c)3
Santa Monica, CA 90405
Ph: 310-453-2492
Fax: 310-453-2744

Amy Santo
Mae Pequena — capoeira@ucla.edu
Amen Santo — Artistic Director

Brasil Brasil presents history, dance, music and knowledge in various art forms emerging from the Afro-Brazilian experience. Brasil Brasil is dedicated to collaborating with diverse organizations to foster creative interchange and serve an ever expanding community.

- Arts Education in the Schools
- Capoeira classes involve martial arts, play, call and response singing, traditional instrumentation and spirituality
- touring and performance ensembles
- general cultural services and events
- rehearsal space/meeting and conference space available

BRASIL BRASIL CULTURAL CENTER (CONTINUED)

As a touring company and in collaboration with the Music Center of Los Angeles County's Educational Division, the Arts Education in the Schools program provides assemblies and residency activities in public schools throughout Southern California.

Pre/K-12 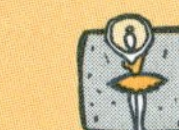 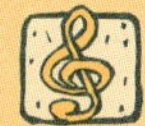

PROGRAMS:	**PERFORMANCES, WORKSHOPS, STUDIO CLASSES RESIDENCIES**
SCHEDULE:	YEAR-ROUND, WEEKDAYS, EVENINGS, WEEKENDS
DETAILS:	PRE/K-12, HISTORY/SOC. SCIENCES VISUAL & PERFORMING ARTS, CREATIVE EXPRESSION, HISTORICAL/CULTURAL CONTEXT, CONNECTIONS/RELATIONS/APPLICATIONS TRAVEL TO SCHOOLS, PROGRAMS ON-SITE BILINGUAL: PORTUGUESE & SPANISH

Youth 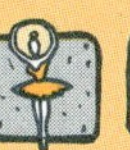 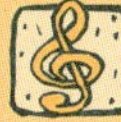

PROGRAMS:	**PERFORMANCES, WORKSHOPS, CLASSES, RESIDENCIES**
SCHEDULE:	YEAR-ROUND, WEEKDAYS, EVENINGS, WEEKENDS

Families 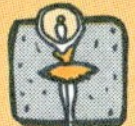 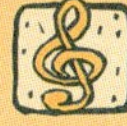

PROGRAMS:	**PERFORMANCES, WORKSHOPS, CLASSES, RESIDENCIES**
SCHEDULE:	YEAR-ROUND, WEEKDAYS, EVENINGS, WEEKENDS

BRAVO! L.A.

SFV

16823 Liggett Street
North Hills, CA 91343
Ph: 818-892-8737
Fax: 818-892-1227

Janice Foy — Director

Bravo! L.A. includes Trio of the Americas, Sierra Chamber Players, New American Quartet, The Harp Trio, and The Ascending Wave; borderless music from all periods, including pop and gypsy!

- workshops that focus on musical issues as they relate to maintaining good mental and physical health
- performances/lectures to demonstrate styles or aspects of a country's music
- master classes that focus on works in progress and encourage young people to participate while being coached by experts
- performances open to the general public—no fee
- lectures on various music topics that incorporate live performances to illustrate the music being discussed

BRAVO! L.A. (CONTINUED)

Bravo! L.A. has a cross-cultural format with bi-lingual aspects that tie in with historical and cultural features of the music. Puppetry and skit dialogue are interspersed between solo and ensemble music. Audience interaction is encouraged with the performances including singing, clapping and playing instruments.

Pre/K-12

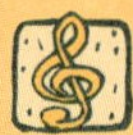

PROGRAMS:	**PERFORMANCES, WORKSHOPS, STUDIO CLASSES RESIDENCIES**
SCHEDULE:	YEAR-ROUND, WEEKDAYS, EVENINGS
DETAILS:	GRADES PRE/K-12, VISUAL & PERFORMING ARTS MULTICULTURAL CREATIVE EXPRESSION, HISTORICAL/CULTURAL CONTEXT TRAVEL TO SCHOOLS, INDIVIDUALLY TAILORED PROGRAMS EDUCATIONAL MATERIALS AVAILABLE, BILINGUAL: SPANISH WORK WITH DEVELOPMENTALLY DISABLED

Youth

PROGRAMS:	**PERFORMANCES, WORKSHOPS, CLASSES, RESIDENCIES**
SCHEDULE:	YEAR-ROUND, WEEKDAYS, EVENINGS

Families

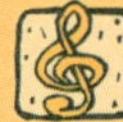

PROGRAMS:	**PERFORMANCES, WORKSHOPS, CLASSES, RESIDENCIES**
SCHEDULE:	YEAR-ROUND, WEEKDAYS, EVENINGS

BRAZILIAN CULTURAL NETWORK

WS

1720 Granville Avenue
Los Angeles, CA 90025
Ph: 310-826-1443
Fax: 310-826-7066
http://artmedia.net/bcn

A.C. Costa — General Manager/Designer Artist

The BCN was created to network the international Brazilian community by listing businesses, individuals, organizations, musicians, and artists serving these communities.

BRAZILIAN NITES PRODUCTIONS

P.O. Box 8327
Universal City, CA 91608
Ph: 818-566-1111
Admin: 818-567-0641
Fax: 818-567-6377
www.artmedia.net/braziliannites

Patricia Leao — Producer — pattyleao@aol.com

We are promoters/producers of Brazilian events such as the once a year Brazilian Summer Festival at the Ford Ampitheater that includes bands, dance, food, and arts and crafts. We also promote/produce events with major Brazilian artists 2-3 times per year.

- Every saturday at El Jardin: live Brazilian bands and dance
- yearly Brazilian Summer Festival
- dance lessons weekly at El Jardin Club
- produce Brazilian artists at Pantages or other theaters 1-3 times per year

BREAD AND JAM CHILDREN'S THEATRE OF LOS ANGELES

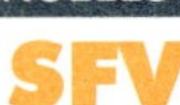

13118 Hartland Street
North Hollywood, CA 91605
Ph: 818-982-1475
www.webbillders.com/breadandjam

Tekla Ackelson-Wright — Founder and Artistic Director

Bread and Jam produces adaptations of acclaimed works of children's literature and original plays. It offers high quality theatre for the young that will appeal to people of all ages.

- productions feature adult actors in plays for young audiences that provide a creative participatory outlet for children 3-7 years of age
- Story and Drama Time programs

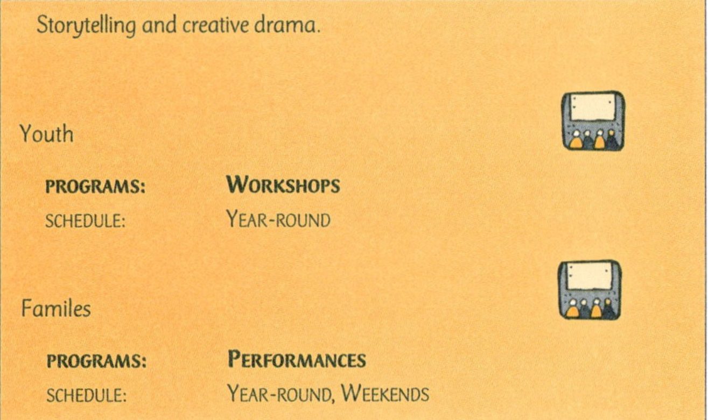

Storytelling and creative drama.

Youth

PROGRAMS:	**WORKSHOPS**
SCHEDULE:	YEAR-ROUND

Familes

PROGRAMS:	**PERFORMANCES**
SCHEDULE:	YEAR-ROUND, WEEKENDS

BRENTWOOD ART CENTER

WS

13031 Montana Avenue
Los Angeles, CA 90049-4891
Ph: 310-451-5657
Fax: 310-395-5403
www.brentwoodart.com

Jo Chandler	Administrator
Ed Buttwinick	Director
Linda Buttwinick	Director
Laura Leyva	Registrar

Brentwood Art Center provides year-round art instruction for adults, teens and children.

- special workshops throughout the year
- Fine Art Day Camp for children in the summer
- birthday parties for children 5-12 years old
- parties for adults may be scheduled for special occasions
- travel abroad program

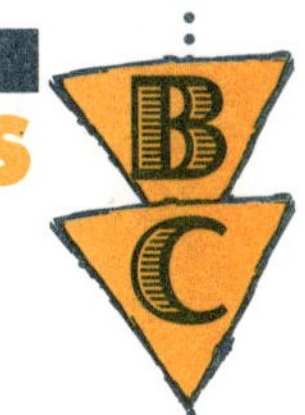

BRENTWOOD ART CENTER (CONTINUED)

The Center has been involved in developing programs and teacher workshops for many community organizations.

Pre/K-12

PROGRAMS:	**WORKSHOPS, STUDIO CLASSES**
SCHEDULE:	YEAR-ROUND, WEEKDAYS, EVENINGS
DETAILS:	PRE/K-12, VISUAL & PERFORMING ARTS
	CREATIVE EXPRESSION
	TEACHER TRAINING PROGRAMS

Youth

PROGRAMS:	**WORKSHOPS, CLASSES**
SCHEDULE:	YEAR-ROUND, WEEKDAYS, EVENINGS
DETAILS:	SOME PROGRAMS FREE

BRIDGE DANCE THEATRE, THE

475 S. Los Robles Avenue, #2 501 (c) 3 **PSG**
Pasadena, CA 91101
Ph: 626-564-9598
www.home.earthlink.net/~thebridgednc

Phyllis Douglass Artistic Director thebridgednc@earthlink.net

The Bridge Dance Theatre is a Los Angeles based modern dance and multimedia performance group.

- live performances
- lecture demonstrations
- dance classes
- workshops

The Bridge Dance Theatre teaches social and cultural significance of dance as an art form, as well as the aesthetic value, and how it applies to every day life.

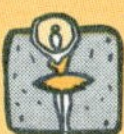

Pre/K-12

PROGRAMS:	**PERFORMANCES, WORKSHOPS, STUDIO CLASSES**
	RESIDENCIES
SCHEDULE:	YEAR-ROUND, WEEKDAYS, EVENINGS
DETAILS:	GRADES PRE/K-12, VISUAL & PERFORMING ARTS
	MULTICULTURAL, AESTHETIC VALUING, CREATIVE EXPRESSION
	TRAVEL TO SCHOOLS
	INDIVIDUALLY TAILORED PROGRAMS

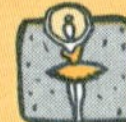

Youth

PROGRAMS:	**PERFORMANCES, WORKSHOPS, CLASSES. RESIDENCIES**
SCHEDULE:	YEAR-ROUND, WEEKDAYS, EVENINGS

BROCKUS PROJECT DANCE COMPANY

5628 Pepperwood Avenue **LB**
Lakewood, CA 90712
Ph/Fax: 562-531-8949

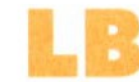

Deborah Brockus Artistic Director

BRONSON FINE ARTS

1410 2nd Street **WS**
Santa Monica, CA 90401
Ph: 310-587-2577
Fax: 310-587-2580

Mark Bronson Director

Specializing in American and European 19th/20th century works of art, antiquities, tribal art. Museum quality conservation and restoration.

BY ANY MEANS NECESSARY ENSEMBLE

3616 Cardiff Avenue, Suite 201 **WS**
Los Angeles, CA 90034
Ph: 310-836-0997
Fax: 310-815-0141

Deborah Kellar Artistic/Executive Director BamnEnsemble@yahoo.com
Byron Nora Associate Artistic Director

By Any Means Necessary Ensemble is a collaborative venture unifying arts organizations, educational institutions, and successful businesses. PEACE provides youth with the skills necessary to gain employment. Youth are responsible for all aspects of theatrical, film, and radio production.

- stage, film, and television production year-round
- acting and voice-overs for stage, film, TV, and radio
- video production workshop
- web site design and maintenance
- sociodrama and psychodrama
- newsletter production
- internet and computer training
- mentor and internship program
- volunteer opportunities

CAFÉ-CLUB FAIS DO-DO

5257 W. Adams Boulevard **HSM**
Los Angeles, CA 90016
Ph: 323-954-8080
Admin: 323-931-4636
Fax: 323-935-9989
www.faisdodo.com

Gary Schwindt General Manager/ x11 gary@faisdodo.com
Belinda Peru Entertainment Manager/ x19 belinda@faisdodo.com
Steven Yablok President/ x10 steve@faisdodo.com

A cross-cultural gathering place in Los Angeles' Mid-City, showcasing music, art, dance, poetry, theater, etc. Café Club Fais Do-Do is host to a monthly Mid-City marketplace, benefitting local charities and producing the annual Street Scene Fair, which raises awareness in the neighborhood about the arts and culture.

- nighly music showcases featuring local and worldly talent
- monthly Mid-City marketplace
- annual Street Scene
- live theater productions
- art exhibits

CAHUENGA PRESS

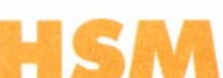

1256 N. Mariposa Avenue
Los Angeles, CA 90029
Ph: 323-664-3640

Holly Prado — Member

Cahuenga Press is a poets' cooperative press devoted to publishing fine books of poetry.

- poetry readings

CALIFORNIA AFRICAN AMERICAN MUSEUM

DSC

600 State Drive, Exposition Park — 501(c)3
Los Angeles, CA 90037
Ph: 213-744-7432
Admin: 213-744-2060
Educ: 213 744-7536
Fax: 213 744-7677
www.caam.ca.gov

Shell Amegah — Director of Communications/213-744-7537
Natasha Gordon — Museum Curator, Visual Arts
Jamesina Henderson — Executive Director/213-744-7513
Evelyn Carter — Education Curator
Rick Moss — Curator of History/213-744-7511

Inside the galleries of CAAM in Los Angeles are living treasures of African-American art, history and culture. CAAM's kaleidoscope of art and history is designed to enhance the public's knowledge of African-American societal contributions of the past and present.

- in-house and travelling exhibitions of African/African-American art
- gift shop
- extensive public programming on saturdays for families
- docent tours
- volunteer/intern positions
- teacher training programs
- film festivals
- archive of books, periodicals, audio and video tapes in our research library

CALIFORNIA AFRICAN AMERICAN MUSEUM (CONTINUED)

Pre/K-12

PROGRAMS: Workshops, Self-guided tours, Guided tours
SCHEDULE: Year-round, Weekdays
DETAILS: Grades Pre/K-12, History/soc. sciences
Visual & performing arts, Language arts
Aesthetic valuing, Creative Expression
Historical/Cultural Context,
Connections/Relations/Applications
Teacher training programs (salary points)
Travel to schools, Programs on-site
Educational materials available, Bilingual: Spanish

Youth

PROGRAMS: Workshops, Classes, Self-Guided Tours, Guided Tours
SCHEDULE: Year-round, weekdays, Evenings

Families

PROGRAMS: Performances, Workshops, Self-Guided Tours, Guided Tours
SCHEDULE: Year-round, Weekdays, Weekends
DETAILS: Some free programs

CALIFORNIA ART CLUB

PSG

P.O. Box 92555 — 501(c)7
Pasadena, CA 91109-2555
Ph: 626-583-9009
Fax: 626-577-9331
www.thespace.com

Paula Delfosse — Office Manager
Peter Adams — President
Elaine Adams — Public Relations

The California Art Club, founded in 1909, has a membership which includes professional artists and patrons interested in the traditional fine arts of painting, drawing, and sculpture.

- monthly meetings featuring prominent guest speakers
- frequent exhibitions of members' works in museums and galleries.
- monthly publication, California Art Club Newsletter
- mentor program
- curriculum development/implementation

CALIFORNIA DESIGN COLLEGE

DSC

3440 Wilshire Boulevard, 7th Floor
Los Angeles, CA 90010
Ph: 213-251-3636
Fax: 213-385-3545
www.cdc.edu

Tony Wong — Placement Coordinator/x 202
Sabrina Kay — Executive Director/x 220
Shideh Shirdel — Dean of Education

Located in the Mid-Wilshire District of Los Angeles, the goal of California Design College is to produce graduates who will pave the way in the dynamic world of fashion, largely by utilizing state-of-the-art fashion computer technology.

- associates of Applied Science Degrees in:
  - apparel Manufactoring (60 weeks)
  - advanced Fashion Design (60 weeks)
  - visual Merchandising (60 weeks)
  - fashion Merchandising (60 weeks)
- certificate programs in:
  - basic Fashion Design (20 weeks)
  - fashion Design (40 weeks)
  - computer Aided Fashion Design (20 weeks)
- ESL programs
  - basic (10 weeks)
  - intermediate (20 weeks)
  - advanced (30 weeks)

CALIFORNIA E.A.R. UNIT, THE

P.O. Box 96374 — 501(c)3
Los Angeles, CA 90086-0374
Ph: 213-488-9788
www.earunit.org

Amy Knoles — Executive Director
Dorothy Stone — Artistic Director

The California E.A.R. Unit, in its twelth year as Ensemble in Residence at the Los Angeles County Museum of Art, is a seven member ensemble dedicated to the performance, promotion and creation of the music of our time.

- four concert series of new chamber music for the public at the Los Angeles County Museum of Art
- international touring ensemble

Yearly performances of 50-75 children's programs in public and private schools. Programs incorporate new and unusual music using exotic as well as every day found objects as instruments in a way that is directly related to melody, rhythm and harmony.

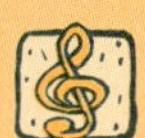

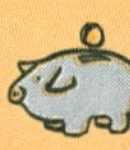

Pre/K-12

PROGRAMS: PERFORMANCES
SCHEDULE: YEAR-ROUND, WEEKDAYS
DETAILS: GRADES PRE/K-12, VISUAL & PERFORMING ARTS
CREATIVE EXPRESSION, HISTORICAL/CULTURAL CONTEXT
CONNECTIONS/RELATIONS/APPLICATIONS
TEACHER TRAINING PROGRAMS (SALARY POINTS)
TRAVEL TO SCHOOLS, PROGRAMS ON-SITE

CALIFORNIA HERITAGE MUSEUM

WS

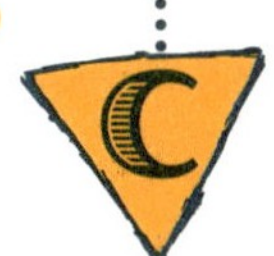

2612 Main Street
Santa Monica, CA 90405
Ph: 310-392-8537

Tobi Smith — Director

CALIFORNIA HUMANITIES ASSOCIATION

SFV

5854 Hillview Park Avenue — 501(c)3
Van Nuys, CA 91401
Ph: 818 780-7387
Educ: 707 839-2974
Admin: 909 882-5641
Fax: 818 780-5254

Nita Corinblit — Secretary
Jacqui Page — President
Fran Cornell — Vice-President
Ron Young — Curriculum Chair
Mark Mrotek — Treasurer

Please see Resources Section for description and programs.

Staff development programs are organized by and for teachers. Sometimes students are included in demonstrations of curriculum development.

Pre/K-12

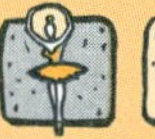 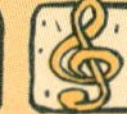 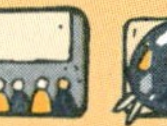 

PROGRAMS: TEACHER TRAINING PROGRAMS
DETAILS: VISUAL & PERFORMING ARTS, AESTHETIC VALUING
HISTORICAL/CULTURAL CONTEXT,
CONNECTIONS/RELATIONS/APPLICATIONS
TRAVEL TO SCHOOLS

CALIFORNIA INSTITUTE OF THE ARTS (CALARTS)

SFV

24700 McBean Parkway — 501(c)3
Valencia, CA 91355
Ph: 805-255-1050
Admin: 805-253-7835
Fax: 805-255-2894
www.calarts.edu

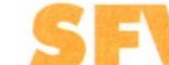

Anita Bonnell — Director of Public Affairs — abonnell@calarts.edu
Steven Lavine — President/x 2120

CalArts is a four-year fully accredited institution of all the visual and performing arts. Located in Valenica, the school offers BFA and MFA degrees.

- tours are given daily at 1:30 p.m. during the school year and by appointment during the summer

Families

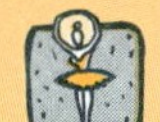 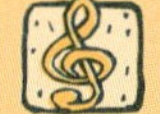 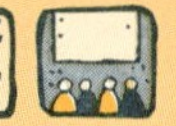 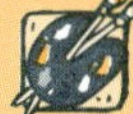

PROGRAMS: PERFORMANCES, GUIDED TOURS
SCHEDULE: SPRING, FALL, WINTER, WEEKDAYS, EVENINGS, WEEKENDS

CALIFORNIA JUNIOR SYMPHONY ASSOCIATION

4420 Boston Avenue 501(c)3 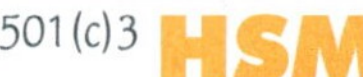
La Crescenta, CA 91214
Ph: 818-249-1285

Ginny Atherton Music Director

Meeting Saturdays in West Hollywood, young musicians ages 8-18 are trained in Orchestra, Chamber Music, and theory.

- masterclasses
- opportunities for talented and disciplined youth

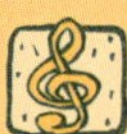

Youth

PROGRAMS: CLASSES
SCHEDULE: YEAR-ROUND, WEEKENDS

CALIFORNIA LAWYERS FOR THE ARTS

1641 18th Street
Santa Monica, CA 90404
Ph: 310 998-5590
Fax: 310 998-5594
www.sirius.com/~cla

WS

Alma Robinson Executive Director UserCLA@aol.com

Please see Resources Section for description and programs.

Spotlight on the Arts is a multi-dimensional program for high school aged, at-risk youth providing summer internships, job training, conflict resolution and communication skills training, mentorships and cultural enrichment.

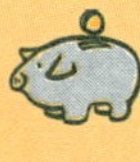

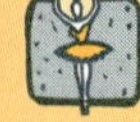 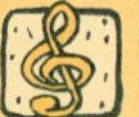 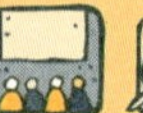

Youth

PROGRAMS: WORKSHOPS
SCHEDULE: SUMMER, WEEKDAYS
DETAILS: CONFLICT RESOLUTION, JOB READINESS AND COMMUNICATIONS SKILLS WORKSHOPS, PAID INTERNSHIPS AND MENTORSHIPS

CALIFORNIA SCIENCE CENTER

700 State Drive
Los Angeles, CA 90037
Ph: 213-744-7400

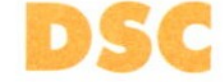

Suzanne Hackett Vice-President of Advancement

CALIFORNIA STATE UNIVERSITY DOMINGUEZ HILLS (CSUDH), UNIVERSITY ART MUSEUM

1000 E.Victoria Street
Carson, CA 90747
Ph: 310-243-3334

SB

Kathy Zimmerer Director

The University Art Gallery supports and enhances the art department program while giving students from other disciplines and interested community members the opportunity to explore and experience contemporary and historical art.

- six exhibitions yearly
- guest lectures
- outreach programming

CALIFORNIA STATE UNIVERSITY LONG BEACH (CSULB) COLLEGE OF THE ARTS

1250 Bellflower Boulevard, LIBE 115 501(c)3 LB
Long Beach, CA 90840
Ph: 562-985-4364
Admin: 562-985-4326
Fax: 562-985-7883

Diana Walti Director of Public Relations dwalti@csulb.edu
Wade Hobgood Dean, College of the Arts whobgood@csulb.edu

One of the nation's most comprehensive arts programs, the College of the Arts is California's largest school for the arts with 2,800 undergraduate and 200 graduate students in its six departments. With seating for 2,400 in six performance halls and the galleries of a renowned art department and museum, the college presents over 350 events annually, drawing thousands of patrons of the arts.

- comprehensive undergraduate and graduate courses in the arts
- community dance program (lessons)
- dance, music and theater performances
- graphic design workshops
- exhibitions in the University Art Museum
- live summer jazz concerts
- performances in the performing arts center
- opera
- art slide registry
- film screenings
- host to arts conferences and meetings

Art Workshop for Youth--this unique Saturday morning workshop is designed to be a creative and enjoyable learning experience for 5-15 year-olds. They will learn about art and artists while creating their own original works of art. Projects include drawing, painting, ceramics, and printmaking.

Youth

PROGRAMS: WORKSHOPS, CLASSES
SCHEDULE: SPRING, FALL, WEEKENDS

CALIFORNIA STATE UNIVERSITY LONG BEACH (CSULB) UNIVERSITY ART MUSEUM

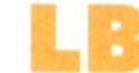

1250 Bellflower Boulevard — 501(c)3
Long Beach, CA 90840
Ph: 562-985-5761
Fax: 562-985-7602
www.csulb.edu/~uam/

Meg Linton	Curator of Exhibitions
Constance Glenn	Director
Liz Harvey	Curator of Education
Ilee Kaplan	Associate Director

Located on the campus of California State University, Long Beach, one of California's largest and most prestigious universities, the University Art Museum (UAM) has played a significant role in achieving international recognition for the arts and artists in Southern California. Since 1973, the UAM has presented diverse, imaginative and cutting-edge exhibitions devoted to the work of the most important artists of our generation.

- present approximately ten exhibitions yearly, focusing on twentieth-century art in all media, with a special interest in works on paper
- hosts exhibitions organized by peer institutions
- collection of site-specific outdoor sculpture
- collaborative projects with community groups
- docent training
- museum tours

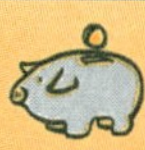

"Art to the Schools" is a joint museum/school program that sends art education graduate students to K-12 classrooms for special workshops and, in turn, brings the classes to the museum for special tours. The "UAM at the Boys and Girls Club" is a model partnership led by museum staff and local artists for groups at club sites and at the museum.

Pre/K-12

PROGRAMS: **GUIDED TOURS**
SCHEDULE: YEAR-ROUND, WEEKDAYS, EVENINGS, WEEKENDS
DETAILS: GRADES PRE/K-12, VISUAL & PERFORMING ARTS
AESTHETIC VALUING, CREATIVE EXPRESSION
TRAVEL TO SCHOOLS, PROGRAMS ON-SITE
EDUCATIONAL MATERIALS AVAILABLE

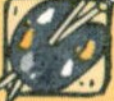

Youth

PROGRAMS: **GUIDED TOURS**
SCHEDULE: YEAR-ROUND, WEEKDAYS, EVENINGS, WEEKENDS

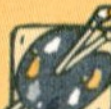

Families

PROGRAMS: **GUIDED TOURS**
SCHEDULE: YEAR-ROUND, WEEKDAYS, EVENINGS, WEEKENDS

CALIFORNIA STATE UNIVERSITY LOS ANGELES (CSULA) LUCKMAN FINE ARTS GALLERY

ELA

5151 State University Drive
Los Angeles, CA 90032
Ph: 323-343 3000
Admin: 323-343-6604
Fax: 323-343-6423

Clifford Harper	Executive Director
Julie Joyce	Director

CALIFORNIA STATE UNIVERSITY LOS ANGELES (CSULA) SATURDAY CONSERVATORY OF MUSIC

ELA

5151 State University Drive
Los Angeles, CA 90032
Ph: 323-343-4109

Mickey Fruchter	University Contact
Art Mautner	Director/562-927-9455

CSULA Conservatory of Music is a Saturday program that includes group lessons on all orchestral instruments, a theory class and an orchestra.

- classes are offered each Saturday from October to June
- class lessons on all orchestral instruments, plus voice 3 choirs, piano and classical guitar
- four orchestras including Youth Symphony West
- concerts presented at the end of each quarter

For fifty dollars a quarter, a student can take up to four classes each Saturday for ten weeks. Children can learn a secondary instrument, sing in a choir or play in an ensemble of like instruments.

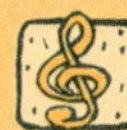

Pre/K-12

PROGRAMS: **PERFORMANCES**
SCHEDULE: SPRING, FALL, WINTER, WEEKENDS
DETAILS: GRADES 5-12, VISUAL & PERFORMING ARTS
CREATIVE EXPRESSION
TEACHER TRAINING PROGRAMS, PROGRAMS ON-SITE
INDIVIDUALLY TAILORED PROGRAMS, EDUCATIONAL MATERIALS

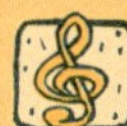

Youth

PROGRASMS: **PERFORMANCES**
SCHEDULE: SPRING, FALL, WINTER, WEEKENDS

CALIFORNIA STATE UNIVERSITY NORTHRIDGE (CSUN) COLLEGE OF ARTS, MEDIA, AND COMMUNICATION

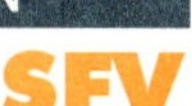

18111 Nordhoff Street
Northridge, CA 91330
Ph: 818-677-2248
Fax: 818-677-2345

Philip Handler	College Dean

CALIFORNIA STATE UNIVERSITY NORTHRIDGE (CSUN) UNIVERSITY ART GALLERIES ML236

18111 Nordhoff Street
Northridge, CA 91330-8236
Ph: 818-677-2226
Admin: 818-677-2156
Fax: 818-677-5910
www.csun.edu/~hfart009

SFV

Ann Burroughs	Exhibition Coordinator	ann.burroughs@csun.edu
Louise Lewis	Director	louise.lewis@csun.edu
Jim Sweeters	Preparator	

The Art Gallery programs art from international and multicultural perspectives featuring historical and contemporary, thematic and media-oriented exhibitions for a broad university and community audience.

- lectures, performances, video and film presentations, symposia and tours
- outreach programs with the diverse cultural communities in the San Fernando Valley and the greater Los Angeles area
- Docent program provides K-12 school tours

Free docent guided tours for K-12 school groups by appointment (818) 677-2156.

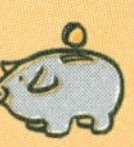

Pre/K-12

PROGRAMS: GUIDED TOURS
SCHEDULE: SPRING, FALL, WINTER, WEEKDAYS, WEEKENDS
DETAILS: GRADES PRE/K-12, VISUAL & PERFORMING ARTS
AESTHETIC VALUING, HISTORICAL/CULTURAL CONTEXT
PROGRAMS ON-SITE

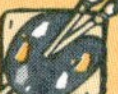

Youth

PROGRAMS: GUIDED TOURS
SCHEDULE: SPRING, FALL, WINTER, WEEKDAYS, WEEKENDS

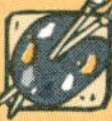

Families

PROGRAMS: GUIDED TOURS
SCHEDULE: SPRING, FALL, WINTER, WEEKDAYS, WEEKENDS

CALIFORNIA TRADITIONAL MUSIC SOCIETY

4401 Trancas Place
Tarzana, CA 91356-5399
Ph: 818-342-7664
Fax: 818-609-0106

501(c)3

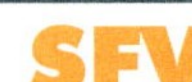

Elaine Weissman	Executive Director	ctms@lafn.org

CTMS fosters and promotes to the public traditional, contemporary and multi-cultural folk music, dance and related performing arts.

- annual "Summer Solstice Folk Music and Dance Festival"
- folk music concerts
- family music and dance camp
- free 48-page magazine published twice a year

CALTECH PUBLIC EVENTS

332 S. Michigan Avenue
Pasadena, CA 91125
Ph: 626-395-4652
Admin: 626-395-3834
Fax: 626-577-0130

501(c)3 **PSG**

Cara Stemen	Marketing Manager/626-395-3841	tickets@caltech.edu
Denise Nelson Nash	Director/626-395-4638	dnn@caltech.edu

Located in Pasadena, Caltech Public Events presents performing arts and lectures in three venues on the campus of the California Institute of Technology.

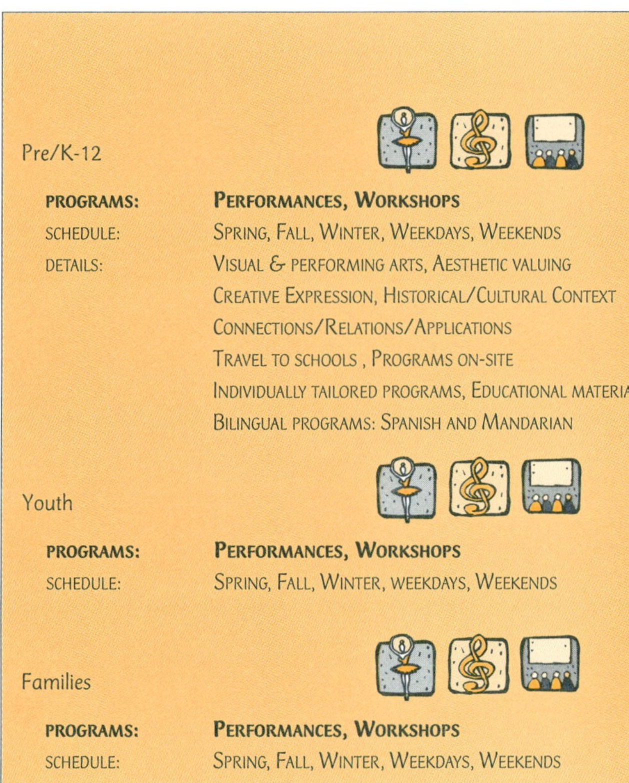

Pre/K-12

PROGRAMS: PERFORMANCES, WORKSHOPS
SCHEDULE: SPRING, FALL, WINTER, WEEKDAYS, WEEKENDS
DETAILS: VISUAL & PERFORMING ARTS, AESTHETIC VALUING
CREATIVE EXPRESSION, HISTORICAL/CULTURAL CONTEXT
CONNECTIONS/RELATIONS/APPLICATIONS
TRAVEL TO SCHOOLS, PROGRAMS ON-SITE
INDIVIDUALLY TAILORED PROGRAMS, EDUCATIONAL MATERIALS
BILINGUAL PROGRAMS: SPANISH AND MANDARIN

Youth

PROGRAMS: PERFORMANCES, WORKSHOPS
SCHEDULE: SPRING, FALL, WINTER, WEEKDAYS, WEEKENDS

Families

PROGRAMS: PERFORMANCES, WORKSHOPS
SCHEDULE: SPRING, FALL, WINTER, WEEKDAYS, WEEKENDS

CAMBRIDGE SINGERS, THE

P.O. Box 92200
Pasadena, CA 91109-2200
Ph: 626-584-0088

501(c)3 **PSG**

Anne Griesel	Administrator
Alexander Ruggieri	Music Director/213-413-4215
Wendy Hunter	Development Director/626-577-4255

The Cambridge singers is a semi-professional chorus whose mission is to inspire audiences to love diverse choral music through exciting, engaging performances that entertain and educate.

- four concerts each year
- concerts feature Russian and Eastern European choral musics
- concerts in retirement homes and hospitals
- pre-concert lectures
- post-concert receptions
- special subscriber/donor events

CAMPUS CONCERTS

2714 Ridgeland Road
Torrance, CA 90505
Ph: 310-326-5761
Admin: 310-541-1280
Educ: 310-544-5592

501(c)3

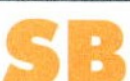

Patricia Maki — Artistic Director
Peggy Sloves — President
Linda Muggeridge — Program Development

Campus Concerts educates, encourages and entertains audiences of all ages. The group promotes school music programs by providing educational concerts and master classes presented by professional teaching/performing musicians.

- live classical chamber music
- live chamber orchestra concerts

Campus Concerts introduces instruments of the orchestra to elementary school students just before they have the opportunity to sign-up for instrumental music classes.

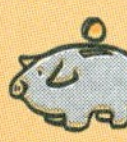

Pre/K-12

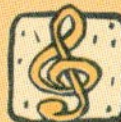

PROGRAMS: **PERFORMANCES, WORKSHOPS**
SCHEDULE: YEAR-ROUND, WEEKDAYS
DETAILS: GRADES PRE/K-12, VISUAL & PERFORMING ARTS
CREATIVE EXPRESSION
TRAVEL TO SCHOOLS, INDIVIDUALLY TAILORED PROGRAMS
EDUCATIONAL MATERIALS AVAILABLE
COST FOR SOME PROGRAMS

Families

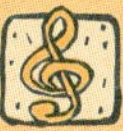

PROGRAMS: **PERFORMANCES, WORKSHOPS**
SCHEDULE: YEAR-ROUND, WEEKENDS
DETAILS: COST FOR SOME PROGRAMS

CANADA GOOSE PROJECT, INC.

11576 Morrison Street
Valley Village, CA 91601
Ph: 818-769-1521
Fax: 818-760-0580

501(c)3

SFV

Rosemarie White — President
Victoria Branch — Artistic Director/Executive Secretary/ 818-789-5679
Arthur Langton — Educational Director/Treasurer/ 818-887-0973
Jonathan Bar-or — Education for Youth/Vice-President/ 310-471-9964

Located in the San Fernando Valley, the Canada Goose Project is an environmental (non-profit) organization dedicated to preserving species and habitat while educating young people about our natural world through art and creativity in nature's classroom.

- volunteer opportunities in nature preserves and wildlife areas observing, drawing, and photographing wildlife and plants
- annual poster contest depicting Chatsworth Nature Preserve, Encino Reservoir, and Sepulveda Wildlife Area
- presentations with slides and art to community organizations
- participation in annual fundraiser
- internships to learn grantwriting and video production

CANADA GOOSE PROJECT, INC. (CONTINUED)

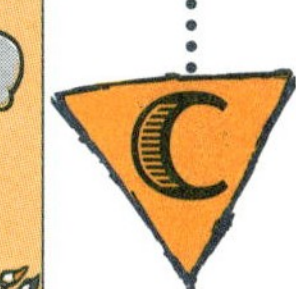

Every year, from October through March, the Canada Goose Project counts migratory geese arriving from Canada. This presents artistic opportunites for artists and photographers as well as writers and presenters/ educators on the natural environment.

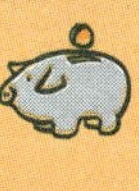

Pre/K-12

PROGRAMS: **PERFORMANCES, WORKSHOPS, SELF-GUIDED TOURS, GUIDED TOURS**
SCHEDULE: FALL, WINTER, EVENINGS, WEEKENDS
DETAILS: PRE/K-12, MATH/SCIENCES, VISUAL & PERFORMING ARTS
AESTHETIC VALUING, CREATIVE EXPRESSION,
HISTORICAL/CULTURAL CONTEXT
CONNECTIONS/RELATIONS/APPLICATIONS
TRAVEL TO SCHOOLS, INDIVIDUALLY TAILORED PROGRAMS
EDUCATIONAL MATERIALS AVAILABLE

Youth

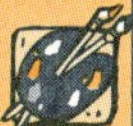

PROGRAMS: **PERFORMANCES, WORKSHOPS, SELF-GUIDED TOURS GUIDED TOURS**
SCHEDULE: FALL, WINTER, EVENINGS, WEEKENDS

Families

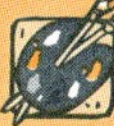

PROGRAMS: **PERFORMANCES, WORKSHOPS, SELF-GUIDED TOURS, GUIDED TOURS**
SCHEDULE: FALL, WINTER, EVENINGS, WEEKENDS

CARECEN - CENTRAL AMERICAN RESOURCE CENTER

2845 W. Seventh Street
Los Angeles, CA 90005
Ph: 213-385-7800
Fax: 213-385-1094

501(c)3

DSC

Angela Sambrano — Executive Director/ x154
Leda Ramos — Director, Education Department/ x137

Located in Pico-Union, CARECEN is a non-profit community center with three main areas of programming– immigrant legal services, youth and family art education, and civic and cultural participation. The Education Department focuses on art education workshops for youth and families.

- artist led workshops by contemporary Los Angeles artists
- visual art/architecture community design workshops
- visual art and poetry workshops
- youth theater
- scultpture, painting and video technology workshops
- youth leadership internships
- family involvement art workshops

CARECEN - CENTRAL AMERICAN RESOURCE CENTER (CONTINUED)

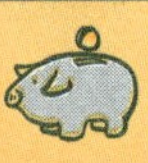

CARECEN's arts and education programs for Central American youth and families focuses on creating visual, technology and language literacy through artist led workshops. CARECEN's visiting Artist/Architecture program engages Los Angeles-based artists/architects to develop curriculum based-arts education in collaboration with the Education Department.

Pre/K-12

 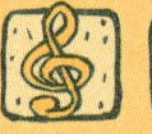 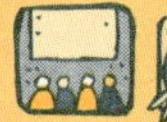

PROGRAMS: Performances, Workshops, Studio classes Residencies

SCHEDULE: Year-round, Weekdays

DETAILS: Grades 5-12, Visual & performing arts
Language arts, Multicultural, Creative Expression
Historical/Cultural Context, architecture/ technology arts
cost for some programs, Programs on-site
Educational materials, Bilingual: Spanish

Youth

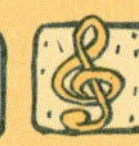 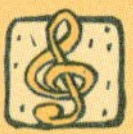

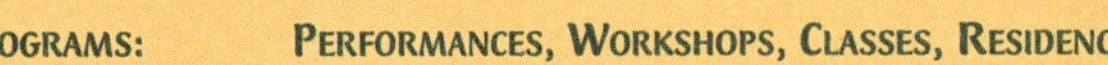

PROGRAMS: Performances, Workshops, Classes, Residencies

SCHEDULE: Year-round, weekdays

Families

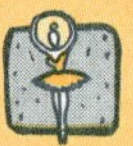 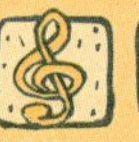 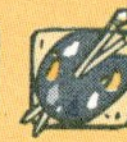

PROGRAMS: Performances, Workshops, Classes, Residencies

SCHEDULE: Year-round, Weekdays, Evenings

CARING STROKES

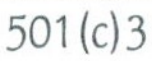

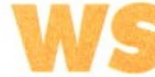

8306 Wilshire Boulevard, #441 501 (c) 3 WS
Beverly Hills, CA 90210
Ph: 800-735-4901
Admin: 323-931-5703
Fax: 213-931-5214

Elizabeth Gorcey
Linda Block
Michele Cait Art Therapist

Caring Strokes holds art workshops in various clinic settings in the Los Angeles area for at-risk and under-privileged youth.

- weekly art workshops
- yearly exhibitions of participants' art works
- workshop focused on the needy and terminally ill

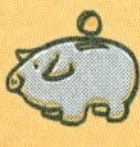

We stress group work to help participants gain self- esteem and knowledge about themselves and the world. Participants work on greeting cards to help raise money for the program.

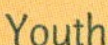

Youth

PROGRAMS: Workshops

SCHEDULE: Year-round, weekdays

CARLA LUNA FLAMENCO ENSEMBLE

P.O. Box 480697 501 (c) 3 HSM
Los Angeles, CA 90048
Ph/Fax: 323-938-4487
www.carlaluna.com

Carla Luna Artistic Director flamenco@carlaluna.com

The Carla Luna Flamenco Dance Ensemble is a professional Flamenco dance and music ensemble composed of 4 to 15 dancers and musicians performing traditional and contemporary Flamenco, as well as Spanish Classical dance and other Folk forms of Provincial Spain.

- lecture demonstrations to colleges and universities
- flexible program to accomodate various performance needs

CAROLE AND BARRY KAYE MUSEUM OF MINIATURES, THE

5900 Wilshire Boulevard HSM
Los Angeles, CA 90036
Ph: 323-937-6464
Admin: 323-937-7766
Fax: 323-937-2123
www.museumof miniatures.com

Enrique Dehesa Director of Sales/ x18
Liliann Hamilton Art Director/x20
Carole Kaye Curator/Owner/x13
Barry Kaye Curator/Owner/x13

Located on Museum Row in the Miracle Mile District, the Carole and Barry Kaye Museum of Miniatures represents works of over 750 contemporary miniature artisans.

- over 350 miniature exhibits

CAROLYN KRUEGER'S GULISTAN DANCE THEATER

1311 N. Brand Boulevard, #7 SFV
Glendale, CA 91202
Ph: 818-244-9398

Carolyn Krueger Artistic Director

Gulistan Dance Theater presents and preserves diverse and historic women's dance traditions of former Soviet Central Asia and the Middle East.

- performances include full-length concerts, concert guesting,festivals, special events and parties
- workshops
- master classes
- private classes
- residencies
- choreography/staging
- lecture-demonstrations
- consulting
- host and promote foreign artists
- research and documentation

CAROLYN KRUEGER'S GULISTAN DANCE THEATER (CONTINUED)

Young audiences travel from Samarkand to Cairo in Gulistan's popular program, "Silk and Sand". This interactive presentation features specialists in the dance and music of the Silk Route and beyond, authentic costumes and audience participation.

Pre/K-12

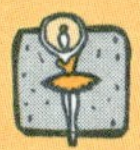
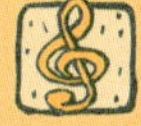

PROGRAMS:	**PERFORMANCES, WORKSHOPS, STUDIO CLASSES, RESIDENCIES**
SCHEDULE:	YEAR-ROUND, WEEKDAYS, EVENINGS, WEEKENDS GRADES PRE/K-12, HISTORY/SOC. SCIENCES VISUAL & PERFORMING ARTS, MULTICULTURAL AESTHETIC VALUING, HISTORICAL/CULTURAL CONTEXT TRAVEL TO SCHOOLS , INDIVIDUALLY TAILORED PROGRAMS EDUCATIONAL MATERIALS AVAILABLE

Youth

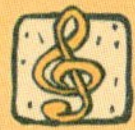

PROGRAMS:	**PERFORMANCES, WORKSHOPS, CLASSES, RESIDENCIES**
SCHEDULES:	YEAR-ROUND, WEEKDAYS, EVENINGS, WEEKENDS

Families

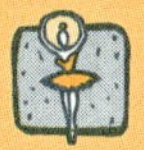
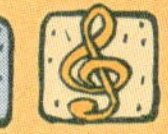

PROGRAMS:	**PERFORMANCES, WORKSHOPS, CLASSES, RESIDENCIES**
SCHEDULE:	YEAR-ROUND, WEEKDAYS, EVENINGS, WEEKENDS

CARPENTER PERFORMING ARTS CENTER

6200 Atherton Street
Long Beach, CA 90815
Ph: 562-985-7098
Admin: 562-985-2488

501 (c) 3 **LB**

Randall Voit	Director of Marketing /562-985-7098
Peter Lesnik	Executive Director/562-985-2488

Conveniently located on the California State University Long Beach campus, The Richard and Karen Carpenter Performing Arts Center is one the Southland's best new theaters for quality entertainment.

- world famous acts
- widescreen film festival

CARPENTER PERFORMING ARTS CENTER (CONTINUED)

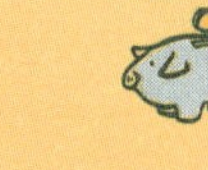

Pre/K-12

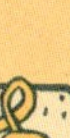
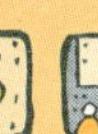
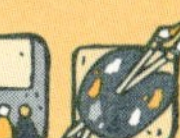

PROGRAMS:	**PERFORMANCES, WORKSHOPS, RESIDENCIES, GUIDED TOURS**
SCHEDULE:	YEAR-ROUND, WEEKDAYS, EVENINGS, WEEKENDS
DETAILS:	GRADES 3-12, VISUAL & PERFORMING ARTS CREATIVE EXPRESSION, CONNECTIONS/RELATIONS/APPLICATIONS PROGRAMS ON-SITE, COST FOR SOME PROGRAMS

Families

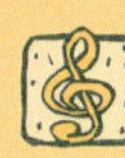
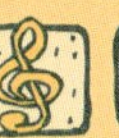
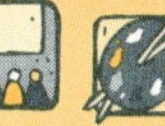

PROGRAMS:	**PERFORMANCES, WORKSHOPS, RESIDENCIES, GUIDED TOURS**
SCHEDULE:	YEAR-ROUND, WEEKDAYS, EVENINGS, WEEKENDS
DETAILS:	COST FOR SOME PROGRAMS

CARSON COMMUNITY SYMPHONY ASSOCIATION

P.O. Box 5425
Carson, CA 90749
Ph: 310-835-0212

501 (c) 3 **SB**

Frances Steiner	Artistic Director/310-833-3442
Alyce Bledsoe	Executive Director/310-675-6178
Gloria Hughes	Clerical Assistant /310-638-4777

Carson Community Symphony Association is a non-profit organization, composed of community musicians and California State Dominguez Hills musicians, which presents free concerts for youth and families in the South Bay area.

Pre/K-12

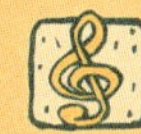

PROGRAMS:	**PERFORMANCES**
SCHEDULE:	SPRING, WEEKDAYS
DETAILS:	GRADES 3-6, VISUAL & PERFORMING ARTS

Families

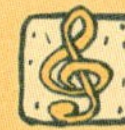

PROGRAM:	**PERFORMANCES**
SCHEDULE:	YEAR-ROUND, EVENINGS

CATALINA ISLAND MUSEUM

Casino Building, #1 Casino Way 501 (c)3 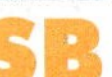
Avalon, CA 90704
Ph: 310-510-2414
Fax: 310-510-2780
www.catalina.com/museum

Stacey Otte Director museum@catalinas.net

Located in the historic Casino Building on beautiful Catalina Island, our museum explores Catalina's 7,000 years of history through exhibits and educational programs for children and adults.

- permanent and rotating exhibits
- gift shop with books, music, t-shirts, notecards
- monthly evening groups (2nd Thursday, 7-9 pm)
- historic house tours (June-October)
- Silent Film Benefit (late May or early June)
- wide variety of volunteer opportunities (including children)
- Holiday Open House at the Inn on Mount. Ada
- free lectures (2-4 times per year)

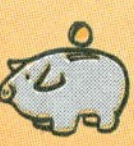

We offer a broad range of educational programming to expose visitors and audiences to Catalina's rich and diverse history: Native Americans, Spanish exploration, mining and ranching, Hollywood celebrities and moviemaking, sportfishing, tourism and big bands.

Pre/K-12

PROGRAMS:	**GUIDED TOURS, LOCAL HISTORY BASED ACTIVITES**
SCHEDULE:	YEAR-ROUND, WEEKDAYS, WEEKENDS
DETAILS:	GRADES 3--6, HISTORY/SOC. SCIENCES TRAVEL TO SCHOOLS, PROGRAMS ON-SITE INDIVIDUALLY TAILORED PROGRAMS

Youth

PROGAMS:	**WORKSHOPS, GUIDED TOURS**
SCHEDULE:	YEAR-ROUND, WEEKDAYS, WEEKENDS

Families

PROGRAMS:	**WORKSHOPS, SELF-GUIDED TOURS, GUIDED TOURS**
SCHEDULE:	YEAR-ROUND, WEEKDAYS, WEEKENDS

CATALINA ISLAND PERFORMING ARTS FOUNDATION

601 Crescent Avenue 501 (c)3 SB
Avalon, CA 90704
Ph: 310-510-7469
Fax: 310-510-2272

David Markowitz Executive Director dmarko@lamg

The Catalina Island Performing Arts Foundation presents educational programs in the performing arts to youth and adults on Catalina Island and operates community radio station KISL.

- Catalina summer arts camps
- community arts residencies
- concerts
- volunteer opportunities
- radio programming

CATHARTIC ARTS CENTER

P.O. Box 64 PO
Pomona, CA 91769-0064
Ph: 909-981-7501

Jeff Colin

CELEBRATION THEATRE

7051 B Santa Monica Boulevard 501 (c)3 HSM
Los Angeles, CA 90038
Ph: 323-957-1884
Fax: 310-271-8870
celetheat@aol.com

Celebration Theatre is the only theater in Los Angeles dedicated to solely producing plays by and for the gay and lesbian communities.

- live plays

CELTIC REGIONAL ARTS INSTITUTE OF CALIFORNIA

P.O. Box 3150 501 (c)3 SB
Rolling Hills, CA 90274
Ph: 310-726-3974
Admin: 310-543-1219
Fax: 310-543-1588
www.craicnet.org

Richard Gee Secretary 104210.3204@compuserve.com
Cait Reed Chairperson

CRAIC integrates the various Celtic folklore traditions, music, languages and dances, offering a community experience through potlucks, language intensives, music and dance sessions. CRAIC offers resources for Celtic Arts in Southern California, including our newsletter and web page.

- eight gatherings (Cruinnithe) per year
- workshops in Celtic music, languages and dance
- traditional music sessions--both intermediate and advanced
- access to concert and events information
- internet website
- festivals and celebrations
- membership and volunteer opportunities

CELTIC REGIONAL ARTS INSTITUTE OF CALIFORNIA (CONTINUED)

Families

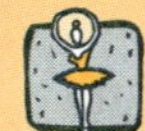 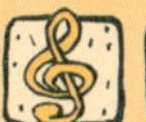 

PROGRAMS: **PERFORMANCES, WORKSHOPS**
SCHEDULE: YEAR-ROUND, WEEKENDS

CENTER FOR JEWISH CULTURE AND CREATIVITY

6399 Wilshire Boulevard, Suite 218 — 501 (c) 3 **WS**
Los Angeles, CA 90048
Ph: 323-658-5824
Fax: 323-658-5826

Ruth Rauch — Executive Vice-President

The Center stimulates the creation of new works in various disciplines and presents new works in a variety of venues.

- fine art and photographic exhibits
- film screenings
- musical performances
- theater performances and readings
- literary evenings
- poetry readings
- lectures
- workshops

Professional artists interact with students in exploring and executing the creative process. Learning and guidance are accompanied by nurturing and individual attention.

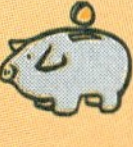

Pre/K-12

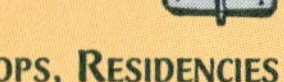

PROGRAMS: **WORKSHOPS, RESIDENCIES**
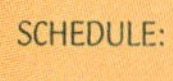
SCHEDULE: SPRING, FALL, WINTER, WEEKDAYS
DETAILS: GRADES 9-12, PHOTOGRAPHY, FILM
VISUAL & PERFORMING ARTS, CREATIVE EXPRESSION
HISTORICAL/CULTURAL CONTEXT
TRAVEL TO SCHOOLS, INDIVIDUALLY TAILORED PROGRAMS
EDUCATIONAL MATERIALS, BILINGUAL: SPANISH

CENTER FOR THE ARTS OF THE AFRICAN DIASPORA (CAAD)

P.O. Box 45543 — 501 (C) 3

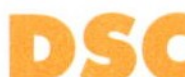

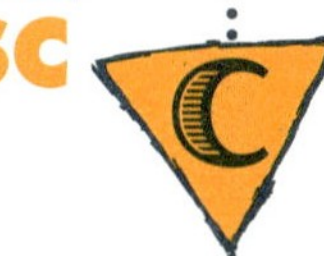

Los Angeles, CA 90045-0543
Ph: 323-532-6974

Toni Johnson — President

CAAD strives to educate the global community on the influence of artists of African decent by supporting, promoting, developing and documenting the arts.

- host annual educational seminar on specific African Diaspora art with exhibition curated in collaboration with art historian, artist or researcher
- curate fine arts exhibitions with nationally and internationally known artists and emerging artists
- conduct/host hands-on workshops (quilt making, mask making, etc.)
- conduct seminars/lectures, workshops, classes with art historians, educators, curators and artists

CENTER FOR THE STUDY OF POLITICAL GRAPHICS

8124 W.Third Street, #24 — 501 (c) 3

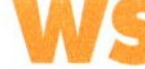

Los Angeles, CA 90048
Ph: 323-653-4662
Fax: 323-653-6991

Liz Fischbach — Administrative Director
Carol Wells — Executive Director

Center for the Study of Political Graphics is a non-profit, tax-exempt educational archive that collects, preserves, documents and exhibits domestic and international posters relating to historical and contemporary movements for peace and social justice.

- traveling exhibitions
- lectures, slide presentations, workshops and panel discussions
- volunteer opportunities
- docent tours
- poster rental
- consultant and research services for artists, scholars, curators, students, filmmakers and playwrights
- customized exhibitions
- annual poster auction
- merchandise for sale includes catalogues, t-shirts, posters and mugs

CENTER FOR THE STUDY OF POLITICAL GRAPHICS (CONTINUED)

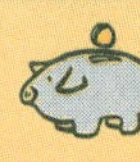

The Center for the Study of Political Graphics produces multicultural poster art exhibitions depicting historical and contemporary events. Docent led tours broaden students' outlook, help them to understand political issues, and reflect on their own responsibilities to society.

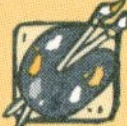

Pre/K-12

PROGRAMS: **GUIDED TOURS, POLITICAL POSTER ART**
SCHEDULE: YEAR-ROUND, WEEKDAYS, EVENINGS, WEEKENDS
DETAILS: GRADES 7-12, HISTORY/SOC. SCIENCES, MULTICULTURAL
HISTORICAL/CULTURAL CONTEXT
TRAVEL TO SCHOOLS

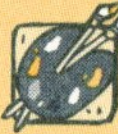

Youth

PROGRAMS: **GUIDED TOURS**
SCHEDULE: YEAR-ROUND, WEEKDAYS, EVENINGS, WEEKENDS

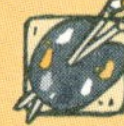

Families

PROGRAMS: **GUIDED TOURS**
SCHEDULE: YEAR-ROUND, WEEKDAYS, EVENINGS, WEEKENDS

CENTRAL NORTH REGIONAL ARTS COUNCIL

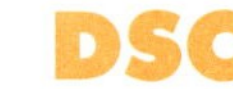

3870 Crenshaw Boulevard, #766
Los Angeles, CA 90008
Ph: 310-854-8909

Developed through the City of Los Angeles Cultural Affairs Department as one of 9 regional arts councils, we are a coalition of arts and community organizations, artists, leaders, business people and all other interested members of the community who have the purpose of assessing, coalescing and acting on the cultural assets and needs of the area. This council serves West Adams-Baldwin Hills, Leimert Park, South Central Los Angeles and Southeast Los Angeles. Goals include:

- develop affordable and accessible local programming that highlights and involves youth and local artists
- develop activities that celebrate the city's cultural diversity and promote community building
- serve as an advisory group to the Cultural Affairs Department on local art and cultural priorities
- strengthen the artistic advancement of the community

CENTRAL SOUTH REGIONAL ARTS COUNCIL

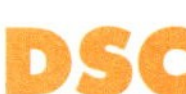

c/o OASIS
Baldwin Hills Crenshaw Plaza
4005 Crenshaw Boulevard
Los Angeles, CA 90008
Ph: 323-291-3414

Developed through the City of Los Angeles Cultural Affairs Department as one of 9 regional arts councils, we are a coalition of arts and community organizations, artists, leaders, business people and all other interested members of the community who have the purpose of assessing, coalescing and acting on the cultural assets and needs of the area. This council serves South Central and Southeast Los Angeles, Westchester and Playa del Rey. Goals include:

- develop affordable and accessible local programming that highlights and involves youth and local artists
- develop activities that celebrate the city's cultural diversity and promote community building
- serve as an advisory group to the Cultural Affairs Department on local art and cultural priorities
- strengthen the artistic advancement of the community

CERRITOS CENTER FOR THE PERFORMING ARTS

12700 Center Court Drive 501(c)3 LB
Cerritos, CA 90703
Ph: 562-916-8500
Admin: 562-916-8510
Educ: 562-916-8542
Fax: 562-916-8514
www.cerritoscenter.com

Wayne Shilkret Executive Director
Stacy Brightman Director of Education and Youth Outreach

The Cerritos Center for the Performing Arts is a presenting organization; we present high quality music, dance and theater events in a comfortable, state-of-the-art moveable theatre.

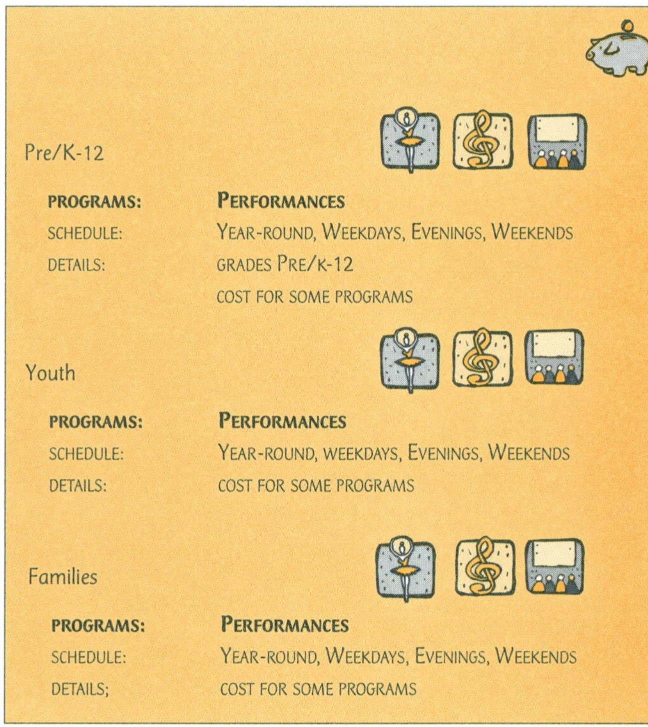

Pre/K-12

PROGRAMS: **PERFORMANCES**
SCHEDULE: YEAR-ROUND, WEEKDAYS, EVENINGS, WEEKENDS
DETAILS: GRADES PRE/K-12
COST FOR SOME PROGRAMS

Youth

PROGRAMS: **PERFORMANCES**
SCHEDULE: YEAR-ROUND, WEEKDAYS, EVENINGS, WEEKENDS
DETAILS: COST FOR SOME PROGRAMS

Families

PROGRAMS: **PERFORMANCES**
SCHEDULE: YEAR-ROUND, WEEKDAYS, EVENINGS, WEEKENDS
DETAILS; COST FOR SOME PROGRAMS

CERRITOS COLLEGE FINE ARTS GALLERY

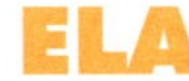

11110 Alondra Boulevard
Norwalk, CA 90650
Ph: 562-860-2451 x2612
Fax: 310-467-5005

Habib Kheradyar — Director
Dan Cautrell — Gallery Coordinator
Geoffrey Allen — Gallery Director

CHAC-MOOL GALLERY

WS

8920 Melrose Avenue
Los Angeles, CA 90069
Ph: 310-550-6792
Fax: 310-550-6872
www.artscenecal.com/ChacMool.html

Esthella Provas — Director — chacmool@earthlink.net

Contemporary fine art, featuring painting and sculptures.

CHAMBER ORCHESTRA OF THE SOUTH BAY

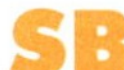

Norris Theatre — 501(c)3
27570 Crossfield Drive
Palos Verdes Peninsula, CA 90274
Ph/Fax: 310-373-3151
www.members.aol.com.RMiller675

Robert Miller — President/310-373-4086
Frances Steiner — Music Director/310-833-3442

The Chamber Orchestra of the South Bay is the only fully professional orchestra serving the South Bay area of Los Angeles, with a full season of concerts. Performances at the Norris Theatre in Palos Verdes, with a repeat performance at El Camino Center for the Arts.

- five-concert season of works for Chamber Orchestra, with national and international - level soloists

CHANNEL ISLANDS NATIONAL PARK

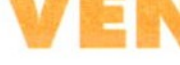

1901 Spinnaker Drive
Ventura, CA 93001
Ph: 805-658-5730
Fax: 805-658-5799

Suzan Brown-Smith — Administrator/ 805-658-5700 — suzan_@nps.gov

CHARLIE COMPANY

WS

1235 Seventeenth Street, Suite E
Santa Monica, CA 90404
Ph: 310-453-4279
Admin: 760-323-4477
Fax: 760-323-3012

Sally Goldin — Business Manager/760-323-4477
Charles Anderson — Artistic Director

Charlie Company was founded to develop a contemporary dance repertoire drawing its technique from classical ballet and motivation from modern dance. The growing repertoire can be performed at a variety of venues and includes works by local choreographers as well as works by Mr. Anderson, the classics, and neo-classics.

- evening performances of solo, duet, trio or full evening work with full cast

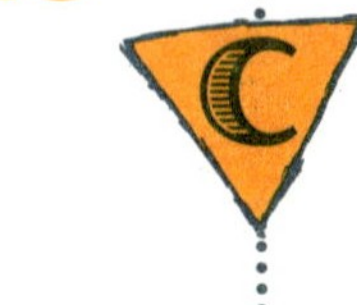

CHICANO RESOURCE CENTER

ELA

4801 E. Third Street
Los Angeles, CA 90022
Ph: 323 263-5807
Admin: 323 264-0155

Brigida Campos — Director

Please see Resource Section for description and programs.

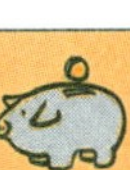

Pre/K-12

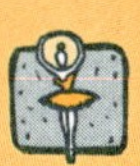

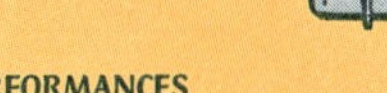

PROGRAMS: **PERFORMANCES**
SCHEDULE: YEAR-ROUND, WEEKDAYS, EVENINGS, WEEKENDS
DETAILS: GRADES PRE/K-12, HISTORICAL/CULTURAL CONTEXT

Youth

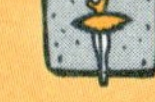

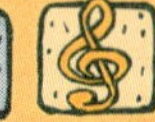

PROGRAMS: **PERFORMANCES**
SCHEDULE: YEAR-ROUND, WEEKDAYS, EVENINGS, WEEKENDS

Families

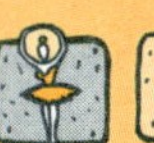

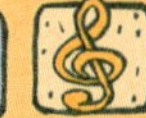

PROGRAMS: **PERFORMANCES**
SCHEDULE: YEAR-ROUND, WEEKDAYS, EVENINGS, WEEKENDS

CHILDREN OF THE WORLD CHOIR, THE

437 S. Wetherly Drive 501(c)3 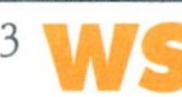
Beverly Hills, CA 90211
Ph: 310-285-9791
Fax: 310-285-9795

Sophie Miller Office Manager
Marrina Waks President/Executive Director

The Children of the World Choir was founded to promote unity and the well-being of humanity through music. The children represent their countries of origin and perform in their international costumes.

- performances at major events, for non-profits, television and film, stage productions, etc.

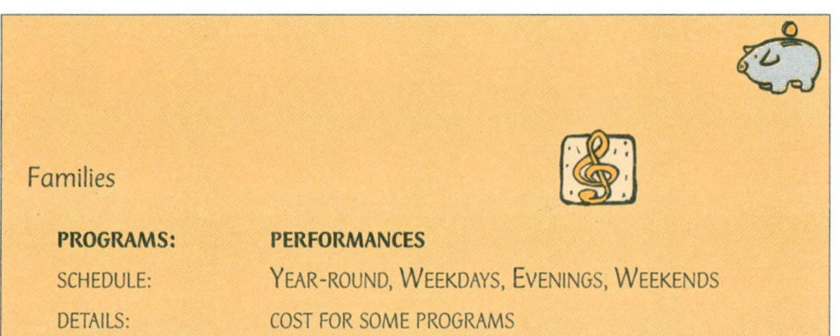

CHINESE CLASSICAL MUSIC ENSEMBLE

1908 Brockwell Ave 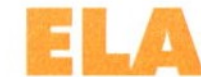
Monterey Park, CA 91754
Ph/Fax: 323-887-0328

Zhiming Han Director han0328@aol.com

The Chinese Classical Music Ensemble, founded by composer Zhiming Han in 1990, performs Chinese instruments (dulcimer, zither, flute, etc) for all occasions. This group has been featured in numerous concerts and movie soundtracks. All members have won national awards and have experience performing internationally. The Ensemble also offers:

- demonstrations on Chinese musical instruments
- concerts at schools, churches, festivals, museums
- quality studio instruction for Yangqin (hammered dulcimer), Zheng (long zither) and Dizi (Chinese bamboo flute)

The Ensemble's demonstration program not only emphasizes live performance and discussion but also audience participation.

Pre/K-12 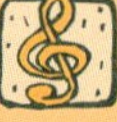

PROGRAMS:	**PERFORMANCES, WORKSHOPS, STUDIO CLASSES**
SCHEDULE:	YEAR-ROUND, WEEKDAYS, EVENINGS, WEEKENDS
DETAILS:	GRADES PRE/K-12, VISUAL & PERFORMING ARTS CREATIVE EXPRESSION TRAVEL TO SCHOOLS, BILINGUAL: CHINESE

Youth 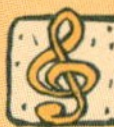

PROGRAMS:	**PERFORMANCES, WORKSHOPS, CLASSES**
SCHEDULE:	YEAR-ROUND, WEEKDAYS, EVENINGS, WEEKENDS

CHOREOGRAPHERS THEATER ENSEMBLE

8665 Burton Way 501(c)3 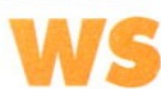
Los Angeles, CA 90048
Ph: 310-248-2687

Elizabeth Ince Executive Director

Choreographers Theater Ensemble employs mature actor/dancers and deals with the issues of the middle-aged and elderly in its dance/theater works.

CHURCH OF SCIENTOLOGY CELEBRITY CENTRE INTERNATIONAL

5930 Franklin Avenue 501(c)3 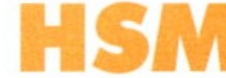
Hollywood, CA 90028
323-960-3100
323-960-3232

Pamela Lancaster-Johnson Artistic and Cultural Affairs Director/x 3170
Susan Watson President
Reinhard Schulte Executive Producer

- career planning
- performance opportunities
- personal counseling
- workshops/seminars/symposia
- rehearsal facilities
- creativity development

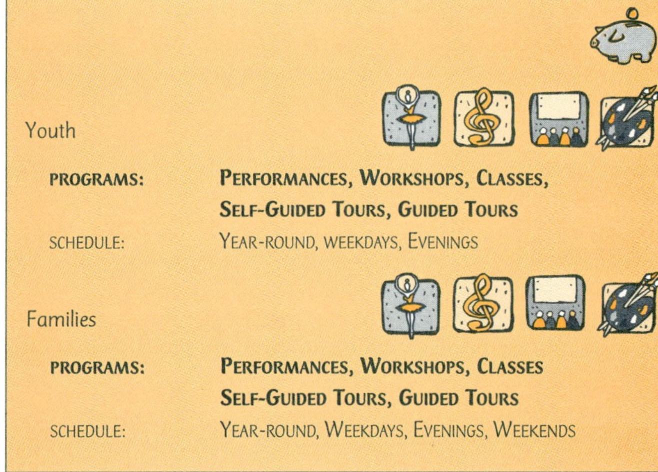

CIRRUS GALLERY

542 S. Alameda Atreet DSC
Los Angeles, CA 90013
Ph: 213-680-3473
Fax: 213-680-0930
CCirrus@aol.com

Contemporary west coast artists and publications from major contemporary artists.

CITY GARAGE

1340 1/2 4th Street (in alley) 501(c)3 **WS**
Santa Monica, CA 90406
Ph: 310-319-9939
Fax: 310-396-1040

Charles Duncomer Managing Director
Frederique Michel Artistic Director

City Garage is a company of fifty actors that focuses on challenging contemporary drama with a particular emphasis on European writing.

- annual season of six to eight productions; new works, modernist classics
- actors workshops and internal training

CITYLIFE

P.O. Box 712574 501(c)3 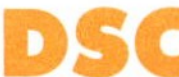
Los Angeles, CA 90071-7574
Ph: 213-687-2267
Fax: 213-687-2191

Jacki Breger Director

CityLife is a program for teenage children of people who live and work Downtown that uses the arts as a tool for the exploration of culture, history and politics in Los Angeles.

CityLife offers unusual, exciting and developmentally appropriate historic and public art tours of Downtown which include well and lesser known landmarks and locations, factual and anecdotal information, public policy and ethnic diversity related issues.

Pre/K-12

PROGRAMS: **GUIDED TOURS, ARCHITECTURE**
SCHEDULE: FALL, WINTER, WEEKDAYS
DETAILS: GRADES 3-12, HISTORY/SOC. SCIENCES,
VISUAL & PERFORMING ARTS, HISTORICAL/CULTURAL CONTEXT
CONNECTIONS/RELATIONS/APPLICATIONS
TRAVEL TO SCHOOLS, INDIVIDUALLY TAILORED PROGRAMS
EDUCATIONAL MATERIALS AVAILABLE

Youth 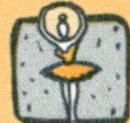 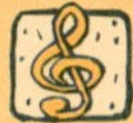 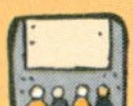 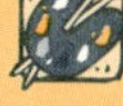

PROGRAMS: **WORKSHOPS, GUIDED TOURS**
SCHEDULE: SUMMER, WEEKDAYS

CITYSCAPE FOTO GALLERY

30 East Colorado Boulevard 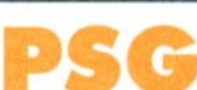
Pasadena, CA 91105
Ph: 626-449-3421
Admin: 626-794-3739
Fax: 626-793-2174

CLICKERS & FLICKERS PHOTO NETWORK

P.O. Box 60508 **PSG**
Pasadena, CA 91116
Ph: 626-794-7447

Dawn Hope Stevens President CandF@juno.com

Clickers & Flickers Photo Network is a group of individuals who range from people with their first 35mm camera to professional photographers. Other members include cinematographers, gallery owners and museum curators. Clickers & Flickers provides an environment in which photography styles, techniques, enjoyment and appreciation can be experienced with people from many fields and levels of expertise.

- bi-monthly newsletter listing events of photographic interest (call for a complimentary issue)
- monthly photo dinners with interesting guest photographers
- public access television shows introducing local photographers
- photography field trips and workshops

COFFEE JUNCTION

19221 Ventura Boulevard **SFV**
Tarzana, CA 91356
Ph: 818-342-3405

Sharon Benson Owner/Partner biheart@artnet.net
Linda Sherlin Owner/Partner

Located in Tarzana, Coffee Junction gives the community a place to meet, hear good music presented in a great environment by local artists, and buy unique handmade wearable art, gifts, gourmet coffees and teas.

- live entertainment Thursdays, Fridays, and Saturdays
- Open Mike on Sundays
- handmade pottery
- handpainted and original greeting cards
- candles, incense, soaps (handmade and organic)
- lots of gourmet coffees (organic and non), teas, and gifts
- custom baskets, gift packs

COLBURN SCHOOL OF PERFORMING ARTS, THE

200 S. Grand Avenue 501(c)3 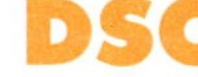
Los Angeles, CA 90012
Ph: 213-621-2200
Fax: 213-621-2110

Wendy Pan-Balderas Registrar
Joseph Thayer Dean
Toby Mayman Executive Director

In its new home a block from the Los Angeles Music Center, the Colburn School of Performing Arts offers early childhood instruction in music, dance, and drama.

- regular instructional offerings in music, dance and drama for pre-college and adult students
- concerts on a regular basis (most are free and open to the public)

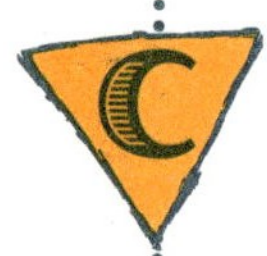

COLBURN SCHOOL OF PERFORMING ARTS, THE (CONTINUED)

Offering the finest training in music, dance and drama, the school's primary focus is pre-college aged students; however adults are welcome as well. Visit our new facility next to MOCA; one block from the Los Angeles Music Center.

Youth 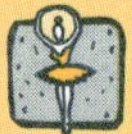 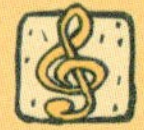 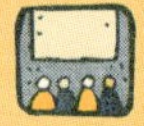

PROGRAMS:	**PERFORMANCES**
SCHEDULE:	YEAR-ROUND, WEEKDAYS, EVENINGS, WEEKENDS

COLEMAN CHAMBER MUSIC ASSOCIATION

202 S. Lake Avenue, Suite 201 501(c)3 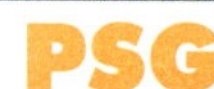
Pasadena, CA 91101
Ph: 626-793-4191
Fax: 626-787-1293
krfccma@aol.com

Founded in 1904 by Alice Coleman, the Association's activities have grown.

- annual series of chamber music concerts in Caltech's Beckman Auditorium
- nationally recognized annual competition for young chamber musicians
- 60 demonstrations and performances each year for children grades K-6 in San Gabriel Valley public schools

Pre/K-12 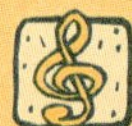

PROGRAMS:	**PERFORMANCES**
SCHEDULE:	YEAR-ROUND
DETAILS:	PRE/K-6, VISUAL & PERFORMING ARTS
	AESTHETIC VALUING
	TRAVEL TO SCHOOLS

COLLAGE DANCE THEATRE

2934 1/2 Beverly Glen Circle, #25 501(c)3 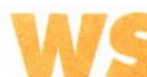
Los Angeles, CA 90077
Ph: 818-784-8669
Fax: 818-981-4116

Kristine Davey Administrator duckler@earthlink.net
Heidi Duckler Artistic Director

Collage Dance Theatre is a collaborative, multimedia, contemporary dance company that creates site-specific works in public spaces such as laundromats, libraries, locker rooms and swimming pools.

- site-specific performances
- residencies
- volunteer opportunities

COLLAGE DANCE THEATRE (CONTINUED)

Collage Dance Theatre creates residencies and workshops specifically designed for the constituency we are serving, and the space in which it resides. 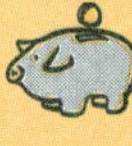

Pre/K-12 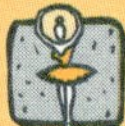

PROGRAMS:	**RESIDENCIES**
DETAILS:	GRADES 9-12, VISUAL & PERFORMING ARTS
	CREATIVE EXPRESSION, CONNECTIONS/RELATIONS/APPLICATIONS
	TRAVEL TO SCHOOLS, INDIVIDUALLY TAILORED PROGRAMS
	BILINGUAL: SPANISH

Youth 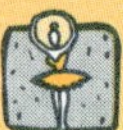

PROGRAMS:	**RESIDENCIES**

COLLAGE ENSEMBLE, INC.

1151 Fifth Avenue 501(c)3 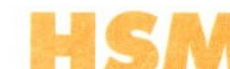
Los Angeles, CA 90019-3439
Ph: 323-766-8780
Fax: 323-766-8472

Brandy Healy Managing Director collage@deltanet.com
Alan Nakagawa Director

Collage Ensemble, Inc. is an inter-disciplinary, inter-ethnic arts collective that creates multi-media installations and performances about the urban experience.

- regional, national, and international installations and performances
- programs coming in 1999 include the Produce Art Center. PAC will be a cultural center for the 7th and Union community. A synthesis between art, education, history, and other cultural denominators will be produced to celebrate and document the rich history the community has to offer.

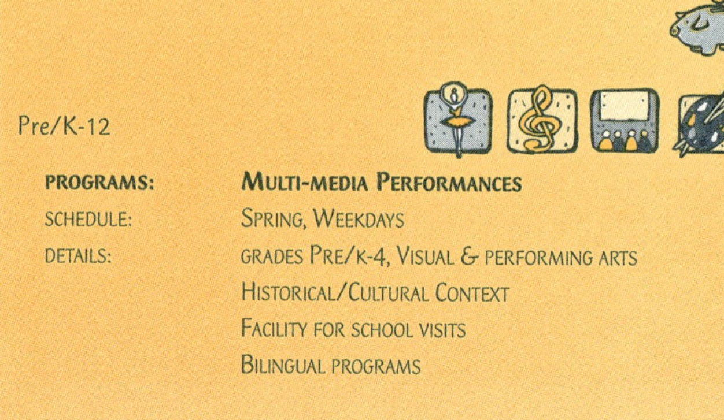

Pre/K-12

PROGRAMS:	**MULTI-MEDIA PERFORMANCES**
SCHEDULE:	SPRING, WEEKDAYS
DETAILS:	GRADES PRE/K-4, VISUAL & PERFORMING ARTS
	HISTORICAL/CULTURAL CONTEXT
	FACILITY FOR SCHOOL VISITS
	BILINGUAL PROGRAMS

COMMUNITY ARTS PARTNERSHIP CALIFORNIA INSTITUTE OF THE ARTS

24700 McBean Parkway 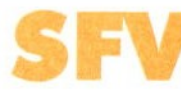
Valencia, CA 91355-2397
Ph: 805-222-2708
Fax: 805-222-2726

Glenna Avila Director

COMMUNITY ARTS RESOURCES, INC. (CARS)

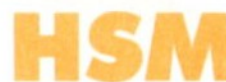

1724 N. Whitley Avenue
Hollywood, CA 90028
Ph: 323-962-1976
Fax: 323-962-6710

Lucy Lin	Operations Manager	carsemail@aol.com
Aaron Paley	President/Executive Director	
Katie Bergin	Executive Director	
Laurel Kishi	Producer	

Community Arts Resources (CARS) produces festivals and consults in Southern California and across the country on a wide range of arts related projects. CARS also acts as a networker and resources for the Los Angeles area, providing a state-of-the-art database of 57,000+ artists, arts organizations, venues and audiences.

- family festivals and programming around Southern California
- mailing lists/labels
- two publications: "Doing it Right In LA" and "Southern California Performing Arts Venues"

Community Arts Resources (CARS) provides tailored workshops at family festivals, a residency program with performing and visual artists at K-12 schools as part of its community outreach programs. CARS also organizes art bus tours for youth, college undergraduates and professionals.

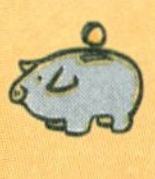

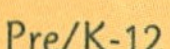

Pre/K-12

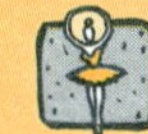 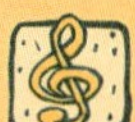 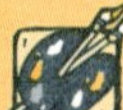

PROGRAMS: RESIDENCIES
SCHEDULE: YEAR-ROUND, WEEKDAYS, WEEKENDS
DETAILS: GRADES 3-12, VISUAL & PERFORMING ARTS
MULTICULTURAL, CREATIVE EXPRESSION
HISTORICAL/CULTURAL CONTEXT
TRAVEL TO SCHOOLS

Families

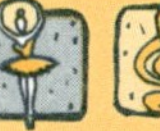 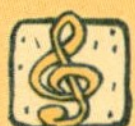 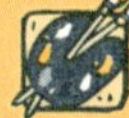

PROGRAMS: PERFORMANCES, WORKSHOPS
SCHEDULE: YEAR-ROUND, WEEKDAYS, WEEKENDS

CONCERNED ARTIST ACTION GROUP

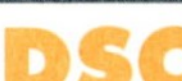

P.O. Box 72341 501(c)3
Watts, CA 90002
Ph: 323-971-5672

Anthony Hamilton	Chairman
Odie Hawkins	Artistic Director
Shirley Hamilton	
Roy Lene Waker	Secretary

- art exhibits by local artists
- poetry by local artists
- dance by local artists
- workshops by local artists
- drumming by local artists

CONCERNED ARTIST ACTION GROUP (CONTINUED)

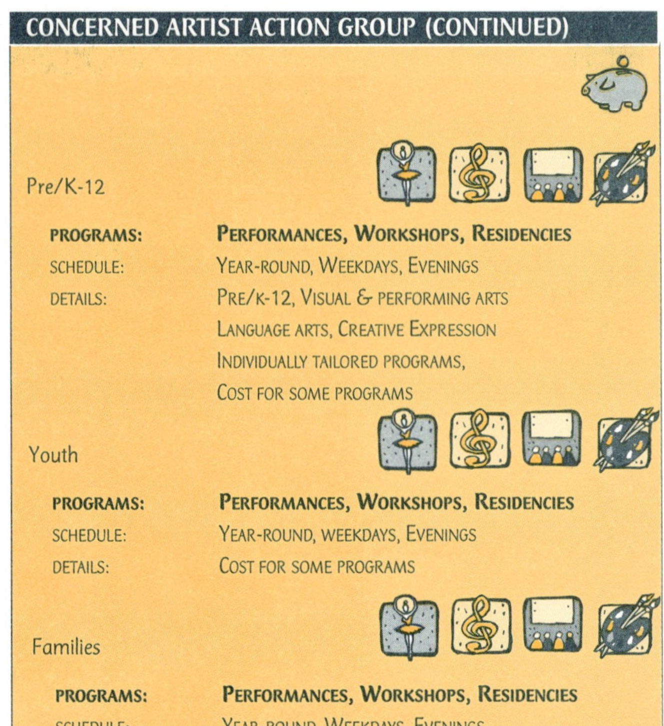

Pre/K-12

PROGRAMS: PERFORMANCES, WORKSHOPS, RESIDENCIES
SCHEDULE: YEAR-ROUND, WEEKDAYS, EVENINGS
DETAILS: PRE/K-12, VISUAL & PERFORMING ARTS
LANGUAGE ARTS, CREATIVE EXPRESSION
INDIVIDUALLY TAILORED PROGRAMS,
COST FOR SOME PROGRAMS

Youth

PROGRAMS: PERFORMANCES, WORKSHOPS, RESIDENCIES
SCHEDULE: YEAR-ROUND, WEEKDAYS, EVENINGS
DETAILS: COST FOR SOME PROGRAMS

Families

PROGRAMS: PERFORMANCES, WORKSHOPS, RESIDENCIES
SCHEDULE: YEAR-ROUND, WEEKDAYS, EVENINGS

CONJUNTO JARDÍN

WS

P.O. Box 603
Pacific Palisades, CA 90272
Ph: 310-454-9888
Fax: 310-454-8108

Libby Harding	Musical Director	Trova9888@aol.com

Updating and reinvigorating the lively Jarocho music of Veracruz, Mexico, Conjuncto Jardín delights audiences with traditional music and dance.

- live concerts
- festival performances
- workshops

C

CONJUNTO JARDÍN (CONTINUED)

Conjuncto Jardín introduces and promotes the lively and colorful Jarocho music and dance of Veracruz, Mexico. The specialized regional folk instruments are explained as well as the intricate percussive dance steps. Students may participate!

Pre/K-12 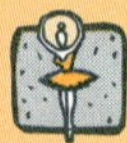 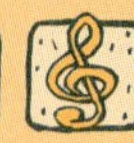

PROGRAMS: **PERFORMANCES, WORKSHOPS**
SCHEDULE: YEAR-ROUND, WEEKDAYS, EVENINGS, WEEKENDS
DETAILS: GRADES PRE/K-12, VISUAL & PERFORMING ARTS
MULTICULTURAL, HISTORICAL/CULTURAL CONTEXT
TRAVEL TO SCHOOLS, INDIVIDUALLY TAILORED PROGRAMS
BILINGUAL: SPANISH

Youth 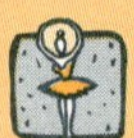 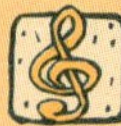

PROGRAMS: **PERFORMANCES, WORKSHOPS**
SCHEDULE: YEAR-ROUND, WEEKDAYS, EVENINGS, WEEKENDS

Families 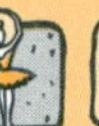 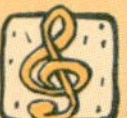

PROGRAMS: **PERFORMANCES, WORKSHOPS**
SCHEDULE: YEAR-ROUND, WEEKDAYS, EVENINGS, WEEKENDS

CORITA ART CENTER, IMMACULATE HEART COMMUNITY

5515 Franklin Avenue 501(c)3 **HSM**
Los Angeles, CA 90028
Ph: 323-466-2157
Fax: 323-466-2150

Peggy Kayser Director ihmla.pacbell.net

The Corita Art Center, part of Immaculate Heart Community, is dedicated to the exhibition, interpretation and care of the works of our country's most celebrated and socially conscious serigraphic artist, Corita.

- gallery (open M-F 1-4 pm and by appointment)
- giftshop
- volunteer opportunties

CORNERSTONE THEATER COMPANY

708 Traction Avenue 501(c)3 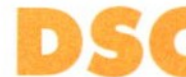
Los Angeles, CA 90013
Ph: 213 613-1700
Fax: 213 613-1714

Daniel Forcey Program Associate
Bill Rauch Artistic Director
Leslie Tamaribuchi Managing Director

Cornerstone Theater Company creates original plays and new adaptions which engage audiences and first-time participants directly in the challenging bridge-building process of crafting innovative inclusive theater.

- live, often site-specific, community-specific, multilingual, performances
- touring presentations
- residencies
- workshops
- technical assistance in fundraising, producing, and volunteer opportunities

CORNERSTONE THEATER COMPANY (CONTINUED)

Cornerstone involves children of all ages in projects onstage and behind the scenes. Our work often includes multiple generations of families working side by side. 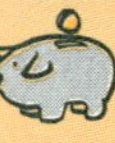

Pre/K-12

PROGRAMS: **PERFORMANCES, RESIDENCIES**
SCHEDULE: YEAR-ROUND, WEEKDAYS, EVENINGS, WEEKENDS
DETAILS: 3-12, VISUAL & PERFORMING ARTS, CREATIVE EXPRESSION
INDIVIDUALLY TAILORED PROGRAMS

Youth

PROGRAMS: **RESIDENCIES**
SCHEDULE: YEAR-ROUND, WEEKDAYS, EVENINGS, WEEKENDS

Families 

PROGRAMS: **PERFORMANCES, RESIDENCIES**
SCHEDULE: YEAR-ROUND, WEEKDAYS, EVENINGS, WEEKENDS

CORONET THEATRE

366 N. La Cienega Boulevard **WS**
Los Angeles, CA 90048
Ph: 310-657-7377
Admin: 310-652-9955
Educ: 310-855-9690
Fax: 310-652-0718

Theodore Rawlins Executive Director amentco@aol.com
Lynne McCreary General Manager
Lani Shipman Director
Kim Gibbs Director

In the last 50 years, the Coronet Theatre has presented over 300 plays and musicals. Featuring such artists as Charles Laughton, Orson Wells, Glenn Close, Charles Chaplin, Woody Harrelson and George C. Scott.

- professional theater productions
- family theater
- rental/rehearsal space
- film/television location
- children's classes
- special events

CORONET THEATRE (CONTINUED)

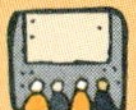

Pre/K-12

PROGRAMS: PERFORMANCES, STUDIO CLASSES
SCHEDULE: YEAR-ROUND, WEEKENDS
DETAILS: GRADES 5-12, VISUAL & PERFORMING ARTS
CREATIVE EXPRESSION
PROGRAMS ON-SITE

Youth

PROGRAMS: PERFORMANCES, CLASSES
SCHEDULE: YEAR-ROUND, WEEKENDS

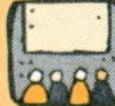

Families

PROGRAMS: PERFORMANCES
SCHEDULE: YEAR-ROUND, WEEKDAYS, EVENINGS, WEEKENDS

CORRIDOR GALLERY OF ART, THE

1024 N. Western Avenue
Los Angeles, CA 90029
Ph: 323-466-7031
www.calendarlive.com/corridor

HSM

Seamus O Dubslaine Owner

COSTA RICAN AMERICAN GROUP (COAG)

1605 W. Olympic Boulevard, Suite 9037 501(c)3
Los Angeles, CA 90015
Ph: 213-918-1114
Admin: 818-342-5721
Fax: 818-342-9007

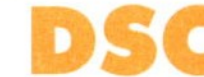

Ruth Garcia President

Located in Los Angeles, COAG is a non-profit organization dedicated to the development of the community in social, cultural and civic areas.

- youth program
- volunteer development
- social events
- individual development
- family development

We train youth to accept their bodies and develop self confidence through beauty pageants.

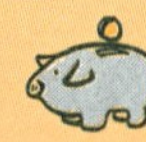

Youth

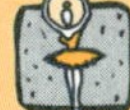 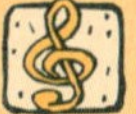 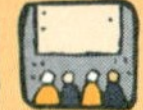

PROGRAMS: PERFORMANCES, CLASSES
SCHEDULE: YEAR-ROUND, EVENINGS, WEEKENDS

COUTURIER GALLERY

166 N. La Brea Avenue
Los Angeles, CA 90036
Ph: 323-933-5557
Fax: 323-933-2357
www.artscenecal.com/Couturier.html

HSM

Darrel Couturier Owner/Director couturier@earthlink.net

Couturier Gallery is a contemporary fine art gallery representing American and Latin American painters, sculptors, photographers and ceramists.

- rotating exhibitions every six weeks
- open and free to the public

COVINA CULTURAL ARTS ADVISORY COMMISSION

150 Hollenbeck Avenue
Covina, CA 91722
Ph: 626-858-7229

PSG

Robert Staples Administrative Assistant
Victoria Stapleton Chair/626-339-9141

The Covina Cultural Arts Advisory Commission is dedicated to nurturing the educational, social and economic growth of the City's cultural environment in which the arts heritage and creativity is supported.

CRAFT AND FOLK ART MUSEUM

5814 Wilshire Boulevard 501(c)3
Los Angeles, CA 90036
Ph: 323-937-4230
Fax: 323-937-5576

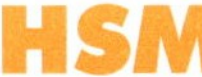

In December 1998, the Folk and Traditional Arts Division of the City of Los Angeles Cultural Affairs Department merged with the Los Angeles Craft and Folk Art Museum. In our newly formed partnership we will continue to exhibit traditional folk art and crafts, as well as continue our regular programs and involvement in the national folk art conferences and publications.

- exhibitions and special events
- biennial national folk arts conference "Living Roots"
- conduct field research, document and publish materials that serve the field
- sponsor regularly scheduled folk & traditional art workshops, craft and traditional design workshops
- museum tours
- award programs for the community and schools
- clearinghouse and database resource for folk & traditional artists, craft & design makers, etc...
- biennial newsletters "Folkways" and "Craft and Design"

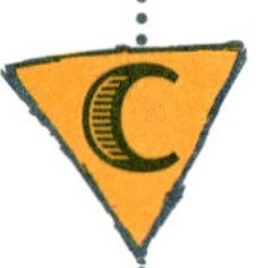

CREATIVE ARTS CENTER

1100 W. Clark Avenue
Burbank, CA 91506
Ph: 818-238-5397
Fax: 818-238-5399
www.flash.net/~faf

SFV

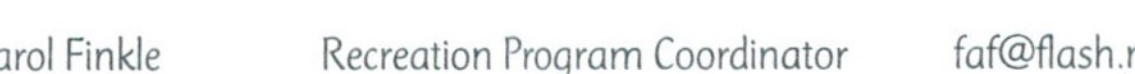

Carol Finkle	Recreation Program Coordinator	faf@flash.net
Claude Hulce	Curator	

The Creative Arts Center is a multidisciplinary municipal gallery and center. In addition to an awe-inspiring gallery, the Center provides over 100 classes weekly in the visual and performing arts.

- monthly exhibitions featuring individuals and groups
- partnerships with schools for education in the arts, Annual Youth Art Expo
- scholarships for young artists and local teachers
- specialty day camps including Art & Music Camp
- bi-annual Arts & Crafts Festival in the park
- oversees performing arts grants for local organizations

We offer low-cost visual and performing arts classes for the entire family. Additionally, we support the schools with scholarships and an exhibition. We monitor a PerformArts Grant program and provide exhibition opportunites for budding artists.

Youth

PROGRAMS: CLASSES
SCHEDULE: YEAR-ROUND, WEEKDAYS, EVENINGS, WEEKENDS

Families

PROGRAMS: CLASSES
SCHEDULE: YEAR-ROUND, WEEKDAYS, EVENINGS, WEEKENDS

CREATIVE PLAYGROUND

619 N. Bronson Avenue
Los Angeles, CA 90004
Ph: 310-636-8089
Fax: 323-464-2554

501(c)3 **HSM**

Elizabeth Tobias	Co-Artistic Director	elizabeth-tobias@tbwachiat.com
Karen Hardcastle	Co-Artistic Director	

CPG is a company of adult, professional artist educators who create and perform affordable, enjoyable, and interactive children's theater. Inspired by the literature and mythology of a diverse and cultural landscape.

- low cost interactive, literature-based performances of 35-45 minute plays
- in residency at the Encino Community Center (or other venues)
- available for in-school visits, arts/family festivals, or private events
- educational workshops in music, writing, creative dramatics

CREATIVE PLAYGROUND (CONTINUED)

The literature-based productions that we develop are performed in-the-round to keep young audience members connected to the piece by proximity, engaging youngsters on a participatory level, and incorporate elements of music and improvisation.

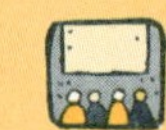

Pre/K-12

PROGRAMS: PERFORMANCES, WORKSHOPS, RESIDENCIES
SCHEDULE: YEAR-ROUND, WEEKDAYS
DETAILS: GRADES PRE/K-4, VISUAL & PERFORMING ARTS
LANGUAGE ARTS, MULTICULTURAL, CREATIVE EXPRESSION
CONNECTIONS/RELATIONS/APPLICATIONS
TRAVEL TO SCHOOLS, FACILITY FOR SCHOOL VISITS
INDIVIDUALLY TAILORED PROGRAMS, EDUCATIONAL MATERIALS
WORK WITH PHYSICALLY CHALLENGED

Youth

PROGRAMS: PERFORMANCES, WORKSHOPS, RESIDENCIES
SCHEDULE: YEAR-ROUND, WEEKENDS
DETAILS: NO COST FOR SOME PROGRAMS

Families

PROGRAMS: PERFORMANCES, WORKSHOPS
SCHEDULE: YEAR-ROUND, WEEKENDS

CROSSROADS SCHOOL FOR ARTS & SCIENCES

1714 21st Street
Santa Monica, CA 90404
Ph: 310-829-7391
Fax: 310-453-7637

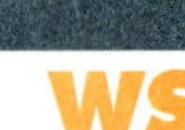

WS

Alva Libuser	Director of Development
Angelica Sotiriou	Creative Director/Arts Outreach Programs
Paul Cummins	President
Pamela Blackwell	Curator

Crossroads School was founded upon five basic commitments: to academic excellence, the arts, the greater community, the development of a student population of social, economic and racial diversity, and to the development of each student's full human potential.

CULVER CITY REDEVELOPMENT AGENCY, CITY OF

4117 Overland Avenue
Culver City, CA 90230
Ph: 310-253-6640
Fax: 310-838-6231

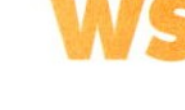

WS

Sid Montz	Supervisor/310-253-6642

Located at the intersection of Venice and Culver Boulevards, the Ivy Substation is a multi-purpose facility. The Substation was built in 1907 as a power switching station for the Pacific Electric Red Car System.

- Summer Sunset Music Festival
- ongoing theatrical performances
- available for public and private events

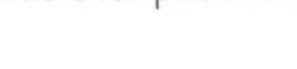

DA CAMERA SOCIETY OF MOUNT ST. MARY'S COLLEGE

12001 Chalon Road 501(c)3 **WS**
Los Angeles, CA 90049
Ph: 310-954-4300
Fax: 310-954-4309
www.msmc.la.edu./dacamera

Eric Eberwein	Marketing/Publications Manager/310-954-4302
Mary Ann Bonino	Founding Director/310-954-4303
Kelly Garrison	General Manager/310-954-4301

The DA Camera Society unites site and sound, producing great music in historic settings across Southern California. Outreach programs are presented in schools, community centers, and juvenile detention facilities.

- six concert series presenting chamber music in historic sites
- children's Concerts in historic sites
- outreach programs
- volunteer opportunities
- newsletter for members
- membership services

Da Camera Society offers interdisciplinary arts eduaction rooted in music which helps kids with aesthetic valuing, critical thinking, math, literacy, and history.

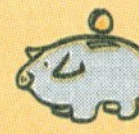

Pre/K-12

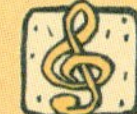

PROGRAMS: **Performances, Workshops, Residencies**
SCHEDULE: Spring, Fall, Winter, Weekdays
DETAILS: Grades Pre/K-12, Visual & performing arts
Aesthetic valuing, Creative Expression
Historical/Cultural Context,
Connections/Relations/Applications
Travel to schools, cost for some programs

Youth

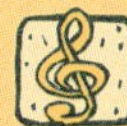

PROGRAMS: **Performances**
SCHEDULE: Spring, Fall, Winter, weekdays
DETAILS: cost for some programs

Families

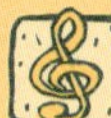

PROGRAMS: **Performances**
SCHEDULE: Spring, Fall, Winter, Weekends
DETAILS: cost for some programs

DA CENTER FOR THE ARTS, THE

252-D S. Main Street 501(c)3 **PO**
Pomona, CA 91766-1630
Ph: 909-397-9716
Fax: 909-629-8697

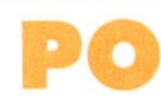

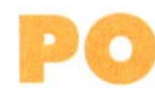

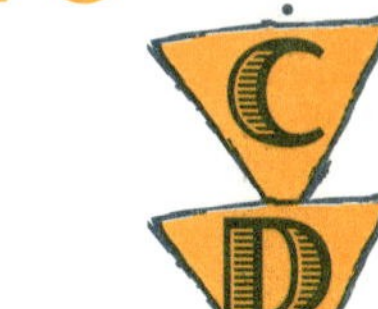

Darlene De Angelo Director

DA Gallery bases its operations on the premise that there is a need and a desire for fine arts that focuses on exhibition and performance. There is a demand and need for a gallery that will show all artists' work, no matter how experimental or conventional.

- visual and performing arts events
- artist's registry
- DA store with artwork
- volunteer opportunities
- Fringe Art Auction
- Fringe of the Fringe Arts Festival
- studio tours
- internship opportunities

DA VINCI ART GALLERY, L.A. CITY COLLEGE

Da Vinci Hall **HSM**
855 N. Vermont Avenue
Los Angeles, CA 90029
Ph: 323-953-4118
Admin: 323-953-4220
Fax: 323-255-9913

John Rand	Gallery Director
Raoul de la Sota	Director

College art gallery serving art school and community.

DAGMAR GALLERY

2525 Michigan Avenue **WS**
G-8 Bergamot Station
Santa Monica, CA 90404
Ph: 310-315-5686
Fax: 310-315-0956
www.onchina.com

Dagmar Tomerlin Director gallery@onchina.com

Representing artists from China and Southeast Asia.

DANCE KALEIDOSCOPE

California State University, Los Angeles — 501(c)3 — **ELA**
Department of Theatre Arts and Dance
5151 State University Drive, K.H. 5104
Los Angeles, CA 90032
Ph: 323-343-MOVE
Admin: 323-343-5124
Fax: 323-343-2670

Donald Hewitt — Executive Director

Dance Kaleidoscope produces an annual festival which presents Southern Californian artists. It also produces an international platform for "Les Grandes Rencontres de Danse" on a bi-annual basis for the West Coast.

- 5 dance performances for general audiences (and families)

Children's performances are narrated. Children are encouraged to participate at intervals.

Pre/K-12

PROGRAMS: PERFORMANCES
SCHEDULE: SUMMER, WEEKENDS
DETAILS: GRADES 5-12, VISUAL & PERFORMING ARTS
CREATIVE EXPRESSION

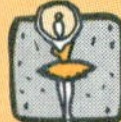

Youth

PROGRAMS: PERFORMANCES
SCHEDULE: WORKSHOPS, SUMMER, WEEKENDS

Families

PROGRAMS: PERFORMANCES
SCHEDULE: SUMMER, WEEKENDS

DANCE SERIES 2000

615 S. Broadway — 501(c)3

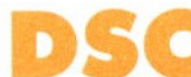

Los Angeles, CA 90014
Ph: 213-629-2939
Fax: 213-629-2999

Nicholas Latimer — General Manager/Executive Director
Marie France Levesque — Creative Director/213-874-1285

Dance Series 2000 is dedicated to the presentation and perpetuation of classical, contemporary, and modern dance performance in Los Angeles.

- seasonal presentations of classical ballet performances by nationally recognized dance companies

Pre/K-12

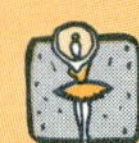 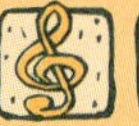 

PROGRAMS: PERFORMANCES
SCHEDULE: SPRING, WINTER, WEEKDAYS, EVENINGS, WEEKENDS
DETAILS: GRADES3-12, HISTORICAL/CULTURAL CONTEXT
FACILITY FOR SCHOOL VISITS

DANIEL SAXON GALLERY

552 Norwich Drive — **WS**
West Hollywood, CA 90048
Ph: 310-657-6033
Fax: 310-657-0273

Daniel Saxon — President

Located in West Hollywood directly opposite the Pacific Design Center, the Daniel Saxon Gallery is the only national gallery devoted exclusively to art by Chicanos.

DANSE CELESTE

844 N. Dillon Street — 501(c)3

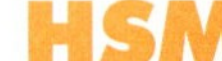

Los Angeles, CA 90026
Ph/Fax: 323-666-3633
www.anaserve.com/~danseceleste

Sophiline Shaprio — Artistic Director — scs@ucla.edu

Danse Celeste is a community-based organization dedicated to the promotion, preservation, and presentation of Cambodian traditional arts.

- master/apprentice workshops
- dance and music concerts
- lecture/demonstrations

We offer individually tailored workshops and lecture/ demonstrations in Cambodian classical dance and music to students of all ages.

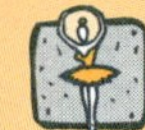

Pre/K-12

PROGRAMS: PERFORMANCES, WORKSHOPS, STUDIO CLASSES
SCHEDULE: YEAR-ROUND, WEEKDAYS, WEEKENDS
DETAILS: GRADES 3-12, VISUAL & PERFORMING ARTS
MULTICULTURAL, AESTHETIC VALUING
CREATIVE EXPRESSION, HISTORICAL/CULTURAL CONTEXT
TRAVEL TO SCHOOLS, INDIVIDUALLY TAILORED PROGRAMS
EDUCATIONAL MATERIALS AVAILABLE, BILINGUAL: KHMER

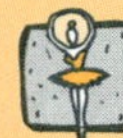

Youth

PROGRAMS: PERFORMANCES, WORKSHOPS, CLASSES
SCHEDULE: YEAR-ROUND, WEEKDAYS, WEEKENDS
DETAILS: NO COST FOR SOME PROGRAMS

DANZA FLORICANTO/USA (AKA FLORICANTO DANCE THEATRE)

4032 S. Overcrest Drive
Whittier, CA 90601-1786
Ph: 562-695-3546

501(c)3 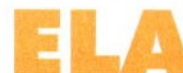

Gema Sandoval — Artistic/Managing Director
Christine Rios — Director School Programs

Danza Floricanto/USA presents the bold, colorful panorama of their Mexican-Chicano heritage through dance. Through research trips and original works, the group, under the direction of Gema Sandoval, has recreated the movement, costume and song of the Mexican and Chicano peoples.

- offers over 150 student assemblies a year thoughout Southern California under the auspices of the Music Center on Tour and the Orange County Performing Arts Center.
- two home-season concerts a year, in the fall at the Luckman Fine Arts Complex and in summer at the John Anson Ford Theater

Floricanto offers a complete cultural experience with food, crafts and dance to children grades K-8, teachers and parents. Lectures/demonstrations are specifically tailored to act as cross-cultural bridges between and among different cultural groups.

Pre/K-12 

PROGRAMS: **Performances, Workshops, Residencies**
SCHEDULE: Year-round, Summer, Fall, Weekdays
DETAILS: Pre/k-8, History/soc. sciences, Visual & performing arts
Multicultural, Historical/Cultural Context
Travel to schools, Educational materials available
Bilingual: Spanish"

Youth 

PROGRAMS: **Performances, Workshops, Residencies**
SCHEDULE: Year-round, Summer, Fall, weekdays

Families 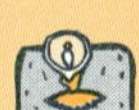

PROGRAMS: **Performances, Workshops, Residencies**
SCHEDULE: Year-round, Summer, Fall, Evenings, Weekends

DAVE WINSTONE MUSIC & ENTERTAINMENT

132 Park View Drive
Oak Park, CA 91301
Ph: 818-889-4158

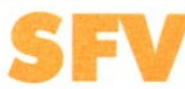

Dave Winstone

From soloists to big bands, Dave Winstone Music and Entertainment entertains Southern California with music from around the world and across the U.S.A.

- live Jazz, Dixieland, Country, Australian folk, Irish and Celtic, Hawaiian Luaus, and Klezmer concerts

DAVE WINSTONE MUSIC & ENTERTAINMENT (CONTINUED)

Alone or with one of my groups, I expose children to LIVE music, introducing, performing and discussing a variety of instruments from around the world and across the U.S.A.

Pre/K-12 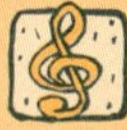

PROGRAMS: **Performances, Workshops**
SCHEDULE: Year-round, Weekdays, Evenings, Weekends
DETAILS: Pre/k-12, Visual & performing arts
Creative Expression, Travel to schools

Youth 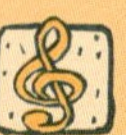

PROGRAMS: **Performances**
SCHEDULE: Year-round, weekdays, Evenings, Weekends

Families 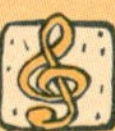

PROGRAMS: **Performances**
SCHEDULE: Year-round, Weekdays, Evenings, Weekends

DAVID ADEN GALLERY

350 Sunset Avenue, Studio 4
Venice, CA 90291
Ph: 310-396-2949
Fax: 310-396-2039

WS

Conrad Hechter — Director — conrad@ fotofactory.com

Specializing in the male nude image; photography and other art forms.

DEAF ARTS COUNCIL

3000 W. Olympic Boulevard, Suite 1464
Santa Monica, CA 90404
Ph: 310-449-4076
TTY: 310-449-4067
Fax: 310-449-4039

501(c)3 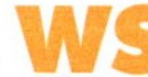

Terrylene T. Sacchetti — Executive Director — DeafArtsCo@aol.com

We are an educational and charitable non-profit organization dedicated to establishing recognition of deaf artists within the professional art world.

- Multimedia Arts Program (MAP)enables deaf and hearing children to learn the arts and develop creatively
- Creative Deaf Consultants (CDC), serving professional deaf artists and the arts/entertainment industry

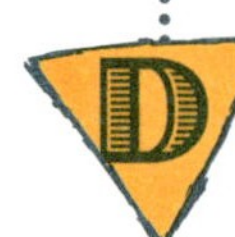

DEAF WEST THEATRE COMPANY

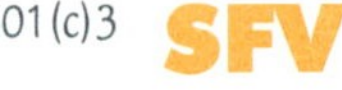

5112 Lankershim Boulevard 501(c)3
North Hollywood, CA 91601-3128
Ph: 818-762-2981
Admin: 818-762-2998
TTD: 818-762-2782
Fax: 323-660-5016

Beverly Nero Director of Development/Marketing DeafWest@aol.com
Ed Waterstreet Artistic Director

DWT was founded in 1991 to directly improve and enrich the cultural lives of the two million deaf and hard of hearing individuals who live in the Los Angeles area.

- Residential Theatre produces two mainstage productions annually
- mainstage children's plays
- Children's Theatre is a series of 12 week workshops in schools throughout Southern California
- professional training workshops for Deaf & Hard of Hearing Artists to prepare them for employment in the entertainment industry

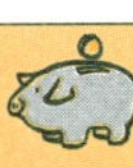

At the conclusion of each workshop, children perform for friends, faculty and families. At least one mainstage children's play is produced per season. A two week summer session is conducted at Camp SignShine for 200 hearing impaired youngsters.

Pre/K-12

PROGRAMS: WORKSHOPS
SCHEDULE: YEAR-ROUND, WEEKDAYS

DEANNA IZEN MILLER GALLERY

13700 Tahiti Way, Studio 331
Marina Del Rey, CA 90292-6537
Ph: 310-822-3333
Fa:; 310-822-7773

Deanna Izen Miller Director izenmillergallery@worldnet.att.net

DEBUSSY TRIO MUSIC FOUNDATION

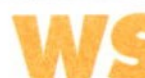

223 S. Bundy Drive, Suite 201 501(c)3
Los Angeles, CA 90049
Ph: 310-472-9740
Fax: 310-472-2911

Diana Steiner Treasurer
Marcia Dickstein Artistic Director

Since 1989, the DTMF has maintained a national program of musical and educational endeavors. It supports the presentation of chamber music concerts to diverse audiences and has a major commitment to the performance and commissioning of American music. The Debussy Trio presents programs that include music of and for the many and varied cultures in our country.

- "Musical Adventures", narrated concerts for families

DEBUSSY TRIO MUSIC FOUNDATION (CONTINUED)

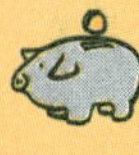

The Debussy Trio provides "Musical Adventures", specially designed concerts for under-served families and also an interactive program for children including works influenced by culture from all around the world.

Pre/K-12

PROGRAMS: PERFORMANCES
SCHEDULE: YEAR-ROUND, WEEKDAYS, WEEKENDS
DETAILS: GRADES 3-12, VISUAL & PERFORMING ARTS, AESTHETIC VALUING, CREATIVE EXPRESSION, HISTORICAL/CULTURAL CONTEXT, TRAVEL TO SCHOOLS, INDIVIDUALLY TAILORED PROGRAMS

Youth

PROGRAMS: PERFORMANCES, WORKSHOPS
SCHEDULE: YEAR-ROUND, WEEKDAYS, WEEKENDS

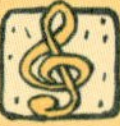

Families

PROGRAMS: PERFORMANCES
SCHEDULE: YEAR-ROUND, EVENINGS, WEEKENDS

DEL MANO GALLERY

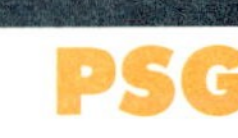

33 E. Colorado Boulevard
Pasadena, CA 91105
Ph: 626-793-6648
Admin: 310-476-8508
Fax: 310-471-0897

Chris Drosse Assistant Director
Ray Leier Director
Jan Peters Director

Founded in 1973; presents works of American artists working in all media of contemporary crafts.

DH INSTITUTE OF MEDIA ARTS

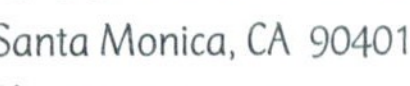

1315 3rd Street Promenade, Suite 300
Santa Monica, CA 90401
Ph: 310-899-9377
www.dhima.com

Joe Cloninger Director joe@dhima.com

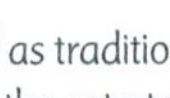

DHIMA offers 2D and 3D computer graphics courses as well as traditional art and animation classes for career-driven individuals entering the entertainment industry and similar visual fields.

- weekend, evening, and day classes, short-term and long-term
- corporate/government training
- industry lectures
- seminars

DIANE DAVISSON DANCERS

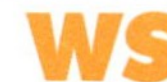

10515 Louisiana Avenue
Los Angeles, CA 90025
Ph/Fax: 310-446-3039

Diane Davisson — Artistic Director

The Diane Davisson Tap Dancers present theatrically-oriented dance shows that reflect the evolution of dance, music styles, and American culture in the 20th Century.

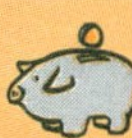

Pre/K-12

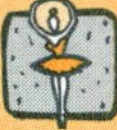

PROGRAMS: PERFORMANCES, WORKSHOPS
SCHEDULE: YEAR-ROUND, WEEKDAYS
DETAILS: GRADES PRE/K-12, VISUAL & PERFORMING ARTS
CREATIVE EXPRESSION, HISTORICAL/CULTURAL CONTEXT
TRAVEL TO SCHOOLS, COST FOR SOME PROGRAMS

Youth

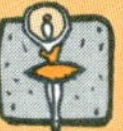

PROGRAMS: PERFORMANCES, WORKSHOPS
SCHEDULE: YEAR-ROUND, WEEKDAYS
DETAILS: COST FOR SOME PROGRAMS

Families

PROGRAMS: PERFORMANCES, WORKSHOPS
SCHEDULE: YEAR-ROUND, WEEKDAYS
DETAILS: COST FOR SOME PROGRAMS

DIRT

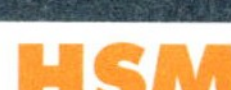

7906 Santa Monica Boulevard, #218
Los Angeles, CA 90046-5169
Ph: 323-822-9359

DONNA STERNBERG & DANCERS

501 (c)3

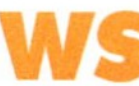

911 9th Street, #206
Santa Monica, CA 90403
310-260-1198

Chris Bradford — Manager/310-446-1383
Donna Sternberg — Artistic Director
Michelle Tatum — President, Board of Directors/213-930-0229

Donna Sternberg & Dancers is committed to developing an appreciation of dance by presenting inspiring, innovative choreography to audiences diverse in age, cultural outlook, and economic background.

- performances
- lecture/demonstrations
- workshops
- master classes
- post-performance discussions

DONNA STERNBERG & DANCERS (CONTINUED)

Our programs include multicultural influences and can be curriculum integrated when requested. The Company also works with other artistic disciplines (theater groups, music) to present a multidisciplinary approach to to the arts.

Pre/K-12

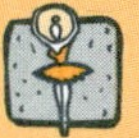

PROGRAMS: PERFORMANCES, WORKSHOPS, STUDIO CLASSES, RESIDENCIES
SCHEDULE: YEAR-ROUND, WEEKDAYS, WEEKENDS
DETAILS: GRADES PRE/K-12, VISUAL AND PERFORMING ARTS
AESTHETIC VALUING, CREATIVE EXPRESSION
TRAVEL TO SCHOOLS , INDIVIDUALLY TAILORED PROGRAMS

Youth

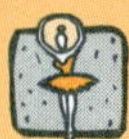

PROGRAMS: PERFORMANCES, WORKSHOPS, CLASSES, RESIDENCIES
SCHEDULE: YEAR-ROUND, WEEKDAYS, WEEKENDS

Families

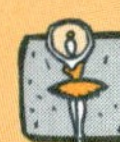

PROGRAMS: PERFORMANCES, WORKSHOPS, CLASSES, RESIDENCIES
SCHEDULE: YEAR-ROUND, WEEKDAYS, WEEKENDS

DOWNEY CIVIC THEATRE

ELA

8435 Firestone Boulevard
Downey, CA 90241-3843
Ph: 562-861-8211
Admin: 562-904-7230
Fax: 562-923-6388

Kevin O'Connor — Theatre Manager — koconnor@downeyca.org
Roger Palmquist — Technical Supervisor

The Downey Theatre, owned and operated by the City of Downey is a proscenium arch theater with a seating capacity of 748 available on a rental basis.

DOWNEY MUSEUM OF ART

ELA

10419 S. Rives Avenue
Downey, CA 90241
Ph: 562-861-0419
Fax: 323-222-9849

The Downey Museum of Art houses a collection of 20th-century California art. The museum strives to support emerging artists and to further the education of a multi-ethnic public.

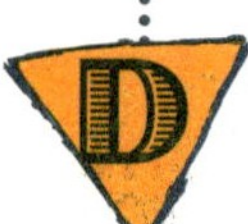

DOWNTOWN ARTS DEVELOPMENT ASSOCIATION (DADA)

315 W. Ninth Street, Suite 201 501(c)3 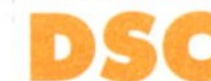
Los Angeles, CA 90015
Ph: 213-624-1196
Fax: 213-627-9914

Michael Tansey President
Amber Pierson Administrative Staff

Art promoter and community builder, DADA generates opportunity through its continually expanding focus; providing venues of exposure and contact for the artist.

- host of the annual Downtown Lives! show, an all-inclusive art and fashion exhibition
- beginning in Summer, 1999, a quarterly publication providing routes to creative achievement for the artist
- quarterly auctions featuring local artists
- volunteer opportunities

DOYLE/LOGAN COMPANY, THE

7836 Santa Monica Boulevard HSM
West Hollywood, CA 90046
Ph: 323-484-8492
Fax: 323-848-8494
www.doylelogan.com

Konrad Kemper	Office Manager	knrad@doylelogan.com
Michael Logan	Designer Director	logan@doylelogan.com
Clay Doyle	Gallery Director	clay@doylelogan.com

Centrally located in West Hollywood, we provide graphic design services for corporate and institutional clients, and feature quarterly exhibitions by emerging and unknown artists.

- graphic design services

DRAMATIC RESULTS

P.O. Box 3532 501(c)3 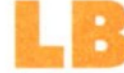
Long Beach, CA 90803
Ph: 562-437-6328
Fax: 562-437-4610
www.ontap657.com

Christi Wilkins Executive Director ontap657.com

DRAMATIC RESULTS is an award-winning nonprofit educational arts-based organization serving at-risk 4th-6th grade students with educational skill building programs on a 1-to-3 facilitator/student ratio.

- volunteer opportunities

DRAMATIC RESULTS (CONTINUED)

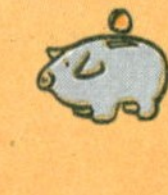
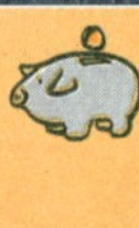

Working with 9-12 year olds with our arts-based educational curriculum, DRAMATIC RESULTS helps 1,000 children each year develop communication and academic skills to experience success in life and an appreciation for how arts can help them accomplish their dreams.

Pre/K-12  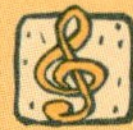 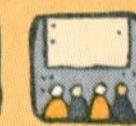 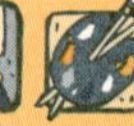

PROGRAMS:	**WORKSHOPS**
SCHEDULE:	YEAR-ROUND, WEEKDAYS
DETAILS:	GRADES 3-8, CONNECTIONS/RELATIONS/APPLICATIONS TRAVEL TO SCHOOLS , INDIVIDUALLY TAILORED PROGRAMS WORK WITH AT-RISK CHILDREN OF SINGLE PARENTS

Youth 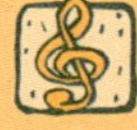 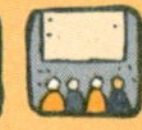 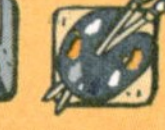

PROGRAMS:	**WORKSHOPS**
SCHEDULE:	YEAR-ROUND, WEEKDAYS

DUO D'AMOUR

2377 Malcolm Avenue WS
Los Angeles, CA 90064-2205
Ph/Fax: 310-470-4724

Patricia Evans Manager/Artistic Director evans@duodamour.com

Duo d'Amour is a flute and classical guitar duo, performing original arrangements of classical, jazz, and pop music for discerning audiences.

- chamber concerts
- performs at special occasion celebrations including business functions, seasonal festivites, weddings, and receptions

DUTTON'S BRENTWOOD BOOKS

11975 San Vicente Boulevard WS
Los Angeles, CA 90049
Ph: 310-476-6263
Fax: 310-471-0399
www.home.earthlink.net/~duttons

Lise Friedman	Events Coordinator	duttons@earthlink.net
Aurora Roman	Children's Books	

Dutton's Brentwood Books is a general independent bookstore with a large children's room. Dutton's Brentwood also has a cafe, friendly staff, and teacher discounts.

- frequent author appearances
- cafe and newsstand

DUTTON'S BRENTWOOD BOOKS (CONTINUED)

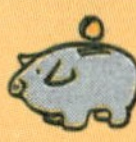

Our children's area features a wide selection for all ages. Our programs of author appearances and readings are fun and we have an annual Preschool Sunday with crafts-characters and a fundraiser.

Pre/K-12

PROGRAMS:	**READINGS AND STORYTELLING**
SCHEDULE:	YEAR-ROUND, WEEKDAYS, EVENINGS, WEEKENDS
DETAILS:	GRADES PRE/K-12, LANGUAGE ARTS, PROGRAMS ON-SITE

Families

PROGRAMS:	**READINGS AND STORYTELLING**
SCHEDULE:	YEAR-ROUND, WEEKDAYS, EVENINGS, WEEKENDS

EAGLE ROCK COMMUNITY CULTURAL ASSOCIATION

SFV

2225 Colorado Boulevard 501(c)3
Los Angeles, CA 90041
Ph: 323-226-1617
Fax: 323-226-0949

Istiharoh Glasgow Community Director
Richard Espinoza Program Director

The Eagle Rock Community Cultural Association provides multi-cultural programming in the form of classes for children and adults, visual art exhibitions, and dance and musical performances.

- monthly exhibitions
- volunteer opportunities
- rental space for art and cultural organizations
- space available for seminars and meetings

Pre/K-12

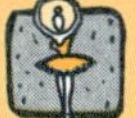
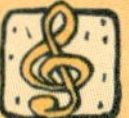
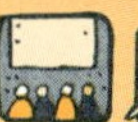
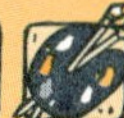

PROGRAMS:	**PERFORMANCES, WORKSHOPS, STUDIO CLASSES SELF-GUIDED TOURS**
SCHEDULE:	YEAR ROUND, WEEKDAYS, WEEKENDS
DETAILS:	GRADES PRE/K-12, VISUAL & PERFORMING ARTS CREATIVE EXPRESSION, TRAVEL TO SCHOOLS FACILITY FOR SCHOOL VISITS, PROGRAMS ON-SITE

Youth

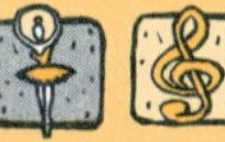
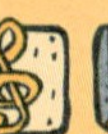
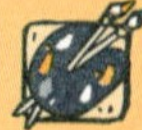

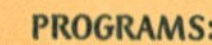

PROGRAMS:	**PERFORMANCES, WORKSHOPS, CLASSES, SELF-GUIDED TOURS**
SCHEDULE:	YEAR-ROUND, WEEKDAYS, EVENINGS, WEEKENDS

Families

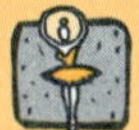
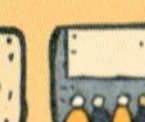

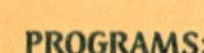

PROGRAMS:	**PERFORMANCES, WORKSHOPS, CLASSES, SELF-GUIDED TOURS**
SCHEDULE:	YEAR-ROUND, WEEKENDS

EAST L.A. CLASSIC THEATRE

ELA

2168 S. Atlantic Boulevard, Suite 378
Monterey Park, CA 91754
Ph: 323-260-8166
Fax: 323-260-8153

Bert Rosario Co-Artistic Director

EAST LOS ANGELES COLLEGE, VINCENT PRICE GALLERY

ELA

1301 Avenida Cesar Chavez
Monterey Park, CA 91754
Ph: 323-265-8841
www.lafn.org/educatiion/elac/gallery.htm

Thomas Silliman Director VPGallery@aol.com
Victor Parra Assistant Director

EAST LOS STREETSCAPERS

PSG

P.O. Box 31460
Los Angeles, CA 90031
Ph: 626-571-6761
Fax: 626-571-6762

Patricia Villagómez Project Managerstscaper@pacbell.net
David Botello Art Director
Wayne Healy Director

Founded in 1975, ELS is a private company that produces public art and related services.

EAST WEST PLAYERS

DSC

120 Judge John Aiso Street 501(c)3
Los Angeles, CA 90012
Ph: 213-625-7000
Fax: 213-625-7111
www.eastwestplayers.com

Suzanne Hee Publicity Director/ x12
Tim Dang Producing Artistic Director/ x11

East West Players, the first and foremost Asian Pacific -American theater, produces a variety of different plays, including traditional classics, huge Broadway productions, and plays specific to the Asian American experience.

- mainstage productions
- theater for youth tour
- David Henry Hulang Writers Institute (writing workshop)
- actors Conservatory
- actors Network
- writer's Gallery
- community outreach

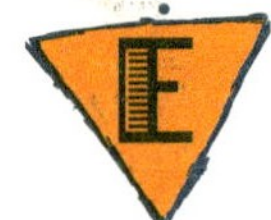

EAST WEST PLAYERS (CONTINUED)

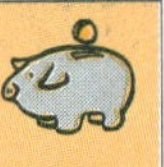

East West Players is the cultural bridge between "East" and "West" through an arts agenda that addresses the needs of all audiences. The artistic programming is educational, provocative, socially relevant, and ultimately enlightening, promoting dialogue which is key to understanding a diverse society.

Pre/K-12  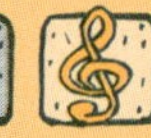 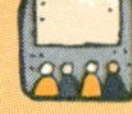

PROGRAMS:	**PERFORMANCES, WORKSHOPS**
SCHEDULE:	SUMMER, WEEKDAYS, EVENINGS
DETAILS:	GRADES PRE/K-12, VISUAL & PERFORMING ARTS MULTICULTURAL, HISTORICAL/CULTURAL CONTEXT TRAVEL TO SCHOOLS

Youth 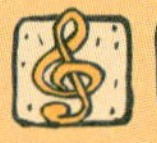

PROGRAMS:	**PERFORMANCES, WORKSHOPS**
SCHEDULE:	SUMMER, WEEKDAYS, EVENINGS

Families  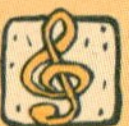 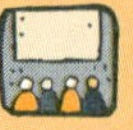

PROGRAMS:	**PERFORMANCES, WORKSHOPS**
SCHEDULE:	SUMMER, WEEKDAYS, EVENINGS

EASTSIDE REGIONAL ARTS COUNCIL

ELA

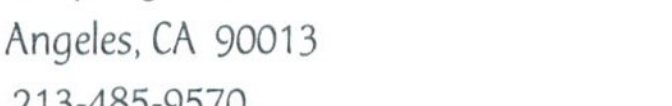

City of Los Angeles Cultural Affairs Department
433 S. Spring Street, 10th Floor
Los Angeles, CA 90013
Ph: 213-485-9570
Fax: 213-485-6835

Julia Williams — cadpublicart@earthlink.net

Developed through the City of Los Angeles Cultural Affairs Department as one of 9 regional arts councils, we are a coalition of arts and community organizations, artists, leaders, business people and all other interested members of the community who have the purpose of assessing, coalescing and acting on the cultural assets and needs of the area. This council serves Northeast Los Angeles, Silver Lake, Echo Park, Lincoln Heights, Westlake, Central City, Central City North and Boyle Heights. Goals include:

- develop affordable and accessible local programming that highlights and involves youth and local artists
- develop activities that celebrate the city's cultural diversity and promote community building
- serve as an advisory group to the Cultural Affairs Department on local art and cultural priorities
- strengthen the artistic advancement of the community

ECLECTIC COMPANY THEATRE

SFV

5312 Laurel Canyon Boulevard — 501(c)3
North Hollywood, CA 91607
Ph: 818-508-3003

Rachel Babcock — President

We are an eclectic group of actors, producers, writers, and directors dedicated to production of interesting and quality theatrical presentations. Our concept is to allow members to produce their shows without artistic interference from an artistic director or artistic board.

- produce "Shakespeare Unbound" which tours Southern California public schools

We present exerpts from Shakespeare in a modern and bilingual format and work with the teachers to prepare their classes.

Pre/K-12 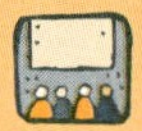

PROGRAMS:	**PERFORMANCES, WORKSHOPS**
SCHEDULE:	SPRING, FALL, WINTER, WEEKDAYS
DETAILS:	GRADES 9-12, VISUAL & PERFORMING ARTS HISTORICAL/CULTURAL CONTEXT, CONNECTIONS/RELATIONS/APPLICATIONS TRAVEL TO SCHOOLS, EDUCATIONAL MATERIALS AVAILABLE

ECLECTIONZ ART GALLERY

PSG

64 N. Raymond Avenue
Pasadena, CA 91103
Ph/Fax: 626-397-2734

Ross Farrell — Owner — eclectionz@aol.com

Located in Old Town, Eclectionz is an art gallery with a fresh outlook, ready to take chances. Always looking for emerging artists. Any medium accepted.

- quarterly exhibits featuring emerging artists

EDENHURST GALLERY

WS

8922 Melrose Avenue
Los Angeles, CA 90069
Ph: 310-247-8151
Admin: 800-611-4545
Fax: 310-247-8167
www.edenhurstgallery.com

Tom Gianetto — Co-Director — edenhurst@earthlink.net
Don Merrill — Co-Director
Dan Nicodemo — Co-Director

California plein air impressionists and early modern masters.

EDUCATIONAL THEATER COMPANY

4477 Hollywood Boulevard, #205 501(c)3 **HSM**
Los Angeles, CA 90027
Ph: 323-666-3240
Fax: 323-666-0733

Ann Greer Managing and Producing Director
Dev Ross Artistic Director

The Educational Theater Company is a dynamic multi-ethnic troupe which tours original stage shows using comedy, drama, music, and movement.

All ETC shows are created with input from educators, parents, and students, reaching 250,000 yearly. Topics include smoking, drug use, violence, teen pregnancy prevention, tolerance, and responsibility. Shows are hip, and entertaining yet gritty and appropriate for the setting.

Pre/K-12

PROGRAMS: **Drug, Alcohol, Violence, and Smoking Prevention**
Performances, Workshops
SCHEDULE: Year-round, Weekdays, Evenings, Weekends
DETAILS: Grades Pre/K-12, Visual & Performing Arts
Creative Expression, Travel to Schools
Individually Tailored Programs, Bilingual: Spanish

Youth

PROGRAMS: **Performances, Workshops**
SCHEDULE: Year-round, weekdays, Evenings, Weekends

EL CAMINO COLLEGE ART GALLERY

16007 Crenshaw Boulevard **SB**
Torrance, CA 90506
Ph: 310-660-3010
Fax: 310-660-3798

Michael Miller Co-Director
Susanna Meiers Co-Director

EL CAMINO COLLEGE CENTER FOR THE ARTS

16007 Crenshaw Boulevard **SB**
Torrance, CA 90506
Ph: 310-329-5345
Admin: 310-660-3748
Fax: 310-660-3734
www.elcamino.cc.ca.us

Tim Van Leer Executive Director Tvanleer@admin.elcamino.cc.ca.us

Located in the South Bay, the Center for the Arts provides high quality, culturally diverse performing arts events for the entertainment and education of its communities.

- a diverse series of events in music, dance, and theater from September-May
- volunteer opportunities

EL CAMINO COLLEGE CENTER FOR THE ARTS (CONTINUED)

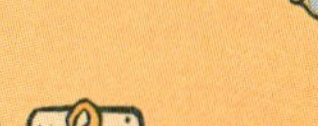

Pre/K-12

PROGRAMS: **Performances, Residencies**
SCHEDULE: Spring, Fall, Winter, Weekdays
DETAILS: Grades 5-12, Visual & Performing Arts
Creative Expression, Facility for School Visits
Programs On-Site, Cost for Some Programs

Families

PROGRAMS: **Performances**
SCHEDULE: Spring, Fall, Winter, Evenings, Weekends
DETAILS: Cost for Some Programs

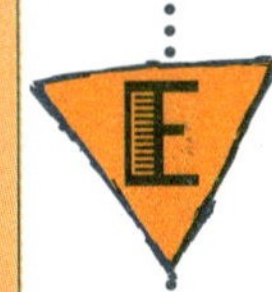

EL CID FLAMENCO SHOW RESTAURANT

4212 W. Sunset Boulevard **HSM**
Los Angeles, CA 90029
Ph: 323-668-0318
Fax: 323-668-0357
www.elcid-ca.com

Jack Haywood Manager

El Cid Flamenco Show Restaurant offers a romantic blend of dining, history, and entertainment that is unique and beautiful, hidden in the heart of Hollywood.

- presents Flamenco—the Performing Arts of Spain

El Cid Flamenco Show Restaurant presents Performing Arts of Spain, "Flamenco".

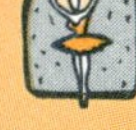

Pre/K-12

PROGRAMS: **Performances**
SCHEDULE: Year-round, Evenings, Weekends
DETAILS: Grades 7-12, History/Soc. Sciences
Visual & Performing Arts, Language Arts
Creative Expression, Historical/Cultural Context
Travel to Schools, Programs On-Site
Individually Tailored Programs, Bilingual: Spanish

Youth

PROGRAMS: **Performances**
SCHEDULE: Year-round, weekdays, Evenings, Weekends

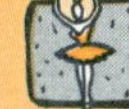

Families

PROGRAMS: **Performances**
SCHEDULE: Year-round, Weekdays, Evenings, Weekends

EL PUEBLO DE LOS ANGELES HISTORIC MONUMENT

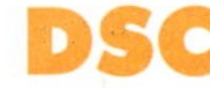

125 Paseo de la Plaza, Suite 400
Los Angeles, CA 90012
Ph: 213-628-1274
Admin: 213-485-6855
Educ: 213-680-2525
Fax: 213-485-8238

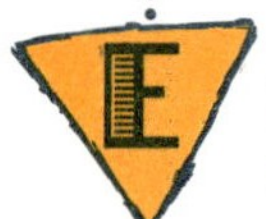

Jean Bruce Poole	Historic Museum Director
Gloria Giangiuli	Visitors' Center Coordinator
Frank Catania	Acting General Manager

El Pueblo de Los Angeles is a multi-ethnic historic monument which reflects the history of Los Angeles to the present and the home of the world-renowned Mexican marketplace on Olvera Street.

- permanent exhibitions on the history of Los Angeles
- temporary exhibits on various subjects
- gift shop
- visitor's Center
- docent tours
- volunteer opportunities
- traditional events

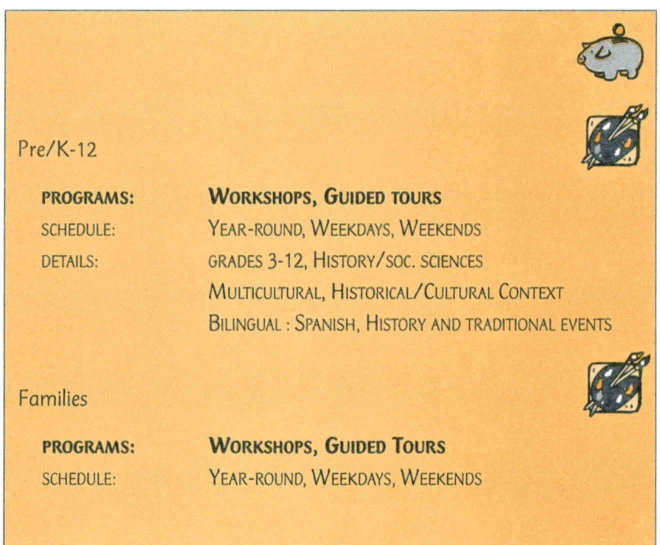

Pre/K-12

PROGRAMS: **Workshops, Guided tours**
SCHEDULE: Year-round, Weekdays, Weekends
DETAILS: grades 3-12, History/soc. sciences
Multicultural, Historical/Cultural Context
Bilingual : Spanish, History and traditional events

Families

PROGRAMS: **Workshops, Guided Tours**
SCHEDULE: Year-round, Weekdays, Weekends

EL TEATRO DE LA REALIDAD (THEATRE OF REALITY)

c/o Hathaway Family Resource Center — 501(c)3 — ELA
840 N. Avenue 66
Los Angeles, CA 90042
Ph: 323-257-9600
Admin: 323-463-7602
Fax: 323-257-8118

Sally Gordon	Project Director/Arts Facilitator
Pat Bowie	Director of Hathaway Family Resource Center
Stacey Michaels	Community Mobilization Coordinator

El Theatre de la Realidad is a community-based organization consisting of volunteers and professional artists who create original plays about the lives of the participants and develop theater works based on ancient myths and folktales.

- live plays
- weekly workshops for women providing them with an opportunity to write, draw, and act out important life experiences; "Life Scripts" is one way in which the participants can feed into the theatre company
- P.A.C.T. (Parents and Children Together) encourages parents and their children to interact creatively together using art and theatre games

A community outreach program of the Hathaway Family Resource Center, El Teatro de la Realidad creates plays about issues affecting the lives of the participants. The Center provides theraputic art programs to examine old patterns and explore new options.

Pre/K-12

PROGRAMS: **Performances, Workshops, Residencies**
SCHEDULE: Year-round, Weekdays, Evenings, Weekends
DETAILS: grades 3-12, Visual & performing arts
Creative Expression
Travel to schools, Programs on-site
Individually tailored programs, Bilingual: Spanish
Work with: At-risk youth

Youth

PROGRAMS: **performances, Workshops, Residencies**
SCHEDULE: Year-round, weekdays, Evenings, Weekends

Families

PROGRAMS: **Performances, Workshops**
SCHEDULE: Year-round, Weekdays, Evenings, Weekends

ELECTRONIC CAFE INTERNATIONAL

1649 18th Street
Santa Monica, CA 90404
Ph: 310-828-8732
Fax: 310-453-4347
www.ecafe.com

501(c)3 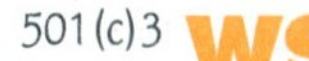

Sherrie Rabinowitz — ecafe@earthlink.net

ELI BROAD FAMILY FOUNDATION, THE

3355 Barnard Way
Santa Monica, CA 90405
Ph: 310-399-4004
Fax: 310-399-7799
www.broadartfdn.org

501(c)3 WS

Andrea Feldman	Assistant Curator	curator@earthlink.net
Joanne Heyler	Curator	
Juliana Hanner	Registrar	
Jeannine Guido	Archivist	

Established in 1984, the Foundation collects the most important art of the last quarter of this century and makes it available to museums and non-profit arts institutions for loan.

ENCINO MEDIA CENTER

16953 Ventura Boulevard
Encino, CA 91426
Ph: 818-784-7266

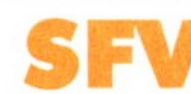

ERNIE WOLFE GALLERY

1655 Sawtelle Boulevard
Los Angeles, CA 90025-3148
Ph: 310-478-2960

WS

Ernie Wolfe — Director

Large scale traditional and architectural sculpture from sub Saharan Africa and tribal furniture, as well as contemporary African paintings and sculpture.

EVERYWOMAN'S VILLAGE

5650 Sepulveda Boulevard
Van Nuys, CA 91411
Ph: 818-787-5100
Fax: 818-994-2331

501(c)3 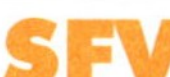

Barbara Beron	Office Manager
Laura Selwyn	Executive Director
Caros Becker	Program Director

In an urban retreat campus setting, the community learning center Everywoman's Village offers adults and youth expert and affordable instruction in a wide curriculum which features small, informal, self-paced learning groups.

- wide curriculum of classes
- student supply store
- artist Co-op 7/ on-going citywide art exhibits
- volunteer opportunities
- drop-in campus tours
- free Course Catalog Mailer
- free Community Service Program lectures

EVERYWOMAN'S VILLAGE (CONTINUED)

Everywoman's Village is an adult and youth community continuing education center offering affordable classes in small, informal groups taught in a supportive, creative, and self-determined learning environment by expert instructors.

Youth 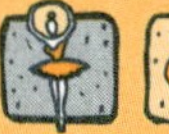 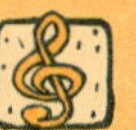 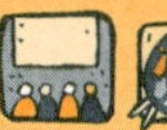 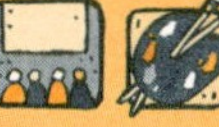

PROGRAMS: Performances, Workshops
SCHEDULE: Year-round, weekdays

Families

PROGRAMS: Performances, Workshops
SCHEDULE: Year-round, Weekdays, Evenings, Weekends
DETAILS: No cost for some programs

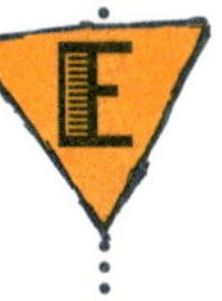

EXCEPTIONAL CHILDREN'S FOUNDATION ART CENTER PROGRAM

3750 W. Martin Luther King Jr. Boulevard
Los Angeles, CA 90008
Ph: 323-298-8230
Admin: 323-290-2000
Fax: 323-298-8202

501(c)3 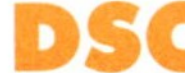

Rohmi Reid	Art Director/ x302
Richard Webb-Msemaji	Program Director/ x259
Carmela Burke	Director of Communications

Established in 1968, the Exceptional Children's Foundation Art Center is a community-based non-profit organization providing adults with developmental disabilites professional art training and studio facilities.

- open to the public
- individual and group tours
- sale of fine arts
- volunteer opportunities
- custom framing services
- local exhibitions and art shows

EZTV

6522 Hollywood Boulevard
Los Angeles, CA 90028
Ph: 323-462-3678
Fax: 323-462-3673
www.eztvmedia.com

501(c)3 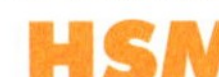

Kate Johnson	President
Michael Masucci	Artistic Director

EZTV is a multifaceted organization that offers media and web services and tools to artists. It is also a center that celebrates, produces and exhibits new media works.

- video editing and production
- image manipulation
- website production
- curated video and new media screenings
- access grants
- media training & seminars
- on-line digital art gallery
- community center for digital filmmakers

FABULOUS MONSTERS PERFORMANCE COMPANY

4401 1/2 Westdale Avenue 501(c)3

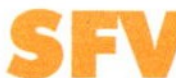

Los Angeles, CA 90041
Ph: 323-857-7512
Admin: 818-409-9136

Mark Compton	Producer/Company Manager
Robert Prior	Artistic Director/323 254-6623

Fabulous Monsters, brainchild of Artistic Director Robert Prior, is an award-winning company of artists, performers and musicians presenting provocative theater adaptations of archetypal myths and classic works.

- workshops for actors
- performances of stage plays
- recruitment of local performance artists including those involved in stage craft such as set builders, lighting designers, stage managers

FAHEY/KLEIN GALLERY

148 N. La Brea Avenue

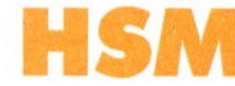

Los Angeles, CA 90036
Ph: 323-934-2250
Fax: 323-934-4243

Randy Klein	Co-Director	fkg@earthlink.net
David Fahey	Co-Director	

Vintage and contemporary photography.

FALCON THEATER

4252 Riverside Drive

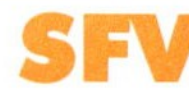

Burbank, CA 91505
Ph: 818-955-8004
Fax: 818-955-7732

Meryl Friedman Executive Producer

FARA FINA COLLECTION

13455 Maxella Avenue, Unit 248

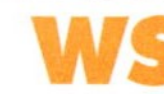

Marina del Rey, CA 90292
Ph: 310-305-1390
Fax: 310-305-0199

Fine African art specializing in Shona sculpture. Many gift items and jewelry.

FASHION INSTITUTE OF DESIGN & MERCHANDISING (FIDM) MUSEUM AND LIBRARY

919 S. Grand Avenue

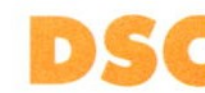

Los Angeles, CA 90015
Ph: 213-624-1200

The museum hosts exhibits on fashion and different aspects of design and merchandising.

FASTFEET/JAMIE NICHOLS

665 E. California Boulevard

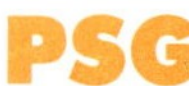

Pasadena, CA 91106
Ph: 626-793-4818

Jamie Nichols Artistic Director

Fastfeet is a diverse contemporary dance company based in Pasadena with an eclectic repertoire directed by Jamie Nichols.

- lecture demonstrations
- performances
- classes
- site-specific works
- performance opportunities

Pre/K-12

PROGRAMS:	**PERFORMANCES, WORKSHOPS, RESIDENCIES**
SCHEDULE:	YEAR-ROUND, WEEKDAYS, EVENINGS, WEEKENDS
DETAILS:	GRADES PRE/K-12, VISUAL & PERFORMING ARTS CREATIVE EXPRESSION TRAVEL TO SCHOOLS, INDIVIDUALLY TAILORED PROGRAMS

Youth

PROGRAMS:	**PERFORMANCES, WORKSHOPS, RESIDENCIES**
SCHEDULE:	YEAR-ROUND, WEEKDAYS, EVENINGS, WEEKENDS

Families

PROGRAMS:	**PERFORMANCES, WORKSHOPS, RESIDENCIES**
SCHEDULE:	YEAR-ROUND, WEEKDAYS, EVENINGS, WEEKENDS

FESTIVALONG BEACH

114 Roycroft Avenue, Apt. A 501(c)3

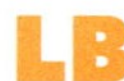

Long Beach, CA 90803-3144
Ph: 562-438-2506

Mark Mantel Executive Director/Founder

FestivaLong Beach serves as an artistic, economic engine, providing continuous and stable opportunities for artists living and working in Long Beach through the public presentation of cutting-edge, experimental, and unique interdisciplinary art and thought. We seek to encourage and nurture the artistic community to remain in Long Beach, and to enlighten, challenge and speak to audiences throughout Southern California with provocative and dynamic presentations and performances.

- performances

FESTIVALONG BEACH (CONTINUED)

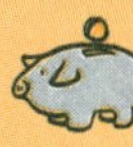

FestivaLong Beach offers direct exposure to the artists making their art and sharing their own unique notions of the creative process.

Pre/K-12

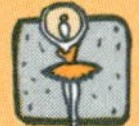
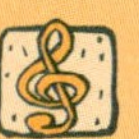
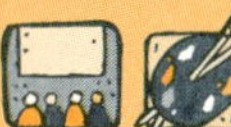

PROGRAMS: PERFORMANCES
SCHEDULE: SPRING, SUMMER, FALL, WEEKDAYS, EVENINGS. WEEKENDS
DETAILS: GRADES PRE/K-12, VISUAL & PERFORMING ARTS
CREATIVE EXPRESSION
TRAVEL TO SCHOOLS, FACILITY FOR SCHOOL VISITS
INDIVIDUALLY TAILORED PROGRAMS

Youth

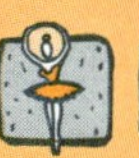
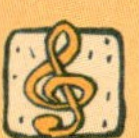
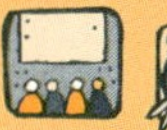
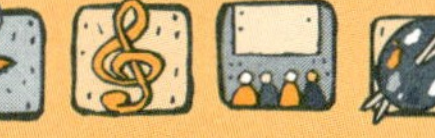

PROGRAMS: PERFORMANCES
SCHEDULE: SPRING, SUMMER, FALL, WEEKDAYS, EVENINGS, WEEKENDS
DETAILS: COST FOR SOME PROGRAMS

Families

PROGRAMS: PERFORMANCES
SCHEDULE: SPRING, SUMMER, FALL, WEEKDAYS, EVENINGS, WEEKENDS
DETAILS: COST FOR SOME PROGRAMS

FIG (FIRST INDEPENDENT GALLERY)

WS

2525 Michigan Avenue
Bergamot Station
Santa Monica, CA 90404
Ph: 310-829-0345
Fax: 310-829-7425
www.netwood.net/~fig

Jeff Gambill Director figgallery@aol.com

Contemporary art.

FILM MUSIC SOCIETY, THE

501(c)3 HSM

P.O. Box 93536
Hollywood, CA 90093
Ph: 818-248-5775
Fax: 818-248-8681
www.filmmusicsociety.org

Jeannie Pool Executive Director

A membership organization devoted to film music preservation and promotion.

- quarterly journal
- bi-monthly newsletter
- books
- annual international film music conference

FILMANTHROPIC

501(c)3 HSM

1722 1/2 Whitley Avenue
Hollywood, CA 90028
Ph: 323-464-9119
Fax: 323-856-8529
www.showbizjobs.com

Nanci Rossov Creative Director

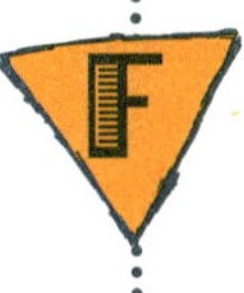

Filmanthropic provides training and opportunities in film (entertainment) production to women, people with disabilities, people over 40, and members of ethnic communities.

- on-the-job training in film production
- script (features) development to same clients
- roundtable discussions on professional development in Entertainment

We provide a school-to-career youth program to train at-risk youth for entry level positions in the entertainment industry.

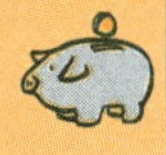

FILMMAKERS ALLIANCE

501(c)3 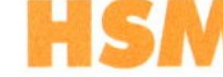

4770 Sunset Boulevard, #716
Los Angeles, CA 90027
Ph: 310-281-6093
www.caryn.com/fa

Filmmakers Alliance is a membership driven non-profit production and support company by and for filmmakers.

- membership productions
- seminars and workshops
- crew & resources databanks
- book, video and script library
- newsletter and website
- writer's workshop
- the PSA program
- production, resources and facilities

FILMMAKERS UNITED

501(c)3 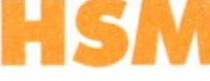

1260 N. Alexandria
Los Angeles, CA 90029

Robert Arentz

We organize the annual Los Angeles International Short Film Festival, which includes variety acts and music performances.

FINEGOOD ART GALLERY

SFV

Bernard Milken Jewish Community Campus
22622 Vanowen Street
West Hills, CA 91307-2646
Ph: 818-587-3218
Fax: 818-716-1773

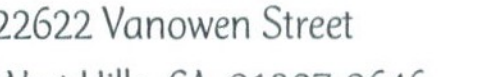

FIREHOUSE THEATRE COMPANY, THE

P.O. Box 69913 501 (c) 3 **WS**
Los Angeles, CA 90069
Ph: 310-659-6744
Fax: 310-659-6644

Irene Oppenheim Artistic Director steinway@worldnet.att.net

The Firehouse particularly strives to be a liaison between artists with disabilities and the mainstream theatrical community.

- workshops
- readings
- consultations
- oriented to and presented by persons with disabilities

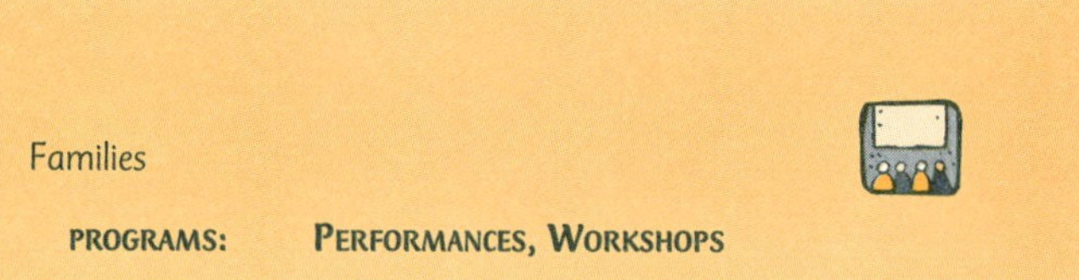

Families

PROGRAMS: **PERFORMANCES, WORKSHOPS**

FLAMENCO ATTRACTIONS INCORPORATED

c/o 11018 Loch Lomond Drive **ELA**
Whittier, CA 90606
Ph/Fax: 562-699-7595
www.geocities.com/Broadway/7793

Juan Talavera Director/Choreographer AlcomPasbueno@webtv.net

Flamenco Attractions Inc. presents the finest Spanish and Flamenco entertainment in Southern California.

- live concerts for colleges and universities
- lectures
- demonstrations
- master classes
- workshops
- group, semi-private and private classes at all levels

Flamenco Attractions Inc. features male Flamenco dancers not usually seen in performances.

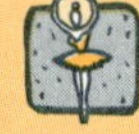

Pre/K-12

PROGRAMS: **PERFORMANCES, WORKSHOPS, STUDIO CLASSES**
SCHEDULE: YEAR-ROUND, WEEKDAYS, WEEKENDS
DETAILS: GRADES PRE/K-12, VISUAL & PERFORMING ARTS
CREATIVE EXPRESSION, HISTORICAL/CULTURAL CONTEXT
TRAVEL TO SCHOOLS, INDIVIDUALLY TAILORED PROGRAMS
EDUCATIONAL MATERIALS AVAILABLE, BILINGUAL: SPANISH

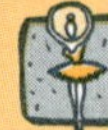

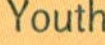

Youth

PROGRAMS: **PERFORMANCES, WORKSHOPS, CLASSES, RESIDENCIES**
SCHEDULE: YEAR-ROUND, WEEKDAYS, WEEKENDS

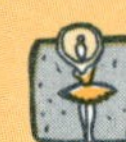

Families

PROGRAMS: **PERFORMANCES, WORKSHOPS, CLASSES, RESIDENCIES**
SCHEDULE: YEAR-ROUND, WEEKDAYS, WEEKENDS

FLIGHTS OF FANTASY STORY THEATER

8048 Le Berthon Street **SFV**
Sunland, CA 91040
Ph/Fax: 818-353-0975

Lorrie Oshatz Artistic Director

Flights of Fantasy Story Theater offers inspired interpretations of multi-cultural folktales and fables using vaudeville comedy format.

- drama and storytelling workshops

We combine a unique blend of storytelling and comedy that encourages children to read and explore world literature. The dynamic presentations provide enriching stories about cultural diversity, shared values and lessons available through literature.

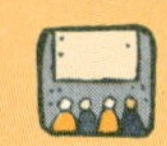

Pre/K-12

PROGRAMS: **PERFORMANCES, WORKSHOPS, RESIDENCIES**
SCHEDULE: YEAR-ROUND, WEEKDAYS, EVENINGS, WEEKENDS
DETAILS: GRADES PRE/K-3-6, VISUAL & PERFORMING ARTS
LANGUAGE ARTS, CREATIVE EXPRESSION
HISTORICAL/CULTURAL CONTEXT,
CONNECTIONS/RELATIONS/APPLICATIONS
TRAVEL TO SCHOOLS, INDIVIDUALLY TAILORED PROGRAMS
EDUCATIONAL MATERIALS AVAILABLE

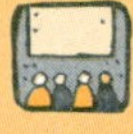

Youth

PROGRAMS: **PERFORMANCES, WORKSHOPS, RESIDENCIES**
SCHEDULE: YEAR-ROUND, WEEKDAYS, EVENINGS, WEEKENDS

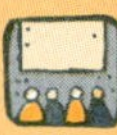

Families

PROGRAMS: **PERFORMANCES**
SCHEDULE: YEAR-ROUND, WEEKDAYS, EVENINGS, WEEKENDS
DETAILS: NO COST FOR SOME PROGRAMS

FLOWERS WEST

2525 Michigan Avenue, E-1 (Bergamot Station) **WS**
Santa Monica, CA 90404
Ph: 310-586-9200
Fax: 310-586-1595
flowerswest@earthlink.net

Sarah Howgate Director

Contemporary European Art.

FOLK DANCE FEDERATION OF CALIFORNIA, SOUTH

236 DeAnza Street 501 (c) 3 **PSG**
San Gabriel, CA 91776
Ph: 626-300-8138
Admin: 818-790-6037
Educ/Fax: 310-478-6600

Sylvia Stachure Publicity Chair
Marilyn Pixler President
Beverly Barr Information Hotline
Dorothy Daw Research

FOLK DANCE FEDERATION, SOUTH (CONTINUED)

Dancing is done around the world. As a Federation of many groups, we can refer you to a specific area and/or type of dance. We also make presentations on request.

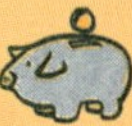

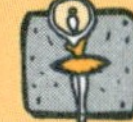

Pre/K-12

PROGRAMS: PERFORMANCES
SCHEDULE: YEAR-ROUND, WEEKDAYS
DETAILS: GRADES PRE/K-12, HISTORY/SOC. SCIENCES
VISUAL & PERFORMING ARTS, MULTICULTURAL
HISTORICAL/CULTURAL CONTEXT
TEACHER TRAINING PROGRAMS, TRAVEL TO SCHOOLS
INDIVIDUALLY TAILORED PROGRAMS

Youth

PROGRAMS: PERFORMANCES, WORKSHOPS
SCHEDULE: YEAR-ROUND, WEEKDAYS, EVENINGS, WEEKENDS
DETAILS: COST FOR SOME PROGRAMS

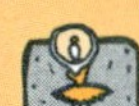

Families

PROGRAMS: WORKSHOPS
SCHEDULE: YEAR-ROUND, WEEKDAYS, EVENINGS, WEEKENDS
DETAILS: COST FOR SOME PROGRAMS

FOLK MUSIC CENTER MUSEUM

220 Yale Avenue
Claremont, CA 91711-4724
Ph: 909-624-2928

501(c)3

Dorothy Chase — Co-owner and Manager
Charles Chase — Co-owner

Folk Music Center Museum gives talks and demonstrations to school-age children in the mornings.

- talks and demonstrations Wednesday mornings
- museum display of instruments
- Folk Festival held in May
- instrument loan program

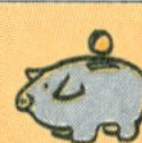

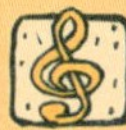

Pre/K-12

PROGRAMS: SELF-GUIDED TOURS
SCHEDULE: YEAR-ROUND, WEEKDAYS
DETAILS: GRADES 3-4, MULTICULTURAL
HISTORICAL/CULTURAL CONTEXT
CONNECTIONS/RELATIONS/APPLICATIONS

FOOTHILL CREATIVE ARTS GROUP

108 N. Baldwin Avenue
Sierra Madre, CA 91024
Ph/Fax: 626-355-8350

501(c)3 PSG

Kathy Foresta — Administrative Assistant
Jacki Raymond — Executive Director

Creative Arts Group is a community art center offering a wide variety of classes in the arts for children and adults. Additionally, it houses a gallery and gift shop featuring the work of Southern Californian artists.

- classes in the arts for children and adults
- art festival and sale
- gallery and gift shop
- home and garden tour
- art exhibitions
- volunteer opportunities
- outreach programs to the community

Creative arts group encourages creative development in children and adults through classes, programs and exhibitions in the arts in a non-competitive environment.

Pre/K-12

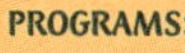

PROGRAMS: STUDIO CLASSES
SCHEDULE: YEAR-ROUND, WEEKDAYS, WEEKENDS
DETAILS: GRADES PRE/K-12, VISUAL & PERFORMING ARTS
CREATIVE EXPRESSION

Youth

PROGRAMS: CLASSES
SCHEDULE: YEAR-ROUND, WEEKDAYS, WEEKENDS

Families

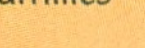

PROGRAMS: CLASSES
SCHEDULE: YEAR-ROUND, WEEKDAYS, EVENINGS, WEEKENDS

FOOTHILL MASTER CHORALE

Westminster Church
1757 N. Lake Avenue
Pasadena, CA 91104
Ph: 626-797-4133

501(c)3

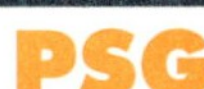

Stefanie Dobrin — Vice-President/626-798-3448
Timothy Howard — Artistic Director/626-583-2726
David Leehy — President/714-680-3800 x277

The 65-voice Foothill Master Chorale is the largest community chorus in the Pasadena area.

- four concerts per season
- performs a wide variety of fine choral music from all periods.

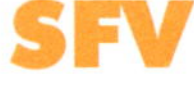

FOREST LAWN MEMORIAL -PARKS & MORTUARIES

SFV

1712 S. Glendale Avenue
Glendale, CA 91205
Ph: 800-204-3131
Fax: 213-344-9035

P. Boger — Community Relations Director/ x4743
Paula Graber — Vice-President, Communications/ x4446

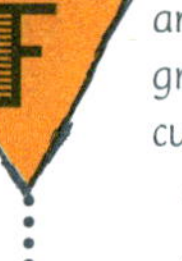

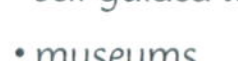

Headquartered in Glendale, with locations in HollywoodHills, Cypress, Covina and Long Beach. Echo Park has its own unique features. Educational programs designed to stimulate young minds in the arts, history, social studies and cultural awareness.

- self-guided tours
- museums
- great collections of art; large size works (mostly originals) of famous European and American sculptures, paintings, and stained glass
- replicas of famous churches for weddings, funerals, and baby christenings
- immense painting, The Crucifixion, by Jan Styka with dramatic audio presentation
- The Last Supper window in stained glass
- patriotic ceremonies: Memorial Day and Veterans Day
- Easter sunrise services
- flower and gift shops
- largest outdoor historical mosaic depicting the Birth of Liberty and more.

We hire professional actors who bring to life noted American Presidents such as Abraham Lincoln and George Washington;; Renaissance greats Michelangelo and Leonardo daVinci; and Montezuma, the last great emperor of Mexico. Students hear fasc inating stories of their lives and view exact replicas of famous works, a life-size statury, paintings and more.

Pre/K-12

PROGRAMS: **PERFORMANCES, SELF-GUIDED TOURS**
SCHEDULE: YEAR-ROUND, WEEKDAYS, WEEKENDS
DETAILS: GRADES 5-6, HISTORY/SOC. SCIENCES
HISTORICAL/CULTURAL CONTEXT
PROGRAMS ON-SITE , INDIVIDUALLY TAILORED PROGRAMS

Families

PROGRAMS: **SELF-GUIDED TOURS**
SCHEDULE: YEAR-ROUND, WEEKDAYS, WEEKENDS

FOREST LAWN PLAZA & MUSEUM OF MEXICAN & AMERICAN HISTORY

SFV

6300 Forest Lawn Drive
Los Angeles, CA 90068
Ph: 800-204-3131

Margaret Burton — Director/ x4737

FORM ZERO ARCHITECTURAL BOOKS AND GALLERY

WS

2433 Main Street - Edgemar
Santa Monica, CA 90405
Ph: 310-450-0222
Fax: 310-450-0071
www.formzero.com

Angela Benson — Public Relations
Andrew Liang — Director — andrew@formzero.com

Form Zero Architectural Books and Gallery is located in the Edgemar Complex designed by Frank Gehry. The bookstore carries over 8000+ titles specifically on architecture.

- four international exhibitions per year
- lecture series in fall and spring

FOUNDATION FOR ART RESOURCES, INC. (FAR)

501 (c)3 **HSM**

P.O. Box 29422
Los Angeles, CA 90029
Ph: 310-289-4181

Rebecca McGrew

The Foundation for Art Resources, Inc. (FAR) was founded in 1977 to facilitate the production and presentation of work not supported by traditional galleries, museums, universities or other arts organizations. FAR's programs and services are organized and administered by a Board of Directors comprised of artists and art professionals who volunteer their services.

- supports and produces programs and exhibitions
- lecture series
- open proposal funds for Los Angeles based art projects and lectures
- variety of public events, programs and exhibitions

FRANK ENTERTAINMENT

c/o Jeanine Frank
P.O. Box 49283
Los Angeles, CA 90049
Ph: 310-476-6735

Jeanine Frank — Director — frankent1@juno.com

Began in 1990 producing theater, comedy and cabaret in livingrooms around Los Angeles, these shows called Parlor Performances received local and national attention and have led to productions booking artists from around the country.

- shows at the Beverly Hills Public Library and the Gindi Auditorium
- book artists into national performing arts venues, non-profit fundraisers and other special events
- performances, workshops and discussions in schools and other institutions

FRANK ENTERTAINMENT (CONTINUED)

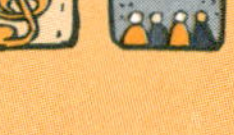
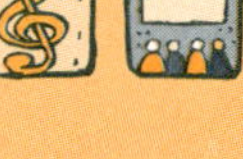
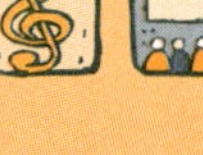
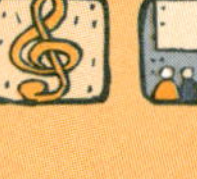
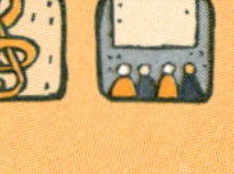
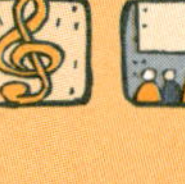
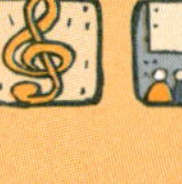

Pre/K-12

PROGRAMS:	**PERFORMANCES**
SCHEDULE:	YEAR-ROUND, EVENINGS
DETAILS:	GRADES PRE/K-12, HISTORY/SOC. SCIENCES VISUAL & PERFORMING ARTS, MULTICULTURAL CREATIVE EXPRESSION, TRAVEL TO SCHOOLS

Families

PROGRAMS:	**PERFORMANCES**
SCHEDULE:	YEAR-ROUND

FRANK LLOYD GALLERY

WS

Bergamot Station
2525 Michigan Avenue, Suite B5b
Santa Monica, CA 90404
Ph: 310-264-3866
Fax: 310-264-3868

Frank Lloyd — Director

Located in the Bergamot Station Arts Center, Frank Lloyd Gallery specializes in modern and contemporary ceramic art.

- monthly exhibitions featuring nationally known ceramic artists
- on-going display of local ceramic artists

FREDERICK R. WEISMAN MUSEUM OF ART, PEPPERDINE UNIVERSITY

WS

24255 Pacific Coast Highway
Malibu, CA 90263
Ph: 310-456-4851
Fax: 310-456-4556

Michael Zakian — Director — mzakian@pepperdine.edu
Nora Halpern — Founding Director

To exhibit art from around the world, both contemporary and historical. Exhibitions of decorative art as well as shows which focus on theatre, film, and performance design.

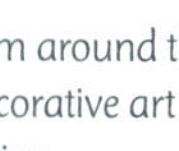
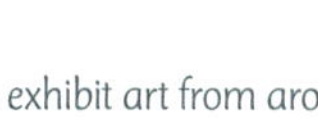

FREE ARTS FOR ABUSED CHILDREN (FAAC)

501(c)3 WS

11965 Venice Boulevard, Suite 402
Los Angeles, CA 90066
Ph: 310-313-4ART
Fax: 310-313-5575

Kris Nieder — Public Relations Administrator — freearts@earthlink.net
Cheryl Silver — Program Director
Kastle Lund — Executive Director

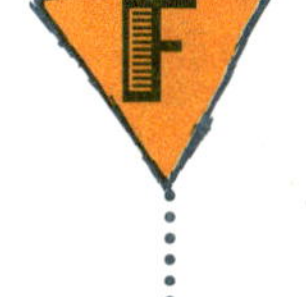

We bring caring volunteers and multidisciplinary arts activities to over 35,000 abused children and families in crisis per year in Los Angeles and Orange County.

- volunteer opportuntie.
- golf tournament to benefit programs
- annual gala events to benefit programs
- monthly volunteer workshops

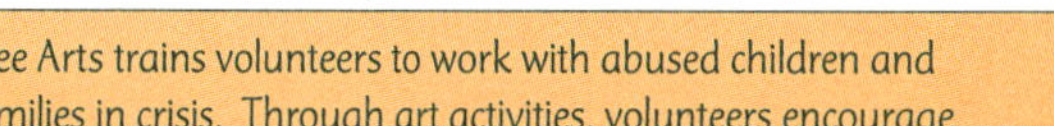
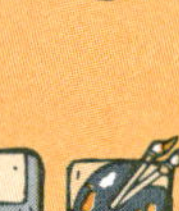
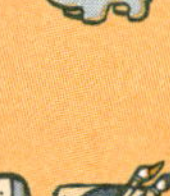

Free Arts trains volunteers to work with abused children and families in crisis. Through art activities, volunteers encourage self-expression and build positive relationships with the children. The motto for Free Arts is as simple as it is effective "Art Heals."

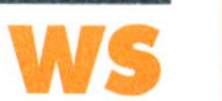
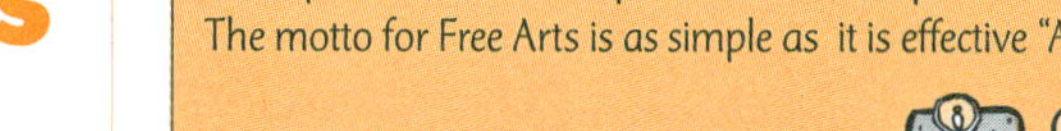

Youth

PROGRAMS:	**PERFORMANCES, WORKSHOPS**
SCHEDULE:	YEAR-ROUND, WEEKDAYS, EVENINGS, WEEKENDS

Families

PROGRAMS:	**WORKSHOPS**
SCHEDULE:	YEAR-ROUND, WEEKDAYS, EVENINGS, WEEKENDS

FRESH PAINT GALLERY

WS

9355 Culver Boulevard, Suite B
Culver City, CA 90232
Ph: 310-558-9355
Fax: 310-558-0553

Helene Brown — Co-Director — freshpaint@earthlink.net
Josetta Sbaglia — Co-Director

Specializing in consulting services for corporate and hotel placement. Contemporary painting, works on paper, mixed media.

FRIDA KAHLO CULTURAL CENTER

DSC

Grupo de Teatro Sinergia
2344 W. Fourth Street
Los Angeles, CA 90057
Ph: 213-382-8133
Fax: 213-639-1573

Ruben Amavizca — Executive Director

- theatre programs in English and Spanish
- Bata visual arts gallery
- classes for children and adults in theater, visual arts, photo, guitar, Afro-Cuban dance, computers and computer animation
- photo lab

FRIENDS OF CERRITOS CENTER FOR THE PERFORMING ARTS

LB

12700 Center Court Drive — 501 (c)3
Cerritos, CA 90703
Ph: 562-916-8510
Fax: 562-916-8514

Stacy Brightman — Director of Education and Youth Outreach/ x8542
Wayne Shilkret — Executive Director

The Friends of the Cerritos Center for the Performing Arts are dedicated to increasing appreciation for the performing arts through education.

- artists-in-the-school residencies
- accredited teacher training and classroom materials
- lectures/demonstrations
- master classes
- student performances, provides as needed students' bus transportation to the performances
- ticket subsidies
- teacher training program

The Friends offers university-accredited teacher training seminars. Our services eliminates the primary obstacles to the students' participation in the arts by providing teacher training, geographic, and financial access.

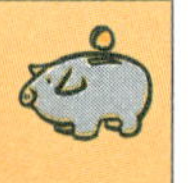

Pre/K-12

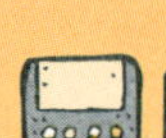
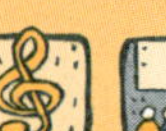
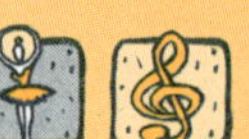
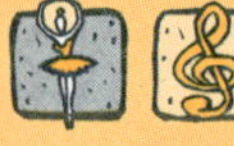

PROGRAMS:	**PERFORMANCES, WORKSHOPS, RESIDENCIES** **GUIDED TOURS**
SCHEDULE:	SPRING, FALL, WINTER, WEEKDAYS
DETAILS:	GRADES PRE/K-12, VISUAL & PERFORMING ARTS CONNECTIONS/RELATIONS/APPLICATIONS TEACHER TRAINING PROGRAMS (SALARY POINTS) TRAVEL TO SCHOOLS, PROGRAMS ON-SITE EDUCATIONAL MATERIALS AVAILABLE

Youth

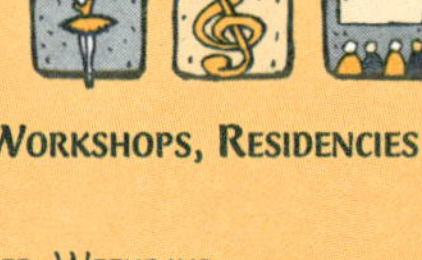

PROGRAMS:	**PERFORMANCES**
SCHEDULE:	SPRING, FALL, WINTER, WEEKDAYS

Families

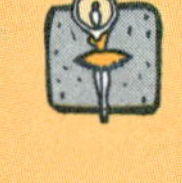

PROGRAMS:	**PERFORMANCES**
SCHEDULE:	SPRING, FALL, WINTER, WEEKDAYS

FRIENDS OF THE JUNIOR ARTS CENTER

HSM

4814 Hollywood Boulevard — 501 (c)3
Los Angeles, CA 90027
Ph: 323-660-3362
Educ: 323-485-4474
Fax: 323-485-7456
www.members.aol.com\fojac1

Stephanie Kimmel — Executive Director — fojac1@aol.com
Patty Sue Jones — Program Director

Friends of the Junior Arts Center (FOJAC) is dedicated to improving arts education for children in Los Angeles.

- K-12 and family programs
- programs for youth with disabilities
- artist residencies for schools and social service agencies
- parent and teacher workshops
- free family workshops
- art academy for older youth
- mentorship opportunities for teens.

Please see organizational description and programs.

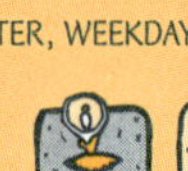

Pre/K-12

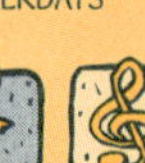

PROGRAMS:	**WORKSHOPS, STUDIO CLASSES, RESIDENCIES**
SCHEDULE:	YEAR-ROUND, WEEKDAYS
DETAILS:	GRADES PRE/K-12, VISUAL & PERFORMING ARTS CREATIVE EXPRESSION, TEACHER TRAINING PROGRAMS (SALARY POINTS) TRAVEL TO SCHOOLS , INDIVIDUALLY TAILORED PROGRAMS EDUCATIONAL MATERIALS AVAILABLE BILINGUA: SPANISH, ARMENIAN, RUSSIAN, SIGN LANGUAGE WORK WITH DISABLED, COST FOR SOME PROGRAMS

Youth

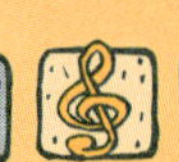
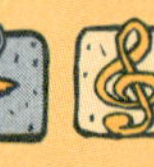
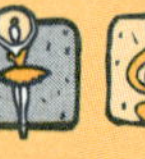
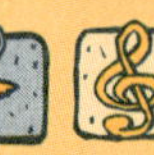
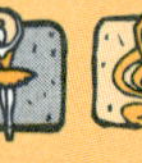

PROGRAMS:	**WORKSHOPS, CLASSES, RESIDENCIES**
SCHEDULE:	YEAR-ROUND, WEEKDAYS, EVENINGS, WEEKENDS
DETAILS:	COST FOR SOME PROGRAMS

Families

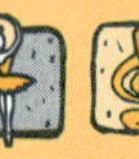
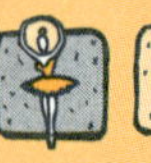
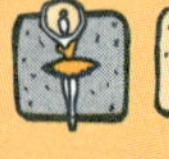
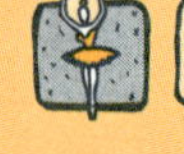
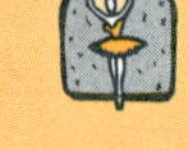
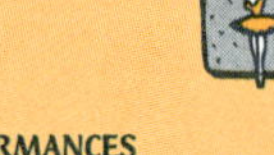

PROGRAMS:	**WORKSHOPS**
SCHEDULE:	YEAR-ROUND, WEEKENDS

FRIENDS OF THE LANKERSHIM CENTER FOR THE ARTS

SFV

5108 Lankershim Boulevard
North Hollywood, CA 91601
Ph: 818-762-8075
www.ar2u.com/LAPS

F. Mooney

G. RAY HAWKINS GALLERY

908 Colorado Avenue **WS**
Santa Monica, CA 90401
Ph: 310-394-5558
Fax: 310-576-2468

Vintage, modern masters and contemporary photography.

GAGOSIAN GALLERY

456 N. Camden Drive **WS**
Beverly Hills, CA 90210
Ph: 310-271-9400
Fax: 310-271-9420
www.artscene.com/Gagosian.html

Candy Coleman Co-Director gagosian@aol.com
Robert Shapazian Co-Director

20th Century painting and sculpture.

GALEF INSTITUTE, THE

11150 Santa Monica Boulevard,3rd Floor **WS**
Los Angeles, CA 90025
Ph: 310-479-8883
Fax: 310-473-9720
www.dwoknet.galef.org

Sue Beauregard Vice-President sue@galef.org

GALERIA SISTER KAREN BOCCALERO

Self-Help Graphics **DSC**
Casa de Sousa
19 W. Olvera Street
Los Angeles, CA 90012
Ph: 323-881-6444
Fax: 323-881-6447

GALLERY 258

258 S. Robertson Boulevard **WS**
Beverly Hills, CA 90211
Ph: 310-659-0741
Fax: 310-360-0548

Molly Barnes

We present contemporary artists of Los Angeles and New York.

GALLERY 825/LA ART ASSOCIATION

825 N. La Cienega Boulevard 501 (c)3 **WS**
Los Angeles, CA 90069-4707
Ph: 310-652-8272
Fax: 310-652-9251

Amy Perez Director

GALLERY AT 777

777 S. Figueroa Street, Suite 3300 **DSC**
Los Angeles, CA 90017
Ph: 213-236-3972
Fax: 213-236-3929

Marie-Claire Peron Director mcperon@777tower.com

GALLERY BY THE SEA

222 W. 6th Street **SB**
San Pedro, CA 90732
Ph: 310-833-3976

Kim Berry Director

Non-profit artists' cooperative dedicated to exhibiting the work of Southern California artists.

GALLERY ELITE

55 N. Venice Boulevard **WS**
Venice, CA 90291
Ph: 310-574-9596
Fax: 310-574-9646

Alana Delon galleryelite@msn.com

GALLERY SOOLIP

550 Norwich Drive **WS**
West Hollywood, CA 90069
Ph: 310-360-0154
Fax: 10-360-0153

Nancy Cahill Director soolipart@aol.com

The gallery presents works on paper

GALVANIC PRESS/GALLERY 7916

7916 Beverly Boulevard **WS**
Los Angeles, CA 90048
Ph: 323-634-7323
Fax: 323-634-7325
www.loop.com/~towey

Mike Towey Owner

Galvanic Press and the associated gallery specializes in 20th-century illustration graphics with a special focus on works originating from 1930 to 1960. Domestic and foreign artists are represented in unique original painting, vintage posters and high quality Iris prints.

- 5-6 exhibitions per year featuring illustration and advertising graphics
- custom designed graphics works
- Iris printmaking, scanning and digital archiving
- custom framing
- resource for set designers, decorators and furniture stores for individualized projects

G

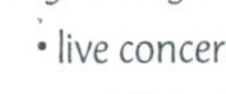

GAMBLE HOUSE, THE

4 Westmoreland Place
Pasadena, CA 91103-3593
Ph: 626-793-3334
Fax: 626-577-7547

501 (c)3 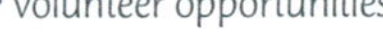

Bobbi Mapstone	Public Relations Manager/ x 10
Edward Bosley	Director
Lee Sanders	Bookstore Manager

Built in 1908, the Gamble House, an internationally recognized masterpiece of the American Arts and Crafts Movement, and a national historic monument, is the best preserved and most complete work of architects Charles and Henry Greene.

- docent led house tours (Thursday - Sunday), 1-hour long
- Gamble House Bookstore
- lectures
- book signings
- special tours of other Greene and Greene houses
- volunteer opportunities and training
- self-guided tours during Thanksgiving and Christmas
- free open house Sunday in May to celebrate National Museum Day with

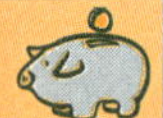

Self-selected seventh-and eighth-grade gifted public school students are trained to tour the house by adult docents. These students, in turn, give house tours to classes of fourth and fifth-graders and their teachers.

Pre/K-12

PROGRAMS: **RESIDENCIES, GUIDED TOURS**
SCHEDULE: SPRING, FALL, WINTER, WEEKDAYS
DETAILS: GRADES 3-8, VISUAL & PERFORMING ARTS
ARCHITECTURE AND DESIGN, HISTORICAL/CULTURAL CONTEXT
FACILITY FOR SCHOOL VISITS, EDUCATIONAL MATERIALS AVAILABLE

GAY MEN'S CHORUS OF LOS ANGELES

8235 Santa Monica Boulevard, Suite 210
West Hollywood, CA 90046-5968
Ph: 323-650-0756
Fax: 323-650-0758
www.gmcla.org

501 (c)3 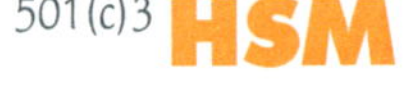

Jon Bailey	Artistic Director	gmclahq@earthlink.net
Peter Massey	Managing Director	

The Gay Men's Chorus of Los Angeles is an ensemble dedicated to excellence in the performance and advancement of a broad range of men's choral literature. GMCLA builds a sense of community and positive self-image among gay men and lesbians, and provides important bridges of understanding to the community-at-large.

- live concerts year-round in Los Angeles, West Hollywood, Glendale, Riverside and Palm Springs
- CD recordings and other merchandise
- special events
- volunteer opportunities

GEFFEN PLAYHOUSE

10886 Le Conte Avenue
Los Angeles, CA 90024
Ph: 310-208-6500
Fax: 310-208-0341

501 (c)3 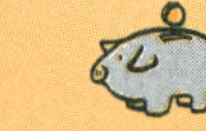

Deborah Warren	Marketing Director
Gil Cates	Producing Director
Lou Moore	Managing Director
Mary Garrett	Artistic Administrator

Located in Westwood, the Geffen Playhouse presents year-round theater productions.

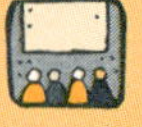

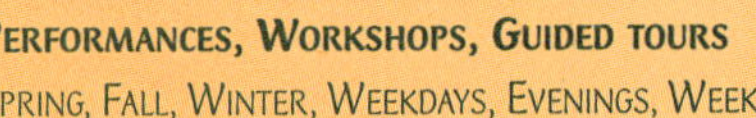

Pre/K-12

PROGRAMS: **PERFORMANCES, WORKSHOPS, GUIDED TOURS**
SCHEDULE: SPRING, FALL, WINTER, WEEKDAYS, EVENINGS, WEEKENDS
DETAILS: GRADES PRE/K-12, VISUAL & PERFORMING ARTS
HISTORICAL/CULTURAL CONTEXT, PROGRAMS ON-SITE
EDUCATIONAL MATERIALS, WORK WITH HEARING IMPAIRED

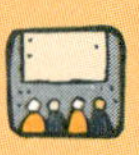

Youth

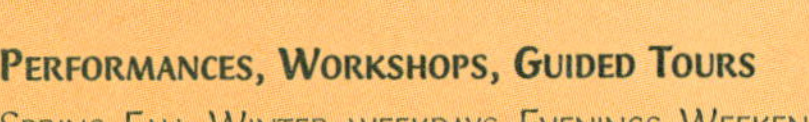

PROGRAMS: **PERFORMANCES, WORKSHOPS, GUIDED TOURS**
SCHEDULE: SPRING, FALL, WINTER, WEEKDAYS, EVENINGS, WEEKENDS

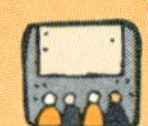

Families

PROGRAMS: **PERFORMANCES, WORKSHOPS, GUIDED TOURS**
SCHEDULE: SPRING, FALL, WINTER, WEEKDAYS, EVENINGS, WEEKENDS

GENE AUTRY MUSEUM OF WESTERN HERITAGE

4700 Western Heritage Way
Los Angeles, CA 90027
Ph: 323-667-2000
Fax: 323-660-5721
www.autry-museum.org

501 (c)3 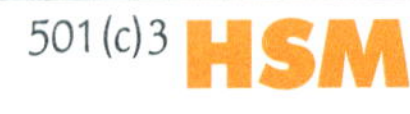

Justin Aldrich	Tourism & Public Relations Director
James Nottage	Vice-President and Chief Curator
Joanne Hale	Chief Executive Officer/Director

Located adjacent to the Los Angeles Zoo, the Gene Autry Western Heritage Museum is a nonprofit cultural and educational institution that acquires, preserves, and interprets art, artifacts, archival materials and published resources to document the history of the American West.

- exhibitions
- research center
- publications
- films
- lectures
- performances
- educational programs and tours

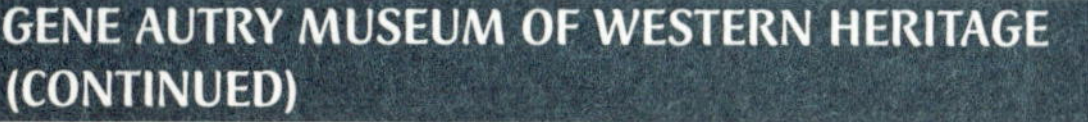

GENE AUTRY MUSEUM OF WESTERN HERITAGE (CONTINUED)

The Autry serves almost a quarter-of-a-million children and adults annually with its public and school programming, workshops, special events, gallery tours and speaker's bureau. Free, guided tours are provided to over 45,000 schoolchildren. "

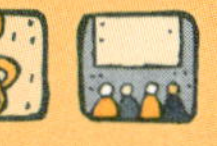
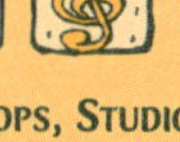

Pre/K-12

PROGRAMS:	**PERFORMANCES, WORKSHOPS, STUDIO CLASSES, GUIDED TOURS**
SCHEDULE:	YEAR-ROUND, WEEKDAYS
DETAILS:	GRADES PRE/K-12, HISTORY/SOC. SCIENCES HISTORICAL/CULTURAL CONTEXT PROGRAMS ON-SITE, BILINGUAL PROGRAMS

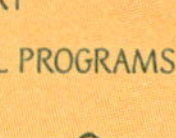
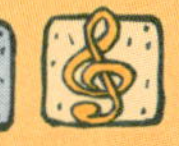
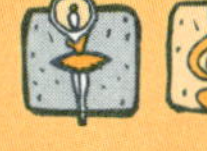

Youth

PROGRAMS:	**PERFORMANCES, WORKSHOPS, CLASSES, GUIDED TOURS**
SCHEDULE:	YEAR-ROUND, WEEKDAYS

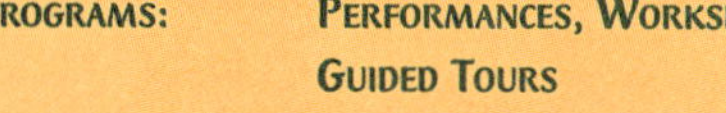

Families

PROGRAMS:	**PERFORMANCES, WORKSHOPS, CLASSES, SELF-GUIDED TOURS, GUIDED TOURS**
SCHEDULE:	YEAR-ROUND, WEEKDAYS, WEEKENDS

GEORGE C. PAGE MUSEUM OF LA BREA DISCOVERIES

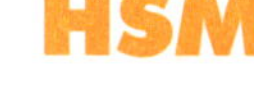

5801 Wilshire Boulevard
Los Angeles, CA 90036
Ph: 323-857-6301
Educ: 323-857-6305
Fax: 323-933-3974

Mark Rodriguez — Chief Deputy Director
James Olson — Exhibits Division Chief

The George C. Page Museum, located at the Rancho La Brea Tar Pits in Hancock Park in the heart of the city, is one of the world's most famous fossil localities, recognized for having the largest and most diverse assemblage of extinct Ice Age plants and animals in the world. Visitors learn about Los Angeles as it was between 10,000 and 40,000 years ago, during the last Ice Age, when animals such as saber-toothed cats and mammoths roamed the Los Angeles basin.

- self-guided tours
- guided tours
- volunteer opportunities

GEORGE C. PAGE MUSEUM OF LA BREA DISCOVERIES (CONTINUED)

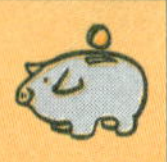

Reservations are required for school visits and must be made through the District Field Trip Representatives for public schools. All other schools may call to obtain a reservation form. Visits must be scheduled at least 3 weeks in advance.

Pre/K-12

PROGRAM:	**SELF-GUIDED TOURS, GUIDED TOURS**
SCHEDULE:	YEAR-ROUND, WEEKDAYS
DETAILS:	GRADES 3-12,HISTORY/SOC. SCIENCES HISTORICAL/CULTURAL CONTEXT, PROGRAMS ON-SITE, EDUCATIONAL MATERIALS

Families

PROGRAMS:	**SELF-GUIDED TOURS, GUIDED TOURS**
SCHEDULE:	WEEKDAYS, WEEKENDS

GEORGE STERN FINE ARTS

WS

8920 Melrose Avenue
Los Angeles, CA 90069
Ph: 310-276-2600
Fax: 310-276-2622
www.sternfinearts.com

George Stern — Director — gsfineart@aol.com

For over 23 years, George Stern Fine Arts has specialized in 19th and 20th century American art, emphasizing the early California Impressionists, American scene painters, and Modernists.

- monthly exhibitions
- books for sale about early California painters

GEORGE'S

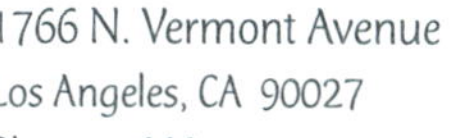

1766 N. Vermont Avenue
Los Angeles, CA 90027
Ph: 323-666-9447
Fax: 323-666-8826

Ann Faison — Director

George's is a store front commercial gallery whose aim is to make fine art affordable to the general public.

- open everyday
- monthly exhibitions featuring local and international artists

Art classes for kids on the second Sunday of each month. All workshops are taught by professional artists in a variety of media.

Pre/K-12

PROGRAMS:	**WORKSHOPS**
SCHEDULE:	YEAR-ROUND, WEEKENDS
DETAILS:	GRADES PRE/K-8, VISUAL & PERFORMING ARTS CREATIVE EXPRESSION

Youth

PROGRAMS:	**WORKSHOPS**
SCHEDULE:	YEAR-ROUND, WEEKENDS

GERMAN-AMERICAN CULTURAL SOCIETY

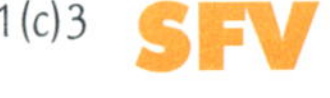
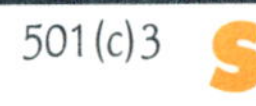
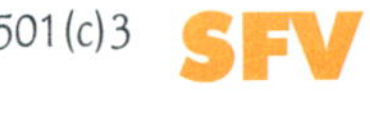
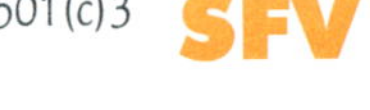

P.O. Box 7894 501(c)3 SFV
Northridge, CA 91327
Ph: 818-360-9309

Charles Bearchell Executive Director

The German-American Cultural Society is a non-profit association devoted to exploration of current and traditional cultural, social and other issues by those interested in Germany, German-American and German-Jewish groups.

- chamber music and recital programs
- dramatic readings
- panel discussions
- current events speakers
- social gatherings
- referral services
- educational and charitable support

GETTY CENTER, THE

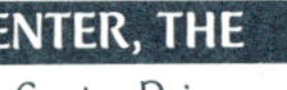
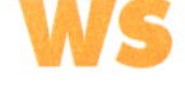
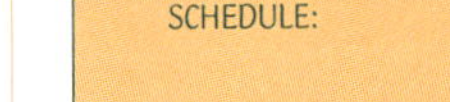

1200 Getty Center Drive WS
Los Angeles, CA 90049-1681
Ph: 310-440-7300
Admin: 310-440-7360
Educ: 310-440-7331
Fax: 310-440-7722
www.getty.edu

Lori Starr	Director of Public Affairs
John Walsh	Vice-President of the J.Paul Getty Trust Director, J. Paul Getty Museum/310-440-7330
Barry Munitz	President and Chief Executive Officer of the J.Paul Getty Trust/310-440-7555
Dianne Brigham	Head of Education
Deborah Marrow	Director, Getty Grant Program/310-440-7320

The Getty Center is the new home of the J. Paul Getty Trust, a foundation devoted to the visual arts and the humanities. The main public destination on the six-building campus is the new J. Paul Getty Museum. The Center also includes the Getty Research Institute, the Getty Conservation Institute, the Getty Education Institute, and the Getty Grant Program.

- exhibitions at the new J. Paul Getty Museum and the Research Institute at the Getty Center
- Getty Villa Museum in Malibu to reopen in the year 2001
- gallery and orientation talks
- art information rooms
- architecture tours, audio guides, and orientation films
- music, performance, and film events
- volunteer opportunities

GETTY CENTER, THE (CONTINUED)

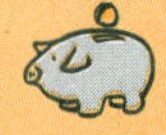
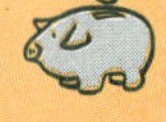

The Getty Center's education programs help visitors look more closely at works of art and deepen their understanding of those works.

Pre/K-12

PROGRAMS:	**PERFORMANCES, WORKSHOPS, STUDIO CLASSES** **SELF-GUIDED TOURS, GUIDED TOURS**
SCHEDULE:	YEAR-ROUND, WEEKDAYS
DETAILS:	PRE/K-12, VISUAL & PERFORMING ARTS AESTHETIC VALUING, CREATIVE EXPRESSION HISTORICAL/CULTURAL CONTEXT TEACHER TRAINING PROGRAMS, PROGRAMS ON-SITE, INDIVIDUALLY TAILORED PROGRAMS, EDUCATIONAL MATERIALS BILINGUA: SPANISH

Youth

PROGRAMS:	**PERFORMANCES, WORKSHOPS, CLASSES,** **SELF-GUIDED TOURS, GUIDED TOURS**
SCHEDULE:	YEAR-ROUND, WEEKDAYS, WEEKENDS

Families

PROGRAMS:	**PERFORMANCES, WORKSHOPS, CLASSES** **SELF-GUIDED TOURS, GUIDED TOURS**
SCHEDULE:	YEAR-ROUND, WEEKDAYS, WEEKENDS

GIDEON GALLERY LTD.

8748 Melrose Avenue WS
Los Angeles, CA 90069
Ph: 310-657-4194
Fax: 310-657-2515

Gideon Gallery is a commercial gallery with over 135,000 works from the16th to 19th century including original etchings, engravings, lithos both hand colored and black/white, hand colored restrikes and reproductions. The gallery services commercial and residential customers.

- framing factory with 2,000 mouldings to choose from

GIRAFFE & STAFF PUPPET CO.

P.O. Box 6898 SB
San Pedro, CA 90734
Ph: 310-831-1198
Fax: 310-831-1102

Sharon Albright Director

Giraffe & Staff Puppet Co. is a pre-school to 4th grade puppet experience that combines laughter and learning.

GIRAFFE & STAFF PUPPET CO. (CONTINUED)

Giraffe & Staff Puppet shows capture even the youngest child's attention and involve them emotionally and verbally with the show that teaches important lessons from graffitti to self-esteem.

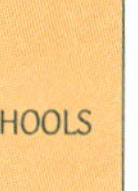

Pre/K-12

PROGRAMS: **PERFORMANCES, WORKSHOPS, STUDIO CLASSES**
SCHEDULE: YEAR-ROUND, WEEKDAYS, WEEKENDS
DETAILS: GRADES PRE/K-4, VISUAL & PERFORMING ARTS
MULTICULTURAL, SOCIAL ISSUES, AESTHETIC VALUING,
CREATIVE EXPRESSION, HISTORICAL/CULTURAL CONTEXT
CONNECTIONS/RELATIONS/APPLICATIONS
TEACHER TRAINING PROGRAMS (SALARY POINTS)
TRAVEL TO SCHOOLS, INDIVIDUALLY TAILORED PROGRAMS

GLAXA STUDIOS

3707 Sunset Boulevard **HSM**
Los Angeles, CA 90026
Ph: 323-663-5295

Richard Kaye

GLOBAL CHILDREN'S ART PARK FOR PEACE

21044 Waveview Drive 501 (c)3 **WS**
Topanga , CA 90290
Ph: 310-455-1458
Fax: 310-455-3658

Kathleen Kaminsky Director

The Global Children's Art Park for Peace, located at the University for Peace, Costa Rica, California, is an outdoor sculpture museum for children and youth expressing their concerns for world peace, human rights, and the environment. In development for the future:

- gift shop
- docent hours
- ongoing workshops for youths and mentors
- meditation center
- volunteer opportunities

Our program, will provide opportunities for creative expression for young people all over the world. Trained teachers will travel to sites to work with youth, local artisans, and mentors, and their works will be installed in the outdoor museums.

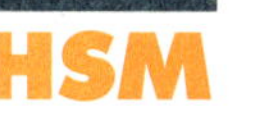

Pre/K-12

PROGRAMS: **WORKSHOPS, STUDIO CLASSES, RESIDENCIES**
SCHEDULE: YEAR-ROUND
DETAILS: GRADES 3-12, VISUAL & PERFORMING ARTS
MULTICULTURAL, AESTHETIC VALUING
CREATIVE EXPRESSION, HISTORICAL/CULTURAL CONTEXT
CONNECTIONS/RELATIONS/APPLICATIONS, TRAVEL TO SCHOOLS
PROGRAMS ON-SIT.E, INDIVIDUALLY TAILORED PROGRAMS
EDUCATIONAL MATERIALS AVAILABLE, BILINGUAL PROGRAMS

Youth

PROGRAMS: **WORKSHOPS, CLASSES, RESIDENCIES**
SCHEDULE: YEAR-ROUND

GOETHE-INSTITUT

5750 Wilshire Boulevard, #100 **HSM**
Los Angeles, CA 90036
Ph: 323-525-3388
Fax: 323-934-3597
www.goethe.de/losangeles

Irmi Maunu-Kocian Office Manager
Margi Kleinman Program Coordinator
Claudia Volkmar-Clarl Director

As a worldwide organization with 135 branches in 73 countries, the Goethe-Institut plays an important role in providing access to German language and culture all over the world.

GOLDEN GENERATION FOUNDATION

540 N. Marengo Avenue, #3 501 (c)3 **PSG**
Pasadena, CA 91101
Ph: 800-839-4983
www.reachout.org

Robert May Director/626-796-9467

Golden Generation Foundation brings developing performers opportunities to benefit needy people in Southern California.

- monthly performances featuring local artists
- volunteer opportunities
- performer support

GRAND PERFORMANCES (FORMERLY CALIFORNIA PLAZA PRESENTS)

350 S. Grand Avene, Suite A4 501 (c)3 **DSC**
Los Angeles, CA 90071
Ph: 213-687-2159
Admin: 213-687-2190
Fax: 213-687-2191
www.grandperformances.org

Michael Alexander Artistic Director malexander@grandperformances.org
Leigh Ann Hahn Associate Director lahahn@grandperformances.org

Grand Performances builds audiences and inclusive communities by bringing together, in a unique urban venue Downtown, the diverse people of Los Angeles through free performing arts programs that reflect our various communities.

- free performances, outdoors June-October
- performances at noon, evenings and weekends
- live performances in dance, music and theater
- volunteer opportunities

Free performances in Downtown Los Angeles.

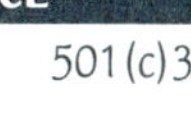

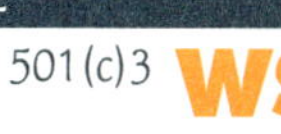

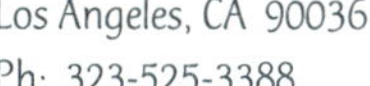

Families

PROGRAMS: **PERFORMANCES**
SCHEDULE: SUMMER, WEEKDAYS, EVENINGS, WEEKENDS

GREAT AMERICAN YANKEE (GAY) FREEDOM BAND OF LOS ANGELES

P.O. Box 460265 501(c)3 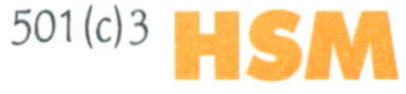
Los Angeles, CA 90046
Ph: 323-734-3472
Admin: 323-465-6274
www.ictus.com

Mark Lane President Bandnut1@aol.com

Formed in 1978, the Great American Yankee (GAY) Freedom Band performs in concerts and parades throughout Southern California. New members always welcome.

- Marching and Concert bands
- corp, twirlers and tall flags
- Brass ensemble
- administrative volunteer opportunities
- event support to assist other groups in fundraising

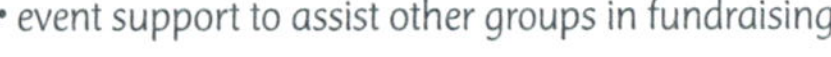

GREAT LEAP, INC.

2912 Colorado Avenue, Suite 204 501(c)3 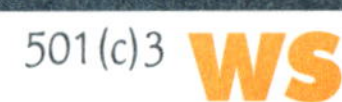
Santa Monica, CA 90404
Ph: 310-264-6696
Fax: 310-264-6699
www.bindurecords.com

Jennifer Kuida Arts Administrator greatleap@anet.net
Nobuko Miyamoto Artistic Director nobuko@bindurecords.com

Great Leap is a non-profit performing arts organization that creates and presents works that give expression to the Asian-American and multi-cultural experience through music, theater, and dance.

- touring theater pieces including "A Slice of Rice," "A Slice of Rice, Frijoles, and Greens", and "A Grain of Sand"
- workshops and concerts

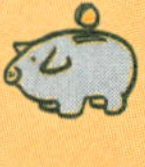

Pre/K-12 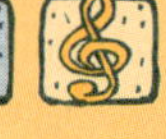 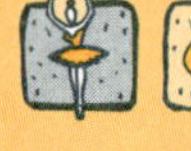 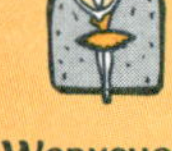

PROGRAMS: **PERFORMANCES, WORKSHOPS, RESIDENCIES**
SCHEDULE: YEAR-ROUND, WEEKDAYS, EVENINGS, WEEKENDS
DETAILS: GRADES PRE/K-12, VISUAL & PERFORMING ARTS
MULTICULTURAL, CREATIVE EXPRESSION
TRAVEL TO SCHOOLS , INDIVIDUALLY TAILORED PROGRAMS
EDUCATIONAL MATERIALS, COST FOR SOME PROGRAMS

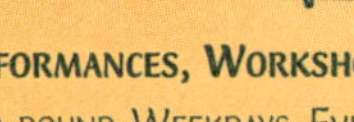

Youth 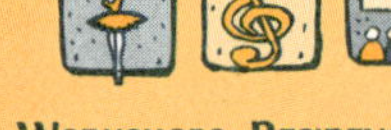

PROGRAMS: **PERFORMANCES, WORKSHOPS, RESIDENCIES**
SCHEDULE: YEAR-ROUND, WEEKDAYS, EVENINGS, WEEKENDS
DETAILS: COST FOR SOME PROGRAMS

Families 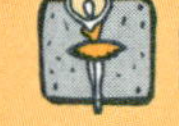

PROGRAMS: **PERFORMANCES, WORKSHOPS, RESIDENCIES**
SCHEDULE: YEAR-ROUND, WEEKDAYS, EVENINGS, WEEKENDS
DETAILS: COST FOR SOME PROGRAMS

GREEK ORTHODOX FOLK DANCE FESTIVAL (FDF)

P.O. Box 2669 501(c)3 SFV
La Mesa, CA 91943-2669
Ph: 888-FDF-YOUTH
Admin/Educ: 619-462-7812
Fax: 619 462-1766
www.greece.org/FDF

Charles Kyriacou Operations Officer/818-354-3824 ChKyriacou@aol.com
Peter Preovolos Chairman of the Board

The Greek Orthodox Greek Dance Festival hosts Greek folk dance competitions and other events for Greek youth under the auspices of the Greek Orthodox Church, Diocese of San Francisco.

- programs offered only to members of the Greek Orthodox Church: dance scholarship to Greece and Musical Apprenticeship Scholarship
- programs offered to the General Public: Folk Dance Festival dance competition and Symposium weekend dance seminars

The Folk Dance Festival inspires Greek youth to learn and preserve their Greek culture using dance as a stepping stone to learning about Greek religion, language, song, customs, etc.

Pre/K-12 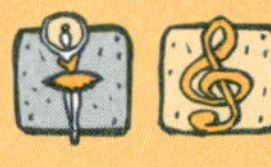

PROGRAMS: **PERFORMANCES, WORKSHOPS**
SCHEDULE: YEAR-ROUND
DETAILS: GRADES PRE/K-12, VISUAL & PERFORMING ARTS
CREATIVE EXPRESSION, HISTORICAL/CULTURAL CONTEXT

GREENE AND GREENE LIBRARY

Huntington Library 501(c)3 PSG
1151 Oxford Road
San Marino, CA 91108
Ph: 626-405-2232

Louise Mills Librarian

The Greene and Greene Library has a concentrated collection of archival material relating to the works of Charles and Henry Greene, their contemporaries and the Arts and Crafts Movement.

GRIER MUSSER MUSEUM

403 S. Bonnie Brae Street DSC
Los Angeles, CA 90057
Ph: 213-413-1814
www.isi.edu/sims/sheila/gm/html

Susan Tejada Owner tejada@isi.edu

Relive the charm of Victorian Los Angeles at the Grier Musser Museum, a 1898 Queen Anne Victorian House located close to Downtown Los Angeles.

- monthly exhibitions
- special holiday events
- docent tours
- gift shop
- postcard show

GRIER MUSSER MUSEUM (CONTINUED)

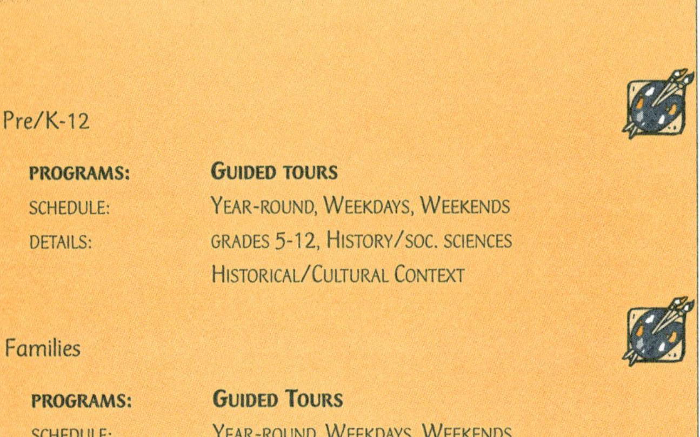

Pre/K-12

PROGRAMS:	**GUIDED TOURS**
SCHEDULE:	YEAR-ROUND, WEEKDAYS, WEEKENDS
DETAILS:	GRADES 5-12, HISTORY/SOC. SCIENCES
	HISTORICAL/CULTURAL CONTEXT

Families

PROGRAMS:	**GUIDED TOURS**
SCHEDULE:	YEAR-ROUND, WEEKDAYS, WEEKENDS

GRIFFIN CONTEMPORARY EXHIBITIONS

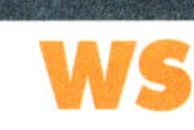

915B Electric Avenue
Venice, CA 90291
Ph: 310-452-1014
Fax: 310-399-0402

GROUP REPERTORY THEATRE

10900 Burbank Boulevard 501(c)3 SFV
North Hollywood, CA 91601
Ph: 818-769-7529
Admin: 818-771-8260

William Arrigon Executive Director
Lenny Chapman Artistic Director/ 818-761-1623

Deep in the heart of North Hollywood, the Group Repertory Theater is committed to theater that entertains, illuminates the human condition and, most importantly, never bores.

- theater production
- free Tuesday and Wednesday projects ten or twelve times a year
- audience members participate in the creative process in open forums on the Tuesday and Wednesday night projects
- internship program for aspiring actors and technicians
- training classes include classical Shakespeare roles
- outreach serves special interests of children and charitable organizations

GUAM COMMUNICATIONS NETWORK (GCN)

3530 Atlantic Avenue, Suite 103 501(c)3 LB
Long Beach, CA 90807
Ph: 562-989-5690
Fax: 562-989-5694
www.guamcomnet.org

Joseph Santos Public Information Officer/ x23
Heidi Chargualaf Cultural Heritage Officer/ x27
Lola Sablan-Santos Executive Director/ x24
Joey Quenga Educational Coordinator/ x26

Located in Long Beach, Guam Communications Network is a multidisciplinary community-based organization that promotes the culture and art forms of the Chamorro people and island of Guam.

- art shows featuring Guamanian artisans
- exhibitions featuring Chamorro folk and traditional arts
- workshops on Chamorro folk and traditional arts
- annual cultural festival
- gift items
- resource library
- volunteer opportunities
- referrals

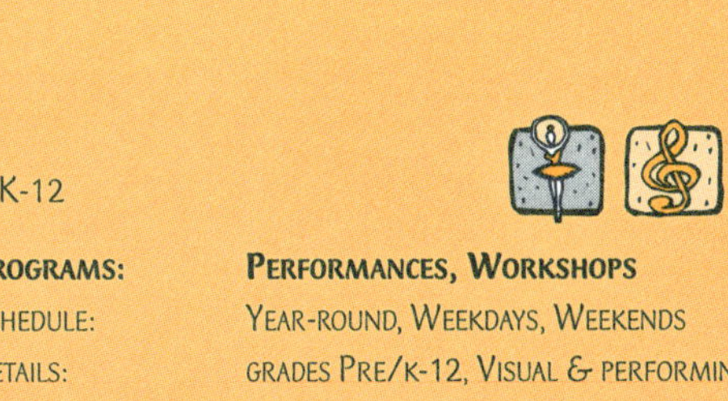

Pre/K-12

PROGRAMS:	**PERFORMANCES, WORKSHOPS**
SCHEDULE:	YEAR-ROUND, WEEKDAYS, WEEKENDS
DETAILS:	GRADES PRE/K-12, VISUAL & PERFORMING ARTS
	CULTURAL PRESERVATION, CREATIVE EXPRESSION
	HISTORICAL/CULTURAL CONTEXT
	TRAVEL TO SCHOOLS, PROGRAMS ON-SITE
	EDUCATIONAL MATERIALS AVAILABLE, BILINGUAL: CHAMORRO

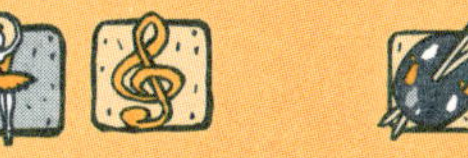

Youth

PROGRAMS:	**PERFORMANCES, WORKSHOPS**
SCHEDULE:	YEAR-ROUND, WEEKDAYS, WEEKENDS

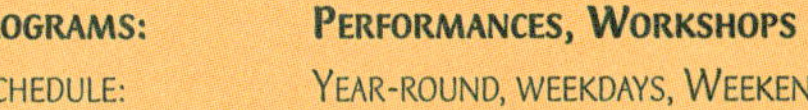
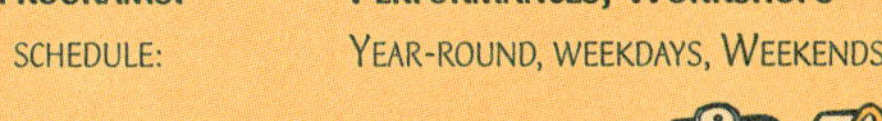
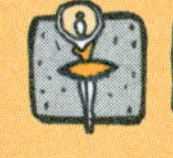
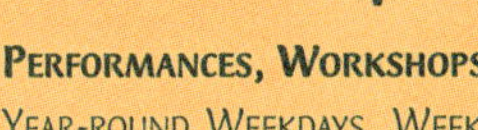

Families

PROGRAMS:	**PERFORMANCES, WORKSHOPS**
SCHEDULE:	YEAR-ROUND, WEEKDAYS., WEEKENDS

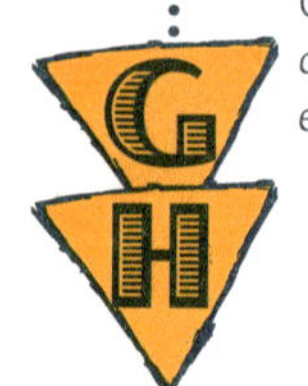

GUILD OPERA COMPANY, INCORPORATED

6425 Hollywood Bouevard, Suite 400 — 501(c)3 **HSM**
Los Angeles, CA 90028
Ph: 323-463-6593
Fax: 323-463-7570

Fran Benedict	Public Information
Paul Gleason	President
Jeannie Brimhall	Vice President, Education
Dorothy Hartshorn	Schools Liaison

Guild Opera Co. was formed in 1949 to produce full-scale opera in English for audiences of school children. Guild Opera provides professional performance experiences for Southern California singers and instrumentalists.

- volunteer opportunities including docents, design of educational materials, administrative
- one or two performances for the general public

Guild Opera creates its productions with children in mind. Preparation matericals are sent to classroom teachers and workshops are presented to music teachers. Trained docents provide props and costumes with a play-script. In addition, Guild Opera tours a contemporary opera with a residency programproviding singing and movement workshops to K-6 students.

Pre/K-12 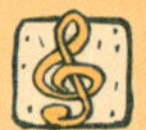

PROGRAMS:	**PERFORMANCES, RESIDENCIES**
SCHEDULE:	YEAR-ROUND, WEEKDAYS
DETAILS:	GRADES PREK-12, VISUAL & PERFORMING ARTS AESTHETIC VALUING, CREATIVE EXPRESSION TRAVEL TO SCHOOLS , INDIVIDUALLY TAILORED PROGRAMS EDUCATIONAL MATERIALS AVAILABLE

GYPSY FOLK ENSEMBLE

P.O. Box 341050 **WS**
Los Angeles, CA 90034
Ph: 310-558-0746
Fax: 310-397-6098

Julie Nelson — Director/ 818-966-4751

The Gypsy Folk Ensemble is an ethnic dance company dedicated to bringing its audience the spirit and exuberance of the folk dances of Europe, the Near East, Polynesia, and America.

- dance concerts
- dance workshops

The programs stress positive aspects of other cultures and peoples through

GYPSY FOLK ENSEMBLE (CONTINUED)

dance and music while placing folk dance in its social and geographic milieu and encouraging active audience participation in dance.

Pre/K-12 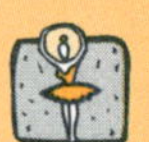 

PROGRAMS:	**PERFORMANCES, WORKSHOPS, RESIDENCIES**
SCHEDULE:	YEAR-ROUND, WEEKDAYS, EVENINGS, WEEKENDS
DETAILS:	GRADES PRE/K-12, HISTORY/SOC. SCIENCES VISUAL & PERFORMING ARTS, MULTICULTURAL PHYSICAL EDUCATION, CREATIVE EXPRESSION HISTORICAL/CULTURAL CONTEXT CONNECTIONS/RELATIONS/APPLICATIONS TRAVEL TO SCHOOLS, INDIVIDUALLY TAILORED PROGRAMS EDUCATIONAL MATERIALS AVAILABLE

Youth

PROGRAMS:	**PERFORMANCES, WORKSHOPS, RESIDENCIES**
SCHEDULE:	YEAR-ROUND, WEEKDAYS, EVENINGS, WEEKENDS

Families

PROGRAMS:	**PERFORMANCES, WORKSHOPS, RESIDENCIES**
SCHEDULE:	YEAR-ROUND, WEEKDAYS, EVENINGS, WEEKENDS

HALF A DOZEN ROSE

6 Rose Avenue **WS**
Venice, CA 90291
Ph: 310-396-0938
Fax: 310-396-1995

Philip Lalonde	Co-Director	plonde@earthlink.net
Sabine Gebser	Co-Director	

Painting, sculpture, photography, performance, and multi-media work.

HAMILTON GALLERIES

130 S. Robertson Boulevard **WS**
Los Angeles, CA 90048
Ph: 310-859-7824
Fax: 310-274-9598

Leigh Hamilton — Director

Emerging California artists.

HAMILTON GALLERIES (AT VILLAGE STUDIO)

15310 Antioch **WS**
Pacific Palisades, CA 90272
Ph: 310-459-1661
Fax: 310-274-9598

Leign Hamilton — Director

Emerging California artists.

HARBOR REGIONAL ARTS COUNCIL

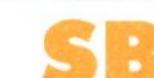

P.O. Box 1874
San Pedro, CA 90731
Ph: 310-354-4080

Developed through the City of Los Angeles Cultural Affairs Department as one of 9 regional arts councils, we are a coalition of arts and community organizations, artists, leaders, business people and all other interested members of the community who have the purpose of assessing, coalescing and acting on the cultural assets and needs of the area. This council serves San Pedro, Port of Los Angeles, Wilmington, Harbor City and Harbor Gateway. Goals include:

- develop affordable and accessible local programming that highlights and involves youth and local artists
- develop activities that celebrate the city's cultural diversity and promote community building
- serve as an advisory group to the Cultural Affairs Department on local art and cultural priorities
- strengthen the artistic advancement of the community

HARBOR UCLA MEDICAL CENTER

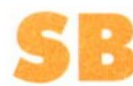

Center for Education, Therapy, and Research in the Medical Arts
1000 W. Carson Street, Box 482
Torrance, CA 90509
Ph: 310-222-3409
Fax: 310-222-4280

Paula Siler	Co-Director, Professional Practice Affairs
Tecla Mickoseff	Administrator/310-222-2101
Jerome Block	Co-Director/310-222-2444

The Center for Education, Therapy, and Research in the Medical Arts (The Center) is an interdisciplinary program at Harbor-UCLA Medical Center dedicated to providing a state-of-the-art nonprofit center for the study of art, art therapy, and creativity in a theraputic and communicative setting. The Center aims to improve the environment as a healing place for patients, families, and staff.

- Artists-in-Residence program employing artists who will work with hospitalized patients in an occupational and rehabilitative mode
- campus and hospital arts beautification and cultural arts identification program to improve the healing aspects of the hospital's structure and environment
- music and performance programs geared to the ethnic/cultural mix of the hospital
- visual and performing arts programs and exhibitions offered to other L.A. County Hospitals and the community-oriented hospitals in the area, and the Torrance Cultural Center

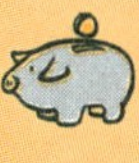

Establishment of The Center for Education, Therapy, and Research in the Medical Arts at Harbor-UCLA Medical Center ilustrates this organization's commitment to improve patient care, improved quality of work life, and continued community outreach efforts.

Families

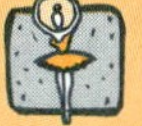 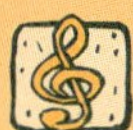 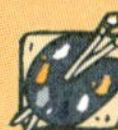

PROGRAMS: **PERFORMANCES, CLASSES**
SCHEDULE: YEAR-ROUND, WEEKDAYS, EVENINGS

HARMONIA BAROQUE PLAYERS

19795 Villager Circle
Yorba Linda, CA 92886
Ph: 714-970-8545
Fax: 714-970-8439

Marika Frankl — Director

Harmonia Baroque Players is a baroque chamber music ensemble, consisting of recorders, baroque violin, baroque oboe, viola da gamba, lute, baroque guitar, and harpsicord. We present public concerts and educational, entertaining lecture-recitals. We have a concert series in Pasadena, Hermosa Beach, and Newport Beach.

- annual three-concert series
- educational, entertaining programs in libraries, community centers, senior centers, and schools

Harmonia Baroque Players presents lecture-recitals for family audiences in libraries and community centers. These are informal programs open to questions and answer, where the musicians talk about their unique instruments and the characteristics of music from many periods. Similar programs are geared to schools from 3rd grade up.

Pre/K-12

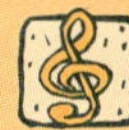

PROGRAMS: **PERFORMANCES**
SCHEDULE: YEAR-ROUND, WEEKDAYS, EVENINGS, WEEKENDS
DETAILS: GRADES 3-12, VISUAL & PERFORMING ARTS
TRAVEL TO SCHOOLS , INDIVIDUALLY TAILORED PROGRAMS

Youth

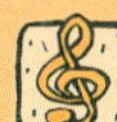

PROGRAMS: **PERFORMANCES**
SCHEDULE: YEAR ROUND, WEEKDAYS, EVENINGS, WEEKENDS

Families

PROGRAMS: **PERFORMANCES**
SCHEDULE: YEAR-ROUND, WEEKDAYS, EVENINGS, WEEKENDS

HAUGH PERFORMING ARTS CENTER

Citrus College
Glendora, CA 91741-1899
Ph: 626-963-9411
Admin: 626-852-8047
Fax: 626-335-4715
www.citrus.cc.ca.us/hpac/hpachtm

PSG

Linda Graves — Promotion and Operation Supervisor/626-852-4045
Greg Hinrichsen — Director of Performing Arts

Located in the heart of the San Gabriel Valley, Haugh Performing Arts Center is a 1400-seat proscenium venue that presents a diverse range of performing arts and artists to the community.

- Evening at Eight: 10-15 performances annually featuring celebrity performers, music ensembles, and theater productions
- Sundays at Two: 6-10 performances and productions
- Passport to Travel: 10 travel/adventure color films featuring live narration by the filmmakers
- Saturday Series for Kids: 6 programs annually, featuring live theater, music, and entertainment designed to introduce children to the theater

Pre/K-12

PROGRAMS:	**PERFORMANCES**
SCHEDULE:	SPRING, FALL, WINTER, WEEKDAYS, EVENINGS, WEEKENDS
DETAILS:	GRADES PRE/K-6, AESTHETIC VALUING

Famlilies

PROGRAMS:	**PERFORMANCES**
SCHEDULE:	SPRING, FALL, WINTER, WEEKDAYS, EVENINGS, WEEKENDS

HBO WORKSPACE

733 N. Seward Street
Hollywood, CA 90038
Ph: 323 993-6099

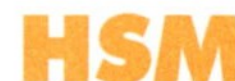

Operated by HBO, a cost-free workspace for the experimental in comedy and otherwise risk-taking performance.

HEART PROJECT, THE

1724 N.Whitley Avenue
Los Angeles, CA 90028
Ph: 323-962-ARTS
Admin: 323-962-6761
Fax: 323-962-6710

HSM

Cynthia Campoy Brophy — Director — heartproj@aol.com

The HeArt project produces a year-long series of multi-disciplinary arts workshops at Los Angeles teen centers with no other access to the arts. The workshops are taught by professional artists and culminate in presentations at L.A.'s cultural centers.

- public presentations at art centers around the city of work created by the students during their workshops

HEART PROJECT, THE (CONTINUED)

The HeArt Project season runs from September through June at four continuation high schools and one housing community center. Students work with artists in disciplines ranging from painting, poetry, folk art, dance, architecture, theater, video and sculpture. The HeArt Project also produces advanced residencies for the more committed students.

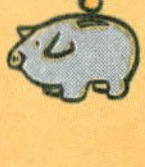

Pre/K-12

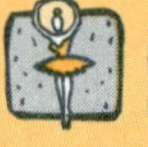 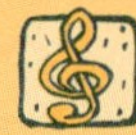 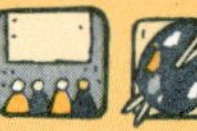

PROGRAMS:	**PERFORMANCES, WORKSHOPS, RESIDENCIES GUIDED TOURS**
SCHEDULE:	YEAR-ROUND, WEEKDAYS
DETAILS:	GRADES 9-12, VISUAL & PERFORMING ARTS, ARCHITECTURE AND VIDEO, MULTICULTURAL CREATIVE EXPRESSION, HISTORICAL/CULTURAL CONTEXT CONNECTIONS/RELATIONS/APPLICATIONS TRAVEL TO SCHOOLS

Youth

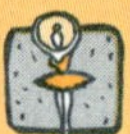 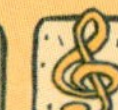 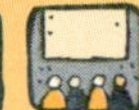 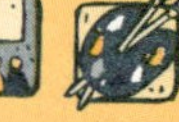

PROGRAMS:	**PERFORMANCES, WORKSHOPS, RESIDENCIES, GUIDED TOURS**
SCHEDULE:	YEAR-ROUND, WEEKDAYS

HEILMAN -C

P.O. Box 49001
Los Angeles, CA 90049
Ph: 310-824-2508
Fax: 310-476-2750
www.heilman-c.com

WS

Julie Heinsohn — Director/ x100 — g@heilman_c.com

Sculpture, painting, performance, and cinema.

HERBERT PALMER GALLERY

9003 Melrose Avenue
Los Angeles, CA 90069
Ph: 310-278-6407
Fax: 310-550-0758

WS

Julie Hopkins — Assistant Director
Herbert Palmer — Director

Modern and contemporary art

HERITAGE GALLERY

718 N. La Cienega Boulevard
Los Angeles, CA 90069
Ph: 310-652-7738

WS

Benjamin Horowitz — Owner
Charlotte Sherman — Associate

The Heritage Gallery exhibits art from the 1930's to the 1990's.

- exhibits artists of California and social realist artists of the world

HERMOSA CIVIC THEATER

City of Hermosa Beach
710 Pier Avenue
Hermosa Beach, CA 90254
Ph: 310-318-0280
Fax: 310-372-4333

SB

Mitch Assumma — Recreation Supervisor
Mary Rooney — Community Resources Director

Owned and operated by the City of Hermosa Beach, the 502-seat Civic Theater serves as a host to everything from town meetings to visiting children's theater and fashion shows.

- community group meetings
- recreational and theater classes for children
- rental facility for gatherings, lectures, surf films, theater, exhibitions and more
- venue for the South Bay Playhouse
- home of the Hermosa Beach Community Center Foundation
- box office and concessions for use
- complete facilities for children's theater

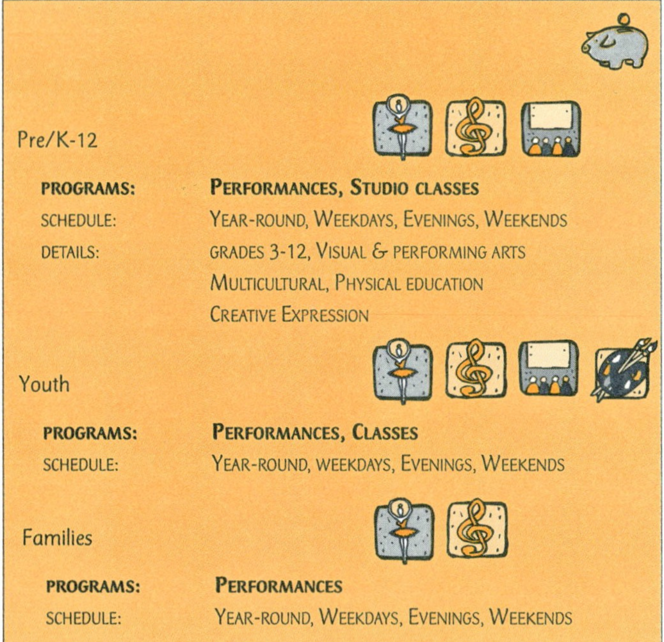

Pre/K-12

PROGRAMS: PERFORMANCES, STUDIO CLASSES
SCHEDULE: YEAR-ROUND, WEEKDAYS, EVENINGS, WEEKENDS
DETAILS: GRADES 3-12, VISUAL & PERFORMING ARTS
MULTICULTURAL, PHYSICAL EDUCATION
CREATIVE EXPRESSION

Youth

PROGRAMS: PERFORMANCES, CLASSES
SCHEDULE: YEAR-ROUND, WEEKDAYS, EVENINGS, WEEKENDS

Families

PROGRAMS: PERFORMANCES
SCHEDULE: YEAR-ROUND, WEEKDAYS, EVENINGS, WEEKENDS

HIGHLAND GROUNDS

742 N. Highland Avenue
Hollywood, CA 90038
Ph: 323-466-1507
www.highlandgrounds.com

HSM

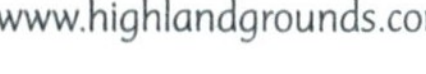

Rich Brenner — Owner

Highland Grounds is a spacious indoor/outdoor Hollywood oasis which emphasizes community. It's a venue for local acoustic singer-songwriters or bands and occasional spoken-word events.

HIGHLAND PARK HERITAGE TRUST

P.O. Box 50894
Los Angeles, CA 90050-0894
Ph: 323-256-4326
Fax: 323-255-0041

501(c)3 **ELA**

Nicole Possert — Vice President/323-255-5792

Located along the historic Arroyo Seco, birthplace of the Arts and Crafts movement, the H.P.H.T. is a community based organization dedicated to historic preservation through education and advocacy.

- annual Home Tour guided by Docent Walking Tours, showcasing the history of the area and the architectural resources, usually in May
- annual Awards Ceremony celebrating people who have improved and or maintained their property in the Highland Park area
- general monthly meetings (second Monday of the month at 7pm)
- special community celebrations dealing with our historic and cultural heritage of Highland Park and Garvanza

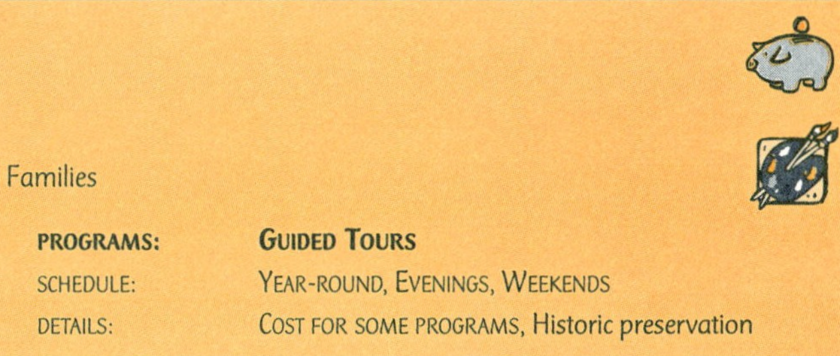

Families

PROGRAMS: GUIDED TOURS
SCHEDULE: YEAR-ROUND, EVENINGS, WEEKENDS
DETAILS: COST FOR SOME PROGRAMS, Historic preservation

HIGHWAYS

1651 18th Street
Santa Monica, CA 90404
Ph: 310-315-1459
Admin: 310-453-1755
Fax: 310-453-4347

501(c)3 **WS**

Mary Milelzcik — Administrative Director/Gallery Curator
Tim Miller — Artistic Director

Located in Santa Monica, Highways celebrates its 10th Anniversary in 1999 as the boldest center for cutting-edge new performance and visual art in Southern California.

- over 200 performances yearly by solo artists, small dance companies, and theatre ensembles
- over 9 contemporary visual art exhibits yearly
- workshops in dance, theater, music and performance
- special events
- see the Highways Calendar for our new website and email address.

HISTORICAL SOCIETY OF LONG BEACH

418 Pine Avenue
Long Beach, CA 90802
Ph: 562-495-1210
Fax: 562-495-1281

501 (c)3 **LB**

Julie Bartolotto Executive Direcrtor

At the Historical Society of Long Beach and through our programs, we promote, develop, exhibit and preserve Long Beach history. We serve those interested in local history, students, educators, and researchers.

- free rotating exhibits featuring Long Beach history
- free monthly programs including an annual cemetary tour, an annual earthquake meeting, and "My Piece of Long Beach History"
- gift shop including photo reproduction
- volunteer opportunities
- research center

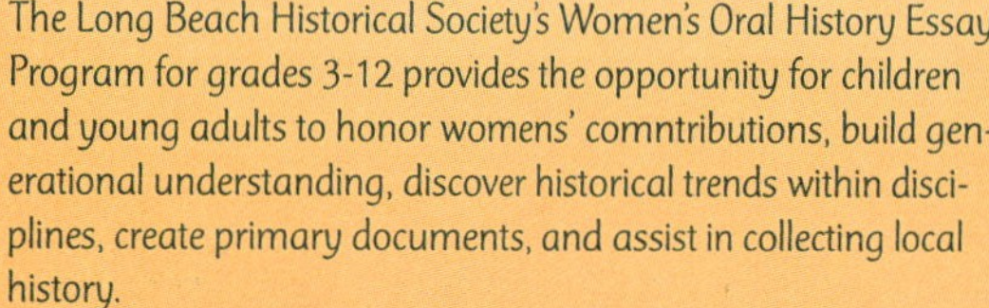

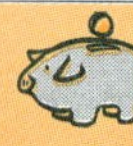

The Long Beach Historical Society's Women's Oral History Essay Program for grades 3-12 provides the opportunity for children and young adults to honor womens' comntributions, build generational understanding, discover historical trends within disciplines, create primary documents, and assist in collecting local history.

Pre/K-12

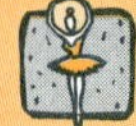
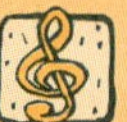
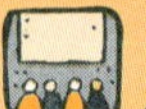
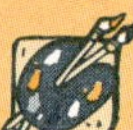

PROGRAMS: **WOMEN'S ORAL HISTORY PROJECT**
SCHEDULE: SPRING
DETAILS: GRADES 3-12, HISTORY/SOC. SCIENCES

HOLLYHOCK HOUSE AND GALLERY

4800 Hollywood Boulevard
Los Angeles, CA 90027
Ph: 323-913-4157
TTD: 323-660-4254
Fax: 213-485-8396

HSM

Thomas Stallman Exhibition Curator
Susan Foley Johannsen Director of Programming
Sara Cannon Education Coordinator
Laurel Granger Event Coordinator

Built between 1919 and 1922, the Hollyhock House is the first Los Angeles project of Frank Lloyd Wright for Aline Barnsdall, as part of her vision to create an arts community in Hollywood. Since 1927, the City of Los Angeles Cultural Affairs Department has maintained Barnsdall's vision by providing a center for the visual and performing arts.

- tours of the historic house
- bookstore
- gallery which features work of Southern California architects and artisans
- volunteer opportunities through "Friends of the Hollyhock House"

HOLLYHOCK HOUSE AND GALLERY (CONTINUED)

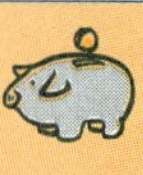

The Hollyhock House and Gallery provides an opportunity for K-12 students, as well as all Los Angeles residents to learn the unique history of architecture and social trends in Los Angeles during the 1920's and to see current architecture of the region exhibited in the Frank Lloyd Wright Gallery.

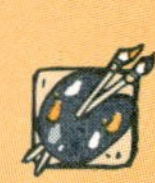

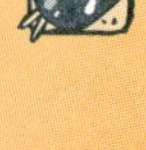

Pre/K-12

PROGRAMS: **WORKSHOPS, GUIDED TOURS**
SCHEDULE: YEAR-ROUND, WEEKDAYS, WEEKENDS
DETAILS: GRADES 3-12, HISTORY/SOC. SCIENCES, PROGRAMS ON-SITE , EDUCATIONAL MATERIALS AVAILABLE

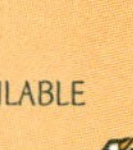

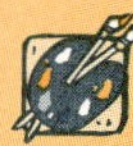

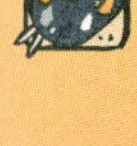

Families

PROGRAMS: **WORKSHOPS, GUIDED TOURS**
SCHEDULE: YEAR-ROUND, WEEKDAYS, WEEKENDS
DETAILS: COST FOR SOME PROGRAMS

HOLLYWOOD BOWL

2301 N. Highland Avenue
Los Angeles, CA 90078
Ph: 323-850-2000
Admin: 213-972-7300
Educ: 213-972-7597
Fax: 213-617-3065
www.hollywoodbowl.org

501 (c)3 **HSM**

Leni Boorstin Public Affairs Director lboorstin@laphil.org
Lindsey Nelson Artistic Administrator/ 323-850-2164
Willem Wijnbergen Executive V.P. and Managing Director
Sue Knussen Director of Education sknussen@laphil.org
Carol Merrill-Mirsky Director, Hollywood Bowl Museum/ 323-850-2058

The 18,000-seat outdoor Hollywood Bowl hosts a summer festival featuring the LA Philharmonic and Hollywood Bowl Orchestras, classical music, jazz, pop, world music, rock, and educational programs. The Hollywood Bowl Museum is open year-round.

- summer home of the Los Angeles Philharmonic
- home of the Hollywood Bowl Orchestra
- classical, pop, jazz, and world music concerts
- Open House at the Bowl (ages 3-9)
- invitational rehearsals
- summer master classes
- E. Edelman Hollywood Bowl Museum (open year-round, free general admission, and school tours)
- volunteer opportunities with "Friends of the Hollywood Bowl"
- Hollywood Bowl Gift Shop
- open rehearsals

HOLLYWOOD BOWL (CONTINUED)

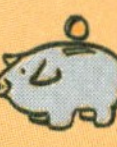

The Open House at the Hollywood Bowl (for ages 3-9) is a six-week music festival from cultures around the world. These interactive programs feature a storyteller, musical performances (sometimes incorporating dance), and culturally relevant crafts workshops. Other summer educational activities are invitational rehearsals and master classes.

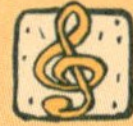

Pre/K-12

PROGRAMS:	**PERFORMANCES, WORKSHOPS, GUIDED TOURS**
SCHEDULE:	SUMMER, WEEKDAYS, WEEKENDS
DETAILS:	GRADES PRE/K-12, VISUAL & PERFORMING ARTS CREATIVE EXPRESSION, HISTORICAL/CULTURAL CONTEXT TEACHER TRAINING PROGRAMS (SALARY POINTS) TRAVEL TO SCHOOLS, PROGRAMS ON-SITE INDIVIDUALLY TAILORED PROGRAMS, EDUCATIONAL MATERIALS COST FOR SOME PROGRAMS

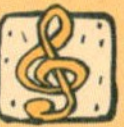

Youth

PROGRAMS:	**PERFORMANCES, GUIDED TOURS**
SCHEDULE:	SUMMER, WEEKDAYS, EVENINGS, WEEKENDS

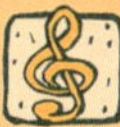

Families

PROGRAMS:	**PERFORMANCES, GUIDED TOURS**
SCHEDULE:	SUMMER, EVENINGS, WEEKENDS

HOLLYWOOD BOWL MUSEUM

2301 N. Highland Avenue
Los Angeles, CA 90078
Ph: 323-850-2058
Fax: 323-850-2066
www.hollywoodbowl.org

501(c)3 **HSM**

Carol Merrill-Mirsky	Director/Curator	museum@laphil.org
Cara Dolan	Museum Assistant	cdolan@laphil.org

The Hollywood Bowl Museum, a department of the Los Angeles Philharmonic Association, is a "music museum" presenting exhibits and public programs on a wide variety of music and culture.

- exhibitions including "The Hollywood Bowl," "Betty Freeman-Music People & Others" and "GTE Resouce Center"
- public programs including lectures, panels, and concerts
- educational programs including school tours, master classes, and additional programs in cooperation with the Los Angeles Philharmonic Education Department
- volunteer programs including gallery hosts and docents
- publications

HOLLYWOOD BOWL MUSEUM (CONTINUED)

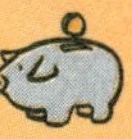

The Hollywood Bowl Museum's program includes a walking tour of the Hollywood Bowl and grounds, music education activities in the museum, and gallery tours.

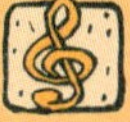

Pre/K-12

PROGRAMS:	**PERFORMANCES, SELF-GUIDED TOURS, GUIDED TOURS**
SCHEDULE:	YEAR-ROUND, WEEKDAYS
DETAILS:	GRADES PRE/K-12, VISUAL & PERFORMING ARTS CREATIVE EXPRESSION, HISTORICAL/CULTURAL CONTEXT CONNECTIONS/RELATIONS/APPLICATIONS PROGRAMS ON-SITE, INDIVIDUALLY TAILORED PROGRAMS

Youth

PROGRAMS:	**PERFORMANCES, SELF-GUIDED TOURS, GUIDED TOURS**
SCHEDULE:	YEAR-ROUND, WEEKDAYS

Families

PROGRAMS:	**PERFORMANCES, SELF-GUIDED TOURS, GUIDED TOURS**
SCHEDULE:	YEAR-ROUND, WEEKDAYS

HOLLYWOOD ENTERTAINMENT MUSEUM

7021 Hollywood Boulevard
Hollywood, CA 90028
Ph: 323-465-7900
Admin: 323-960-4803
Educ: 323-960-4802
Fax: 323-469-9576
www.hollywoodmuseum.org

501(c)3 **HSM**

Ceri Wilson	Marketing Director/ 323-960-4804
Richard Peterson	Curator/ 323-960-4805
Phyllis Caskey	President & CEO/ 323-960-4801
Ernest Dailey	Education Director
Rachel Smookler	Director of Admissions

The Hollywood Entertainment Museum celebrates Hollywood the place and the industry, with technologically advanced hands-on exhibits, and tours through a studio backlot, original sets, and educational programs.

- screening rooms
- editing suite
- foley suite
- permanent and changing exhibits
- facility rental for special events
- group and youth tours
- curriculum development
- educational and family programs
- special events
- Academy Award party
- Celebrity Golf Tournament

HOLLYWOOD ENTERTAINMENT MUSEUM (CONTINUED)

Hollywood Entertainment Museum brings Los Angeles' largest export and most distinctive art form to life in the setting from which it originated.

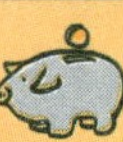

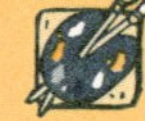

Pre/K-12

PROGRAMS:	**WORKSHOPS, SELF-GUIDED TOURS, GUIDED TOURS**
SCHEDULE:	YEAR-ROUND, WEEKDAYS, EVENINGS, WEEKENDS
DETAILS:	GRADES PRE/K-12, VISUAL & PERFORMING ARTS MULTICULTURAL, CREATIVE EXPRESSION HISTORICAL/CULTURAL CONTEXT CONNECTIONS/RELATIONS/APPLICATIONS TRAVEL TO SCHOOLS, PROGRAMS ON-SITE INDIVIDUALLY TAILORED PROGRAMS, EDUCATIONAL MATERIALS BILINGUA: SPANISH, COST FOR SOME PROGRAMS

Youth

PROGRAMS:	**WORKSHOPS, SELF-GUIDED TOURS, GUIDED TOURS**
SCHEDULE:	YEAR-ROUND, WEEKDAYS, EVENINGS, WEEKENDS
DETAILS:	COST FOR SOME PROGRAMS

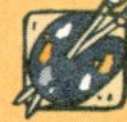

Families

PROGRAMS:	**WORKSHOPS, SELF-GUIDED TOURS, GUIDED TOURS**
SCHEDULE:	YEAR-ROUND, WEEKDAYS, EVENINGS, WEEKENDS
DETAILS:	COST FOR SOME PROGRAMS

HUAYUCALTIA

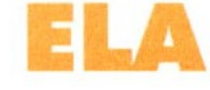

4700 Baltimore Street
Los Angeles, CA 90042
Ph/Fax: 323-258-6903

Antonio Ezkauriatza	Administrative Manager	ezeka@earthlink.com
Ciro Hurtado	Musical Director	ihti@ixnetcom.com

Huayucaltia is a multi-national musical group that utilizes Latin American styles and instruments in order to create a unique world sound that transcends geographical and cultural barriers.

- indoor and outdoor live concerts
- workshops and demonstrations

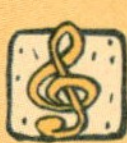

Youth

PROGRAMS:	**PERFORMANCES, WORKSHOPS**
SCHEDULE:	YEAR-ROUND, EVENINGS, WEEKENDS

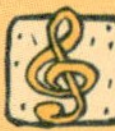

Families

PROGRAMS:	**PERFORMANCES**
SCHEDULE:	YEAR-ROUND, EVENINGS, WEEKENDS

HUDSON THEATRES

6539 Santa Monica Boulevard — 501(c)3 — HSM
Hollywood, CA 90038
Ph: 323-856-4249
Admin: 323-856-4252
Fax: 323-856-4316

Marc Alvarado	Managing Director
Elizabeth Reilly	Artistic Director

Located on Theatre Row in Hollywood, the Hudson Theatres are devoted to the development and production of new works by American playwrights. We are committed to doing our part to raise the level of excellence of theatre in Los Angeles while hopefully providing a growing interest in gratifying live theatre.

HUNTINGTON BEACH ART CENTER

538 Main Street — 501(c)3
Huntington Beach, CA 92648
Ph: 714-374-1650
Admin: 714-374-1659
Fax: 714-374-1654
www.hbcoca.org

Tyler Stallings	Curator of Programs
Naida Osline	Director/ x1661
Maria Babaccia	Education Coordinator

Located on the beach, the Huntington Beach Art Center is a multidisciplinary community-based organization that presents contemporary art and popular culture in all of its forms.

- classes and workshops
- movement
- dance
- readings

We specialize in intensive projects with high schools that culminate in exhibitions and catalogues.

Pre/K-12

PROGRAMS:	**STUDIO CLASSES, RESIDENCIES**
SCHEDULE:	SPRING, WEEKDAYS
DETAILS:	GRADES 9-12, VISUAL & PERFORMING ARTS CREATIVE EXPRESSION, HISTORICAL/CULTURAL CONTEXT TRAVEL TO SCHOOLS, INDIVIDUALLY TAILORED PROGRAMS

HUNTINGTON LIBRARY, ART COLLECTIONS & BOTANICAL GARDENS

1151 Oxford Road
San Marino, CA 91108
Ph: 626-405-2141
Admin: 626-405-2100
Educ: 626-405-2126
Fax: 626-405-0225
www.huntington.org

501(c)3 **PSG**

Catherine Bobcock — Communications Director/ 626-405-2147
Edward Nygren — Director of the Art Collections/ 626-405-2226
Robert Skotheim — President/ 626-405-2115
Lee Devereux — Volunteer Services Director/ 626-405-2105

The Huntington is a museum and research center surrounded by 150 acres of gardens. Collections emphasize English and American history and literature, as well as British, French, and American art.

- permanent collections
- changing exhibitions
- garden tours
- gift shop
- English tea
- chamber music concerts
- exhibit lectures
- garden shows and sales
- volunteer opportunities

Garden workshops for children

Pre/K-12

PROGRAMS:	**GUIDED TOURS**
SCHEDULE:	SPRING, FALL, WINTER, WEEKDAYS
DETAILS:	GRADES 3-12, HISTORY/SOC. SCIENCES VISUAL & PERFORMING ARTS, AESTHETIC VALUING HISTORICAL/CULTURAL CONTEXT, TEACHER TRAINING PROGRAMS , FACILITY FOR SCHOOL VISITS EDUCATIONAL MATERIALS AVAILABLE

Youth

PROGRAMS:	**WORKSHOPS**
SCHEDULE:	YEAR-ROUND, WEEKENDS
DETAILS:	COST FOR SOME PROGRAMS

IGUANA GALLERY, THE

107 N. Myrtle Avenue
Monrovia, CA 91016
Ph: 626-358-0783
Admin: 626-357-2924
Fax: 626-358-0783

PSG

By appointment only

IKON LIMITED FINE ARTS

170 S. La Brea Avenue
Los Angeles, CA 90036
Ph: 323-937-3220
Fax: 323-937-3229

HSM

Kay Koch-Richards — Director — ikonltd@artnet.net

Contemporary and modern works on paper

IMAGINATION STATION

4712 Admiralty Way #515
Marina del Rey, CA 90292
Ph: 310-854-4196

501(c)3 **WS**

Jennifer Brandt — Director
Jake Eberle — Director
Shari Getz — Director

Imagination Station, a nonprofit children's theater company, is first and foremost dedicated to providing quality, non-violent entertainment which children and parents can share and enjoy together.

- volunteer opportunities: ushering programs, backstage crew set construction and costuming

Imagination Station's Performance Program offers highly interactive and unique new versions of familiar classics, encouraging children to question underlying thematic and moral issues. The company's Acting Workshops offer a fun, safe environment in which children can explore and create.

Pre/K-12

PROGRAMS:	**PERFORMANCES**
SCHEDULE:	YEAR-ROUND, WEEKDAYS
DETAILS:	GRADES PRE/K-6, VISUAL & PERFORMING ARTS CREATIVE EXPRESSION, CONNECTIONS/RELATIONS/APPLICATIONS FACILITY FOR SCHOOL VISITS, PROGRAMS ON-SITE

Youth

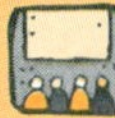

PROGRAMS:	**WORKSHOPS**
SCHEDULE:	YEAR-ROUND, WEEKDAYS

Families

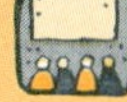

PROGRAMS:	**PERFORMANCES**
SCHEDULE:	YEAR-ROUND, EVENINGS

INCA, THE PERUVIAN ENSEMBLE

P.O. Box 39813 501(c)3
Los Angeles, CA 90039
Ph: 323-662-0074
Fax: 323-662-1941

Guillermo Bordarampe Director pervinca@earthlink.net

"INCA", the Peruvian Ensmble provides music and music & dance programs from Peru. INCA was founded in 1981 and has been touring the midwest and the western states ever since.

- presents a variety of performances and educational activities
- INCA performs at theaters, festivals, schools (K-12), universities, colleges, museums, public libraries, as well as private and corporate events
- programs include music and dances from the Incas, the Hispanic communities of Coastal Peru, the Black communities from Peru's southern coast, and the natives from the Peruvian Amazon jungle

Every year INCA provides about 200 shows at schools all over the L.A. Unified and L.A. County's School Districts through I.C.A.P. and Performing Tree. INCA offers three different programs in schools: "INCA", music from Peru, "Amazonas," music from South America and "Ritmo Caliente" music from Central America, the Caribbean, and Mexico.

Pre/K-12 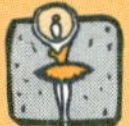 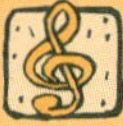

PROGRAMS: **Performances, Workshops, Residencies**
SCHEDULE: Year-round, Weekdays, Evenings, Weekends
DETAILS: Grades Pre/K-12, History/Soc. Sciences
Visual & Performing Arts, Language Arts
Multicultural, Aesthetic Valuing
Creative Expression, Historical/Cultural Context
Travel to Schools, Individually Tailored Programs
Educational Materials, Bilingual: Spanish"

Youth 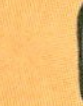 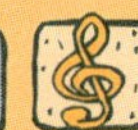

PROGRAMS: **Performances, Workshops, Residencies**
SCHEDULE: Year-round, Weekdays, Evenings, Weekends

Families 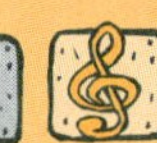

PROGRAMS: **Performances, Workshops, Residencies**
SCHEDULE: Year-round, Weekdays, Evenings, Weekends

INDEPENDENT COMPOSERS ASSOCIATION

P.O. Box 45134 501(c)3
Los Angeles, CA 90045-5134
Ph: 310-828-3004
Fax: 310-829-5923

Burt Goldstein President drburt@aol.com

The Independent Composers Association produces concerts of chamber music composed primarily of Los Angeles-area composers.

INEZ FINE ART & FRAMES

ELA

3229 Cesar Chavez Avenue
Los Angeles, CA 90063
Ph: 323-261-2535
Fax: 323-261-5361
www.ifaf.com
ifaf@ifaf.com

Contemporary painting, sculpture, and works on paper by emerging artists. Museum quality conservation framing services.

INNER-CITY ARTS

DSC

720 Kohler Street 501(c)3
Los Angeles, CA 90021
Ph: 213-627-9621
F ax: 213 627-6469

Beth Tishler Director of Education & Community Programs
Bob Bates Artistic Director
Cynthia Harnisch Executive Director

Inner-City Arts is dedicated to providing ethnically diverse, at-risk youth with positive experiences through the arts. ICA builds self-esteem and provides enriching experiences in the arts which lead to increased self-confidence, creativity and academic success.

INNER CITY CULTURAL CENTER

DSC

514 S. Spring Street, Suite B114 501(c)3
Los Angeles, CA 90014
Ph: 213-627-7670
F ax: 213 622-5881

Inner City Cultural Center's mission is to explore the arts as a tool which bridges the communication gap between LA's diverse communities. Inner City Cultural Center produces and presents a wide variety of programming in all media.

INSIDE OUT

WS

819 Milwood Avenue 501(c)3
Los Angeles, CA 90064
Ph: 310-306-6825
Fax: 310-306-9747

Camille Ameen Co-Artistic Director NsideOut98@aol.com
Johnathan Zeichner Co-Artistic Director

To build self-esteem and community, Inside Out provides interdisciplinary arts programming to at-risk and underserved middle schoolers throughout L.A., culminating in theater pieces written, cast, designed and performed by participants.

- volunteer opportunities for performances, camping retreat, fundraising events, and in the office
- public invite to see and support children's original theater pieces in the spring
- professional artists from all disciplines can train to join our staff

INSIDE OUT (CONTINUED)

Currently in five LAUSD middle schools, our programs assemble a diverse cultural, socio-economic mix. Working in teams, kids create topical art and theater pieces on themes of importance to them. The School Project includes a three-day camping retreat.

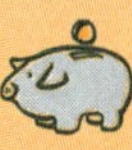

Pre/K-12

 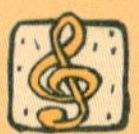 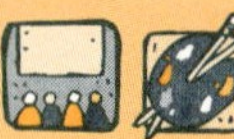

PROGRAMS: **PERFORMANCES, WORKSHOPS**
SCHEDULE: SPRING, FALL, WINTER, WEEKDAYS., WEEKENDS
DETAILS: GRADES 5-8, VISUAL & PERFORMING ARTS
CREATIVE EXPRESSION, TRAVEL TO SCHOOLS
INDIVIDUALLY TAILORED PROGRAMS
EDUCATIONAL MATERIALS AVAILABLE, BILINGUAL: SPANISH

Youth

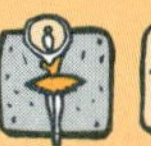 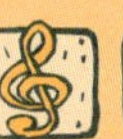 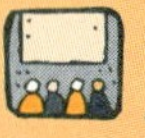

PROGRAMS: **PERFORMANCES, WORKSHOPS**
SCHEDULE: SPRING, FALL, WINTER., WEEKDAYS, WEEKENDS

Families

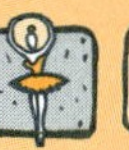 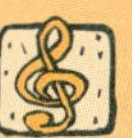 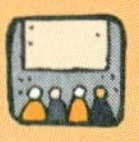 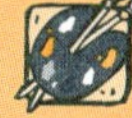

PROGRAMS: **PERFORMANCES, WORKSHOPS**
SCHEDULE: SPRING, FALL, WINTER, WEEKENDS

INSTITUTE OF CULTURAL INQUIRY

1708 Berkeley Street
Santa Monica, CA 90404
Ph: 310-828-5622
Fax: 310-315-9334
www.culturalinquiry.org

501(c)3 **WS**

Lisa Patt Director institute@culturalinquiry.org

The Institute of Cultural Inquiry is an educational and cultural organization which responds to and explores the many facets of visual culture.

- changing exhibits and displays
- publications
- AIDS-related visual projects
- Day Without Art (December 1) activites
- interactive installations and environments
- internet performances
- seminars and symposiums
- Artist-in-Residence program
- ongoing discussion groups centered on visual culture
- educational outreach for grades 7-12
- library
- volunteer opportunities
- gift shop

INSTITUTE OF CULTURAL INQUIRY (CONTINUED)

Our educational programs are centered on visual projects which are used to initiate a discussion about AIDS. Students are exposed to a non-verbal language as a way to respond to the contradictory emotions that this pandemic has unleashed.

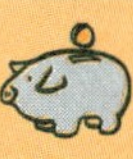

Pre/K-12

PROGRAMS: **WORKSHOPS**
SCHEDULE: YEAR-ROUND, WEEKDAYS, WEEKENDS
DETAILS: GRADES 7-12, HISTORY/SOC. SCIENCES
VISUAL & PERFORMING ARTS, MULTICULTURAL
HISTORICAL/CULTURAL CONTEXT
TRAVEL TO SCHOOLS, FACILITY FOR SCHOOL VISITS
INDIVIDUALLY TAILORED PROGRAMS EDUCATIONAL MATERIALS

INTERGROUP CULTURAL AWARENESS PROGRAM (ICAP)

Office of the Intergroup Relations Specially Funded Los Angeles Unified School District Programs
1320 W. Third Street, Room 800
Los Angeles, CA 90280
Ph: 213-625-6436
Fax: 213-482-7622

ELA

Marilyn Johnson Smith Specialist
Winston Tan Editor: ICAP Friends/ 213-462-6409

The purpose of ICAP is to foster the concepts of cultural pluralism, intergroup relations, and human dignity through active participation in the multiethnic and cross-cultural performing and fine arts.

- schedules over 4,000 programs in more than 300 schools each year
- provides hands-on, feet-on, and brain-on workshops for students and teachers in their disciplines in conjunction with academic achievement

ICAP's uniqueness is that it is a series of performances, not a one shot endeavor, and it has always emphasized the wonderful diversity of its performers, matched to those of its communities."

Pre/K-12

 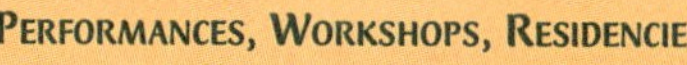

PROGRAMS: **PERFORMANCES, WORKSHOPS, RESIDENCIES**
SCHEDULE: YEAR-ROUND, WEEKDAYS
DETAILS: GRADES PRE/K-12, HISTORY/SOC. SCIENCES
MATH/SCIENCES, VISUAL & PERFORMING ARTS
LANGUAGE ARTS, MULTICULTURAL, PHYSICAL EDUCATION
HISTORICAL/CULTURAL CONTEXT
TRAVEL TO SCHOOLS, INDIVIDUALLY TAILORED PROGRAMS,
EDUCATIONAL MATERIALS, BILINGUAL: SPANISH

INTERNATIONAL CITY THEATER

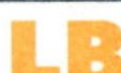

4901 E. Carson Street — 501 (c) 3
Long Beach, CA 90808
Ph: 562-938-4128
Admin: 562-938-4051
Fax: 562-938-4118

Caryn Morse Desai — General Manager
Shashin Desai — Artistic Director/ 562-938-4277

International City Theatre produces professional, award-winning new plays, classics, and musicals at two locations in Long Beach.

- two seasons of plays and musicals at two locations in Long Beach
- internship oportunities
- volunteer opportunities
- readings
- workshops
- educational outreach

International City Theatre brings years of experience to the training and teaching of young people. Some projects are new and specifically produced for a wide range of children.

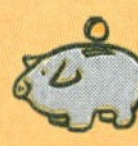

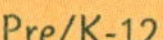

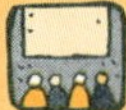

Pre/K-12

PROGRAMS:	**PERFORMANCES**
SCHEDULE:	YEAR-ROUND, WEEKDAYS, EVENINGS, WEEKENDS
DETAILS:	GRADES 3-12, VISUAL & PERFORMING ARTS
	AESTHETIC VALUING, CREATIVE EXPRESSION
	TRAVEL TO SCHOOLS, FACILITY FOR SCHOOL VISITS
	EDUCATIONAL MATERIALS, COST FOR SOME PROGRAMS

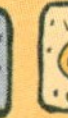
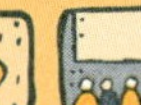
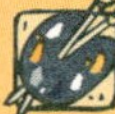

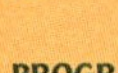

Youth

PROGRAMS:	**PERFORMANCES, WORKSHOPS**
SCHEDULE:	SUMMER, WEEKDAYS, EVENINGS, WEEKENDS
DETAILS:	COST FOIR SOME PROGRAMS

INTERNATIONAL DOCUMENTARY ASSOCIATION

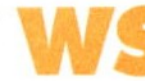

1551 S. Roberston Boulevard, Suite 201 — 501 (c) 3
Los Angeles, CA 90035-4257
Ph: 310-284-8422
Fax: 310-785-9334
www.documentary.org

Joshua Travierso — Office Manager/ x8
Betsy McLane — Executive Director/ x3
Dale Zackery — Membership Coordinator/ x32

The International Documentary Association is a nonprofit association established in 1982 to promote nonfiction film and video and to support the efforts of documentary makers around the world.

- publish "International Documentary", featuring in-depth articles and interviews as well as monthly listings of events and articles
- offer screenings, advocacy, awards within the industry, workshops, community events, and fiscal sponsors for aspiring documentarians
- publish a membership directory

ISTITUTO ITALIANO DI CULTURA

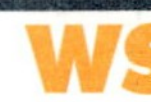

Italian Government Cultural Office
1023 Hilgard Avenue
Los Angeles, CA 90024
Ph: 310-443-3250
Fax: 310-443-3254
www.iicusa.org

Italian cultural institute.

- film screenings
- literary lecture series
- lectures
- exhibitions
- workshops
- music and theatre performances
- italian language courses

ITURRALDE GALLERY

HSM

154 N. La Brea Avenue
Los Angeles, CA 90036
Ph: 323-937-4267
Fax: 323-937-4269

Ana Iturralde — Co-Owner — itugal@ni.net
Teresa Iturralde — Co-Owner

Iturralde Gallery has been exhibiting contemporary art by Latin American artists since 1987.

- Changing exhibitions every six weeks, featuring contemporary art by Latin American artists

IVRI-NASAWI

WS

1033 N. Orlando Avenue — 501 (c) 3
Los Angeles, CA 90069
Ph/Fax: 323-650-3157
Admin: 718-997-5571
www.ivri-nasawi.org

Jordan Elgrably — Creative Director
Joyce Allegra Maio — New York Director/ 212-362-9074
Ammiel Alcalay — CoFounder
Ruth Behar — Literary Editor

Headquartered in Los Angeles, Irvi-NASAWI is a national Jewish arts organization which emphasizes Sephardic and Mizrahi (Middle Eastern) cultures, education, and community outreach.

- annual Sephardic Arts Festival
- National Sephardic Literary Contest
- annual group art exhibits
- concerts
- symposia
- salons
- volunteer opportunities
- artists and writers guild

IVRI-NASAWI (CONTINUED)

Irvi-NASAWI is the only Jewish cultural association in the United States which educates the Jewish and general communities about the Sephardic/Mizrahi experience, and represents artists, writers, and intellectuals from these communities.

Families 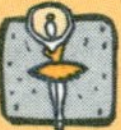 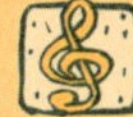

PROGRAMS:	**PERFORMANCES**
SCHEDULE:	SUMMER, WEEKENDS

JACK RUTBERG FINE ARTS INC.

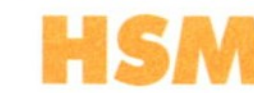

357 N. La Brea Avenue
Los Angeles, CA 90036
Ph: 323-938-5222
Fax: 323-938-0577

Jack Rutberg Director JFineArts@aol.com

Jack Rutberg Fine Arts, Inc. is one of Los Angeles' leading galleries dealing in major Modern and Contemporary, American and European works of art. Centrally located, the gallery regularly features significant historical exhibitions in its spacious galleries located on La Brea Avenue.

- important solo, group, and thematic exhibitions of works available for sale by 20th century artists including Marc Chagall, Pablo Picasso, Georges Rouault, Joan Miro, Alexander Calder, Edward Hopper, Roy Lichtenstein, Hans Burkhardt, and Sam Francis
- published catalogues and videos are available for purchase
- group docent tours for schools and organizations available
- internship opportunities available

The gallery presents major art exhibitions that offer individuals and groups an opportunity to experience and acquire historically important works of art in an intimate and informative manner. 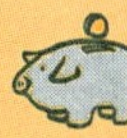

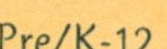

Pre/K-12

PROGRAMS:	**GUIDED TOURS**
SCHEDULE:	YEAR-ROUND, WEEKDAYS
DETAILS:	GRADES PRE/K-12, VISUAL & PERFORMING ARTS AESTHETIC VALUING, HISTORICAL/CULTURAL CONTEXT FACILITY FOR VISITS, INDIVIDUALLY TAILORED PROGRAMS

Youth 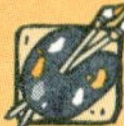

PROGRAMS:	**GUIDED TOURS**
SCHEDULE:	YEAR-ROUND, WEEKDAYS

Families 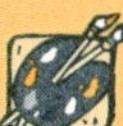

PROGRAMS:	**GUIDED TOURS**
SCHEDULE:	YEAR-ROUND, WEEKDAYS

JAN BAUM GALLERY

HSM

170 S. La Brea Avenue
Los Angeles, CA 90036
Ph: 323-932-0170
Fax: 323-932-0245

Jan Baum Director

International/Contemporary art/Primitive art.

JAN KESNER GALLERY

HSM

164 N. La Brea Avenue
Los Angeles, CA 90036
Ph: 323-938-6834
Fax: 323-938-1106

Jan Kesner Director

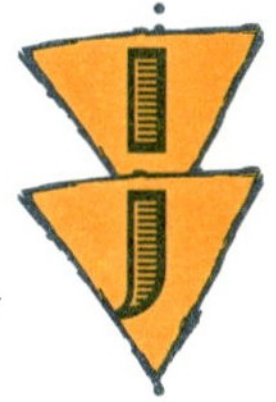

As a well-established fine art photography gallery, the Jan Kesner Gallery has developed a sophisticated exhibition program which continually explores relationships between 20th-century masters and the exciting new visions of contemporary artists.

- monthly exhibitions featuring national and international gallery artists

JAPAN FOUNDATION, LOS ANGELES OFFICE

WS

2425 Olympic Boulevard, Suite 650 E
Santa Monica, CA 90404
Ph: 310-449-0027
Fax: 310-449-1127
www.jflalc.org

Alan Kita	Program Associate/ x104	Akita@jflalc.org
Isao Tsujimoto	Director	jflalc@jflalc.org

Representing the Western U.S. territory, the Japan Foundation provides promotional assistance to present the arts, culture, language, and sciences of Japan.

- awards grants to artists, arts presenters, filmmakers and visual artists

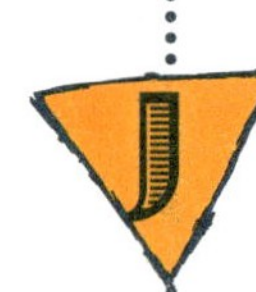

JAPANESE AMERICAN CULTURAL & COMMUNITY CENTER (JACCC)

244 S.San Pedro Street, Suite 505
Los Angeles, CA 90012
Ph: 213-628-2725
Fax: 213-617-8576

DSC

Brian Yamami	Grants and Programs Administrator yamami@jaccc.org
Robert Hori	Director of Visual & Cultural Arts Programs/ x105

Located in Little Tokyo in downtown Los Angeles, the JACCC is a unique ethnic cultural center, dedicated to preserving and promoting the Japanese American cultural heritage and to encourage greater understanding of the culture of Japan in the U.S.

- exhibitions of traditional and contemporary artists
- library with over 10,000 pieces about Japan and Japanese America
- James Irvine Garden—award-winning Japanese American garden
- Center Shop—craft and gift items and work by local Asian-American artists
- the Japan America Theatre presents the finest performing artists from Japan and Asian/Japanese-American artists
- Japanese Cultural Room—display of Japanese calligraphy and authentic tea room
- hosts summer festivals on the Plaza such as Nisei Week Festival, Tofu Festival, and Taiko Gatherings

We offer the finest programs directed towards our JapaneseAmerican community, for all ages and families, and accessible to all.

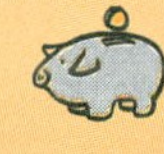

Pre/K-12

PROGRAMS:	**PERFORMANCES**
SCHEDULE:	SUMMER, WINTER, WEEKDAYS
DETAILS:	GRADES PRE/K-12, INDIVIDUALLY TAILORED PROGRAMS
	EDUCATIONAL MATERIALS AVAILABLE, BILINGUAL: JAPANESE

Youth

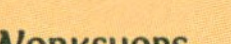

PROGRAMS:	**WORKSHOPS**
SCHEDULE:	YEAR-ROUND, WEEKDAYS
DETAILS:	COST FOR SOME PROGRAMS

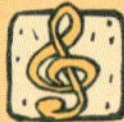

Families

PROGRAMS:	**WORKSHOPS**
SCHEDULE:	SPRING, SUMMER, WINTER, WEEKDAYS, WEEKENDS
DETAILS:	COST FOR SOME PROGRAMS

JAPANESE AMERICAN NATIONAL MUSEUM

369 E. First Street
Los Angeles, CA 90012
Ph: 213-625-0414
Fax: 213-625-1770

501(c)3 **DSC**

Chris Komai	Public Information Officer/ x240
Karin Higa	Art Curator/ x217
Irene Hirano	Executive Director/ x299
Pamela Funai	Education Manager/ x268
Sara Iwahashi	Publications Manager/ x281

The Japanese American National Museum is the first U.S. museum dedicated to sharing the experience of Americans of Japanese ancestry. Through building a comprehensive collection of Japanese American objects, images, and documents and through a multi-faceted program of exhibitions, educational programs, films, and publications the museum tells the story of Japanese Americans around the country to a national and international audience.

- guided tours for schools and general groups
- workshops, lectures, and other activities
- volunteer opportunities
- National Resource Center
- cafe
- garden
- gift shop

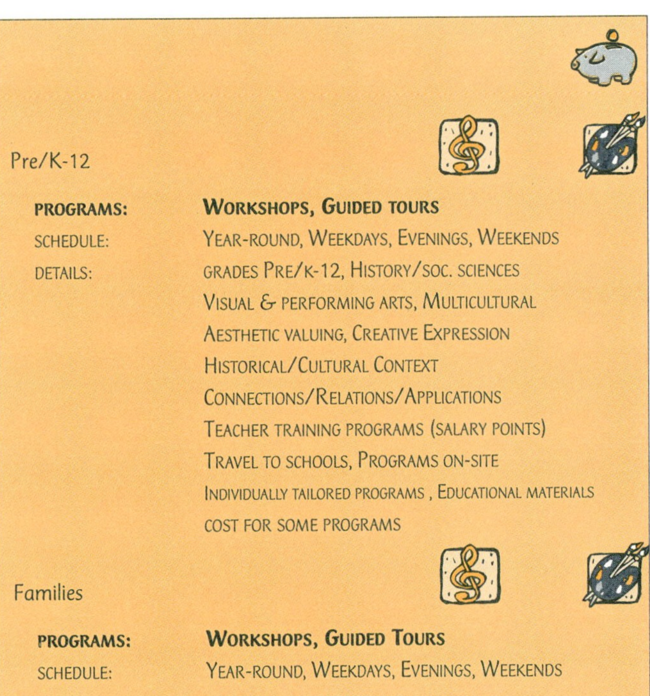

Pre/K-12

PROGRAMS:	**WORKSHOPS, GUIDED TOURS**
SCHEDULE:	YEAR-ROUND, WEEKDAYS, EVENINGS, WEEKENDS
DETAILS:	GRADES PRE/K-12, HISTORY/SOC. SCIENCES
	VISUAL & PERFORMING ARTS, MULTICULTURAL
	AESTHETIC VALUING, CREATIVE EXPRESSION
	HISTORICAL/CULTURAL CONTEXT
	CONNECTIONS/RELATIONS/APPLICATIONS
	TEACHER TRAINING PROGRAMS (SALARY POINTS)
	TRAVEL TO SCHOOLS, PROGRAMS ON-SITE
	INDIVIDUALLY TAILORED PROGRAMS , EDUCATIONAL MATERIALS
	COST FOR SOME PROGRAMS

Families

PROGRAMS:	**WORKSHOPS, GUIDED TOURS**
SCHEDULE:	YEAR-ROUND, WEEKDAYS, EVENINGS, WEEKENDS
DETAILS:	COST FOR SOME PROGRAMS

JASON VASS GALLERY

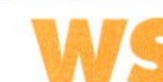

1210A Montana Avenue
Santa Monica, CA 90403
Ph: 310-395-2048
Fax: 310-395-4541

Jason Vass	Owner	jvass@gte.net
Donald Barrett	Assistant	

Jason Vass Gallery, international vintage poster gallery, shows lithographs (posters) from 1880-1960 covering propaganda, film, product, transportation, and music.

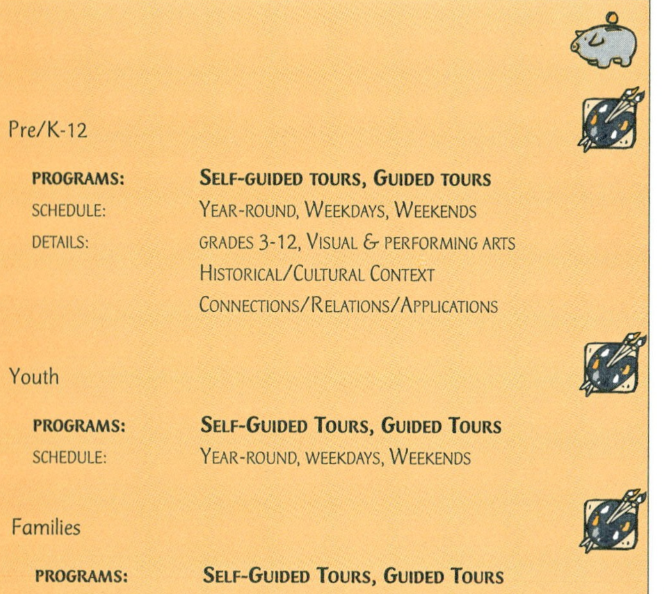

Pre/K-12

PROGRAMS: **SELF-GUIDED TOURS, GUIDED TOURS**
SCHEDULE: YEAR-ROUND, WEEKDAYS, WEEKENDS
DETAILS: GRADES 3-12, VISUAL & PERFORMING ARTS
HISTORICAL/CULTURAL CONTEXT
CONNECTIONS/RELATIONS/APPLICATIONS

Youth

PROGRAMS: **SELF-GUIDED TOURS, GUIDED TOURS**
SCHEDULE: YEAR-ROUND, WEEKDAYS, WEEKENDS

Families

PROGRAMS: **SELF-GUIDED TOURS, GUIDED TOURS**
SCHEDULE: YEAR-ROUND, WEEKDAYS, WEEKENDS

JAZZ DANCE L.A. FOUNDATION

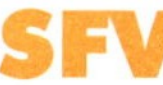

12117 Moorpark Street 501(c)3
Studio City, CA 91602
Ph: 818-980-3006
Fax: 818-980-3185

Judy Lam	Chairperson/ 310-284-2279	jlam@ccnlaw.com
Takeshi Hamagaki	Artistic Director	

Jazz Dance L.A. Foundation is dedicated to promoting the art of jazz dance in all forms, i.e. balletic, lyrical, ethnic, modern, blues, etc... through public performances and other special events.

- annual Jazz Dance L.A. concert series—a theatrical forum for choreographers to display their works and diversity of jazz dance styles
- master classes

JAZZANTIQUA DANCE & MUSIC ENSEMBLE

DSC

c/o The Dance Collective 501(c)3
4327 Degnan Boulevard
Los Angeles, CA 90008
Ph: 323-292-1538
Admin: 310-271-0789
Fax: 310-276-6139
www.jazzantiqua.org

Jeanne Taylor	Publicist/ 310-657-7115
Pat Taylor	Artistic Director

JazzAntiqua is a fourteen-member ensemble of dancers and musicians dedicated to sharing the art of jazz with audiences of all ages and backgrounds.

- concert performances
- weekly jazz dance classes
- annual community outreach program: The Art of Jazz includes master classes, clinics, lecture-demonstrations, free mini-performances
- dance studio rental

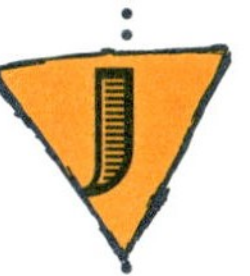

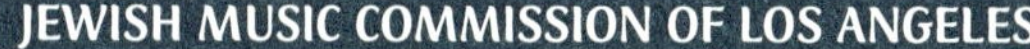

JEWISH MUSIC COMMISSION OF LOS ANGELES

SFV

13351-D Riverside Drive 501(c)3
Sherman Oaks, CA 91423
Ph: 818-907-7194
Fax: 818-789-2567

David Kates	Executive Director	jewshmsc@aol.com
Richard Braun	Chairman	

The Jewish Music Commission of Los Angeles creates new opportunities for the performance of Jewish music, encourages composition of Jewish music and offers education seminars for composers. One of the seminars, "Ten Lessons in Composing Jewish Music", is a unique opportunity for professionally advanced composers to attend a master class with one of the most prominent composers of Jewish music in America.

- Dr. Michael Isaacson's seminar "Ten Lessons in Composing Jewish Music", audiotape also available
- concerts and recitals of new and important Jewish music
- audiotapes of American Jewish song festivals

JIM GAMBLE PUPPET PRODUCTIONS

SB

6777 Vallon Drive
Rancho Palos Verdes, CA 90275
Ph: 310-541-1921
Admin: 310-541-8041
Fax: 310-541-2195
www.jimgamble.com

Jim Gamble	Chief Executive Officer	jimgamble@aol.com
Marty Gamble	Promotions Manager	martygambl@aol.com

Internationally known for innovative performance styles, Jim Gamble Puppet Productions gives 2000 shows annually to foster music education, cultural enrichment and family fun. Named one of the top world authorities on trick marionettes. Productions have toured Japan, Hong Kong, Singapore, Europe, Turkey and Iran.

- music programs: Peter and the Wolf, Carnival of the Animals, Nutcracker, Hansel & Gretel, Peer Gynt
- cultural enrichment programs: Tales of the Ashanti
- family fun programs: Wonderful World of Puppets, Monster Mash, Witch's Brew, Circus!, Night Before Christmas, Santa's Workshop, Enchanted Toyshop
- shows available in various languages
- show travels to schools, theaters, fairs, festivals and fundraisers

Jim Gamble Puppet Productions' marionette and rod puppet productions foster music education through informative entertaining programs. Audiences meet puppet composers, hear their musical works, and are enthralled as puppet characters in the hands of highly trained and skilled puppeteers interpret the musical classics.

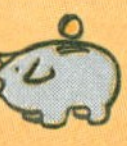

Pre/K-12

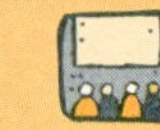

PROGRAMS: Performances, Workshops, Residencies
SCHEDULE: Year-round, Weekdays, Evenings, Weekends
DETAILS: grades Pre/K-6, Visual & performing arts
Multicultural, Aesthetic valuing
Historical/Cultural Context
Teacher training programs, Travel to schools
Individually tailored programs , Educational materials
Bilingual: Japanese, cost for some programs

Youth

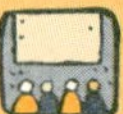

PROGRAMS: Performances
SCHEDULE: Year-round, weekdays, Evenings, Weekends

Families

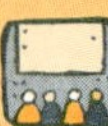

PROGRAMS: Performances
SCHEDULE: Year-round, Weekdays, Evenings, Weekends

JIM MCAULEY ENSEMBLE

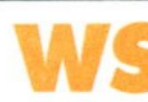

P.O. Box 66279
Los Angeles, CA 90066
Ph: 310-391-3777

Jim McAuley

Jim McAuley is a composer and musician whose work reflects the improvisational traditions of jazz, ethnic, and experimental music.

- the ensemble is available for performances and collaborations with dance, theatre, video artists, etc.

Utilizing over a dozen unique ethnic instruments, "Guitars from Renaissance to Rap" traces the history of American music with an emphasis on African and Latino influences. Children particularly enjoy the opportunity to play the insturments.

Pre/K-12

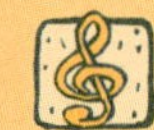

PROGRAMS: Performances, Workshops, Residencies
SCHEDULE: Year-round, Weekdays, Evenings, Weekends
DETAILS: grades 3-12, History/soc. sciences
Visual & performing arts, Multicultural
Creative Expression, Historical/Cultural Context
Travel to schools, Individually tailored programs

Youth

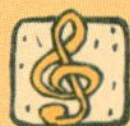

PROGRAMS: Performances, Workshops., Residencies
SCHEDULE: Year-round, weekdays, Evenings, Weekends
DETAILS: Cost for some programs

Families

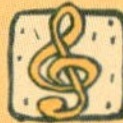

PROGRAMS: Performances, Workshops
SCHEDULE: Year-round, Weekdays, Evenings, Weekends

JUDSON STUDIOS/GALLERY, THE

ELA

200 S. Avenue 66
Los Angeles, CA 90042
Ph: 323-255-2800
Admin: 323-255-0131
Fax: 323-255-8529
www.judsonstudios.com

David Judson	Director	djudson@judsonstudios.com
Walter Judson	President	wjudson@judsonstudios.com

The Judson Studios, founded in 1897, is located on the banks of the Arroyo Seco. The stained glass studio housed USC's School of Fine Arts until 1920. Today, the Judson Gallery exhibits artists from around the world.

- bi-monthly exhibitions of artists working in various mediums
- guided tours of the stained glass studio
- gift shop
- lectures

JUDSON STUDIOS/GALLERY, THE (CONTINUED)

Pre/K-12

PROGRAMS:	**GUIDED TOURS**
SCHEDULE:	YEAR-ROUND, WEEKDAYS, WEEKENDS
DETAILS:	GRADES 3-8, VISUAL & PERFORMING ARTS HISTORICAL/CULTURAL CONTEXT

Families

PROGRAMS:	**GUIDED TOURS**
SCHEDULE:	YEAR-ROUND, WEEKDAYS, WEEKENDS

JUNIOR ARTS CENTER

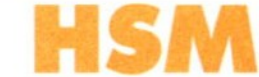

4814 Hollywood Boulevard
Los Angeles, CA 90027
213-485-4474
213-485-7456

Richard Ellis	JAC Director
Patty Sue Jones	Program Director

The art centers in Barnsdall Art Park provide instruction in a unique and beautiful park site. The Barnsdall Art Center is for adults and the Junior Arts Center is for children.

- daytime, evening, and Saturday classes for adults
- exhibition schedules for adults and children
- special events for all ages

The Junior Arts Center offers after school, Saturday and summer classes for children and youth. The Cultural Affairs Department funding allows low cost, high quality instruction in fine facilities and in a beautiful park.

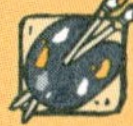

Pre/K-12

PROGRAMS:	**STUDIO CLASSES**
SCHEDULE:	YEAR-ROUND, WEEKDAYS, WEEKENDS
DETAILS:	GRADES PRE/K-12, VISUAL & PERFORMING ARTS CREATIVE EXPRESSION TEACHER TRAINING PROGRAMS (SALARY POINTS) PROGRAMS ON-SITE

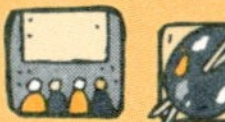

Youth

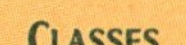

PROGRAMS:	**CLASSES**
SCHEDULE:	YEAR-ROUND, WEEKDAYS, WEEKENDS

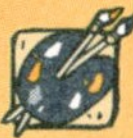

Families

PROGRAMS:	**CLASSES**
SCHEDULE:	YEAR-ROUND, WEEKDAYS, EVENINGS, WEEKENDS

JUST IMAGINE RESEARCH LIBRARY

SFV

6910 Farmdale Avenue
North Hollywood, CA 91605
Ph: 818-764-5644
Fax: 818-764-6655

Aeryn Donnelly	Researcher

The Just Imagine Research Library is a private collection specializing in architecture, interior design, art, photography, graphic design and more. By appointment only, please.

- research

KANTOR GALLERY

WS

8642 Melrose Avenue, Suite 100
Los Angeles, CA 90069
Ph: 310-659-5388
Fax: 310-659-3169

kantorart@earthlink.net

KAOS NETWORK/VIDEO 3333

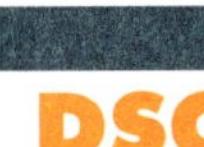

4343 Leimert Boulevard
Los Angeles, CA 90008
Ph: 323-296-5717
Fax: 323-291-3856

Ben Caldwell	Director

KÁRPÁTOK HUNGARIAN FOLK ENSEMBLE

501 (c)3

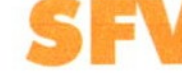

16051 Yarnell Street
Sylmar, CA 91342
Ph: 310-540-7261
Fax: 818-833-6960

La'szlo Gáspár	General Manager	lazgasp@pacificnet.net
Marianna Toghia	Secretary	toghia@aol.com

Kárpátok's main goal is to contribute to the multi-ethnic American cultural landscape through the perpetuation of the performing arts of the Hungarian people, by performing and teaching traditional dances, songs, and music.

- beginner and intermediate recreational workshop
- intermediate and advanced improvisational workshop
- master classes
- lecture demonstrations and concerts
- children's programming

J K

KÁRPÁTOK HUNGARIAN FOLK ENSEMBLE (CONTINUED)

Kárpátok's educational program brings to life dances, rituals, and celebrations of Hungarian peasant life, with universal appeal. The program encompasses dance presentations, cultural tradition discussions, language arts, history, and dance dialect.

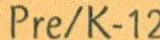

Pre/K-12  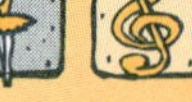

PROGRAMS:	**PERFORMANCES, WORKSHOPS, RESIDENCIES**
SCHEDULE:	YEAR-ROUND, EVENINGS, WEEKENDS
DETAILS:	GRADES PRE/K-12, VISUAL & PERFORMING ARTS MULTICULTURAL, CREATIVE EXPRESSION HISTORICAL/CULTURAL CONTEXT TRAVEL TO SCHOOLS, INDIVIDUALLY TAILORED PROGRAMS EDUCATIONAL MATERIALS AVAILABLE

Youth 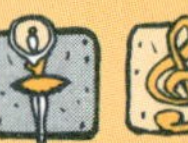

PROGRAMS:	**PERFORMANCES, WORKSHOPS, RESIDENCIES**
SCHEDULE:	YEAR-ROUND, EVENINGS, WEEKENDS

Families 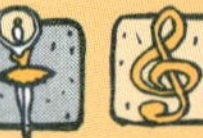

PROGRAMS:	**PERFORMANCES, WORKSHOPS, RESIDENCIES**
SCHEDULE:	YEAR-ROUND, EVENINGS, WEEKENDS

KAYAMANAN NG LAHI PHILIPPINE FOLK ARTS

11338 Braddock Drive
Culver City, CA 90230
Ph: 310-391-2357
Fax: 310-398-1644
www.kayamanan.com

501(c)3 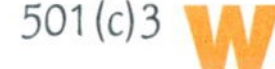

Ave Jacinto — Administrative Director — kayamanan@earthlink.com
Barabara Ele — Dance Director/ 818-762-3240
Joel Jacinto — Cultural Program Director
Leonilo Angos — Music/Technical Director/ 818-762-3240

Based in the westside of L.A., Kayamanan Ng Lahi is a folk arts organization that preserves, presents, and promotes the richness and diversity of the Philippine culture through dance and music.

- weekly workshops in dance
- weekly rondalla (Philippine stringed instrument) classes
- annual concerts
- live performances for public and private events
- quarterly recitals
- Philippine dance and music consultation
- lecture/demonstrations
- residency in dance and music
- technical assistance and training

KAYAMANAN NG LAHI PHILIPPINE FOLK ARTS (CONTINUED)

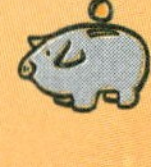

Dances taught are based upon anthropological research and strict attention is given to the appropriate native costumes and accompanying music. Prior to learning actual dances, students are first required to take and pass a six week Basics I course where they learn the fundamentals of Philippine dance movement.

Pre/K-12 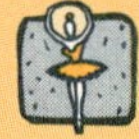 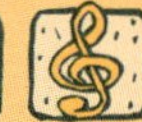

PROGRAMS:	**PERFORMANCES, WORKSHOPS, RESIDENCIES**
SCHEDULE:	YEAR-ROUND, EVENINGS, WEEKENDS
DETAILS:	GRADES 5-12, VISUAL & PERFORMING ARTS MULTICULTURAL, HISTORICAL/CULTURAL CONTEXT TRAVEL TO SCHOOLS, PROGRAMS ON-SITE INDIVIDUALLY TAILORED PROGRAMS, EDUCATIONAL MATERIALS BILINGUAL : FILIPINO, COST FOR SOME PROGRAMS

Youth 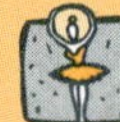 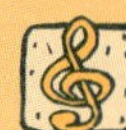

PROGRAMS:	**PERFORMANCES, WORKSHOPS, RESIDENCIES**
SCHEDULE:	YEAR-ROUND, EVENINGS, WEEKENDS
DETAILS:	COST FOR SOME PROGRAMS

Families 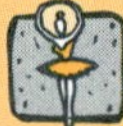 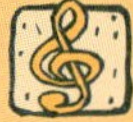

PROGRAMS:	**WORKSHOPS, RESIDENCIES**
SCHEDULE:	YEAR-ROUND, EVENINGS, WEEKENDS

KCRW, 89.9 FM

1900 Pico Boulevard
Santa Monica, CA 90405
Ph: 310-450-5183
Fax: 310-450-7172
www.kcrw.org

501(c)3 WS

Sarah Spitz — Publicity Director — sarahspitz@kcrw.org
Ruth Seymour — General Manager
Jennifer Ferro — Assistant General Manager
Ariana Morgenstern — Assistant Musical Director

KCRW is National Public Radio's Southern California flagship station, presenting an eclectic mix of news, music, public affairs, and cultural and radio drama programming.

- volunteer opportunities such as the Summer Sign Up Pledge Drive, office and partial program and production assistance, Summerday Auction, food and wine event, and the Winter on-air Subscription.

KELLOGG UNIVERSITY ART GALLERY, W. KEITH AND JANET

California Polytechnic University, Pomona **PO**
Pomona, CA 91768
Ph: 909-869-4302
Admin: 909-869-4301
Educ: 909-869-3508
Fax: 909-869-4939
www.csupomona.edu/~art/artgal.html

Patrick Merrill Director

The Kellogg Gallery's exhibitions focus on the evolving issues of contemporary art as practiced in Southern California. Special exhibits bring attention to important national artists and issues of art historical/critical interests spanning ideological and cultural boundaries.

- group docent tours available with appointment
- opening receptions are free and open to the public
- every year on the Thursday before Halloween a combined music and dance performance begins at 5:00 to celebrate "harvest" festivals around the world

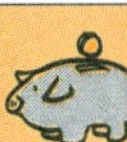

Pre/K-12

PROGRAMS:	**GUIDED TOURS**
SCHEDULE:	SPRING, FALL, WINTER, WEEKDAYS, WEEKENDS
DETAILS:	GRADES 9-12, VISUAL & PERFORMING ARTS
	AESTHETIC VALUING, HISTORICAL/CULTURAL CONTEXT
	PROGRAMS ON-SITE

KENTWOOD PLAYERS

8301 S. Hindrey Avenue 501(c)3 **WS**
Los Angeles, CA 90045
Ph: 310-645-5156
Fax: 310-280-0943

Charlotte Lee Schildkret President
Michelle Rosen Plays Committee Chairman/ 818-342-9617

For forty-nine years, in a theater wholly owned by Kentwood Players, a year-round season of highly acclaimed productions has been provided for the community, one of which is a musical.

KESHET CHAIM DANCE ENSEMBLE

4155 Dixie Canyon Avenue 501(c)3 **SFV**
Sherman Oaks, CA 91423
Ph: 818-784-0344
Fax: 818-986-1496

Genie Benson Managing Director kcdancers@earthlink.net
Eyton Avisar Artistic Director

Keshet Chaim, "Rainbow of Life", is an American-Israeli contemporary dance troupe celebrating the spirit of Judaism and Israeli culture throughout the world. This touring company has become a pioneer in the development of Jewish dance.

- festivals
- stage performances
- collaborations
- workshops
- performances for churches
- performances for schools
- touring
- representing Israeli government

Keshet Chaim is the sole company providing dance of the Israeli culture to the community on a performance level.

Pre/K-12

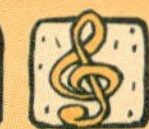

PROGRAMS:	**PERFORMANCES, WORKSHOPS**
SCHEDULE:	YEAR-ROUND, WEEKDAYS, EVENINGS, WEEKENDS
DETAILS:	GRADES PRE/K-12, VISUAL & PERFORMING ARTS
	MULTICULTURAL, CREATIVE EXPRESSION
	HISTORICAL/CULTURAL CONTEXT
	TRAVEL TO SCHOOLS , INDIVIDUALLY TAILORED PROGRAMS

Youth

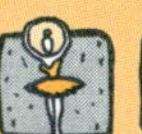

PROGRAMS:	**PERFORMANCES, WORKSHOPS**
SCHEDULE:	YEAR-ROUND, EVENINGS, WEEKENDS

Families

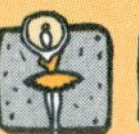

PROGRAMS:	**PERFORMANCES, WORKSHOPS**
SCHEDULE:	YEAR-ROUND, EVENINGS, WEEKENDS

KIDS IN MOTION

19201 Parthenia Street, Suite J
Northridge, CA 91324
Ph: 818-727-7878
Fax: 818-727-0009

SFV

Ellen Friend	Administrator
Janeece Flint	Theatre Director/ 818-727-7619
Carol Maldonado	Area Director

Servicing the Los Angeles Unified School District and the surrounding areas, Kids in Motion is a leader in providing After School Enrichment, Touring Theater, Artists In Residence programs and camps.

- winter, spring, and summer camp
- day camps throughout the year
- touring Children's Theatre
- artist In Residence programs
- after School Enrichment

The organization specializes in bringing a variety of programs to school sites. We offer enrichment programs that are presented in fun, educational ways.

Pre/K-12

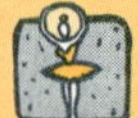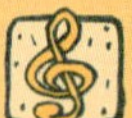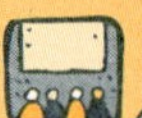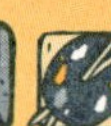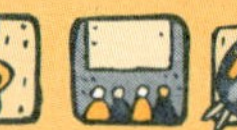

PROGRAMS: **Performances, Workshops, Residencies**
SCHEDULE: Year-round, Weekdays, Evenings, Weekends
DETAILS: grades Pre/k-8, Math/sciences,
Visual & performing arts, Language arts
Physical education, Creative Expression
Connections/Relations/Applications
Teacher training programs, Travel to schools
Educational materials available, Bilingual: Spanish

Youth

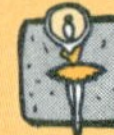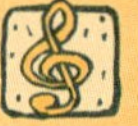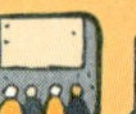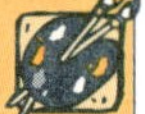

PROGRAMS: **Performances, Workshops, Residencies**
SCHEDULE: Year-round, weekdays, Evenings, Weekends

Families

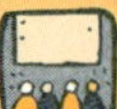

PROGRAMS: **Performances**
SCHEDULE: Year-round, Weekdays, Evenings, Weekends

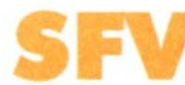

KIDSPACE MUSEUM

390 S. El Molino Avenue
Pasadena, CA 91101
Ph: 626-449-9143
Admin: 626-499-9144
Fax: 626-449-9985
www.kidspacemuseum.org

501(c)3 PSG

Angels Parris	Marketing and Special Events/ x15
Sherry Caisley	Public Programs Coordinator/ x16
Carol Scott	Executive Director/ x10
Roy Mueller	Director of Education/ x23
Jessica Ruskin	School Programs Coordinator/ x20

Located in beautiful Pasadena, Kidspace is a participatory museum designed for children ages 2-10. Visitors are invited to explore interactive exhibits and programs centered around the arts, sciences, and humanities.

- participatory exhibits and programs
- art exhibits
- four community-centered special events: Eco Arts Festival (April), Critter Expo (summer), Haunted House (Octoner), Rosebud Parade (November)
- summer camp
- "No Nap Club" and "Mommy and Me"- pre-K education programs
- parent education
- teacher development
- gift shop
- birthday parties
- volunteer opportunities

The hands-on, minds-on nature of "The Kidspace Experience" offers children and parents multiplte ways to relate to the real world. With exhibits built to scale and programs that pique a child's curiosity, "The Kidspace Experience" is both fun and educational!

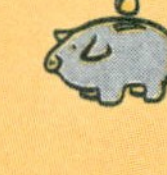

Pre/K-12

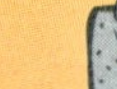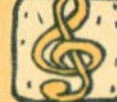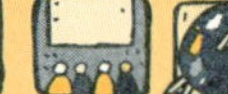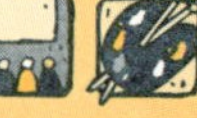

PROGRAMS: **Performances, Workshops, Studio classes, Self-guided tours, Guided tours**
SCHEDULE: Year-round, Weekdays, Weekends
DETAILS: grades Pre/k-6, History/soc. sciences, Math/sciences
Visual & performing arts, Language arts,
Multicultural, Creative Expression
Connections/Relations/Applications
Teacher training programs (salary points)
Travel to schools, Programs on-site
Individually tailored programs, Educational materials
work with disabled, cost for some programs

Youth

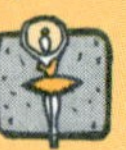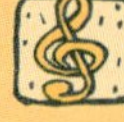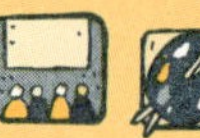

PROGRAMS: **Performances, Workshops, Classes**
Self-Guided Tours, Guided Tours
SCHEDULE: Year-round, weekdays, Weekends
DETAILS: cost for some programs

Families

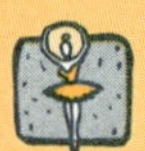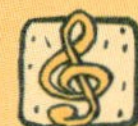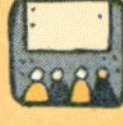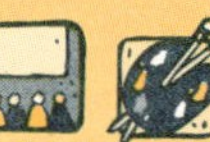

PROGRAMS: **Performances, Workshops, Classes**
Self-Guided Tours, Guided Tours
SCHEDULE: Year-round, Weekdays, Evenings, Weekends

KIYO HIGASHI GALLERY

WS

8332 Melrose Avenue
Los Angeles, CA 90069-5240
Ph: 323-655-2482
Fax: 323-655-7016

Kiyo Hagashi

Contemporary art.

KLON, 88.1 FM

501 (c) 3 LB

1288 N. Bellflower Boulevard
Long Beach, CA 90815
Ph: 562-985-5566
Fax: 562-597-8453
www.klon.org

Tina Thompson	Office Manager
Judy Jankowski	General Manager

KLON FM 88.1 is an 8000 watt radio station focusing on jazz and blues.

- volunteer opportunities
- jazz education
- Long Beach Blues Festival
- caravans to local clubs

KNIGHTSBRIDGE THEATRE

PSG

35 S. Raymond Avenue
Pasadena, CA 91105
Ph/Fax: 626-440-0821
Admin: 626-440-0894
Educ: 626-300-8138

Joseph Paul Stachura	Artistic Director/Producer
Amanda Karr	Theatre Operations/ 818-993-7063
Sylvia Stachura	Publicity Volunteer

The Knightsbridge Theatre can be found down the spiral staircase in the Braley Building, 35 S. Raymond Street, Old Pasadena. The theater is a professional live theater with a nonprofit classical wing: the National American Shakespeare Company.

- live drama performed on weekends (offers senior and student rates)
- weekday dramas are added for special occasions.

KOPLIN GALLERY

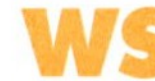

464 N. Robertson Boulevard
Los Angeles, CA 90048
Ph: 310-657-9843
Fax: 310-657-9849
www.home.earthlink.net/~koplin/

Marti Koplin	Director	koplin@earthlink.net
Eleana Del Rio	Co-Director	

Located in West Hollywood, Koplin Gallery exhibits fine art, sculpture, painitngs, and drawings. New exhibitions are shown every eight weeks.

- Eight week exhibition schedule featuring artists from the U.S. and Europe
- Docent tours are available to art groups and others
- Intern program is available

KOREAN AMERICAN MUSEUM

501 (c) 3 HSM

P.O. Box 741879
Los Angeles, CA 90004
Ph: 213-388-4229
Fax: 213-250-7654
www.lacn.org/kam/

Sunnie Hong	Program Coordinator	kamuseum@juno.com
You-kyong Kim	Executive Director	youkyong@aol.com
Anne Choi	Research Developer	

Located in the heart of Los Angeles' Koreatown, the Korean American Museum's mission is to preserve and interpret the history, experiences, culture, and achievements of Americans of Korean ancestory. KAM shares the achievements of the Korean American culture with people of other cultures as a way of promoting the inter-cultural dialogue without which diversity cannot flourish.

- monthly exhibitions featuring local and overseas artists
- gift shop
- volunteer opportunities
- group tours
- reception openings

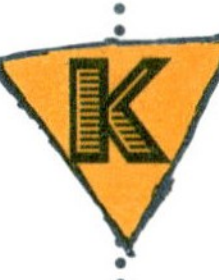

KOREAN CULTURAL CENTER

501 (c) 3
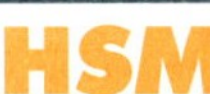

5505 Wilshire Boulevard
Los Angeles, CA 90036
Ph: 323-936-7141
Fax: 323-936-5712
www.kccla.org

In addition to an art museum, featuring a permanent collection of traditional and contemporary Korean art, the Center offers a library and video library.

KOREAN PHILHARMONIC ORCHESTRA

501 (c) 3
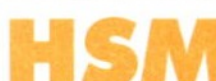

3123 West 8th Street, #208
Los Angeles, CA 90005
Ph: 213-387-4632
Fax: 213-387-7025

Raymond Cho	Music Director/Conductor
Steven Du	Chairman of the Board

Korean Philharmonic Orchestra's primary aim is to foster a mutual respect for different cultures, and a meeting of minds through a joint appreciation of music.

- two to four concerts per year

KPCC, 89.3 FM

501 (c) 3 PSG

1570 E. Colorado Boulevard
Pasadena, CA 91106
Ph: 626-585-7000
Fax: 626-585-7916
www.kpcc.org

Ilsa Setziol	Producer/ x5764

KPCC is an affiliate of National Public Radio and provides regular coverage of the arts.

- Two locally produced talk shows- "Larry Mantle's Airtalk" and "Talk of the City"

KPFK PACIFICA RADIO 90.7 FM

3729 Cahuenga Boulevard West
North Hollywood, CA 91604
Ph: 818-985-2711
Fax: 818-763-7526

501(c)3 **SFV**

Kathy Lo	Program Director
Mark Schubb	General Manager
Candy Capel	Development Director

KPFK Pacifica Radio for all of Southern California is a public radio broadcast station.

- national programming from Pacifica Radio
- local/community public affairs programs
- local/community news broadcasts
- local/community cultural and music programs
- public service announcements
- wide variety of volunteer opportunities

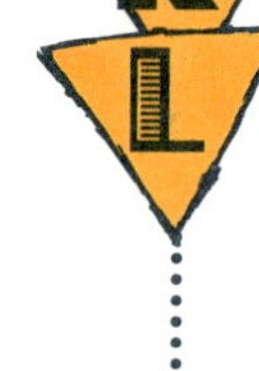

KUSC CLASSICAL KIDS

P.O. Box 77913
Los Angeles, CA 90007
Ph: 213-514-1400
Fax: 213-747-9400

501(c)3 **DSC**

Patricia Rich	Director/ 213-514-1416	prich@kusc.org
Mary Castillo	Editor/ 213-740-7656	marycast@mizar.usc.edu

The KUSC Classical Kids Club is a partnership with USC, KUSC, and arts and cultural organizations throughout Southern California. Our mission is to educate the next generation of classical music audiences.

- publish a bi-monthly calendar of events that features articles on classical music figures and history and highlights our cultural partners and major events in Southern California
- work with arts, cultural, and educational organizations to promote events for children and families
- information resource for families and educators

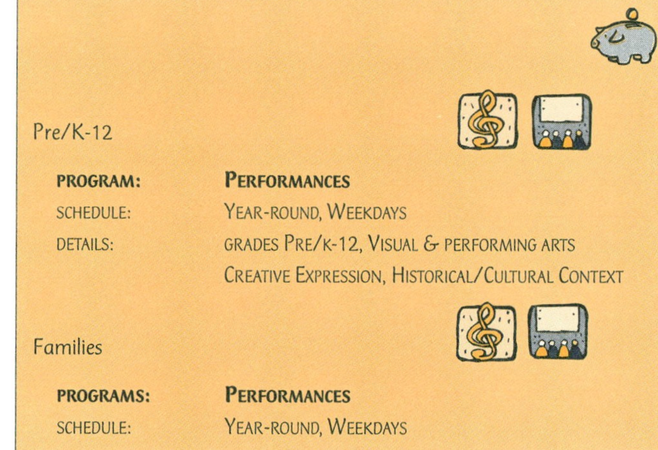

Pre/K-12

PROGRAM: PERFORMANCES
SCHEDULE: YEAR-ROUND, WEEKDAYS
DETAILS: GRADES PRE/K-12, VISUAL & PERFORMING ARTS
CREATIVE EXPRESSION, HISTORICAL/CULTURAL CONTEXT

Families

PROGRAMS: PERFORMANCES
SCHEDULE: YEAR-ROUND, WEEKDAYS

KUSC, 91.5 FM

P.O. Box 77913
Los Angeles, CA 90007-0913
Ph: 213-514-1400
Fax: 213-747-9400
www.kusc.org

501(c)3 **DSC**

Amy Iwata	Office Manager/ x462
Branda Pennell	General Manager/ x450
Sheila Rue	Program Director/ x430

KUSC is a non-commercial, listener supported, classical radio station serving Southern California.

KXLU, 88.9 FM

7900 Loyola Boulevard
Los Angeles, CA 90045
Ph: 310-338-2866
Fax: 310-338-5959

WS

Olivia Torres — General Manager

L.A. ARTCORE CENTER/BREWERY ANNEX

420 E. 3rd Street, Suite 110
Los Angeles, CA 90013-1645
Ph: 213-617-3274
Fax: 213-617-0303

DSC

Lydia Takeshita — Executive Director

L.A. BRIDGES THEATRE COMPANY OF THE DEAF

P.O. Box 55521
Sherman Oaks, CA 91413
Ph: 323-460-2886
Fax: 818-997-7335
www.members.aol.com/LABTCDeaf

501(c)3 **SFV**

Jennifer Delora	President	LABTCDeaf@aol.com

L.A. Bridges Theatre Company of the Deaf is a nonprofit theatrical organization providing an outlet for deaf/hh disabled artists, and educates maintstream audiences about deafness and deaf culture through theater arts.

- on-going referral services for deaf/hh performers to mainstream media
- children's sign music program for Pre/K-12 hearing and deaf children
- acting classes and workshops ages 3 and up for deaf/hh artists
- concerts in ASL music
- sign language theatre
- "Deaf Perspectives" talk show on cable TV

L.A. BRIDGES THEATRE COMPANY OF THE DEAF (CONTINUED)

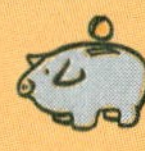

We make our programs specially designed for each group, school, etc. Fees are negotiable. We provide equal access and bring our programs, shows, and workshops to both hearing and deaf audiences.

Pre/K-12

 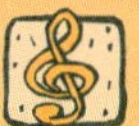 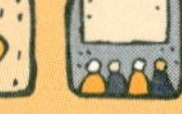

PROGRAMS: **PERFORMANCES, WORKSHOPS**
SCHEDULE: YEAR-ROUND, WEEKDAYS, EVENINGS, WEEKENDS
DETAILS: GRADES PRE/K-12, VISUAL & PERFORMING ARTS
LANGUAGE ARTS, CREATIVE EXPRESSION
CONNECTIONS/RELATIONS/APPLICATIONS
TRAVEL TO SCHOOLS, INDIVIDUALLY TAILORED PROGRAMS
BILINGUAL: ASL

Youth

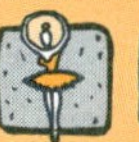 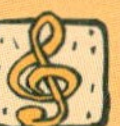 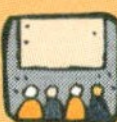

PROGRAMS: **PERFORMANCES, WORKSHOPS**
SCHEDULE: YEAR-ROUND, WEEKDAYS, EVENINGS ,WEEKENDS

Families

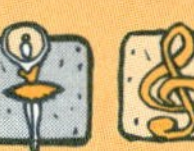 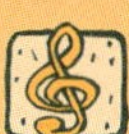 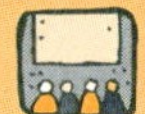

PROGAMS: **PERFORMANCES, WORKSHOPS**
SCHEDULE: YEAR-ROUND, WEEKDAYS, EVENINGS, WEEKENDS

L.A. FREEWAVES

2151 Lakeshore Avenue
Los Angeles, CA 90039
Ph: 213-617-3950
Admin: 323-664-1510
Fax: 323-664-1577
www.freewaves.org

501 (c)3 **HSM**

Anne Bray	Executive Director	freewaves@aol.com
Ming-Yuen Ma	Program Director	info@freewaves.org

L.A. Freewaves is an energetic multicultural media arts network that produces festivals, curriculum materials, workshops and a website dedicated to independent video and new media as accessible tools for artists and audiences.

- festival of video and new media
- internet workshops
- web site of media arts resources
- free tapes to high schools and public libraries

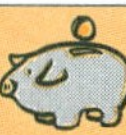

We provide short thematic compilation reels of artists videos organized around themes with curriculum guides for High School humanities and media arts classes.

Pre/K-12

PROGRAMS: **MEDIA ARTS**
DETAILS: GRADES 9-12, LANGUAGE ARTS, MULTICULTURAL
CONNECTIONS/RELATIONS/APPLICATIONS
TRAVEL TO SCHOOLS

L.A. GAY AND LESBIAN CENTER THE VILLAGE AT ED GOULD PLAZA

1125 N. McCadden Place
Los Angeles, CA 90028
Ph: 323-461-2633
Admin: 323-860-7337
Fax; 323-860-7340

501 (c)3 **HSM**

Cirilo Domine — Arts Coordinator

Located in Hollywood, the Advocate Gallery is a unique artists' space that promotes and exhibits the works of lesbian, gay, bisexual, and transgender artists as well as artists living with AIDS.

- monthly exhibitions and receptions
- performance art
- artist talks
- free slide documentation for artists living with AIDS through the Robert D. Farber Living Arts Project
- volunteer opportunities

L.A. HARBOR COLLEGE ART GALLERY

1111 Figueroa Place
Wilmington, CA 90744
Ph: 310-522-8474

SB

L.A. LOUVER GALLERY

45 N. Venice Boulevard
Venice, CA 90291
Ph: 310-822-4955
Fax: 310-821-7529

WS

Kimberly Davis	Co-Director	info@lalouver.com
Peter Goulds	Co-Director	

Contemporary American and European Art.

L.A. OPERA

135 N. Grand Avenue
Los Angeles, CA 90012
Ph: 213-972-8001
Admin: 213-972-7219
Educ: 213-972-7258
Fax: 213-687-3490
www.laopera.org

501 (c)3 **DSC**

Rosemarie Marquez	Community Relations Manager	rmarquez@laopera.com
Peter Hemmings	General Director	
Patricia Mitchell	Executive Director	
Llewellyn Crain	Director, Community Programs	lcrain@laopera.com

L.A. Opera is a world-class opera company in residence at the Dorothy Chandler Pavilion of the Music Center of Los Angeles.

- eight operas performed at the Dorothy Chandler Pavilion per season
- gift shop
- volunteer opportunities through several support groups
- internship opportunities
- unique programs that introduce new audiences to opera

L.A. OPERA (CONTINUED)

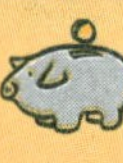

L.A. Opera's innovative educational and community programs are internationally renowned for their participatory, in-depth approach. L.A. Opera engages participants in the making and performing of opera, as well as examining operas in their cultural contexts.

Pre/K-12 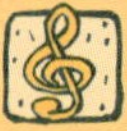

PROGRAMS: **OPERA PERFORMANCES, WORKSHOPS, RESIDENCIES**
SCHEDULE: SPRING, FALL, WINTER, WEEKDAYS
DETAILS: GRADES 3-12, VISUAL & PERFORMING ARTS
AESTHETIC VALUING, CREATIVE EXPRESSION
HISTORICAL/CULTURAL CONTEXT
CONNECTIONS/RELATIONS/APPLICATIONS
TEACHER TRAINING PROGRAMS (SALARY POINTS)
TRAVEL TO SCHOOLS, PROGRAMS ON-SITE
INDIVIDUALLY TAILORED PROGRAMS, EDUCATIONAL MATERIALS

Families 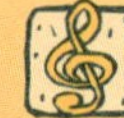

PROGRAMS: **PERFORMANCES**
SCHEDULE: EVENINGS, WEEKENDS

L.A. THEATRE WORKS

681 Venice Boulevard
Venice, CA 90291
Ph: 310-827-0808
Fax: 310-827-4949
www.kcrw.org/latw

501(c)3 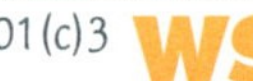

Stephen Gutwillig — Managing Director — latworks@aol.com
Susan Loewenberg — Producing Director
Gale Cohen — Arts and Children Program Director

Founded in 1974, L.A. Theatre Works is committed to the presentation and preservation of work for theater and radio and to extensive outreach programs for at-risk and incarcerated youth in L.A. County.

- "The Play's the Thing" live-in-performance radio theater series offers 14 productions each year of contemporary and classic plays performed before live subscription audiences and recorded for future broadcast on KCRW
- Audio Theatre Collection— the largest library of plays recorded for broadcast in the nation, available to the public through catalog and retail sales

L.A. THEATRE WORKS (CONTINUED)

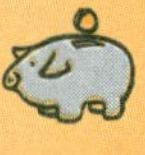

The Arts & Children Program recruits professional artists for residencies with incarcerated youngsters and at-risk youth in underserved communities. Alive & Aloud: Radio Plays for Learning in the Classroom makes our Audio Theatre Collection accessible to public secondary schools nationwide.

Pre/K-12 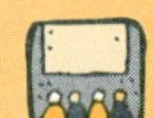

PROGRAMS: **AUDIO THEATER**
DETAILS: GRADES 7-12 HISTORY/SOC. SCIENCES
VISUAL & PERFORMING ARTS, AESTHETIC VALUING
HISTORICAL/CULTURAL CONTEXT,
CONNECTIONS/RELATIONS/APPLICATIONS
EDUCATIONAL MATERIALS AVAILABLE

Youth 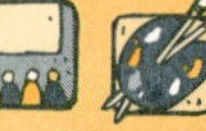

PROGRAMS: **WORKSHOPS, CLASSES, RESIDENCIES**
SCHEDULE: YEAR-ROUND, WEEKDAYS

L.A. TROUPE, THEATRE-IN-EDUCATION

1118 W. Magnolia Boulevard, A-201
Burbank, CA 91506
Ph: 818-563-3092
Fax: 818-563-4933

501(c)3 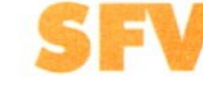

Cherie Brown — Co-Director — LATROUPE@aol.com
Koni McCurdy — Co-Director

The L.A. Troupe, Theatre-In-Education is a professional company touring into schools with 45 minute adaptations of classical plays.

- workshops and residencies for students and teachers pre-K-12

The L.A. Troupe offers professional on-site productions that are true to the original plot and language of the piece. Workshops and residencies allow students to discover the joy of language and the excitement of performance.

Pre/K-12 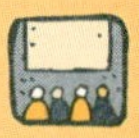

PROGRAMS: **PERFORMANCES, WORKSHOPS, RESIDENCIES**
SCHEDULE: YEAR-ROUND, WEEKDAYS
DETAILS: GRADES PRE/K-12, VISUAL & PERFORMING ARTS
AESTHETIC VALUING, CREATIVE EXPRESSION
HISTORICAL/CULTURAL CONTEXT
TRAVEL TO SCHOOLS, INDIVIDUALLY TAILORED PROGRAMS
EDUCATIONAL MATERIALS AVAILABLE

LA ALTERNATIVE MEDIA NETWORK

8124 W. 3rd Street, Room 208
Los Angeles, CA 90048
Ph: 323-655-5720
Fax: 310-458-6566
www.home.labridge.com/`laamn/

501 (c) 3 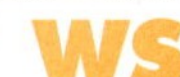

Joan Sekler — Director/ 310-458-6566 — sekler@labridge.com

The LA Alternative Media Network is a group of independent media-makers creating a democratic media as an alternative to corporate-controlled media.

- video group—camcorder activists, writers, editors are producing a video series "Our Jobs Our Lives"
- internet group—producing on-line the "LA Free Press" composed of articles which the mainstream media ignores
- radio group—producing news segments at KPFK-Pacifica Radio
- print media group—composed of individuals who write for independent newspapers, magazines,' zines, etc.

LA ARTCORE

120 Judge John Aiso Street
Los Angeles, CA 90012
Ph: 213-617-3274
Fax; 213-617-0303
www.laartcore.com

501 (c) 3 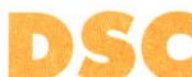

Lydia Takeshita — Exective Director
Sun Mi Choe — Assistant to Executive Director

LA Artcore is dedicated to reforging the relationship between artists and the public for an exchange of information, ideas, and feelings in an open forum to promote discussions and understanding about artists' creative work.

- monthly exhibtions featuring local artists
- international exchange shows
- conversation with exhibiting artists
- art workshops
- community development
- Annual Award Benefit
- California Artist Directory
- sponsors monthly exhibition of non-professional artists at the Union Cafe
- panel discussion on art issues
- symposiums on business of the arts
- collaboration with CS Fine Art in graphic arts and printing
- sponsors Julia and David Fellowship
- volunteer opportunites

LA ARTCORE (CONTINUED)

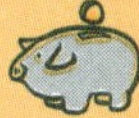

Education programs include art workshops, seminars,and panel discussions which are all presented by professional artists.

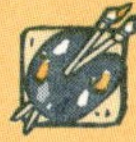

Pre/K-12

PROGRAMS: **WORKSHOPS, GUIDED TOURS**
SCHEDULE: YEAR-ROUND, WEEKDAYS, EVENINGS, WEEKENDS
DETAILS: GRADES PRE/K-6, VISUAL & PERFORMING ARTS
AESTHETIC VALUING, CREATIVE EXPRESSION
HISTORICAL/CULTURAL CONTEXT
CONNECTIONS/RELATIONS/APPLICATIONS
TRAVEL TO SCHOOLS, FACILITY FOR SCHOOL VISITS

Youth

PROGRAMS: **WORKSHOPS, GUIDED TOURS**
SCHEDULE: YEAR-ROUND, WEEKDAYS, EVENINGS, WEEKENDS

Families

PROGRAMS: **WORKSHOPS, GUIDED TOURS**
SCHEDULE: YEAR-ROUND, WEEKDAYS, EVENINGS, WEEKENDS

L

LA CASA DE LA CULTURA DE EL SALVADOR EN LOS ANGELES

1605 W. Olympic Boulevard, Suite 404
Los Angeles, CA 90015
Ph: 213-382-5218
Fax; 323-581-3205

DSC

Ricardo Escobar — Communications — Pipiles4u@aol.com
Dagoberto Reyes — Director
Mauricio Cortez — Education
Thelma Garcia — Administrator

LA COUNTY CENTURY GALLERY

13000 Sayre Street
Sylmar, CA 91342
Ph: 818-362-3220
Fax: 818-364-7755
www.artscenecal.com/Century.html

SFV

John Cantley — Director

The L.A. County Century Gallery presents art exhibits which are of educational value to the community.

LA LUZ

406 East 1st Street
Long Beach, CA 90802
Ph: 562-437-1591

LB

LA LUZ DE JESUS GALLERY

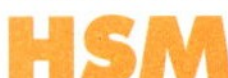

4633 Hollywood Gallery
Los Angeles, CA 90027
Ph: 323-666-7667
Fax: 323-663-0243
www.laluzdejesus.com

Leslie Napoles — Gallery Director — laluzde@pacbell.net
Billy Shire — Owner/ 213-663-0122

Established in 1986, La Luz de Jesus Gallery showcases a variety of artists, from the undiscovered underground to the very famous post-pop heroes.

- monthly exhibitions of art
- opening receptions first Friday of the month, 8-11 p.m.
- gift shop
- book signings

LA MARCA MUSIC AND PERFORMING ARTS SCHOOL

2655 W. 230th Place
Torrance, CA 90505
Ph/Fax: 310-325-8708

Priscilla LaMarca-Kandel — Owner/Director — LaMarcaMusic@hotmail.com

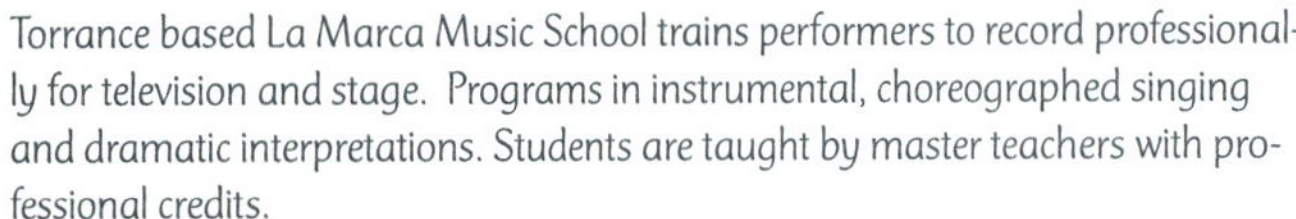

Torrance based La Marca Music School trains performers to record professionally for television and stage. Programs in instrumental, choreographed singing and dramatic interpretations. Students are taught by master teachers with professional credits.

- periodic recitals and on-site performances
- touring performances for pre-schools, public schools, community events, business conventions, and parties
- All-American and popular music by spirited choirs and bands
- volunteer opportunities
- full service party planning available includes catering and entertainment

Children age birth to six culminate in total understanding of all music concepts including note reading and keyboard playing through original stories and game-like activities. Ages 7-18 have opportunities to work with the L.A. Music Center's Orchestra, in international tours and at major theme parks. Many students record for children's albums and commercials.

Pre/K-12

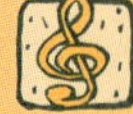
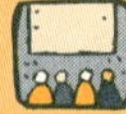

PROGRAMS: Performances, Workshops, Studio classes, Residencies
SCHEDULE: Year-round, Weekdays, Evenings, Weekends
DETAILS: Grades Pre/K-12, Visual & performing arts
Creative Expression, Travel to schools
Facility for school visits, Programs on-site
Individually tailored programs, Educational materials

Youth

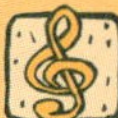
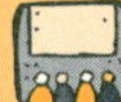

PROGRAMS: Performances, Workshops, Classes
SCHEDULE: Year-round, weekdays, Evenings, Weekends

Families

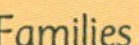
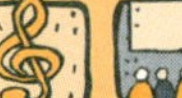

PROGRAMS: Performances
SCHEDULE: Year-round, Weekdays, Evenings, Weekends

LA MIRADA ARTS GALLERY AND ARTS COLONY OF LA MIRADA

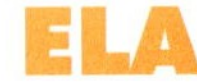

15040 Imperial Highway — 501(c)3
La Mirada, CA 90638
562-943-5846

Mellody Anderson — President
Dorothy Benedict — Gallery Director

We are the arts colony of La Mirada which is a community based organization of artists with an art gallery. La Mirada Art Gallery features multi-media art work such as watercolors, oils, jewelery, sculptures, ceramics, pottery, and gifts.

- large gallery with monthly exhibtions featuring local artists
- volunteer opportunitites
- gift shop
- publication of local art shows to members
- open juried show yearly with prize money and art supply gift certificates
- showcase art work in local libraries and banks
- participate in local and public celebrations
- free monthly art demonstrations

We have a high school art show for all art students in La Mirada. We give out two or more scholarships each year to graduating high school art majors for college expenses. We have an elementary and middle school art show in our gallery.

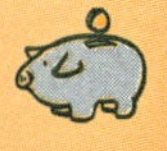

Pre/K-12

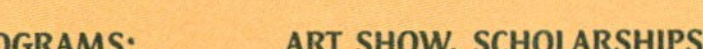

PROGRAMS: Art show, Scholarships
SCHEDULE: Spring, Fall, Winter, Weekdays, Evenings, Weekends
DETAILS: Grades Pre/K-12, Visual & performing arts
Aesthetic valuing, Creative Expression
Programs on-site, Individually tailored programs

Families

PROGRAMS: Workshops
SCHEDULE: Spring, Fall, Winter, Weekdays, Evenings, Weekends

LABAND ART GALLERY, LOYOLA MARYMOUNT UNIVERSITY

7900 Loyola Boulevard — 501(c)3 — WS
Los Angeles, CA 90045
Ph: 310-338-2880
Fax: 310-338-6024
www.lmu.edu/colleges/cfa/art/laband/laband.html

Gordon Fuglie — Director — gfuglie@popmail.lmu.edu

Constructed in 1984, the Laband Gallery exhibits thematic projects featuring traditional and non-traditional spirituality, the exploration of social and political issues, and ethnological and anthropological displays.

- five annual exhibits, for the LMU community and the greater L.A. public
- host the National Biennial Exhibition of the Los Angeles Printmaking Society

LANCASTER PERFORMING ARTS CENTER

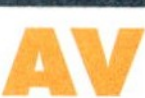

750 West Lancaster Boulevard
Lancaster, CA 93534
Ph: 805-723-5950
Fax: 805-723-5945

The mission of the Lancaster Performing Arts Center is to present high quality arts programming to the surrounding community.

LANKERSHIM ARTS CENTER

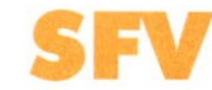

5108 Lankershim Boulevard
North Hollywood, CA 91601
Ph: 818-761-8838
Fax: 818-752-2682

The Lankershim Arts Center provides classes, lectures/symposia, performances, and exhibitions for the community.

- low-cost arts instruction in theatre, dance, and visual art
- performances
- exhibitions

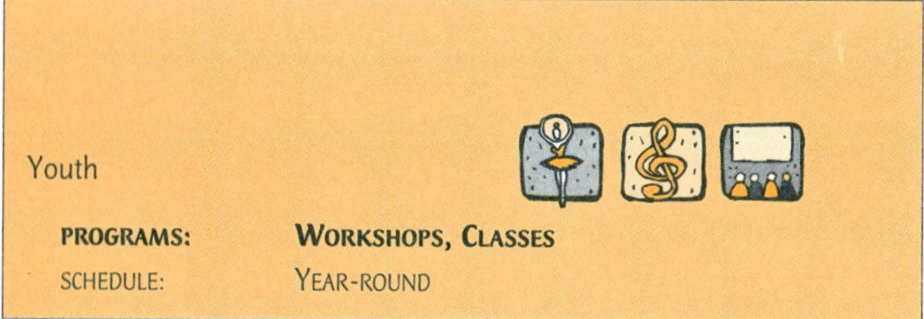

Youth

PROGRAMS:	**Workshops, Classes**
SCHEDULE:	Year-round

LANTERMAN HOUSE

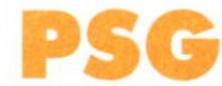

4420 Encinas Drive
La Cañada, CA 91011
Ph: 818-790-1421

501 (c)3

Frances Hill	Volunteer/ 818-249-8411
Melissa Patton	Executive Director

Lanterman House is a municipally owned historic house museum. Completed in 1915, the Arts and Crafts style home retains all of its original furnishings and interiors.

- docent led tours
- museum shop
- public lectures and programs
- volunteer opportunities
- special events

LANTERMAN HOUSE (CONTINUED)

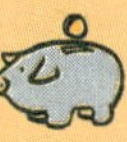

Our programs deal specifically with the history and development of the Crescenta-Cañada Valley as well as Arts and Crafts architecture and interior design.

Pre/K-12

PROGRAMS:	**Guided tours**
SCHEDULE:	Year-round, Weekdays
DETAILS:	Grades 3-12, History/soc. sciences, Architecture and design, Historical/Cultural Context Travel to schools, Programs on-site Educational materials available

Families

PROGRAMS:	**Guided Tours**
SCHEDULE:	Year-round, Weekdays, Weekends
DETAILS:	Cost for some programs

LARRY SMITH FINE ARTS

WS

8642 Melrose Avenue
Los Angeles, CA 90069
Ph: 310-360-9135
Fax: 310-360-9166
www.larrysmithfineart.com

Naomi Pringle	Director	lsfa@ix.netcom.com

Larry Smith FIne Art, across from the Pacific Design Center, is the exclusive L.A. distributor for famed landscape artist Eyvind Earle and "Art for the Blind" by Volk and more.

LATIN AMERICAN MASTERS

WS

264 N. Beverly Drive
Beverly Hills, CA 90210
Ph: 310-271-4847
Fax: 310-278-3932

William Sheehy	Director

Latin American Masters specializes in 20th Century Latin American art. This art gallery organizes exhibits, publishes catalogs, and sells works by Latin America's most important artists.

- one-man shows for major artists
- group shows
- docent tours
- a forum for Latin America's great masters

LATINO MUSEUM OF HISTORY, ART AND CULTURE, THE

112 S.Main Street
Los Angeles, CA 90012
Ph: 213-626-7600
Fax: 213-626-3830

501(c)3 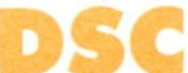

Alicia Marquez — Receptionist
Margerita Madina — Curator/ 213-633-1998
Denise Lugo — Executive Director/ 213-626 7676

The Latino Museum is a community oriented organization that works to bring Latino art and contribution to the community through art and education.

- exhibitions featuring Latino artists from around the world
- film and video presentations for exhibitions and documentaries on artistic and historical subjects
- volunteer opportunities

Our educational program has been created with the help of the Los Angeles County Museum of Art and the Los Angeles Unified School District..

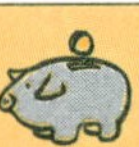

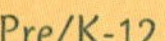

Pre/K-12

PROGRAMS: WORKSHOPS, SELF-GUIDED TOURS, GUIDED TOURS
SCHEDULE: YEAR-ROUND, WEEKDAYS
DETAILS: GRADES PRE/K-12, VISUAL & PERFORMING ARTS
AESTHETIC VALUING, CREATIVE EXPRESSION
HISTORICAL/CULTURAL CONTEXT
CONNECTIONS/RELATIONS/APPLICATIONS
TEACHER TRAINING PROGRAMS, FACILITY FOR SCHOOL VISITS
EDUCATIONAL MATERIALS AVAILABLE, BILINGUAL: SPANISH

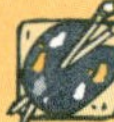

Youth

PROGRAMS: WORKSHOPS, SELF-GUIDED TOURS, GUIDED TOURS
SCHEDULE: YEAR-ROUND, WEEKDAYS

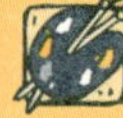

Families

PROGRAMS: WORKSHOPS, SELF-GUIDED TOURS, GUIDED TOURS
SCHEDULE: YEAR-ROUND, WEEKDAYS

LATINO THEATER INITIATIVE PROGRAM

Mark Taper Forum/Center Theatre Group
Music Center of L.A.
135 N. Grand Avenue
Los Angeles, CA 90012
Ph: 213-972-7588
Fax: 213-972-0746

501(c)3 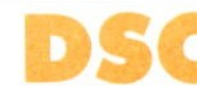

Diane Rodriguez — Co-Director/ 213-972-7586
Luis Alfaro — Co-Director

LTI provides access opportunitites and advocacy for Latino art audiences.

- productions
- readings
- workshops
- performances

LATINO THEATER INITIATIVE PROGRAM (CONTINUED)

Youth

PROGRAMS: PERFORMANCES, WORKSHOPS
SCHEDULE: YEAR-ROUND, WEEKDAYS
DETAILS: COST FOR SOME PROGRAMS

Families

PROGRAMS: PERFORMANCES., WORKSHOPS
SCHEDULE: YEAR-ROUND, WEEKDAYS
DETAILS: COST FOR SOME PROGRAMS

LAWRENCE GALLERY

9507 Santa Monica Boulevard, #310
Beverly Hills, CA 90210
Ph: 310-278-0882

WS

David Lawrence — Director

Lawrence Gallery is an art gallery with an extensive inventory of contemporary fine art prints available.

- gallery space for rent for shows by artists
- juried shows

LEIMERT PARK FINE ART GALLERY

3351 W. 43rd Street
Los Angeles, CA 90008
Ph: 323-299-0319
Fax: 323-299-0320

DSC

LESLIE SACKS FINE ART

Brentwood Town and Country
11640 San Vicente Boulevard
Brentwood, CA 90049
Ph: 310-820-9448
Fax: 310-207-1757
www.artscenecal.com/sacks.html

WS

Lee Spiro — Co-Director — lesliesacks@earthlink.net
Leslie Sacks — Director

Modern and Contemporary masters, Impressionists, Post Impressionists, German Expressionists, Illustrated artists' books, and African Art.

LICIA PEREA Y DANZANTES

2159 Lyric Avenue
Los Angeles, CA 90027
Ph/Fax: 323-669-3302

501(c)3 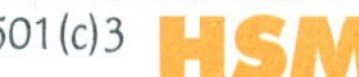

Licia Perea — Artistic Director — llperea@earthlink.net
Frankie Estrada — alexbassin@aol.com

Licia Perea y Danzantes is dedicated to performance and education in contemporary dance, theater within the concert, and film/video mediums. Feminist, Latino, and Native American perspectives color the work.

- live performance
- touring (national and internationel)
- master classes
- lectures/demonstrations
- volunteer opportunities
- video/film

LIVING ROOM, THE

1132 Broadway
Santa Monica, CA 90401
Ph: 310-451-2647

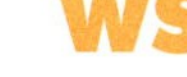

A non-profit exhibition space committed to showing contemporary artwork by emerging and established artists.

LLOYD E. RIGLER - LAWRENCE E. DEUTSCH FOUNDATION, THE / CLASSIC ARTS SHOWCASE

P.O. Box 828
Burbank, CA 91503-0828
Ph: 323-878-0283
Fax: 323-878-0329
www.classicartstv.org

Lloyd Rigler — Executive Director
Jamie Rigler — Artistic Director

Designed to build an audience, Classic Arts Showcase is a non-commercial satellite arts service presenting clips of classical arts performances at no cost to the public or broadcasters. Videos include:

- dance, ballet
- animation
- classical film
- theater
- chamber, orchestra, solo instrument music
- architecture, folk and museum art
- archival documentary
- opera, choral, solo voice

LLOYD E. RIGLER - LAWRENCE E. DEUTSCH FOUNDATION, THE / CLASSIC ARTS SHOWCASE (CONTINUED)

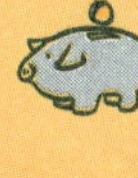

As the arts become less available in school and at home, less children are exposed to them. Classic Arts Showcase presents an opportunity to see and learn about the arts which resonates throughout a child's life, inspiring them to attend live performances.

Pre/K-12 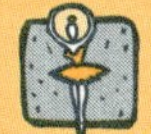 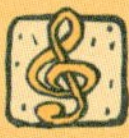 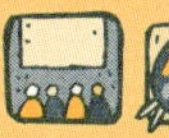 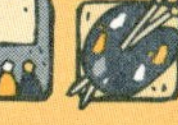

PROGRAMS: PERFORMANCES
DETAILS: VISUAL & PERFORMING ARTS, AESTHETIC VALUING

Youth 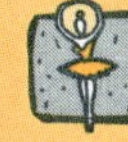 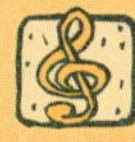 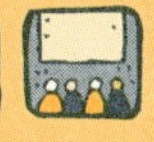 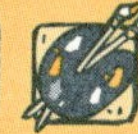

PROGRAMS: PERFORMANCES

Families 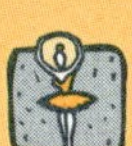 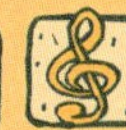 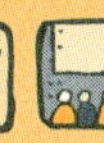 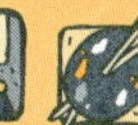 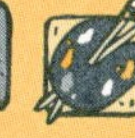

PROGRAMS: PERFORMANCES

LO CAL COMPOSERS

P.O. Box 4368
Culver City, CA 90230-4368
Ph: 310-398-8302

501(c)3 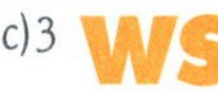

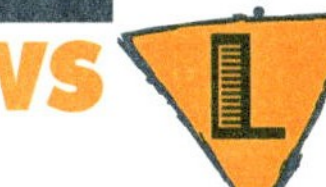

Carlos Rodriguez — President

The Lo Cal Composers Ensemble was founded in 1984 to provide a venue for new works of serious contemporary music by Los Angeles composers, to expand the audience for such compositions, and to enlighten a broad constituency of Los Angeles citizens with regards to the diverse and fascinating domain of newly composed music.

LOLA MONTES FOUNDATION FOR DANCES OF SPAIN & THE AMERICAS

1529 N.Commonwealth Avenue
Los Angeles, CA 90027
Ph: 323-664-3288
Fax: 323-663-7742

501(c)3 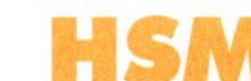

Lola Montes — President/Artistic Director
Susana Kobritz — Vice President

Lola Montes Foundation supports Lola Montes and her Spanish dancers, which is dedicated to preserving Hispanic culture through the arts. A panorama of performances offers dance, music, song of Spain and Latin America.

- live programs of dances of Spain and Latin America
- guest appearances with symphony orchestras
- ballet scenes from operas
- fair and festival programs
- concert programs
- California heritage
- master classes
- workshops
- youth and family programs

LOLA MONTES FOUNDATION FOR DANCES OF SPAIN & THE AMERICAS (CONTINUED)

Through the medium of dance, music, song, and commentary as well as authentic costuming, the tradition and culture of settlers from Spain and Latin America are shown to have influenced our life style today. Hispanic youth are put in touch with their roots and take pride in their contribution to California and the Southwest. Commentary is in English and Spanish.

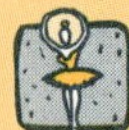

Pre/K-12

PROGRAMS: PERFORMANCES, WORKSHOPS, RESIDENCIES
SCHEDULE: YEAR-ROUND, WEEKDAYS, EVENINGS, WEEKENDS
DETAILS: GRADES PRE/K-12, VISUAL & PERFORMING ARTS
CREATIVE EXPRESSION, HISTORICAL/CULTURAL CONTEXT
TRAVEL TO SCHOOLS , INDIVIDUALLY TAILORED PROGRAMS
EDUCATIONAL MATERIALS AVAILABLE, BILINGUAL: SPANISH
WORK WITH HANDICAPPED

Youth

PROGRAMS: PERFORMANCES, WORKSHOPS, RESIDENCIES
SCHEDULE: YEAR-ROUND, WEEKDAYS, EVENINGS, WEEKENDS

Families

PROGRAMS: PERFORMANCES
SCHEDULE: YEAR-ROUND, WEEKDAYS, EVENINGS, WEEKENDS

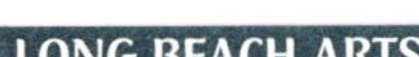

LONG BEACH ARTS

447 Long Beach Boulevard
Long Beach, CA 90803
Ph: 562-435-5995

501(c)3 LB

Paul Dominguez — Gallery Coordinator
Karl Weber — President

Founded in 1924, Long Beach Arts continuously supports emerging artists and provides a space to display their work.

- 11-12 exhibitions yearly, juried by prominent experts
- classes for adults and juniors
- gallery staffed by volunteers

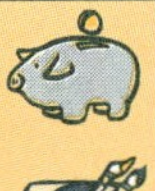

Youth

PROGRAMS: WORKSHOPS, CLASSES
SCHEDULE: FALL, WEEKDAYS

LONG BEACH CITY COLLEGE, ART DEPARTMENT

4901 E. Carson Street
Long Beach, CA 90808-1706
Ph: 562-938-4319
Admin: 562-938-4492
Fax: 562-938-4118
www.art.lbcc.cc.ca.us

LB

Marcia Netteberg — Department Secretary
Larry White — Chair

Long Beach City College Art and Photography offers foundation classes in the major fine arts disciplines.

- classes offered in jewelery, applied design, art history, sculpture, ceramics, photography, print making, graphic design, computer graphics, drawing, painting, illustration, and exhibition designs.

LONG BEACH CITY COLLEGE, ART GALLERY

4901 E. Carson Street
Long Beach, CA 90808
Ph: 562-938-4319

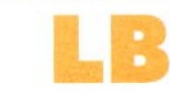

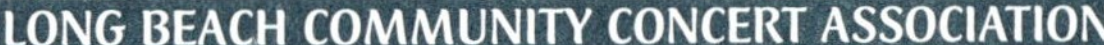

LONG BEACH COMMUNITY CONCERT ASSOCIATION

P.O. Box 6379
Lakewood, CA 90714
Ph: 310-764-2823
Admin: 562-421-2624
Fax: 562-421-4767

501(c)3 LB

Linda Kimberly — Executive Director
B.J. Sherwin — President/ 310-638-6655

The Long Beach Community Concert Association presents five variety shows per season at the Terrace Theater in Long Beach, California. Shows include orchestral, choral, magic, Russian folk festival, and jazz, all of which are family orient-

LONG BEACH MUSEUM OF ART

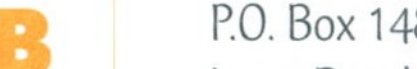

2300 E.Ocean Boulevard 501(c)3
Long Beach, CA 90803
Ph: 562-439-2119
Admin: 562-439-2119 x 32
Fax: 562-439-3587
www.lbma.com

Jeri Vaughn	Marketing/Public Relations Manager/ x40	jeri@lbma.com
Harold Nelson	Director / x27	haln@lbma.com
Sue Ann Robinson	Director of Education and Outreach/ x35	
Martin Betz	Director of Exhibitions/Special Programs/ x22	

Located in a historic home overlooking the Pacific Ocean the Long Beach Museum of Art hosts exhibits ranging from contemporary to American decorative arts that change quarterly .

- changing exhibition featuring 100 years of American and European works, decorative arts, and media arts with a focus on Southern California artists
- docent tours
- volunteer and intern opportunities
- summer Concert Series
- café
- ground rentals
- artist-led gallery talks
- NewVisions: video annual grant program
- artmaking workshops
- video art education and production

All programs are free. School tours are followed by hands-on artmaking workshops. Programs are designed to reach traditionally under-served populations and at-risk youth.

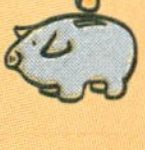

Pre/K-12

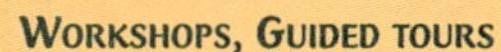

PROGRAMS: **WORKSHOPS, GUIDED TOURS**
SCHEDULE: YEAR-ROUND, WEEKDAYS, WEEKENDS
DETAILS: GRADES PRE/K-12, VISUAL & PERFORMING ARTS
AESTHETIC VALUING, CREATIVE EXPRESSION
HISTORICAL/CULTURAL CONTEXT
CONNECTIONS/RELATIONS/APPLICATIONS
TEACHER TRAINING PROGRAMS
TRAVEL TO SCHOOLS, PROGRAMS ON-SITE
INDIVIDUALLY TAILORED PROGRAMS , EDUCATIONAL MATERIALS
WORK WITH AT-RISK YOUTH

Youth

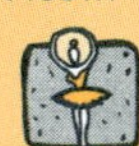
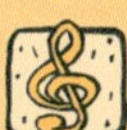
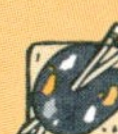

PROGRAMS: **PERFORMANCES, WORKSHOPS, CLASSES, GUIDED TOURS**
SCHEDULE: YEAR-ROUND, WEEKDAYS, WEEKENDS
DETAILS: COST FOR SOME PROGRAMS

Families

PROGRAMS: **PERFORMANCES, WORKSHOPS, SELF-GUIDED TOURS GUIDED TOURS**
SCHEDULE: YEAR-ROUND, WEEKENDS
DETAILS: COST FOR SOME PROGRAMS

LONG BEACH OPERA

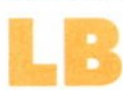

P.O. Box 14895 501(c)3
Long Beach, CA 90803
Ph: 562-439-2580
Fax: 562-683-2109

Michael Milenski	General Director	mmilenski@aol.com

The Long Beach Opera was founded in 1978 as an operatic producing company for the Long Beach Convention and Entertainment Center. The Opera produces highly theatrical and sometimes risky productions of both well-known and long-forgotten operas.

LONG BEACH SYMPHONY

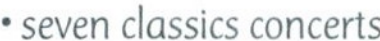

555 E. Ocean Boulevard, Suite 106 501(c)3
Long Beach, CA 90802
Ph: 562-436-3203
Admin: 562-436-3202
Fax: 562-491-3599
www.lbso.org

Cindy Loeffler	Marketing Director/ x234	cindy@lbso.org
Priscilla Munson	Artistic Director/ x230	pris@lbso.org
Fran Spears	Executive Director/ x221	fran@lbso.org

Music Director JoAnn Falletta leads the orchestra in a spectacular season of classics concerts. Principal POPS! Conductor Michael Krajewski conducts lively "musical indoor picnic" POPS! concerts. Exciting guest artists also featured.

- seven classics concerts
- fair festive POPS! concerts

LOREN L. ZACHARY SOCIETY FOR THE PERFORMING ARTS, THE

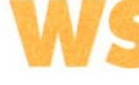

2250 Gloaming Way 501(c)3
Beverly Hills, CA 90210
Ph: 310-276-2731

Nedra Zachary	Director
Loren Zachary	President/Founder

The Loren L. Zachary Society for the Performing Arts sponsors a National Vocal Competition for young opera singers to assist in launching careers on the opera stages of America and abroad.

- General public is welcome to attend the Grand Finals Concert of the National Vocal Competition

LORETTA LIVINGSTON & DANCERS

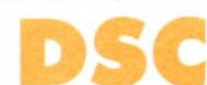

1318 E.Seventh Street, Suite 201 501(c)3
Los Angeles, CA 90021
Ph: 213-627-4684
Fax: 213-627-5875

David Plettner	Treasurer
Loretta Livingston	Artistic Director

Loretta Livingston & Dancers produces Loretta Livingston's dance and educational projects and brings them to the widest possible audience.

- choreographic commissions for Livingston
- solo performances by Livingston
- group performances of Livingston's choreography
- guest artist and collaborative projects
- dance workshops

LOS ANGELES BALLET

P.O. Box 712462 501(c)3
Los Angeles, CA 90071-7462
Ph: 213-833-3610
Admin: 714-991-8050

Andrew Deneau General Manager
Caitlin Goddard Ballet Mistress

The new Los Angeles Ballet has been organized to offer performances and educational programs throughout the greater Los Angeles area.

- Dance In Schools, grades 3-5 educational program
- ballet productions
- special events

Dance In Schools consists of a lecture demonstration concert, twice weekly ballet technical class, field trips to ballet performances, and final student concert performances. The program is made available to children in grades 3-5 throughout the greater L.A. area at schools at low cost or no cost based on need. It is the only in-school ballet training program in the U.S.

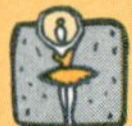

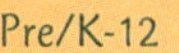

Pre/K-12

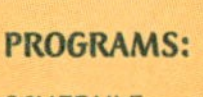

PROGRAMS:	**PERFORMANCES, STUDIO CLASSES, RESIDENCIES**
SCHEDULE:	YEAR-ROUND, WEEKDAYS, EVENINGS, WEEKENDS
DETAILS:	GRADES PRE/K-6, VISUAL & PERFORMING ARTS CREATIVE EXPRESSION, TRAVEL TO SCHOOLS INDIVIDUALLY TAILORED PROGRAMS

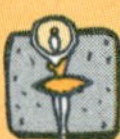

Youth

PROGRAMS:	**PERFORMANCES, CLASSES, RESIDENCIES**
SCHEDULE:	YEAR-ROUND, WEEKDAYS, EVENINGS, WEEKENDS

Families

PROGRAMS:	**PERFORMANCES**
SCHEDULE:	YEAR-ROUND, WEEKDAYS, EVENINGS

LOS ANGELES CENTER FOR PHOTOGRAPHIC STUDIES (LACPS) AT RE: SOLUTION GALLERY

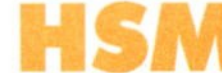

6518 Hollywood Boulevard 501(c)3 HSM
Los Angeles, CA 90028
Ph: 323-466-6232
Fax: 323-466-3203

Tania Martinez-Lemke Director

The Los Angeles Center for Photographic Studies offers programs which stimulate progressive dialogue and diverse representation in the media arts. A nationally regarded nonprofit, LACPS's educational mission is to encourage and present creative communication with photography and related arts.

- cultural events
- annual exhibitions
- lectures
- workshops
- publications

LOS ANGELES CHAMBER BALLET

1060 20th Street, Studio 18 501(c)3 WS
Santa Monica, CA 90403
Ph: 310-453-4952
Fax: 310-829-5049

Raiford Rogers Director

The Los Angeles Chamber Ballet is a contemporary dance company with an eclectic repertoire and roots in traditional ballet. The emphasis is on producing original work, often in collaboration with other Los Angeles artists.

- ballet concerts

The Los Angeles Chamber Ballet is the only professional ballet company in Los Angeles to offer student outreach.

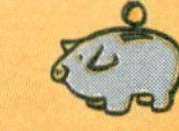

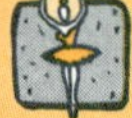

Pre/K-12

PROGRAMS:	**PERFORMANCES, WORKSHOPS, STUDIO CLASSES** **RESIDENCIES**
SCHEDULE:	YEAR-ROUND, WEEKDAYS
DETAILS:	GRADES 3-6, VISUAL & PERFORMING ARTS TRAVEL TO SCHOOLS

LOS ANGELES CHAMBER ORCHESTRA

611 W. 6th Street, Suite 2710 501(c)3 DSC
Los Angeles, CA 90017
Ph: 213-622-7001
Fax: 213-955-2071
www.laco.org

Michelle Weger	Executive Staff Assistant/ x200	lacham@earthlink.net
Jeffrey Kahane	Artistic Director	
Ruth Eliel	Executive Director/ x207	
Andrea Laguni	Director of Artistic Administration and Education/ x213	
Sherrie Course	Manager, Marketing and Box Office/ x203	

The Los Angeles Chamber Orchestra performs high-quality concerts, from Baroque and early classical works to the compositions from the 19th and 20th centuries, including many works by living composers.

- monthly concerts, September through April
- volunteer opportunities
- special summer concerts
- family programming
- silent film gala
- solo recitals and small ensembles

LOS ANGELES CHAMBER ORCHESTRA (CONTINUED)

L.A. Chamber Orchestra's education programs provide in-depth docent lectures and professional concerts free of charge to elementary school students in greater Los Angeles. Music Director Jeffrey Kahane conducts the concerts and engages students in the process of active listening.

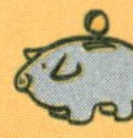

Pre/K-12

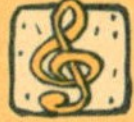

PROGRAMS:	**PERFORMANCES, WORKSHOPS**
SCHEDULE:	YEAR-ROUND, WEEKDAYS
DETAILS:	GRADES PRE/K-12, VISUAL & PERFORMING ARTS AESTHETIC VALUING, HISTORICAL/CULTURAL CONTEXT TRAVEL TO SCHOOLS, EDUCATIONAL MATERIALS AVAILABLE

Youth

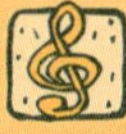

PROGRAMS:	**PERFORMANCES, WORKSHOPS**
SCHEDULE:	YEAR-ROUND, WEEKDAYS, WEEKENDS
DETAILS:	COST FOR SOME PROGRAMS

Families

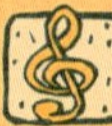

PROGRAMS:	**PERFORMANCES**
SCHEDULE:	YEAR-ROUND, WEEKENDS
DETAILS:	COST FOR SOME PROGRAMS

LOS ANGELES CHILDREN'S CHORUS

54 N. Oakland Avenue
Pasadena, CA 91101
Ph: 626-793-4231
Fax: 626-793-0173
www.homeearthlink.net/~lachldchorus/index.html

501(c)3 **PSG**

Becky Smith	Business Manager	
Anne Tomlinson	Artistic Director	lachldchorus@earhtlink.com

The Los Angeles Children's Chorus is an educational and performance program for children throughout L.A. County and has built an outstanding reputation for the quality of its musical performances.

- presents two independent home concerts annually
- performs with other groups in many venues throughout L.A.

Choristers are chosen by annual June opening auditions and participate in weekly rehearsals and musicianship classes.

Youth

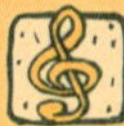

PROGRAMS:	**PERFORMANCES, CLASSES**
SCHEDULE:	SPRING, FALL, WINTER, WEEKDAYS, EVENINGS, WEEKENDS

LOS ANGELES CHILDREN'S MUSEUM

310 N. Main Street
Los Angeles, CA 90012
Ph: 213-687-8800
Admin: 213-687-8825
Fax: 213-687-0319
www.lacm.org

501(c)3 **DSC**

Mary Kay Wilson	Reservation Manager	lacm@lacm.org
Frank Pittarese	Director of Exhibits, Pgms & Operations	
Candace Barrett	Executive Director	candace@earthlink.net
Dawn Martinez	Program Manager	candelita_1@hotmail.com

The Los Angeles Children's Museum offers a hands-on, participatory environment in which children, ages 2 to 12, learn by doing. Fifteen permanent exhibits help to demystify everyday experiences. Monthly programming allows children to interact with artists and create their own artwork, experience live performances by professional entertainers, and attend a variety of "drop- in" workshops.

- "hands on" exhibits
- performances
- workshops
- membership opportunities
- gift shop

In addition to our public hours and events, our theater-based literacy program, Reader's Theater is available for tour to schools.

Pre/K-12

PROGRAMS:	**PERFORMANCES, RESIDENCIES, GUIDED TOURS**
SCHEDULE:	YEAR-ROUND, WEEKDAYS
DETAILS:	GRADES PRE/K-12, HISTORY/SOC. SCIENCES MATH/SCIENCES, VISUAL & PERFORMING ARTS LANGUAGE ARTS, CREATIVE EXPRESSION CONNECTIONS/RELATIONS/APPLICATIONS TRAVEL TO SCHOOLS, PROGRAMS ON-SITE

Youth

PROGRAMS:	**PERFORMANCES, WORKSHOPS, CLASSES, GUIDED TOURS**
SCHEDULE:	YEAR-ROUND, WEEKDAYS

Families

PROGRAMS:	**PERFORMANCES, GUIDED TOURS**
SCHEDULE:	YEAR-ROUND, WEEKENDS

LOS ANGELES CHOREOGRAPHERS & DANCERS

351 S. Virgil Avenue — 501(c)3 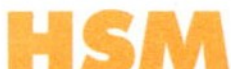
Los Angeles, CA 90020-1315
Ph/Fax: 213-385-1171
www.usc.edu/dept/dance

Louise Reichlin	Artistic/Managing Director
Alfred Desio	Associate Director
Jodi Barthiaume	Administrative Assistant to Director

Founded in 1979, Los Angeles Choreographers & Dancers, a nonprofit organization, has presented multiple educational programs and created many new works through its two professional dance companies Louise Reichlin & Dancers (modern) and Zapped Taps™/Alfred Desio (electronic and acoustic tap).

- approximately 100 performances and workshops yearly at various venues
- new dance works by Louise Reichlin (modern) and by Alfred Desio (tap)
- programs with special themes including technology and dance, cross cultural themes, and world music
- choreography for company and special commissions including concert, theater, musicals, orchestra, circus, video, and opera
- Colburn Kids Tap/L.A., a special youth company project
- classes in both modern and tap dance
- Tap-Tronic™ systems
- internships

One workshop series is based on modern dance warm-ups, followed by an improvisational movement exploration which includes objects brought from home. Using the movement factors of Time, Space, and Energy, Reichlin and the students create a dance with the theme of shared activities that cross cultural, age, and gender boundaries.

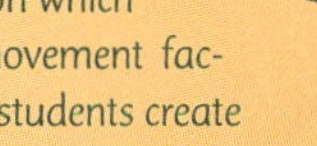

Pre/K-12

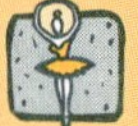

PROGRAMS: Performances, Workshops, Studio classes, Residencies
SCHEDULE: Year-round, Weekdays, Evenings, Weekends
DETAILS: grades Pre/k-12, Visual & performing arts, Multicultural, Creative Expression, Travel to schools, Individually tailored programs, Educational materials, cost for some programs

Youth

PROGRAMS: Performances, Workshops, Classes, Residencies
SCHEDULE: Year-round, weekdays, Evenings, Weekends
DETAILS: cost for some programs

Families

PROGRAMS: Performances, Workshops, Classes, Residencies
SCHEDULE: Year-round, Weekdays, Evenings, Weekends

LOS ANGELES CITY COLLEGE THEATRE ACADEMY

HSM

855 N. Vermont Avenue
Los Angeles, CA 90029
Ph: 323-953-4528
Admin: 323-953-4336
Fax: 323-953-4500
www.citywww.lacc.cc.ca.us/theatre/index.htm

Cliff O'Connell	Theatre Manager
Fred Fate	Academy Chair

The Theatre Academy provides each Academy student in Acting, Technical Theatre, and Costuming with the principles and techniques, discipline, organization, and dedication to training required for success in the entertainment industry. The Theatre Academy is one of the most highly recommended training programs for actors and technicians seeking professional training.

- 8 full theatre productions each academic year, September through May
- summer Shakespeare production

The Los Angeles City College Theatre Academy has an Upward Bound Program.

Pre/K-12

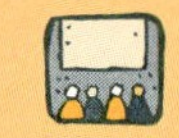

PROGRAMS: Workshops
SCHEDULE: Year-round, Weekdays, Evenings, Weekends
DETAILS: grades 9-12, History/soc. sciences, Math/sciences, Visual & performing arts, Multicultural

Youth

PROGRAMS: Workshops
SCHEDULE: Year-round, weekdays, Evenings, Weekends

Families

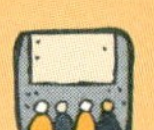

PROGRAMS: Workshops
SCHEDULE: Year-round, Weekdays, Evenings

LOS ANGELES CONSERVANCY

523 W. Sixth Street, Suite 1216 — 501(c)3 DSC
Los Angeles, CA 90014-1218
Ph: 213-623-CITY
Fax: 213-623-3909

Linda Dishman — Executive Director — info@laconservancy.org

The largest membership-based historic preservation organization in the West, dedicated to the recognition, preservation and revitalization of the architectural heritage of greater Los Angeles.

LOS ANGELES CONSERVATION CORPS

605 W. Olympic Boulevard, Suite 450 501(c)3
Los Angeles, CA 90015
Ph: 213-362-9000
Admin: 213-749-3601
Fax: 213-362-7958

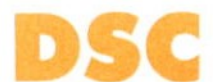

Bruce Saito Executive Director/ x203
Phil Matero Program Director/ 213-749-9769

The LACC is a nonprofit community based organization which employs inner-city youth to perform various community beautification projects throughout Los Angeles. The Mural Team, in an effort to remove and prevent graffiti, paints murals and involves local residents and schools and participates in community events.

- community beautification
- mural painting
- tree planting
- graffiti removal
- special event participation

The after-school program provides a safe environment, structured activities, and instruction in goal setting, life skills, and environmental and cultural awareness.

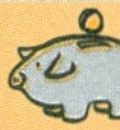

Youth

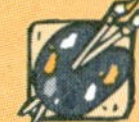

PROGRAMS: PLEASE SEE DESCRIPTION ABOVE FOR PROGRAMS

LOS ANGELES CONTEMPORARY EXHIBITIONS (LACE)

6522 Hollywood Boulevard 501(c)3
Hollywood, CA 90028
Ph: 323-957-1777
Fax: 323-957-9025

HSM

Bridget DuLong Managing Director
Irene Tsatsos Director/Curator

LACE is a contemporary visual arts center that fosters rigorous investigation of contemporary art practices, encourages artistic research, presents the results of these ideas in exhibitions and other forms and serves as a forum for the exchange of ideas between artists and their audiences.

- regular exhibitions of contemporary visual art in all media
- lectures
- literary events
- performance
- film and video screenings

LOS ANGELES COUNTY HIGH SCHOOL FOR THE ARTS FOUNDATION

5151 State University Drive 501(c)3
Los Angeles, CA 90032
Ph: 323-343-2554
Admin: 323-343-2787
Fax: 323-343-2549

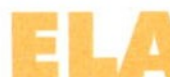

Ben Fonseca Recruitment Coordinator/ 323-343-2565
Judith Din Executive Director

Arts High is a comprehensive arts high school which allows students to fulfill high school graduation and college entrance requirements while studying the arts. Admission is open to the public. Students in grades 9-12 are admitted upon successful completion of application and audition.

- public, tuition-free high school education, 9-12
- comprehensive arts education in dance, theatre, music, and visual arts
- performances open to the public
- docent tours
- volunteer opportunities

Arts High is located on the Cal State University, L.A. Campus and provides a quality education to students in grades 9-12, free of charge. Annually, 90% of graduates continue their education at the nation's major universities and conservatories.

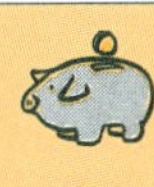

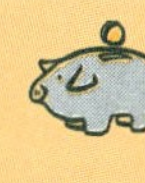

Pre/K-12

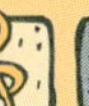

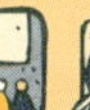

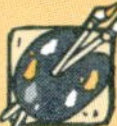

PROGRAMS: PERFORMANCES, GUIDED TOURS

SCHEDULE: SPRING, FALL, WINTER, WEEKDAYS, EVENINGS, WEEKENDS

DETAILS: GRADES 5-12, HISTORY/SOC. SCIENCES, MATH/SCIENCES
VISUAL & PERFORMING ARTS, LANGUAGE ARTS
MULTICULTURAL, PHYSICAL EDUCATION
AESTHETIC VALUING, CREATIVE EXPRESSION
HISTORICAL/CULTURAL CONTEXT
CONNECTIONS/RELATIONS/APPLICATIONS
TRAVEL TO SCHOOLS, FACILITY FOR SCHOOL VISITS
BILINGUAL PROGRAMS, COST FOR SOME PROGRAMS

LOS ANGELES COUNTY MUSEUM OF ART

5905 Wilshire Boulevard
Los Angeles, CA 90036
Ph: 323-857-6000
Admin: 323-857-6512
Fax: 323-931-7347
www.lacma.org

HSM

Keith McKeown Assistant Vice-President, Communications and Marketing
Andrea Rich CEO

One of the country's largest art museums, the Los Angeles County Museum of Art features an encyclopedic collection from prehistory to present day.

- internationally renowned collection
- presents more than 25 special exhibitions each year
- music, film and educational programs

LOS ANGELES COUNTY MUSEUM OF ART, EDUCATION DEPARTMENT

5905 Wilshire Boulevard
Los Angeles, CA 90036
Ph: 323-857-6000
Admin: 323-857-6512
Fax: 323-931-7347
www.lacma.org

HSM

Lisa Weintraub	Education Coordinator/ x6512
Jane Burrell	Chief, Museum Education/ x 6137
Maritza Galdamez	Secretary, Education/ x 6505

The Education Department of LACMA offers several in-house and outreach programs for the public.

- special exhibition lectures
- films (educational)
- Teacher's Academy
- Evenings for Educators
- symposia
- audio tours (permanent collections and special exhibitions)
- internships (high school, graduate, and undergraduate)
- docent tours

LACMA has been serving the public of L.A. County (and beyond) for over thirty years. Our large array of programs suits all ages, races, and abilities and are well-loved.

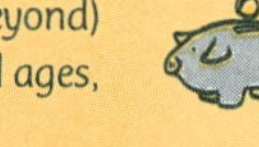

Pre/K-12

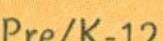
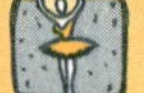
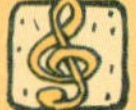
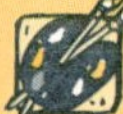

PROGRAMS:	**PERFORMANCES, WORKSHOPS, STUDIO CLASSES, RESIDENCIES, SELF-GUIDED TOURS, GUIDED TOURS**
SCHEDULE:	YEAR-ROUND, WEEKDAYS, WEEKENDS
DETAILS:	GRADES PRE/K-12, VISUAL & PERFORMING ARTS AESTHETIC VALUING, CREATIVE EXPRESSION TEACHER TRAINING PROGRAMS (SALARY POINTS) TRAVEL TO SCHOOLS, PROGRAMS ON-SITE INDIVIDUALLY TAILORED PROGRAMS, EDUCATIONAL MATERIALS BILINGUAL: SPANISH, WORK WITH DISABLED COST FOR SOME PROGRAMS

Youth

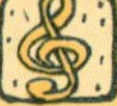
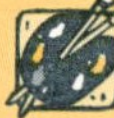

PROGRAMS:	**PERFORMANCES, WORKSHOPS, CLASSES, RESIDENCIES SELF-GUIDED TOURS, GUIDED TOURS**
SCHEDULE:	YEAR-ROUND, WEEKDAYS, WEEKENDS
DETAILS:	COST FOR SOME PROGRAMS

Families

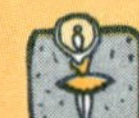
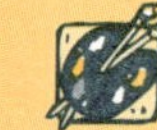

PROGRAMS:	**PERFORMANCES, WORKSHOPS, CLASSES, RESIDENCIES SELF-GUIDED TOURS, GUIDED TOURS**
SCHEDULE:	YEAR-ROUND, WEEKDAYS, WEEKENDS
DETAILS:	COST FOR SOME PROGRAMS

LOS ANGELES COUNTY MUSEUM OF ART MUSIC PROGRAMS

5905 Wilshire Boulevard
Los Angeles, CA 90036
Ph: 323-857-6000
Educ: 323-857-6512
Fax: 323-857-6214
www.lacma.org

501(c)3 **HSM**

Annissa Lui	Coordinator/ 323-857-6234
Dorrance Stalvey	Director, Music Programs

The museum's department of Music Programs, national winner of the AS, CAP/Chamber Music America Award for Adventurous Programming in 1991, 1994, and 1996, annually offers concert series' featuring distinguished ensembles and soloists in programs with repertoires that range from established masterworks to important new compositions.

LOS ANGELES CULTURAL AFFAIRS DEPARTMENT, CITY OF

433 S. Spring Street, 10th Floor
Los Angeles, CA 90013
Ph: 213-485-2433
Fax: 213-485-6835

DSC

Eve Rappoport	Manager, Community Relations
Adolfo V. Nodal	General Manager
Roella Louie	Director, Grants, Public Art & Cultural Planning
Ernest Dillihay	Director of Performing Arts

Through its programs and activities, the Department improves the quality of life for the residents of Los Angeles and vistors to the city by stimulating and supporting cultural activities.

- cultural grants
- historic preservation
- exhibitions
- performing and visual arts events
- public arts
- arts instruction
- festivals

LOS ANGELES DESIGNERS' THEATRE

P.O. Box 1883
Studio City, CA 91614-0883
Ph: 323-650-9600
TTD: 323 654-2700
Fax: 323-654-3260
www.ladesigners@juno.com

501(c)3 **SFV**

Richard Niederberg Artistic Director

Los Angeles Designers' Theatre is a theatrical producer of over 5,000 performances of over 400 productions since 1970.

- live music, theater, dance, opera, etc.
- internships/training in theater design and theater law/administration

LOS ANGELES DOCTORS SYMPHONY ORCHESTRA

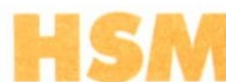

2337 N. Berendo Street
Los Angeles, CA 90027
Ph/Fax: 323-662-1045
www.netcom.com/~ivans/ladso.html

Ethel McClatchey	Vice President, Orchestra Council	ehtelred2@aol.cm
Ivan Shulman	Music Director	ivans@ix.netcom.com
Richard Chen	President, Orchestra Council	rychen@ucla.edu

Founded in 1953, Los Angeles Doctors Symphony Orchestra, presently under leadership of conductor Ivan Shulman, is one of the oldest community orchestras in the U.S. with medical origins still presenting concerts.

- live concerts in a variety of venues
- low cost or free admission; proceeds benefit medical and other charities

LOS ANGELES EDUCATIONAL PARTNERSHIP, HUMANITAS

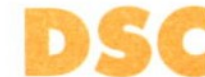

315 W. Ninth Street — 501 (c) 3
Los Angeles, CA 90015
Ph: 213-622-5237
Fax: 213-629-5288
www.lalc.k12.ca.us

Lili Barsha	Humanitas Project Coordinator	
Barbara Golding	Director	bgolding@laep.lalc.k12.ca.us

LAEP is engaged in public school restructuring and reform. Humanitas facilitates interdisciplinary humanities teaching and learning with art at the center which includes curriculum design and facilitation with arts organizations in support of high school art programs.

- network of over 400 secondary teachers united in their committment to creating access to the humanities in 38 Los Angeles High Schools
- 3 teachers' centers provide on-going training for LAUSD secondary teachers interested in the Humanitas model of instruction
- Summer Academy for teachers with salary points
- Teacher led in-services with salary point credit

Pre/K-12

PROGRAMS: **WORKSHOPS**
SCHEDULE: YEAR-ROUND, WEEKDAYS
DETAILS: GRADES PRE/K-12, HUMANITIES, AESTHETIC VALUING
CREATIVE EXPRESSION, HISTORICAL/CULTURAL CONTEXT
CONNECTIONS/RELATIONS/APPLICATIONS
TEACHER TRAINING PROGRAMS (SALARY POINTS)

LOS ANGELES FORUM FOR ARCHITECTURE AND URBAN DESIGN

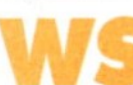

835 N. Kings Road — 501 (c) 3
West Hollywood, CA 90069
Ph: 323-852-7145
Fax: 323-954-9409

The Los Angeles Forum for Architecture and Urban Design provides a framework for design professionals and members of the general public to explore, evaluate, and impact the development of architecture in Los Angeles.

LOS ANGELES MODERN DANCE AND BALLET

HSM

Hollywood-Los Feliz Jewish Community Center — 501 (c) 3
1110 Bates Avenue
Los Angeles, CA 90029
Ph: 323-663-9130
Fax: 323-664-5474

Naomi Goldberg — Artistic Director

Los Angeles Modern Dance and Ballet, a seasonal company, brings dance experiences to all ages throughout Southern California.

- performances in community centers, schools, and in traditional theaters
- workshops in dance for all ages in sites throughout Los Angeles
- classes at the Hollywood-Los Feliz Jewish Community Center
- mentor dance program for high school students
- volunteer opportunities

L

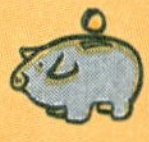

LAMD&B educational programs feature in-depth collaborations with teachers and students in an integrated partnership exploring contemporary dance.

Pre/K-12

PROGRAMS: **PERFORMANCES, WORKSHOPS, STUDIO CLASSES RESIDENCIES**
SCHEDULE: SPRING, WEEKDAYS, EVENINGS, WEEKENDS
DETAILS: GRADES PRE/K-12, VISUAL & PERFORMING ARTS
CREATIVE EXPRESSION, TEACHER TRAINING PROGRAMS
(SALARY POINTS), TRAVEL TO SCHOOLS
PROGRAMS ON-SITE, INDIVIDUALLY TAILORED PROGRAMS
EDUCATIONAL MATERIALS, WORK WITH DISABLED
COST FOR SOME PROGRAMS

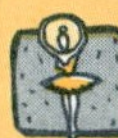

Youth

PROGRAMS: **PERFORMANCES, WORKSHOPS, CLASSES, RESIDENCIES**
SCHEDULE: SPRING, WEEKDAYS, EVENINGS, WEEKENDS

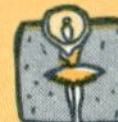

Families

PROGRAMS: **PERFORMANCES, WORKSHOPS, CLASSES, RESIDENCIES**
SCHEDULE: SPRING, WEEKDAYS, EVENINGS, WEEKENDS

LOS ANGELES MOZART ORCHESTRA

P.O. Box 17643
Los Angeles, CA 91416-7643
Ph: 818-705-5860
Fax: 818-342-1431

501(c)3 **SFV**

Julie Campbell	Operations Manager	jecucla@aol.com
Lucinda Carver	Music Director and Conductor	

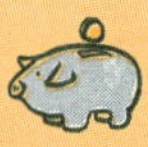

Pre/K-12

PROGRAMS:	**PERFORMANCES**
SCHEDULE:	YEAR-ROUND, WEEKDAYS, EVENINGS, WEEKENDS
DETAILS:	GRADES 3-6, VISUAL & PERFORMING ARTS CREATIVE EXPRESSION, HISTORICAL/CULTURAL CONTEXT TRAVEL TO SCHOOLS

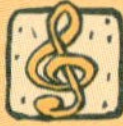

Youth

PROGRAMS:	**PERFORMANCES**
SCHEDULE:	YEAR-ROUND, WEEKDAYS, EVENINGS, WEEKENDS

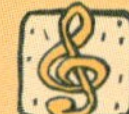

Families

PROGRAMS:	**PERFORMANCES**
SCHEDULE:	YEAR-ROUND, WEEKDAYS, EVENINGS, WEEKENDS
DETAILS:	COST FOR SOME PROGRAMS

LOS ANGELES MUNICIPAL ART GALLERY

4804 Hollywood Boulevard
Los Angeles, CA 90027
Ph: 213-485-4581
TTD: 323-660-9254
Fax: 213-485-8396

HSM

Scott Canty	Curator/Director of CAO Slide Registry
Noel Korten	Exhibitions Coordinator
Susan Foley Johannson	Director of Museum Education
Sidney Taylor	Registrar

The Los Angeles Municipal Art Gallery is devoted to the exhibition, interpretation and documentation of emerging, mid-career, and senior artists of the area in group and individual presentation formats. The curatorial focus includes painting, sculpture, photography, architecture, video, installation, design, and related disciplines that reflect the cultural fabric of Los Angeles.

- variety of exhibitions including: theme, solo, biennial, annual individual artists grants, guest curator, and local artist exhibitions
- volunteer opportunities
- docent, school, and disabled children gallery tours
- Cultural Affairs Department Slide Registry
- children's film series
- conversations with the artists
- family art and teacher workshops
- Museum Education Intern Program
- Teacher Resource Center
- night readings

LOS ANGELES MUNICIPAL ART GALLERY (CONTINUED)

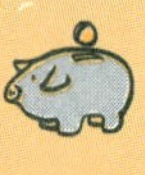

Tours encourage viewers to analyze and refine their appreciation of contemporary art. For student tours, the educators use interactive inquiry methods, role-playing, theater techniques, and guided art projects to promote enjoyment and understanding.

Pre/K-12

PROGRAMS:	**PERFORMANCES, WORKSHOPS, SELF-GUIDED TOURS GUIDED TOURS**
SCHEDULE:	YEAR-ROUND, WEEKDAYS, EVENINGS, WEEKENDS
DETAILS:	GRADES 3-12, VISUAL & PERFORMING ARTS AESTHETIC VALUING, CREATIVE EXPRESSION HISTORICAL/CULTURAL CONTEXT TEACHER TRAINING PROGRAMS (SALARY POINTS) PROGRAMS ON-SITE, EDUCATIONAL MATERIALS AVAILABLE BILINGUAL: SPANISH, ARMENIAN, WORK WITH DISABLED

Youth

PROGRAMS:	**PERFORMANCES, WORKSHOPS, SELF-GUIDED TOURS GUIDED TOURS**
SCHEDULE:	YEAR-ROUND, WEEKDAYS, EVENINGS, WEEKENDS

Families

PROGRAMS:	**PERFORMANCES, WORKSHOPS, SELF-GUIDED TOURS GUIDED TOURS**
SCHEDULE:	YEAR-ROUND, WEEKDAYS, EVENINGS, WEEKENDS

LOS ANGELES MUSEUM OF THE HOLOCAUST MARTYRS MEMORIAL

6006 Wilshire Boulevard
Los Angeles, CA 90048
Ph: 323-761-8170
Fax: 323-761-8076

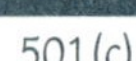

501(c)3

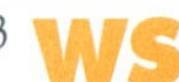

WS

LOS ANGELES PHILHARMONIC ASSOCIATION

135 N. Grand Avenue 501(c)3 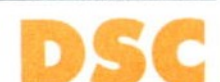
Los Angeles, CA 90012
Ph: 213-972-7300
Admin: 213-972-7597
Fax: 213-972-7650
www.laphil.org

Leni Boorstin	Public Affairs Director	lboorstin@laphil.org
Esa-PekkaSalonen	Music Director	
Willem Wijnbergen	Exec. Vice-President/Managing Director	
Sue Knussen	Director of Education	sknussen@laphil.org

The L.A. Philharmonic, with its administrative organization, performs and presents music in its varied forms at the Music Center, the Hollywood Bowl, and in community venues throughout Los Angeles.

- orchestra and recital concerts in the Dorothy Chandler Pavilion
- classical, pops, jazz and world music concerts at the Hollywood Bowl
- chamber music concerts at Gindi Auditorium
- new music concerts at the Japan America Theatre
- neighborhood concerts in community venues
- symphonies for youth and symphonies for schools
- recordings
- regional, national and international concert tours
- E. Edelman Hollywood Bowl Museum and Hollywood Bowl gift shop
- volunteer opportunities with Philharmonic affiliates

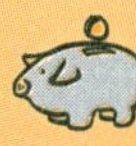

Los Angeles Philharmonic education programs include exposure to and interaction with a world-class orchestra and its musicians. Programs include Music for Educators, L.A. Philharmonic High School Honor Orchestra, Invitational Rehearsals and more.

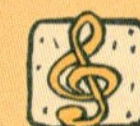

Pre/K-12

PROGRAMS: **Performances, Residencies, Guided tours**
SCHEDULE: Year-round, Weekdays, Weekends
DETAILS: Grades Pre/K-12, Visual & performing arts
Creative Expression, Historical/Cultural Context
Teacher training programs (salary points)
Travel to schools, Programs on-site
Individually tailored programs, Educational materials
Cost for some programs

Youth

PROGRAMS: **Performances, Residencies, Guided Tours**
SCHEDULE: Year-round, weekdays, Evenings, Weekends
DETAILS: cost for some programs

Families

PROGRAMS: **Performances, Guided Tours**
SCHEDULE: Year-round, Weekdays, Evenings, Weekends
DETAILS: cost for some programs

LOS ANGELES POVERTY DEPARTMENT

1226 Alvarado 501(c)3 HSM
Los Angeles, CA 90026
Ph/Fax: 213-413-1077

Sonya Mims	Administrative Director
John Malpede	Artistic Director
Emmanuel Deleage	Administrative Director

LA Poverty Department is a theater company comprised of mainly homeless and formerly homeless people with a limited number of local artists.

- open workshops
- transitional homeless workshop
- group collaborative shows
- individual projects
- residencies

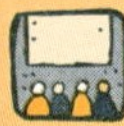

Pre/K-12

PROGRAMS: **Workshops**
SCHEDULE: Year-round, Evenings, Weekends
DETAILS: Visual & performing arts, Creative Expression
Travel to schools, Individually tailored programs
Work with Homeless

LOS ANGELES PUBLIC LIBRARY, ART, MUSIC, RECREATION, RARE BOOKS AND ADULT OUTREACH

630 W. Fifth Street DSC
Los Angeles, CA 90071
Ph: 213-228-7240
Fax: 213-228-7239
www.lapl.org

Romaine Ahlstrom	Department Manager	rahlstro@lapl.org

The Art, Music, Recreation and Rare Books Department of the Los Angeles Public Library has an extensive collection of books, journals and online databases on all aspects of the arts.

LOS ANGELES PUBLIC LIBRARY, CULTURAL PROGRAMS DEPARTMENT

630 W. 5th Street 501(c)3 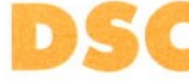
Los Angeles, CA 90071
Ph: 213-228-7326
Fax: 213-228-7289
www.lapl.org

Louise Steinman	Cultural Programs Director/ 213-228-7472
Toria Aiken	Exhibitions Coordinator/ 213-228-7287

LAPL established a Cultural Programs Department in 1993. The Cultural Programs Department is under the aegis of the Library Foundation of Los Angeles, a non-profit organization which seeks and provides funding for projects which complement, but do not supplant, the City's responsibility for the operation of LAPL..

- live music, dance, art, theater, and literary programs by poets, authors, musicians, artists, world leaders, and scholars
- Mark Taper Auditorium, galleries, and children's story theater

LOS ANGELES REPERTORY COMPANY, INC.

6560 Hollywood Boulevard, 2nd Floor — 501(c)3 **HSM**
Los Angeles, CA 90028-6217
Ph: 323-464-8542
Fax: 323-464-6130

Peter Ellenstein — Producing Director/ x3
Robert Ellenstein — Artistic Director/ x3

Founded in 1966, the L.A. Repertory Company, Inc. is known for its world-class theatrical productions and professional training. A dues-paying collective of theatre artists creates each production through an ensemble production.

- theatre productions
- theatre workshops and classes
- rehearsal studio rentals
- performance rentals

We tour socially relevant plays to the schools and create study guides for teachers. We often do productions of classic plays which fit in well with school curriculum.

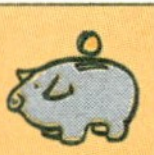

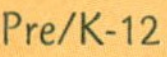

Pre/K-12

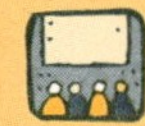

PROGRAMS: PERFORMANCES, WORKSHOPS
SCHEDULE: YEAR-ROUND, WEEKDAYS, EVENINGS
DETAILS: GRADES PRE/K-12, VISUAL & PERFORMING ARTS
CREATIVE EXPRESSION, TRAVEL TO SCHOOLS
PROGRAMS ON-SITE, INDIVIDUALLY TAILORED PROGRAMS
EDUCATIONAL MATERIALS, COST FOR SOME PROGRAMS

Youth

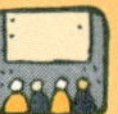

PROGRAMS: PERFORMANCES
SCHEDULE: YEAR-ROUND, WEEKDAYS, EVENINGS
DETAILS: COST FOR SOME PROGRAMS

Families

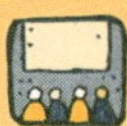

PROGRAMS: PERFORMANCES, WORKSHOPS, CLASSES
SCHEDULE: YEAR-ROUND, WEEKDAYS, EVENINGS

LOS ANGELES THEATRE CENTER

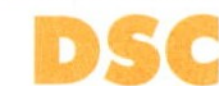

514 S. Spring Street
Los Angeles, CA 90013
Ph: 213-485-1624
Fax: 213-847-3169

Joan deBruin — Director, Folk/Traditional Arts & Exhibitions
Michael Sahhar — Booking/Literary Manager
Ernest Dillihay — Performing Arts Director
Earl Sherburn — Community Arts Director

Our primary goal with LATC remains to help create opportunities for you and your family to attend live performances without "breaking the household bank.

LOS ANGELES-ST. PETERSBURG RUSSIAN FOLK ORCHESTRA

199 S. Los Robles, Suite 711 — 501(c)3 **PSG**
Pasadena, CA 91101
Ph: 626-568-9979
Educ: 626-799-2773
Fax: 626-584-8807
www.geocities.com/Vienna/Choir/2574/LASPRFO.html

Peggy Propper — Board Member — peggypropper@worldnet.att.net
Anatoly Manialyga — Artistic Director
Iryna Orlova — Music Director — IOrlova@aol.com

The Los Angeles-St. Petersburg Russian Folk Orchestra is comprised of an orchestra, chamber ensemble, and soloists dedicated to education, production, and performance of music written and arranged for Russian folk instruments such as balalaika, domra, bayan, and guisli.

- live concerts
- workshops
- private and group lessons
- master classes
- senior citizen concerts

We are an orchestra traditional in nature but unusual in sound in that balalaikas sit where cellos are generally placed, and domras sit where violins are usually placed. The result is a warm tremolb sound.

Youth

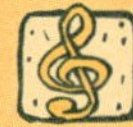

PROGRAMS: PERFORMANCES
SCHEDULE: YEAR-ROUND, EVENINGS, WEEKENDS

Families

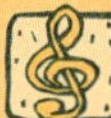

PROGRAMS: PERFORMANCES
SCHEDULE: YEAR-ROUND, EVENINGS, WEEKENDS

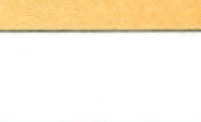

LOUIS STERN FINE ARTS

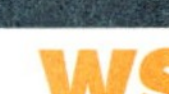

9002 Melrose Avenue
West Hollywood, CA 90069
Ph: 310-276-0147
Fax: 310-276-7740
www.artnet.com/1stern.html

Louis Stern — President — lstern613@aol.com
Rachel Breslin — Registrar

Specializing in Impressionist, Post-Impressionist, Modern, and Latin American art, our exhibition program also features work by select contemporary artists. Opening receptions are held in conjunction with the West Hollywood Galleries.

LUCKMAN FINE ARTS COMPLEX

California State University, Los Angeles 501 (c) 3 **ELA**
5151 State University Drive
Los Angeles, CA 90032
Ph: 323-343-6611
Admin: 323-343-6615
Fax: 323-343-6423

Judy Brickham	Office Manager/ 323-343-6613
Clif Harper	Executive Director
Ronnie Cavalluzzi	Director of Outreach and Education
Wendy Baker	Business Manager/ 323-343-6619

Situated on the campus of California State University, Los Angeles, the Luckman Complex is a multidisciplinary arts facility dedicated to the presentation and exhibition of traditional and contemporary art forms.

- diverse programming including dance, music, and theatrical presentations
- gallery exhibitions

We're Creating Opportunites for Learning Through the Arts (COLTA). This stimulating arts education program is designed to provide a wide variety of culturally diverse performing and visual arts experiences for students.

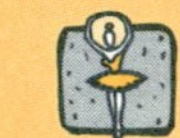 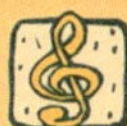 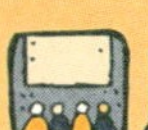 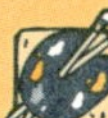

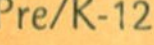

Pre/K-12

PROGRAMS:	**PERFORMANCES, GUIDED TOURS**
SCHEDULE:	SPRING, FALL, WINTER, WEEKDAYS
DETAILS:	GRADES PRE/K-12, VISUAL & PERFORMING ARTS
	MULTICULTURAL, CREATIVE EXPRESSION
	HISTORICAL/CULTURAL CONTEXT
	TRAVEL TO SCHOOLS, PROGRAMS ON-SITE
	INDIVIDUALLY TAILORED PROGRAMS, EDUCATIONAL MATERIALS

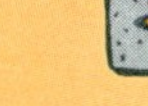 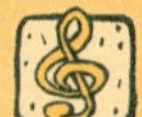 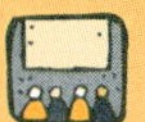 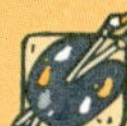

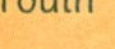

Youth

PROGRAMS:	**WORKSHOPS**
SCHEDULE:	SPRING, FALL, WINTER, WEEKDAYS

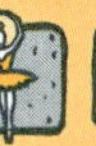 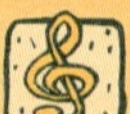 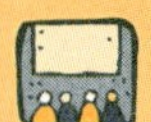 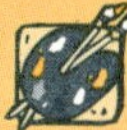

Families

PROGRAMS:	**PERFORMANCES**
SCHEDULE:	SPRING, FALL, WINTER, WEEKENDS

LULA WASHINGTON'S LOS ANGELES CONTEMPORARY DANCE THEATRE

5041 W. Pico Boulevard 501 (c) 3

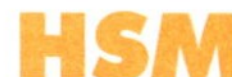

Los Angeles, CA 90019
Ph: 323-936-6591
Admin: 323-678-6250
Fax: 323-671-4572
www.lacn.org\lulawashington\

Erwin Washington	Executive Director	lwdt@netroplex.com
Lula Washington	Artistic Director	

To provide a creative outlet for African American dance artists in the under-served, economically depressed areas of South-Central Los Angeles.

- performance ensemble
- dance classes

LULA WASHINGTON'S LOS ANGELES CONTEMPORARY DANCE THEATRE (CONTINUED)

We offer a program titled "I do dance not drugs" as an extracurricular youth activity. We also offer daily dance classes at our studio as well as a summer dance camp

Pre/K-12

PROGRAMS:	**PERFORMANCES, WORKSHOPS**
SCHEDULE:	YEAR-ROUND, WEEKDAYS
DETAILS:	PRE/K-12, VISUAL & PERFORMING ARTS
	CREATIVE EXPRESSION
	HISTORICAL/CULTURAL CONTEXT
	TRAVEL TO SCHOOLS

Youth

PROGRAMS:	**WORKSHOPS, CLASSES**
SCHEDULE:	YEAR-ROUND, SUMMER, WEEKDAYS, EVENINGS

LUNAPARK

665 N. Robertson Boulevard **WS**
Los Angeles, CA 90069
Ph: 310-652-0611
Fax: 310-652-7121

Laura Connelly	PR Director
Jean-Pierre Boccara	Owner

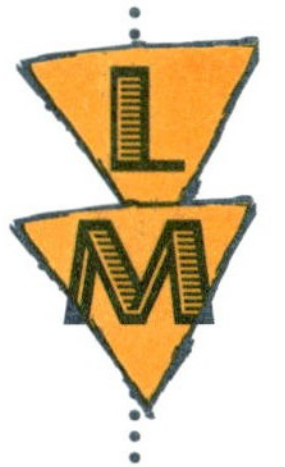

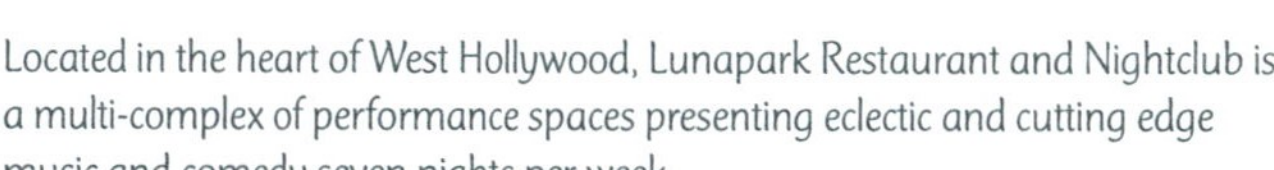

Located in the heart of West Hollywood, Lunapark Restaurant and Nightclub is a multi-complex of performance spaces presenting eclectic and cutting edge music and comedy seven nights per week.

- live music and comedy seven nights per week

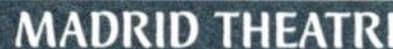

MADRID THEATRE

21622 Sherman Way **SFV**
Canoga Park, CA 91303
Ph: 818-347-9938

Anisa Olazabol	Performing Arts Program Coordinator

MAK CENTER FOR ART AND ARCHITECTURE

Friends of the Schindler House 501 (c)3 **WS**
835 N. Kings Road
West Hollywood, CA 90069
Ph: 323-651-1510
Fax: 323-651-2340

Lou Anne Greenwald	Program Coordinator/ x10
Carol McMichael-Reese	Director/ x11
Angelica Fuentes	Docent Coordinator/ x10

The MAK Center, a nonprofit organization which focuses on the intersection of contemporary art and architecture, creates exhibitions and lectures and manages a residency program for emerging artists and architects.

- public tours of the historic Schindler House
- docent and volunteer program
- bookstore specializing in books on contemporary art and architecture including publications by the MAK Center L.A. and the MAK, Vienna
- ongoing schedule of exhibitions of contemporary art and architecure
- lectures, panel discussions, and symposia
- architecture tours
- exhibitions and lectures by MAK Center artists and architects in residence

MALIBU STAGE COMPANY

29243 Pacific Coast Highway 501 (c)3 **WS**
Malibu, CA 90265
Ph: 310-456-8226
Fax: 310-456-8170
www.winomar@aol.com

Jane Windsor	Secretary
Charles Marowitz	Artistic Director

The Malibu Stage Company is a professional theater ensemble specializing in chamber-versions of the classics.

- childrens, teenage, and professional acting classes
- regular theater performances

The Malibu Stage Company offers professional training for actors and teen-agers as well as for businessmen and executives desiring public speaking tuition.

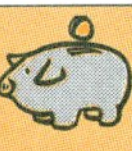

Youth

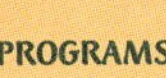

PROGRAMS: WORKSHOPS
SCHEDULE: YEAR-ROUND, WEEKDAYS, WEEKENDS

MANHATTAN BEACH, CULTURAL ARTS DIVISION, CITY OF

1400 Highland Avenue **SB**
Manhattan Beach, CA 90266
Ph: 310-545-5621
Educ: 310-376-9511
Fax: 310-545-5234
www.ci.manhattan-beach.ca.us

Howard Spector	Cultural Arts Mgr/ x326	hspector@ci.manhattan-beach.ca.us
Barbara Johnson	Education Supervisor	bjohnson@ci.manhattan-beach.ca.us
Christine Johnson	Perf. Arts Supervisor/x348	cjohnson@ci.manhattan-beach.ca.us

The City of Manhattan Beach's Cultural Arts Division fulfills the needs of the community by providing instruction in and presentation of music, dance, literature, visual arts and theater.

- year-round music concerts
- dance performances
- visual arts classes
- performing arts classes
- artist residencies
- artist in schools programs
- arts education masterplan with school district
- theater productions
- literary publications
- public art
- creative writing
- internships
- volunteer opportunities

The Cultural Arts Division is in its third year of implementing the Arts Education Masterplan in conjunction with the Manhattan-Beach Unified School District. It is designed to integrate arts into the core curriculum.

Pre/K-12

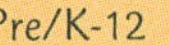
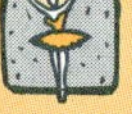
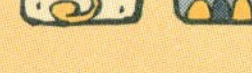
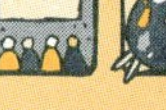

PROGRAMS: PERFORMANCES, WORKSHOPS, STUDIO CLASSES, RESIDENCIES
SCHEDULE: YEAR-ROUND, WEEKDAYS
DETAILS: GRADES PRE/K-12, VISUAL & PERFORMING ARTS
AESTHETIC VALUING, CREATIVE EXPRESSION
HISTORICAL/CULTURAL CONTEXT
CONNECTIONS/RELATIONS/APPLICATIONS
TEACHER TRAINING PROGRAMS, TRAVEL TO SCHOOLS
PROGRAMS ON-SITE , INDIVIDUALLY TAILORED PROGRAMS

Youth

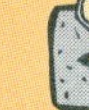
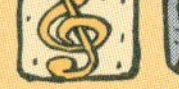
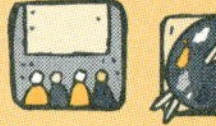

PROGRAMS: PERFORMANCES, WORKSHOPS, CLASSES
SCHEDULE: YEAR-ROUND, WEEKDAYS, EVENINGS, WEEKENDS

MANNY SILVERMAN GALLERY

610 N. Almont Drive **WS**
Los Angeles, CA 90069
Ph: 310-659-8256
Fax: 310-659-1001

Linda Hooper	Director	msgallery@aol.com

Modern and contemporary art specializing in American abstract art of the Post-War Period.

MARC RICHARDS GALLERY

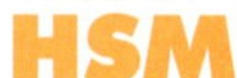

170 S. La Brea Avenue
Los Angeles, CA 90036
Ph: 323-634-0838
Fax: 310-858-0688

Marc Richards — Director — cardova@mail.artnet.net

Chinese antiquities and contemporary works of art.

MARILYN PINK/MASTER PRINTS & DRAWINGS/FINE

P.O. Box 491446
Los Angeles, CA 90049
Ph: 310-395-1465
www.artscenecal.com/Pink.html

Marilyn Pink — Director — finartla@aol.com

Fine works of art on paper, 15th-20th century. Private dealer.

MARK TAPER FORUM/CENTER THEATRE GROUP

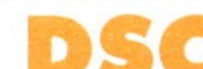

Music Center of Los Angeles — 501(c)3
135 N. Grand Avenue
Los Angeles, CA 90012
Ph: 213-628-2772
Admin: 213-972-7353
Fax: 213-972-0746
www.TaperAhmanson.com

Jim Royce — Managing Director/ 213-972-7324
Gordon Davidson — Artistic Director
Charles Dillingham — Managing Director
Dolores Chavez — Director PLAY

A 752-seat theater with a thrust stage, the Taper has built a reputation for excellence both in the development of new plays, voices for the theater and in its continuing commitment to serve the broadest possible audience. The Taper was founded in 1967 as an outgrowth of UCLA's Theatre Group.

Pre/K-12

PROGRAMS: PERFORMANCES
SCHEDULE: YEAR-ROUND, WEEKDAYS, EVENINGS, WEEKENDS
DETAILS: GRADES 7-12, VISUAL & PERFORMING ARTS
FACILITY FOR SCHOOL VISITS

Youth

PROGRAMS: PERFORMANCES
SCHEDULE: YEAR-ROUND, WEEKDAYS, EVENINGS, WEEKENDS

Families

PROGRAMS: PERFORMANCES
SCHEDULE: YEAR-ROUND, WEEKDAYS, EVENINGS, WEEKENDS

MCGROARTY ARTS CENTER

7570 McGroarty Terrace — 501(c)3 — SFV
Tujunga, CA 91042
Ph: 818-352-5285
www.mcgroartyarts.org

Isabella Barone — Director — director@mcgroartyarts.org
Larelle Geils — Artistic Director

Located in the Northeast Valley, the McGroarty Arts Center is a multidisciplinary community based organization that presents contemporary art in all of its various forms. Programs offer events that promote and preserve local historical and cultural traditions. The Center is State Historical Monument #63.

- exhibitions by local artists every two months
- docent tours of the home by appointment
- assortment of concert types varying by funder

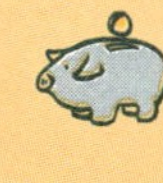

McGroarty Arts Center provides a full curriculum of arts instruction for children and adults. Special programs include performances and exhibitions that showcase visual, literary and performing artists.

Youth

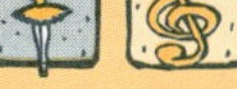
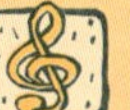
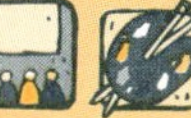

PROGRAMS: PERFORMANCES, WORKSHOPS, CLASSES, SELF-GUIDED TOURS, GUIDED TOURS
SCHEDULE: YEAR-ROUND, WEEKDAYS, EVENINGS, WEEKENDS
DETAILS: COST FOR SOME PROGRAMS

Families

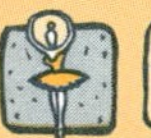
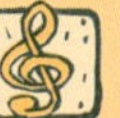
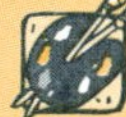

PROGRAMS: PERFORMANCES, WORKSHOPS, CLASSES SELF-GUIDED TOURS, GUIDED TOURS
SCHEDULE: YEAR-ROUND, WEEKDAYS, EVENINGS, WEEKENDS

MCLEAN GALLERY

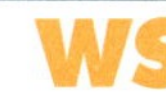

Malibu Country Mart
23410 Civic Center Way, D3
Malibu, CA 90265
Ph: 310-456-2226
Fax: 310-456-1875
www.mcleangallery.com
art@mcleangallery.com

MENDENHALL GALLERY WHITTIER COLLEGE

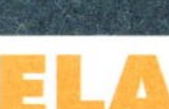

13406 Philadelphia Street
Whittier, CA 90608
Ph: 562-907-4200 x4311
Fax: 562-698-4067

Kim Russo — Art Department

M

METROPOLITAN ASSOCIATES

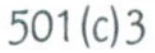
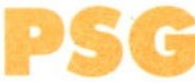

535 S. Grand Avenue 501(c)3 PSG
Pasadena, CA 91105
Ph: 626-796-4165
Fax: 626-449-5041

Alice Coulombe   President

We raise funds for performing arts experiences for children. We support the performing arts by buying blocks of tickets for group attendance at performances.

- summer film festival

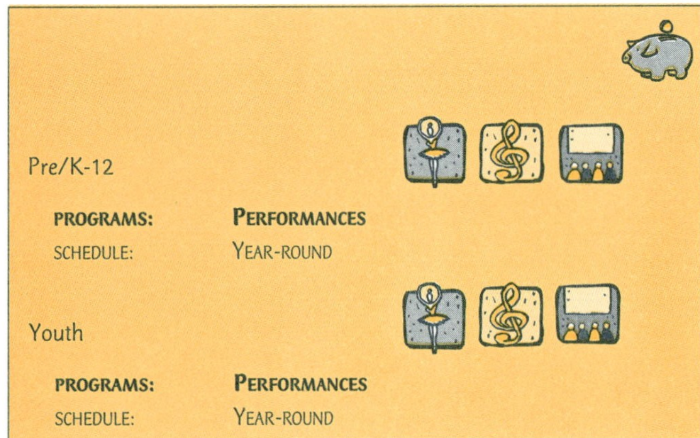

Pre/K-12

PROGRAMS: PERFORMANCES
SCHEDULE: YEAR-ROUND

Youth

PROGRAMS: PERFORMANCES
SCHEDULE: YEAR-ROUND

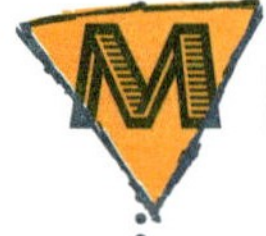

MEXICAN CULTURAL INSTITUTE OF LOS ANGELES

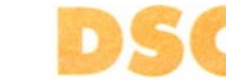

125 Paseo de la Plaza, Suite 300 501(c)3 DSC
Los Angeles, CA 90012
Ph: 213-624-3660
Fax: 213-624-9387

Leticia Quezada   President and CEO

The Mexican Cultural Institute fosters a better understanding between the people of Mexico and the U.S. through comprehensive programs in art, education, and culture.

- conference on Mexican history and culture
- visual art exhibits
- dance and musical performances
- bookstore containing materials from Mexico written in Spanish
- Mexican folk arts gift shop
- festivals commemorating traditional Mexican holidays
- lectures by visiting scholars from Mexico
- volunteer opportunities

MEXICAN CULTURAL INSTITUTE OF LOS ANGELES

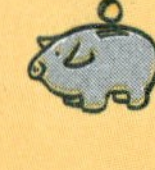

All our educational programs include participation by the audience and are easy to understand. The quality of the programs is consistent and it makes people come back when new programs are presented.

Pre/K-12

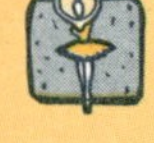
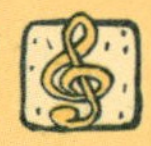
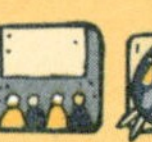

PROGRAMS: PERFORMANCES, WORKSHOPS, SELF-GUIDED TOURS
SCHEDULE: YEAR-ROUND, WEEKDAYS, WEEKENDS
DETAILS: GRADES 3-12, HISTORY/SOC. SCIENCES
VISUAL & PERFORMING ARTS, LANGUAGE ARTS
MULTICULTURAL, CREATIVE EXPRESSION
HISTORICAL/CULTURAL CONTEXT
TEACHER TRAINING PROGRAMS, TRAVEL TO SCHOOLS
PROGRAMS ON-SITE, INDIVIDUALLY TAILORED PROGRAMS
EDUCATIONAL MATERIALS AVAILABLE, BILINGUAL : SPANISH
COST FOR SOME PROGRAMS

Youth

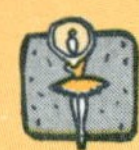
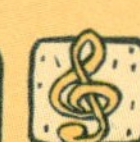
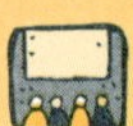
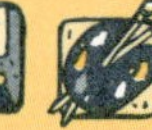

PROGRAMS: PERFORMANCES, WORKSHOPS, SELF-GUIDED TOURS
SCHEDULE: YEAR-ROUND, WEEKDAYS, WEEKENDS
DETAILS: COST FOR SOME PROGRAMS

Families

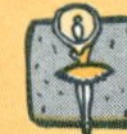
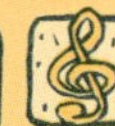
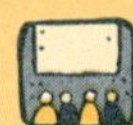
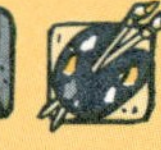

PROGRAMS: PERFORMANCES, WORKSHOPS, SELF-GUIDED TOURS
SCHEDULE: YEAR-ROUND, WEEKDAYS, EVENINGS, WEEKENDS
DETAILS: COST FOR SOME PROGRAMS

MICHAEL HITTLEMAN GALLERY

8797 Beverly Boulevard, #302 WS
Los Angeles, CA 90048
Ph: 323-655-5364
Fax: 323-659-0211

Michael Hittleman

Fine Israeli art/contemporary Israeli masters.

MICHAEL KIZHNER FINE ART

1010 Palm Avenue, #307 WS
Los Angeles, CA 90069
Ph: 310-659-5222
Fax: 310-659-0838

By appointment only

MICHAEL LEVY GALLERY

115 Pine Avenue, Suite 240 LB
Long Beach, CA 90802
Ph: 562-983-9717
Fax: 562-983-9988

Michael Levy   Director

Modern and emerging Masters.

MICHELLE BERNE/CELEBRATION ARTS

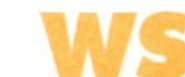

1653 18th Street, Studio 1
Santa Monica, CA 90404
Ph: 310-828-5353
Fax: 310-453-4347

Michelle Berne — Artistic Director — celarts@earthlink.net
Joshua Fontanez — Associate Artist

Located at the 18th Street Arts Complex in Santa Monica, Celebration Arts is a multidisciplinary community-based organization that aids communities in unique artistic expressions and visions. Celebration Arts began with an inspiration by Michelle Berne, who is dedicated to the idea that art, in all its forms is a viable response to life; that celebrating life belongs at the core of our experience.

- large scale papier mache sculpture
- large people-powered "floats"
- giant puppets, masks, costumes, and body adornments
- dance, music, and choreography to co-create imaginative and colorful events
- workshops developed for children, teens, and adults
- slide presentation--intro. to Celebration Arts
- site-specific performance
- consultation and commissions
- produce large-scale events that bring together thousands of performers and tens of thousands of spectators.
- school residencies that build continuity between the curriculum and projects students will work on

MID-CITY REGIONAL ARTS COUNCIL

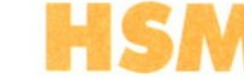

City of Los Angeles Cultural Affairs Department
433 S. Spring Street, 10th Floor
Los Angeles, CA 90013
Ph: 213-485-9570
Fax: 213-485-6835

Julia Williams — cadpublicart@earthlink.net

Developed through the City of Los Angeles Cultural Affairs Department as one of 9 regional arts councils, we are a coalition of arts and community organizations, artists, leaders, business people and all other interested members of the community who have the purpose of assessing, coalescing and acting on the cultural assets and needs of the area. This council serves Hollywood and Wilshire. Goals include:

- develop affordable and accessible local programming that highlights and involves youth and local artists
- develop activities that celebrate the city's cultural diversity and promote community building
- serve as an advisory group to the Cultural Affairs Department on local art and cultural priorities
- strengthen the artistic advancement of the community

MIRIAM REED PRODUCTIONS

P.O. Box 2781
Beverly Hills, CA 90213
Ph/Fax: 310-859-8385
www.reed prod@lalc.k12.ca.us

Miriam Reed — President

Miriam Reed Productions offers powerful one-woman performances for all locales to inspire women and young women to claim their individual power and personal identity.

- One-woman performances, 40-90 minutes in length, easily set up, accommodating most spaces. Performances include: "Margaret Sanger: Radiant Rebel,""Louisa May Alcott: Living 'Little Women'", and "Elizabeth Cady Stanton and Susan B. Anthony: Mrs. Stanton and Susan"

Miriam Reed Productions arouse women to a recognition of how recently won are their human rights, including the right to vote and the right to available contraception information and supplies.

Pre/K-12

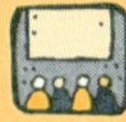

PROGRAMS: **PERFORMANCES, WORKSHOPS**
SCHEDULE: YEAR-ROUND
DETAILS: GRADES 9-12, HISTORY/SOC. SCIENCES
VISUAL & PERFORMING ARTS,
HISTORICAL/CULTURAL CONTEXT
TRAVEL TO SCHOOLS, INDIVIDUALLY TAILORED PROGRAMS
EDUCATIONAL MATERIALS AVAILABLE

Families

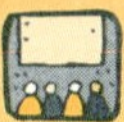

PROGRAMS: **PERFORMANCES, WORKSHOPS**
SCHEDULE: YEAR-ROUND

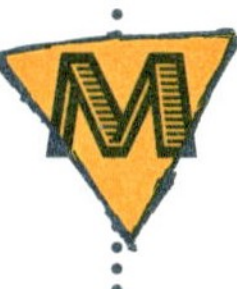

MOB RULE, INC.

P.O. Box 7024 — 501(c)3
Santa Monica, CA 90406
Ph: 310-285-8823

Lee Costello — Artistic Director — ba117@lafn.org
Kate Moore — Executive Director
Eric Vollmen — Development Director

Traveling to various under-serviced communities, we offer free theater games workshops. We also mount presentations (interactional) in an effort to build community ties.

- weekly improvisational theater games workshops for senior citizens
- storytelling workshops for children
- periodical presentations including workshops and professional presentations by our staff of pro volunteers

MOB RULE, INC. (CONTINUED)

Our staff will travel to the school or institution and provide a single or series of workshops in improvisational theater or storytelling.

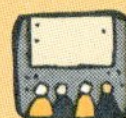

Pre/K-12

PROGRAMS:	**RESIDENCIES**
SCHEDULE:	YEAR-ROUND, WEEKDAYS
DETAILS:	GRADES PRE/K-12, VISUAL & PERFORMING ARTS CREATIVE EXPRESSION, TRAVEL TO SCHOOLS INDIVIDUALLY TAILORED PROGRAMS WORK WITH SENIOR CITIZENS

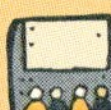

Youth

PROGRAM:	**RESIDENCIES**
SCHEDULE:	YEAR-ROUND, WEEKDAYS

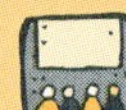

Families

PROGRAMS:	**PERFORMANCES**
SCHEDULE:	YEAR-ROUND, WEEKDAYS

MOLLY BARNES GALLERY

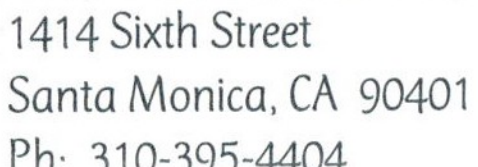

WS

1414 Sixth Street
Santa Monica, CA 90401
Ph: 310-395-4404
Fax: 310-395-0431

Molly Barnes — Director

Contemporary art.

MONART SCHOOL OF THE ARTS

WS

3316 Pico Boulevard
Santa Monica, CA 90405
Ph: 310-396-5990

Janice Purnell — Owner/Director — Monart3@aol.com
Karen Jackson — Owner/Director

The Monart School for the Arts is a westside private art school providing classes for ages four to adult, inservices for classroom teachers, and outreach programs in public schools and at-risk youth in greater L.A.

MONART SCHOOL OF THE ARTS (CONTINUED)

For twenty years the Monart School of the Arts has been in public and private sectors teaching realistic drawing. We use high quality artist materials and teach media usage and techniques. We provide a multiple intelligence approach to drawing for classroom teachers.

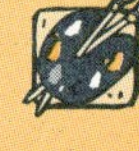

Pre/K-12

PROGRAMS:	**STUDIO CLASSES**
SCHEDULE:	YEAR-ROUND, WEEKDAYS, WEEKENDS
DETAILS:	GRADES PRE/K-12, VISUAL & PERFORMING ARTS CREATIVE EXPRESSION, TEACHER TRAINING PROGRAMS (SALARY POINTS) TRAVEL TO SCHOOLS, INDIVIDUALLY TAILORED PROGRAMS EDUCATIONAL MATERIALS AVAILABLE

Youth

PROGRAMS:	**WORKSHOPS, CLASSES**
SCHEDULE:	YEAR-ROUND, WEEKDAYS, WEEKENDS

Families

PROGRAMS:	**WORKSHOPS, CLASSES**
SCHEDULE:	YEAR-ROUND, WEEKDAYS, WEEKENDS

MONKEY KING PRODUCTIONS

ELA

125 Gladys Avenue #F
Monterey Park, CA 91755
Ph: 626-573-5534

Alex Luu — Artistic Director/Performer — alexluu@yahoo.com

Monkey King Productions is a community-based organization that presents contemporary theater for various art venues and high school/elementary campuses.

- one-man theater performances for community centers and schools
- summer festival performances/shows that feature local artists/performers
- writing/performing workshops for youth, especially at-risk youth
- performances specifically catered for youth/parents conferences dealing with cultural, familial, and interpersonal issues/conflicts

MONKEY KING PRODUCTIONS (CONTINUED)

Monkey King Productions' performances/workshops address and satisfy the appreciation and tolerance of cultural differences within the community with an emphasis on empowerment within autobiographical writing/performing skills.

Pre/K-12

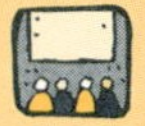

PROGRAMS:	**PERFORMANCES, WORKSHOPS, STUDIO CLASSES, RESIDENCIES**
SCHEDULE:	YEAR-ROUND, WEEKDAYS, EVENINGS, WEEKENDS
DETAILS:	GRADES 5-12, HISTORY/SOC. SCIENCES VISUAL & PERFORMING ARTS MULTICULTURAL, CREATIVE EXPRESSION HISTORICAL/CULTURAL CONTEXT CONNECTIONS/RELATIONS/APPLICATIONS TRAVEL TO SCHOOLS , INDIVIDUALLY TAILORED PROGRAMS Bilingual:Chinese,Work with Asians/Asian-Americans

Youth

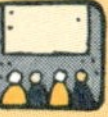

PROGRAMS:	**PERFORMANCES, WORKSHOPS, CLASSES, RESIDENCIES**
SCHEDULE:	YEAR-ROUND, WEEKDAYS, EVENINGS, WEEKENDS

MONROVIA ARTS FESTIVAL ASSOCIATION

P.O. Box 92
Monrovia, CA 91017
Ph: 626-397-3797
Fax: 626-359-2295

501 (c) 3

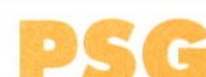

NancySims President/ 626-358-6106
Lilias Coombs Volunteer Center

The Monrovia Arts Festival Association presents "Celebrate the Arts", an annual juried show featuring fine arts, crafts, food, entertainment and a school art exhibit.

- annual juried arts and crafts show
- donations to Monrovia public schools from show proceeds
- art gallery for local artists

MONTGOMERY GALLERY, POMONA COLLEGE

333 North College Avenue
Claremont, CA 91711-6344
Ph: 909-621-8283
Fax: 909-621-8989
www.pomona.edu/montgomery

501 (c) 3

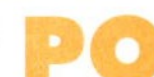

Barbara Senn Administrative Assistant
Marjorie Harth Director mharth@pomona.edu

Montgomery Gallery oversees the permanent collections of Pomona College. During the academic year, temporary exhibitions are presented, and students train and participate in museum practices.

- docent tours
- receptions
- temporary exhibitions
- public lectures

MONTGOMERY GALLERY, POMONA COLLEGE (CONTINUED)

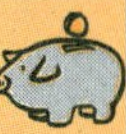

An extended program for fifth and sixth grade students as a means for them to actively participate in a gallery situation. Students make several two-hour visits to the gallery during the de-installation of an exhibition, and observe, design and install the Pomona Student Show.

Pre/K-12

PROGRAMS:	**SELF-GUIDED TOURS, GUIDED TOURS**
SCHEDULE:	SPRING, FALL
DETAILS:	GRADES 3-12, VISUAL & PERFORMING ARTS AESTHETIC VALUING, INDIVIDUALLY TAILORED PROGRAMS EDUCATIONAL MATERIALS AVAILABLE

MOSAICO ART

12511 Mitchell Avenue
Los Angeles, CA 90066
Ph: 310-737-1797
Fax: 310-737-1198

WS

Marcella Harvey Director

Mosaico Art promotes diverse artists who work in community-based projects and offers expressive arts workshops to make art more accessible to all.

- community-based projects
- quarterly exhibits
- volunteer opportunities
- art and healing workshops
- gift shop

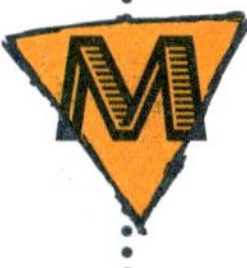

We offer mostly arts and healing workshops that aim to improve an individual's quality of life by assisting them to express themselves through the use of art; aiding artists and non-artists in promoting their creativity, and supporting artists in their processes.

Youth

PROGRAMS:	**WORKSHOPS, CLASSES**
SCHEDULE:	YEAR-ROUND, WEEKDAYS, EVENINGS, WEEKENDS

Familes

PROGRAMS:	**WORKSHOPS, CLASSES**
SCHEDULE:	YEAR-ROUND, WEEKDAYS, EVENINGS, WEEKENDS

MOUNT SAN ANTONIO COLLEGE ART GALLERY

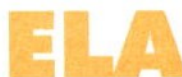

1100 N. Grand Avenue
Walnut, CA 91789
Ph: 909-594-5611/ x4328
Fax: 909-468-3954

Bob Orso — Asst. Director
Fatemeh Burnes — Director

MOUNT ST. MARY'S COLLEGE-JOSE DRUDIS-BIADA GALLERY

WS

12001 Chalon Road
Los Angeles, CA 90049
Ph: 310-954-4360
Admin: 310-954-4361
Fax: 310-440-1397

Jody Baral — Director

MOXIE!

501 (c)3 WS

Santa Monica Film Festival
4127 Via Marina, #206
Marina del Rey, CA 90292
Ph: 310-289-7144
Fax: 310-823-3323
santamonicafilmfest.com

Albert de Quay — Founder/Director — smfilmfest@aol.com

Twelve monthly film festivals, one annual award.

- monthly exhibition featuring indie filmmakers from across the country and around the world.
- question and answer sessions.
- Moxie! awards for Best film/filmmaker.

We introduce new topics closely related to young people to ignite new aspirations toward filmmaking.

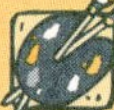

Youth

PROGRAMS: **FILMSCREENINGS**
SCHEDULE: YEAR-ROUND, WEEKDAYS

MTA METRO ART

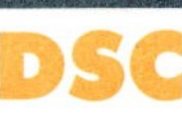
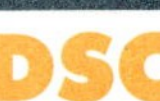
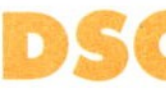
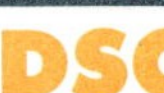
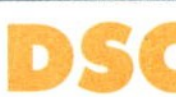
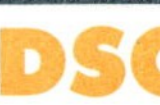

1 Gateway Plaza
Los Angeles, CA 90012
Ph: 213-922-4ART
Admin: 213-922-2720
Fax: 213-922-2719
www.mta.net

Maya Emsden — Director — emsdenm.mta.net

Metro Art commissions artists to create works which enhance the public transit environment. Artists are selected by panels comprised of arts professionals and community members.

- permanent public art at Metro Rail stations, Metro Link stations, Metro Bus transit centers, and Gateway Transit Center
- temporary public art including poetry, bus cards, performing arts, and metro Bus Division murals
- volunteer opportunities including docent tours, internships, and events
- conservation/maintenance
- informational materials

MURAL CONSERVANCY OF LOS ANGELES

501 (c)3 HSM

P.O. Box 861176
Los Angeles, CA 90086
Ph: 213-481-1186
Fax: 213-482-4357
www.lamurals.org

Bill Lasarow — President

MCLA helps to preserve, maintain and document public mural art in the greater Los Angeles area.

- mural rescue program
- mural bus tours
- website documents over 1,000 public murals in Los Angeles
- quarterly newsletter

MUSEUM OF AFRICAN AMERICAN ART

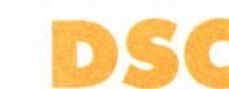

4005 Crenshaw Boulevard, Third Floor
Crenshaw Plaza
Los Angeles, CA 90008-2534
Ph: 323-294-7071
Fax: 323-294-7084

MUSEUM OF ARTS DOWNTOWN LOS ANGELES (MADLA)

DSC

605 W. Olympic Boulevard
Los Angeles, CA 90015
Ph: 213-627-7849
Fax: 213-627-0772
www.madla.org

Aria Gannon — Community Relations — madla@earthlink.net
Madla Hruza — Director

Contemporary paintings, photography, sculpture, mixed media, and performing arts.

MUSEUM OF CONTEMPORARY ART (MOCA)

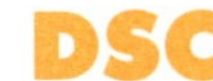

250 S. Grand Avenue
Los Angeles, CA 90012
Ph: 213-62-MOCA2
Fax: 213-620-8674
www.MOCA-LA.org

DSC

Katherine Lee	
Paul Schimmel	Chief Curator
Richard Koshalek	Director

MOCA's mandate is to bring new and unmistakable vitality to the contemporary art scene of Los Angeles and to the arts in general.

MUSEUM OF CULTURAL DIVERSITY, THE

20700 Avalon Boulevard
Carson, CA 90747
Ph: 310-324-4702
Fax: 310-639-6662

501 (c)3 SB

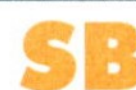

Cheryl Roberts	Public Relations
Deborah Williams	Executive Director

Located in the most diverse community in the United States, the Museum of Cultural Diversity showcases the cultures of the world on a daily basis. A weekly calendar exposes the public to the existence, suffering, and contributions made to the world from our culturally diverse society, through contemporary and traditional art forms.

- musical performances on Sundays
- workshops and lectures on Saturdays
- volunteer opportunities
- board opportunities
- art exhibitions quarterly featuring local and international artists
- artist opportunities

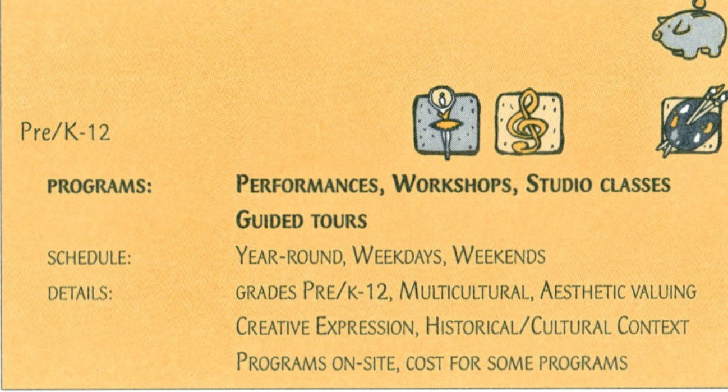

Pre/K-12

PROGRAMS: PERFORMANCES, WORKSHOPS, STUDIO CLASSES
GUIDED TOURS
SCHEDULE: YEAR-ROUND, WEEKDAYS, WEEKENDS
DETAILS: GRADES PRE/K-12, MULTICULTURAL, AESTHETIC VALUING
CREATIVE EXPRESSION, HISTORICAL/CULTURAL CONTEXT
PROGRAMS ON-SITE, COST FOR SOME PROGRAMS

MUSEUM OF JURASSIC TECHNOLOGY

9341 Venice Boulevard
Culver City, CA 90232-2621
Ph: 818-836-6131
Fax: 818-287-2267
www.mjt.org

501 (c)3 WS

M.A. Peers	Organizational Head
David Wilson	Artistic Director
Diana Wilson	Treasurer
Sara Velas	Curatorial and Administrative Assistant
Bridget Marrin	Resident Mineaturist

The Museum of Jurassic Technology in Los Angeles, California is an educational institution dedicated to the advancement of knowledge and the public appreciation of the lower Jurassic.

- gift shop with commemorative china
- curiosities and wonder
- ongoing and rotating exhibits
- publications of museum exhibitions
- library for the diffusion of useful knowledge
- lecture series

MUSEUM OF LATIN AMERICAN ART

628 Los Alamitos Avenue
Long Beach, CA 90802
Ph: 562-437-1689
Admin: 562-901-9162
Fax: 562-437-7043
www.molaa.com

501 (c)3 LB

Susan Golden	Public Relations Coordinator	rgfa@ix.netcom.com
Cynthia McMullin	Director of Collections and Exhibits	
David Wood	Managing Director	

Located in Long Beach, the MoLAA is the only museum in the Western United States dedicated to the exhibition, interpretation and study of the contemporary art of Mexico, Central and South America, and the Spanish speaking Caribbean.

- major solo exhibitions of leading Latin American artists
- group exhibitions defining contemporary art movements
- lectures, presentations, films, and art workshops
- museum store and retail art galleries
- performing arts space
- restaurant

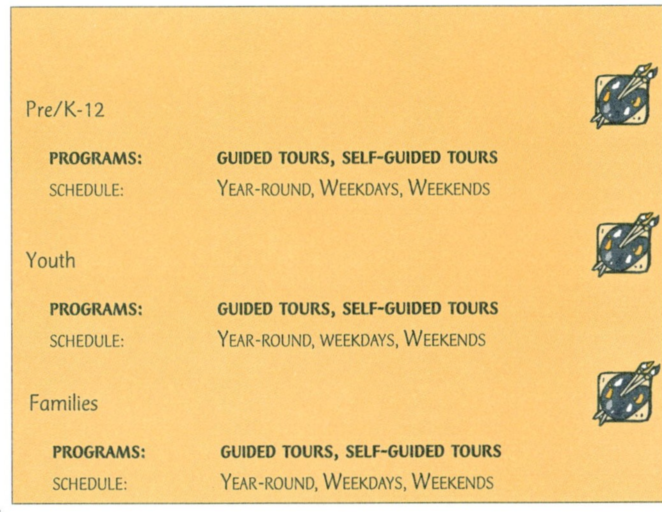

Pre/K-12

PROGRAMS: GUIDED TOURS, SELF-GUIDED TOURS
SCHEDULE: YEAR-ROUND, WEEKDAYS, WEEKENDS

Youth

PROGRAMS: GUIDED TOURS, SELF-GUIDED TOURS
SCHEDULE: YEAR-ROUND, WEEKDAYS, WEEKENDS

Families

PROGRAMS: GUIDED TOURS, SELF-GUIDED TOURS
SCHEDULE: YEAR-ROUND, WEEKDAYS, WEEKENDS

MUSEUM OF NEON ART

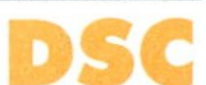

501 W. Olympic Boulevard
Los Angeles, CA 90015
Ph: 213-489-9918
Fax: 213-489-9932

Mary Carter Curator

MONA exhibits fine art in electric and kinetic media and documents and preserves outstanding examples of neon signs and marquees. MONA fosters appreciation of the electric arts and art history through classes in neon design and techniques and through guided tours of the city's sign and electric fine art installations.

MUSEUM OF TELEVISION AND RADIO

465 N. Beverly Drive
Beverly Hills, CA 90210
Ph: 310-786-1000
Admin: 310-786-1070
Educ: 310-786-1034
Fax: 310-786-1086
www.mtr.org

501 (c)3 WS

Romy David	Museum Manager/ 310-786-1030
Steve Bell	Director
Coria Fantozzi	Education Director

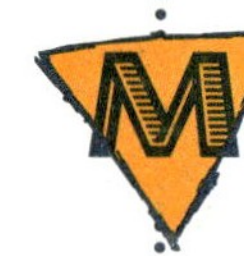

Located in the heart of Beverly Hills, the Museum of Television and Radio was founded to preserve the history and creativity of television and radio.

- Recreating Radio—workshops that introduce kids and parents to the wonders of classical radio
- Television Together—a workshop for parents and children 4-8, that explores creative ways to watch TV with kids
- Movies of the Month screenings
- gallery exhibitions
- gift shop with TV and radio themed products
- docent tours and screenings of the collection
- volunteer opportunities in visitor services
- senior and student tours

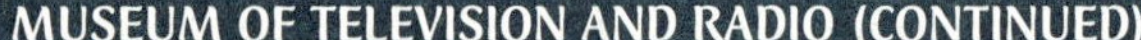

MUSEUM OF TELEVISION AND RADIO (CONTINUED)

Using programs from the collection, museum educators teach 90-minute interactive classes that encourage active observation and critical thinking about issues and events. While the medium is television or radio, the subject may be advertising, science fiction, the changing role of women, politics, global ecology and many others.

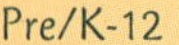

Pre/K-12

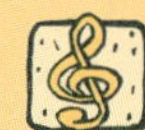

PROGRAMS: WORKSHOPS, GUIDED TOURS
SCHEDULE: YEAR-ROUND, WEEKDAYS, EVENINGS, WEEKENDS
DETAILS: GRADES PRE/K-12, HISTORY/SOC. SCIENCES
HISTORICAL/CULTURAL CONTEXT
PROGRAMS ON-SITE

Youth

 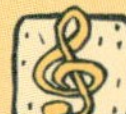 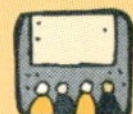 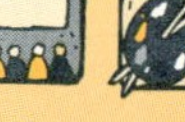

PROGRAMS: WORKSHOPS, GUIDED TOURS
SCHEDULE: YEAR-ROUND, WEEKDAYS, EVENINGS, WEEKENDS

Families

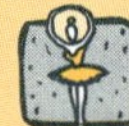 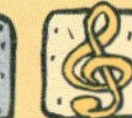 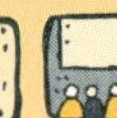 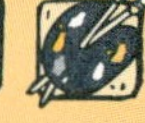

PROGRAMS: WORKSHOPS, GUIDED TOURS
SCHEDULE: YEAR-ROUND, WEEKDAYS, EVENINGS, WEEKENDS
DETAILS: COST FOR SOME PROGRAMS

MUSEUM OF TOLERANCE

9760 W. Pico Boulevard
Los Angeles, CA 90035
Ph: 310-553-8403
Admin: 310-553-9036
Fax: 310-553-4521
www.wiesenthal.com

501 (c)3 WS

Felice Richter	Marketing Director/ 310-772-2457	frichter@wiesenthal.com
Rabbi Meyer May	Executive Director	
Janet Garfinkle	Youth Education/ 310-772-2502	janetg@wiesenthal.com

Established to help visitors understand and experience discrimination, the Museum of Tolerance is a high-tech interactive look at hate, tolerance, and one's own biases.

- Holocaust survivor lectures
- gift shop and book store
- social action agenda
- volunteer classes and opportunities
- docent-lead tours
- monthly arts and lectures program
- Tools for Tolerance© programs for law enforcement, educators, and professionals
- teaching Tools for Tolerance© for educators

MUSEUM OF TOLERANCE (CONTINUED)

The programs offered by the Museum of Tolerance are tailored to each group's issues. There is a combined focus on issues of tolerance and the Holocaust taught from an historical frame of reference. The programs offer access to the library, scholars and experts in the field as well as offer quality and variety in the supporting staff and materials.

 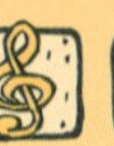 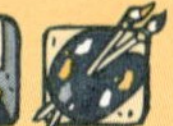

Pre/K-12 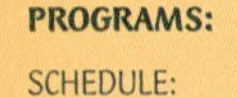

PROGRAMS:	**WORKSHOPS, SELF-GUIDED TOURS, GUIDED TOURS**
SCHEDULE:	YEAR-ROUND, WEEKDAYS, WEEKENDS
DETAILS:	GRADES 3-12, HISTORY/SOC. SCIENCES
	MULTICULTURAL, HISTORICAL/CULTURAL CONTEXT
	TEACHER TRAINING PROGRAMS (SALARY POINTS)
	TRAVEL TO SCHOOLS, PROGRAMS ON-SITE
	INDIVIDUALLY TAILORED PROGRAMS, EDUCATIONAL MATERIALS

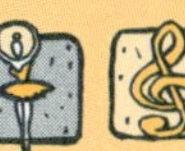 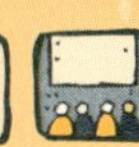 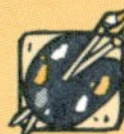

Youth

PROGRAMS:	**WORKSHOPS, SELF-GUIDED TOURS, GUIDED TOURS**
SCHEDULE:	YEAR-ROUND, WEEKDAYS, WEEKENDS

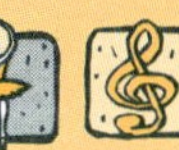 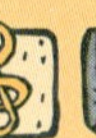 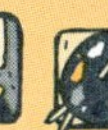 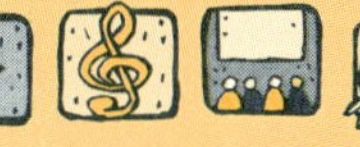

Families

PROGRAMS:	**WORKSHOPS, SELF-GUIDED TOURS, GUIDED TOURS**
SCHEDULE:	YEAR-ROUND, WEEKDAYS, WEEKENDS

MUSIC CENTER EDUCATION DIVISION

717 W. Temple Street, Suite 400
Los Angeles, CA 90012
Ph: 213-250-ARTS
Admin: 213-202-2275
Educ: 213-202-2278
Fax: 213-481-7597

501(c)3 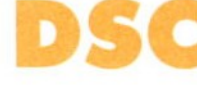 DSC

Karen Wood	Managing Director	mced@earthlink.net
Barbara Leonard	Artistic Development/ 213-202-2256	
Joan Boyett	Vice President for Education/ 213-202-2280	
Melinda Williams	Director of Education/ 213-202-2278	

Established in 1979 by The Music Center of Los Angeles County, the mission of the Education Division is to provide lifelong learning opportunities in the arts and in particular, to enrich the lives and education of children by bringing the arts into their daily environment.

- more than 150 performances available for touring
- art partnerships
- artist residency
- Individually Designed Art Packages
- admission free, "Very Special Arts Festival," features continuous performances and workshops and an art exhibition
- various other programs for teachers, students, and schools

MUSIC CENTER EDUCATION DIVISION (CONTINUED)

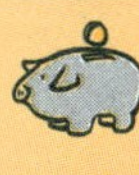

More than 750 schools throughout Southern California look to the Music Center Education Division as a primary source of in-school workshops, performances, with programs designed for students and educators at all levels of experience.

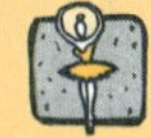 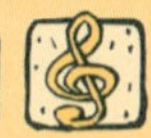 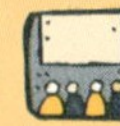 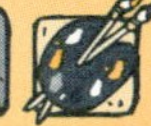

Pre/K-12

PROGRAMS:	**PERFORMANCES, WORKSHOPS**
SCHEDULE:	YEAR-ROUND, WEEKDAYS
DETAILS:	GRADES PRE/K-12, VISUAL & PERFORMING ARTS
	AESTHETIC VALUING, CREATIVE EXPRESSION
	HISTORICAL/CULTURAL CONTEXT
	CONNECTIONS/RELATIONS/APPLICATIONS
	TEACHER TRAINING PROGRAMS (SALARY POINTS)
	TRAVEL TO SCHOOLS, PROGRAMS ON-SITE
	INDIVIDUALLY TAILORED PROGRAMS, EDUCATIONAL MATERIALS
	BILINGUAL: 20 LANGUAGES

 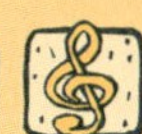 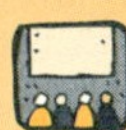 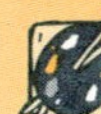 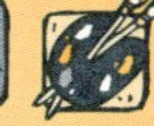

Youth

PROGRAMS:	**PERFORMANCES, WORKSHOPS**
SCHEDULE:	YEAR-ROUND, WEEKDAYS, WEEKENDS

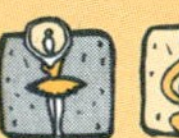 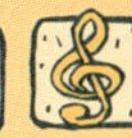 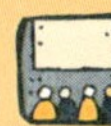 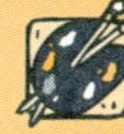 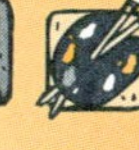

Families

PROGRAMS:	**WORKSHOPS**
SCHEDULE:	YEAR-ROUND, WEEKDAYS, WEEKENDS

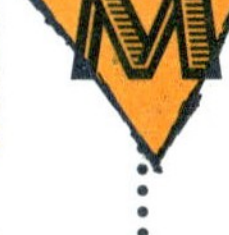

MUSIC CENTER OF LOS ANGELES COUNTY, THE

717 W. Temple Street, Suite 400
Los Angeles, CA 90012
Ph: 213-202-2200
Fax: 213-481-1176

DSC

Joanne Kozberg	President

The Music Center, a performing arts center for Los Angeles, includes four resident companies: Los Angeles Philharmonic, Center Theatre Group/Mark Taper Forum and Ahmanson Theatre, Los Angeles Music Center Opera, Los Angeles Master Chorale, along with the Music Center Education Division and hundreds of community activities.

MUSIC CIRCLE, THE

625 S. Madison Avenue
Pasadena, CA 91106
Ph/Fax: 626-405-9759

501(c)3 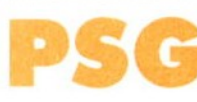 PSG

Kaye Lubach	Managing Director	MusiCircle@aol.com
Harihar Rao	Executive/Artistic Director/ 626-449-6987	

Founded in 1973 by Ravi Shankar and Harihar Rao, the Music Circle has been the dominant force in bringing the finest Indian classical music and dance to Southern California audiences.

- six to twelve concerts each year between September and July
- festivals of Indian classical music and dance
- multi-ethnic Asian arts events
- volunteer opportunites

MUSIC CIRCLE, THE (CONTINUED)

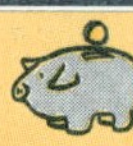

The Music Circle offers presentations of Indian arts and culture. Educational materials include coloring books based on India's epics and folktales are available.

Pre/K-12

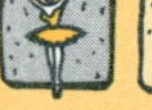

PROGRAMS: **PERFORMANCES**
DETAILS: VISUAL & PERFORMING ARTS, CREATIVE EXPRESSION
HISTORICAL/CULTURAL CONTEXT, TRAVEL TO SCHOOLS
EDUCATIONAL MATERIALS AVAILABLE

MUSIC THEATRE OF SOUTHERN CALIFORNIA, THE

PSG

P.O. Box 5004
San Gabriel, CA 91778-5004
Ph: 626-308-2868
Admin: 626-281-9444
Fax: 626-281-3750
www.musictheatre.org

Bill Shaw — Artistic Director
Roger Lockie — Executive Director

The Music Theatre of Southern California is committed to artistic excellence in the presentation and preservation of the unique American art form—musical theater. We have successfully evolved from a community theater to an award-winning, critically acclaimed professional regional theater company serving over 60,000 patrons a year.

- four productions annually
- 18 public performances at 2 venues, the San Gabriel Civic Auditorium and the Alex Theatre in Glendale
- 3 free studio presentations
- summer student Performing & Fine Arts Workshops
- youth and dance education programs
- scholarships for performers
- year-round dance classes
- student mentoring and career education activities
- Guild membership and volunteer opportunities

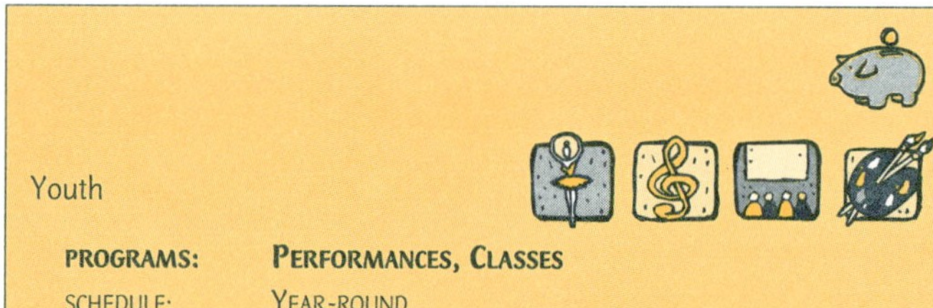

Youth

PROGRAMS: **PERFORMANCES, CLASSES**
SCHEDULE: YEAR-ROUND
DETAILS: COST FOR SOME PROGRAMS

MUSICAL THEATRE GUILD

501(c)3 **SFV**

P.O. Box 2612
Toluca Lake, CA 91610-0612
Ph: 818-848-6844

Eric Andrist — Co-founder
Jeff Rizzo — Co-founder

mfguild@aol.com

Musical Theatre Guild is a membership based musical theatre performance company.

MUSICAL THEATRE GUILD (CONTINUED)

We offer free tickets to high school and college students in musical theatre programs to come to our shows.

Pre/K-12

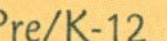

PROGRAMS: **PERFORMANCES**
SCHEDULE: YEAR-ROUND, EVENINGS, WEEKENDS
DETAILS: GRADES 7-12, VISUAL & PERFORMING ARTS
CREATIVE EXPRESSION, PROGRAMS ON-SITE

MUSICAL YOUTH ARTIST REPERTORY (MYART)

501(c)3 **LB**

7835 Ritchie Street
Long Beach, CA 90808
Ph: 800-400 2985
Admin: 562-431-1842
www.myart.org

John Erratt — President, Board of Directors
Dana Hanstein-Hanlen — Executive/Artistic Director
Gale Bull — Member, Board of Directors

Musical Youth Artist Repertory Theatre is a youth musical theater company producing four fully staged musicals, usually Broadway shows, each year with casts of 100-200 actors ranging in age from five through college. Rehearsals and performances are in the Long Beach/West Orange County areas.

- four fully staged Broadway musicals each year
- training in acting, song, and dance incorporated into the rehearsal program

We offer reduced price tickets for schools to mid-week morning shows open only to schools and senior groups. Weekend matinee performances have reduced-price tickets for youth groups and include a backstage tour after the performance.

Pre/K-12

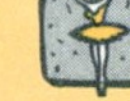
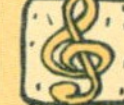
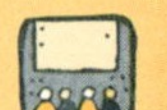

PROGRAMS: **PERFORMANCES**
SCHEDULE: YEAR-ROUND, WEEKENDS
DETAILS: GRADES PRE/K-12, VISUAL & PERFORMING ARTS
CREATIVE EXPRESSION
PROGRAMS ON-SITE, EDUCATIONAL MATERIALS AVAILABLE

Youth

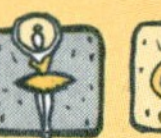
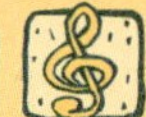
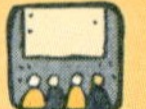

PROGRAMS: **PERFORMANCES, GUIDED TOURS**
SCHEDULE: YEAR-ROUND, WEEKENDS

MUSIQUE L.A.

DSC

4621 W. 63rd Street
Los Angeles, CA 90043-3516
Ph: 323-299-1392

Brice Martin
Natalie Martin

Featuring trained Julliard musicians in flute and piano, Musique L.A. performs classical recitals and plays folk instruments.

- performances for children and adults
- variety of instruments played

MUSIQUE L.A. (CONTINUED)

Pre/K-12

PROGRAMS:	**PERFORMANCES**
SCHEDULE:	YEAR-ROUND, WEEKDAYS, EVENINGS, WEEKENDS
DETAILS:	GRADES PRE/K-12, VISUAL & PERFORMING ARTS AESTHETIC VALUING, CREATIVE EXPRESSION HISTORICAL/CULTURAL CONTEXT CONNECTIONS/RELATIONS/APPLICATIONS TRAVEL TO SCHOOLS, INDIVIDUALLY TAILORED PROGRAMS

Youth

PROGRAMS:	**PERFORMANCES**
SCHEDULE:	YEAR-ROUND, WEEKDAYS, EVENINGS, WEEKENDS

Families

PROGRAMS:	**PERFORMANCES**
SCHEDULE:	YEAR-ROUND, WEEKDAYS, EVENINGS, WEEKENDS

NAILING THE KIPPER PRESENTS, INC.

P.O. Box 291220
Los Angeles, CA 90029-1220
Ph: 323-969-4814
Fax: 323-625-3501

Rhonda Reynolds Artistic Director NTKipper@aol.com
Mark Salamon Associate Artistic Director

As a professional nonprofit theater ensemble, Nailing the Kipper Presents provides an accessible forum in which people of diverse cultures converge to share the immediacy and passion of live performance.

- play reading series- an opportunity for emerging Los Angeles writers to have plays read and considered for production
- workshops
- volunteer opportunities

NATIONAL ACADEMY OF SONGWRITERS

6255 Sunset Boulevard, Suite1023 501(c)3
Hollywood, CA 90028
Ph: 323-463-7178
Fax: 323-463-2146
www.nassong.org

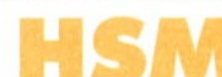

Beth Galicia Director of Operations
Dawn Dagucon Executive Director
John Feins Director of Programs

The National Academy of Songwriters is an educational nonprofit whose mission is to educate and protect songwriters.

- educational panels- seminars about the craft of songwriting and the business of the music industry
- Acoustic Underground Live Showcase
- Songwriters Expo Conference
- NAS Lifetime Achievement Awards Concert
- NAS Songwriters Musepaper publication

NATIONAL ACRYLIC PAINTERS ASSOCIATION, USA

2525 E. 5th Street 501(c)3
Long Beach, CA 90814
Ph: 562-439-3276
Fax: 562-597-3750

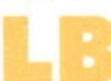

Linda Gunn USA Director

NAPA USA is the only professional artist group that gives its members international exposure through exhibitions in the U.S. and Great Britian. Our goal is to promote the use of the acrylic medium, as well as to educate the public through quality exhibitions. Catalogs are kept on file in the archives of the Tate Museum, London.

- exhibitions in the U.S.
- members receive newsletters and a prospectus from both NAPA in England and NAPA USA
- U.K. exhibitions held at the Royal Birmingham Society of Artists yearly

NATIONAL AMERICAN SHAKESPEARE COMPANY

35 S. Raymond Avenue 501(c)3
Pasadena, CA 91105
Ph: 626-440-0821
Admin/Fax: 626-440-0894
Educ: 626-300-8138

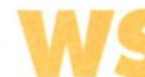

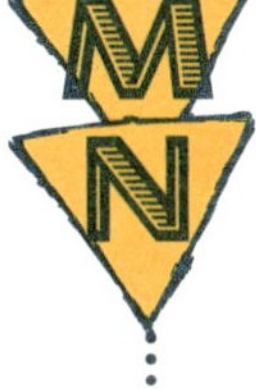

Joseph Paul Stachura Artistic Director/Producer
Amanda Karr Theatre Operations/ 818-993-7063
Sylvia Stachura Publicity Volunteer

The National American Shakespeare Company is the nonprofit classic wing of the Knightsbridge Theatre located in Pasadena.

- live drama performed on weekends (senior and student discounts)
- weekday dramas are added for special occasions.

NATIONAL ASSOCIATION OF COMPOSERS/ USA, THE

Box 49256 Barrington Station 501(c)3
Los Angeles, CA 90049
Ph: 310-541-8213
Fax: 310-373-3244
www.thebook.com/nacusa

WS

Marshall Bialosky President
Deon Price Secretary/ 310-838-4465

Headquartered in Los Angeles, we are the second oldest serious music composers' organization in the U.S. We perform concerts of members' music, hold an annual young composers' competition, and publish a national newsletter.

- at least four concerts a year of chamber music in various L.A. locales
- other concerts throughout the year from our branch chapters

NATURAL HISTORY MUSEUM OF LOS ANGELES COUNTY

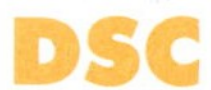

900 Exposition Boulevard
Los Angeles, CA 90007
Ph: 213-763-DINO
Fax: 213-744-2999
www.nhm.org

Jim Powell	President and Director
	School Tours Coordinator/ 213-763-3333
	Public Programs Coordinator/ 213-763-3535
	Outreach Office/ 213-763-3344

The Natural History Museum, located in Exposition Park near downtown Los Angeles assembles, conserves, interprets, and holds collections of irreplaceable objects from nature and human history. These collections reveal the history of the Earth and the evolution and diversity of life and culture.

- self-guided tours of exhibits/guided tours on various topics
- publications
- Discovery Center and Insect Zoo
- hands-on programs
- travelling insect zoo for schools
- Earthmobile and Seamobile for LAUSD schools
- Artifact Loan Programs for classrooms
- Educator's Open House
- teacher workshops for salary point credit
- scouting group sleepovers
- venue available for corporate events, weddings and parties
- volunteer opportunities

N

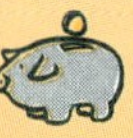

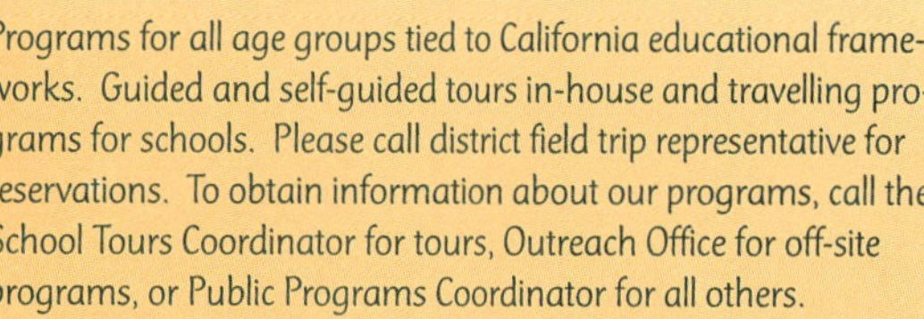

Programs for all age groups tied to California educational frameworks. Guided and self-guided tours in-house and travelling programs for schools. Please call district field trip representative for reservations. To obtain information about our programs, call the School Tours Coordinator for tours, Outreach Office for off-site programs, or Public Programs Coordinator for all others.

Pre/K-12

PROGRAMS:	**WORKSHOPS, SELF-GUIDED TOURS, GUIDED TOURS**
SCHEDULE:	YEAR-ROUND, WEEKDAYS
DETAILS:	GRADES PRE/K-120, HISTORY/SOC. SCIENCES
	MATH/SCIENCES, HISTORICAL/CULTURAL CONTEXT
	CONNECTIONS/RELATIONS/APPLICATIONS
	TEACHER TRAINING PROGRAMS (SALARY POINTS)
	TRAVEL TO SCHOOLS, PROGRAMS ON-SITE
	EDUCATIONAL MATERIALS AVAILABLE, FEE FOR SOME PROGRAMS

Families

PROGRAMS:	**WORKSHOPS, SELF-GUIDED TOURS, GUIDED TOURS**
SCHEDULE:	YEAR-ROUND, WEEKENDS

NEW ALCHEMY GALLERY

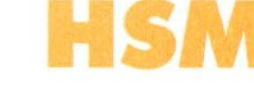

6909 Melrose Avenue
Los Angeles, CA 90038
Ph: 323-933-6912
Fax: 323-933-8538
www.calendarlive.com/newalchemy

NEW IMAGE ART

HSM

7906 Santa Monica Boulevard, #208
Los Angeles, CA 90046
Ph: 323-654-2192
Educ: 818-567-5395
Fax: 323-654-2192

Stanley Somers	Director
Marseta Goldberg	Co-Director

This artist-run gallery is dedicated to the concept of "New Image Art" as an art movement and was founded by the Richard Marshall Whitney Museum in 1978. The primary emphasis is on American Avant Garde contemporary artists working in minimalism, performance, and symbolism.

- exhibition schedule of known and new artists in one person and group show formats

NEWPORT BEACH RECITAL SERIES

501(c)3

109 Cottage Lane
Aliso Viejo, CA 92525
Ph: 949-643-8171
Admin/Fax: 949-640-6276
www.ocnow.com

Nan Morisseau	Executive Director
Leonid Levitsky	Artistic Director
Brenda Kiser	Publicist/ 949-898-9099

Newport Beach Recital Series "World Classical Musicians" perform repertoire from Bach to Rach. Programs include a concert series, student scholarships, senior and community outreach, advance cultural literacy, diversity, and music appreciation.

- six classical chamber music concerts in Los Angeles and Orange Counties
- Neptune Summer Music Festival and Symposium with celebrity artists and spokespeople
- Pacific Virtuosi- tours, trains, sponsors, and escorts gifted California youth
- Anne Ulseth Weston Scholarships
- SenioReach- youngsters perform in elderly facilities
- Adopt A Cause- charities are treated to concerts
- Friends Guild- volunteer and intern opportunities

NEWSPACE GALLERY

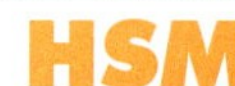

5241 Melrose Avenue
Los Angeles, CA 90038
Ph: 323-469-9353
Fax: 323-469-1120

Suzanne Vielmetter	Associate Director
Joni Gordon	Director

Contemporary Los Angeles Painting and Sculpture; 20th Century Masterworks

NON-PROFIT WORLD CONTEMPORARY ART

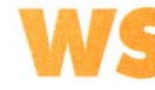

1355 Westwood Boulevard, Suite 217
Los Angeles, CA 90024
Ph: 310-312-2400
Fax: 310-477-1414
caliart@aol.com

NORRIS THEATRE FOR THE PERFORMING ARTS

27570 Crossfield Drive
Rolling Hills Estates, CA 90274
Ph: 310-544-0403
Fax: 310-544-2473
www.norristheatre.org

501(c)3

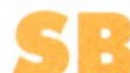

Susan Swarthout   Executive Director/ x17   sswarthout@norristheatre.org

The Norris Theatre for the Performing Arts provides a performing arts center which enriches the South Bay community by fostering the performing arts through professional performances, community informed cultural activites, and the provision of educational and outreach programs.

- performances by professional artists
- volunteer opportunities
- rental to community arts organizations

The Norris currently offers a Student Matinee series. With the opening of the Harlyne J. Norris Pavilion, we will be offering a range of classes and workshops in the arts for youth and adults.

Pre/K-12

 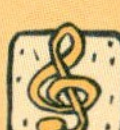 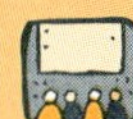

PROGRAMS:	**PERFORMANCES, GUIDED TOURS**
SCHEDULE:	SPRING, FALL, WINTER, WEEKDAYS
DETAILS:	GRADES PRE/K-12, VISUAL & PERFORMING ARTS AESTHETIC VALUING, CREATIVE EXPRESSION EDUCATIONAL MATERIALS AVAILABLE

Families

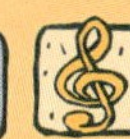 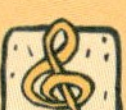 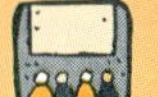

PROGRAMS:	**PERFORMANCES**
SCHEDULE:	SPRING, FALL, WINTER, WEEKENDS

NORTH WIND QUINTET

21134 Celtic Street
Chatsworth, CA 91311
Ph: 818-701-1700
Fax: 818-701-1787

501(c)3

SFV

Jenice Rosen   Artistic Director   musicservice@earthlink.net

The North Wind Quintet is Los Angeles' premiere chamber ensemble, celebrating the 29th season, devoted to developing new audience awareness for the performing arts through chamber music by presenting their exclusive "audience friendly" programming.

- general public, "audience friendly" programming include standard chamber music as well as familiar music and new compositions by Los Angeles composers at a variety of venues

NORTH WIND QUINTET (CONTINUED)

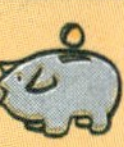

Classic Fun! With the North Wind Quintet is an interactive, educational program about chamber music, composition, orchestration, and the wind instruments of the orchestra. The program includes the music of Mozart, Bach, and television/movie themes. It is a hands-on programs for young listeners.

Pre/K-12

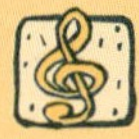

PROGRAMS:	**PERFORMANCES, WORKSHOPS, RESIDENCIES**
SCHEDULE:	YEAR-ROUND, WEEKDAYS
DETAILS:	GRADES PRE/K-12, VISUAL & PERFORMING ARTS CREATIVE EXPRESSION, TRAVEL TO SCHOOLS INDIVIDUALLY TAILORED PROGRAMS, EDUCATIONAL MATERIALS WORK WITH DEVELOPMENTALLY/PHYSICALLY CHALLENGED

Families

PROGRAMS:	**PERFORMANCES, WORKSHOPS**
SCHEDULE:	YEAR-ROUND, WEEKDAYS, EVENINGS, WEEKENDS

NORTHEAST VALLEY REGIONAL ARTS COUNCIL

7747 Foothill Boulevard
Tujunga, CA 91042
Ph: 818-352-3287

SFV

Developed through the City of Los Angeles Cultural Affairs Department as one of 9 regional arts councils, we are a coalition of arts and community organizations, artists, leaders, business people and all other interested members of the community who have the purpose of assessing, coalescing and acting on the cultural assets and needs of the area. This council serves Mission Hills, Panorama City, North Hills, Sun Valley, Arleta, Pacoima, Sylmar, Lakeview Terrace, Shadow Hills, Sunland, and Tujunga. Goals include:

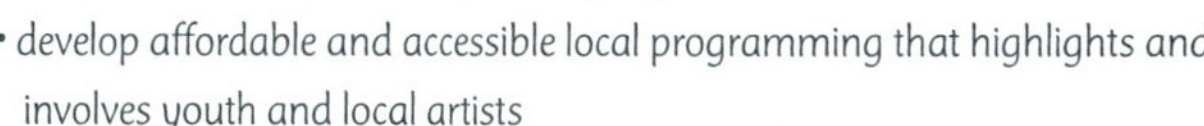

- develop affordable and accessible local programming that highlights and involves youth and local artists
- develop activities that celebrate the city's cultural diversity and promote community building
- serve as an advisory group to the Cultural Affairs Department on local art and cultural priorities
- strengthen the artistic advancement of the community

NORTON SIMON MUSEUM OF ART

411 W. Colorado Boulevard
Pasadena, CA 91105
Ph: 626-449-6840
Fax: 626-796-4978

PSG

Kimberly Gilholly   Public Information
Walter Timoshuk   Executive Vice President

Seven Centuries of European Art from the Renaissance to the 20th century including works by such famous artists as Raphael, Botticelli, Rubens, Rembrandt, Zurburan, Watteau, Fragonard, and Goya. Particularly celebrated are the collection of Impressionist and Post-Impressionist paintings and 20th century works by Picasso, Matisse, and the German Expressionists.

NORWALK CULTURAL ARTS CENTER, CITY OF

13200 Clarkdale Avenue 501(c)3 **LB**
Norwalk, CA 90701
Ph: 562-929-5521
Admin: 562-929-5665
Educ: u562-929-5570
Fax: 562-929-5773

Aya Sugano	Arts Center Manager
Joel Tapper	Recreation Leader II
Elsa Garcia	Recreation Supervisor
Eunice Castaneda	Arts Education Coordinator

Located in southeastern Los Angeles County, the Cultural Arts Center is the hidden gem of Norwalk. Art classes, gallery space and family activities abound seasonally.

- changing exhibits in the Mary Paxon Gallery
- hallway exhibits
- Arte Nights
- seasonal/summer children's museum
- artist buddies
- volunteer opportunities
- language classes
- art resource room

We have an incredible staff comprised of energetic, resourceful, caring, passionate, creative and fun- loving people who have a skill for bringing out the best in others' creativity.

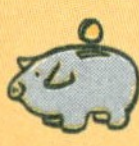

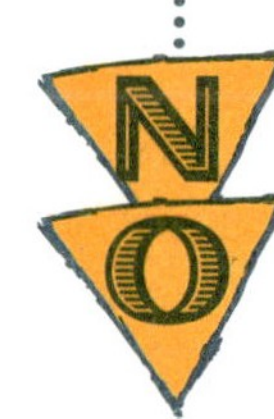

Pre/K-12

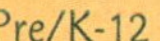

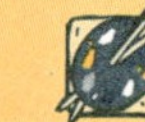

PROGRAMS:	**WORKSHOPS, STUDIO CLASSES**
SCHEDULE:	YEAR-ROUND, WEEKDAYS
DETAILS:	GRADES PRE/K-12, VISUAL & PERFORMING ARTS
	AESTHETIC VALUING, CREATIVE EXPRESSION
	CONNECTIONS/RELATIONS/APPLICATIONS
	PROGRAMS ON-SITE , INDIVIDUALLY TAILORED PROGRAMS
	BILINGUAL: SPANISH, WORK WITH DEVELOPMENTALLY DISABLED

Youth

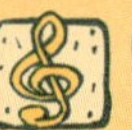

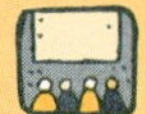

PROGRAMS:	**PERFORMANCES, WORKSHOPS, CLASSES**
SCHEDULE:	YEAR-ROUND, WEEKDAYS

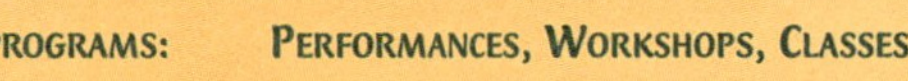

Families

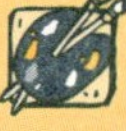

PROGRAMS:	**WORKSHOPS, CLASSES**
SCHEDULE:	YEAR-ROUND, WEEKDAYS, WEEKENDS

NOSOTROS THEATRE

1314 N. Wilton Place **HSM**
Hollywood, CA 90029
Ph: 323-466-8566
Admin: 310-472-7167
Fax: 323-466-8540

Alma Beltran	
Jerry-Velasco	Artistic Director
Gil Avila	President

Promoting Hispanics in the entertainment field— actors, writers, directors, etc. A large segment of our membership consists of aspiring artists, just entering the field. For these individuals, one of the primary benefits of membership is the opportunity to meet with members who are established professionals.

NUCLEAR FAMILY, THE

2438 Silver Lake Boulevard **HSM**
Los Angeles, CA 90039-3236
Ph: 323-669-0827

Rika Ohara	Director

Rika Ohara and the Nuclear Family create interdisciplinary (time-based visual media and dance-theater) works of sociopsychological significance.

- exhibitions (installation)
- screenings
- performances of interdisciplinary and musical pieces

OCCIDENTAL COLLEGE

Performing Arts Facilities **SFV**
1600 Campus Road
Los Angeles, CA 90041
Ph: 323-259-2737
Fax: 323-341-4987

Ellen Ketchum	Director

OCCIDENTAL COLLEGE, WEINGART GALLERIES & COONS ADMINISTRATION CENTER GALLERIES

1600 Campus Road **SFV**
Los Angeles, CA 90041
Ph: 323-259-2749
Fax: 323-259-2930

Linda Lyke	Professor/Curator
Hendrik Stooker	(Retired)

The galleries of Occidental College are the Weingart Galleries and the Coons Administration Center Galleries. Their mission is to exhibit innovative contemporary work in every medium, mostly by artists from Southern California with an emphasis on those working in Eagle Rock, Highland Park, and Mount Washington.

OCEANS GALLERY

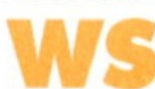

9144 Sepulveda Boulevard
Los Angeles, CA 90045
Ph: 310-670-2503
Fax: 310-645-3645
www.primenet.com/~oceans/

Alan Broder   Director   oceans@primenet.com

Limited and open edition fine art photographic prints of images by today's leading photographers of the ocean realm.

ODALISQUE FINE ART

1638 Abbot Kinney Boulevard
Venice, CA 90291
Ph: 310-314-7217
Fax: 310-314-7257

Hillar Kaplan   Director   odalisque@earthlink.net

Specializing in contemporary paintings, photgraphy, and sculpture by local artists.

ODYSSEY THEATRE ENSEMBLE

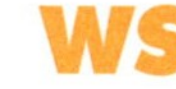

2055 S. Sepulveda Boulevard
Los Angeles, CA 90025
Ph: 310-477-2055
Fax: 310-444-0455

Jerry Charlson   Director of Publicity
Lucy Pollak   Director of Development
Ron Sossi   Artistic Director

The mission of the Odyssey Theatre Ensemble is to produce theater in Los Angeles which incorporates the creation of new American work, the re-exploration of classical material, experimentation with the most current developments in the international theater.

OJAI FESTIVALS, LTD.

501 (c)3

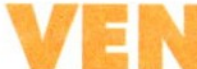

201 S. Signal Street
Ojai, CA 93023
Ph: 805-646-2094
Fax: 805-646-6037

Karen Collins   Marketing and Development Associate
Ernest Fleischmann   Artistic Director
Jacqueline Saunders   Executive Director
Celeste Matesevac   Outreach Program Director

The Ojai Music Festival, presented annually for over 50 years in the scenic Ojai Valley, is a world-class music festival known for adventurous programming of twentieth-century and traditional classical music.

- free Festival Previews and Audience Development concerts and Meet the Artists Concert in Ventura, Santa Barbara, and Los Angeles counties
- free classical music lectures
- low-cost community concerts

OJAI FESTIVALS, LTD. (CONTINUED)

Ojai Festival's education program is the only arts organization offering free music education activities in our area. Programs are developed in cooperation with a teacher's panel in order to integrate the programs to the school curriculum. Multicultural activities are included. There are over 50 free presentations annually to over 6,000 schoolchildren including Music Van, Musical Time Machine Series, Musicians Meet Musicians, field trips to the symphony and mentoring programs.

Pre/K-12

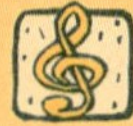

PROGRAMS: **PERFORMANCES, WORKSHOPS, STUDIO CLASSES**
SCHEDULE: SPRING, FALL, WINTER
DETAILS: GRADES PRE/K-12, AESTHETIC VALUING
CREATIVE EXPRESSION, HISTORICAL/CULTURAL CONTEXT
CONNECTIONS/RELATIONS/APPLICATIONS
TRAVEL TO SCHOOLS, PROGRAMS ON-SITE
EDUCATIONAL MATERIALS AVAILABLE

Youth

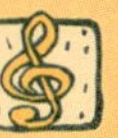

PROGRAMS: **PERFORMANCES, WORKSHOPS, CLASSES**
SCHEDULE: SPRING, FALL, WINTER

Families

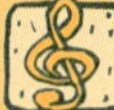

PROGRAMS: **PERFORMANCES**
SCHEDULE: YEAR-ROUND

OPERA ENCORES

SFV

P.O. Box 68
Woodland Hills, CA 91365
Ph: 818-716-7372
Fax: 818-884-9795

Rena Dictor LeBlanc   Founder/President

Opera Encores offers opera parties once a month for single music lovers ages 21-55. The parties are held in private houses and music halls.

- once a month opera parties

ORLANDO GALLERY

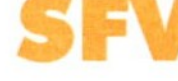

14553 Ventura Boulevard
Sherman Oaks, CA 91403
Ph: 818-789-6012
www.artscenecal.com/Orlando.html

Don Grant   Director   orlando2@earthlink.net
Bob Gino   Director

Features California contemporary art and art from Africa.

OTHER SIDE OF THE HILL PRODUCTIONS, INC., THE (AKA THE ROAD THEATRE COMPANY)

5108 Lankershim Boulevard
North Hollywood, CA 91601
Ph: 818-761-8838
Fax: 818-761-1378

501 (c)3 **SFV**

The Road Theatre produces original and innovative material as well as classic plays that deal with social and political issues relevant to today's world.

- mainstage productions
- outreach classes, benefit performances

OTIS COLLEGE OF ART AND DESIGN

9045 Lincoln Boulevard
Los Angeles, CA 90045-3550
Ph: 310-665-6800
Fax: 310-665-6805

501 (c)3 **WS**

Mark Denton	Vice President Development/ 310-665-6855
Mark Salmon	Vice President Academic Affairs/ 310-665-6939
Chris Alford	Vice President Finance and Administration
Neil Hoffman	President/ 310-665-6936

Otis College of Art and Design is a community committed to integrating visual and critical thinking to educate future professionals. Otis offers the Bachelor of Fine Arts degree in ceramics, communication arts, illustration, environmental arts, fashion design, fine arts, photography, surface design and a Master of Fine Arts degree. Evening and weekend courses are offered through Otis Continuing Education.

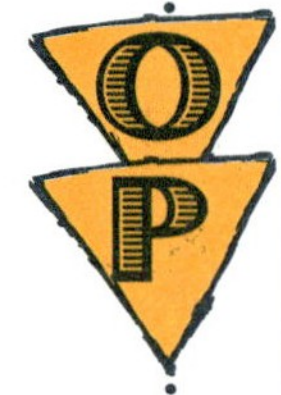

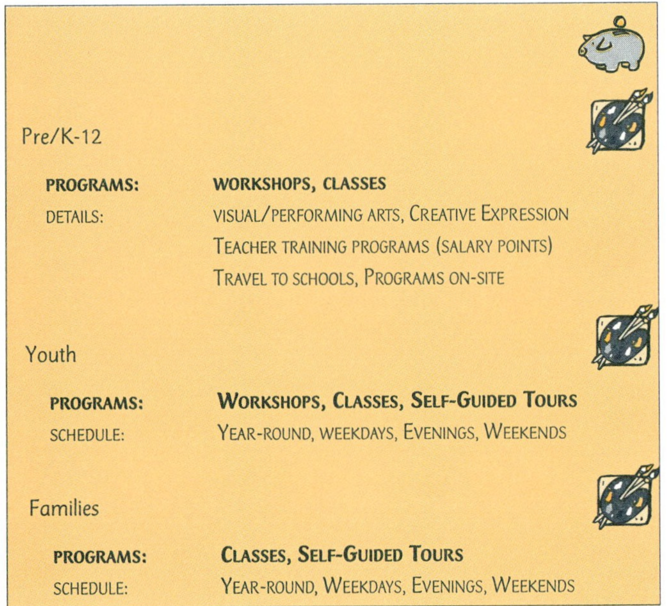

Pre/K-12

PROGRAMS: WORKSHOPS, CLASSES
DETAILS: VISUAL/PERFORMING ARTS, CREATIVE EXPRESSION
TEACHER TRAINING PROGRAMS (SALARY POINTS)
TRAVEL TO SCHOOLS, PROGRAMS ON-SITE

Youth

PROGRAMS: WORKSHOPS, CLASSES, SELF-GUIDED TOURS
SCHEDULE: YEAR-ROUND, WEEKDAYS, EVENINGS, WEEKENDS

Families

PROGRAMS: CLASSES, SELF-GUIDED TOURS
SCHEDULE: YEAR-ROUND, WEEKDAYS, EVENINGS, WEEKENDS

OUTFEST: THE LOS ANGELES GAY AND LESBIAN FILM FESTIVAL

1125 N. McCadden Place, #235
Los Angeles, CA 90038
Ph: 323-960-9200
Fax: 323-960-2397
www.outfest.org

501 (c)3 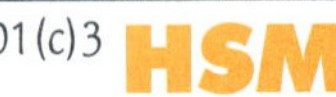

Morgan Rumpf	Executive Director

OUTFEST aims to establish the premiere lesbian, gay, bisexual, and transgender film festival by building bridges among audiences, filmmakers, and the entertainment industry through high quality programs and events that enlighten, educate, and entertain the diverse communities of Los Angeles County.

- volunteer, membership, and sponsorship opportunities
- panels and seminars
- takes place in July at the Directors Guild of America and other exciting venues in and around Los Angeles

P.E.A.C.E. 2000 PROMOTING EDUCATIONAL, ARTISTIC AND CAREER EXCELLENCE

3616 Cardiff Avenue
Los Angeles, CA 90034
Ph: 310-836-0997
Fax: 310-815-0141

WS

Deborah Kellar	Artistic/Executive Director	PeaceProject@yahoo.com
Byron Nora	Program Manager	

P.E.A.C.E. 2000 is an African-American theatrical ensemble devoted to freedom of speech, freedom of expression, and is a contemporary voice in professional theater. BAMN provides theatrical productions year-round providing performing opportunities for actors, and experience for writers, directors, and technical people.

- full theatrical productions
- staged readings
- new works festival
- community outreach programs
- theatrical workshops
- casting director seminars
- agent workshops
- classes
- director workshops
- apprenticeships
- volunteer opportunities

P.E.A.C.E. 2000 PROMOTING EDUCATIONAL, ARTISTIC AND CAREER EXCELLENCE (CONTINUED)

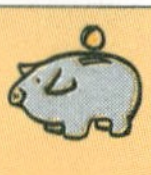

Youth are responsible for all technical and creative aspects of radio, stage, tv, and film production including scriptwriting, acting, directing, camera, light and sound operation, set design and construction, news reporting, and interviewing. P.E.A.C.E. produces productions year-round.

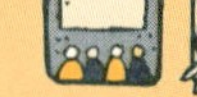

Pre/K-12

PROGRAMS:	**PERFORMANCES, WORKSHOPS, RESIDENCIES**
SCHEDULE:	YEAR-ROUND, WEEKDAYS, WEEKENDS
DETAILS:	GRADES 5-12, VISUAL & PERFORMING ARTS
	LANGUAGE ARTS, CREATIVE EXPRESSION
	TRAVEL TO SCHOOLS, INDIVIDUALLY TAILORED PROGRAMS
	EDUCATIONAL MATERIALS AVAILABLE
	WORK WITH MENTALLY/PHYSICALLY CHALLENGED

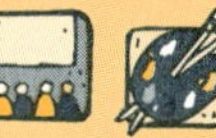

Youth

PROGRAMS:	**PERFORMANCES, WORKSHOPS, RESIDENCIES**
SCHEDULE:	YEAR-ROUND, WEEKDAYS, WEEKENDS

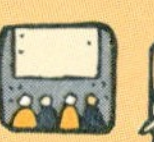

Families

PROGRAMS:	**PERFORMANCES, WORKSHOPS, RESIDENCIES**
SCHEDULE:	YEAR-ROUND, EVENINGS

PACEWILDENSTEIN

9540 Wilshire Boulevard
Beverly Hills, CA 90212
Ph: 310-205-5522
Admin: 310-278-3633
Fax; 310-205-5527
www.pacewildenstein.com

WS

Modern and contemporary paintings, sculpture, drawings and photography

PACIFIC ASIA MUSEUM

46 N. Los Robles Avenue
Pasadena, CA 91101
Ph: 626-449-2742
Fax: 626-449-2754
www.westmuse/pacasiamuseum

501 (c)3

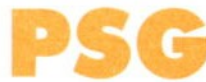

Paul Little	Director of Communications/ x18
David Kamansky	Executive Director and Senior Curator/ x35
James Hanley	Director of Administration/ x13
Lucia Yang	Education Coordinator/ x31
Nancy Davis	Director of Strategic Planning/ x33

Pacific Asia Museum preserves and presents the art and culture of Asia and the Pacific Islands. The museum's programs are designed to promote cross-cultural understanding of the people and cultures of the Pacific and Asian regions.

- docent led tours of galleries and garden
- special programs including monthly Family Free Days, classes, lectures, and performances related to Asia and Pacific cultures
- monthly Authors on Asia program
- volunteer opportunities

PACIFIC ASIA MUSEUM (CONTINUED)

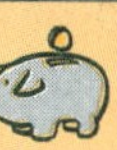

The museum offers a variety of educational programs for schools, visitors, and specialized audiences. Educational activites provide a variety of learning experiences in a postive enviroment to enhance the participants' understanding of the people and cultures of Asia and the Pacific.

Pre/K-12

PROGRAMS:	**PERFORMANCES, WORKSHOPS, GUIDED TOURS**
SCHEDULE:	YEAR-ROUND, WEEKDAYS, WEEKENDS
DETAILS:	GRADES PRE/K-12, VISUAL & PERFORMING ARTS
	MULTICULTURAL, HISTORICAL/CULTURAL CONTEXT
	CONNECTIONS/RELATIONS/APPLICATIONS
	TEACHER TRAINING PROGRAMS, PROGRAMS ON-SITE
	COST FOR SOME PROGRAMS

Youth

PROGRAMS:	**PERFORMANCES, WORKSHOPS, CLASSES, SELF-GUIDED TOURS, GUIDED TOURS**
SCHEDULE:	YEAR-ROUND, WEEKDAYS, WEEKENDS
DETAILS:	COST FOR SOME PROGRAMS

Families

PROGRAMS:	**PERFORMANCES, WORKSHOPS, CLASSES SELF-GUIDED TOURS, GUIDED TOURS**
SCHEDULE:	YEAR-ROUND, WEEKDAYS, WEEKENDS
DETAILS:	COST FOR SOME PROGRAMS

PACIFIC COMPOSERS FORUM

2054 Midvale Avenue
Los Angeles, CA 90025
Ph: 310-475-0501
www.composersforum.com

501 (c)3

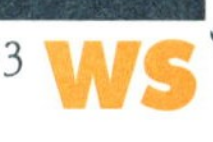

P

Mark Ruttle	composerpcf@aol.com

The Pacific Composers Forum is a 200-plus service organization that fosters the development, performance, and public awareness of its members' music. We promote the composers of Southern California and their music to the world.

- present 6-8 concerts of members' music each year
- offer 10-12 composer study sessions focusing on the music of prominent living composers on topics of interest to composers
- 3-4 membership meetings which feature a guest artist
- occasional workshops, readings, and recording sessions
- quarterly newsletter
- website where members without internet sites can maintain a presence

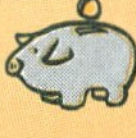

Children are given access and musical empowerment to realize that anyone can create. They acquire this through composing their own music using MIDI equipment and an excellent teaching program. This program requires only one session.

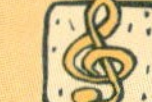

Pre/K-12

PROGRAMS:	**PERFORMANCES, WORKSHOPS, RESIDENCIES**
SCHEDULE:	YEAR-ROUND, WEEKDAYS
DETAILS:	VISUAL & PERFORMING ARTS, CREATIVE EXPRESSION
	TRAVEL TO SCHOOLS

PACIFIC SERENADES

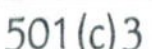
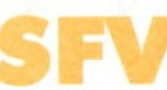

1440 Melwood Drive
Glendale, CA 91207
Ph: 323-852-0260

501(c)3 **SFV**

Mark Carlson	Artistic Director	PacSer@aol.com
Libby Slatkin	Media Liasion/ 323-939-9670	

Pacific Serenades is a chamber music ensemble committed to generating music ensemble committed to generating new works primarily by Southern California composers and presenting them in the context of standard repertoire.

- four programs presented between January and June, performed in three different locations

PACIFIC STUDIO FOR DANCE

1123 N. Pacific Avenue
Glendale, CA 91202
Ph: 818-240-2393
www.gledaleplus.com

SFV

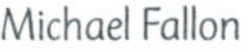

Michael Fallon	Manager-Administrator
Laura Fremont	Owner-Director

Pacific School for Dance offers a fine arts curriculum of movement theater based in ballet, jazz, tap, musical theatre, and host Cole-Link Dance Theatre and In Sync Dance Ensemble.

- studio rentals
- workstudy and scholarship program
- Cole-Link Dance Theatre— professional company researching Jack Cole jazz roots of theatre dance and its continued development in jazz today
- In Sync Dance Ensemble— student company offering events including a benefit spring concert

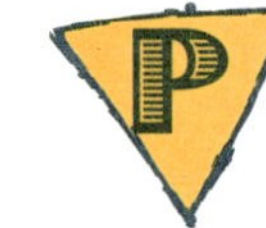

The education programs have a strong emphasis on technique as a foundation for life. Student creations are founded on learned fundamentals and educated decision making. The programs include access to and support from the professional field.

Pre/K-12

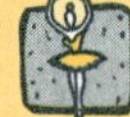
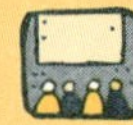

PROGRAMS: **PERFORMANCES, WORKSHOPS, STUDIO CLASSES**
SCHEDULE: SPRING, FALL, WINTER, WEEKDAYS, EVENINGS, WEEKENDS
DETAILS: GRADES PRE/K-12, VISUAL & PERFORMING ARTS
CREATIVE EXPRESSION, PROGRAMS ON-SITE
INDIVIDUALLY TAILORED PROGRAMS

Youth

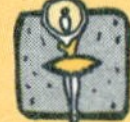
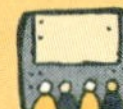

PROGRAMS: **PERFORMANCES, WORKSHOPS, CLASSES**
SCHEDULE: SPRING, FALL, WINTER, WEEKDAYS, EVENINGS, WEEKENDS
DETAILS: COST FOR SOME PROGRAMS

Families

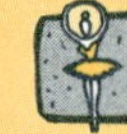
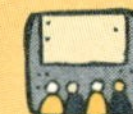

PROGRAMS: **PERFORMANCES, WORKSHOPS, CLASSES**
SCHEDULE: SPRING, FALL, WINTER, WEEKDAYS, EVENINGS, WEEKENDS

PALMDALE PLAYHOUSE

38334 Tenth Street East
Palmdale, CA 93550
Ph: 805-267-5684
Admin: 805-267-5100
Educ: 805-267-ARTS
Fax: 805-267-5672

501(c)3 **AV**

Dea McAllister	Cultural Arts/Theater Manager

The Palmdale Playhouse provides a place for the enjoyment of professional and community-based theatre. We offer an opportunity for citizens of the Greater Antelope Valley to volunteer their time and talents to the arts and to serve as a learning center for people of all ages and abilities to explore the many crafts that come under the umbrella of theater.

- youth and community choir
- youth and community orchestra
- visual arts program
- youth and community dance company
- writer's roundtable
- summer theater camp
- volunteer opportunities

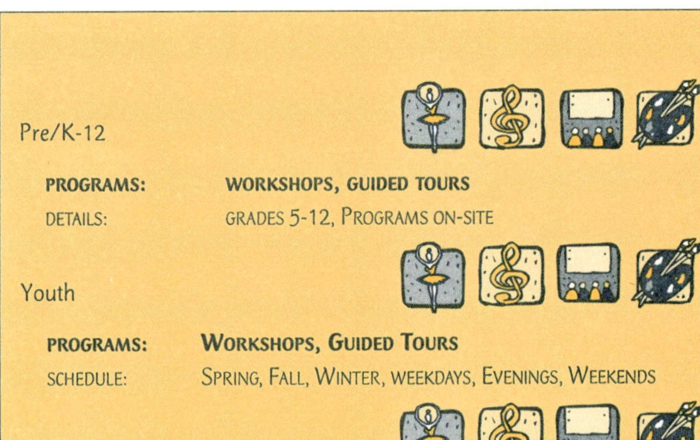

Pre/K-12

PROGRAMS: **WORKSHOPS, GUIDED TOURS**
DETAILS: GRADES 5-12, PROGRAMS ON-SITE

Youth

PROGRAMS: **WORKSHOPS, GUIDED TOURS**
SCHEDULE: SPRING, FALL, WINTER, WEEKDAYS, EVENINGS, WEEKENDS

Families

PROGRAMS: **WORKSHOPS, GUIDED TOURS**
SCHEDULE: SPRING, FALL, WINTER, WEEKDAYS, EVENINGS, WEEKENDS

PALOS VERDES ART CENTER

5504 W. Crestridge Road
Rancho Palos Verdes, CA 90275
Ph: 310-541-2479
Fax: 310-541-9520
www.palosverdes.com/artcenter

501(c)3 **SB**

Kathy Shinkle	Public Relations Director	artcenter@palosverdes.com
Scott Canty	Exhibitions Director	
Janene Ferguson	Education Director	
Gail Phinney	Program Director	

The Palos Verdes Art Center inspires individuals to celebrate, appreciate, and create art through its exhibition, education, and outreach programs.

- over 20 exhibitions annually featuring Southern California artists
- 200 classes a year
- Art for Fun(d)s Sake— juried arts and crafts street fair
- Concours d'Elegance— classic car show
- gift shop
- volunteer opportunities
- scholarships

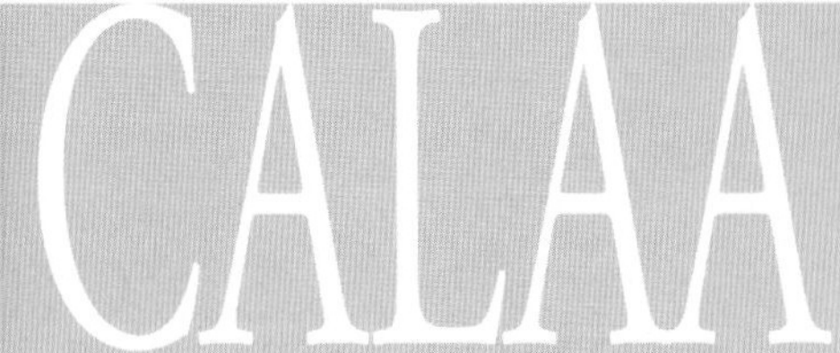

California Assembly of Local Arts Agencies.

Championing Local Arts in California Since 1988.

CALAA is the largest umbrella service organization for arts organizations operating at the local level of any state in the country. We offer:

STATEWIDE AND NATIONAL NETWORK

- Network of professional arts administrators, artists, businesses and people interested in supporting and helping to strengthen the arts in California
- Benefit of statewide partnerships with other arts service organizations such as California Confederation of the Arts, California Lawyers for the Arts, California Presenters, the Nonprofit Policy Council, etc.
- Americans for the Arts affiliated discounts on membership, events, publications.

PROFESSIONAL DEVELOPMENT AND LEADERSHIP TRAINING

- Consultancies to meet the priority needs of each district
- Workshops and seminars co-sponsored with organizations such as the California Arts Council, the National Assembly of Local Arts Agencies, and the California Lawyers for the Arts
- Annual Convocation designed to address the most current issues and needs of the local arts agency field
- Technical assistance through our Peer Advisor Network, Advanced Leadership Roundtable and Arts 101 programs

INFORMATION RESOURCES

- Radius Magazine: published periodically, each issue highlights LAA activity across the state of California
- Website with the latest information in the field, and partnership with California CultureNet
- Access to other information, databases, publications on a national and regional level

ADVOCACY

- In cooperation with the California Confederation of the Arts, CALAA orchestrates grass roots advocacy for the arts at the local, state and national levels
- Represents the field to government, industry, business, the public and to regional, statewide and national arts organizations. Provides visibility and advocacy for the arts at the local level with groups such as the California League of Cities and the California State Association of Counties
- Coordination of on-going media campaigns to increase local art agency visibility. Technical assistance in press and public relations.

Who joins CALAA?

- Local Arts Agencies
- Local Arts Administrators
- Individual Artists
- Community Leaders
- Foundations and Non-Profits
- Elected Officials
- Professional Organizations
- Corporations and Businesses
- Local Visual and Performing Arts Organizations
- Local Arts Touring and Presentation Groups

Join the Network Today!

Write, call or fax us at:

693 Sutter Street, Third Floor,
San Francisco, CA 94102
Telephone: 415/441-5900
Fax: 415/441-5938

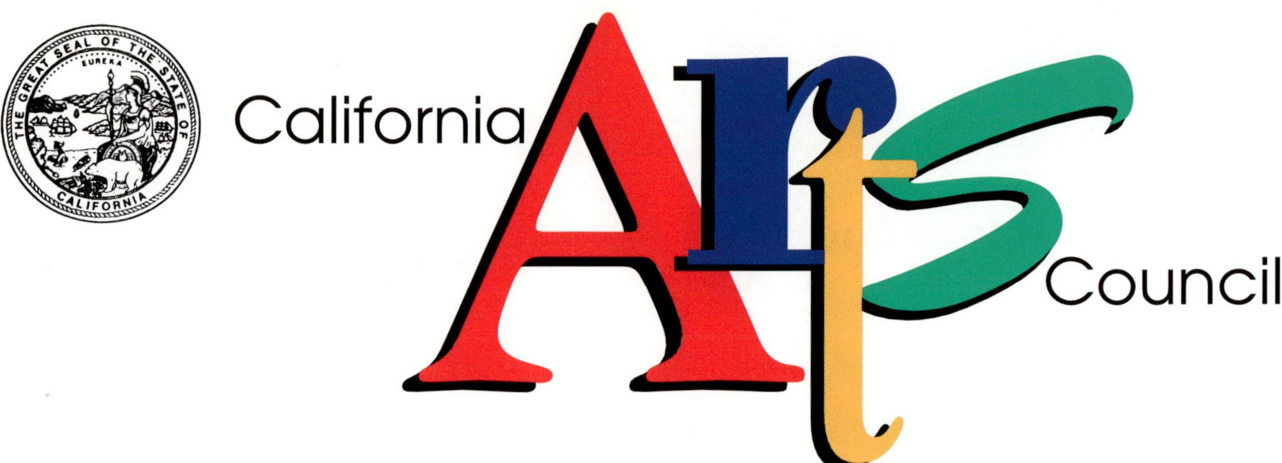

The CAC is a state agency, funded primarily through the state's annual budget process, supplemented with funds from the National Endowment for the Arts. Its grants are usually matched by foundations, individuals, earned income, government agencies, or other organizations.

The mission of the CAC is to make quality art reflecting all of California's diverse cultures available and accessible; to support the state's broad economic, educational, and social goals through the arts; to provide leadership for all levels of the arts community; and to present effective programs that add a further dimension to our cities, our jobs, and our creative spirit.

The Director is the Chief Executive Officer and reports directly to the Governor. The Director and Deputy Director for Partnerships are appointed by, and serve at the pleasure of the Governor. The Director and Deputy Director manage a professional staff headquartered in Sacramento.

The appointed Council of the CAC consists of 11 members who serve four-year staggered terms. The Governor appoints nine members; the Legislature appoints two. Council members serve without salary, elect their own chair, and meet throughout the state to encourage public attendance. This body has final approval of CAC grants.

The California Arts Council provides funding in the following categories:

Organizational Support Program
Local Arts Education Program
Artists In Residence Program
California Challenge Program
Artists Fellowship Program
Performing Arts Touring and Presenting Program
Multi-cultural Arts Advancement Program
Technical Assistance Program
State and Local Partnership Program
Traditional Folk Arts Program

To find out more about the California Arts Council's funding programs, you may request a Guide to Programs by calling 1-800-201-6201. Specific information about each grant program is available in this publication. You can also access information about the California Arts Council on our Website located at http://www.cac.ca.gov.
1300 I Street, Suite 930, Sacramento, CA 95814 Tel: 916 .322.6555 Fax: 916.322.6575

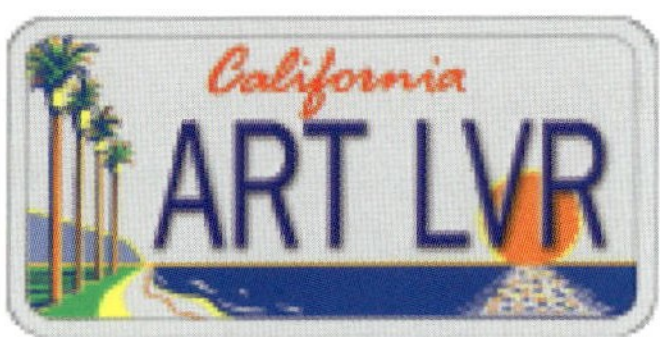

©Thiebaud ♡1993

The California Arts Council is pleased to offer this California Coastline license plate designed by world renowned California Artist, Wayne Thiebaud. Now you may order your California Coastline license plate for only $30.* Your contribution will help fund arts education and local arts programming in the state that would not otherwise be possible. Call the number below for an application.

1. 800 . 201 . 6201

* The standard plate is $30 with a $15 annual renewal fee. You may order personalized plates for $70.

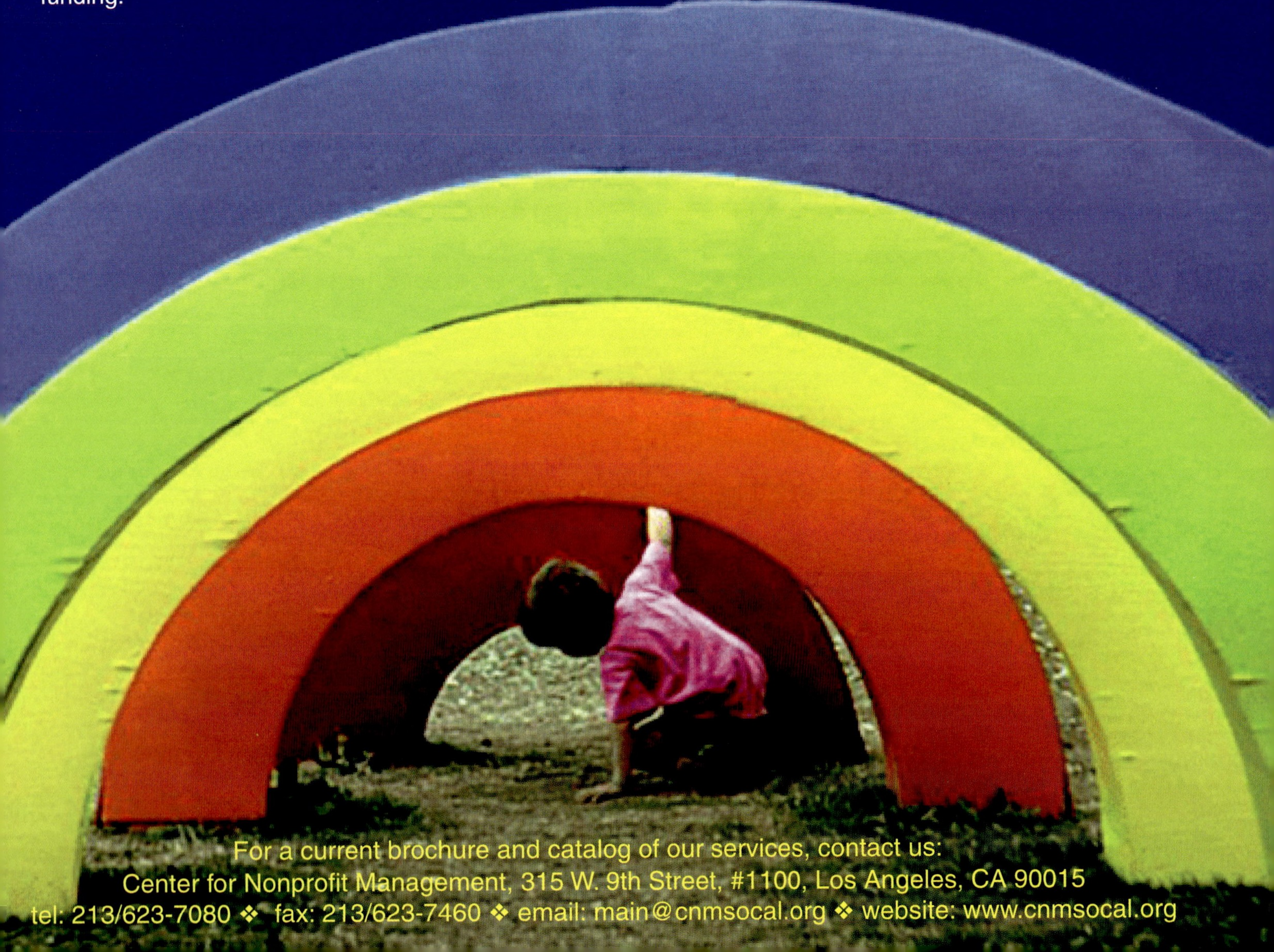

Alert Your Community To

Classic Arts Showcase

and We Will Put a New Audience in Your Unsold Seats.

If not available in your area ask your City Councilman to get CAS on one of your local community channels.

Classic Arts Showcase, a non-profit, non-commercial 24 hour satellite arts service, is a monumental audience development project designed for one purpose only, to inspire viewers to go out and experience that arts in their own community. We are, in a very real sense, an audience building tool for your organization.

We are available in over 52 million cable homes nationwide, but we may not yet be on in your area. We need your help in spreading the word. Contact your local cable provider or broadcast and ask them to do an air check of Classic Arts Showcase over satellite G1R-5, and then fax us for an application to air our broadcast offer their public access, educational or PBS channel. Or contact your local school organization and have them do the same for their school channel. Help us to help you build a future audience for your organization, and all the classic arts.

CAS is available 24 hours a day via satellite G1R-5 to all cable operators, broadcasters and individual large dish owners and brought to you via hundreds of public access channels nationwide. For an application to air CAS fax us at (323) 878-0329.

Clip after clip of great classic arts performances from the worlds of
BALLET * OPERA * DANCE * RECITAL * CHAMBER AND CHORAL MUSIC * ORCHESTRAL MUSIC * CLASSIC FILM * ARCHITECTURAL ART * SOLO VOICE * ANIMATION * FOLK ART * THEATRE * MUSEUM ART * CLASSIC FILM * ARCHIVAL DOCUMENTARY * SOLO INSTRUMENT
All Classic Arts! 24 Hours a Day! Free and Unscrambled!

Where to see Classic Arts Showcase in the Los Angeles Area:

Seen in Los Angeles on:
KCET-PBS Ch28
Nightly at the end of their broadcast day from either 1am, 1:30am or 2am until 5am excepting for Wednesday
LA CHANNEL Ch36
7 nights a week 1-6am

Seen in Beverly Hills on:
BEVERLY HILLS SCHOOL DISTRICT Ch36
24 hours a day, 7 days a week

Seen in the Fullerton area on:
CAL STATE/FULLERTON
Various Titan Channels
Mon: 8-10am, 2-7pm / Tues: 4-6pm, 7-10pm /
Wed: 8-10am, 2-10pm / Thu: 7-10pm /
Fri, Sat, Sun: 8:30am-10pm

Seen in La Crescenta, Burbank and Glendale on:
GLENDALE UNIFIED SCHOOL DISTRICT Ch15
Mon-Sun: 7pm-7am

Seen in Long Beach on:
CAL STATE LONG BEACH Ch68
Mon-Fri: 10am-12noon / Sat & Sun: 8am-12noon

Seen in Malibu and Pacific Palisades on:
PEPPERDINE UNIVERSITY Ch3
7 days a week, 9pm-4am

Seen in Pasadena on:
PASADENA UNIFIED SCHOOL DISTRICT
Channels 64/ 55/47
Fri: 12noon-5pm, 7:30pm-12midnight
Mon: 12midnight-9am

Seen in Thousand Oaks on:
CALIFORNIA LUTHERAN UNIVERSITY Ch67
Monday through Friday 12noon-6pm

Seen in West Hollywood on:
CIT OF WEST HOLLYWOOD Ch35
24 hours a day, 7 days a week

Classic Arts Showcase
PERFORMING - VISUAL - FILM
PO Box 828 Burbank, CA 91503-0828

If you'd like to be seen on CAS send us a VHS tape. If accepted we'll need a copy of the master on digital BetCam SP tape.

www.culturela.org 213.485.2433
433 South Spring Street, 10th Floor Los Angeles, CA 90013

City of Los Angeles

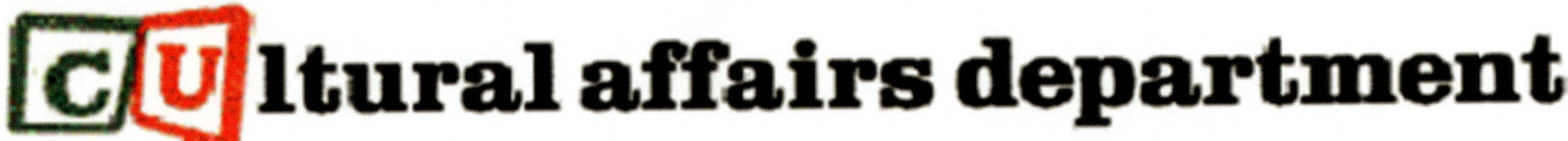

Adolfo V. Nodal
General Manager

performing arts

festivals

grants

public art

architecture/historic preservation

community arts

calendar of events

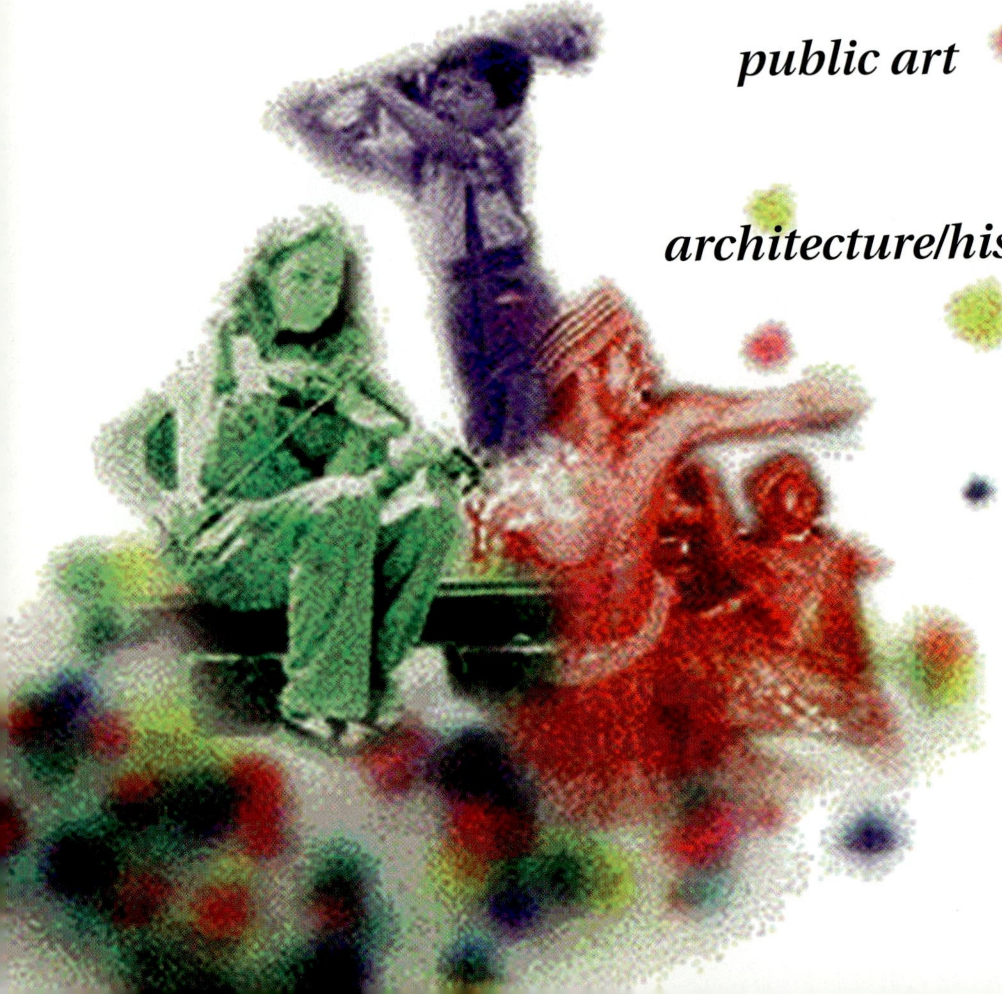

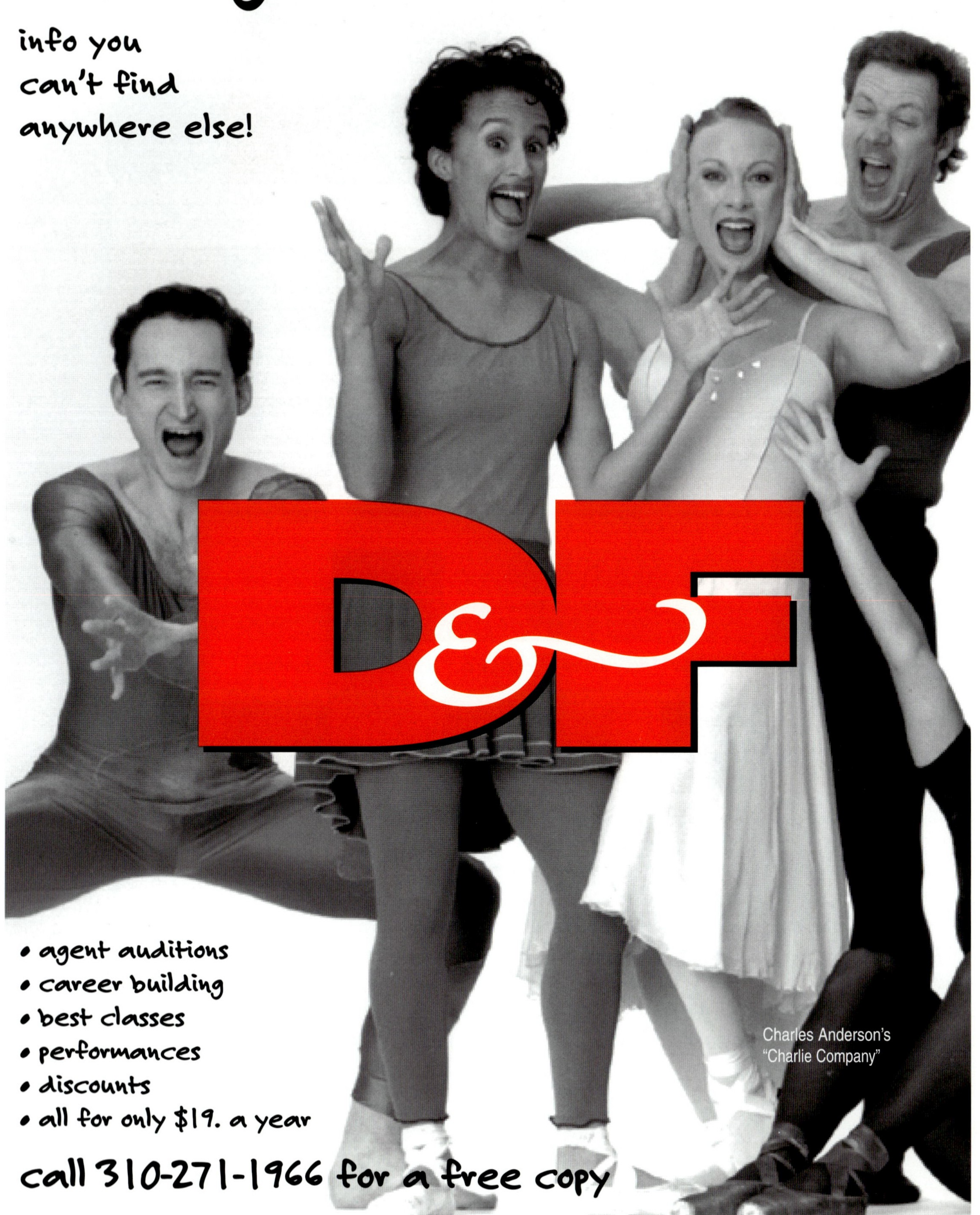
gotta have it!
info you
can't find
anywhere else!
D&F
• agent auditions
• career building
• best classes
• performances
• discounts
• all for only $19. a year
call 310-271-1966 for a free copy
Charles Anderson's
"Charlie Company"

The mission of the Los Angeles County Arts Commission is to foster excellence, diversity, vitality and accessibility of the arts of the County of Los Angeles. The Commission plays a leadership role in cultural services for the County, providing information and resources to the community, artists, arts organizations and municipalities.

Grant Programs

The **Small Organizational Grant Program (OGP I)** funds artistic or administrative advancement projects for arts organizations with budgets under $100,000 and two years of producing history.

The **Mid-Size Organizational Grant Program (OGP II)** funds artistic or administrative sustainability projects for arts organizations with budgets between $100,000 and $800,000 and two years of producing history.

The **Large Organizational Grant Program (OGP III)** provides annual support for arts organizations with budgets over $800,000, including major Los Angeles County institutions.

Performance Opportunities

Summer Nights at the Ford
late June-Labor Day
outdoor performing arts series at the John Anson Ford Amphitheatre

Inside at the Ford
November-April
theater in the Ford's renovated 87-seat space

Los Angeles County Holiday Celebration
December 24
music and dance broadcast live from the Dorothy Chandler Pavilion of the Music Center on KCET, Channel 28

Los Angeles County-Wide Arts Open House
first Saturday in October
more than 100 free events throughout the county celebrating national arts and humanities month

Los Angeles County Arts Commission

For applications and guidelines contact:
Los Angeles County Arts Commission
374 Kenneth Hahn Hall of Administration
500 West Temple Street
Los Angeles, CA 90012
Tel. (213) 974-1343
FAX (213) 625-1765
Email: acampbell@bos.co.la.ca.us
Internet: www.lacountyarts.org

MUSIC CENTER EDUCATION DIVISION

Expand Creativity

Have fun with our Arts Programs for

Teachers

Parents

Kids

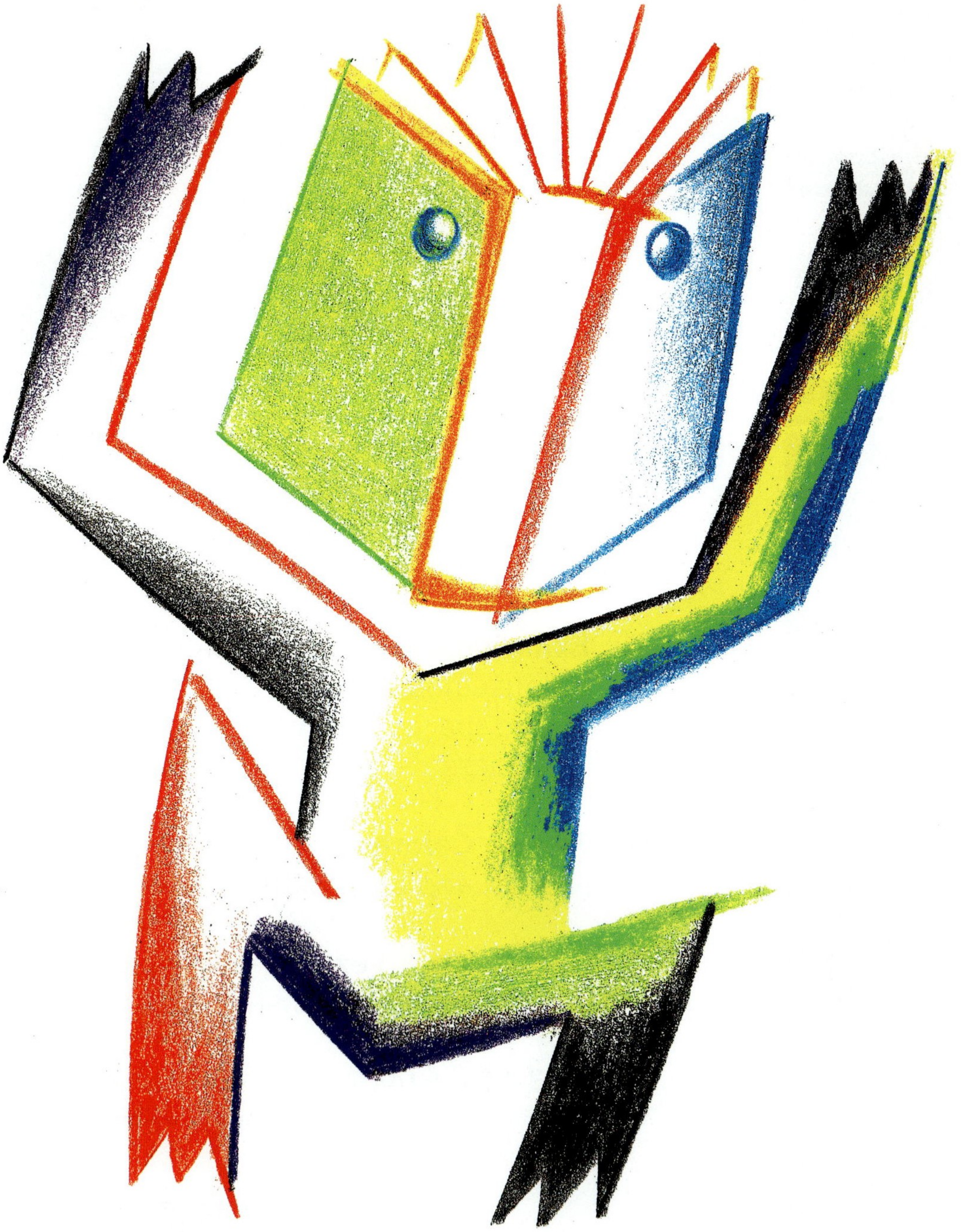

Dance

Music

Theatre

Visual Art

the arts@ucla

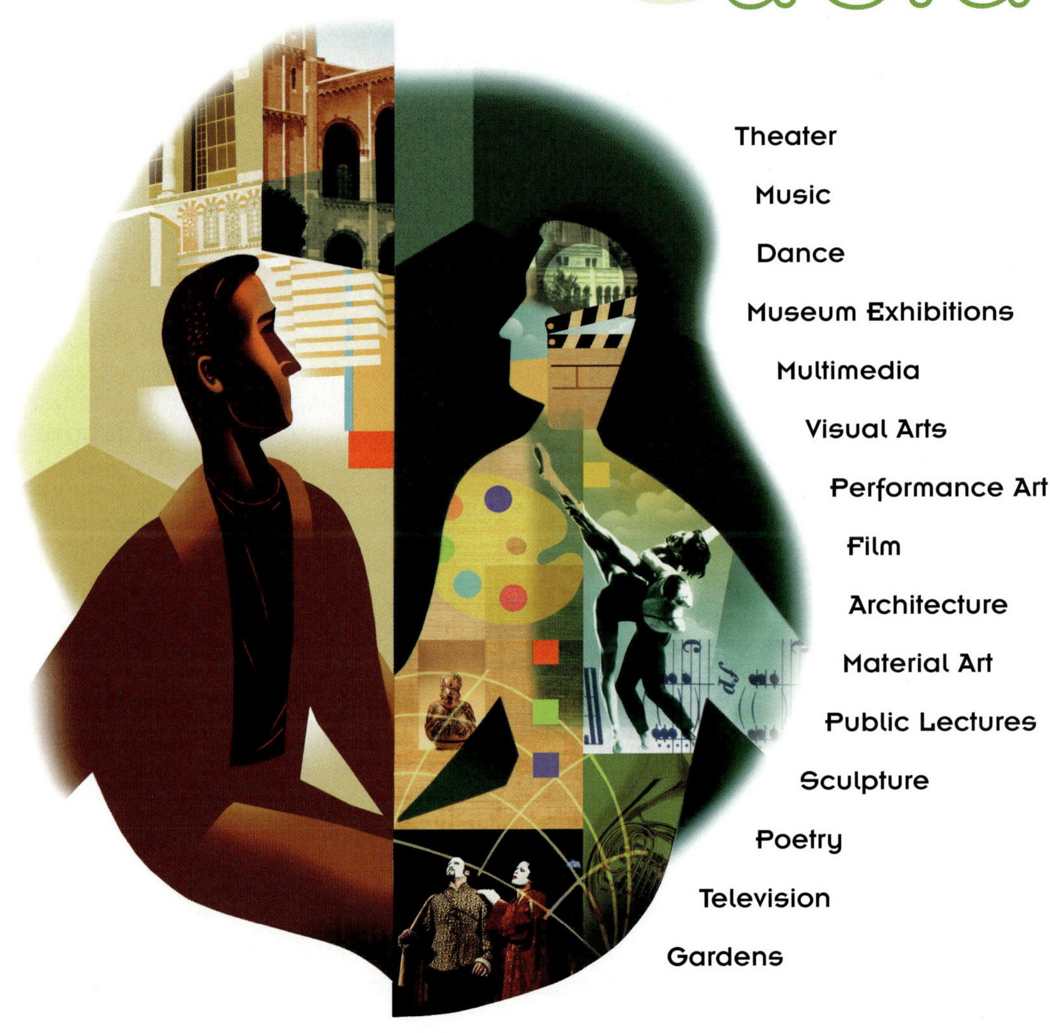

THE LEADING ARTS AND CULTURAL CENTER OF THE WEST

UCLA offers everything from the ancient to the avant-garde. With an unparalleled depth and range of cultural events on the Westwood campus or nearby, arts enthusiasts can find something to do every day of the year.

You will find a complete listing of UCLA's theaters, museums, professional schools, film and television archives, gardens, and continuing education programs in this guide. See pages 178–181

www.ucla.edu

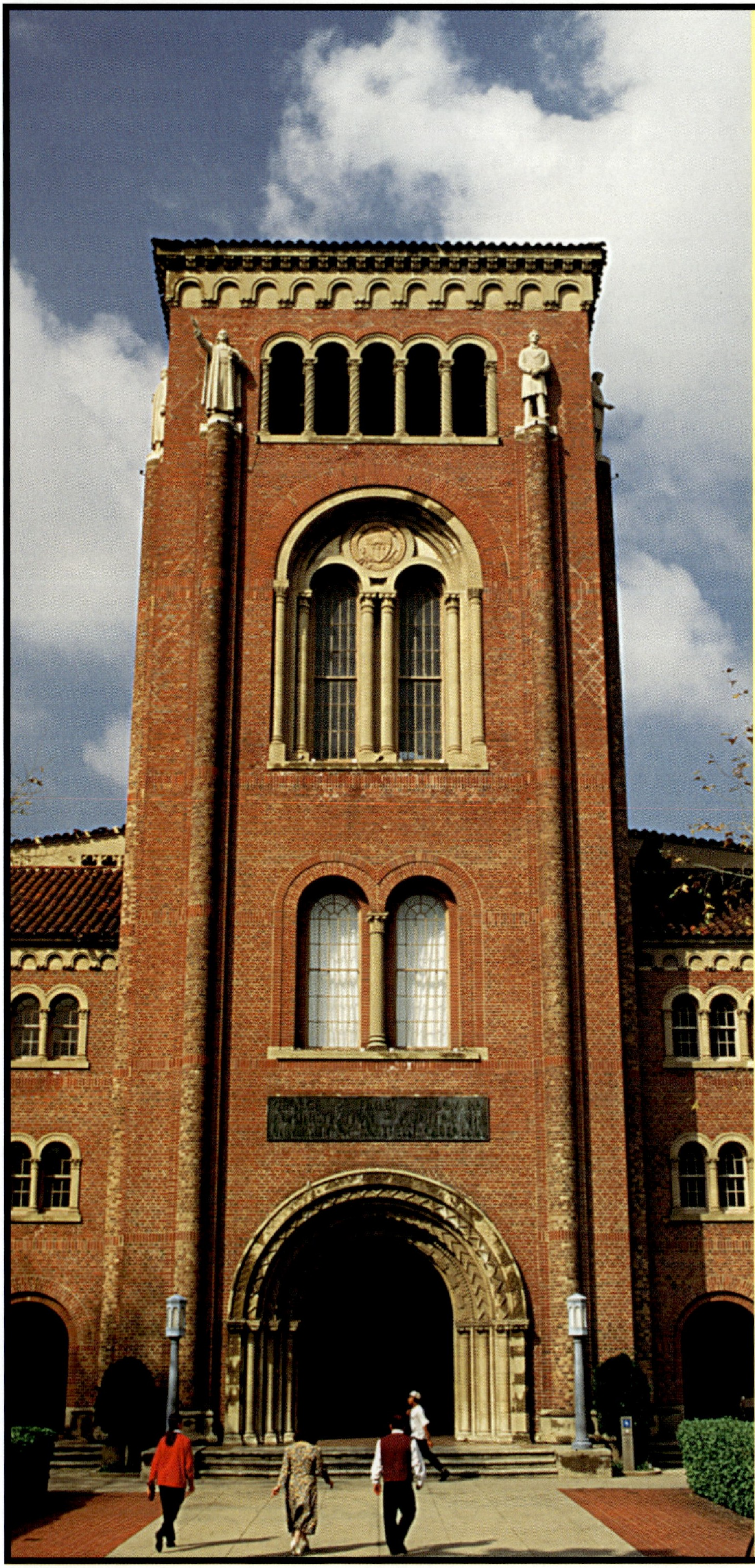

KUSC, 91.5 FM

Celebrating more than 50 years as a leading Southern California cultural resource, KUSC provides the best in classical music and news programs while serving as a voice for the regional arts community.

USC Fisher Gallery

Fisher Gallery offers exhibitions ranging from antiquities to Old Master artists through contemporary works of local, national and international artists.

USC Helen Lindhurst Architecture Gallery

Recent shows have included such important international architects as Renzo Piano, Santiago Calatrava, Herman Hertzberger, Alvaro Siza, and Carlos Diniz.

USC School of Music

The USC School of Music is the most active producer of live music performances in all of Southern California, offering more than 500 concerts and recitals every year.

USC Spectrum

Spectrum produces a sixty-event season that presents the finest in arts and lecture events including appearances by the St. Paul Chamber Orchestra, Aquila Theatre Company of London, Teatro de Danza Espanol and the Alvin Ailey Repertory Ensemble.

USC Symphony

One of the preeminent ensembles of its kind in the country, the USC Symphony has enjoyed a long tradition in Southern California built upon exciting performances and innovative programming.

USC School of Theatre

Founded in 1945 by William C. de Mille, the USC School of Theatre has a long history of training in drama and theatre arts. The School offers an active calendar of productions from a wide selection of major historical periods and dramatic styles.

USC Warner Brothers Archives

Presented to USC by Warner Communications in 1977, the USC Warner Bros. Archives is the largest and possibly the richest single studio collection in the world.

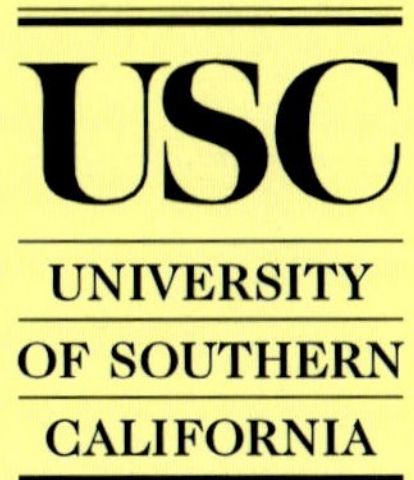

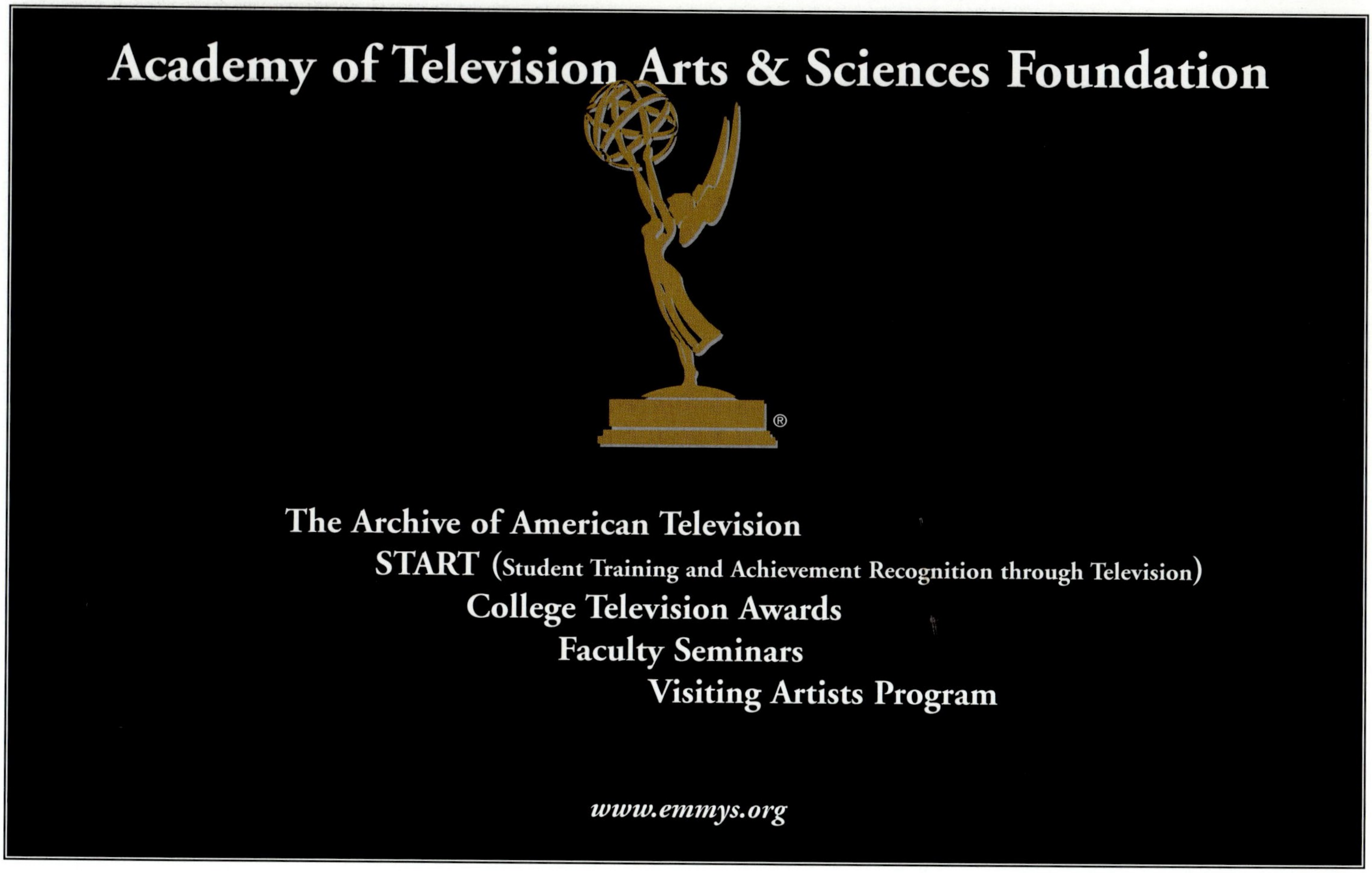

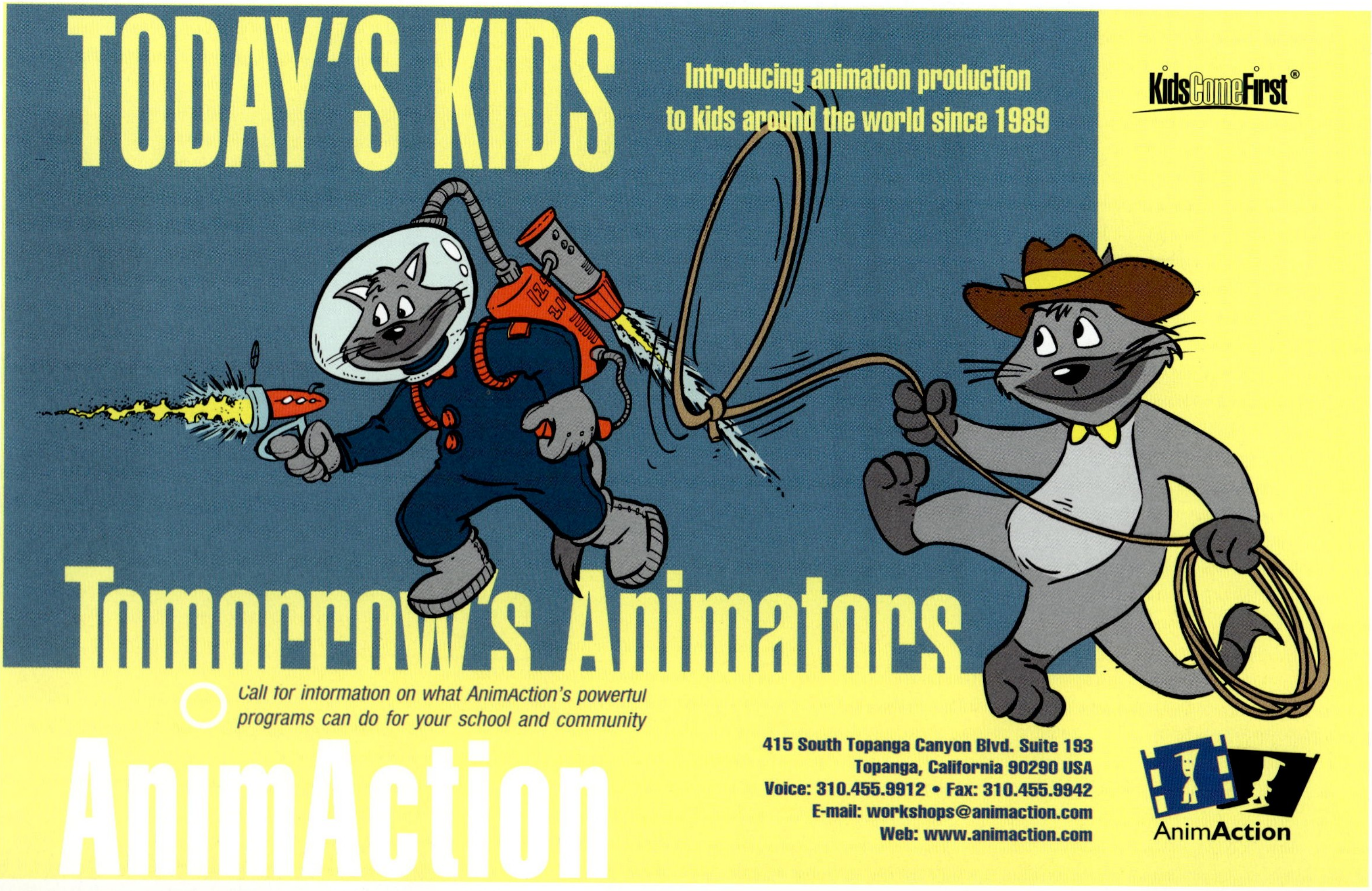

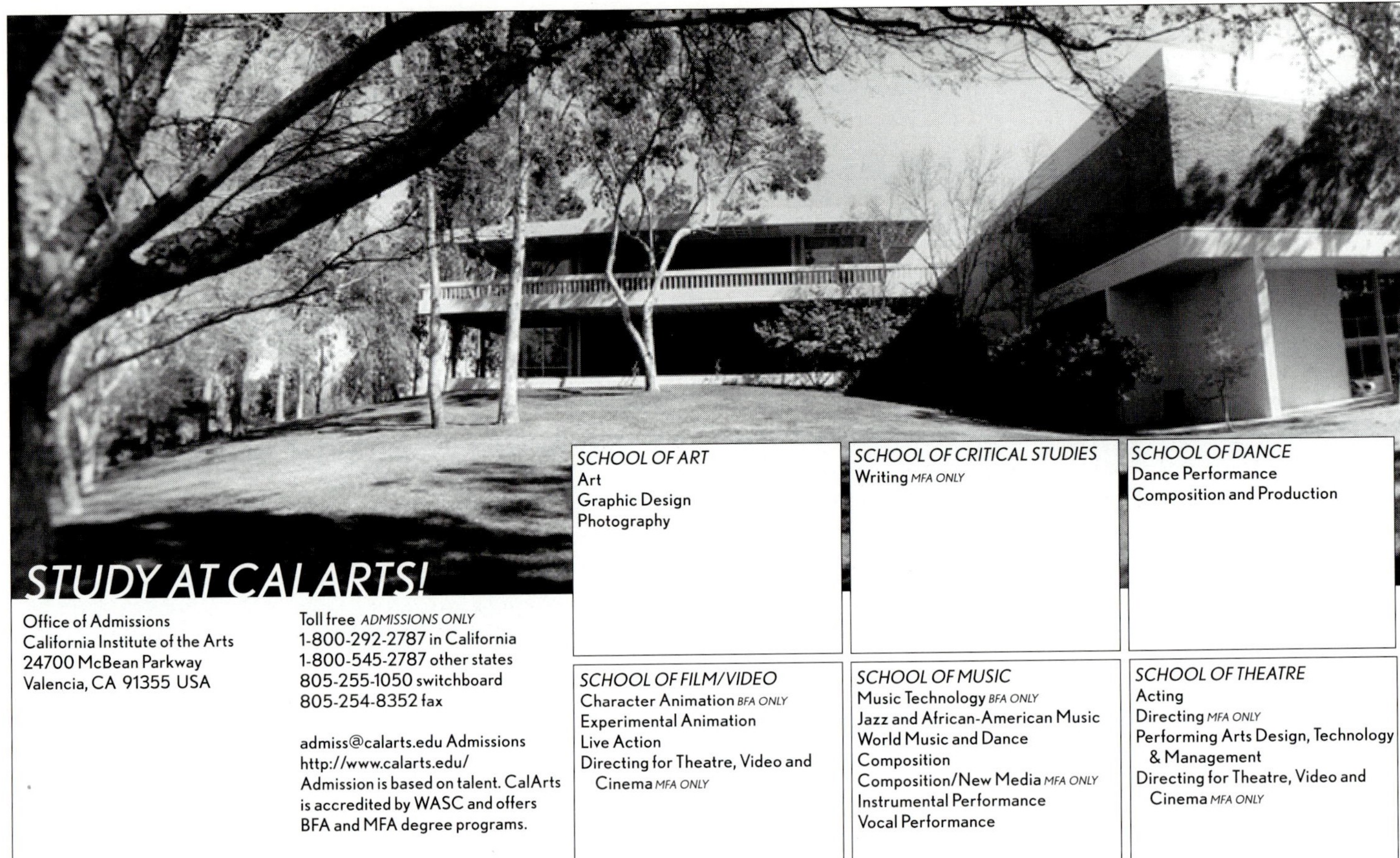

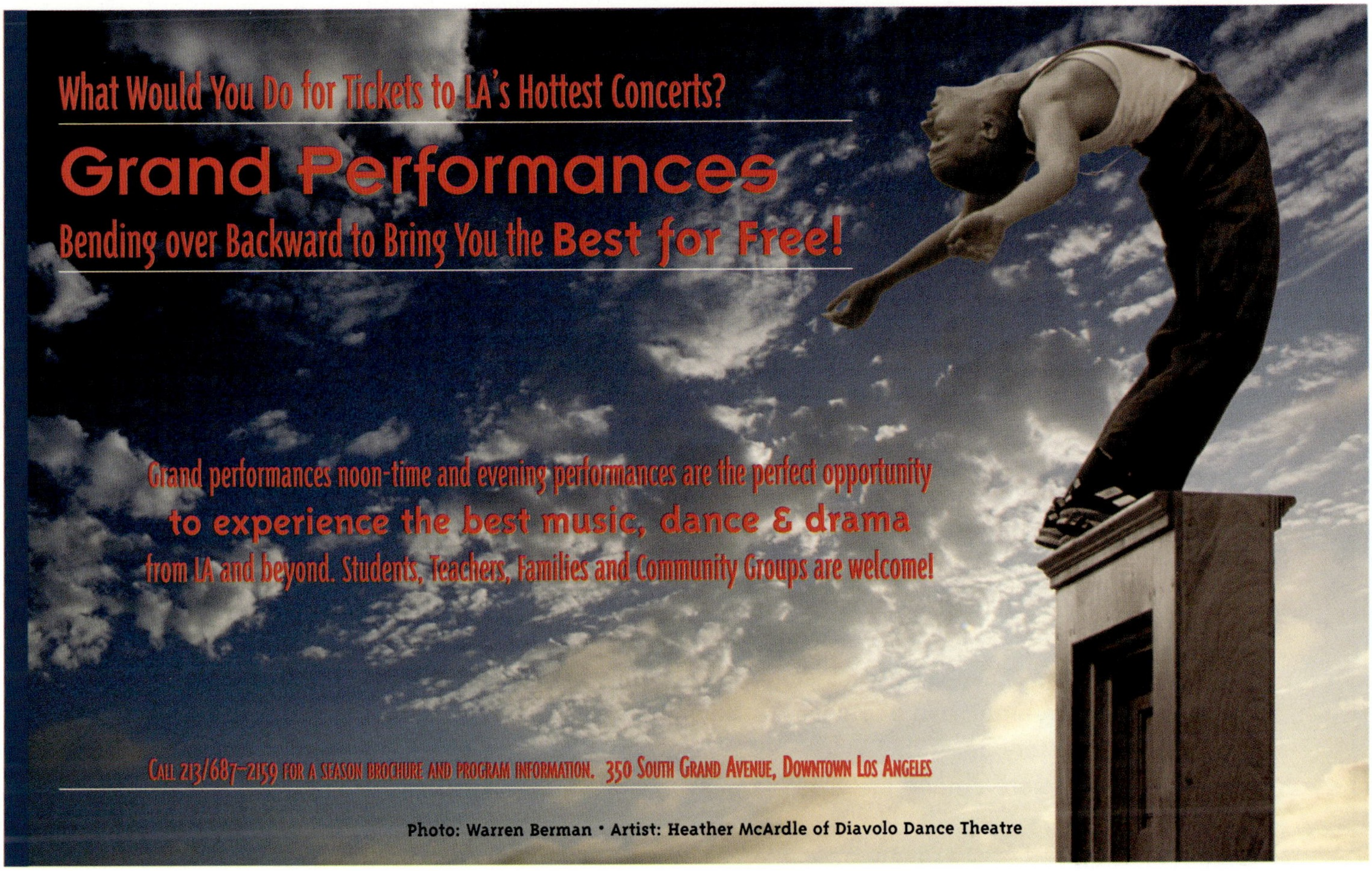

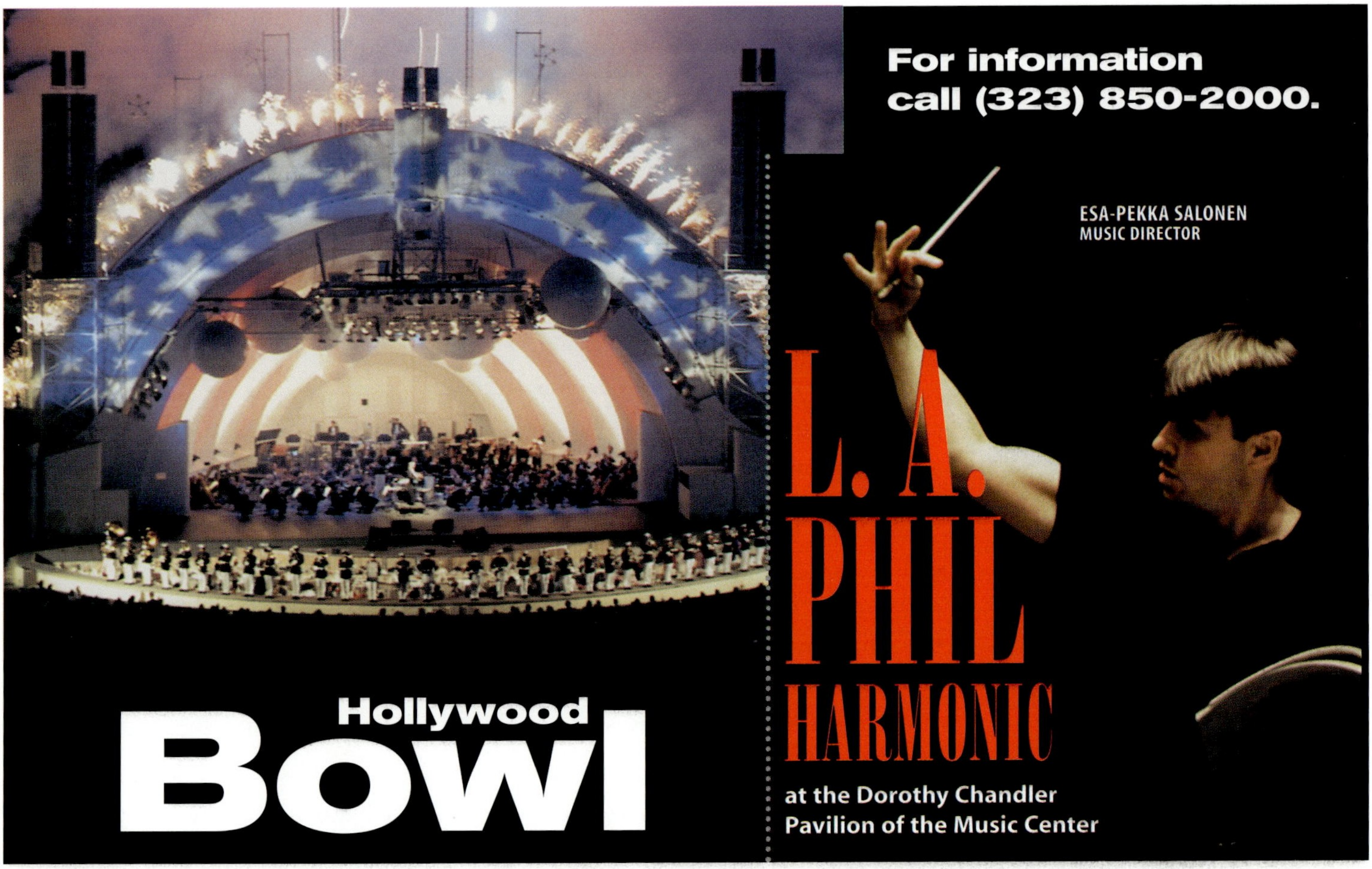

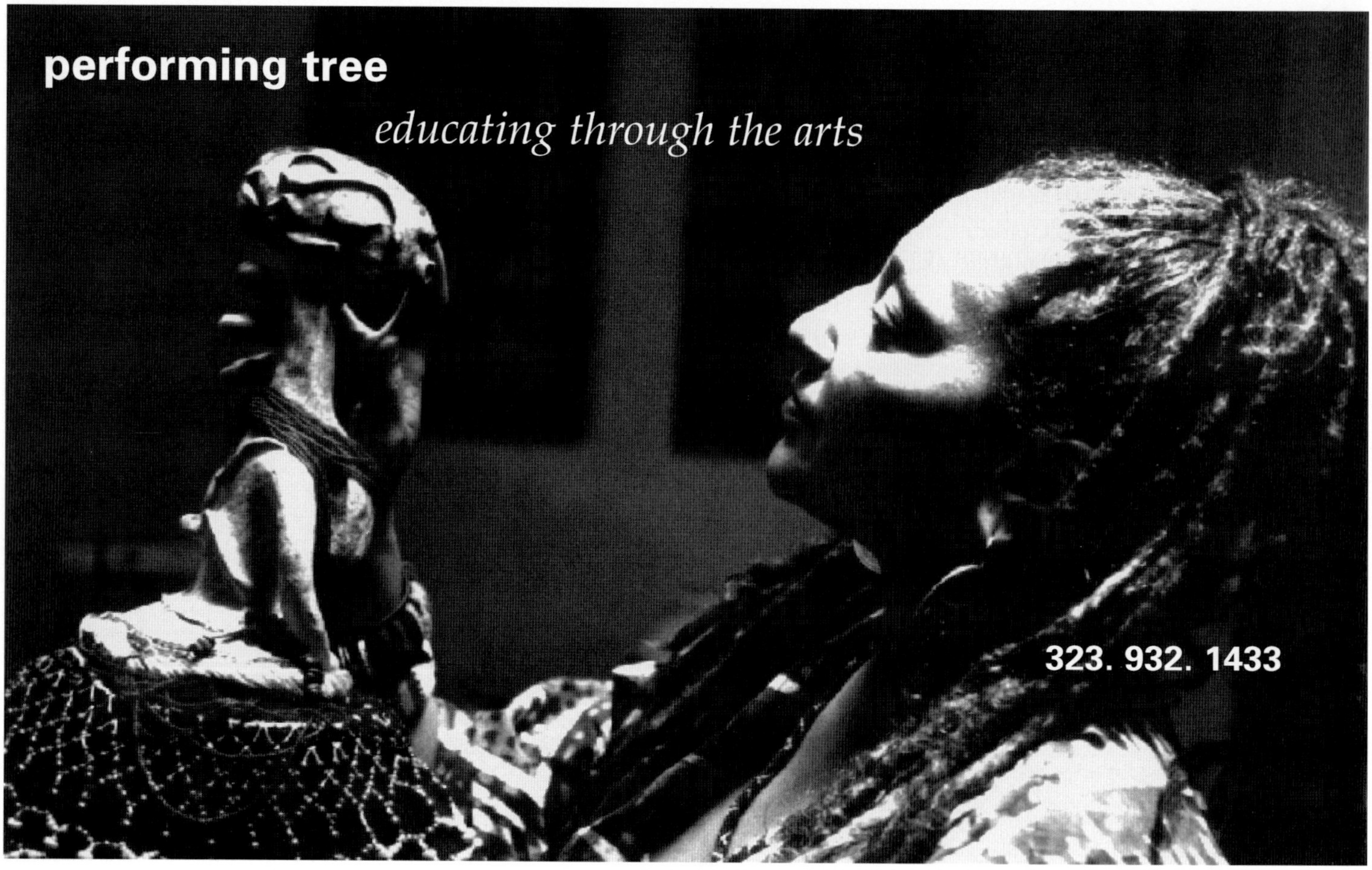

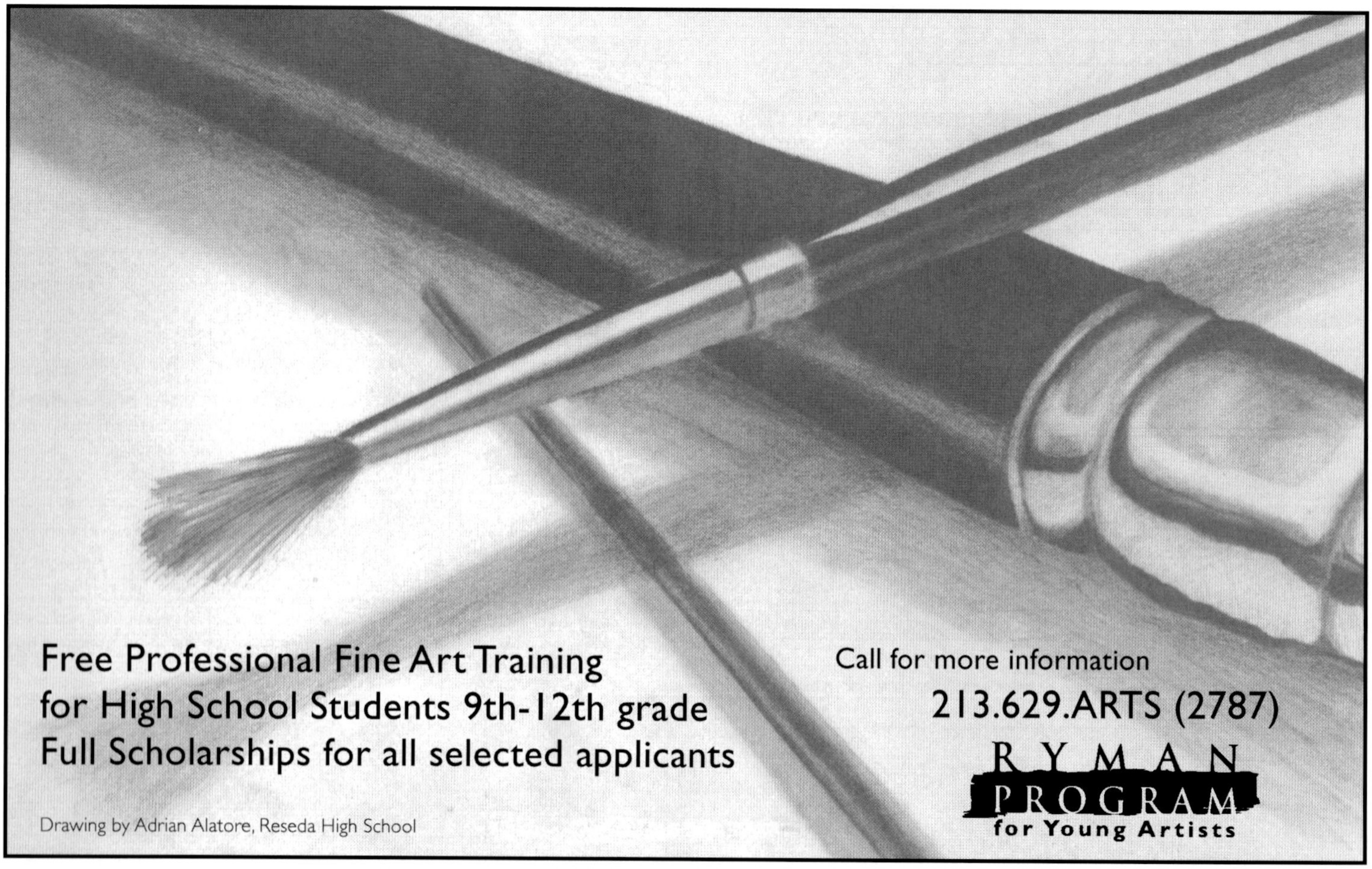

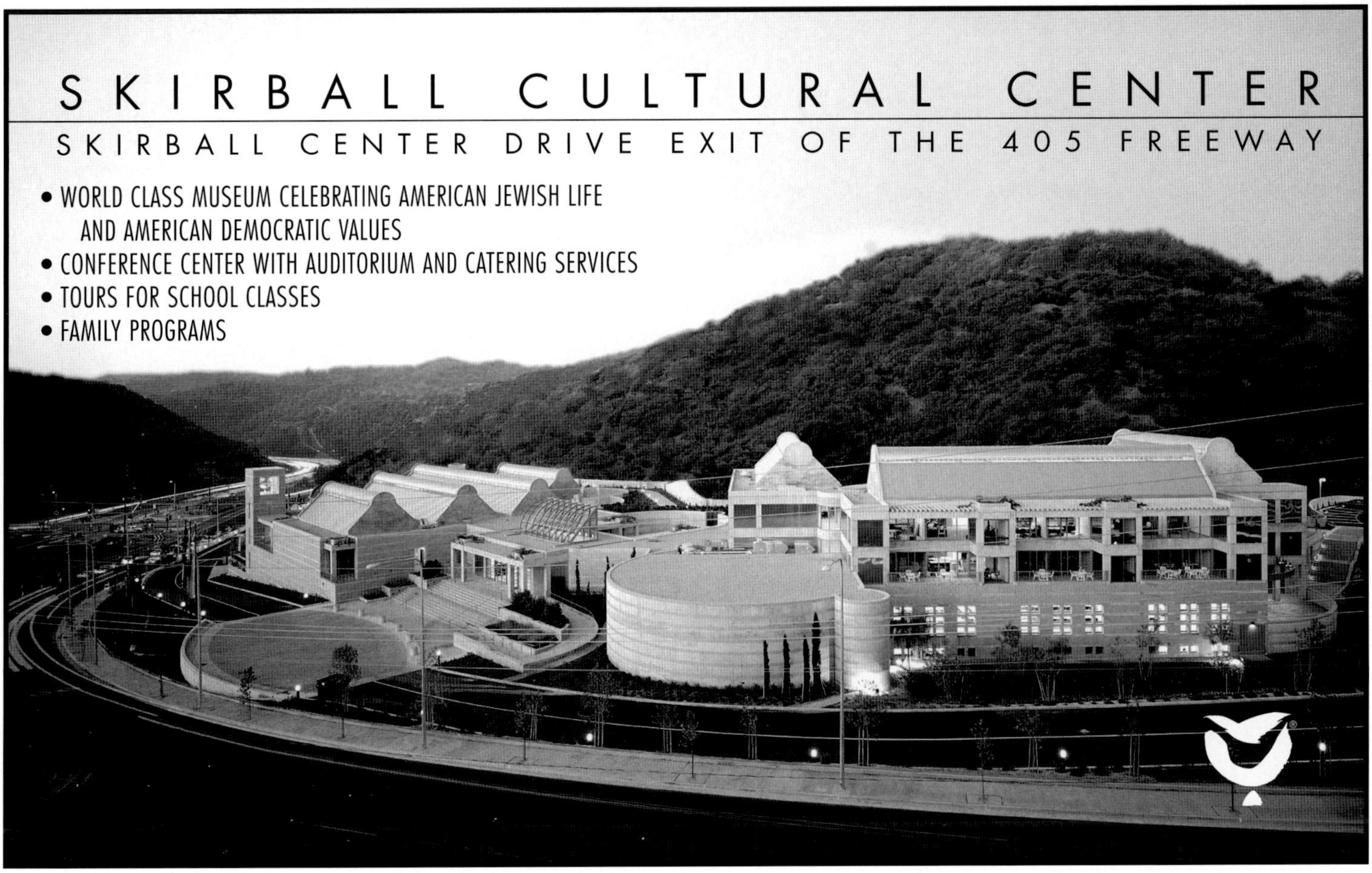

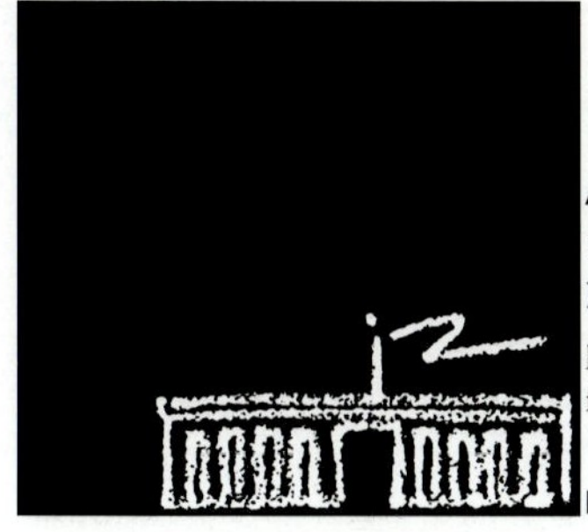

Armory Center for the Arts
145 N. Raymond Ave.
Pasadena, CA 91103
phone: 626.792.5101
fax: 626.449.0139

Programs for Schools

■ **Cultural Traditions/ New Visions:** Field trips to the Armory combining the experience of viewing contemporary art in a professional gallery or traditional art objects from around the world with related art-making studio activities. *Grades 1–12.*

■ **Gallery Tours:** One hour free guided tours led by trained artist/educators through the Armory gallery. *All grades.*

■ **Walk to Art:** Site specific, individually designed after school art classes and artist residencies taught by professional artists for children. *Grades K–8.*

■ **Project FLARE (Fun with Language, Arts and Reading):** An in-school program that brings together classroom teachers and artists to create effective interdisciplinary instruction using both language arts and visual arts. *Grades 5–8.*

■ **Teacher Training:** Specialized in-service workshops for classroom teachers to learn innovative and interactive teaching techniques integrating the arts with other core curriculum.

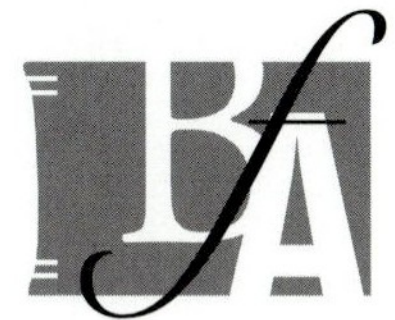

BILINGUAL FOUNDATION OF THE ARTS

THEATRE TEATRO TEATRO PARA LOS NIÑOS **BILINGUAL** THEATRE FOR CHILDREN TEATRO PARA LOS JÓVENES THEATRE FOR YOUNG PEOPLE TEATRO LEÍDO/READER'S THEATRE TRANSLATIONS **THEATRE**

CELEBRATING HISPANIC DRAMA ONE LANGUAGE AT A TIME

323.225.4044
421 North Avenue 19
Los Angeles, California 90031

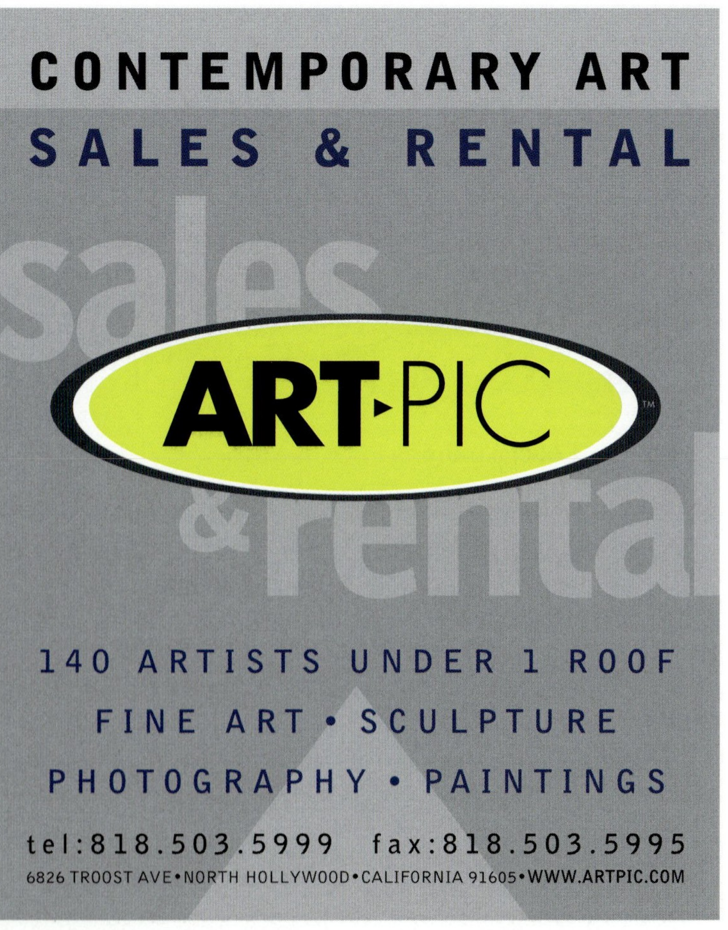

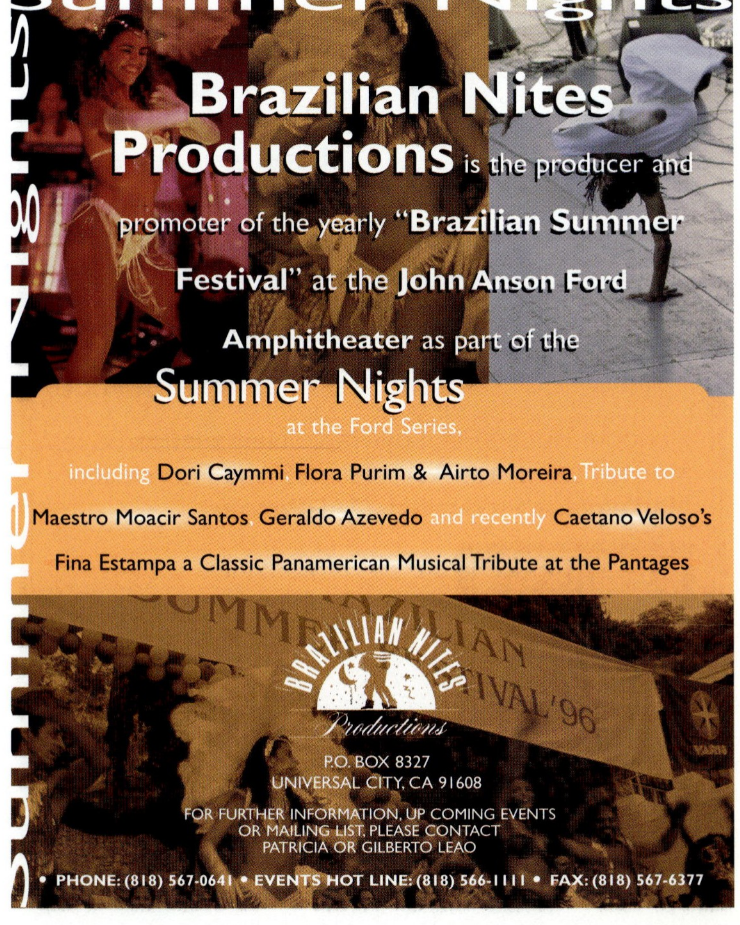

PALOS VERDES ART CENTER (CONTINUED)

The educational programs offer age appropriate instruction, summer/school holiday Arts Camps, and Sunday Family Programs (low-cost children's workshops geared to current exhibitions).

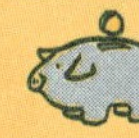

Pre/K-12

PROGRAMS: **Workshops, Studio classes**
SCHEDULE: Year-round, Weekdays, Evenings, Weekends
DETAILS: grades Pre/K-12, Visual & performing arts
Creative Expression, Teacher training programs
(salary points), Facility for school visits
Work with Developmentally disabled, cost for some programs

Youth

PROGRAMS: **Workshops, Classes**
SCHEDULE: Year-round, weekdays, Evenings, Weekends
DETAILS: cost for some programs

Families

PROGRAMS: **Workshops, Classes**
SCHEDULE: Year-round, Weekdays, Evenings

PALOS VERDES PLAYERS

2433 Moreton Street
Torrance, CA 90505
Ph: 310-326-2287
Admin: 310-541-5591
Fax: 310-377-0169
www.falsh.net/~bville/

501(c)3 **SB**

Louis Janicich	Business Director/213-267-5844
Tony Torrisi	Artistic Director/310-391-4488
Roxanne Bettonville	President

Located in Torrance, Palos Verdes Players is a community theatre presenting a diverse selection of quality productions and providing a venue for talented people in all facets of theatre production.

- opportunities for new playwrights to showcase their work
- live performances ranging from classics to modern theatre

Palos Verdes Players offers training in production of theatrical staging, sound, light, and stage mangement.

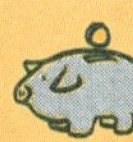

Youth

PROGRAMS: **Performances**
SCHEDULE: year-round, Evenings

PAN AFRICAN FILM FESTIVAL, THE

P.O. Box 2418
Beverly Hills, CA 90213
Ph: 323-295-1706
Fax: 323-295-1952

501(c)3 **DSC**

Ayuko Babu	Executive Director
Asantewa Olatunji	General Manager
Melvonna Ballenger	Student Fest Coordinator
Media Brown	Director of Development

The Pan African Film Festival exhibits over 60 new films made by or about black people and exhibits the works of over 100 prominent and emerging black fine artists.

- major international film festival
- art show
- poetry readings
- panel discussions and seminars
- music concerts
- docent tours
- volunteer opportunities
- fundraiser for social and community organizations
- senior citizen screenings
- fashion shows
- art and dance workshops

We use film to commence discussion on topics important to youth (cultural diversity, literacy, teen pregnancy, and AIDS prevention).

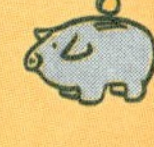

Pre/K-12

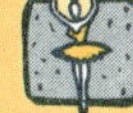

PROGRAMS: **Performances, Workshops, Self-guided tours Guided tours**
SCHEDULE: Winter, Weekdays, Weekends
DETAILS: grades Pre/K-12, Visual & performing arts
Aesthetic valuing, Connections/Relations/Applications
Programs on-site, cost for some programs

Youth

PROGRAMS: **Performances, Workshops, Classes Self-Guided Tours, Guided Tours**
SCHEDULE: Winter, weekdays

Families

PROGRAMS: **Workshops, Classes, Self-Guided Tours Guided Tours**
SCHEDULE: Weekdays, Evenings, Weekends

PANAMANIAN CULTURAL ARTS CENTER OF CALIFORNIA

P.O. Box 207
Canoga Park, CA 91305
Ph: 818-410-1236

501(c)3

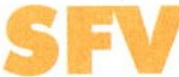

Victor Grimaldo Director vivapanama@earthlink.net

Located in the San Fernando Valley, the Panamanian Cultural Arts Center of California provides a sample of the different faces of the Panamaniam culture through its music, dance, arts and crafts, literature, and painting.

- participates in local and international events organized by government institutions, universities, community organizations, and private institutions

This is the only educational organization that performs dances linked with different periods of history of Panama. This program can be performed in English or Spanish by people well documented about history and dance.

Pre/K-12

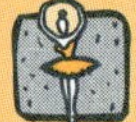 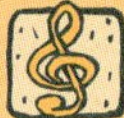 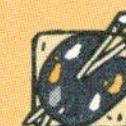

PROGRAMS: **Performances, Workshops, Studio classes**
SCHEDULE: Year-round, Evenings, Weekends
DETAILS: Grades Pre/K-12, History/Soc. Sciences
Visual & Performing Arts, Historical/Cultural Context
Teacher training programs (salary points)
Travel to schools, Educational materials available
Bilingual: Spanish

Youth

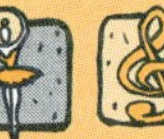 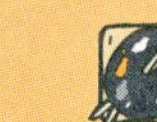

PROGRAMS: **Performances, Workshops, Classes**
SCHEDULE: Year-round, Evenings, Weekends

Families

 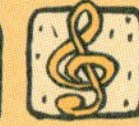 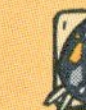

PROGRAMS: **Performances, Workshops, Classes**
SCHEDULE: Year-round, Evenings, Weekends

PARS ART CENTER

7412 Balboa
Van Nuys, CA 91406
Ph: 818-904-0765
Fax: 818-904-0048

501(c)3 SFV

Abdollah Nazemi Artistic Director
Linda Fidell President

Pars Art Center perserves, performs, exhibits, and teaches art and culture. The center fosters intercultural exchanges promoting understanding through art and education.

- 2,000 square foot space for exhibitions and performances
- theater lighting and excellent acoustics
- two 400 square foot studios for rehearsals and classrooms
- friendly, supportive atmosphere and reasonable rates
- capacity for 3/4" videotaping
- library of Iranian dance, music, costumes, pictures, books and folk art
- a big welcome to members of all arts communities

PARS NATIONAL BALLET

7412 Balboa
Van Nuys, CA 91406
Ph: 818-904-0765
Fax: 818-904-0048

SFV

Abdollah Nazemi Artistic Director

Pars National Ballet presents Persian ethnic dance, ballet and ethnic theater.

- programs based on Iranian culture and history
- Persian ethnic dances and costumes
- Persian ballet
- ethnic dance classes to children and adults
- Persian music collection
- taped interviews with expatriated Persian artists
- picture library

PAS D'ASL

P.O. Box 1086
Manhattan Beach, CA 90266
Ph: 310-289-7493
www.pasdasl.com

SB

Mona Jean Cedar Director MonaJeanCedar@pasdasl.com

Pas d'ASl offers performances of original dance choreographed with American Sign Language (ASL) and original spoken word poems composed in ASL. Workshops are given that experiment with the combining of these three communicative arts (dance, ASL, poetry).

Pas d'ASL encourages students to express themselves holistically by thinking in the conceptual nature of ASL to see the whole idea, and then to dance with the whole body, including hands, fingers, face, and voice. The experience of creating and performing physically with dance, mentally with language and spiritually with poetry simultaneously is deeply powerful.

Youth

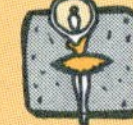

PROGRAMS: **Performances, Workshops**
SCHEDULE: Year-round, Weekdays, Evenings, Weekends

PASADENA ARTS COUNCIL

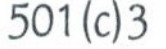

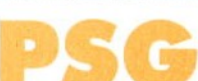

116 Plaza Pasadena
Pasadena, CA 91101
Ph: 626-795-0825
Fax: 626-795-1009

501(c)3 PSG

Kelly Crowe	Membership Coordinator
Barbara Cole	Executive Director

Located on the Green Street side of the Plaza Pasadena across from the Pasadena Civic Auditorium and the Convention Center, the Pasadena Arts Council is an information center for arts and culture in the northwest San Gabriel Valley.

- monthly calendar of cultural events
- monthly art exhibits
- meeting facilities
- mail drop and fiscal receivership services
- Spring and Fall fine art and crafts fairs
- "Guide to Cultural Resources" publication
- telephone/in-office referrals to cultural resources and arts & cultural events
- sponsor of intorductory, multi-disciplinary art education program for elementary school children

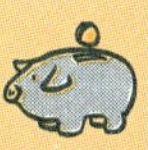

The Children's Center for the Arts program provides classes to every third and fourth grade student in participating Pasadena Unified School District elementary schools. Participation is part of the students' educational experience to awaken creative thought processes, interest in the arts and greater feelings of self-worth.

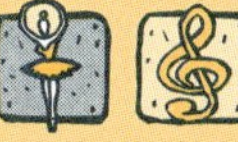

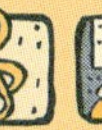

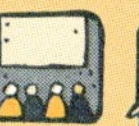

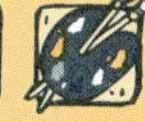

Pre/K-12

PROGRAMS: **PERFORMANCES, WORKSHOPS, STUDIO CLASSES**
SCHEDULE: SPRING, FALL, WINTER, WEEKDAYS
DETAILS: GRADES 3-4, VISUAL & PERFORMING ARTS
CREATIVE EXPRESSION, FACILITY FOR SCHOOL VISITS
BILINGUAL : SPANISH

PASADENA CITY COLLEGE DIVISION OF ART

1570 E. Colorado Boulevard
Pasadena, CA 91106
Ph: 626-585-7238
Fax: 626-585-7914
www.paccd.cc.ca.us

PSG

Mark Wallace	Public Information Officer/626-585-7315
Linda Malm	Dean, Art Department

A California Community College with an exceptionally highly regarded Division of Art. Over 100 sections offered each semester. Our instructors are committed to the teaching/learning process, actively involved in their specialized field, and exceptionally accomplished professionally.

- concentrations in Studio art, Ceramics, Design, Art History, Photography and Cinematography
- Artist-in-Residency program
- sculpture Garden
- computer Lab
- gallery

PASADENA CONSERVATORY OF MUSIC

845 Atchison Street
Pasadena, CA 91104
Ph: 626-798-9426
Fax: 626-798-9487
www.home.earthlink.net/~pasmusic/

501(c)3 PSG

Beverly Lafontaine	Director of Community Relations/Marketing
Stephen McCurry	Executive Director
Karen Smith	Registrar

Located in two historical California bungalows, the Pasadena Conservatory of Music is a pre-college school of music providing instruction to 800 students per year, from toddlers to adults.

- music for young children (toddler-6)
- individual instrumental instruction
- performance classes
- elementary string orchestra
- middle school coaching
- student recitals
- faculty recitals
- volunteer opportunities
- Mansions, Music, and Cabarets— unique performances in unique settings

Music is for everyone. Pasadena Music Conservatory works from the premise that music education is a necessary and vital part of life and should be available to all who want it.

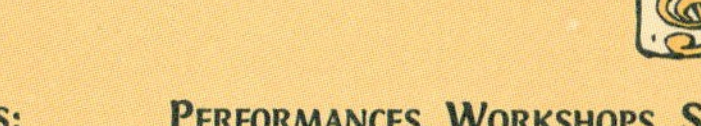

Pre/K-12

PROGRAMS: **PERFORMANCES, WORKSHOPS, STUDIO CLASSES**
SCHEDULE: YEAR-ROUND, WEEKDAYS, EVENINGS, WEEKENDS
DETAILS: GRADES PRE/K-12, VISUAL & PERFORMING ARTS
CREATIVE EXPRESSION, INDIVIDUALLY TAILORED PROGRAMS

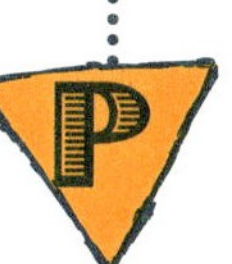

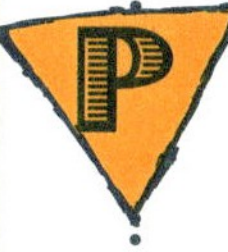

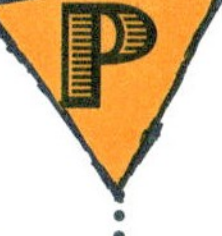

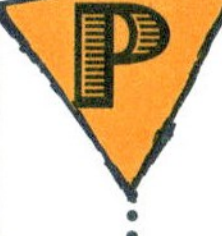

Youth

PROGRAMS: **PERFORMANCES, WORKSHOPS, CLASSES**
SCHEDULE: YEAR-ROUND, WEEKDAYS, EVENINGS, WEEKENDS

Families

PROGRAMS: **PERFORMANCES**
SCHEDULE: YEAR-ROUND, EVENINGS, WEEKENDS

PASADENA CROWN CITY CHORUS

Michelinda Presbyterian Church
225 S. Hill Avenue
Pasadena, CA 91106-3402
Ph: 626-797-6075

501(c)3 PSG

Len Gold	Public Relations Chair	goldcrest/@juno.com
Joan King	Chorus Director	
Clyde Yocum	President/ 626-449-2882	
Jack Wheatley	Past President/ 909-593-4321	

The Pasadena Crown City Chorus performs sing-outs for various organizations including fundraisers at restaurants or community centers. Our music is geared to all age groups.

- live performances

PASADENA CROWN CITY CHORUS (CONTINUED)

The educational programs encourage appreciation for our form of singing.

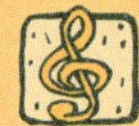

Pre/K-12

PROGRAMS: PERFORMANCES
DETAILS: GRADES PRE/K-12, VISUAL & PERFORMING ARTS
CREATIVE EXPRESSION

Families

PROGRAMS: PERFORMANCES

PASADENA CULTURAL PLANNING, CITY OF

175 N. Garfield Avenue
Pasadena, CA 91109
Ph: 626-744-6770
Fax: 626-793-5937
www.ci.pasadena.ca.us/arts

PSG

Rochelle Branch   Public Arts Coordinator/ 626-744-6915

The City of Pasadena Cultural Planning Division serves as the administrative arm for city-sponsored arts and cultural programming and activities.

- quarterly exhibitions
- Pasadena Art Space at One Colorado
- music concerts
- performance events
- artists in the schools
- community Arts Partnership
- public art projects
- artist and arts organization mailing list maintenance
- archive of public art in Pasadena
- website--virtual tour of public art in Pasadena

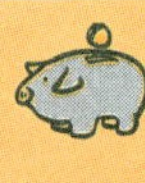

Artists in the Schools program provides opportunities for artists to work with young people at participating schools in the Pasadena area. Artists and arts organizations may apply for up to $10,000 which is matched $1 for $1 from the school.

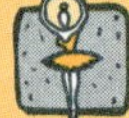
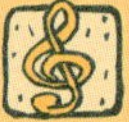
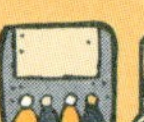

Pre/K-12

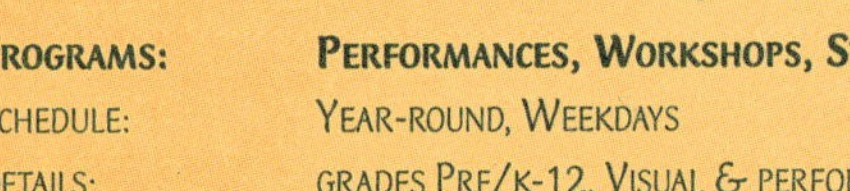

PROGRAMS: PERFORMANCES, WORKSHOPS, STUDIO CLASSES
SCHEDULE: YEAR-ROUND, WEEKDAYS
DETAILS: GRADES PRE/K-12, VISUAL & PERFORMING ARTS
CREATIVE EXPRESSION, HISTORICAL/CULTURAL CONTEXT
CONNECTIONS/RELATIONS/APPLICATIONS
TRAVEL TO SCHOOLS, FILM AND VIDEO

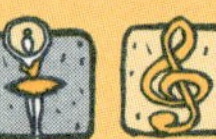
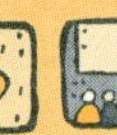
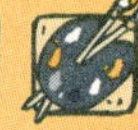

Youth

PROGRAMS: PERFORMANCES, WORKSHOPS, CLASSES
SCHEDULE: YEAR-ROUND, WEEKDAYS

PASADENA PLAYHOUSE

39 S. El Molino Avenue   501(c)3
Pasadena, CA 91101
Ph: 626-792-8672
Fax: 626-792-7343
www.pasadenaplayhouse.com

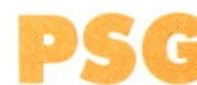

Lars Hansen   Executive Director/ x201   lhansen@PasadenaPlayhouse.com
Sheldon Epps   Artistic Director/ x283

The Pasadena Playhouse is the state theater of California founded in 1917 by Silmor Brown. This 686-seat historical landmark building is listed on the national register of historic places.

- annual season of 6 plays or musicals which give 306 performances, playing

PASADENA POPS ORCHESTRA

20 S. Altadena Drive   501(c)3
Pasadena, CA 91107
Ph: 626-792-7677
Admin: 626-792-POPS
Fax: 626-792-3410

PSG

Lori Baumann   Office Manger   Pops@mail.serve.com
Lucas Richman   Principal Conductor
Trudi Benford   Executive Director

The Pasadena POPS Orchestra presents a 5-concert summer series of pops and light classical at Descanso Gardens in La Cañada, and also presents special concerts throughout the year.

- Summer Picnic Concert Series at Descanso Gardens
- children's concerts and carnival
- Winter Concert Series
- annual fundraiser/gala
- Volunteer Guild and youth volunteer opportunities

PASADENA PRESBYTERIAN CHURCH

585 E. Colorado Boulevard   501(c)3
Pasadena, CA 91101
Ph: 626-568-2608
Admin: 626-793-2191
Fax: 626-584-6544
www.PPC.net

PSG

Anita Protich   Secretary
Gregory Norton   Minister of Music   ggnorton@earthlink.net

Located in the Playhouse District of downtown Pasadena, Pasadena Presbyterian Church is a busy performing venue for community-based ensembles and church-sponsored concerts.

- choral/orchestral concerts
- weekly music at noon concerts (Wednesdays at 12:10)
- organ recitals
- visiting ensembles
- choirs for all ages, open to all

PASADENA SHAKESPEARE COMPANY, THE

Suite 296 The Plaza Pasadena 501(c)3 **PSG**
300 E. Colorado Boulevard
Pasadena, CA 91109
Ph: 626-564-8564
www.home.earthlink.net/~psc2000

Gillian Bagwell	Artistic Director
David Paul Needles	Associate Director

The Pasadena Shakespeare Company (PSC)is a nonprofit professional theater presenting the works of Shakespeare and other playwrights. The PSC has a resident acting company.

- five productions each year
- readings
- workshops and classes

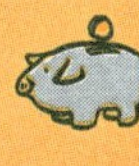

The PSC offers groups discounts to its performances for schools. Many groups participate in post-performance discussions with the actors. The PSc aims to make its performances accessible to young audiences who have not attended a Shakespeare play.

Pre/K-12

PROGRAMS:	**PERFORMANCES, WORKSHOPS**
SCHEDULE:	YEAR-ROUND, WEEKDAYS, EVENINGS, WEEKENDS
DETAILS:	COST FOR SOME PROGRAMS

Youth

PROGRAMS:	**PERFORMANCES, WORKSHOPS**
SCHEDULE:	YEAR-ROUND, WEEKDAYS, EVENINGS, WEEKENDS
DETAILS:	COST FOR SOME PROGRAMS

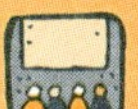

Families

PROGRAMS:	**PERFORMANCES**
SCHEDULE:	YEAR-ROUND, WEEKDAYS, EVENINGS, WEEKENDS

PATRICIA CORREIA GALLERY

Bergamot Station **WS**
2525 Michigan Avenue, Space E2
Santa Monica, CA 90404
Ph/Fax: 310-264-1762

Patricia Correia	Gallery Director/Owner

The gallery is committed to providing a forum for contemporary artists to reach the public and make a difference through the ideas generated from fine art. The gallery represents 15-20 artists— emerging, mid-career, and established. In its choice of artwork to exhibit, the gallery responds to innovative, well conceived and mature creative talent, regardless of the artist's chosen medium.

PAUL KOPEIKIN GALLERY

138 N. La Brea Avenue **HSM**
Los Angeles, CA 90036-2912
Ph: 323-937-0765
Fax: 323-937-5974
www.paulkopeikingallery.com

Pilar Graves	Associate Director	pkgallery@aol.com
Paul Kopeikin	Director	

Fine art photography representing California Pictorialism and Modernism.

PAUL MORSE PRODUCTIONS

P.O. Box 5331 **PSG**
West Covina, CA 91791
Ph: 626-576-0040
Admin: 323-256-3236

Susan Devlin	Programs Director
Jaime Ferrar	Artistic Director
Berta Stevens	Executive Director

Since 1980, Paul Morse Productions has been dedicated to the interests of bringing high quality, live theater to audiences of all ages.

Cultural awareness, historical significance, and bringing great literature to life are the focus of our four unique programs. The programs are suitable for audiences of all ages.

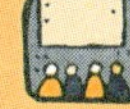

Pre/K-12

PROGRAMS:	**PERFORMANCES, WORKSHOPS**
SCHEDULE:	YEAR-ROUND, WEEKDAYS, EVENINGS, WEEKENDS
DETAILS:	GRADES PRE/K-12, HISTORY/SOC. SCIENCES VISUAL & PERFORMING ARTS, MULTICULTURAL CREATIVE EXPRESSION, TRAVEL TO SCHOOLS EDUCATIONAL MATERIALS AVAILABLE, BILINGUAL: SPANISH

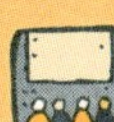

Youth

PROGRAMS:	**PERFORMANCES, WORKSHOPS**
SCHEDULE:	YEAR-ROUND, WEEKDAYS, EVENINGS, WEEKENDS

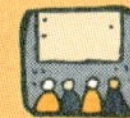

Families

PROGRAMS:	**PERFORMANCES**
SCHEDULE:	YEAR-ROUND, WEEKDAYS, EVENINGS, WEEKENDS

PEN CENTER USA WEST

672 S. Lafayette Park Place, #41 501(c)3
Los Angeles, CA 90057
Ph: 213-365-8500
Fax: 213-365-9616

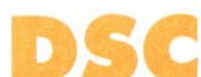

Christina Apeles	Coordinator of Membership/Literary Awards
Sherrill Britton	Executive Director
Sarah Jacobus	Program Coordinator
Larry Siems	Freedom to Write Director

PEN Center USA West is a professional writers organization that fosters a vital literary culture in the West and defends freedom of expression.

- readings
- pragmatic seminars for writers

"PEN in the Classroom" brings writers into high school classrooms for ten to twelve creative writing workshops.

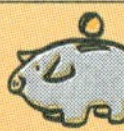

Pre/K-12

PROGRAMS:	**WORKSHOPS**
SCHEDULE:	YEAR-ROUND, WEEKDAYS
DETAILS:	GRADES 9-12, LANGUAGE ARTS, TRAVEL TO SCHOOLS INDIVIDUALLY TAILORED PROGRAMS

PEPPERDINE UNIVERSITY CENTER FOR THE ARTS

24255 Pacific Coast Highway 501(c)3
Malibu, CA 90263-4594
Ph: 310-456-4594
Educ: 310-456-4055
Fax: 310-456-4556
www.pepperdine.edu

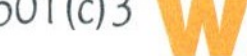
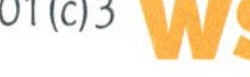

Brad Cope	Marketing-Publicity Manager/ARTSReach Coordinator
Marnie Mitze	Managing Director
Linda Ball	Office Manager

The Pepperdine University Center for the Arts is located on the spectacular Malibu campus, includes Smothers Theatre, Raitt Recital Hall and the Frederick R. Weisman Museum of Art.

- host to over 250 public events
- performances and exhibitions by international entertainers and visual artists
- student productions
- exhibitions and performances by community groups such as the Malibu Ballet Society, Children's Theatre Experience and the Malibu Art Association

PEPPERDINE UNIVERSITY CENTER FOR THE ARTS (CONTINUED)

Pepperdine's ARTSReach Program works in partnership with Crossroads Community Foundation's PS Arts Program. From PS Arts, students receive music, theatre, dance and art instruction. Pepperdine's program supplements their classroom work with free performances and exhibitions by world-class artists on Pepperdine's campus.

Pre/K-12

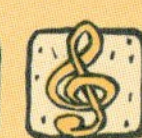
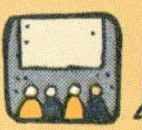
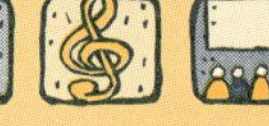
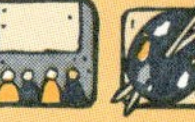

PROGRAMS:	**PERFORMANCES**
SCHEDULE:	SPRING, FALL, WINTER, WEEKDAYS, WEEKENDS
DETAILS:	GRADES PRE/K-6, VISUAL & PERFORMING ARTS AESTHETIC VALUING, CREATIVE EXPRESSION

Youth

PROGRAMS:	**WORKSHOPS**
SCHEDULE:	SPRING, FALL, WINTER, WEEKDAYS, WEEKENDS

Families

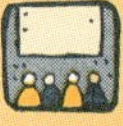

PROGRAMS:	**PERFORMANCES**
SCHEDULE:	SPRING, FALL, WINTER, WEEKENDS
DETAILS:	COST FOR SOME PROGRAMS

PERFORMING ARTS FOR LIFE AND EDUCATION FOUNDATION

6425 Hollywood Boulevard, Suite 300 501(c)3
Hollywood, CA 90028
Ph: 323-463-8236
Fax: 310-604-3324

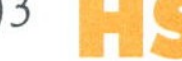

Charles Douglass	Artistic Director
Michael Barnes	Executive Director

Performing Arts for Life and Education Foundation trains young people in all aspects of the perfoming arts disciplines.

- after-school and summer arts training
- two shows annually
- tour all summer long
- assembly programs
- master classes using the work of Shakespeare as a conduit

We are unique in that we allow the youth participants to create and perform their own works based on Shakespeare. We are multi-cultural and we seek to provide college scholarships for our participants.

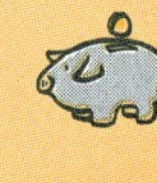

Pre/K-12

PROGRAMS:	**PERFORMANCES**
SCHEDULE:	YEAR-ROUND, WEEKDAYS
DETAILS:	CREATIVE EXPRESSION, TRAVEL TO SCHOOLS

Youth

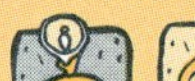
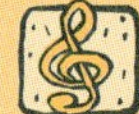
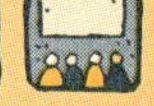

PROGRAMS:	**PERFORMANCES, WORKSHOPS, CLASSES**
SCHEDULE:	YEAR-ROUND, WEEKDAYS, WEEKENDS

PERFORMING TREE

4201 Wilshire Boulevard, Suite 407 501(c)3 **HSM**
Los Angeles, CA 90010
Ph: 323-932-1433
Fax: 323-932-1542

Frances Carrillo — Associate Director/ x19
Laurie Schell — Executive Director/ x12
Leslie Johnson — Director of Education Programs/ x16

The mission of Performing Tree is to educate through the arts, believing that the arts have the power to inform, enrich, and transform the learning experience for every individual.

Through strong and ongoing collaborations with artists, educators, community organizations, social service providers, and families, Performing Tree's performances, workshops, and multi-day residencies serve to spark imaginations and unlock creative spirits, encouraging every learner to reach for success.

Pre/K-12

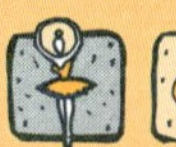
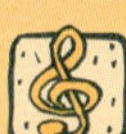
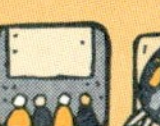
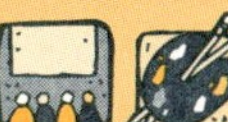

PROGRAMS: PERFORMANCES, WORKSHOPS, RESIDENCIES, GUIDED TOURS
SCHEDULE: YEAR-ROUND, WEEKDAYS
DETAILS: GRADES PRE/K-12, HISTORY/SOC. SCIENCES
VISUAL & PERFORMING ARTS, LANGUAGE ARTS
MULTICULTURAL, CREATIVE EXPRESSION
HISTORICAL/CULTURAL CONTEXT
CONNECTIONS/RELATIONS/APPLICATIONS
TEACHER TRAINING PROGRAMS, TRAVEL TO SCHOOLS
INDIVIDUALLY TAILORED PROGRAMS, EDUCATIONAL MATERIALS
BILINGUAL: SPANISH, WORK WITH AT-RISK & SPECIAL NEEDS

Youth

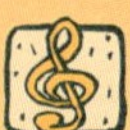
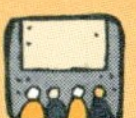
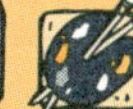

PROGRAMS: PERFORMANCES, WORKSHOPS, RESIDENCIES, GUIDED TOURS
SCHEDULE: YEAR-ROUND, WEEKDAYS, EVENINGS, WEEKENDS
DETAILS: NO COST FOR SOME PROGRAMS

Families

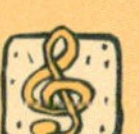
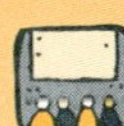
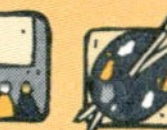

PROGRAMS: PERFORMANCES, WORKSHOPS, RESIDENCIES
SCHEDULE: YEAR-ROUND, WEEKDAYS, EVENINGS, WEEKENDS
DETAILS: NO COST FOR SOME PROGRAMS

PERSONALIZED TRAVEL

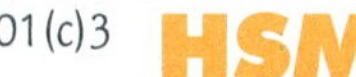

5455 Sylmar Avenue, Suite 902 **SFV**
Sherman Oaks, CA 91401
Ph: 818-994-2402

Roberta Kritzia — Owner

Personalized Travel organizes sketching/painting trips on location in Italy. This is a unique opportunity to visit and paint the hidden medieval hilltowns of Umbria, Tuscany and the Venice regions.

- painting and sketching in small groups with well known art teachers such as Corrine Hartly, Glenn Villpu and Glen Knowles
- opportunity to visit Italian artists' and craftsmen's studios in combination with the production of their own artwork while sampling the regional cuisine and wine of Italy
- daily art demos and critiques
- all services such as hotels, transportation and most meals are provided by Personalized Travel
- bilingual travel guides

PETER FETTERMAN GALLERY

Bergamot Station **WS**
2525 Michigan Avenue- Building B
Santa Monica, CA 90404
Ph: 310-453-6463
Fax: 310-453-6959

Peter Fetterman — Director — pfgallery@earthlink.net

Gallery - Contemporary fine art photography

PETER MEREMBLUM YOUTH ORCHESTRAS

4420 Boston Avenue 501(c)3 **WS**
La Crescenta, CA 91214
Ph: 818-249-1285

Ginny Atherton — Music Director

Meeting Saturdays in West Hollywood, young musicians ages 8-18 are trained in Orchestra, Chamber Music and theory.

- master classes
- opportunities for talented and disciplined youth

Youth

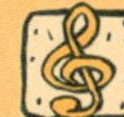

PROGRAMS: CLASSES
SCHEDULE: YEAR-ROUND, WEEKENDS

PETERSEN AUTOMOTIVE MUSEUM

6060 Wilshire Boulevard 501(c)3 **HSM**
Los Angeles, CA 90036
Ph: 323-930-CARS
Admin: 323-964-6356
Educ: 323-964-6347
Fax: 323-930-6642
www.peterson.org

Dave Linden — Public Relations Manager/ 323-964-6344
Leslie Kendall — Curatorial Manager/ 323-964-6340
Ken Gross — Director
Helen Praks — Education Coordinator

Located in the heart of Los Angeles' famed Miracle Mile, the Petersen Automotive Museum is one of the world's largest and most innovative automotive museums. Three floors of automotive history take the visitor through time and trace the development of the automobile and its influence on the culture of Los Angeles.

- five rotating galleries with over 150 historical, classic and fantasy vehicles
- interactive exhibits
- May Family Children's Discovery Center
- teacher preview nights
- penthouse conference center available for corporate or private functions
- volunteer opportunities

The 6,500 square-foot May Family Discover Center is designed to spark children's interest in science through the automobile. Teacher preview nights help integrate classroom curriculum with a museum visit. Reservations required for school groups.

Pre/K-12

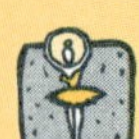
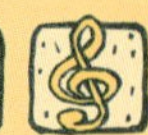
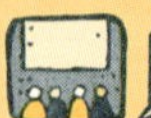
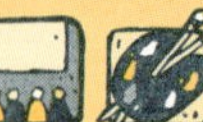

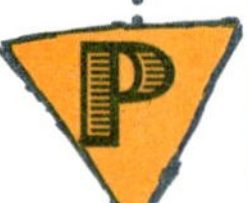

PROGRAMS: GUIDED TOURS
SCHEDULE: YEAR-ROUND, WEEKDAYS
DETAILS: GRADES 3-12, VISUAL & PERFORMING ARTS
CREATIVE EXPRESSION, HISTORICAL/CULTURAL CONTEXT
FACILITY FOR SCHOOL VISITS
INDIVIDUALLY TAILORED PROGRAMS, EDUCATIONAL MATERIALS

Youth

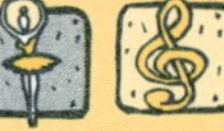
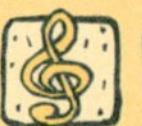
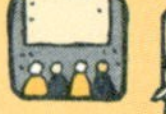

PROGRAMS: GUIDED TOURS
SCHEDULE: YEAR-ROUND, WEEKDAYS, WEEKENDS

Families

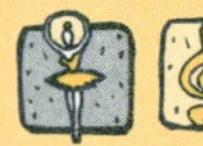
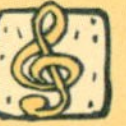
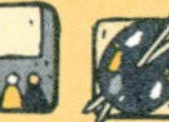

PROGRAMS: GUIDED TOURS
SCHEDULE: YEAR-ROUND, WEEKDAYS, WEEKENDS

PETTERSON MUSEUM OF INTERCULTURAL ART AT PILGRIM PLACE, THE (CONTINUED)

730 Plymouth Road 501(c)3 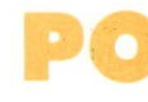

Claremont, CA 91711
Ph: 909-399-5544

Sandra Tygum — Museum Coordinator

Located at Pilgrim Place in Claremont, the Petterson Museum fulfills today's need for a center devoted to developing an awareness of diverse cultures and appreciation of "arts of the people".

- changing exhibits of intercultural arts and from our permanent collection
- docent tours
- volunteer opportunities
- monthly lectures
- annual "Spring Celebration of the Arts"
- two-day Fall festival in conjunction with Pilgrim Places
- special tours can be arranged
- free admission to museum and events
- FRIENDS membership available

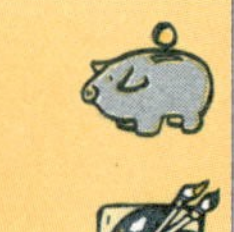

Families

PROGRAMS: SELF-GUIDED TOURS, GUIDED TOURS
SCHEDULE: YEAR-ROUND, WEEKENDS

PHANTOM PROJECTS EDUCATIONAL THEATRE GROUP

P.O. Box 250 **ELA**
La Mirada, CA 90637-0250
Ph: 562-902-0019
Fax: 562-943-0869

Steve Cisneros — Owner/Executive Producer — PhantomProjects@prodigy.net

Phantom Projects is owned by and features high school and college students who bring educational messages to students across Southern California. The program travels to middle/high school, churches and youth conferences.

PHANTOM PROJECTS EDUCATIONAL THEATRE GROUP (CONTINUED)

Phantom Projects provides three different programs on abstinence education, drug and alcohol prevention and equality among the races. All programs incorporate live theater, silde presentations and open-forum discussions. All shows written by award winning teacher turned playwright Bruce Gevirtzman.

Pre/K-12

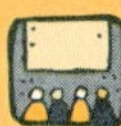

PROGRAMS:	**PERFORMANCES, WORKSHOPS**
SCHEDULE:	YEAR-ROUND, WEEKDAYS, EVENINGS, WEEKENDS
DETAILS:	GRADES 5-6, DRUGS/ALCOHOL PREVENTION, ABSTINENCE EDUCATION, HISTORICAL/CULTURAL CONTEXT MULTICULTURAL, TRAVEL TO SCHOOLS FACILITY FOR SCHOOL VISITS, EDUCATIONAL MATERIALS

Youth

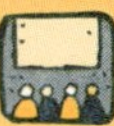

PROGRAMS:	**PERFORMANCES, WORKSHOPS**
SCHEDULE:	YEAR-ROUND, WEEKDAYS, EVENINGS, WEEKENDS

Families

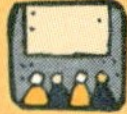

PROGRAMS:	**PERFORMANCES, WORKSHOPS**
SCHEDULE:	YEAR-ROUND, WEEKDAYS, EVENINGS, WEEKENDS

PICO RIVERA CENTRE FOR THE ARTS

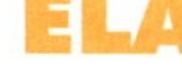

9200 Mines Avenue
Pico Rivera, CA 90660
Ph: 562-801-4300
Admin: 562-801-4430
Fax: 562-801-0671

Annette Johnson	Manager Public Art, Cultural Planning and Marketing
Cindy-Lu Gans	Director Recreation and Community Service

The Pico Rivera Centre for the Arts is a working gallery that offers a minimum of four exhibitions per year and four 8-10 week art instruction workshops.

- summer concert series
- art instruction
- gallery exhibits

PICO RIVERA CENTRE FOR THE ARTS (CONTINUED)

The Pico Rivera Centre for the Arts programs have small class sizes, experienced art instructors, a convenient location and a friendly atmosphere.

Pre/K-12

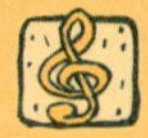
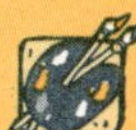

PROGRAMS:	**STUDIO CLASSES**
SCHEDULE:	YEAR-ROUND
DETAILS:	GRADES 5-12, VISUAL & PERFORMING ARTS CREATIVE EXPRESSION, HISTORICAL/CULTURAL CONTEXT TRAVEL TO SCHOOLS, FACILITY FOR SCHOOL VISITS

Youth

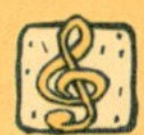
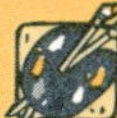

PROGRAMS:	**CLASSES**
SCHEDULE:	YEAR-ROUND, EVENINGS, WEEKENDS

Families

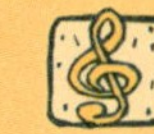
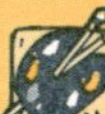

PROGRAMS:	**CLASSES**
SCHEDULE:	YEAR-ROUND, EVENINGS, WEEKENDS

PIERCE COLLEGE ART GALLERY

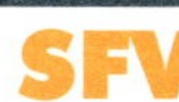

6201 Winnetka Avenue
Woodland Hills, CA 91371
Ph: 818-719-6498
saulart@worldnet.att.net

PLATT GALLERY, UNIVERSITY OF JUDAISM

WS

15600 Mulholland Drive
Los Angeles, CA 90077
Ph: 310-476-9777
Fax: 310-471-1278

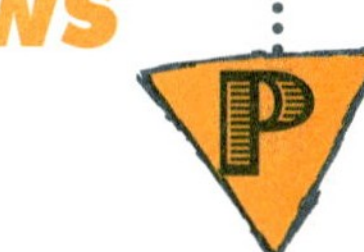

Judith Samuel	Gallery Coordinator/ x276

The Platt Gallery exhibits the work of local and international contemporary and modern artists with an emphasis on Judaica and other multicultural areas. The gallery is located on the University of Judaism and provides outreach through special forums and exhibition related events.

PLAYWRIGHTS' KITCHEN ENSEMBLE

501(c)3 WS

368 N. La Cienega Boulevard
Los Angeles, CA 90048
Ph: 310-652-9602
Fax: 310-652-6401

Lynne McCreary	General Manager/ 310-652-9955
Dan Lauria	Artistic Director
Ted Rawlins	Executive Director/ 310-652-9955

The mission of the Playwrights' Kitchen Ensemble is to develop, promote, and produce new works by American playwrights and to nurture and encourage artistic voices.

- weekly readings of new plays, free to the public
- classes in acting and writing
- internships in arts administration and production

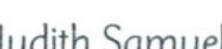

PLAZA DE LA RAZA

3540 N. Mission Road
Los Angeles, CA 90031
Ph: 323-223-2475
Fax: 323-223-1804
www.plazaraza.org

501(c)3 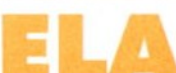

Rose Cano — Executive Director
Maria Jimenez-Torrez — Education Coordinator — mjtorres@plazaraza

Plaza de la Raza is a cultural and educational center which provides cultural, artistic, and educational expression of thoughts, actions, and heritage of the Mexican/Chicano/Latino community for the enrichment of all society through its school of performing and visual arts, workshops, theater performances, and exhibitions for all ages.

- School of Performing and Visual Arts
- Community Arts Partnership
- Summer concerts
- virtual online museum of the Plaza's permanent art collection

School of Performing and Visual Arts (SPVA) provides quality arts education to Los Angeles students. A wide variety of ten-week courses are offered Monday-Friday after school and on Saturdays, in three major disciplines: visual art, dance, music.

Pre/K-12 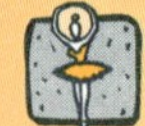 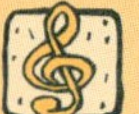 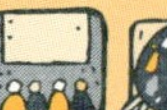

PROGRAMS: **Performances, Workshops, Self-guided tours Guided tours**
SCHEDULE: Year-round, Weekdays
DETAILS: grades Pre/K-12, Visual & performing arts
Creative Expression, Bilingual: Spanish

Youth  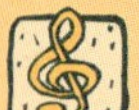 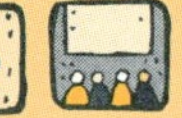  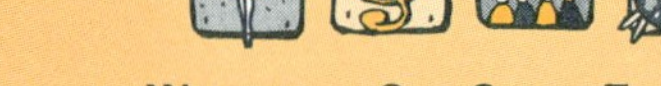

PROGRAMS: **Performances, Workshops, Self-Guided Tours Guided Tours**
SCHEDULE: Year-round, weekdays

Families 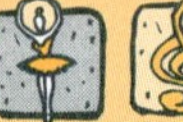 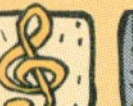 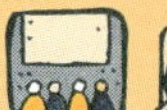 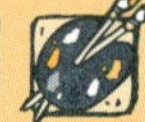

PROGRAMS: **Performances, Workshops, Self-Guided Tours, Guided Tours**
SCHEDULE: Year-round, Weekdays

POETRY SOCIETY OF AMERICA

P.O. Box 3761
Palos Verdes, CA 90274
Ph: 310-669-2369
Admin: 212-254-9628
Fax: 310-514-0302

Elena Burke — Director — ekduende@aol.com

We are the local chapter of the Poetry Society, the oldest national nonprofit poetry organization in the United States offering a broad range of public cultural programs diverse in style and type.

- contests
- occasional library tributes
- poetry in public places
- Poetry in Motion™ (poetry on buses and subways)
- public readings
- bookmark, books, poster sales, and free distribution available
- membership

Pre/K-12

PROGRAMS: **Poetry Performances**
SCHEDULE: Year-round, Weekdays, Evenings, Weekends
DETAILS: grades 9-12, Language arts
Travel to schools , Individually tailored programs
Educational materials, Bilingual : Spanish

POETS & WRITERS, INCORPORATED (CALIFORNIA OFFICE)

580 Washington Street, Suite 308
San Francisco, CA 94111
Ph: 415-986-9577
Fax: 415-986-9575
www.pw.org

501(c)3

Ryan Tranquilla — Program Associate — ryan@pw.org
Karen Clark — Director of California Programs — kc@pw.org

Poets & Writers (P&W) is a nonprofit national service organization dedicated to fostering the professional development of poets and fiction writers, promoting-communication throughout the U.S. literary community, and helping to create an environment in which literature can be appreciated by the widest possible public.

- California Readings/Workshops Program, provides matching fees for poets and fiction writers to give readings and workshops in community settings
- Writers on Site Program, offers short-term residencies for writers in partnership with visual and literary arts organizations in California
- techincal assistance services for literary presenters, includes publications, workshops and individual consultations
- P & W Online offers information about P & W programs, technical assistance information, and online forums for writers

POMONA CULTURAL ARTS COMMISSION

P.O. Box 660
Pomona, CA 91769
Ph: 909-620-2332
Fax: 909-620-2326

PO

Douglas Bridges — Superintendant of Recreation

POST

1904 E. 7th Place
Los Angeles, CA 90021
Ph: 213-488-3379

DSC

Gallery

POWERHOUSE THEATER

3116 2nd Street
Santa Monica, CA 90405
Ph: 310-392-6529
Admin: 310-396-3680

WS

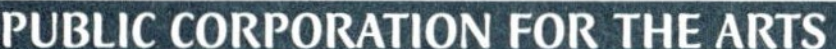

PUBLIC CORPORATION FOR THE ARTS

434 E. Broadway — 501(c)3
Long Beach, CA 90802-4908
Ph: 562-570-1930
Admin: 562-570-1927
Fax: 562-983-3814

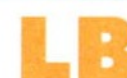

LB

Deborah Robinson	Administrative Coordinator	artpca@aol.com
Jorge Pardo	Director of Visual Art and Design/ 562-570-1924	
Robb Hankins	Executive Director	
Cathy Carpenter	Community Arts and Education Manager	
Wendy Chang	Director, Training and Advancement	

The Public Corportation for the Arts (PCA) is a private, non-profit arts enterprise which supports and promotes the development of diverse artistic and cultural resources in Long Beach and its surrounding regions. Designated by the City of Long Beach as its arts advisory body, the PCA assists over 95 cultural arts organizations and more than 700 emerging, mid-career, and professional artists in the region.

- programs service needs of arts organizations, individual artists in all disciplines, and the community-at-large
- overall promotional and advocacy support
- marketing expertise
- technical assistance

PURPLE CIRCUIT

2025 Griffith Park Boulevard, #4
Los Angeles, CA 90039
323-666-0693

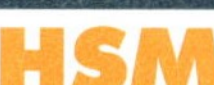

HSM

Bill Kaiser — Coordinator/ 323-661-1982 — purplecir@aol.com

The Purple Circuit promotes gay, lesbian, queer, bi, and transgendered theater and performance throughout the world.

- quarterly newsletter
- directory of venues
- hotline listing current productions in CA (323) 666-0693

RACHEL ROSENTHAL COMPANY, THE

2847 S. Robertson Boulevard — 501(c)3
Los Angeles, CA 90034
Ph: 310-839-0661
Fax: 310-837-4511
www.rachelrosenthal.org

WS

Rochelle Fabb	Publicist/Booking Manager	
Rachel Rosenthal	Artistic Director	
Tad Cougherour	Executive Director	tad@rachelrosenthal.org

The Rachel Rosenthal Company is a renowned, interdisciplinary performance company of actors, dancers, vocalists, video, and visual artists. They perform multi-media and site-specific works under the direction of internationally acclaimed performer Rachel Rosenthal.

- the DBD Experience—a weekend intensive performance workshop in all aspects of improvisional theater (voice, movement, text, set building, lights, sound, and costume)
- an eight-week workshop in advanced performance training to learn improvisational techniques and/or develop your own solo performance
- workshops taught by Company members in prop-driven performance, voice and body integration, butoh, and mind-body movement
- Rachel Rosenthal solo performances and Company performances of full theatrical pieces including: Ur Boor, Timepiece, and The Unexpurgated Virgin
- site-specific performances
- volunteer and intern opportunities (earn college credit)

Rachel Rosenthal has been teaching her heralded brand of improvisational theater training nationally and internationally to students since the 1950's. This creative method is applicable to high school students and adults, actors and artists of all disciplines who seek to cross over into performance.

Youth

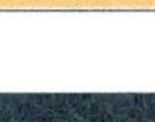

PROGRAMS: PERFORMANCES, WORKSHOPS, RESIDENCIES
SCHEDULE: YEAR-ROUND, EVENINGS, WEEKENDS

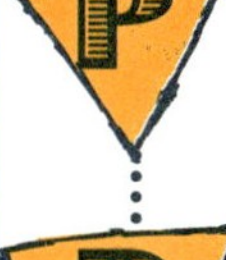

RADICAL CRAFTSMAN GALLERY

365 W. Seventh Street
San Pedro, CA 90731
Ph: 310-521-9012

SB

Contemporary Art/Contemporary Crafts.

RAGTIME ART GALLERY

696 E. Colorado Boulevard, Suite 8
Pasadena, CA 91101
Ph: 626-792-2404
Fax: 626-792-8891

PSG

Kim Ward — Director — ragtimeart@aol.com

RATTLE, A LITERARY JOURNAL

SFV

13440 Ventura Boulevard, #200
Sherman Oaks, CA 91423
Ph: 818-788-3232
Fax: 818-788-2831

Stellasue Lee — Poetry Editor — stellasuel@aol.com
Alan Fox — Editor

Rattle is published in June and December and includes poetry, essays, reviews, and interviews.

RATTLE UP

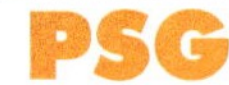

665 E. California Boulevard
Pasadena, CA 91106
Ph: 626-793-4818

Steven Woodruff — Artistic Director

Rattle Up is a traditional English dance company performing with live music. The all male dance company performs dances drawn on the sword dance tradition of Northern England and the Morris of the Welsh/English border.

- live dances with live music
- outdoor performances
- street dancing
- pageants
- audience participation

REMBA GALLERY, THE

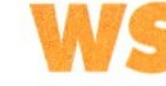

462 N. Robertson Boulevard
Los Angeles, CA 90048
Ph: 310-657-1101
Fax: 310-657-1153

Carl Berg — Associate Director — remba@earthlink.net
Lea Remba — Director

Contemporary American, European, and Latin American artists. Mixografias on handmade paper and sculptures in copper.

REPERCUSSION UNIT

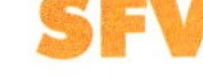

P.O. Box 220808
Newhall, CA 91322
Ph: 805-259-3195
Fax: 805-259-3388
www.smartlink.net/~artskids

Larry Stein — Art Director — kids@smartlink.net
John Bergamo
Gregg Johnson — Education Director

Since 1976, the Repercussion Unit has delighted audiences of all ages in the U.S. and Europe with its eclectic blend of music for found objects and percussion instruments from all over the world.

- concerts
- workshops
- film, dance, and theater scoring

REPERCUSSION UNIT (CONTINUED)

Inspirations & Influences" traces the roots of the Repercussion Unit's music to the traditional music of India, Bali, Africa, the Caribbean, and the United States. The audience discovers connections between the music of these cultures and the ensemble's unique blend of sounds.

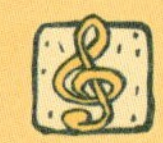

Pre/K-12

PROGRAMS: PERFORMANCES, WORKSHOPS
SCHEDULE: YEAR-ROUND, WEEKDAYS, EVENINGS, WEEKENDS
DETAILS: GRADES PRE/K-12, VISUAL & PERFORMING ARTS
MULTICULTURAL, AESTHETIC VALUING
CREATIVE EXPRESSION, HISTORICAL/CULTURAL CONTEXT
TRAVEL TO SCHOOLS, EDUCATIONAL MATERIALS AVAILABLE

Youth

PROGRAMS: PERFORMANCES, WORKSHOPS
SCHEDULE: YEAR-ROUND, WEEKDAYS, EVENINGS, WEEKENDS

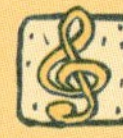

Families

PROGRAMS: PERFORMANCES, WORKSHOPS
SCHEDULE: YEAR-ROUND, WEEKDAYS, EVENINGS, WEEKENDS

RHAPSODY IN TAPS

501 (c)3

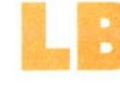

4812 Matney Avenue
Long Beach, CA 90807
714-838-3318
714-838-4660

Kay Davis — Adminstrative Director
Linda Sohl-Donnell — Artistic Director/ 562-428-6411

Rhapsody in Taps is a touring company of seven dancers and five jazz musicians who perform a diverse repertoire of traditional and contemporary choreography.

- rhythm tap dance with live jazz concerts
- children's in-theater lecture/demonstration/mini-performance
- master classes

RICO GALLERY, INC.

WS

208 Pier Avenue
Santa Monica, CA 90405
Ph: 310-399-5353
Fax: 310-399-3534

Julie Rico — President

- monthly exhibitions featuring local artists

RIO HONDO COLLEGE ART GALLERY

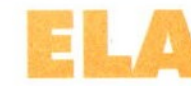

3600 Workman Mill Road
Whittier, CA 90608
Ph: 562-692-0921

RIO HONDO SYMPHONY ASSOCIATION

P.O. Box 495
Whittier, CA 90608
Ph: 562-947-5907

501(c)3

ELA

Dorothea Cummings — Publicity and Advertising Manager
Wayne Reinecke — Conductor and Music Director

The Rio Hondo Symphony is a nonprofit community symphony orchestra that performs four free concerts each season in the Whittier High School Auditorium for the benefit of the entire community.

- four free concerts per season

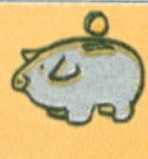

Two musicians give performance-demonstration programs to introduce the students to the instruments of the orchestra. The programs are entertaining and educational, and accent audience particpation. The programs are for fouth and fifth graders.

Pre/K-12

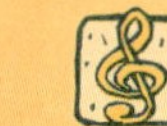

PROGRAMS: **PERFORMANCES**
SCHEDULE: WEEKDAYS
DETAILS: GRADES 3-6, VISUAL & PERFORMING ARTS
TRAVEL TO SCHOOLS, INDIVIDUALLY TAILORED PROGRAMS

RITMO FLAMENCO! Y DANZAS DE ESPAÑA

2946 Francis Avenue
Los Angeles, CA 90005-1505
Ph: 213-382-6928
Fax: 323-851-1194

501(c)3

HSM

Carolyn Berger — Artistic Director

Ritmo Flamenco! is a traditional Spanish dance and music performing company that performs, teaches, and represents Spanish culture in the new world for the L.A. community.

- family and general audience music and dance programs
- master classes in flamenco and related arts for high schools and colleges
- studio instruction in Spanish dance

These programs include colorful costumes, compelling rhythms, and lots of movement. Spanish dance and music have an exotic quality, and flamenco, in particular includes influences from cultures all over the world which appeal to culturally diverse L.A.

Pre/K-12

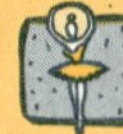
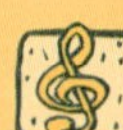

PROGRAMS: **PERFORMANCES**
SCHEDULE: YEAR-ROUND, WEEKDAYS, EVENINGS, WEEKENDS
DETAILS: GRADES PRE/K-12, VISUAL & PERFORMING ARTS
CREATIVE EXPRESSION, HISTORICAL/CULTURAL CONTEXT
TRAVEL TO SCHOOLS

Youth

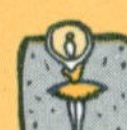
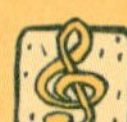

PROGRAMS: **PERFORMANCES, WORKSHOPS, CLASSES**
SCHEDULE: YEAR-ROUND, WEEKDAYS, EVENINGS, WEEKENDS

Families

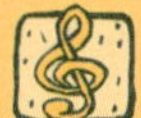

PROGRAMS: **PERFORMANCES, CLASSES**
SCHEDULE: YEAR-ROUND, WEEKDAYS, EVENINGS, WEEKENDS

ROBERT BERMAN GALLERY

2525 Michigan Avenue - Building C
Santa Monica, CA 90404
Ph: 310-315-9506
Admin: 310-453-9195
Fax: 310-315-9508

WS

Robert Berman — Director — berman@cybrport.com

Contemporary artists.

ROBEY THEATRE COMPANY

4444 Riverside Drive, Suite 110
Burbank, CA 91505
Ph: 818-567-3294
Fax: 818-567-3296
www.robeytc.aol.com

501(c)3

SFV

Bennet Guillory — Artistic Director
Lia Johnson — Administrative Assistant

Founded in December 1994 by Danny Glover and Bennet Guillory, Robey Theatre Company (RTC) encourages new plays written about the black experience for the American theater through readings, labs, and productions.

- RTC's Acting Workshop focuses on creating a comfortable work environment and sharpening the actor's awareness through exercises, monologues, and scene work by using different techniques to immerse the actor in the world of the character and scene
- Robey's Playwright's Lab develops new scripts and nurtures playwrights in a workshop setting by giving each playwright a "resource team" (director, actors, etc.) to help explore and strengthen the playwright's intention; a final public reading concludes the workshop, followed by audience discussion

ROCK A MOLE MUSIC

P.O. Box 341305
Los Angeles, CA 90034
Ph: 310-398-4477
Fax: 310-398-8190

WS

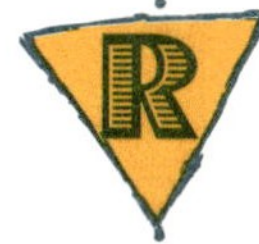

Ernie Perez — Public Information Officer — reztop@aol.com

Rock A Mole Music produces festivals that feature music, art, poetry, and video by or about at-risk youth, the homeless, prisoners, and welfare recipients.

- cultural festivals

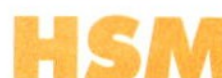
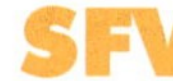

ROCK A MOLE MUSIC (CONTINUED)

Rock A Mole festivals attract a large and broad cross-section of people of all ages, races, and walks of life.

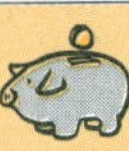

Pre/K-12

 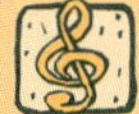 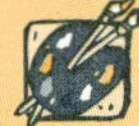

PROGRAMS: PERFORMANCES
SCHEDULE: YEAR-ROUND, WEEKENDS
DETAILS: GRADES PRE/K-12, VISUAL & PERFORMING ARTS
CREATIVE EXPRESSION, BILINGUAL: SPANISH

Youth

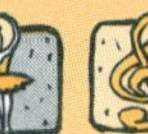 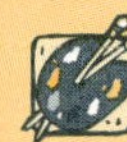

PROGRAMS: PERFORMANCES
SCHEDULE: YEAR-ROUND, WEEKENDS

Families

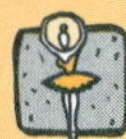 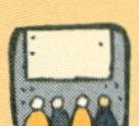 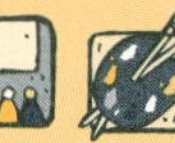

PROGRAMS: PERFORMANCES
SCHEDULE: YEAR-ROUND, WEEKENDS

ROSAMUND FELSEN GALLERY

WS

Bergamot Station B4
2525 Michigan Avenue
Santa Monica, CA 90404
Ph: 310-828-8488
Fax: 310-828-1075
www.strikingdistance.com

Gordon Haines Assistant Director rosamund@gte.net
Rosamund Felsen Owner/Director

The Rosamund Felsen Gallery is a contemporary art gallery that represents artists by exhibiting their work for sale to collectors and museums.

- approximately twelve exhibitions a year that include painting, sculpture, drawings, photography, video, and installation art

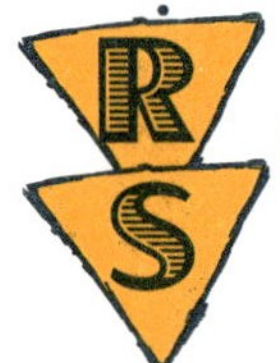

RTKL INTERNATIONAL EXHIBITION GALLERY

DSC

333 S. Hope Street, Suite C200
Los Angeles, CA 90071
Ph: 213-627-7373
Fax: 213-627-9815
www.rtkl.com
aeshelman@la.rtkl.com

RUDY PEREZ/LOS ANGELES

WS

1721 W. 8th Street, #409
Los Angeles, CA 90017
Ph: 213-483-4079

Rudy Perez Artistic Director
Don Bondi Associate/ 213-644-8777

Rudy Perez/L.A. operates at the facilities at the Westside Academy of Dance and the S.M. and L.A. County High School for the Arts. The premise is to offer mentorships in contemporary dance to the unique young professional/student.

RUDY PEREZ/LOS ANGELES (CONTINUED)

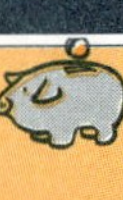
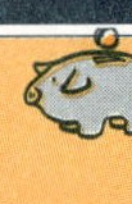
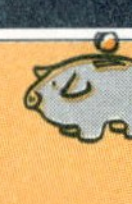
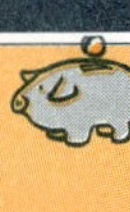
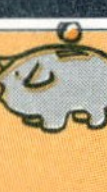

The program utilizes the expertise, knowledge, and skills of the director. In part, the director's vast repertory will be restaged as a teaching tool toward the preservation of the historical work created in Los Angeles.

Youth

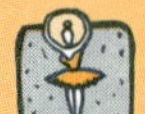

PROGRAMS: WORKSHOPS, CLASSES
SCHEDULE: YEAR-ROUND, WEEKDAYS, WEEKENDS

RUSSIAN SCHOOL FOR THE PERFORMING ARTS, THE

HSM

c/o Brickell
343 1/2 N. Curson Avenue
Los Angeles, CA 90036
Ph: 323-931-5292
Fax: 323-938-8898

Claude Brickell Director

The Russian School for the Performing Arts offers professional-level training in classical ballet featuring Russian technique. Only dancers with strong professional potential are accepted. All instructors were formerly with major Russian ballet companies.

- classical ballet training and method acting for the professional dancer

RUTH BACHOFNER GALLERY

WS

2525 Michigan Avenue, #G2
Santa Monica, CA 90404-4014
Ph: 310-829-3300
Fax: 310-449-0070
www.bachofner.com
la_art@ix.netcom.com

Contemporary artists.

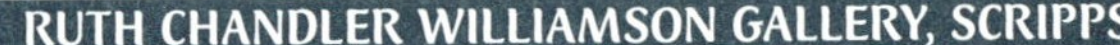

RUTH CHANDLER WILLIAMSON GALLERY, SCRIPPS

PO

Box 1030 Columbia Avenue
Claremont, CA 91711-3948
Ph: 909-607-3397
Fax: 909-607-4691
www.scrippscol.edu/~dept/gallery/GalleryPg.html

Mary MacNaughton Director mmacnaug@scrippscol.edu

SAM FRANCIS GALLERY, THE CROSSROADS SCHOOL OF ARTS & SCIENCES

WS

1714 21st Street
Santa Monica, CA 90404
Ph: 310-829-7391
Fax: 310-453-7637

Pamela Blackwell Curator/ x402

The Sam Francis Gallery, as a community exhibition space representing Crossroads School for Arts and Sciences, will focus on presenting strong visual work and concepts that reflect contemporary issues important to the Crossroads community, current artistic issues, and diverse media.

SAN FERNANDO VALLEY ARTS COUNCIL

P.O. Box 261541 501(c)3 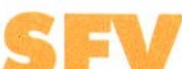
Encino, CA 91426
Ph: 818-986-7266
Admin: 818-986-ARTS
Fax: 818-597-9652

Roslyn Wolin President

The San Fernando Valley Arts Council has supported the arts and educated the public for 30 years. This organization is part of the Arts Partners program with the L.A. Cultural Affairs Department, and administers the Encino Media Center.

- beginning and intermediate animation program is offered in 10 week sessions for youths 14-19
- photography darkroom is open 20 hours a week to amateur photographers
- variety of art classes as well as photography for children and adults

Pre/K-12 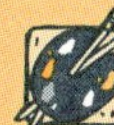

PROGRAMS:	**WORKSHOPS**
SCHEDULE:	YEAR-ROUND, WEEKDAYS, EVENINGS, WEEKENDS
DETAILS:	GRADES 9-12, VISUAL & PERFORMING ARTS

SAN PEDRO ART ASSOCIATION

222 W. Sixth Street 501(c)3 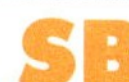
San Pedro, CA 90731
Ph: 310-833-3976

Loa Sprung Membership/ 310-832-0593
Jim Robertson President/ 909-244-5002

The San Pedro Art Association is an art club founded in 1936.

- monthly meetings and demos
- monthly gallery exhibits and two open shows
- art classes
- Colored Pencil Society

SANDAKA GALLERY

316 N. La Brea Avenue 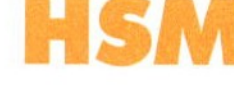
Los Angeles, CA 90036
Ph: 323-938-7836
Fax: 323-938-7883
hbahsoon@aol.com

Original fine African art. Masks, statues, ritual objects.

- appraisal services
- consultation services
- consignment services

SANDRONI REY CONTEMPORARY ART

1224 Abbot Kinney Boulevard WS
Venice, CA 90291
Ph: 310-392-3404
Fax: 310-399-0184

Contemporary art.

SANGEET SCHOOL OF WORLD MUSIC AND DANCE

5241 York Boulevard 501(c)3 ELA
Los Angeles, CA 90042
Ph: 323-258-1424
www.shplang.org

Paul Livingstone Director paul@shplang.org

The Sangeet School, located in the diverse Highland Park neighborhood of northeast Los Angeles, is dedicated to presenting and teaching world music and dance, while increasing awareness of cultural diversity.

- six-week sessions and special workshops in traditional music and dance, from North and South India, West Africa, Mexico, Cuba, Brazil, the Middle East and Ireland are taught by master, professional and international artists
- classes open to all skill levels
- world music and dance concert series
- quality ethnic instruments and recordings available for sale

Sangeet School is the first community-based school for diverse traditional arts in Los Angeles. With an emphasis on practical applications, Sangeet School is dedicated to making world music education accessible to all.

Pre/K-12 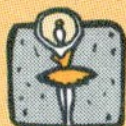 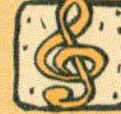

PROGRAMS:	**PERFORMANCES, WORKSHOPS, STUDIO CLASSES**
SCHEDULE:	YEAR-ROUND, EVENINGS, WEEKENDS
DETAILS:	GRADES PRE/K-12, VISUAL & PERFORMING ARTS
	CREATIVE EXPRESSION

Youth 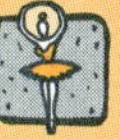 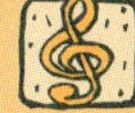

PROGRAMS:	**PERFORMANCES, WORKSHOPS, CLASSES**
SCHEDULE:	YEAR-ROUND, EVENINGS, WEEKENDS

Families 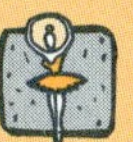 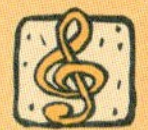

PROGRAMS:	**PERFORMANCES, WORKSHOPS, CLASSES**
SCHEDULE:	YEAR-ROUND, EVENINGS, WEEKENDS

SANTA CLARITA BALLET COMPANY

26798 Oak Avenue 501(c)3 SFV
Santa Clarita, CA 91351
Ph: 805-251-6844

Corinne Glover Executive Director
Carol Guidry Artistic Director

The Santa Clarita Ballet Company provides quality ballet theater to the community through the blending in of performances with professional guest artists and local students.

- annual "Nutcracker" ballet in December
- annual Spring performance

SANTA CLARITA BALLET COMPANY (CONTINUED)

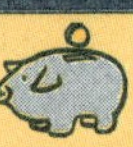

The Santa Clarita Ballet offers a comprehensive dance program with an emphasis on classical ballet. A professional atmosphere is provided along with a positive learning environment in which students discover the beauty of the art of ballet.

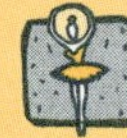

Pre/K-12

PROGRAMS:	**STUDIO CLASSES**
SCHEDULE:	YEAR-ROUND, WEEKDAYS, EVENINGS, WEEKENDS
DETAILS:	GRADES PRE/K-12, VISUAL & PERFORMING ARTS CREATIVE EXPRESSION, TRAVEL TO SCHOOLS

SANTA CLARITA, THE CITY OF

23920 Valencia Boulevard, Suite 120
Santa Clarita, CA 91355
Ph: 805-255-4910
Admin: 805-255-4945
Educ: 805-255-4910
Fax: 805-255-1996
www.santa-clarita.com

Gail Ortiz	Public Information Officer/ 805-255-4314
Michael Marks	Cultural Arts Coordinator/ 805-286-4078
Rick Putnam	Director
Sean Morgan	Cultural Arts Coordinator/ 805-286-4034

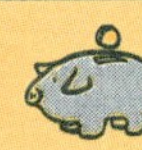

The City of Santa Clarita offers basic classes that are entry level arts, music, theater, and dance instruction.

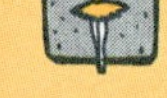 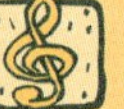 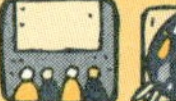 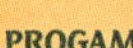

Pre/K-12

PROGAMS:	**PERFORMANCES, WORKSHOPS**
SCHEDULE:	YEAR-ROUND, WEEKDAYS
DETAILS:	GRADES PRE/K-12, VISUAL & PERFORMING ARTS PHYSICAL EDUCATION, CREATIVE EXPRESSION

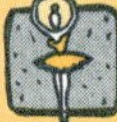 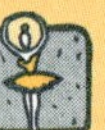 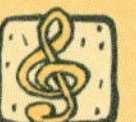 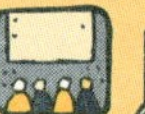

Youth

PROGRAMS:	**CLASSES**
SCHEDULE:	YEAR-ROUND, WEEKDAYS

SANTA CLARITA INTERNATIONAL FILM FESTIVAL (SCIFF)

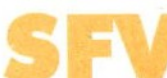

P.O. Box 801507 501(c)3
Santa Clarita, CA 91380-1507
Ph: 805-257-3131
Admin: 805-250-9901
Fax: 805-257-8989
www.sciff.org

Mitch Matovich	Chairman/ 805-250-0644	pattemitch@aol.com
Patte Dee	Program Director	
Chris Shoemaker	Executive Director/ 805-259-5494	actsre8@earthlink.net

The Santa Clarita International Film Festival sponsors the "Celebration of Famly Entertainment" film festival in Santa Clarita. It is the only film festival for film and screenplay competitions with guidelines of no gratuitous sex, violence and nudity.

- the festival includes international films and screenplays from features, animation and documentaries
- student film shorts competition
- seminars, "Directors on Directing", "Producers on Producing", "the Art of Animation", "Writing the Winning Screenplay"
- awards ceremony and dinner on video for television broadcast

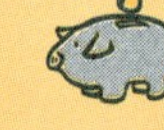

Over 600 students attend film screenings of foreign films with English subtitles, documentaries on children, animation films that use innovative approaches to storytelling.

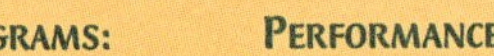

Pre/K-12

PROGRAMS:	**PERFORMANCES**
SCHEDULE:	YEAR-ROUND, WEEKDAYS
DETAILS:	GRADES 5-6, VISUAL & PERFORMING ARTS MULTICULTURAL, CREATIVE EXPRESSION CONNECTIONS/RELATIONS/APPLICATIONS FACILITY FOR SCHOOL VISITS

SANTA CLARITA VALLEY ARTISTS' ASSOCIATION

SFV

P.O. Box 55101
Valencia, CA 91380
Ph: 805-296-2ART
www.scvleon.com/scvaa/

SCV Artists' Association was founded in 1989 by local artists dedicated to Community Visual Arts Appreciation. We exist to further the interests of artists and provide a scholarship fund for graduating high school seniors intent on continuing their art education upon graduation.

SANTA CLARITA VALLEY YOUTH ORCHESTRA

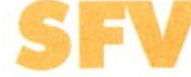

College of the Canyons 501(c)3
26455 Rockwell Canyon Road
Santa Clarita, CA 91355
Ph: 805-253-3604
Admin: 805-254-8225
Educ: 805-259-7800 x3254
Fax: 818-846-1338

Sue Bozman	Public Information Officer	
Robert Lawson	Director	
Sally Angel	President/ 818-846-8988	svangel@aol.com

The Youth Orchestra provides instrumental education for students ages 8-21. It has three ensembles accommodating varying skill and talent levels.

SANTA CLARITA VALLEY YOUTH ORCHESTRA (CONTINUED)

We are the only orchestral program that provides classical music training in the Santa Clarita Valley.

Youth 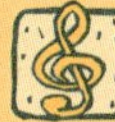

PROGRAMS: **PERFORMANCES**
SCHEDULE: YEAR-ROUND, EVENINGS, WEEKENDS

SANTA FE ART COLONY

ELA

2401 S. Santa Fe Avenue, Suite #22
Los Angeles, CA 90058
Ph: 323-587-5513
Fax: 323-587-5902

Jett Jackson — Open Studio Director
Richard Gerrish — Manager

Located in downtown Los Angeles, SFAC provides live/work space for visual artists in a Laisséz-faire environment, and provides access to groups, organizations, curators, and collectors directly to artists in their studios.

- tours available by appointment for all groups and collectors
- annual open studio event each spring, open to the public as announced
- other special arrangements possible, providing direct contact with artists in their studios

SANTA MONICA COLLEGE ART GALLERY

1900 Pico Boulevard
Santa Monica, CA 90405-1644
Ph: 310-452-9231

SANTA MONICA COLLEGE PHOTOGRAPHY GALLERY

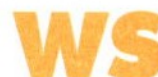

1900 Pico Boulevard
Santa Monica, CA 90405
Ph: 310-452-9289
Fax: 310-396-4970

Robert Jones — Gallery Director

An important public venue dedicated exclusively to photographic art. Exhibits the work of international artists working in the traditional and avant garde.

SANTA MONICA HERITAGE MUSEUM

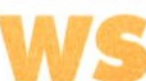

2612 Main Street
Santa Monica, CA 90405-3515
Ph: 310 392-8537

Tobi Smith — Executive Director

SANTA MONICA MUSEUM OF ART

501(c)3 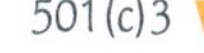

Bergamot Station
2525 Michigan Avenue, Building G1
Santa Monica, CA 90404
Ph: 310-586-6488
Admin: 310-586-6488 x16
Fax: 310-586-6487
www.netvip.com/smmoa

Ashley Emenegger — Museum Coordinator/ x12
Thomas Rhoads — Executive Director/ x15 — smmuseum@netvip.com
Carole Ann Klonarides — Curator of Programming/ x16

Santa Monica Museum of Art is a non-collecting nonprofit arts organization. SMMOA presents the work of mid-career, underecognized, and emerging artists, primarily from Southern California, and sponsors the creation of new work through its Artist Projects Series.

- thematic and group exhibitions
- solo exhibitions
- commissioned site-specific installations of the Artist Projects Series

The Museum's education programs include Art Partners (an outreach program for at-risk youth in the local public schools), Friday Evening Salons, Lectures/Artist Talks, and Kids Art Station (multi-session classes introducing young artists, ages 7-12, to artmaking, art history and art appreciation) 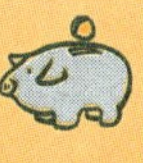

Pre/K-12 

PROGRAMS: **GUIDED TOURS**
SCHEDULE: SPRING, FALL
DETAILS: GRADES 3-6, VISUAL & PERFORMING ARTS
AESTHETIC VALUING, CREATIVE EXPRESSION
CONNECTIONS/RELATIONS/APPLICATIONS
FACILITY FOR SCHOOL VISITS

Youth 

PROGRAMS: **WORKSHOPS, CLASSES, GUIDED TOURS**
SCHEDULE: SPRING, FALL

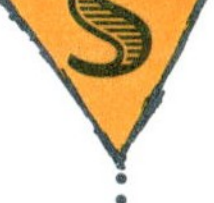

SANTA MONICA PLAYHOUSE

1211 4th Street
Santa Monica, CA 90401
Ph: 310-394-9779
Fax: 310 393-5573
www.home1.gte.net.theatre

501 (c) 3 WS

Sandra Zeitzew	Public Relations Director/ x651
Chris DeCarlo	Artistic Director
Evelyn Rudie	Artistic Director
Cheryl Jennings	Director of Education/ x616
Rachel Galper	Development Director/ x630

Santa Monica Playhouse is Los Angeles's oldest professional repertory theater, providing evening shows, family theatre, workshops, school tours, writing and performance labs, international and cultural exchange for over 35 years.

- professional stage plays in two theaters
- weekend family theater matinees
- host birthday parties
- weekly acting workshops for adults and children
- café
- concerts
- play readings
- international tours
- volunteer opportuntities
- summer acting camps

From beginners to students with serious career intent, Santa Monica Playhouse offers workshops, interships, immersion programs, school field trips and educator seminars taught in a working theater environment by professional artists and playwrights.

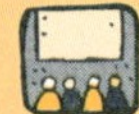

Pre/K-12

PROGRAMS: **Performances, Workshops, Studio classes, Residencies**
SCHEDULE: Year-round, Weekdays, Evenings, Weekends
DETAILS: grades Pre/k-12, Visual & performing arts
Integrating literature with art, Creative Expression
Historical/Cultural Context
Connections/Relations/Applications
Teacher training programs, Travel to schools
Programs on-site, Individually tailored programs
Educational materials available

Youth

PROGRAMS: **Performances, Workshops, Classes, Residencies**
SCHEDULE: Year-round, weekdays, Evenings, Weekends

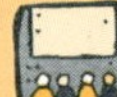

Families

PROGRAMS: **Performances, Workshops, Classes, Residencies**
SCHEDULE: Year-round, Weekdays, Evenings, Weekends

SANTA MONICA SYMPHONY ASSOCIATION

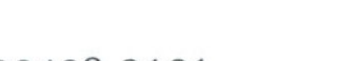

P.O. Box 3101
Santa Monica, CA 90408-3101
Ph: 310-996-3260
Admin: 310-278-5657
Educ: 310-394-4176
Fax: 310-395-1014
www.web.mit.edu/markwang/www/SMSymphony.html.

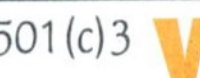

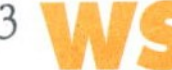

David Bendett	President
Allen Gross	Music Director/Conductor/ 626-796-8966
David Bendett	Acting Executive Director
Sheila Wells	Vice President
Sonia Luna	Treasurer/ 310-206-4213

The Santa Monica Symphony presents four admission-free, semi-professional classical symphonic concerts at the Santa Monica Civic Auditorium on Sundays from October through May with outstanding solo performers.

- pre-concert lectures
- youth outreach concerts
- "Artists in the Schools" performances at local public schools

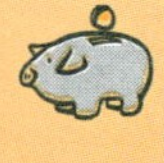

The "Artists in the Schools" program is unique and popular due to the talents of a virtuoso violinist who mesmerizes the classroom with extemporaneous, interactive presentations;; he encourages all students to attend special Youth/Family concerts with their families.

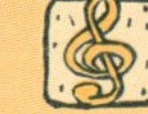

Pre/K-12

PROGRAMS: **Performances**
SCHEDULE: Spring, Fall, Winter, Weekdays, Evenings, Weekends
DETAILS: grades Pre/k-12, Visual & performing arts
Creative Expression, Travel to schools

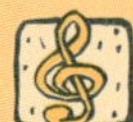

Youth

PROGRAMS: **Performances**
SCHEDULE: Spring, Fall, Winter, weekdays, Evenings, Weekends

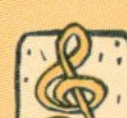

Families

PROGRAMS: **Performances**
SCHEDULE: Spring, Fall, Winter, Weekdays, Evenings, Weekends

SANTA MONICA TRADITIONAL FOLK MUSIC CLUB

1642 Voorhees Avenue
Manhattan Beach, CA 90266-7044
Ph: 310-376-8760
Fax: 310-379-4523

501(c)3 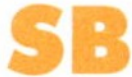

April Halprin Wayland — Founder — rabbitt101@aol.com
Ross Altman — President/ 213-931-9321

Santa Monica Traditional Folk Music Club members love American and International folk music. Established in 1978, the club meets the first Saturday of each month to share songs accompanied by guitars, banjos, fiddles, concertinas, penny whistles, and other folk instruments.

- monthly gatherings
- folk music and storyteller concerts
- annual showcase, "Birthday Jubilee Grandslam Celebration Concert"
- participation in the L.A. County-wide Arts Open House
- camp outs
- folk music library
- newsletter

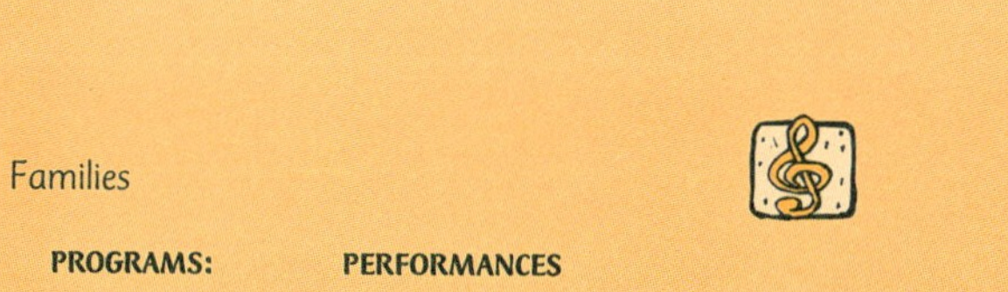

Families

PROGRAMS: PERFORMANCES
SCHEDULE: YEAR-ROUND, EVENINGS, WEEKENDS

SATURDAY NIGHT BATH CONCERT FUND

19723 Ronald Avenue
Torrance, CA 90503-1242
Ph: 310-542-1239
Fax: 310-371-5270

501(c)3 SB

Howard Rich — Artistic Director

Saturday Night Bath Concert Fund is a mobile six piece Jazz/Blues ensemble performing for at-risk youth at their facilities.

- youth concerts

SATURDAY NIGHT BATH CONCERT FUND (CONTINUED)

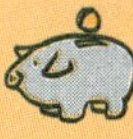

Saturday Night Bath Concert Fund performs youth concerts for at-risk youth, pregnant teens and continuation high school students, performing their style of music; includes 35mm/ slide visuals and acoustical musical instrument histories in one-on-one clinic format. Students often join performances and become "guest rappers" and instrumentalists, improving interaction and self-esteem.

Pre/K-12

PROGRAMS: PERFORMANCES, WORKSHOPS
SCHEDULE: YEAR-ROUND, WEEKDAYS, EVENINGS, WEEKENDS
DETAILS: GRADES 9-12, VISUAL & PERFORMING ARTS
LANGUAGE ARTS, MULTICULTURAL
AESTHETIC VALUING, CREATIVE EXPRESSION
HISTORICAL/CULTURAL CONTEXT, TRAVEL TO SCHOOLS
EDUCATIONAL MATERIALS, Work with at-risk youth

Youth

PROGRAMS: PERFORMANCES, WORKSHOPS
SCHEDULE: YEAR-ROUND, WEEKDAYS, EVENINGS, WEEKENDS

SAVING AND PRESERVING ARTS AND CULTURAL ENVIRONMENTS (SPACES)

1804 N. Van Ness Avenue
Los Angeles, CA 90028
Ph/Fax: 323-463-1629

501(c)3 HSM

Seymour Rosen — Director

SPACES is a nonprofit arts organization concerned with the identification, documentation, and preservation of large-scale contemporary art environments in the United States. It seeks recognition for the creators of these environments and recognition for the genre. SPACES educates and informs the public and also functions as an arts advocacy group and an information resource.

SCREEN ACTORS GUILD (SAG) FOUNDATION

5757 Wilshire Boulevard
Los Angeles, CA 90036-3600
Ph: 323-954-1600
Fax: 323-549-6710

501(c)3 HSM

Janice Sands — Executive Director

The SAG Foundation is the charitable, educational and humanitarian adjunct to the Screen Actors Guild. It offers services to the membership and opportunities to members interested in community outreach.

- AIDS Fund
- Book PALS (Performing Artists for Literacy in Schools)
- Catastrophic Health Fund
- financial seminars
- John L. Dales Scholarship Fund
- legacy documentation
- membership assistance

SCREEN ACTORS GUILD (SAG) FOUNDATION (CONTINUED)

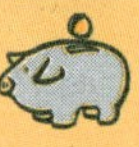

The Foundation coordinates and sponsors a literacy program, which sends volunteer professional performers into educational facilities in "at risk" neighborhoods to read to children. The goal is to stimulate students to further develop their reading and communication skills

Pre/K-12

PROGRAMS: LITERATURE WORKSHOPS
SCHEDULE: YEAR-ROUND
DETAILS: GRADES PRE/K-12, LANGUAGE ARTS, TRAVEL TO SCHOOLS

Youth

PROGRAMS: LITERATURE WORKSHOPS
SCHEDULE: YEAR-ROUND

SELF-HELP GRAPHICS & ART

3802 Cesar Chavez Avenue
Los Angeles, CA 90063
Ph: 323-881-6444
Admin: 323-881-6442
Fax: 323-881-6447
www.selfhelpgraphics.com

501(c)3

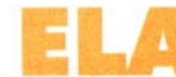

Bertha Velasquez — Office Manager
Tomas Benitez — Director
Pat Gomez — Assistant Director/ 323-881-6441
Christina Ochoa — Gallery Director/ 323-881-6442

Located in the heart of East Los Angeles, Self-Help Graphics is a community arts center presenting the work of Chicano artists to local, regional, national and international audiences.

- exhibitions featuring emerging and established artists (Galeria Otra Vez)
- Tienda Colores featuring artist-made jewelry, niches, cards and gifts
- limited edition serigraphs, mono-silkscreen prints available for purchase, featuring the work of emerging and established Chicano artists
- annual Day of the Dead exhibition and celebration
- local, national and international exhibition print program

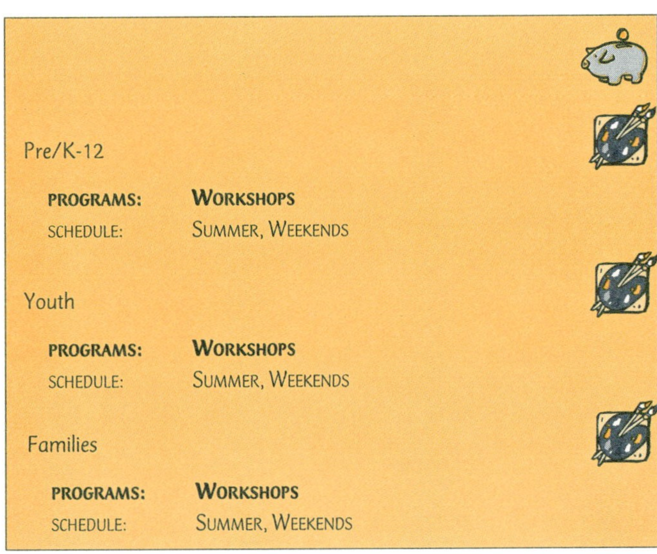

Pre/K-12

PROGRAMS: WORKSHOPS
SCHEDULE: SUMMER, WEEKENDS

Youth

PROGRAMS: WORKSHOPS
SCHEDULE: SUMMER, WEEKENDS

Families

PROGRAMS: WORKSHOPS
SCHEDULE: SUMMER, WEEKENDS

SENIOR EYE GALLERY

LB

Palmcrest House Senior Residency
3501 Cedar Avenue, Palmcrest House
Long Beach, CA 90807
Ph: 562-595-4551
Fax: 562-426-1099

Julian Finegold — Director

SHAKESPEARE AND FRIENDS FOUNDATION

11824 Dorothy Street
Los Angeles, CA 90049
Ph: 310-820-2292

501(c)3 WS

Dee Marie Nieto — Founder/Director

Shakespeare and Friends Foundation is a California nonprofit, educational organization devoted to innovative methods for teaching today's junior high and high school students key principles of productive living through the power and insight of Shakespeare's writings.

Shakespeare and Friends targets inner-city schools and exposes them to the theater and the classics. Each presentation is structured as a lesson with a specific theme relevant to the students' lives.

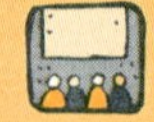

Pre/K-12

PROGRAMS: PERFORMANCES
DETAILS: GRADES 9-12, VISUAL & PERFORMING ARTS
CREATIVE EXPRESSION
CONNECTIONS/RELATIONS/APPLICATIONS
TRAVEL TO SCHOOLS, INDIVIDUALLY TAILORED PROGRAMS
EDUCATIONAL MATERIALS AVAILABLE

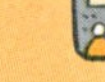

Youth

PROGRAMS: PERFORMANCES
SCHEDULE: YEAR-ROUND, WEEKDAYS, EVENINGS

SHAKESPEARE FESTIVAL/LA

411 W. Fifth Street, Suite 815
Los Angeles, CA 90013
Ph: 213-489-1121
Fax: 213-489-7850

501(c)3

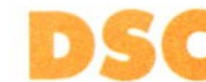

Joel Kimmel — Director of Development/ x12
Ben Donenberg — Artistic Director/ x11 — bdonenberg@aol.com
Dani Bedau — Youth Outreach Director/ x13
Kate Harris — Director of Administration/ x10

Shakespeare Festival/LA enchants, enriches, and builds community through professional theatrical traditions that are accessible to all.

- free union-contracted productions of Skakespeare's plays every summer
- screenings of Shakespeare films
- celebrity play readings
- volunteer opportunities

SHAKESPEARE FESTIVAL/LA (CONTINUED)

The festival is the only Los Angeles Shakespeare company to offer free union-contracted productions to the public, while doing educational outreach and other social service programs.

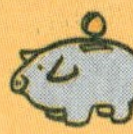

Pre/K-12

PROGRAMS: **PERFORMANCES, WORKSHOPS**
SCHEDULE: YEAR-ROUND, WEEKDAYS, EVENINGS, WEEKENDS
DETAILS: GRADES 7-12, VISUAL & PERFORMING ARTS
AESTHETIC VALUING, CREATIVE EXPRESSION
HISTORICAL/CULTURAL CONTEXT
CONNECTIONS/RELATIONS/APPLICATIONS
TEACHER TRAINING PROGRAMS (SALARY POINTS)
EDUCATIONAL MATERIALS, WORK WITH AT-RISK YOUTH

Youth

PROGRAMS: **WORKSHOPS, CLASSES**
SCHEDULE: YEAR-ROUND, WEEKDAYS, EVENINGS, WEEKENDS

Families

PROGRAMS: **PERFORMANCES**
SCHEDULE: YEAR-ROUND, WEEKDAYS, EVENINGS ,WEEKENDS

SHAKESPEARE LEAGUE OF PASADENA

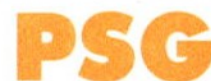

171 S. Grand Avenue
Pasadena, CA 91105
Ph: 626-793-5714
501(c)3

Sally Gilmore	Director/ 626-578-7544
Leah Bessey	Drama Chairman/ 213-662-7252
Barbara Sakuma-Germain	Programs/ 626-282-8924
Peggy Schmid	Membership/ 626-289-9982

The Shakespeare League is a philanthropic organization in the West San Gabriel Valley. Its members, a diverse group of women, join together to preserve American musical theater as as an art form and in the process help those in the community who are less fortunate.

- yearly full scale Broadway musical with full orchestra
- cabaret show
- monthly skits at meetings
- educational programs
- yearly musical profits benefit charity

SHARON TRUAX FINE ART

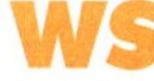

1625 Electric Avenue
Venice, CA 90291-4803
Ph/Fax: 310-396-3162

Exhibition and project space for regional, national and international artists.

SHERRY FRUMKIN GALLERY

WS

Bergamot Station T-1
2525 Michigan Avenue
Santa Monica, CA 90404
Ph: 310-453-1850
Fax: 310-453-8370

Sherry Frumkin	Director	SFRUG310@aol.com
Christine Duval	Co-Director	

Contemporary artists

SHINING STONE FOUNDATION

SB

1414 E. Mariposa Avenue
El Segundo, CA 90245
Ph: 562-494-1120
501(c)3

Gail Davis	Secretary
Willard Krick	Director of Culture
Mary Jacalyn Gage	President

Shining Stone Foundation consists of homeless, formerly homeless, and concerned citizens. We do weekly workshops and exhibitions, festivals, parades, and events on an ongoing basis.

- weekly workshops
- weekly exhibitions
- art projects at festivals

We exhibit creations from workshops for sale at festivals and provide free art projects to participating children.

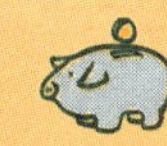

Pre/K-12

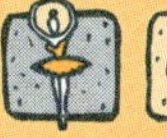
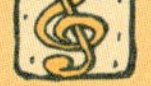
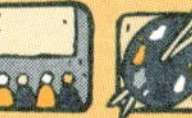

PROGRAMS: **PERFORMANCES, WORKSHOPS, SELF-GUIDED TOURS GUIDED TOURS**
SCHEDULE: YEAR-ROUND, WEEKDAYS, EVENINGS, WEEKENDS
DETAILS: GRADES PRE/K-12, HISTORY/SOC. SCIENCES
MATH/SCIENCES, VISUAL & PERFORMING ARTS
LANGUAGE ARTS, MULTICULTURAL, CREATIVE EXPRESSION
HISTORICAL/CULTURAL CONTEXT
CONNECTIONS/RELATIONS/APPLICATIONS
WORK WITH HOMELESS, DEVELOPMENTALLY DISABLED

Youth

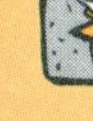
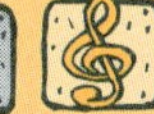
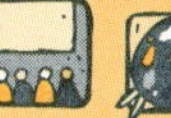

PROGRAMS: **PERFORMANCES, WORKSHOPS. SELF-GUIDED TOURS GUIDED TOURS**
SCHEDULE: YEAR-ROUND, WEEKDAYS, EVENINGS, WEEKENDS

Families

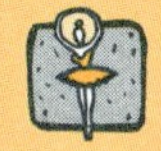
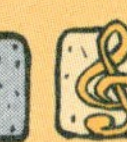
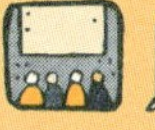
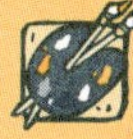

PROGRAMS: **PERFORMANCES, WORKSHOPS, SELF-GUIDED TOURS, GUIDED TOURS**
SCHEDULE: YEAR-ROUND, WEEKDAYS, EVENINGS, WEEKENDS

SHOOTING BACK

1630 Shell Avenue
Venice, CA 90291
Ph: 310-823-8333
Educ: 310-823-2999
Fax: 310-823-6783

501 (c) 3 **WS**

Jim Hubbard — Director

Shooting Back provides photography and writing workshops for at-risk youth as a creative outlet to teach skills, and to exhibit their work in order to educate the public about issues related to youth.

- volunteer opportunities
- exhibitions
- books and videos
- workshops
- seminars
- public speaking

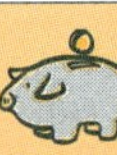

Youth love opportunities to express themselves through photography and writing—Shooting Back provides these opportunities. In addition, participants have the opportunity to have their works exhibited and published. Mentors offer unique support to the youth.

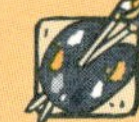

Pre/K-12

PROGRAMS:	**WORKSHOPS**
DETAILS:	GRADES 7-12, VISUAL & PERFORMING ARTS
	CREATIVE EXPRESSION, TRAVEL TO SCHOOLS
	EDUCATIONAL MATERIALS AVAILABLE

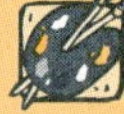

Youth

PROGRAMS:	**WORKSHOPS**
SCHEDULE:	YEAR-ROUND, WEEKDAYS, WEEKENDS

SHOSHANA WAYNE GALLERY

2525 Michigan Avenue, B1
Santa Monica, CA 90404
Ph: 310-453-7535
Fax; 310-453-1595

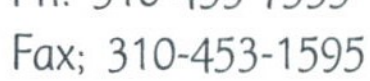

WS

Shoshana Blank — Director

Located at Bergamot Station Arts Center, Shoshana Wayne Gallery presents exhibitions of contemporary art in various media.

- changing contemporary art exhibitions

SIDE STREET PROJECTS

1629 18th Street, #3
Santa Monica, CA 90404-3807
Ph: 310-829-0779
Fax: 310-828-0620
www.artmedia.com/organizations.sidestreet/

501 (c) 3 **WS**

Karen Atkinson — Director — sidest@ix.netcom.com
Katie Sivers — Associate Director

Located in Santa Monica, Side Street Projects is a multi-disciplinary, artist-run organization dedicated to supporting the creation and presentation of work by artists and creative education programs for youth.

- exhibtions featuring work by local internation artists
- full woodworking facilities
- rehearsal, meeting or workshop space
- darkroom
- online magazine for artists
- free web listings for members
- Alternate Routes: education on wheels to all areas of Los Angeles teaching wooodworking and creative skills to kids
- performance space
- fiscal receivership

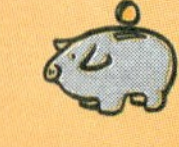

The Alternate Routes program is education on wheels featuring a renovated transit bus with 10 woodworking stations, which travels to after-school programs, community centers, and birthday parties.

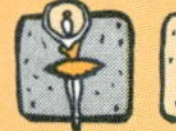

Pre/K-12

PROGRAMS:	**WORKSHOPS, STUDIO CLASSES, GUIDED TOURS**
SCHEDULE:	YEAR-ROUND, WEEKDAYS, WEEKENDS
DETAILS:	GRADES 5-12, VISUAL & PERFORMING ARTS
	CREATIVE EXPRESSION, TEACHER TRAINING PROGRAMS
	TRAVEL TO SCHOOLS, PROGRAMS ON-SITE
	INDIVIDUALLY TAILORED PROGRAMS, EDUCATIONAL MATERIALS
	BILINGUAL: SPANISH, COST FOR SOME PROGRAMS

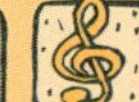
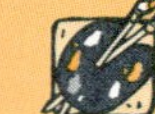

Youth

PROGRAMS:	**WORKSHOPS, CLASSES, GUIDED TOURS**
SCHEDULE:	YEAR-ROUND, WEEKDAYS, WEEKENDS
DETAILS:	COST FOR SOME PROGRAMS

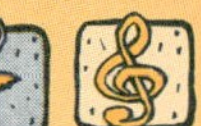
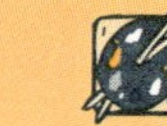

Families

PROGRAMS:	**WORKSHOPS, GUIDED TOURS**
SCHEDULE:	YEAR-ROUND, WEEKDAYS, WEEKENDS

SIERRA MADRE CHORALE

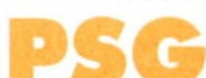

PSG

605 W. Huntington Drive, #518 — 501(c)3
Monrovia, CA 91016
Ph: 626-798-0850

Kathy Branson	Secretary/ 626-285-5868	
Fred Copeland	Musical Director/ 626-579-0075	
Susan Ruble	President/ 626-357-0560	
Steve Hawkins	Booking Agents	thawkins@jps.net

The Sierra Madre Chorale is a community chorale which performs throughout the San Gabriel Valley, Los Angeles, and Orange counties. Membership is open to those who love to sing and want to perform.

- two community concerts per year
- two festival performances per year
- weekly rehearsals
- performances at community events such as the Annual Memorial Day Ceremony, Annual Frontier Days and the Fourth of July Parade
- free summer concerts at Central Park in Sierra Madre

SIERRA MADRE PUBLIC LIBRARY

PSG

440 W. Sierra Madre Boulevard
Sierra Madre, CA 91024
Ph: 626-355-7186
Fax: 626-355-6218

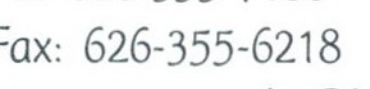

www.sierramadre@lib.ca.us

Toni Buckner	City Librarian	
Catriona Shafer	Library Technician II	circ@sierramadre.lib.ca.us

Sierra Madre Public Library is the city library for the City of Sierra Madre and is a member of the Metropolitan Cooperative Library System.

- "Listening to Voices"
- monthly poetry reading series

SILAYAN DANCE COMPANY

HSM

316 N. Reno Street — 501(c)3
Los Angeles, CA 90026
Ph: 323-957-4778
Fax: 213-738-7844

Dulce Capadocia	Artistic Director
Sonia Capadocia	Founder

Located in the heart of "Temple Street" community, Silayan Dance Company produces and presents acclaimed, original dance works inspired by Filipino legends, folklore, and themes throughout greater Los Angeles.

- public presentations
- workshops in schools, colleges and universities

SILAYAN DANCE COMPANY (CONTINUED)

The Silayan Dance Company programs are fun, enriching and give students of all ages an opportunity to learn Philippine culture in a non-competive and nuturing environment. The tailor-made programs incorporate creative movement, lecture/demonstrations, storytelling, music, folk culture, and more.

Pre/K-12

PROGRAMS:	**PERFORMANCES, WORKSHOPS, RESIDENCIES**
SCHEDULE:	YEAR-ROUND, WEEKDAYS
DETAILS:	GRADES PRE/K-12, VISUAL & PERFORMING ARTS MULTICULTURAL, HISTORICAL/CULTURAL CONTEXT TRAVEL TO SCHOOLS , INDIVIDUALLY TAILORED PROGRAMS

Youth

PROGRAMS:	**PERFORMANCES, WORKSHOPS, RESIDENCIES**
SCHEDULE:	YEAR-ROUND, WEEKDAYS

Families

PROGRAMS:	**PERFORMANCES, WORKSHOPS, RESIDENCIES**
SCHEDULE:	YEAR-ROUND, WEEKDAYS

SILK ROADS DESIGN GALLERY

HSM

834 N. La Brea Avenue
Los Angeles, CA 90038
Ph: 323-871-8885
Fax: 323-871-8883

Specializing in fine antiques, art, furniture, accessories, textiles, fold and tribal art from jamor cultural center from around the Pacific Rim.

SIMON RODIA WATTS TOWERS MUSIC & ART FESTIVAL

Please refer to Watts Towers Arts Center

SIMON/SCHADE GALLERY

HSM

828 N. La Brea Avenue
Los Angeles, CA 90038
Ph: 323-466-4099
Fax: 323-466-4255
www.simonschadegallery.com
jim@enclavegallery.com

Exhibits progressive paintings in a welcoming atmosphere.

SIQUEIROS-KOLL GALLERY

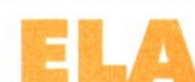

ELA

2103 Humbolt Street
Los Angeles, CA 90031
Ph: 323-222-1555
Fax: 323-222-1605
artworld1@yahoo.com

SITE (SEEING IT THROUGH EXHIBITIONS)

8033 Sunset Boulevard, #92 — 501 (c) 3
Los Angeles, CA 90046

Laura Larson	Co-President
Cindy Bennett	Co-President

SITE (Seeing It Through Exhibitions) is a nonprofit arts organization that exhibits art, organizes critique groups and art talks.

SKIDMORE CONTEMPORARY ART

3835 Cross Creek Road, #21
Malibu, CA 90265
Ph: 310-456-5070
Fax: 310-456-3925

WS

Lia Skidmore	Director

Contemporary art.

SKIRBALL MUSEUM AND CULTURAL CENTER

2701 N. Sepulveda Boulevard — 501 (c) 3 WS
Los Angeles, CA 90049
Ph: 310-440-4500
Admin: 310-440-4554
Educ: 310-440-4652
Fax: 310-440-4695
www.skirball.org

Jocelyn Tetel	Director of Advancement/ 310-440-4560	jtetel@skirball.com
Nancy Berman	Director of Museum/ 310-440-4611	nberman@skirball.com
Uri Herscher	President and CEO/ 310-440-4540	
Adele Lander Burke	Director of Education	aburke@skirball.com

Located in Los Angeles, this "oasis in the city," designed by Moshe Safdie seeks to interpret the Ameican Jewish experience and to strengthen American society through a range of cultural programs.

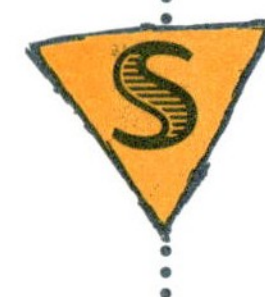

- ongoing festivals and programs celebrating the holidays, special programs, exhibitions, and seasons
- film festivals
- live concert series including jazz, classical, R&B, etc.
- live theater, dance, and literary readings
- docent-led tours of the museum's exhibits in various languages and for the visually impaired
- two-three changing exhibitions a year
- classes in music, film, writing, history, art, archaeology, architecture, etc...
- scholars, dignitaries, writers, artists, and experts lecture on a variety of subjects including culture and current events
- amenities include a gift store and cafe

SKIRBALL MUSEUM AND CULTURAL CENTER (CONTINUED)

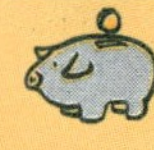

The Skirball Cultural Center's educational programs provide extensive pre-visit curricular materials free of charge to area teachers. All school touring programs include hands-on experimental activities such as art production, historical simulations, and dramatic expression.

Pre/K-12

PROGRAMS:	**PERFORMANCES, SELF-GUIDED TOURS, GUIDED TOURS**
SCHEDULE:	YEAR-ROUND, WEEKDAYS, WEEKENDS
DETAILS:	GRADES PRE/K-12, HISTORY/SOC. SCIENCES VISUAL & PERFORMING ARTS, MULTICULTURAL CREATIVE EXPRESSION, HISTORICAL/CULTURAL CONTEXT CONNECTIONS/RELATIONS/APPLICATIONS TEACHER TRAINING PROGRAMS (SALARY POINTS) PROGRAMS ON-SITE, INDIVIDUALLY TAILORED PROGRAMS EDUCATIONAL MATERIALS AVAILABLE WORK WITH VISUALLY IMPAIRED, COST FOR SOME PROGRAMS

Youth

PROGRAMS:	**SELF-GUIDED TOURS, GUIDED TOURS**
SCHEDULE:	YEAR-ROUND, WEEKDAYS, WEEKENDS

Families

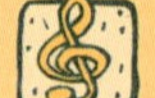
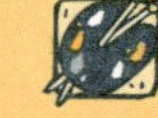

PROGRAMS:	**WORKSHOPS, SELF-GUIDED TOURS, GUIDED TOURS**
SCHEDULE:	YEAR-ROUND, WEEKDAYS, EVENINGS, WEEKENDS

SKITZO'S

10525 Encino Avenue — 501 (c) 3 SFV
Granada Hills, CA 91344
Ph: 818-360-7125
Fax: 818-360-1725

Debra Clark	Executive Producer	DCLARK0704@aol.com
Patsy Keating	Producer	

Skitzo's, a professional community theater group, specializes in sketch comedy and children's theater.

- performances of children's theater and sketch comedy
- charities
- on-site performances for schools

SKITZO'S (CONTINUED)

Focusing on the special needs of talents of the individual child for children's theater allows them to express themselves creatively and emotionally to build self-esteem.

Pre/K-12 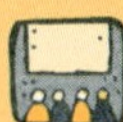

PROGRAMS:	**PERFORMANCES**
SCHEDULE:	YEAR-ROUND, WEEKDAYS, EVENINGS, WEEKENDS
DETAILS:	GRADES PRE/K-12, VISUAL & PERFORMING ARTS CREATIVE EXPRESSION, TRAVEL TO SCHOOLS INDIVIDUALLY TAILORED PROGRAMS WORK WITH: AT-RISK YOUTH

Youth 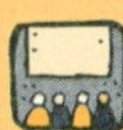

PROGRAMS:	**PERFORMANCES**
SCHEDULE:	YEAR-ROUND, WEEKDAYS, EVENINGS, WEEKENDS
DETAILS:	COST FOR SOME PROGRAMS

Families 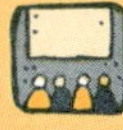

PROGRAMS:	**PERFORMANCES**
SCHEDULE:	YEAR-ROUND, WEEKDAYS, EVENINGS, WEEKENDS

SLAMDANCE

6381 Hollywood Boulevard, #520
Los Angeles, CA 90028
Ph: 323-466-1786
Fax: 323-466-1784
www.slamdance.com

HSM

Larry Hansen	Festival Operations
Peter Baxter	Executive Director
Dan Miruish	Co-Founder

Slamdance is by filmmakers for filmmakers. It supports new filmmakers whose work appears in all styles and formats.

- Slamdance offers an annual film festival
- screenplay competition
- "On the Road" screenings
- L.A. based education on new independent filmmaking

SMOKIN' JOHNNIE'S BBQ

11720 Ventura Boulevard
Studio City, CA 91604
Ph: 818-760-6631

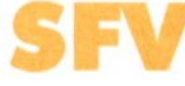

Bobby Cottonwood   Manager   smokinjohnnies@webtv.net

Located at Ventura Boulevard and Colfax, Smokin' Johnnie's BBQ is a full service restaurant and bar with no age limit on entry. Smokin' Johnnie's features the best BBQ this side of town, live blues six nights a week, comedy nights Monday, and smoking patios.

- live blues performances Tuesday through Sunday
- cover charge for special performances only
- monday night Comedy Showcase
- sunday's acoustic blues, bluegrass, Celtic, and experimental music

SOCIAL AND PUBLIC ART RESOURCE CENTER (SPARC)

685 Venice Boulevard
Venice, CA 90291
Ph: 310-822-9560
Fax; 310 827-8717
www.sparcmurals.org

501(c)3 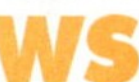

Deborah Padilla	Managing Director/ x13
Judith Baca	Founder/Artistic Director/ x14
Marcos Sanchez	Program Manager/ x12
Linda Delgado	Office Manager/ x15

Located in the heart of Venice, SPARC is a multi-cultural arts center that produces, exhibits, distributes, and preserves public art works (murals). Founded in 1976, SPARC is dedicated to public art projects citywide that involve artists, community groups and youth.

- monthly public art exhibitions in the Gallery
- mural commissions to artists
- mural Resource & Education Center
- gift shop
- mural tours
- internships
- volunteer opportunities
- performance space facilities
- digital mural commission opportunities
- digital mural lab
- seminars and readings
- largest image bank of murals

SPARC's Mural Resource and Education Center offers the largest archive of murals and public art in the world. Teachers, students, and scholars utilize the MREC in a variety of ways; research, curriculum development and publication. SPARC also has a digital workshop and training facilities.

Pre/K-12 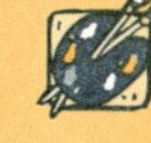

PROGRAM:S:	**WORKSHOPS, SELF-GUIDED TOURS, GUIDED TOURS**
SCHEDULE:	YEAR-ROUND, WEEKDAYS
DETAILS:	GRADES 9-12, VISUAL/PERFORMING ARTS, MULTICULTURAL CREATIVE EXPRESSION, HISTORICAL/CULTURAL CONTEXT TEACHER TRAINING PROGRAMS (SALARY POINTS) TRAVEL TO SCHOOLS, PROGRAMS ON-SITE INDIVIDUALLY TAILORED PROGRAMS, EDUCATIONAL MATERIALS BILINGUAL: SPANISH

Youth 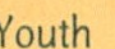 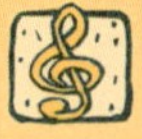 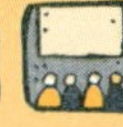 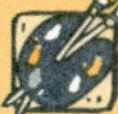

PROGRAMS:	**PERFORMANCES, WORKSHOPS, RESIDENCIES, SELF-GUIDED TOURS, GUIDED TOURS**
SCHEDULE:	YEAR-ROUND, WEEKDAYS, EVENINGS, WEEKENDS

Families 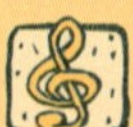 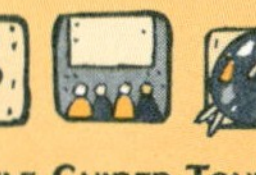 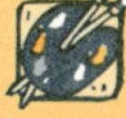

PROGRAMS:	**PERFORMANCES, WORKSHOPS, SELF-GUIDED TOURS, GUIDED TOURS**
SCHEDULE:	YEAR-ROUND, WEEKDAYS, EVENINGS, WEEKENDS
DETAILS:	NO-COST FOR SOME PROGRAMS

SOCIETY OF ARCHITECTURAL HISTORIANS, SOUTHERN CALIFORNIA CHAPTER

P.O. Box 92224 501(c)3
Pasadena, CA 91109-2224
Ph: 800-972-4722
www.cacr.caltech.edu/~mac/sah/index.htm

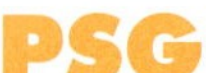

Ted Wells — President/ 949-495-6009

The Society of Architectural Historians seeks to inform and educate a wider public about the history and function of architecture & design, as well as support preservation activities to protect significant buildings, landscapes, urban areas and documents.

- local, national, and international architectural tours
- lectures and symposia
- publications
- special events
- volunteer opportunities
- book signings

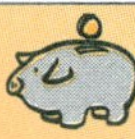

Pre/K-12

PROGRAMS:	**GUIDED TOURS (ARCHITECTURE & DESIGN)**
SCHEDULE:	YEAR-ROUND
DETAILS:	GRADES 7-12, HISTORICAL/CULTURAL CONTEXT

SOCIETY OF ILLUSTRATORS OF LOS ANGELES

116 The Plaza Pasadena 501(c)3
Pasadena, CA 91101
Ph: 818-551-1760
www.geocities.com/MadisonAvenue/7602

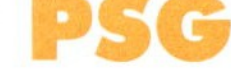

Alyce Heath	Executive Director	slLA1@aol.com
Fred Smith	President	
Brad Weinman	Scholarship Chair	
Brian White	Program Chair	

SILA is a society of illustrators desiring to promote, foster, and stimulate interest in the art of illustration. The society uses programs, competitions, and exhibitions to broaden horizons of practicing illustrators and offers scholarships to student illustrators.

- annual Illustration West Competition
- various programs during the year
- Air Force Program

SOUTH BAY CONSERVATORY

Torrance Cultural Center 501(c)3 SB
3320 Civic Center Drive
Torrance, , CA 90503
Ph: 310-618-6364
Fax: 310-325-0458

Geetha Balakrisna	Registrar
DeBorah Green-Rogers	Director
Carole Ross	Office Manager

Located in the Joslyn Fine Arts Gallery at the Torrance Cultural Arts Center, South Bay Conservatory (School of Music-Dance-Art-Drama) is a nonprofit school of fine arts dedicated to providing quality performing and visual arts education.

- private and group lessons
- classes for ages 18 months to adult, at all levels of ability
- Music Together® for 18 months to 4 years old
- instruction in all orchestral and band instruments including piano, voice, guitar, and percussion
- Chamber Music Institute
- ballet, tap, jazz and performance companies
- drawing, painting and mixed-media art
- junior and advanced acting and adult scene study
- musical theatre productions and summer camp
- performance opportunities
- experienced faculty members

We offer private and group classes and performances. We also specialize in early childhood arts education for children 18 months and up.

Youth

PROGRAMS:	**CLASSES**
SCHEDULE:	YEAR-ROUND, WEEKDAYS, EVENINGS, WEEKENDS

Families

PROGRAMS:	**CLASSES**
SCHEDULE:	YEAR-ROUND, WEEKDAYS, EVENINGS, WEEKENDS

SOUTH COAST CHORALE

P.O. Box 92524 501(c)3 LB
Long Beach, CA 90809
Ph: 562-439-6919

Bob Phibbs — Artistic Director

The South Coast Chorale is a 35 voice community chorus dedicated to providing a positive image of the gay and lesbian community. SCC is the artistic voice of the gay community.

- three concerts per season held at the Carpenter Performing Arts Center in Long Beach

SOUTH VALLEY REGIONAL ARTS COUNCIL

5651 Vineland Avenue
North Hollywood, CA 91601
Ph: 818-655-7000

Developed through the City of Los Angeles Cultural Affairs Department as one of 9 regional arts councils, we are a coalition of arts and community organizations, artists, leaders, business people, and all other interested members of the community who have the purpose of assessing, coalescing and acting on the cultural assets and needs of the area. This council serves Encino, Tarzana, Sherman Oaks, Studio City, Toluca Lake, North Hollywood, Valley Village and Van Nuys. Goals include:

- develop affordable and accessible local programming that highlights and involves youth and local artists
- develop activities that celebrate the city's cultural diversity and promote community building
- serve as an advisory group to the Cultural Affairs Department on local art and cultural priorities
- strengthen the artistic advancement of the community

SOUTHEAST SYMPHONY ASSOCIATION, INC.

501(c)3 DSC
Los Angeles, CA 90008-8801
Ph: 323-293-SESA
Admin: 818-504-0600
Educ: 323-295-9578
Fax: 818-504-9291

Lorraine Julian	Public Relations Director/ 323-735-6211
Jacqueline Broussard	Artistic Director
Rosemarie Cook-Glover	President
Frank Harris	Executive Director

The Southeast Symphony Association promotes wide exposure of the Southeast Symphony Orchestra, identifies, develops and presents new musical talent, and sponsors educational program opportunities for youth.

- four free concerts
- pre-concert presentations at various sites for senior citizens

The Southeast Symphony Association sponsors the S.E.S.A. Music Conservatory, a program providing differentiated instruction with a broad and varied music curriculum to motivate students. Students are offered the opportunity to learn to play an instrument, as well as expand and refine their talents.

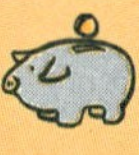

Pre/K-12

PROGRAMS:	**WORKSHOPS**
SCHEDULE:	SPRING, FALL, WINTER, WEEKDAYS
DETAILS:	GRADES 3-12, VISUAL & PERFORMING ARTS AESTHETIC VALUING, CREATIVE EXPRESSION HISTORICAL/CULTURAL CONTEXT TRAVEL TO SCHOOLS

Youth

PROGRAMS:	**PERFORMANCES, CLASSES**
SCHEDULE:	SPRING, FALL, WINTER, WEEKENDS

SOUTHERN CALIFORNIA ART THERAPY ASSOCIATION

P.O. Box 4455 501(c)3
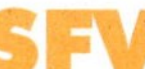

Sunland, CA 91041-4455
Ph: 818-759-8014
Admin: 818-353-0129
Fax: 818-361-8095

Dorothy Shepherd	Corresponding Secretary
Angeline Leonard	President/ 818-344-4555
Terry Tibbetts	President-Elect/ 909-481-4547

Southern California Art Therapy Association is a chapter of American Art Therapy Association which supports students and professional members and educates the general public about art therapy through conferences and programs of the training institute.

- continuing education programs for licensed professional mental health workers and the general public
- members participate in community activities such as Kids Care Fairs which uses art activites to relieve children's stress and anxiety
- members participate in art shows and projects using art to raise money for community programs, such as Project Achieve in Glendale

SOUTHERN CALIFORNIA BLUES SOCIETY

13337 E. South Street, Suite 249 501(c)3
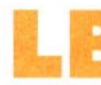

Cerritos, CA 90703
Ph: 714-527-0232
Fax: 714-527-6411

Allen Brown	President
Melvin Eddy	Vice President/Artistic Director
James Friss	Executive Director
Kathryn Alesandrini	Education Manager

The Southern California Blues Society (SCBS) is a community-based organization involved in educating our young, presenting free Blues performances and special programs designed to sustain Blues music as an American art form.

- Blues in the Schools
- the Willie Dixon Scholarship Award
- live summer Blues concerts in locations throughout Southern California
- volunteer opportunities

Progam explores the history of the Blues.

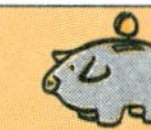

Pre/K-12

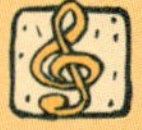

PROGRAMS:	**PERFORMANCES, WORKSHOPS**
SCHEDULE:	YEAR-ROUND, WEEKDAYS
DETAILS:	GRADES PRE/K-12, HISTORY/SOC. SCIENCES HISTORICAL/CULTURAL CONTEXT, TRAVEL TO SCHOOLS COST FOR SOME PROGRAMS

S

SOUTHERN CALIFORNIA CONSERVATORY OF MUSIC

245 Berkshire
La Cañada, CA 91011
Ph: 818-767-6554
Fax: 818-768-6242

501(c)3 **PSG**

Lurrine Burgess	Director
Grant Horrocks	Chairman, Conservatory Division
Richard Taesch	Chairman, Braille Music Division

SCCM provides specialized training by expert teachers to serious students in the field of music. Performance training includes ensembles, musical theater for young singers, frequent student recitals, and concerts.

- quarterly recitals
- solo and chamber music concerts

The Preparatory Division (non-credit) prepares the beginning student of all ages for the Conservatory Division. The Conservatory Division has 12 levels with performance, examination, and jury requirements. All classes are credited towards SCCM Conservatory Diploma. Placement auditions are required. The Degree Division offers a Bachelor of Music.

Pre/K-12

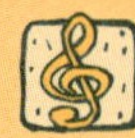

PROGRAMS: **Performances, Workshops, Studio classes**
SCHEDULE: Year-round, Weekdays, Evenings
DETAILS: grades 3-12, Visual & performing arts
Creative Expression, Individually tailored programs

Youth

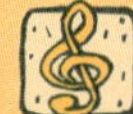

PROGRAMS: **Performances, Workshops, Classes**
SCHEDULE: Year-round, weekdays, Evenings

Families

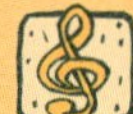

PROGRAMS: **Performances, Workshops, Classes**
SCHEDULE: Year-round, Weekdays, Evenings

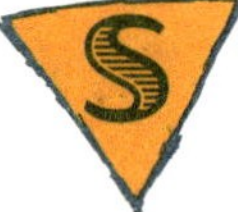

SOUTHERN CALIFORNIA DANCE THEATRE

4410 Greenmeadow Road
Long Beach, CA 90808
Ph: 562-496-1766
www.scdt.com

501(c)3

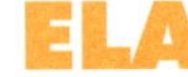

Paula Vreulink	Artistic Director	paula@scdt.com
Susan Nalicat	Administrator	susan@acdt.com

The Southern California Dance Theatre (SCDT) is a Long-Beach-based dance company encouraging people, especially youth, to become involved in the arts through dance, choreography, stage productions and arts education.

- ballet performances
- Young Choreographers Festival

SOUTHERN CALIFORNIA DANCE THEATRE (CONTINUED)

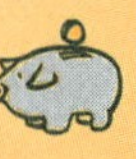

The Pre/K-2 program and workshop is an entertaining ballet performance with a message about our society, followed by a workshop for the children. The 7-12 program is a young choreographers workshop in a three-week intensive program. Students attend dance-related classes, and choreograph and perform their own works.

Pre/K-12

PROGRAMS: **Performances, Workshops**
SCHEDULE: Year-round, Weekdays
DETAILS: grades 7-12, Visual & performing arts
Aesthetic valuing, Creative Expression
Historical/Cultural Context
Connections/Relations/Applications
Travel to schools, Educational materials
Cost for some programs

Youth

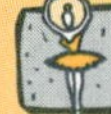

PROGRAMS: **Performances, Workshops**
SCHEDULE: Year-round, weekdays
DETAILS: Cost for some programs

Families

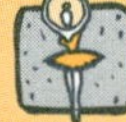

PROGRAMS: **Performances**
SCHEDULE: Year-round, Weekends
DETAILS: cost for some programs

SOUTHERN CALIFORNIA EARLY MUSIC SOCIETY

P.O. Box 544
Pacific Palisades, CA 90272-0544
Ph: 310-358-5967
Fax: 310-277-5798

501(c)3 **WS**

Mimi Fisher	President/ 310-277-1757
Bim Erlendotter	Vice President/ 310-394-8926

Serving the Southland, SCEMS is a nonprofit, all-volunteer, membership organization which supports the study, performance, and enjoyment of Medieval, Renaissance, Baroque, and Classical music through publications and events.

- early Music News magazine
- monthly calendar of early music concerts and events
- directory of early music ensembles and Society members
- varied season of workshops, lectures, and courses
- co-sponsorship of early music events
- early music-related social gatherings
- ticket discounts to selected early music events for Society members
- volunteer opportunities

SOUTHERN CALIFORNIA FESTIVAL FOR CHILDREN

4912 Tujunga, Suite 6 501(c)3 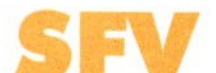
North Hollywood, CA 91601
Ph: 818-753-8040
Fax: 818-753-8899

Andy Walker Education Director
Tami Tirgrath Executive Director

We are a group of artists, educators, and cultural agencies dedicated to presenting an international theater festival for youth. The festival will celebrate many diverse cultures through their art and promote the power of live theater.

- a multitude of cultural performances from around the world
- theater, dance, art, music
- theater workshops: costuming, stage combat, directing, writing, stage design, puppetry, stage technology, etc...
- highlights of local groups from around Southern California

Every spring, we produce a citywide celebration to provide the children of Los Angeles with the finest youth theater possible.

Pre/K-12 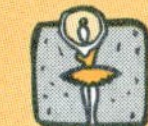 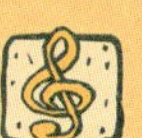 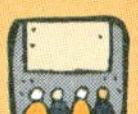

PROGRAMS: PERFORMANCES, WORKSHOPS
SCHEDULE: SPRING, WEEKDAYS, WEEKENDS
DETAILS: GRADES PRE/K-12, VISUAL & PERFORMING ARTS
LANGUAGE ARTS, MULTICULTURAL, CREATIVE EXPRESSION
PROGRAMS ON-SITE, EDUCATIONAL MATERIALS AVAILABLE

Youth 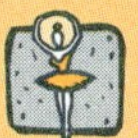 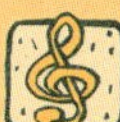 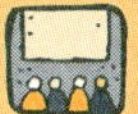

PROGRAMS: PERFORMANCES, WORKSHOPS
SCHEDULE: SPRING, WEEKDAYS, WEEKENDS

Families 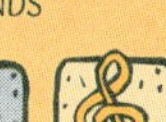 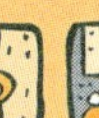 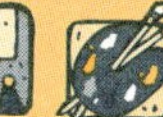

PROGRAMS: PERFORMANCES, WORKSHOPS
SCHEDULE: SPRING, WEEKDAYS, WEEKENDS

SOUTHERN CALIFORNIA MUSIC OUTREACH CORPORATION

1031 Bienveneda Avenue 501(c)3 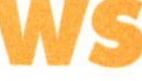
Pacific Palisades, CA 90272
Ph: 310-573-7787
Fax: 310-573-7421

Thomas Neenan Music Director/Conductor/ #127
Connie Grisham Administrator/ #114

The Southern California Music Outreach Corporation works in conjunction with St. Matthew's Music Guild which is a self-supporting organization for music at St. Matthew's Episcopal Church. The chamber music series has been in existence for sixteen years and enjoys a reputation as a center for outstanding programs of choral, instrumental, and keyboard music.

- chamber music series

SOUTHERN CALIFORNIA MUSIC OUTREACH CORPORATION (CONTINUED)

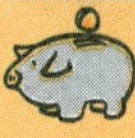

Pre/K-12 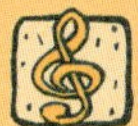

PROGRAMS: PERFORMANCES
SCHEDULE: SPRING, FALL, WINTER, WEEKDAYS
DETAILS: GRADES 3-8, Visual & performing arts
CREATIVE EXPRESSION, TRAVEL TO SCHOOLS

SOUTHERN CALIFORNIA WOMEN'S CAUCUS FOR ART (SCWCA)

315 W. Ninth Street, Suite 1100 501(c)3 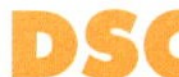
Los Angeles, CA 90015
www.scwa.org

Ada Brown President/ 626-457-5972 adapbrown@aol.com
Jean Towgood Membership/Conference Chair/ 714-842-6066 jtowgood@aol.com
Diana Hobstetter Secretary/ 310-827-5768
Janice DeLoof Treasurer/ 714-526-5071

SCWCA is the local Southern California chapter of the Women's Caucus for Art, a national organization for women actively engaged in visual arts professions.

- exhibitions featuring art by women from the local and regional area
- lectures and professional workshops
- conferences
- newsletter
- research on equity in the arts
- peer review and critique groups
- web site
- volunteer opportunities
- documentation of Southern California women artists

SOUTHLAND OPERA

174 W. Foothill Boulevard, #338 501(c)3 PSG
Monrovia, CA 91016
Ph: 626-256-3222
Fax: 626-357-9156

Ann Noriel General Director
Steve Parkin Artistic Director

Using the talent and skills of local Southern California artists since September 1997, Southland Opera has had over 300 musical performances, 270 of which were student educational outreach programs.

- "Amahl and the Night Visitors", a one-act Christmas opera, fully staged with a set and costumes, adaptable to a variety of different performance situations. It may be performed with piano or chamber orchestra
- operatic and musical theatre concerts, tailored to fit the presenter's needs
- other fully-staged operatic productions for both students and adults

S

SOUTHLAND OPERA (CONTINUED)

Without sacrificing the intgrity of the music, Southland Opera keeps productions innovative and exciting,to keep the attention of students. The company's singers/actors have a long history of working together, making the production quality extremely high.

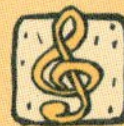

Pre/K-12

PROGRAMS: PERFORMANCES, WORKSHOPS
SCHEDULE: YEAR-ROUND, WEEKDAYS, EVENINGS, WEEKENDS
DETAILS: GRADES PRE/K-12, HISTORY/SOC. SCIENCES
VISUAL & PERFORMING ARTS, LANGUAGE ARTS, MULTICULTURAL
CREATIVE EXPRESSION, TRAVEL TO SCHOOLS
EDUCATIONAL MATERIALS AVAILABLE

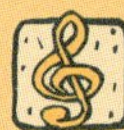

Families

PROGRAMS: PERFORMANCES, WORKSHOPS
SCHEDULE: YEAR-ROUND, WEEKDAYS, EVENINGS, WEEKENDS

SOUTHWEST CHAMBER MUSIC

595 E. Colorado Boulevard, Suite 211 501(c)3
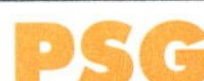

Pasadena, CA 91101
Ph: 626-685-4455
Fax: 626-685-4458
www.swmusic.org

Inka Bujalski Program Director
Jeff Von Der Schmidt Artistic Director
Jan Karlin Executive Director

Southwest Chamber Music is Southern California's most active professional chamber music ensemble, providing innovative concerts and educational programs in Pasadena and Los Angeles.

- Sunday and Tueday concert series at Zipper Concert Hall
- Tueday evening commuter concerts at Zipper Concert Hall
- Saturday evening concert series at the Pasadena Presbyterian Church
- open rehearsals on Friday evenings in the Gallery Space of the Armory Center
- pre-concert talks and post-concert receptions at all of the above venues with access to performers, composers, and artists
- Beethovan Birthday Marathon, a full day and evening of music celebrating the composer
- summer concerts at the Huntington Art Gallery Loggia
- guest appearances at various sites throughout California

SOUTHWEST CHAMBER MUSIC (CONTINUED)

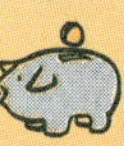

Members of Southwest Chamber Music provide a mentorship program of weekly coachings and scholarship lessons to young musicians at high schools in the Pasadena and Los Angeles Unified School District's "Project Muse" in-school concerts and "Breaking the Code of Contemporary Music: Open Rehearsals" for families and students of all ages.

Pre/K-12

PROGRAMS: PERFORMANCES, RESIDENCIES
SCHEDULE: YEAR-ROUND, WEEKDAYS, WEEKENDS
DETAILS: GRADES PRE/K-12, VISUAL & PERFORMING ARTS
AESTHETIC VALUING, CREATIVE EXPRESSION
CONNECTIONS/RELATIONS/APPLICATIONS
TEACHER TRAINING PROGRAMS, TRAVEL TO SCHOOLS
INDIVIDUALLY TAILORED PROGRAMS , EDUCATIONAL MATERIALS
WORK WITH AT-RISK YOUTH

Youth

PROGRAMS: PERFORMANCES, RESIDENCIES
SCHEDULE: YEAR-ROUND, WEEKDAYS, WEEKENDS

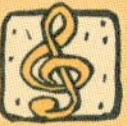

Families

PROGRAMS: PERFORMANCES
SCHEDULE: YEAR-ROUND, WEEKDAYS, WEEKENDS
DETAILS: COST FOR SOME PROGRAMS

SOUTHWEST MUSEUM

234 Museum Drive 501(c)3 SFV
Los Angeles, CA 90065
Ph: 323-221-2164
Fax: 323-224-8223

Jeannette O'Malley Assistant Director/Curator of Exhibits
Duane King Executive Director

The Southwest Museum is a major educational center dedicated to the preservation and presentation of the history and culture of Native American Indians. The Southwest Museum collects, preserves and protects ethnographic objects, art and archival materials that represent American Indian heritage.

SOUTHWEST MUSEUM AT LACMA WEST

6067 Wilshire Boulevard 501(c)3
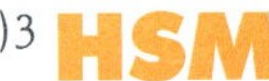

Los Angeles, CA 90036
Ph: 323-933-4510

Jeannette O'Malley Assistant Director/Curator of Exhibits
Duane King Executive Director

SPOKEN WORD FESTIVAL

1873 Lucretia Avenue
Los Angeles, CA 90026-1807
Ph/Fax: 323-662-8173

501(c)3 **HSM**

Eric Trules — Executive and Artistic Director — trules@mizar.usc.edu

The Spoken Word Festival is a mult-disciplinary presenting and producing organization that brings the richness, diversity, sound of language and the spoken word to the diverse, multi-lingual people of the Los Angeles area, both on and off the page.

- festivals, readings, films, and videos featuring poetry and the spoken word

ST. ELMO VILLAGE

4830 St. Elmo Drive
Los Angeles, CA 90019
Ph: 323-931-3409
Fax; 323-931-2065

501(c)3 **HSM**

Roderick Sykes — Founder/Director
Jacqueline Alexander — Administrator

We provide a place to explore and develop creativity, direct youth in our community to pursue achievable goals, and to help adults rediscover the creative spirit in us all.

- Saturday workshops in painting and drawing, computer graphics, drama, and drumming
- Thursday evening clay workshop
- exhibits of painting and photography in the Cafe de Art Coffee Shop
- annual Festival of the Arts of Creative Survival on Memorial Day Weekend
- tours

STAGES, INC.

1540 N. McCadden Place
Hollywood, CA 90028
Ph: 310-463-5356
Fax: 310-440-3989

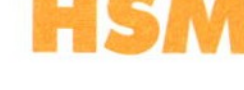

Sonia Lloveras — Managing Director
Paul Verdier — Artistic Director

STAGES' presents theater works of universal themes of marked originality, to reach out and touch people of all ethnic and cultural heritage. Productions are performed in English and other languages.

STANDER ENTERTAINMENT

6309 Ben Avenue
North Hollywood, CA 91606
Ph/Fax: 818 769-6365

SFV

Jacqueline Stander — General Manager

Stander Entertainment represents national recording/touring acts and is a consultant for festivals, line-ups, and artists.

STANDER ENTERTAINMENT (CONTINUED)

Tailored to educational programs, Stander Entertainment offers an empowerment, creativity seminar through music.

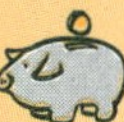

Pre/K-12

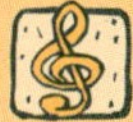

PROGRAMS: PERFORMANCES, WORKSHOPS
SCHEDULE: YEAR-ROUND, WEEKDAYS, EVENINGS, WEEKENDS
DETAILS: GRADES 7-12, TRAVEL TO SCHOOLS
INDIVIDUALLY TAILORED PROGRAMS, BILINGUAL: SPANISH
COST FOR SOME PROGRAMS

STEED WOODWIND QUINTET

12811 Matteson Avenue, #7
Los Angeles, CA 90066
Ph: 310-391-4061

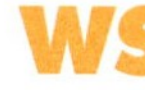

William Steed — Leader

STEEN ART STUDY

961 E. California Boulevard, Suite 329
Pasadena, CA 91106-4057
Ph: 323-681-6343
Fax: 626-577-2384
www.steenartstudy.com

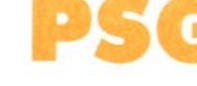

Ronald Steen — Professor — steen@steenartstudy.com

Steen Art Study is an entity for university degreed Ronald E. Steen as Independent Art Historian and Art Educator, founded in 1983, for the purposes of conducting research, publishing, curating, lecturing, and conducting classes, and educational trips.

- art research
- publish essays, catalogs, and reviews on art history
- lectures
- curating
- Art History Series- a ten week illustrated lecture series
- Contemporary Art Series- a six week summer series
- study trips
- newsletter

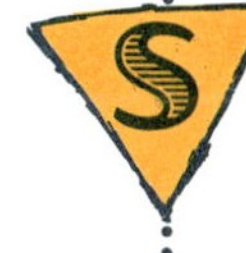

STEPHEN COHEN GALLERY

7358 Beverly Boulevard
Los Angeles, CA 90036
Ph: 323-937-5525

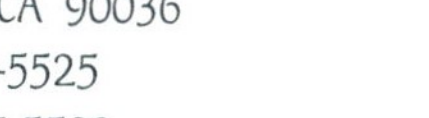

Fax: 323-937-5523
www.stephencohengallery.com

HSM

Stephen Cohen — Director — stephen@stephencohengallery.com

Fine vintage and contemporary photography, American and European.

STOP-GAP

1570 Brookhollow Drive
Santa Ana, CA 92705
Ph: 714-979-7061
Fax: 714-979-7065
www.stopgap.org

501 (c) 3

Joy LePatner	Director of Administration	JoyLePatner@stopgap.org
Don Laffoon	Co-founder and Exetuive Director	DonLaffoon@stopgap.org
Victoria Bryan	Co-founder/Managing Director	VictoriaBryan@stopgap.org
Fionnuala Kenny	Director of Education	FionnualaKenny@stopgap.org

Stop-Gap is Southern California's award-winning theater company dedicated to using drama as an educational and therapeutic tool to make a positive difference in individuals lives.

- interactive touring plays for classrooms, youth and adults, eleven issue-oriented plays for youth, and one play on breast cancer for adults
- drama therapy workshops for special populations, twelve on-going weekly workshops with groups including battered women, abused children, frail elderly, and children in the hospital
- Stop-Gap Institute Training programs are for drama therapists, or allied professionals to use the Stop-Gap method, and for school districts to replicate Stop-Gap touring plays
- Emergency Response programs, individually designed for natural disasters and traumatic situations in schools and communities

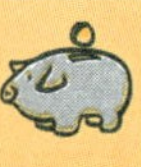

Not only does Stop-Gap provide interactive theater programs to schools and sites, but through the Stop-Gap Institute, the program also trains allied professionals to use the Stop-Gap Method of Interactive Theatre in their own schools, groups, agencies and teen theater programs.

Pre/K-12

PROGRAMS: PERFORMANCES, WORKSHOPS
SCHEDULE: YEAR-ROUND, WEEKDAYS, EVENINGS, WEEKENDS
DETAILS: GRADES 3-12, WIDE RANGE OF ISSUE-ORIENTED, INTERACTIVE THEATER PROGRAMS, TRAVEL TO SCHOOLS
INDIVIDUALLY TAILORED PROGRAMS, BILINGUAL: SPANISH
COST FOR SOME PROGRAMS

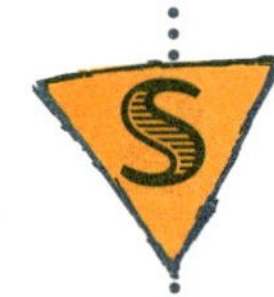

Youth

PROGRAMS: PERFORMANCES, WORKSHOPS
SCHEDULE: YEAR-ROUND, WEEKDAYS, EVENINGS, WEEKENDS
DETAILS: COST FOR SOME PROGRAMS

Families

PROGRAMS: PERFORMANCES, WORKSHOPS
SCHEDULE: YEAR-ROUND, WEEKDAYS, EVENINGS, WEEKENDS
DETAILS: COST FOR SOME PROGRAMS

STORYTELLERS AND TROUBADOURS

1202 W. Collins Avenue
Orange, CA 92867
Ph: 714 771-1981
Fax: 714 771-2456

Ken Frawley — Information Officer/ 888-499-1270

Storytellers and Troubadours provides a wide variety of storytelling/family music programs to schools, libraries, fairs, and other community events.

Storytellers and Troubadours offers programs that provide a view of American History by combining stories, true facts, songs, western arts and dance. Some programs create music and songs, while others give a multicultural view of prople from around the world as found in their stories.

Pre/K-12

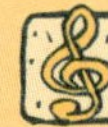
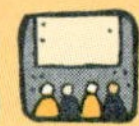

PROGRAMS: PERFORMANCES, WORKSHOPS, RESIDENCIES
SCHEDULE: YEAR-ROUND, WEEKDAYS, EVENINGS, WEEKENDS
DETAILS: GRADES PRE/K-8, HISTORY/SOC. SCIENCES
VISUAL & PERFORMING ARTS, MULTICULTURAL
CREATIVE EXPRESSION, TEACHER TRAINING PROGRAMS
TRAVEL TO SCHOOLS, INDIVIDUALLY TAILORED PROGRAMS
EDUCATIONAL MATERIALS AVAILABLE, BILINGUAL: SPANISH

Youth

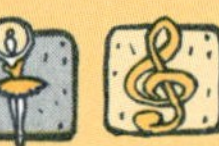
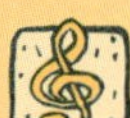
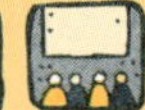

PROGRAMS: PERFORMANCES, WORKSHOPS
SCHEDULE: YEAR-ROUND, WEEKDAYS, EVENINGS, WEEKENDS

Families

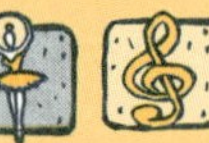
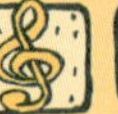
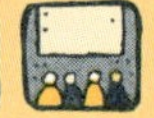

PROGRAMS: PERFORMANCES
SCHEDULE: YEAR-ROUND, WEEKDAYS, EVENINGS, WEEKENDS

STORYTELLING, MUSIC AND MORE

1165 S. Sierra Bonita Avenue
Los Angeles, CA 90019
Ph: 323-933-4614
Fax: 323-937-0869

HSM

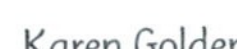

Karen Golden — kargolden@aol.com

Karen Golden delights audiences of all ages with her unique blend of stories and music.

- performances of folk, personal, and family stories with music
- keynote addresses
- storytelling "How to" workshops
- teachers training

STORYTELLING, MUSIC AND MORE (CONTINUED)

Special programs include folktales and footwear, stories from Jewish tradition, stories of immigration, tales from around the world, and "How to Tell Stories" workshops for kids.

Pre/K-12

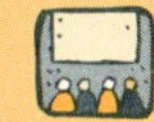

PROGRAMS: PERFORMANCES, WORKSHOPS, RESIDENCIES
SCHEDULE: YEAR-ROUND, WEEKDAYS, EVENINGS, WEEKENDS
DETAILS: GRADES PRE/K-12, HISTORY/SOC. SCIENCES
VISUAL & PERFORMING ARTS, LANGUAGE ARTS, MULTICULTURAL
CREATIVE EXPRESSION, HISTORICAL/CULTURAL CONTEXT
TEACHER TRAINING PROGRAMS, TRAVEL TO SCHOOLS
INDIVIDUALLY TAILORED PROGRAMS , EDUCATIONAL MATERIALS
WORK WITH AT-RISK YOUTH

Youth

PROGRAMS: PERFORMANCES, WORKSHOPS, RESIDENCIES
SCHEDULE: YEAR-ROUND, WEEKDAYS, EVENINGS, WEEKENDS

Families

PROGRAMS: PERFORMANCES, WORKSHOPS, RESIDENCIES
SCHEDULE: YEAR-ROUND, WEEKDAYS, EVENINGS, WEEKENDS

STUDIO 202

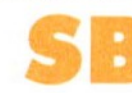

112 N. Catalina Avenue
Redondo Beach, CA 90277
Ph/Fax: 310-372-4001

STUDIO 324

WS

324 Sunset Avenue, Studio D
Venice, CA 90291
Ph: 310-392-4272
Admin: 310-396-0262
Fax: 310-392-1717

Helen Garber — Director — hkgphoto@aol.com
David Schoffman — Director, Art School

Located three blocks from Venice Beach, Studio 324 is a group studio space with annual exhibits and arts workshops for adults. David Schoffman, transplanted New York artist, directs the painting/drawing program. The environment, three-blocks from the beach, envelops the class participant in creative juices inspiring New York cool vibe.

- workshops in painting, drawing, museum tours, and art history
- annual exhibition

STUDIO OF PERFORMING ARTS

WS

8558 W. Third Street
Los Angeles, CA 90048
Ph: 310-275-4683

Michael Lipson — President
Peri Rogovin — Director

Ballroom Dance Studio, located near the Beverly Center, offers group and private dance lessons in Swing, Lingy Hop, Latin-Salsa, Argentine Tango and Wedding Preparations.

- five studios
- validated parking
- air-conditioning

SUNLAND TUJUNGA BRANCH LIBRARY

SFV

7771 Foothill Boulevard
Tujunga, CA 91042
Ph: 818-352-4481

Vivian Fielder — Branch Manager

The Sunland Tujunga Branch of the Los Angeles Public Library offers a broad selection of books, books on tape, videos, magazines, compact discs for adults, teens, and children; computers with Internet access, on-line databases, word processing; and a community room where programs for all ages are presented by the library and community groups.

- monthly exhibitions featuring local artists and collectors
- Friends of the Library Book Store
- poetry readings
- writer's groups
- Foothill Gem & Mineral Society
- LaLeche League
- Sunland Tujunga Art Association
- Crescenta Valley Sierra Club
- weekly internet workshops

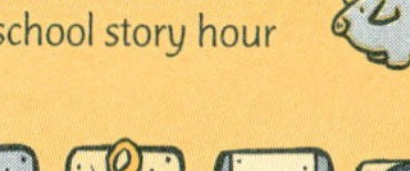

The Sunland Tujunga Branch Library offers children and teen programs in crafts, reading, performances, pre-school story hour and summer reading programs.

Pre/K-12

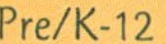

PROGRAMS: PERFORMANCES, WORKSHOPS
SCHEDULE: YEAR-ROUND, WEEKDAYS, EVENINGS, WEEKENDS
DETAILS: GRADES PRE/K-12, VISUAL & PERFORMING ARTS
LANGUAGE ARTS, MULTICULTURAL, TRAVEL TO SCHOOLS
PROGRAMS ON-SITE , EDUCATIONAL MATERIALS AVAILABLE

Youth

PROGRAMS: PERFORMANCES, WORKSHOPS
SCHEDULE: YEAR-ROUND, WEEKDAYS, EVENINGS, WEEKENDS

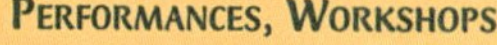

Families

PROGRAMS: PERFORMANCES, WORKSHOPS
SCHEDULE: YEAR-ROUND, WEEKDAYS, EVENINGS, WEEKENDS

SUNYATA GALLERY

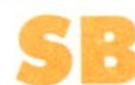

331 W. 7th Street
San Pedro, CA 90731
Ph/Fax: 310-832-5516

Don O'Melveny

Emerging artists; eclectic, cool, progressive sensibilities. Launch pad for the next generation.

SYMPHONY IN THE GLEN

4655 Kingswell Avenue, #209 — 501(c)3 — HSM
Los Angeles, CA 90027
Ph: 323-955-6976
Admin: 323-644-5600
Fax: 323-644-8208
www.symphonyintheglen.org

Barbara Ferris	Managing Director
Arthur Rubinstein	President and Music Director

Based in Griffith Park, Symphony In The Glen provides free symphonic concerts in outdoor settings. Family attendance is encouraged and children are welcome.

- children's activites precede the concerts and include "The Junior Maestro Conducting Class" and "Learning about the Orchestra"
- all concerts, parking, and kid's activites are free

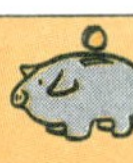

The outdoor setting allows parents of all cultures to introduce themselves and their children to classical music in a relaxed and welcoming atmosphere. Families who attend over time are exposing thier children to live symphonic music in their most formative years. Mentally and physically disabled children can easily take part in the activities.

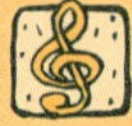

Families

PROGRAMS:	**PERFORMANCES, WORKSHOPS**
SCHEDULE:	SUMMER, WEEKENDS

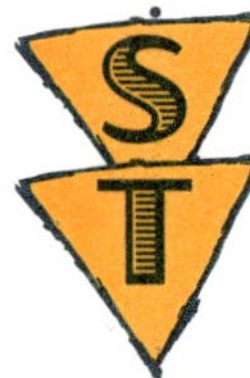

T.A.G., THE ARTISTS' GALLERY

2903 Santa Monica Boulevard — 501(c)3 — WS
Santa Monica, CA 90404
Ph: 310-829-9556
Fax: 310-829-0655
www.artscenecal.com/TAG.html

Riva Weinstein	Director
Kaija Keel	President

We are a nonprofit membership organization where members have the opportunity to exhibit their work. We also serve as a resource for collectors.

T. HERITAGE GALLERY

1109 Gayley Avenue
Los Angeles, CA 90024
Ph: 310-208-1896
Fax: 310-476-8331

Tim Heritage	Director

Original contemporary art dedicated to further the awareness of our world's environment and promote positive changes in society. Museum quality picture framing and restoration.

TAMARIND THEATRE

HSM

5919 Franklin Avenue
Hollywood, CA 90028
Ph: 323-465-7980
Admin: 323-465-7989
Fax: 323-465-8093

Tom Kendall	Producing Artistic Director
Nick Alan	Managing Director

The Tamarind Theatre is a 99-seat charming theatre located on the Franklin Avenue strip with five wonderful restaurants and easy valet parking.

- original plays and musicals
- classes
- comedy sportz

TANGUERO PRODUCTIONS

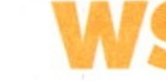

8075 W. 3rd Street, Suite 410
Los Angeles, CA 90048
Ph: 323-930-1244
Fax: 323-930-0186

Jenny Pinedo	Administrative Assistant/PR Promotions/ x21
Loreen Arbus	Owner/ x10
Monica Suyo	Assistant/ x10

Tanguero Productions produces Ritmo Tango, the first and only Argentine Tango Theatrical presentation in the U.S., as well as workshops, choreography, and lectures.

- group and private tango classes
- coaching
- Ritmo Tango products
- special events and exhibitions
- available for travel

TANI AND FRIENDS

6030 Romaine Street
Los Angeles, CA 90038-3010
Ph: 323-462-6409

501(c)3 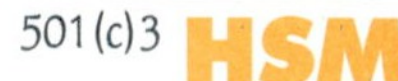

Tani — Artistic Director

Tani and Friends are dancers who specialize in dances of Asia primarily with music and relevant cultural historical information included.

- group and solo performances for schools, clubs, and festivals
- master classes and lecture demonstrations for colleges
- workshops on request

We include lively, bright material, and balance this with thoughtful, slow material. The performances are colorful, authentic, informative, cheerful, inspiring, and from very diverse cultures for comparison and contrast.

Pre/K-12 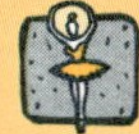

PROGRAMS: PERFORMANCES, WORKSHOPS, STUDIO CLASSES
SCHEDUE: LYEAR-ROUND, WEEKDAYS, EVENINGS, WEEKENDS
DETAILS: GRADES PRE/K-12, VISUAL & PERFORMING ARTS
HISTORICAL/CULTURAL CONTEXT, TRAVEL TO SCHOOLS
INDIVIDUALLY TAILORED PROGRAMS, EDUCATIONAL MATERIALS
WORK WITH SPECIAL SPECIAL EDUCATION

Youth 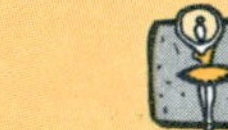

PROGRAMS: PERFORMANCES, WORKSHOPS, CLASSES
SCHEDULE: YEAR-ROUND, WEEKDAYS, EVENINGS, WEEKENDS

Families 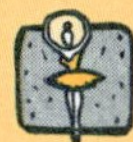

PROGRAMS: PERFORMANCES, WORKSHOPS, CLASSES
SCHEDULE: YEAR-ROUND, WEEKDAYS, EVENINGS, WEEKENDS

TARA'S GALLERY

22311 Ventura Boulevard, #118
Woodland Hills, CA 91364
Ph: 818-992-0809
Fax: 818-713-1791
www.taras-gallery.com

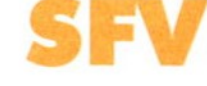

Tara Mozafarian — Gallery Director/Art Teacher — tarasgallery@protonet.com

Located on Ventura Boulevard in Woodland Hills, Tara's Gallery is a studio gallery that presents contemporary painting and offers workshops for experienced artists as well as painting classes.

- monthly exhibitions featuring mostly local artists (individuals and groups)
- over the weekend mini shows
- painting workshops for experienced independent artists
- painting classes for adults and youths

TARA'S GALLERY (CONTINUED)

Tara's Gallery offers classes that teach many different techniques, in small groups with individual attention. Workshops are also offered in a friendly and supportive environment with opportunities to become professional.

Youth 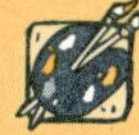

PROGRAMS: CLASSES
SCHEDULE: YEAR-ROUND, WEEKDAYS, EVENINGS

Families

PROGRAMS: CLASSES
SCHEDULE: YEAR-ROUND, WEEKDAYS, EVENINGS

TASENDE

8808 Melrose Avenue
Los Angeles, CA 90069
Ph: 310-276-8686
Fax: 310-276-8576
www.artscenecal.com/tasende.html

WS

Aitor Tasende — Gallery Manager — tasende@aol.com
Mary Hynes — Director

Contemporary drawings, paintings and sculpture

TEATRO YERBA BUENA

615 Romulo Street
Los Angeles, CA 90065
Ph: 323-763-1960
Admin: 323-221-9735
Educ: 323-740-1480
Fax; 323-763-1969
www.nexusdimension.com

501(c)3 SFV

Jose Montes — Artistic Director
Edward Moya — Executive Director
Annette Cordova — Educational Programs Manager/ 213-223-4994

Teatro Yerba Buena, based in the Cypress Park community of Los Angeles, combines comedy skits, music, and dance in street theater form for audiences of all ages.

TEATRO YERBA BUENA (CONTINUED)

TYB uses the three disciplines (theater, music, and dance) as an avenue to teach young children. We also use comedy and satire to reach adult audiences. We write and create our own material.

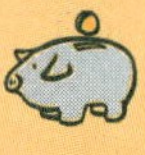

Pre/K-12

 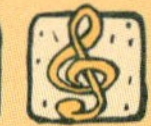 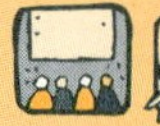

PROGRAMS: PERFORMANCES
SCHEDULE: YEAR-ROUND, WEEKDAYS, WEEKENDS
DETAILS: GRADES PRE/K-12, HISTORY/SOC. SCIENCES
VISUAL & PERFORMING ARTS, MULTICULTURAL
CREATIVE EXPRESSION, TRAVEL TO SCHOOLS
FACILITY FOR SCHOOL VISITS, COST FOR SOME PROGRAMS
INDIVIDUALLY TAILORED PROGRAMS, BILINGUAL: SPANISH

Youth

 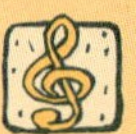 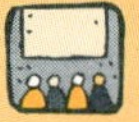 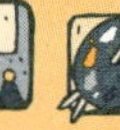

PROGRAMS: PERFORMANCES
SCHEDULE: YEAR-ROUND, WEEKDAYS, EVENINGS
DETAILS: COST FOR SOME PROGRAMS

Families

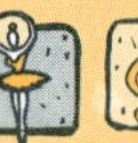 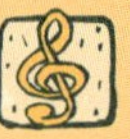 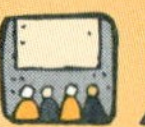 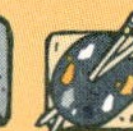

PROGRAMS: PERFORMANCES
SCHEDULE: YEAR-ROUND, EVENINGS, WEEKENDS

TELEPOETICS, INC.

1939 1/4 W. Washington Boulevard — 501(c)3 **WS**
Los Angeles, CA 90018-1635
Ph: 323-766-1266
Fax: 323-734-7055
www.this.is/telepoetics

Merilene Murphy — Poet/President — PeazRitr@ix.netcom.com

Telepoetics, Inc. is a tele-arts service provider of fun literary-based audio/video projects in the classroom, studio and theatrical settings (page-to-stage live and/or webcast interactive).

- live and interactive web casts and video conferences connecting poets and audiences worldwide
- talent showcases
- literary workshops
- tele-art workshops
- collaborators welcome for various projects such as building on the concept "world peace by any medium necessary"
- interested in working with scientists to explore alternative paper products for publishing

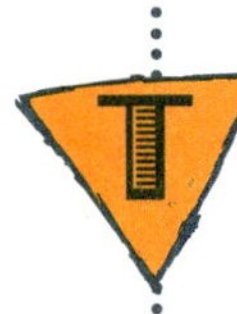

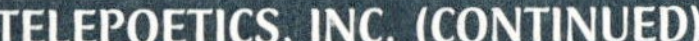

TELEPOETICS, INC. (CONTINUED)

Telepoetics, Inc. uses arts and technology to dazzle the audience with cheap-to-free high tech production of live webcasts with the end result connecting people to the poetry each person has inside.

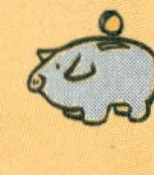

Pre/K-12

 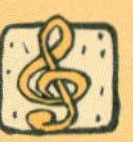 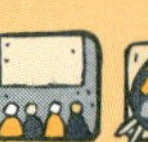

PROGRAMS: PERFORMANCES, WORKSHOPS, POETRY-BASED TELECOMMUNICATIONS
SCHEDULE: YEAR-ROUND, WEEKDAYS, EVENINGS, WEEKENDS
DETAILS: GRADES PRE/K-12, VISUAL & PERFORMING ARTS
MULTICULTURAL, CONNECTIONS/RELATIONS/APPLICATIONS
TRAVEL TO SCHOOLS , INDIVIDUALLY TAILORED PROGRAMS
COST FOR SOME PROGRAMS

Youth

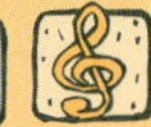 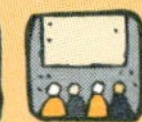 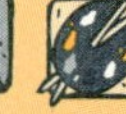

PROGRAMS: PERFORMANCES, WORKSHOPS, POETRY-BASED TELECOMMUNICATIONS
SCHEDULE: YEAR-ROUND, WEEKDAYS, EVENINGS, WEEKENDS
DETAILS: COST FOR SOME PROGRAMS

Families

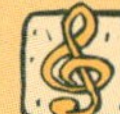 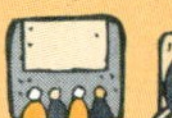 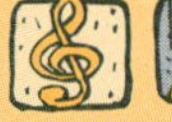 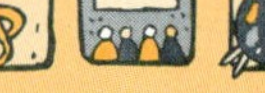

PROGRAMS: PERFORMANCES, WORKSHOPS, POETRY-BASED TELECOMMUNICATIONS
SCHEDULE: YEAR-ROUND, WEEKDAYS, EVENINGS, WEEKENDS
DETAILS: COST FOR SOME PROGRAMS

TEXTILE MUSEUM ASSOCIATES OF SOUTHERN CALIFORNIA, INC.

P.O. Box 49160 — 501(c)3
Los Angeles, CA 90049
Ph: 310-454-8221

Cheri Hunter — Program Co-Chair
Tom Rutherford — President/ 818-242-7576
Bunny Rutherford — Membership Chair/ 818-242-7576

The largest non-commercial textile and rug society in the U.S., Textile Museum Associates of Southern California, Inc. presents educational programs on antique and contemporary handmade ethnic and art textiles of the world, and oriental rugs.

- monthly slide lectures by nationally and internationally renowned rug and textile scholars, museum curators, collectors, and dealers
- field trips to museum exhibitions, galleries, and private collections
- hands-on study and analysis of rugs and textiles
- receptions and openings
- exhibitions
- textile conservation advicce
- newsletter

THAI COMMUNITY ARTS AND CULTURAL CENTER

P.O. Box 2105 501(c)3
Venice, CA 90294
Ph: 310-827-2910

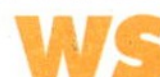

Vibul Wonprasat Artistic Director
Terisa Chung Administrative Assistance

The Thai Community Arts and Cultural Center seeks to promote Thai arts, Thai culture, education, and entertainment in L.A.

- annual Thai Cultural Day

The Thai Community Arts And Cultural Center offers lessons in Thai traditional painting, drawing and painting, and ornamental design.

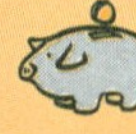

Families

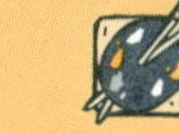

PROGRAMS: **CLASSES**
SCHEDULE: YEAR-ROUND, WEEKENDS

THEATRE ARTS FESTIVAL FOR YOUTH (TAFFY)

P.O. Box 2665 501(c)3
Winnetka, CA 91309-2665
Ph: 818-998-2339
Fax: 818-709-1461

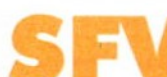

Pamela Wood Director

Theatre Arts Festival For Youth presents the best in multicultural and multi-disciplinary arts entertainment and education for youth and their families.

TAFFY offers classes for K-5 in music, drama, and visual arts that follow a timeline from primitive to modern and can be adopted to fit a school's curriculum. Performance workshops are also available in reading, writing and music appreciation.

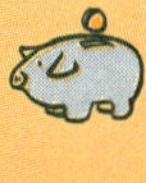

Pre/K-12

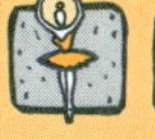
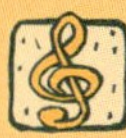
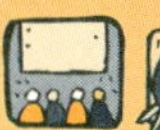

PROGRAMS: **PERFORMANCES, WORKSHOPS, STUDIO CLASSES, RESIDENCIES**
SCHEDULE: YEAR-ROUND, WEEKDAYS, EVENINGS, WEEKENDS
DETAILS: GRADES PRE/K-12, VISUAL & PERFORMING ARTS
LANGUAGE ARTS, MULTICULTURAL, CREATIVE EXPRESSION
HISTORICAL/CULTURAL CONTEXT
TEACHER TRAINING PROGRAMS, TRAVEL TO SCHOOLS
PROGRAMS ON-SITE, INDIVIDUALLY TAILORED PROGRAMS
Educational materials, cost for some programs

Youth

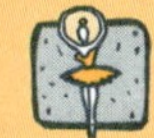
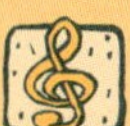
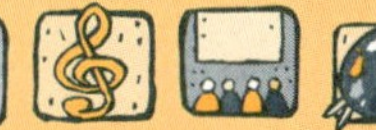

PROGRAMS: **PERFORMANCES, WORKSHOPS, CLASSES, RESIDENCIES**
SCHEDULE: YEAR-ROUND, WEEKDAYS, EVENINGS, WEEKENDS
DETAILS: COST FOR SOME PROGRAMS

Families

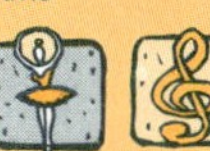
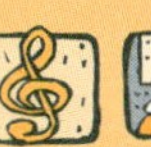
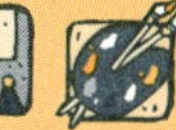

PROGRAMS: **PERFORMANCES, WORKSHOPS, CLASSES, RESIDENCIES**
SCHEDULE: YEAR-ROUND, WEEKDAYS, EVENINGS, WEEKENDS
DETAILS: COST FOR SOME PROGRAMS

THEATRE OF HEARTS/YOUTH FIRST

400 S. Lafayette Park Place, Suite 307 501(c)3
Los Angeles, CA 90057
Ph: 213-384-6878
Fax: 213-351-9883

DSC

Sheila Scott-Wilkinson Executive Director sscottwilk@aol.com

The mission of Youth First, the preeminent Artist-In-Residence program of Theatre of Hearts, is to prevent and intervene in youth-on-youth violence by involving youth, 7-18 years of age (inclusive of grades K-12) and their families in on-going, high quality, multidisciplinary fine arts educational workshops offered at schools and community-based sites in neighborhoods throughout Los Angeles County. Residencies are customized to suit the needs of each community and/or school site. Youth First works collaboratively with site personnel and professional artists to build a core curriculum based on the developmental needs of the youth.

- art educational workshops 13-15 weeks in length ending with a work-in-progress presentation open to the public; workshops offered in theater, choral, dance, music, creative writing, storytelling, visual arts, and video production
- county-wide youth exhibitions/performances arranged yearly
- volunteer opportunities for special events

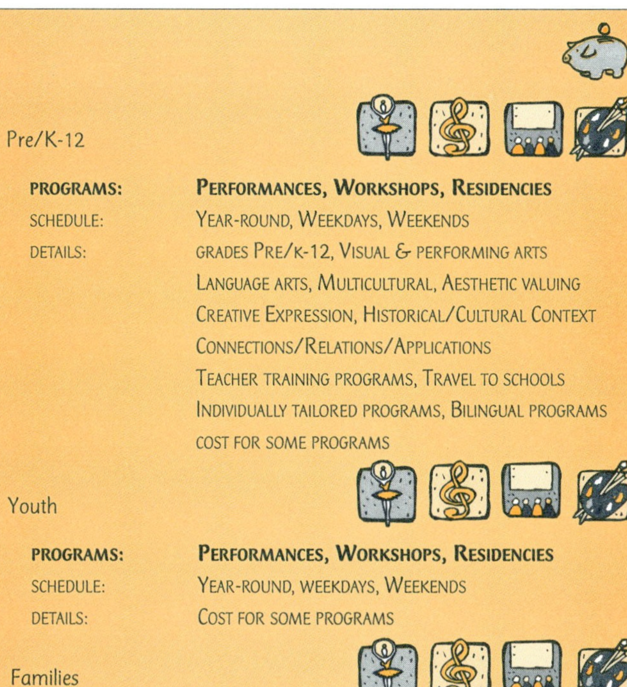

Pre/K-12

PROGRAMS: **PERFORMANCES, WORKSHOPS, RESIDENCIES**
SCHEDULE: YEAR-ROUND, WEEKDAYS, WEEKENDS
DETAILS: GRADES PRE/K-12, VISUAL & PERFORMING ARTS
LANGUAGE ARTS, MULTICULTURAL, AESTHETIC VALUING
CREATIVE EXPRESSION, HISTORICAL/CULTURAL CONTEXT
CONNECTIONS/RELATIONS/APPLICATIONS
TEACHER TRAINING PROGRAMS, TRAVEL TO SCHOOLS
INDIVIDUALLY TAILORED PROGRAMS, BILINGUAL PROGRAMS
COST FOR SOME PROGRAMS

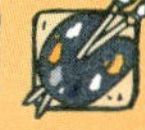

Youth

PROGRAMS: **PERFORMANCES, WORKSHOPS, RESIDENCIES**
SCHEDULE: YEAR-ROUND, WEEKDAYS, WEEKENDS
DETAILS: COST FOR SOME PROGRAMS

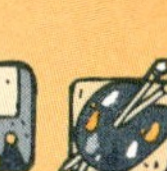
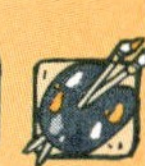

Families

PROGRAMS: **PERFORMANCES, WORKSHOPS, RESIDENCIES**
SCHEDULE: YEAR-ROUND, WEEKDAYS, WEEKENDS
DETAILS: COST FOR SOME PROGRAMS

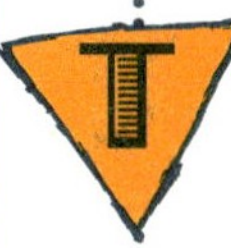

THEATRE OF NOTE

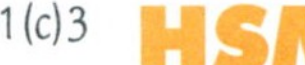
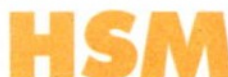

1517 Cahuenga Boulevard
Hollywood, CA 90028
Ph: 323-856-8611

501(c)3 HSM

David Bickford — President, Art Board

Theatre of NOTE is called, "the best place in town for new work to get on its feet and kick," by Backstage West. Theatre of NOTE produces innovative new plays and reworkings of classics.

- productions of edgy and innovative new plays
- productions of classic plays
- late night cabarets and short plays
- reading series of new plays
- Performance Marathon (early spring), a 12-hour extravaganza of theater, dance, spoken word, and music
- rehearsal space

Theatre of NOTE offers matinee performances of appropriate plays for high schools. Discussion and theater games follow the performance.

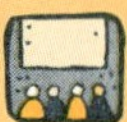

Pre/K-12

PROGRAMS:	**PERFORMANCES**
SCHEDULE:	YEAR-ROUND, WEEKDAYS
DETAILS:	GRADES 9-12, VISUAL/PERFORMING ARTS
	AESTHETIC VALUING, CREATIVE EXPRESSION
	HISTORICAL/CULTURAL CONTEXT
	INDIVIDUALLY TAILORED PROGRAMS

THEATRE PALISADES

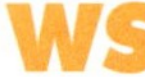

941 Temescal Canyon
Pacific Palisades, CA 90272
Ph: 310-454-1970
Admin: 310-454-8040

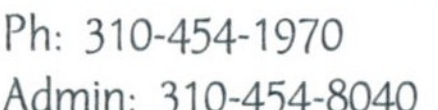

501(c)3 WS

Eva Holberg — Vice President, Administration
Sherry Coon — President

Theatre Palisades, an all volunteer community theater, mounts five major productions per year, including one musical. We are located in Pacific Palisades in our own home, the Pierson Playhouse.

- five shows annually, 18-25 performances each
- classic motion pictures once a month
- kid's shows, by and for children, once a year
- teen shows occassionally
- chamber music 6 times per year
- membership shows
- special shows
- youth pageant

THEATRE THEATER HOLLYWOOD

6425 Hollywood Boulevard, Suite 410
Hollywood, CA 90028
Ph: 323-871-9433
Admin: 323-871-0210
Fax: 323-871-9433
www.thtrethter.org

501(c)3 HSM

Nicolette Chattey — Executive Director
Jeff Murray — Artistic Director
Nicolette Chattey — Executive Director

Theatre Theater located on Hollywood Boulevard is an umbrella theater arts organization dedicated to supporting new work or work new to Los Angeles.

- on-going live performance
- theater, music, comedy, improv
- original script submission and readings
- classes in acting, voice, fencing, movement, and improv
- rehearsal facilities
- video editing facilities
- video studio recording
- class space

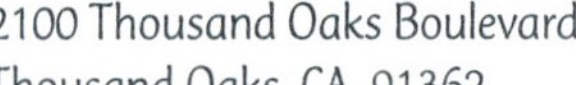

THOUSAND OAKS CIVIC ARTS PLAZA

2100 Thousand Oaks Boulevard
Thousand Oaks, CA 91362
Ph: 805-449-ARTS
Admin: 805-449-2700
Educ: 805-449-2707
Fax: 805-449-2750

VEN

Kathie Harrison — Media Services Coordinator/ 805-449-2765
Thomas Mitze — Theaters Director

Located approximately 25 minutes from the 101/405 freeway interchange, the Thousand Oaks Civic Arts Plaza consists of the 1800-seat Fred Kavli Theatre and the 400-seat Forum Theatre. Presentations range from world-class ballet, contemporary entertainers, Broadway touring productions, and symphonies to family-oriented shows, local Civic Light Opera, chamber music, and recitals.

- big band series
- Foundation Dance series
- Broadway touring season presented by Theatre League
- local Braodway season presented by Cabrillo Music Theatre
- New West Symphony season
- Camerata Pacifica season
- Gold Coast Plays
- Santa Susana Repertory Company
- 15 to 20 contemporary entertainers presented by Avalon
- numerous local musical, choral, and dramatic presentations
- rotating visual arts exhibits in the lobby areas of the Fred Kavli Theatre

THOUSAND OAKS CIVIC ARTS PLAZA (CONTINUED)

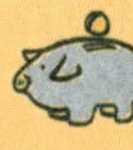

Performance seasons are presented by the Conejo Valley Children's Concert Series (under the Conejo Valley Adult School) and the Ventura County Superintendent of Schools, and include nationally recognized talent.

Pre/K-12

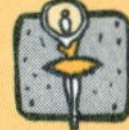 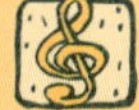

PROGRAMS:	**PERFORMANCES**
SCHEDULE:	SPRING, FALL, WINTER, WEEKDAYS, EVENINGS, WEEKENDS
DETAILS:	GRADES PRE/K-12, VISUAL & PERFORMING ARTS MULTICULTURAL, AESTHETIC VALUING, CREATIVE EXPRESSION HISTORICAL/CULTURAL CONTEXT, COST FOR SOME PROGRAMS

Families

PROGRAMS:	**PERFORMANCES**
SCHEDULE:	SPRING, FALL, WINTER, WEEKDAYS, EVENINGS, WEEKENDS

TOBEY C. MOSS GALLERY

HSM

7321 Beverly Boulevard
Los Angeles, CA 90036-2534
Ph: 323-933-5523
Fax: 323-933-7618
www.tobeymoss.com

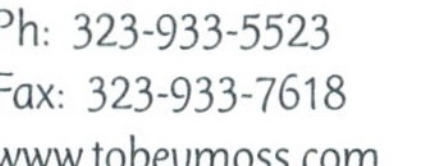

Marni Mahaffey	Office Manager	tobeymoss@earthlink.net
Tobey Moss	Director	

The gallery presents fine arts in all media with a focus upon California modernist and abstractionist artists active in the 1930s-1960s who are of art historical influence.

- twelve months of art exhibits featuring California artists of the 1930s-1960s
- docent tours
- occasional lecture programs

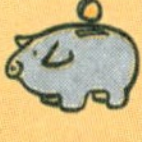

I tailor programs in my art gallery to the appropriate age, grade level, and curriculum. I cover art techniques, the history of those developments, the relationships to social history, and sometimes the music and literature of the period.

Pre/K-12

PROGRAMS:	**GUIDED TOURS**
SCHEDULE:	YEAR-ROUND, WEEKDAYS, WEEKENDS
DETAILS:	GRADES 5-12, VISUAL & PERFORMING ARTS AESTHETIC VALUING, HISTORICAL/CULTURAL CONTEXT CONNECTIONS/RELATIONS/APPLICATIONS PROGRAMS ON-SITE, INDIVIDUALLY TAILORED PROGRAMS

TOLUCA LAKE PLAYERS

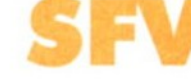

4301 N. Cahuenga Boulevard — 501(c)3
Toluca Lake, CA 91602
Ph: 818-508-7084
Fax: 818-508-0243

Suthern Hayes	Artistic Director/ x3	grrr8plays@aol.com

As the only live theater in Toluca Lake. We produce original as well as published works by playwrights.

- live theatre

TOMLIN-ACHESON FINE ARTS

WS

216 Pier Avenue
Santa Monica, CA 90405
Ph: 310 396-1592
Fax: 310 396-1833

American artists from 1920-1940.

TORRANCE CULTURAL ARTS CENTER

SB

3330 Civic Center Drive
Torrance, CA 90503
Ph: 310-781-7150
Admin: 310-618-2376
Fax: 310-781-7199
www.tcac.torrnet.com

Dan Watt	Public Relations Coordinator/ 310-781-7173
Phil Tilden	General Services Director/ 310-781-7140
Robert Myers	Cultural Services Director/ 310-618-2376

The Torrance Cultural Arts Center is a community facility which provides the public with quality cultural and artistic programs.

- art exhibitions featuring well-known and emerging local artists
- visual and performing arts, aerobics and martial arts classes for all ages
- community and professional theater performances
- free summer concerts
- annual arts festival
- rental facilities for art shows, performances, parties, weddings, seminars, etc

Students of all ages and levels are encouraged to develop their artistic and creative skills through a wide variety of affordable visual and performing arts courses.

Youth

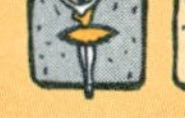 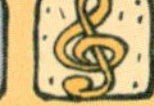 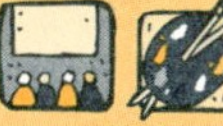 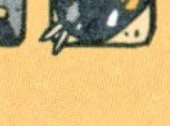

PROGRAMS:	**PERFORMANCES, CLASSES**
SCHEDULE:	YEAR-ROUND, WEEKDAYS, EVENINGS, WEEKENDS

Families

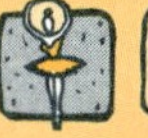 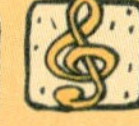 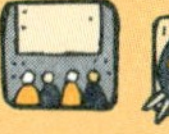 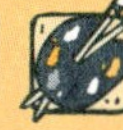

PROGRAMS:	**CLASSES**
SCHEDULE:	YEAR-ROUND, WEEKDAYS, EVENINGS, WEEKENDS

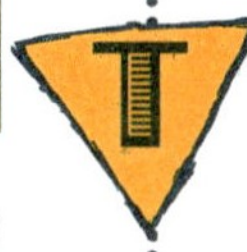
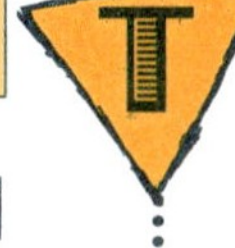

TORRANCE HISTORICAL SOCIETY & MUSEUM

SB

1345 Post Avenue
Torrance, CA 90501
Ph: 310-328-5392

Grace Elgin	Museum Volunteer Chair

TORRANCE JOSLYN FINE ARTS GALLERY

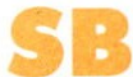

3320 Civic Center Drive
Torrance, CA 90503
Ph: 310-781-7159
Fax: 310-781-7106
www.torrnet.com

Sandy Choi	Public Relations Specialist	schoi@tornet.com
Megumi Sando	Curator/ 310-618-6341	msando@torrnet.com
Robert Myers	Cultural Services/ 310-618-2380	rmyers@torrnet.com

We promote the arts and art education and provide a common ground for artists and the community to learn, create, and interact. Through exhibits and workshops the gallery seeks to enhance personal and social well-being in the community.

- approximately 8 exhibitions yearly featuring local artists
- live summer noon concerts
- volunteer opportunities
- docent tours
- art talks
- art lectures
- festivals

Our "Stories in Art" program provides children with the opportunity to discover both the visual and the literary arts, and to nurture this discovery through readings, workshops, gallery tours, lectures and discussions.

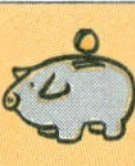

Pre/K-12

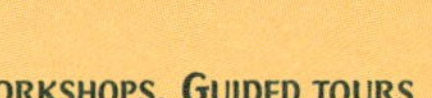

PROGRAMS: WORKSHOPS, GUIDED TOURS
SCHEDULE: SPRING, FALL, WEEKDAYS
DETAILS: GRADES 3-12, VISUAL & PERFORMING ARTS
AESTHETIC VALUING, CREATIVE EXPRESSION
HISTORICAL/CULTURAL CONTEXT
CONNECTIONS/RELATIONS/APPLICATIONS
PROGRAMS ON-SITE

Youth

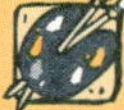

PROGRAMS: WORKSHOPS, GUIDED TOURS
SCHEDULE: SPRING, FALL, WEEKDAYS

Families

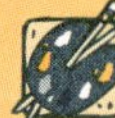

PROGRAMS: WORKSHOPS, GUIDED TOURS
SCHEDULE: YEAR-ROUND, WEEKDAYS, WEEKENDS

TOWNE STREET THEATRE

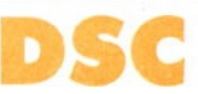

799 S. Towne Avenue, Loft 301 501(c)3
Los Angeles, CA 90021
213-624-4796
213-637-6290

Nancy Davis Artistic/Producing Director/ 213-637-7290

Located in the Fashion District Downtown, Towne Street Theatre presents original work, as well as revivals of older works of plays relative to the African-American experience.

- two shows per year
- classes in acting, directing, screenwriting, playwriting, and improvisation
- workshops in theater
- staged readings

Our classes are structured for the African-American student and the issues they will face in the performing arts arena that others will not. Classes are taught by working professionals in each field.

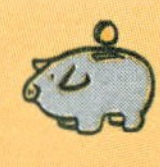

Youth

PROGRAMS: PERFORMANCES, WORKSHOPS, CLASSES
SCHEDULE: FALL, WINTER, EVENINGS, WEEKENDS

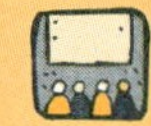

Families

PROGRAMS: PERFORMANCES, WORKSHOPS, CLASSES
SCHEDULE: FALL, WINTER, WEEKENDS

TRACK 16 GALLERY

Bergamot Station
2525 Michigan Avenue C-1
Santa Monica, CA 90404
Ph: 310-264-4678
Fax: 310-264-4682
www.track16.com
reception@track16.com

Vintage Americana and contemporary art.

TRADITIONAL ARTISTS' GUILD OF PARAMOUNT

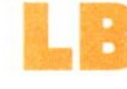

15500 Downey Avenue 501(c)3
Paramount, CA 90723
Ph: 562-925-9134

John Nowlin	President
Lea Myles	IVP
Ryo Terasaki	Co-President/ 562-803-5857

The Traditional Artists' Guild of Paramount is a community-based organization that presents traditional art .

- annual show displaying artwork of Southern Califronia Artists (late March)
- monthly exhibitions featuring local artists

TRADITIONAL ARTISTS' GUILD OF PARAMOUNT (CONTINUED)

The Traditional Artists' Guild of Paramount displays student art in the city-wide, county-wide annual show.

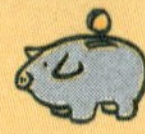

Pre/K-12

PROGRAMS:	**WORKSHOPS**
SCHEDULE:	SPRING, WEEKENDS
DETAILS:	GRADES PRE/K-12, VISUAL & PERFORMING ARTS CREATIVE EXPRESSION

TRIP DANCE THEATER

401 N. Genesee Avenue, #106
Los Angeles, CA 90036
Ph/Fax: 323-655-2464

501 (c) 3 **HSM**

Monica Favand Artistic Director TRIPDance@mci2000.com

L.A. based TRIP Dance Theatre is a company of contemporary modern dance choreographers who collaborate with musicians and visual artists to perform multi-media, social-political dance theater, and offer classes in modern dance, pilates, and improvisation.

- evening-length performances
- showcase performances
- lecture demonstrations
- improvisational performances
- pilates training
- modern dance classes
- residencies for children and professionals
- chinese dance workshops
- improvisational workshops
- Butoh-based body training/workshops

TRIP Dance Theatre offers several tailored programs for youth and adults with an overriding emphasis on the creative, expressive, and communicative possibilities of dance and movement. Company members offer workshops in their particular areas of expertise which include, modern dance, creative movement, improvisation, Butoh dance, Chinese dance, and Pilates training.

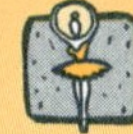

Pre/K-12

PROGRAMS:	**PERFORMANCES, WORKSHOPS**
SCHEDULE:	YEAR-ROUND, WEEKDAYS, EVENINGS, WEEKENDS
DETAILS:	GRADES PRE/K-12, VISUAL & PERFORMING ARTS CREATIVE EXPRESSION, TRAVEL TO SCHOOLS INDIVIDUALLY TAILORED PROGRAMS

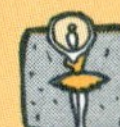

Youth

PROGRAMS:	**PERFORMANCES, WORKSHOPS**
SCHEDULE:	YEAR-ROUND, WEEKDAYS, EVENINGS, WEEKENDS

TRUST FOR PRESERVATION OF CULTURAL HERITAGE

2655 Glendower Avenue
Los Angeles, CA 90027
Ph: 323-668-0234
Admin: 323-660-0607
Fax: 323-660-3646
www.ennisbrownhouse.org

501 (c) 3 **HSM**

Janet Tani	Associate Curator
Franklin de Groot	Executive Director
Norma Gross	Program Director

The Ennis Brown House is a historic site designed by master architect Frank Lloyd Wright. The Trust for Preservation of Cultural Heritage is dedicated to educational purposes for the general public.

- the Ennis Brown House is available for docent tours by reservation
- gift shop
- volunteer opportunities
- site available for educational seminars and similar gatherings

The Trust for Preservation of Cultural Heritage exposes students of all ages to the importance of historic preservation and great works of architecture.

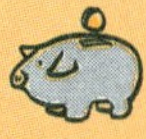

Pre/K-12

PROGRAMS:	**GUIDED TOURS**
SCHEDULE:	YEAR-ROUND, WEEKDAYS, WEEKENDS
DETAILS:	GRADES 3-12, ARCHITECTURE HISTORICAL/CULTURAL CONTEXT CONNECTIONS/RELATIONS/APPLICATIONS COST FOR SOME PROGRAMS

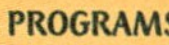

Families

PROGRAMS:	**GUIDED TOURS**
SCHEDULE:	YEAR-ROUND, WEEKDAYS, WEEKENDS
DETAILS:	COST FOR SOME PROGRAMS

TWO ROADS THEATRE

4348 Tujunga Avenue
Studio City, CA 91604
Ph: 818-766-9381
Fax: 818-762-9840

501 (c) 3 **SFV**

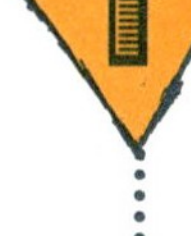

Edmund Gaynes	Producing Artistic Director
Pamela Hall	Associate Artistic Director

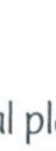

The Two Roads Theatre has produced and developed many original plays and musicals, including several that have gone on to New York for successful runs.

- acting classes
- writer workshops
- involvement opportunites for children and seniors

U.P., INC.

352 S. Camden Drive
Beverly Hills, CA 90212
Ph: 310-277-5163

501(c)3 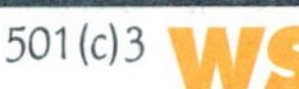

Lisa Janti — Executive Director

U.P., Inc. is a community-based public benefit arts organization whose primary mission is to revitalize, unify, and inspire all segments of the community through the arts, especially the youth.

- arts instruction for youth in a variety of fields including photography, dance, theater production, video and film production, painting, and other visual arts
- general arts programs for all ages in a variety of art forms

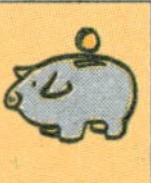

U.P., Inc. works primarily with high-risk youth offering a variety of inspiring programs designed to provide skills development and creatively engage them in positive educational experiences that can lead to employment and career goals.

Youth 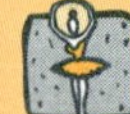 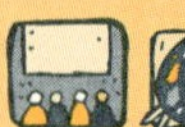

PROGRAMS: PERFORMANCES, WORKSHOPS, CLASSES
SCHEDULE: YEAR-ROUND, WEEKDAYS, WEEKENDS

Families 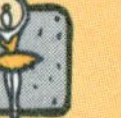 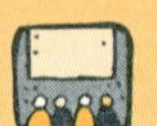

PROGRAMS: PERFORMANCES, WORKSHOPS, CLASSES
SCHEDULE: YEAR-ROUND, EVENINGS
DETAILS: COST FOR SOME PROGRAMS

UCLA AT THE ARMAND HAMMER MUSEUM OF ART AND CULTURAL CENTER

10899 Wilshire Boulevard
Los Angeles, CA 90024-4201
Ph: 310-443-7000
Admin: 310-443-7020
Fax: 310-443-7099
www.hammer.ucla.edu

501(c)3 WS

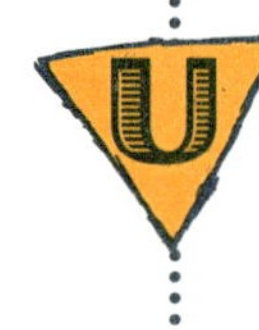

Terry Morello	Director of Public Information/ 310-443-7047	tmorello@ucla.edu
Ann Philbin	Director/ 310-443-7033	aphilbin@ucla.edu
Cindi Dale	Director of Education/ 310-443-7056	cdale@ucla.edu
Mary Ann Sears	Director, Marketing/Special Events/ 310-443-7030	msears@ucla.edu

Located in the heart of Westwood Village, UCLA at the Armand Hammer Museum of Art and Cultural Center showcases diverse and contemporary art exhibitions and a variety of art and education programs for people of all ages.

- art rental and sales gallery
- poetry readings
- symposia
- art history courses
- summer festivals
- bookstore/gift shop
- live summer jazz concerts
- docent tours
- volunteer opportunities
- on-going permanent collection exhibition
- year-round schedule of temporary art exhibitions ranging from the Renaissance to contemporary

UCLA AT THE ARMAND HAMMER MUSEUM OF ART AND CULTURAL CENTER (CONTINUED)

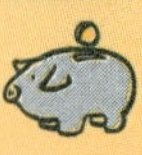

The UCLA/Armand Hammer Museum promotes multidisciplinary humanities-based learning about art. Contemporary exhibitions with strong social and political bases, and opportunities for under-represented artists are presented. The Museum provides a forum for critical dialogue on art and issues surrounding the exhibitions.

Pre/K-12 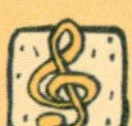 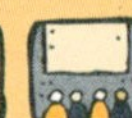 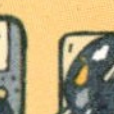

PROGRAMS: STORYTELLING, POETRY READINGS, SELF-GUIDED TOURS, GUIDED TOURS
SCHEDULE: YEAR-ROUND, WEEKDAYS
DETAILS: GRADES PRE/K-12, HISTORY/SOC. SCIENCES, VISUAL & PERFORMING ARTS, LANGUAGE ARTS
AESTHETIC VALUING, CREATIVE EXPRESSION
HISTORICAL/CULTURAL CONTEXT
CONNECTIONS/RELATIONS/APPLICATIONS
TEACHER TRAINING PROGRAMS (SALARY POINTS)
PROGRAMS ON-SITE, EDUCATIONAL MATERIALS AVAILABLE
BILINGUAL PROGRAMS: SPANISH

Youth 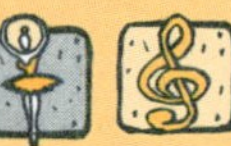 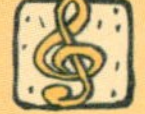 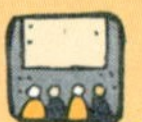 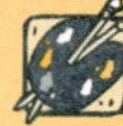

PROGRAMS: PERFORMANCES, WORKSHOPS, SELF-GUIDED TOURS, GUIDED TOURS
SCHEDULE: YEAR-ROUND, WEEKENDS

Families

PROGRAMS: PERFORMANCES, WORKSHOPS, SELF-GUIDED TOURS, GUIDED TOURS
SCHEDULE: YEAR-ROUND, EVENINGS, WEEKENDS

UCLA, DEPARTMENT OF ETHNOMUSICOLOGY

2539 Shoenberg Hall
Los Angeles, CA 90095
Ph: 310-206-3033
Admin: 310-206-5184
Fax: 310-206-9593
www.ethnomusic.ucla.edu

WS

Betty Price	Management Services Officer/ 310-206-5184	
Timothy Rice	Chairman/ 310-825-8381	
Miriam Gerberg	Outreach Director/ 310-206-9593	mgerberg@arts.ucla.edu

The Ethnomusicology Department at UCLA offers degrees and study opportunites in all types of world music. Additional programming includes community outreach.

- concerts of world music ensembles led by masters of each tradition
- residencies in K-12 schools and community colleges
- on campus visits
- instrument collection tours
- arranged use of world famous archives of world music
- publications include journals, video and audio recordings

UCLA, DEPARTMENT OF ETHNOMUSICOLOGY (CONTINUED)

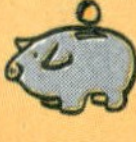

Outreach educational programs offer hands-on musical learning in a wide array of world musical cultures as well as performers. Small classes offer opportunities to work and perform with outstanding internationally known instructors.

Pre/K-12 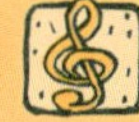

PROGRAMS:	**PERFORMANCES, WORKSHOPS, RESIDENCIES** **GUIDED TOURS**
SCHEDULE:	SPRING, FALL, WINTER, WEEKDAYS
DETAILS:	GRADES PRE/K-12, HISTORY/SOC. SCIENCES VISUAL & PERFORMING ARTS, MULTICULTURAL CREATIVE EXPRESSION, HISTORICAL/CULTURAL CONTEXT TEACHER TRAINING PROGRAMS (SALARY POINTS) TRAVEL TO SCHOOLS, PROGRAMS ON-SITE EDUCATIONAL MATERIALS AVAILABLE BILINGUAL: SIGN LANGUAGE

Families 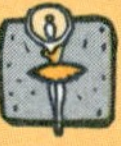 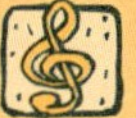

PROGRAMS:	**PERFORMANCES**
SCHEDULE:	SPRING, FALL, WINTER, EVENINGS, WEEKENDS
DETAILS:	COST FOR SOME PROGRAMS

UCLA, DEPARTMENT OF FILM AND TELEVISION

405 Hilgard Avenue
Los Angeles, CA 90024
Ph: 310-206-0426
Fax: 310-825-7782
www.tft.ucla.edu

Teri B. Michael	Director, Marketing/ 310-206-3235	terim@emelnitz.ucla.edu
Robert Rosen	Dean/ 310-825-7741	brosen@emelnitz.ucla.edu

The Department of Film and Television is an assemblage of elite students selected from hundreds of applicants each year in film and television production, animation and screenwriting, producing 80 to 100 new works annually.

- week-long student film festival held every June at the Melnitz Theater, open to the public

UCLA, DEPARTMENT OF MUSIC

1309 Schoenberg Hall
Westwood, CA 90024-1505
Ph: 310-825-4761
Admin: 310-206-5430
Fax: 310-206-4738
www.music.ucla.edu

501(c)3 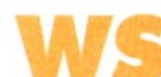

Betty Price	Management Services Officer/ 310-206-5184
Jon Robertson	Department Chair/ 310-825-1839 Outreach Office

Located in Westwood, UCLA offers undergraduate and graduate degrees in music with an emphasis in performance and composition. Classes are small with world-class faculty teaching.

- classical music concerts (orchestral, choral, opera and chamber music)
- wind ensembles and jazz concerts
- one or more yearly performances of opera and musical theater
- free master classes with artists performing with UCLA Performing Arts

UCLA, DEPARTMENT OF THEATER

UCLA Campus
405 Hilgard Avenue
Los Angeles, CA 90024
Ph: 310-206-3235
Fax: 310-825-7782
www.tft.ucla.edu

501(c)3 WS

Teri B. Michael	Director, Marketing/Communications	terim@emelnitz.ucla.edu
Robert Rosen	Dean/ 310-825-7741	brosen@emelnitz.ucla.edu

Focusing on comprehensive training for the profession as well as serious study of history and literature, the department incorporates diverse cultures and traditions to explore theater as a forum for reflecting the human experience.

- production season features 25 to 30 public performances
- performances are presented by students with professional direction

UCLA, DEPARTMENT OF WORLD ARTS & CULTURES

124 Dance Building, Box 951608
Los Angeles, CA 90095-1608
Ph: 310-825-3951
Fax: 310-825-7507
www.wac.ucla.edu

501(c)3 WS

Carl Patrick	Office Administrator
Angelia Leung	Vice-Chair
Judy Alter	Associate Professor

A multidisciplinary department, World Arts & Cultures is rooted in the generation of insights into human creativity; the relationship between art and cultural identity; and the creation and study of dance.

UCLA, DESIGN FOR SHARING

10920 Wilshire Boulevard, Suite 750
Los Angeles, CA 90024-1529
Ph: 310-825-7681
Fax: 310-206-3843
www.performingarts.ucla.edu/outreach.htm

501(c)3 WS

Nancy Papalexis	Director	npapalex@ucla.edu
Anna Cross	DFS Assistant	across@ucla.edu

Design for Sharing is the community outreach program for the UCLA Center for Performing Arts. It provides special programs for school children, master classes for talented youngsters and free tickets for community organizations to attend performances.

- presents public programs for youngsters and families in the spring on the UCLA campus
- "Picnic and Concert" introduces children to orchestral instruments and music
- volunteers needed to assist with the K-12 programs on show days preparing educational materials and helping in the office

UCLA, DESIGN FOR SHARING (CONTINUED)

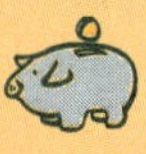

Design for Sharing presents Demonstration Performances where students see performances by leading musical artists. Artists appearing at the UCLA Center for the Performing Arts present hour-long morning shows in Royce Hall and other venues.

Pre/K-12 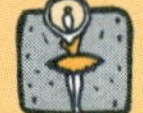 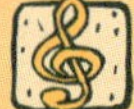

PROGRAMS:	**PERFORMANCES, WORKSHOPS**
SCHEDULE:	SPRING, FALL, WINTER, WEEKDAYS
DETAILS:	GRADES PRE/K-12, VISUAL & PERFORMING ARTS PROGRAMS ON-SITE, EDUCATIONAL MATERIALS AVAILABLE

Youth 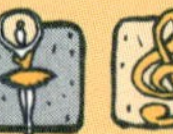 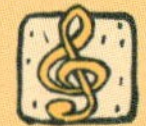

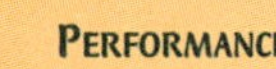

PROGRAMS:	**PERFORMANCES**
SCHEDULE:	YEAR-ROUND, EVENINGS, WEEKENDS

Families 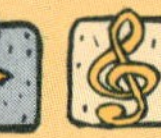 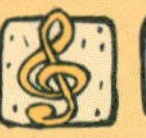 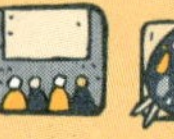

PROGRAMS:	**PERFORMANCES**
SCHEDULE:	SPRING, WEEKENDS

UCLA EXTENSION

10995 Leconte Avenue
Los Angeles, CA 90024
Ph: 310-825-9971
Fax: 310-206-3223
www.unex.ucla.edu

501(c)3 **WS**

Richard Macales	Public Information Representative/ 310-825-1901
Robert Lapiner	Dean/ 310-825-2361

UCLA Extension is a global leader in continuing higher education. We offer the largest selection of continuing education courses in the United States. We offer more than 1000 career and enrichment programs each quarter. Classes are held in dozens of sites throughout greater Los Angeles.

- Art History and Theory programs
- Art Studio workshops
- Photography
- Architecture
- Interior and Environmental Design
- Landscape Architecture
- Entertainment Studies and Performing Arts
- New Media
- Acting
- Film, Television and Video
- Music
- Computer Graphics
- Graphic Design
- Creative Writing
- Screenwriting
- Culinary Arts
- Functional Arts and Crafts
- Animation
- Figure Drawing

...and more

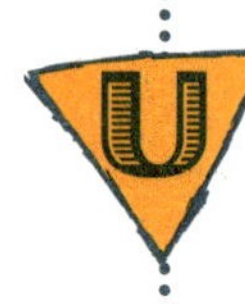

UCLA FILM AND TELEVISION ARCHIVE

302 East Melnitz
Los Angeles, CA 90024-1323
Ph: 310-206-8013
Educ: 310-206-5388
Fax: 310-206-3129
www.ucla.cinema.ed

501(c)3 **WS**

Cornelia Emerson	Development and Public Affairs Officer/ 310-206-1477
Andrea Alsberg	Head of Programming/ 310-206-1475
Robert Rosen	Director/ 310-206-8013
Steven Ricci	Head of Research and Study/ 310-206-5388
Edward Richmond	Curator/ 213-462-4921

The UCLA Film and Television Archive is one of the world's major media archives, with a collection of 200,000 titles, a research and study center, and a major exhibition program.

- over 200 yearly screenings of archival, independent and international film and video
- national and international touring programs
- research and study center serving 13,000 scholars annually
- world renowned program in film preservation
- scholarly publications
- electronic publishing

UCLA FOWLER MUSEUM OF CULTURAL HISTORY

UCLA Campus
405 Hilgard Avenue
Los Angeles, CA 90024
Ph: 310-206-5663
Admin: 310-825-9672
Fax: 310-206-7007
www.fmch.ucla.edu

501(c)3 **WS**

Christine Sellin	Director of Public Information/ 310-825-4288	csellin@fmch.ucla.edu
Doran Ross	Director/ 310-825-4259	dross@fmch.ucla.ecu
Clarissa Coyoca	Assistant Director/ 310-825-5289	ccoyoca@fmch.ucla.edu
Betsy Quick	Director of Education/ 310-825-9341	bquick@fmch.ucla.edu
Stacey Hong	Assistant Director of Education/ 310-825-7325	

The UCLA Fowler Museum of Cultural History collects, preserves, studies, interprets, exhibits and publishes the past and present art and material culture from Africa, Asia, Oceania, Native and Latin America.

- programs include lecture series, symposia, gallery talks and workshops
- public exhibitions, publications and programs
- dynamic educational resource for students, faculty, and staff of the university and for the diverse communities of greater Los Angeles

UCLA FOWLER MUSEUM OF CULTURAL HISTORY (CONTINUED)

The UCLA Fowler Museum of Cultural History provides educational experiences for school audiences and facilitates public understanding of the world's richly varied artistic traditions. The museum emphasizes active learning approaches that embody the perspectives of cultures represented.

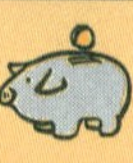

Pre/K-12

PROGRAMS: PERFORMANCES, WORKSHOPS, SELF-GUIDED TOURS GUIDED TOURS
SCHEDULE: YEAR-ROUND, WEEKDAYS, WEEKENDS
DETAILS: GRADES PRE/K-2, HISTORY/SOC. SCIENCES
VISUAL & PERFORMING ARTS, MULTICULTURAL
AESTHETIC VALUING, CREATIVE EXPRESSION
HISTORICAL/CULTURAL CONTEXT
CONNECTIONS/RELATIONS/APPLICATIONS
TEACHER TRAINING PROGRAMS (SALARY POINTS)
PROGRAMS ON-SITE , EDUCATIONAL MATERIALS AVAILABLE
BILINGUAL: SPANISH, COST FOR SOME PROGRAMS

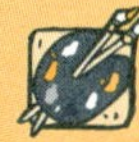

Youth

PROGRAMS: PERFORMANCES, WORKSHOPS, SELF-GUIDED TOURS GUIDED TOURS
SCHEDULE: YEAR-ROUND, WEEKDAYS, WEEKENDS
DETAILS: COST FOR SOME PROGRAMS

Families

PROGRAMS: PERFORMANCES, WORKSHOPS, SELF-GUIDED TOURS GUIDED TOURS
SCHEDULE: YEAR-ROUND, WEEKDAYS, WEEKENDS
DETAILS: COST FOR SOME PROGRAMS

UCLA PERFORMING ARTS

Royce Hall
Los Angeles, CA 90024
Ph: 310-825-4401
Admin: 310-206-8745
Educ: 310-825-8025
Fax: 310-206-3843
www.performingarts.ucla.edu

501(c)3 **WS**

Michael Blachly Director mblachly@ucla.edu
Linda Timmons Manager ltimmons@ucla.edu

Located in West Los Angeles on the UCLA campus, the UCLA Center for the Performing Arts presents an annual program of music, dance, and theater of the highest standard. We support the development of new and emerging artists and art forms, promote audience development through community outreach programs and host non-performance lectures, artists' residencies, discussions, and workshops.

- Design for Sharing program
- artist residency
- pre-performance lectures
- public performances

UCLA PERFORMING ARTS (CONTINUED)

Pre/K-12

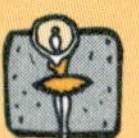
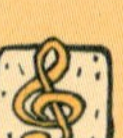

PROGRAMS: PERFORMANCES, RESIDENCIES
SCHEDULE: YEAR-ROUND, WEEKDAYS
DETAILS: GRADES 3-6, VISUAL & PERFORMING ARTS

Families

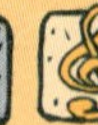

PROGRAMS: PERFORMANCES
SCHEDULE: YEAR-ROUND, EVENINGS, WEEKENDS

UCLA, SCHOOL OF THE ARTS AND ARCHITECTURE

303 East Melnitz, Box 951427
Los Angeles, CA 90095-1427
Ph: 310-206-6465
Fax: 310-267-0110
www.arts.ucla.edu

501(c)3 **WS**

Carolyn Campbell Director of Communications/ 310-825-6540
Daniel Neuman Dean/ 310-206-6469

The UCLA School of the Arts and Architecture is a professional school for visual and performing artists, architects, and scholars who will be well prepared to serve as cultural leaders of the 21st century.

- year-round variety of free and ticketed events open to the public
- lectures, symposia, exhibitions, concerts, and performances presented by the departments of Architecture and Urban Design, Art, Design, Ethnomusicology, Music and World Arts and Cultures
- see additional listings in guide for UCLA Performing Arts, UCLA at Armand Hammer Museum of Art and Cultural Center, and UCLA Fowler Museum of Cultural History

UCLA SCHOOL OF THEATER, FILM AND TELEVISION

UCLA Campus
405 Hilgard Avenue
Los Angeles, CA 90024-1622
Ph: 310-206-0426
Fax: 310-206-1686
www.tft.ucla.edu

501(c)3 **WS**

Teri Bond Michael Director, Marketing/Communications/ 310-206-3235
Robert Rosen Dean

The UCLA School of Theater, Film and Television is the only major university recognizing the close relationship of theater, film, and television in an integrated academic program. Aspiring screenwriters, theater actors, filmmakers and designers explore every aspect of the visual.

- offers broad range of opportunities throughout the year for the public to view professional quality student theatrical productions, original motion-picture and animation work and screenings of classic films and television

UDUA LONG BEACH

121 Linden Avenue, Suite B110 501(c)3 **LB**
Long Beach, CA 90802-4990
Ph: 562-733-0184
Fax: 562-495-0755

Charles Udoma	Executive Director
Pauline Jones	Art/Craft Director
Sally Smith	Culture Analyst

Udna Long Beach is a cultural arts organization that promotes, educatse and presents African lifestyles in Long Beach through African festivals and concerts.

- Drum Festival in Long Beach in April
- Taste of Africa in August
- poetry readings all summer
- Black Business Seminar in May
- Anaheim Street Festival held the first Saturday in October

UKRAINIAN ART CENTER, INC.

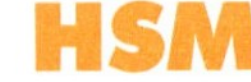

4315 Melrose Avenue
Los Angeles, CA 90029
Ph: 323-668-0172

Daria Chaikovsky	President/Executive Director
Natalie Orlins-Gebet	Program Director

The Ukrainian Art Center is a nonprofit organization with the purpose of preserving, developing, and displaying Ukrainian folk and fine art. One goal is to establish the West Coast's first museum of Ukrainian folk and fine art.

UNITED LATINOS FOR THE ARTS- LOS ANGELES (ULA-LA)

P.O. Box 25575 501(c)3 **WS**
Los Angeles, CA 90025
Ph: 310-477-4481

Angelica Gonzalez	President
Eriberto	Art Program Director/Curator
Teddi Mercure	Vice President

ULA-LA was established as an organization to lend support to artists and artistic projects, and to assist artists in exhibiting and marketing their works in a professional environment.

- exhibitions address and acknowledge the creative potential of raw talent, create cultural appreciation, and provide an educational experience
- tours to selected museums, galleries, and murals

U

UNIVERSITY OF LA VERNE, HARRIS ART GALLERY

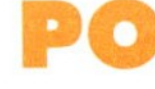

1950 Third Street
La Verne, CA 91750
Ph: 909-593-3511 x4763

USC FISHER GALLERY

823 Exposition Boulevard 501(c)3 **DSC**
Los Angeles, CA 90089-0292
Ph: 213-740-4561
Fax: 213-740-7676
www.usc.edu/dept/Fisher_Gallery

Kay Allen	Associate Director	kallen@mizer.usc
Selma Holo	Director	
Jeanette LaVere	Educator	
Jennifer Jaskowiak	Collections Curator	

Fisher Gallery, established in 1939, is the accredited art museum of the University of Southern California. The gallery offers exhibitions ranging from antiquities, to old master artists to contemporary works by local, national, and international artists.

- docent tours
- volunteer opportunities

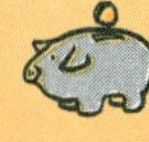

The popular "Tuesdays at Fisher" program held from 12-1 pm focuses on the current exhibition. "Wake-up call! addresses special issues related to our exhibition and "Family at Fisher" day includes art workshops, music and performances.

Pre/K-12

PROGRAMS: **Performances, Workshops, Guided tours**
SCHEDULE: Spring, Fall, Winter, Weekdays, Weekends
DETAILS: Grades Pre/k-12, Visual & performing arts
Aesthetic valuing, Creative Expression
Historical/Cultural Context
Connections/Relations/Applications
Travel to schools, Programs on-site
Individually tailored programs, Educational materials
Bilingual: Spanish

Youth

PROGRAMS: **Performances, Workshops, Guided Tours**
SCHEDULE: Spring, Fall, Winter, weekdays, Weekends

Families

PROGRAMS: **Performances, Workshops, Guided Tours**
SCHEDULE: Spring, Fall, Winter, Weekdays, Weekends

USC HELEN LINDHURST FINE ARTS GALLERY

Watt Hall 103
Los Angeles, CA 90089-0292
Ph: 213-740-2787
Admin: 213-740-9153
Fax: 213-740-8938
www.usc.edu

501(c)3 DSC

Kathleen Sweeney	Development Director/ 213-740-6261	
Ruth Weisberg	Dean	
Penelope Jones	Director of Admissions	

The Helen Lindhurst Fine Arts Gallery shows graduate and undergraduate student exhibitions throughout the academic year. In spring, the gallery showcases community-based art projects.

- monthly exhibitions featuring work of graduate and undergraduate students
- additional exhibitions include works created by faculty and community-based art programs

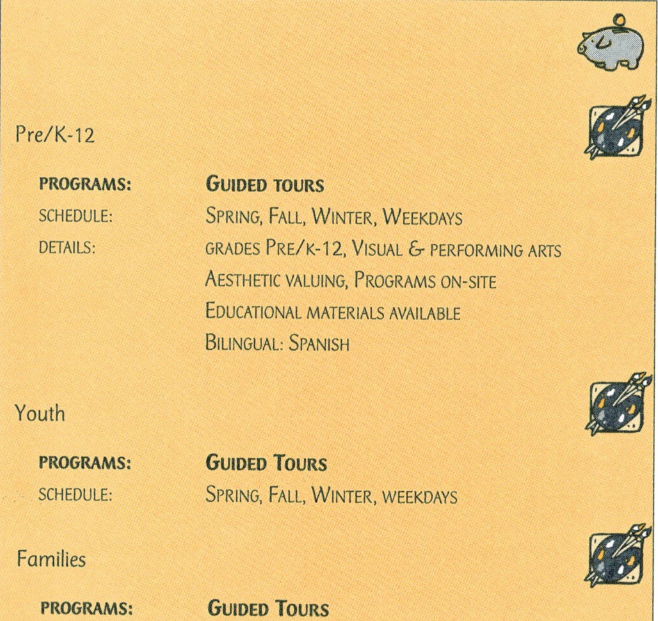

Pre/K-12

PROGRAMS: GUIDED TOURS
SCHEDULE: SPRING, FALL, WINTER, WEEKDAYS
DETAILS: GRADES PRE/K-12, VISUAL & PERFORMING ARTS
AESTHETIC VALUING, PROGRAMS ON-SITE
EDUCATIONAL MATERIALS AVAILABLE
BILINGUAL: SPANISH

Youth

PROGRAMS: GUIDED TOURS
SCHEDULE: SPRING, FALL, WINTER, WEEKDAYS

Families

PROGRAMS: GUIDED TOURS
SCHEDULE: SPRING, FALL, WINTER, WEEKDAYS

USC SCHOOL OF ARCHITECTURE

University of Southern California
Los Angeles, CA 90007
Ph: 213-740-2723
Admin: 213-740-2083
Fax: 213-740-8884
www.usc.edu/dept/architecture

501(c)3 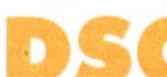

The USC School of Architecture offers degrees in architecture, landscape architecture, and building science at the undergraduate and graduate levels. Coursework often incorporates interdisciplinary topics. The curriculum is both "high tech" and "high touch" combining powerful computers with the fundamentals of beauty, proportion, and harmony.

- exhibits top architectural work
- regular tours of USC's Gamble House in Pasadena
- summer series of short courses in Historic Preservation
- 3 semester abroad programs in France, Italy, and Malaysia
- Helen Topping Architecture and Fine Arts Library
- community design studio
- lecture series with outstanding practitioners

USC SCHOOL OF FINE ARTS

University Park Campus
Watt Hall 103
850 West 37th Street
Los Angeles, CA 90089-0292
Ph: 213-740-2787
Fax: 213-740-8938

501(c)3 DSC

Kathleen Sweeney	Director of Development/ 213-740-6261	kens@mizar.usc.edu
Ruth Weisberg	Dean	
Penny Jones	Director of Admissions/ 213-740-9153	
Russ Barclay	Office Manager	barclay@usc.edu

Located in the heart of Los Angeles, the USC School of Fine Arts combines both traditional and experimental approaches to art studies at the graduate and undergraduate levels.

- monthly exhibitions featuring the work of students and faculty artists
- tours of art facilities
- lectures, workshops and symposia with artists, critics and art professionals

Art workshops led by USC students are offered on select days at the campus for elementary and middle schools in the USC area. High school students may attend intensive Saturday classes through a partnership with the Ryman Program for Young Artists.

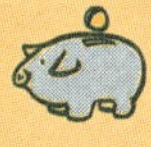

Pre/K-12

PROGRAMS: WORKSHOPS, GUIDED TOURS
SCHEDULE: YEAR-ROUND, WEEKDAYS
DETAILS: GRADES 3-12, VISUAL & PERFORMING ARTS
CREATIVE EXPRESSION, TRAVEL TO SCHOOLS
PROGRAMS ON-SITE, INDIVIDUALLY TAILORED PROGRAMS
EDUCATIONAL MATERIALS, BILINGUAL: SPANISH

Youth

PROGRAMS: WORKSHOPS, CLASSES, GUIDED TOURS
SCHEDULE: YEAR-ROUND, WEEKDAYS, WEEKENDS

USC SCHOOL OF THEATRE

University Park
1029 Childs Way
Los Angeles, CA 90089-0791
Ph: 213-743-1967
Admin: 213-740-8686
Educ: 213-740-1286
Fax: 213-740-8888
www.usc.edu/dept/theatre/dramanet

501(c)3 DSC

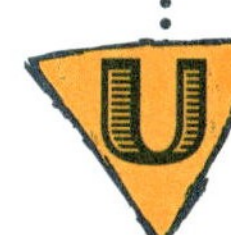

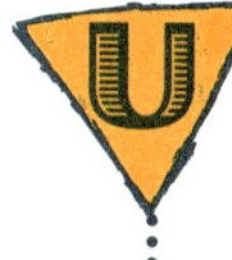

Jon White-Spunner	Theatre Mgmt Assoc./ 213-743-1967	spunner@mizar.usc.edu
Robert Scales	Dean/ 213-740-8686	rscale@mizar.usc.edu
Lori Fisher	Director, Academic Services/ 213-740-1286	lfisher@mizar.usc.edu
Jack Rowe	Production Coordinator/ 213-740-5905	jrowe@mizar.usc.edu

Located on the campus of the University of Southern California, the USC School of Theatre prepares students to perform professionally, with integrity and confidence in the theatre, film, television, and related professions.

- offers an exciting range of classical and contemporary plays and musicals
- fall and spring semester performances

USC SCHOOL OF THEATRE (CONTINUED)

The Theatre for Youth Program explores learning in the various aspects of theatre such as performance training, conducting theater workshops, observing performances, and performing with youth of all ages. Performances take place on campus and at local schools.

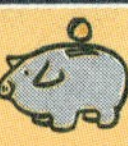

Pre/K-12

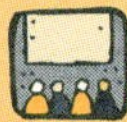

PROGRAMS: **PERFORMANCES, WORKSHOPS**
SCHEDULE: SPRING, FALL, WEEKDAYS
DETAILS: GRADES PRE/K-12, VISUAL & PERFORMING ARTS
MULTICULTURAL, CREATIVE EXPRESSION
HISTORICAL/CULTURAL CONTEXT
PROGRAMS ON-SITE

USC SPECTRUM

University of Southern California
STU-B7
Los Angeles, CA 90089-0898
Ph: 213-740-2167
Fax: 213-740-5293

501 (c) 3 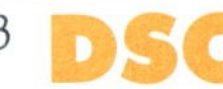

Craig Spinger — Assistant Dean

USC Spectrum, a program of the Division of Student Affairs, presents the finest in arts and lecture programs by internationally known artists for education and entertainment of the USC community and its neighbors in Los Angeles.

- concerts
- theatrical performances
- poetry readings
- lectures
- dance performances

USC SUMMER PROGRAM

Bovard Hall 113
Los Angeles, CA 90089-0291
Ph: 213-740-5679
Fax: 213-740-6417

501 (c) 3 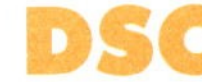

Verlena Irvin — Assistant to Director
Ric Abramson — Arts Coordinator/ 213-740-2723
Lynn Goodnight — Director of Summer Programs

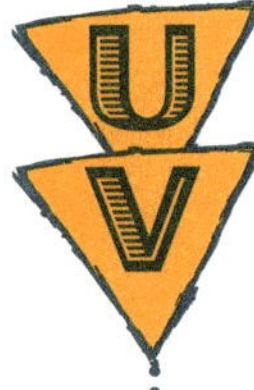

Part of USC's summer program, "Interaction in the Arts", brings together four disciplines: architecture, fine arts, music, and theater, in order to explore the creative formation of environments. Open to college-bound high school students, this program attempts to identify and produce interdisciplinary themes, programs, concepts, and events that emerge from common spatial investigations within the arts.

VALENTINA OUMANSKY DRAMATIC DANCE FOUNDATION

3433 Cahuenga Boulevard West
Los Angeles, CA 90068
Ph: 323-850-9497

501 (c) 3 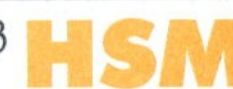

Marilyn Carter — Treasurer
Valentina Oumansky — Artistic Director
Tarumi Takagi-Inouye — Media Specialist

Located on the southside of Universal Center Drive in Los Angeles, Valentina Oumansky Dramatic Dance Foundation produces interdisciplinary live concerts and video for all.

- dramatic dance workshops
- seminars
- video production
- Footprint Folio—a news bulletin
- artist-in-residence program for public and private schools and colleges

Pre/K-12

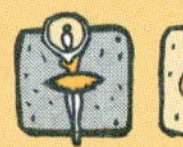 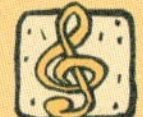

PROGRAMS: **PERFORMANCES, WORKSHOPS, RESIDENCIES**
SCHEDULE: YEAR-ROUND, WEEKDAYS, EVENINGS, WEEKENDS
DETAILS: GRADES PRE/K-12, VISUAL & PERFORMING ARTS
MULTICULTURAL, CREATIVE EXPRESSION
TEACHER TRAINING PROGRAMS (SALARY POINTS)
TRAVEL TO SCHOOLS, PROGRAMS ON-SITE
INDIVIDUALLY TAILORED PROGRAMS, EDUCATIONAL MATERIALS

Youth

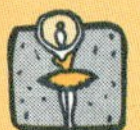 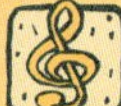

PROGRAMS: **PERFORMANCES, WORKSHOPS, CLASSES, RESIDENCIES**
SCHEDULE: YEAR-ROUND, WEEKDAYS, EVENINGS, WEEKENDS

Families

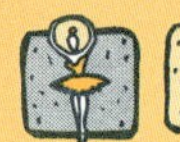 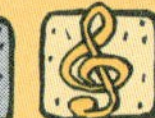

PROGRAMS: **PERFORMANCES, WORKSHOPS**
SCHEDULE: YEAR-ROUND, WEEKDAYS, EVENINGS, WEEKENDS

VALLEY CULTURAL CENTER

21550 Oxnard Street, Suite 470
Woodland Hills, CA 91367-7110
Ph: 818-704-1587
Admin: 818-704-1358
Fax: 818-704-1604
www.valleycultural.org

501(c)3 **SFV**

Suzanne Hackett — Executive Director — yetilvft@valleyculturalorg
Pamela Peterson — Office Manager

The Valley Cultural Center seeks to enlighten, educate, and enrich present and future generations by providing diverse programs through the performing and visual arts.

- "Concerts in the Park", a free 14-week performing arts series
- artist-in-residence program
- music-in-the-schools program
- children's concert series
- scholarship programs
- arts services organization offering technical assistance and informational services to the arts community in the San Fernando Valley
- volunteer opportunities

Valley Cultural Center programs, residencies, and outreach are offered free of charge to ensure the greatest level of participation by those in the community with the fewest resources.

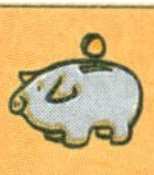

Pre/K-12

PROGRAMS: PERFORMANCES, RESIDENCIES
SCHEDULE: YEAR-ROUND, WEEKDAYS
DETAILS: GRADES 3-6, VISUAL & PERFORMING ARTS
CREATIVE EXPRESSION, TRAVEL TO SCHOOLS
PROGRAMS ON-SITE, INDIVIDUALLY TAILORED PROGRAMS

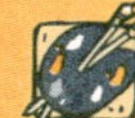

Youth

PROGRAMS: PERFORMANCES, RESIDENCIES
SCHEDULE: YEAR-ROUND, WEEKDAYS

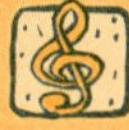
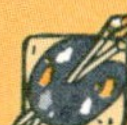

Families

PROGRAMS: PERFORMANCES
SCHEDULE: YEAR-ROUND, WEEKENDS

VALLEY INSTITUTE OF VISUAL ART

8516 Reseda Boulevard
Northridge, CA 91324
Ph: 818-576-0775
Admin: 818-769-0748

501(c)3 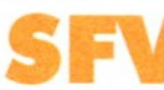

Connie Larson — President/ 818-769-0748
Beverly Grossman — Scheduling and Exhibition Chair/ 818-343-7157

Valley Institute of Visual Art (VIVA) is dedicated to the advancement of the visual arts through exhibition, education, and outreach.

- monthly exhibitions featuring local artists and art organizations
- volunteer opportunities

VALLEY SYMPHONY ORCHESTRA

Los Angeles Valley College
Van Nuys, CA 91401
Ph: 818-947-2346
Fax: 818-783-1777

501(c)3 **SFV**

Robert Chauls — Artistic Director/Music Director/ 818-947-2775

The Valley Symphony Orchestra is San Fernando Valley's premiere community orchestra giving five annual concerts of traditional and contemporary music.

- five concerts per year
- annual composition competition open to all composers in greater L.A.
- annual vocal concert
- opportunities for instrumental concerts

VALLEY WATERCOLOR SOCIETY

c/o Jean Sadler
P.O. Box 4623
Valley Village, CA 91607
Ph: 818-980-6418

501(c)3 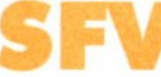

Jean Sadler — President
Joyce Lipshultz — Program Chairman/ 818-344-4032

Valley Watercolor Society is a nonprofit organization devoted to promoting interest, knowledge, and appreciation of watermedia through meetings, exhibitions, paint-outs, and other appropriate activities.

- monthly meetings and demonstrations by exceptional and well known watercolor artists
- two juried exhibits each year
- art workshops
- bus trips to juried exhibits by the National Watercolor Society and Watercolor West
- some members available to teach art to children in public schools
- yearly scholarships to student artists in college
- monthly newsletter
- monthly paint-outs

Members who travel to public schools to give art instruction bring a fresh view to students through creative expression.

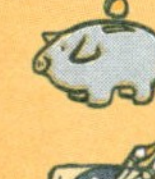

Pre/K-12

PROGRAMS: WORKSHOPS, STUDIO CLASSES
SCHEDULE: SPRING, FALL, WINTER, WEEKDAYS
DETAILS: GRADES 3-8, VISUAL & PERFORMING ARTS
AESTHETIC VALUING, CREATIVE EXPRESSION
HISTORICAL/CULTURAL CONTEXT, TRAVEL TO SCHOOLS
EDUCATIONAL MATERIALS AVAILABLE

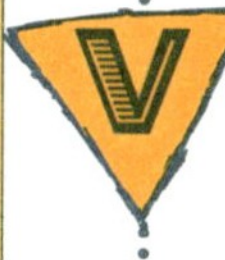

VENICE ARTS MECCA

610 California Avenue
Venice, CA 90291
Ph: 310-578-1745

501 (c) 3

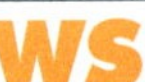

Andrea Hairston Locke	Artistic Director
Jim Hubbard	Photography and Multi-media Director
Natalie Bates	Writing Coordinator

The Venice Arts Mecca is a multi-disciplinary youth arts organization providing free arts workshops to low-income youth. Areas of emphasis are writing, performing arts, photography, and multi-media.

Youth have an opportunity to work as youth arts mentors under the tutelage of professional artists. Guest artists, master classes, and field trips expose youth to career opportunities in the arts.

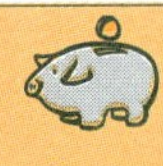

Youth

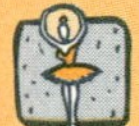
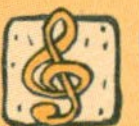
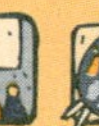

PROGRAMS: PERFORMANCES, WORKSHOPS, CLASSES
SCHEDULE: YEAR-ROUND, WEEKDAYS, EVENINGS, WEEKENDS

VENTURA CHAMBER MUSIC FESTIVAL ASSOCIATION

89 S. California Street, Suite D
Ventura, CA 93001
Ph: 805-648-3146
Fax: 805-648-4103
www.vcmfa.org

501 (c) 3

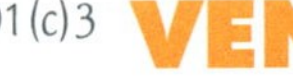

Karyll Lynn Burns	Executive Director	klburns@aol.com
Burns Taft	Artistic Director	
Julianne Gwin	Development Associate	

The Ventura Chamber Music Festival Association offers a variety of Chamber music concerts and themed receptions in unique and historic venues in downtown Ventura.

The Ventura Chamber Music Festival provides an educational outreach program for 4th and 5th grade students in the Ventura Unified School District and 6th grade students countywide. On occasion, concerts are provided to at-risk 4th grade students.

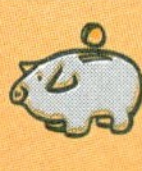

Pre/K-12

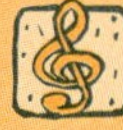
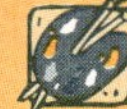

PROGRAMS: PERFORMANCES
SCHEDULE: WEEKDAYS, EVENINGS, WEEKENDS
DETAILS: GRADES 3-8, VISUAL & PERFORMING ARTS
AESTHETIC VALUING, CREATIVE EXPRESSION
HISTORICAL/CULTURAL CONTEXT
CONNECTIONS/RELATIONS/APPLICATIONS
TRAVEL TO SCHOOLS, PROGRAMS ON-SITE
EDUCATIONAL MATERIALS AVAILABLE

Youth

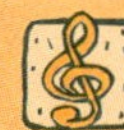
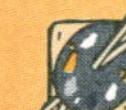

PROGRAMS: PERFORMANCES
SCHEDULE: WEEKDAYS, EVENINGS, WEEKENDS

Families

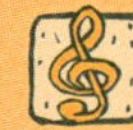
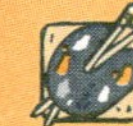
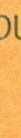

PROGRAMS: PERFORMANCES
SCHEDULE: WEEKDAYS, EVENINGS, WEEKENDS
DETAILS: COST FOR SOME PROGRAMS

VENTURA COURT THEATRE ALLIANCE

12417 Ventura Court
Studio City, CA 91604
Ph: 818-763-3856

SFV

Shannon Monahan Managing Director/ 818-888-2619

Youth

PROGRAMS: PERFORMANCES, WORKSHOPS
SCHEDULE: YEAR-ROUND, WEEKDAYS, WEEKENDS

VENTURE WEST THEATRE COMPANY

9680 Yoakum Drive
Beverly Hills, CA 90210
Ph: 310-275-5027
Admin: 310-234-9111
Educ: 310-271-7442
Fax; 310-275-0510

501 (c) 3

WS

Marcia Messing	Managing Director
Drew Snyder	Artistic Director
Barbara Berkowitz	Dramature

- performances of new plays (full productions)
- readings of new plays in their developmental stage
- community outreach programs and workshops
- volunteer opporutnities to work on productions

Families

PROGRAMS: PERFORMANCES, WORKSHOPS
SCHEDULE: YEAR-ROUND, WEEKDAYS, EVENINGS, WEEKENDS
DETAILS: COST FOR SOME PROGRAMS

VERDUGO HILLS SWEET ADELINES

P.O. Box 721
Glendale, CA 91209
Ph: 626-500-1063

501 (c) 3

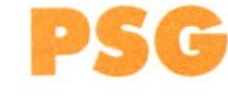

Nancy Branam	Team Manager/ 818-363-5867	
Carolyn Butler	Co-Director	wilbut269@delphi.com
Bill Butler	Co-Director	
Bunny Ankney	Chorus Manager/ 626-917-5690	

The Verdugo Hills Chorus is an organization of female singers dedicated to the musical art form of barbershop harmony through education, competition, and entertainment.

- visitors welcome to rehearsals and performances
- membership open to females who love to sing and perform

VERY SPECIAL ARTS GALLERY WEST

184 N. Cañon Drive
Beverly Hills, CA 90210
Ph: 310-385-0499
Fax: 310-385-0867
www.vsarts.org

501 (c) 3 **WS**

Rachel Schneir	Gallery Manager	vsawest@earthlink.net
Nina Tatum	Gallery Director	
Lisa Insana	Community Relations Mgr/ 310-385-0297	lisai@vsarts.org

Through art exhibitions and shows, the VSA Gallery West in Beverly Hills cultivates disability awareness and education by showcasing the exceptional contributions artists with disabilities make to the world of art.

- exhibitions featuring artists with disabilities
- private reception space
- private and corporate art consultation
- one-of-a-kind arts and crafts, including handmade jewelry, ceramic sculpture, and textiles by artists with disabilities
- limited edition prints

VICTORY THEATRE/THE LITTLE VICTORY, THE

3326 W. Victory Boulevard
Burbank, CA 91505
Ph: 818-843-9253
Admin: 818-841-4404
Fax: 818-841-6328

501 (c) 3 **SFV**

Maria Gobetti	Artistic Co-Director/Executive Director, Acting Studio	
Tom Ormeny	Artistic Co-Director	thevictory@mindspring.com

The Victory and The Little Victory Theatre was chartered to present West Coast premieres of mainly American playwrights.

- acting studio
- training of professional actors
- playwright workshops attended by the public
- workshops for the Verdugo Health Clinic
- volunteer programs for the elderly and disabled

The Theatre in Education (TIE) program offers low cost and free seating to rehabilitation organizations, and junior and senior high school students.

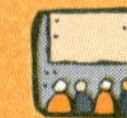
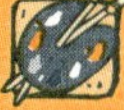

Youth

PROGRAMS: PERFORMANCES, CLASSES
SCHEDULE: YEAR-ROUND, EVENINGS, WEEKENDS

VIRGINIA AVENUE PROJECT, THE

1653 18th Street, #2
Santa Monica, CA 90404
Ph: 310-828-7443
Fax: 310-828-1433

501 (c) 3 **WS**

Kendis Marcotte	Executive Director/ 626-792-2283	vapjt@lalc.kiz.ca.us
Leigh Curran	Artistic Director	
Monica Brunt	Production Manager	

The Virginia Avenue Project brings at-risk youth between the ages of six and eighteen together with professional writers, actors, and directors to create evenings of theater.

- four free preformances a year

The Project is composed of six core programs all sharing the common discipline and hard work one can achieve. The One- On-One Program pairs an adult writer-performer with a child. In the Playmaking Program, the tables are turned and the children write plays for the adults, Successive programs build up skills gained from the previous programs.

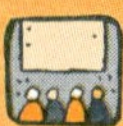

Youth

PROGRAMS: PERFORMANCES
SCHEDULE: YEAR-ROUND

VISUAL ARTISTS ASSOCIATION CELEBRITY CENTRE INTERNATIONAL

1550 N. Verdugo Road, #45
Glendale, CA 91208
Ph: 818-543-3240
Fax: 818-545-8801

501 (c) 3 **SFV**

Lynn Sagner	President	vaa@kscn.net

Located in the historic "Chateau Elyseé" in Hollywood, the Celebrity Centre International Visual Artists Association is a personal and community outreach group, continually working to improve conditions in the environment.

- performance and rehearsal opportunities at Celebrity Centre International, including guided tours of the facility
- volunteer and/or paid performances for and with other community groups
- art exhibitions and festivals at Celebrity Centre and in the community
- volunteer opportunities

VISUAL ARTISTS ASSOCIATION CELEBRITY CENTRE (CONTINUED)

The Visual Artists Association education program uses Hubbard standard technology of study so that the artist fully understands and applies what he/she has learned in his/her chosen field in order to flourish and prosper.

Pre/K-12

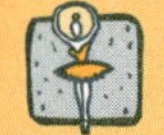 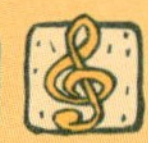 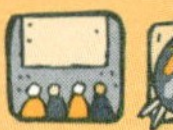 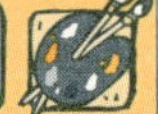

PROGRAMS: PERFORMANCES, WORKSHOPS, STUDIO CLASSES
SCHEDULE: YEAR-ROUND, WEEKDAYS, EVENINGS, WEEKENDS
DETAILS: GRADES PRE/K-12, VISUAL & PERFORMING ARTS
HUMANITIES, SPIRITIAL COUNSELING, AESTHETIC VALUING
CREATIVE EXPRESSION, HISTORICAL/CULTURAL CONTEXT
CONNECTIONS/RELATIONS/APPLICATIONS, PROGRAMS ON-SITE
INDIVIDUALLY TAILORED PROGRAMS, EDUCATIONAL MATERIALS
BILINGUAL : SPANISH

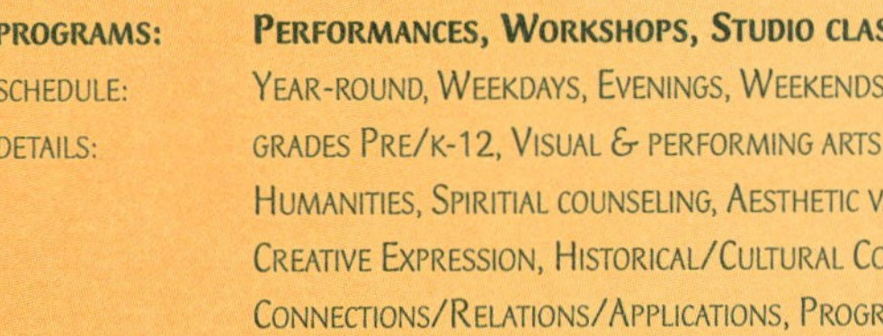

Youth

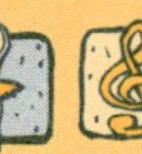 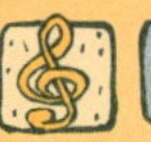 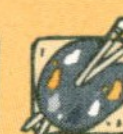

PROGRAMS: PERFORMANCES, WORKSHOPS, CLASSES
SCHEDULE: YEAR-ROUND, WEEKDAYS, EVENINGS, WEEKENDS

Families

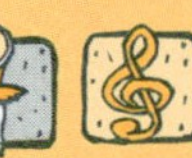 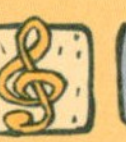 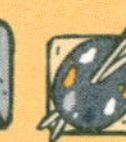

PROGRAMS: PERFORMANCES, WORKSHOPS, CLASSES
SCHEDULE: YEAR-ROUND, WEEKDAYS, EVENINGS, WEEKENDS

VISUAL ARTS AND DESIGN ACADEMY

2925 E. Sierra Madre Boulevard
Pasadena, CA 91107
Ph: 626-798-8901
Fax: 626-798-1875

PSG

Mark Williams — Coordinating Teacher/ x228
Jeannine Savedra — Studio Arts Instructor/ x338
Ben Ramirez — Principal/ x231

VADA is a partnership, career academy inside Pasadena High School for students 10-12th grade. We are a school-to-career program offering foundation skills in a variety of visual arts disciplines.

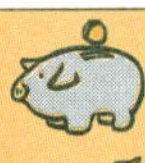

Pre/K-12

PROGRAMS: CLASSES
SCHEDULE: SPRING, FALL, WINTER, WEEKDAYS
DETAILS: GRADES 9-12, VISUAL & PERFORMING ARTS
AESTHETIC VALUING, CREATIVE EXPRESSION
HISTORICAL/CULTURAL CONTEXT
CONNECTIONS/RELATIONS/APPLICATIONS

VISUAL COMMUNICATIONS

120 Judge John Aiso Street, Basement Level — 501(c)3 — DSC
Los Angeles, CA 90012
Ph: 213-680-4462
Fax: 213-687-4848

Linda Mabalot — Executive Director

Visual Communication is the nation's oldest Asian Pacific American media arts center providing programs and services for production of independent, community service and organizational videos; distribution of film, video and publications; and exhibitions.

VIVA! LESBIAN AND GAY LATINO ARTISTS

1125 N. McCadden Place, Suite 148 — 501(c)3
Hollywood, CA 90038
Ph: 323-468-1097
Fax: 323-468-1098

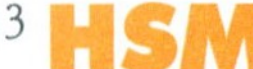

Monica Palacios — Director

Viva! Lesbian and Gay Latino Artists is a nonprofit arts agency that works to discover, empower and promote lesbian and gay latino art and artists since 1987.

VOICES IN HARMONY

P.O. Box 64516 — 501(c)3
Los Angeles, CA 90064
Ph: 310-854-4545
Admin: 310-204-0321
Fax: 323-655-1071

Dina Howard — Executive Director
Melissa Fitzgerald — Artistic Director
David Ackert — Artistic Director

Voices in Harmony pairs inner-city teenagers with theater professionals to examine issues such as intolerance, racism, and child abuse; teens and mentors collaborate to write and perform original pieces of theater.

- teenagers can participate as mentees
- adults can be mentors, directors, writing consultants, producers, or volunteers
- shows are open to the general public

VOICES IN HARMONY (CONTINUED)

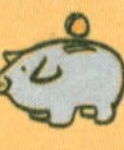

While there are many wonderful programs that encourage teens to express themselves through theater, Voices in Harmony is unique in that we focus on providing the teens with mentor/role models with whom the collaboration takes place.

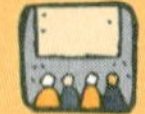

Pre/K-12

PROGRAMS:	**PERFORMANCES**
SCHEDULE:	SUMMER, EVENINGS, WEEKENDS
DETAILS:	GRADES 7-12, VISUAL & PERFORMING ARTS DRUG ABUSE AND PREVENTION, STEREOTYPING AND INTOLERANCE EDUCATION, CREATIVE EXPRESSION CONNECTIONS/RELATIONS/APPLICATIONS WORK WITH INNER-CITY TEENS

Youth

PROGRAMS:	**PERFORMANCES**
SCHEDULE:	SUMMER, EVENINGS, WEEKENDS

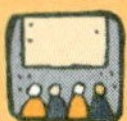

Families

PROGRAMS:	**PERFORMANCES**
SCHEDULE:	SUMMER, EVENINGS, WEEKENDS

WARNER GRAND THEATRE

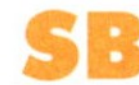

478 W. 6th Street
San Pedro, CA 90731
Ph: 310-548-7672
Fax: 310-548-2493

WATTS LABOR COMMUNITY ACTION COMMITTEE (WLCAC)

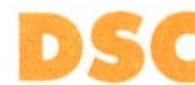

10950 S. Central Avenue
Los Angeles, CA 90059
Ph: 323-563-5639
Fax: 323-563-7307

Sandra Jones	Director of Arts & Culture
Teryl Watkins	President

WATTS PROPHETS, THE

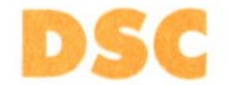

1106 W. 64th Street
Los Angeles, CA 90044
Ph: 323-971-5672

Shirley Hamilton

The members of the Watts Prophets draw upon their years of working as poet/performers/ambassadors for the community of Watts. They have performed for and collaborated with every conceivable segment of the population; children, families, college students, and the incarcerated. Lecture/Demonstrations, performances and poetry workshops tailored for young people, children at-risk, or college students. Participatory workshops/Master Classes in:

- Contemporary Musical Poetics—Rap as Modern Art
- African-American history
- African-American art
- the art of poetry
- race relations

WATTS PROPHETS, THE (CONTINUED)

The Watts Prophets, tempered by thirty plus years of working and living in Watts, bring to the stage the same fire that ignited their birth but with the added perspective of time that brings depth and wisdom.

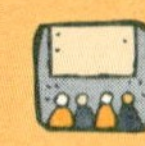

Pre/K-12

PROGRAMS:	**PERFORMANCES, WORKSHOPS, RESIDENCIES**
SCHEDULE:	YEAR-ROUND, WEEKDAYS
DETAILS:	GRADES PRE/K-12, VISUAL & PERFORMING ARTS LANGUAGE ARTS, POETRY/SPOKEN WORD CREATIVE EXPRESSION, TEACHER TRAINING PROGRAMS (SALARY POINTS), TRAVEL TO SCHOOLS INDIVIDUALLY TAILORED PROGRAMS

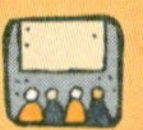

Youth

PROGRAMS:	**PERFORMANCES, WORKSHOPS, RESIDENCIES**
SCHEDULE:	YEAR-ROUND, WEEKDAYS, EVENINGS, WEEKENDS

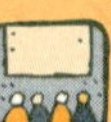

Families

PROGRAMS:	**PERFORMANCES, WORKSHOPS, RESIDENCIES**
SCHEDULE:	YEAR-ROUND, WEEKDAYS, EVENINGS, WEEKENDS

WATTS TOWERS ARTS CENTER

DSC

1727 E. 107th Street
Los Angeles, CA 90002
Ph: 323-847-4646
Admin: 323-485-1795
Fax: 323-564-7030

Mark Greenfield	Director

Adjacent to the Watts Towers of Simon Rodia (also administered by the Cultural Affairs Department), the arts center offers special programs for children, such as a Saturday dance workshop, and hosts community workshops and meetings. Annual events are the Watts Towers Music and Arts Festival and the Day of the Drum Festival.

WEDNESDAY'S HOUSE

WS

2409 Main Street
Santa Monica, CA 90405
Ph: 310-452-4486

Robyn Zielan	Entertainment Coordinator
Daniel DaRocha	Owner

Established in 1993, Wednesday's House, a local coffeehouse, has been a center for new and up-and-coming musicians, poets, and artists.

- bi-monthly talent night hosted by editor of Interbang poetry magazine.
- revolving original movie memorabilia poster show from 40's to 60's.
- gift shop
- live music from local artists
- new music and poetry from up-and-coming artists by way of a monthly updated listening station
- Internet access

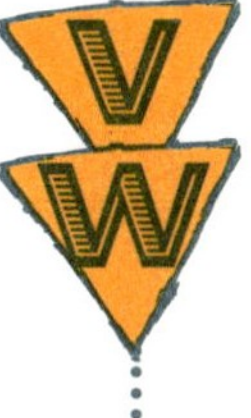

WEST COAST ENSEMBLE

522 N. La Brea Avenue
Los Angeles, CA 90036
Ph: 323-525-0022
Admin: 310-449-1447
Fax: 310-453-2254

501 (c)3 **HSM**

Anne Etue	Public Relations/ 310-453-9004
Les Hanson	Artistic Director
Claudia Jaffee	Managing Director/ 310-829-2289
Richard Israel	Managing Director

Located on La Brea in Hollywood, West Coast Ensemble is a 150-member company under the artistic direction of Les Hanson.

- full season of eight plays per year
- original and published plays
- advanced training, workshops
- accessible production environment

WEST VALLEY REGIONAL ARTS COUNCIL

c/o Valley Cultural Center
21550 Oxnard Street, Suite 470
Woodland Hills, CA 91367
Ph: 818-704-1358
Fax: 818-704-1604

SFV

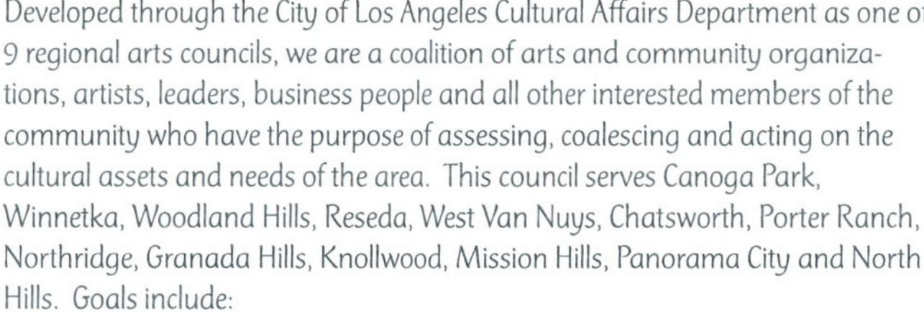

Developed through the City of Los Angeles Cultural Affairs Department as one of 9 regional arts councils, we are a coalition of arts and community organizations, artists, leaders, business people and all other interested members of the community who have the purpose of assessing, coalescing and acting on the cultural assets and needs of the area. This council serves Canoga Park, Winnetka, Woodland Hills, Reseda, West Van Nuys, Chatsworth, Porter Ranch, Northridge, Granada Hills, Knollwood, Mission Hills, Panorama City and North Hills. Goals include:

- develop affordable and accessible local programming that highlights and involves youth and local artists
- develop activities that celebrate the city's cultural diversity and promote community building
- serve as an advisory group to the Cultural Affairs Department on local art and cultural priorities
- strengthen the artistic advancement of the community

WESTCHESTER SYMPHONY SOCIETY

P.O. Box 4846
Culver City, CA 90231
Ph: 310-839-5537
Fax: 310-822-8660

501 (c)3 **WS**

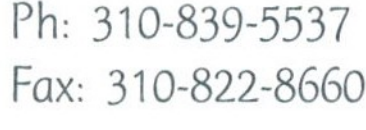

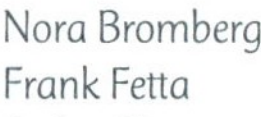

Nora Bromberg	Executive Vice-President/ 310-839-5537
Frank Fetta	Music Director/Conductor/ 323-255-7884
Arthur Danner	Youth Chairman/ 310-287-4209
A.E. Maersch	President/ 213-955-5632

The Culver City-Marina del Rey-Westchester Symphony presents a season of free or moderately priced concerts in the Westchester-Culver City area.

- a season of 3-4 free concerts plus one gala benefit concert
- a youth program in which winners of our concerto competition play as soloists at a symphony concert
- volunteers are welcome to assist at concerts and to participate in the administrative functions of the symphony
- membership in the Symphony Society welcomed

WESTSIDE REGIONAL ARTS COUNCIL

324 Sunset Avenue
Venice, CA 90291
Ph: 310-392-2328

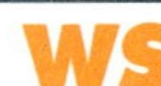

WS

Developed through the City of Los Angeles Cultural Affairs Department as one of 9 regional arts councils, we are a coalition of arts and community organizations, artists, leaders, business people and all other interested members of the community who have the purpose of assessing, coalescing and acting on the cultural assets and needs of the area. This council serves Brentwood, Pacific Palisades, Beverly Crest, Bel Air, Westwood, Mar Vista, Marina Del Rey, Palms and West Los Angeles. Goals include:

- develop affordable and accessible local programming that highlights and involves youth and local artists
- develop activities that celebrate the city's cultural diversity and promote community building
- serve as an advisory group to the Cultural Affairs Department on local art and cultural priorities
- strengthen the artistic advancement of the community

WHITTIER ART ASSOCIATION

8035 S. Painter Avenue
Whittier, CA 90601
Ph: 562-698-8710

501 (c)3 **ELA**

Dorothea Boyd	Curator

The Whittier Art Association is a nonprofit organization that has served Whittier for 60 years. The WAA maintains a gallery with continuous exhibits of the best available arts and crafts. Admission is free.

- monthly exhibitions featuring local artists
- rental space for art exhibits
- juried shows
- gift shop
- annual "Walnut Tree Festival" of arts and crafts
- monthly public program

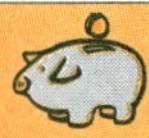

Summer art classes are offered to students from elementary through high school. Teachers are WAA members who are professional artists and art educators.

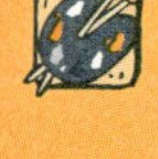

Youth

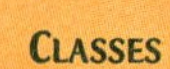

PROGRAMS:	**CLASSES**
SCHEDULE:	SUMMER, WEEKDAYS
DETAILS:	COST FOR SOME PROGRAMS

WHITTIER CULTURAL ARTS FOUNDATION, CITY OF

7630 S. Washington Avenue
Whittier, CA 90602
Ph: 562-464-3430
Fax: 562-464-3581

ELA

Kimberly Powell Albarian   Cultural Arts Supervisor/ 562-464-3440

The Whittier Cultural Arts Foundation was founded in 1987 by the City of Whittier as a fundraising entity to help the Whittier Cultural Arts Commission realize its objectives of encouraging and developing the arts in the community and schools of Whittier.

- Arts Alive Program provides field trips for students from the Whittier Union High School District to visit major museums in the Los Angeles area
- Art Reach Program provides training in arts instruction and curriculum development to Whittier and East Whittier Elementary school districts
- Music Enrichment Program for elementary school children
- membership in the Foundation is offered

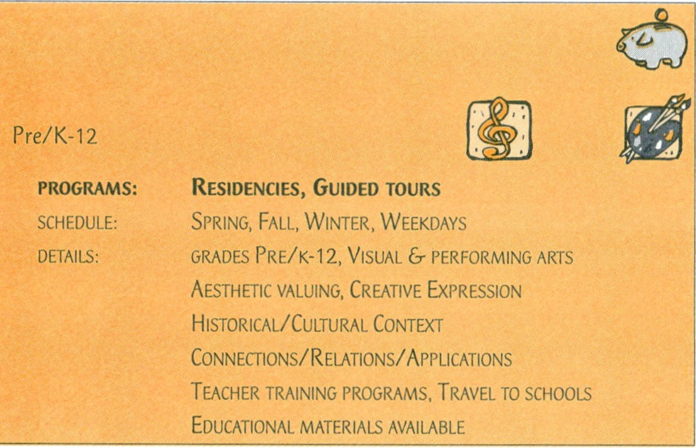

Pre/K-12

PROGRAMS: **RESIDENCIES, GUIDED TOURS**
SCHEDULE: SPRING, FALL, WINTER, WEEKDAYS
DETAILS: GRADES PRE/K-12, VISUAL & PERFORMING ARTS
AESTHETIC VALUING, CREATIVE EXPRESSION
HISTORICAL/CULTURAL CONTEXT
CONNECTIONS/RELATIONS/APPLICATIONS
TEACHER TRAINING PROGRAMS, TRAVEL TO SCHOOLS
EDUCATIONAL MATERIALS AVAILABLE

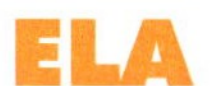

WHITTIER MUSEUM

6755 Newlin Avenue
Whittier, CA 90601
Ph: 562-945-3871

ELA

Debi Sherwood   Museum Manager

WILL GEER THEATRICUM BOTANICUM

1419 N. Topanga Canyon Boulevard
Topanga, CA 90290
Ph: 310-455-2322
Fax: 310-455-4373

WS

Karen Reed   Youth Programs   theatricum@aol.com
Phillip Arnold
Ellen Geer   Artistic Director
Karen Hardcastle   School Days & Enrichment Programs
Susan Angelo   Academy Programs

We are dedicated to the belief that theater, music and education are an integral and necessary part of life for all individuals to experience on a regular and inexpensive basis. We are a nonprofit professional repertory theater with a strong educational wing.

- annual season of musical events and play productions of both new works and the classics
- youth programs
- high school programs
- academy classes
- school days
- classroom enrichment programs
- adult academy classes

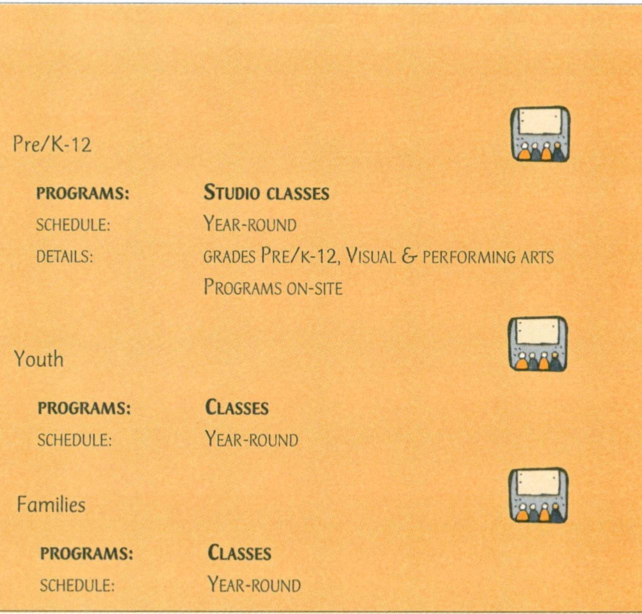

Pre/K-12

PROGRAMS: **STUDIO CLASSES**
SCHEDULE: YEAR-ROUND
DETAILS: GRADES PRE/K-12, VISUAL & PERFORMING ARTS
PROGRAMS ON-SITE

Youth

PROGRAMS: **CLASSES**
SCHEDULE: YEAR-ROUND

Families

PROGRAMS: **CLASSES**
SCHEDULE: YEAR-ROUND

WILLIAM A. KARGES FINE ART

9001 Melrose Avenue
Los Angeles, CA 90069
Ph: 310-276-8551
Fax: 310-276-7980
www.kargesfineart.com

WS

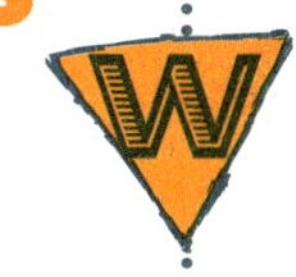

Coby Taylor   Sales   kargesfineart@worldnet.att.net
Whitney Ganz   Director
Susan Schomburg   Research Director

Early Californian and American paintings.

WILLIAM GRANT STILL COMMUNITY ARTS CENTER

2520 W. View Street
Los Angeles, CA 90016
Ph: 213-237-1540
Admin: 323-734-1164
Fax: 213-485-1610

HSM

James Burks Director african_marketplace@juno.com

Named after composer William Grant Still, the center presents year-round exhibitions, workshops, and performing arts events. The center's support group co-sponsors the African Marketplace, which has grown from a modest performing and visual arts festival into a major event.

WILLIAM TURNER GALLERY

77 Market Street
Venice, CA 90291
Ph: 310-392-8399
Fax: 310-392-7348

WS

William Turner Director

WOLFRYD-SELWAY FINE ART

8678 Melrose Avenue
West Hollywood, CA 90069
Ph: 310-657-1711
Fax: 310-657-7771
www.art_service.com
cforney@art_service.com

WS

WOMEN IN THEATRE

11684 Ventura Blvd., Ste. 444
Studio City, CA 91601
Ph: 818-763-5222
Fax: 818-763-5255
www.womenintheatre.org

501(c)3 SFV

Bette Rae Brown Membership Chair
Carol Kiernan President
Gena Gilcrease Outreach Committee Chair

Women in Theatre is a nonprofit organization that networks artists and professional staffs, nurturing and empowering individuals while encouraging positive images of women and providing outreach to the Los Angeles community through theater arts.

- monthly newsletter of events
- playreadings with audience discussion
- "Actor's Work-It" acting workshops with diverse instructors
- networking luncheons/mixers
- community outreach programs feature workshops and readings for Los Angeles community groups
- "Angel Project" offers audience discussions after live theatrical productions
- discounts to local theatrical events
- group health insurance opportunities

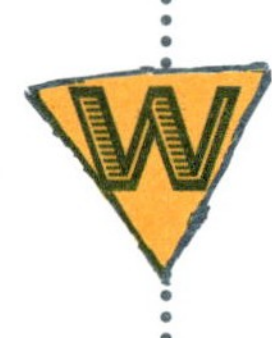

WOMEN IN THEATRE (CONTINUED)

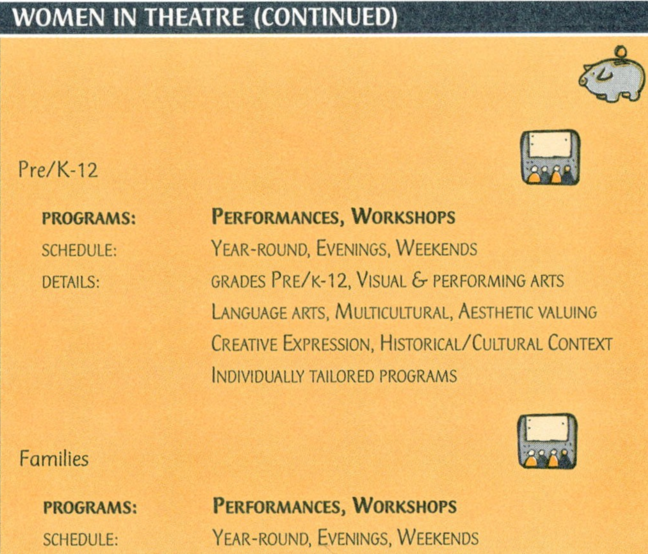
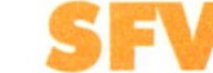

Pre/K-12

PROGRAMS:	**PERFORMANCES, WORKSHOPS**
SCHEDULE:	YEAR-ROUND, EVENINGS, WEEKENDS
DETAILS:	GRADES PRE/K-12, VISUAL & PERFORMING ARTS LANGUAGE ARTS, MULTICULTURAL, AESTHETIC VALUING CREATIVE EXPRESSION, HISTORICAL/CULTURAL CONTEXT INDIVIDUALLY TAILORED PROGRAMS

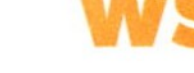

Families

PROGRAMS:	**PERFORMANCES, WORKSHOPS**
SCHEDULE:	YEAR-ROUND, EVENINGS, WEEKENDS

WOODBURY UNIVERSITY ART GALLERY

7500 Glenoaks Boulevard
Burbank, CA 91510-7846
Ph: 818-767-0888
Fax: 818-540-9320

SFV

University, fashion design, marketing, costume design, visual arts.

WORKMEN'S CIRCLE/ARBETER RING

1525 S. Robertson Boulevard
Los Angeles, CA 90035-4231
Ph: 310-552-2007
Fax: 310-552-3417
www.circle.org

WS

Mary Koukhab Assistant Director
Eric Gordon Director

The Workmen's Circle/Arbeter Ring is a national membership organization offering Jewish, especially Yiddish, arts, cultural, and educational programs and activities. We also emphasize social and economic justice for all people.

- six art exhibitions yearly in A Shenere Velt Gallery with related panels, concerts, lectures, and docent tours
- Yiddish classes
- Yiddish chorus
- concerts, theater
- lectures, discussions, forums
- charitable fundraising
- healthcare, cemetary benefits

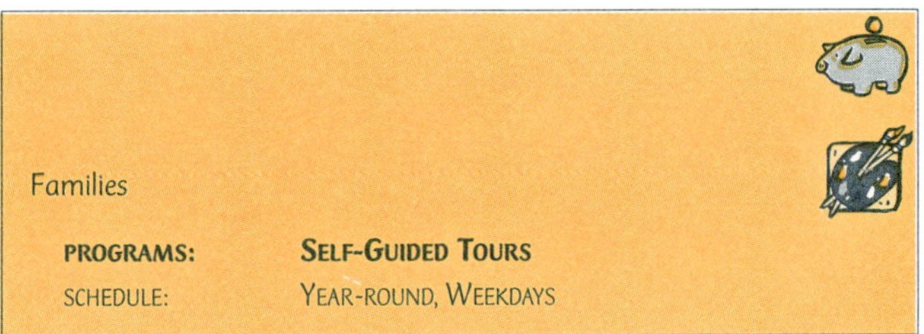

Families

PROGRAMS:	**SELF-GUIDED TOURS**
SCHEDULE:	YEAR-ROUND, WEEKDAYS

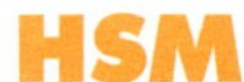
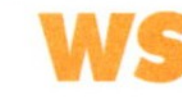
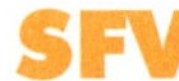

WORLD STAGE

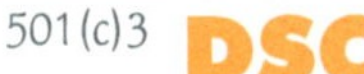

4344 Degnan Boulevard 501(c)3 **DSC**
Los Angeles, CA 90008
Ph: 323-293-2451

Michael Datcher Literary Director
Kamau Daáood Artistic Director

- Monday night drumming session
- Tuesday night jazz vocal workshop
- Wednesday night poetry workshop
- Thursday night jazz jam session
- Friday and Saturday jazz concert series

Pre/K-12

PROGRAMS: PERFORMANCES, WORKSHOPS
SCHEDULE: YEAR-ROUND, WEEKDAYS, EVENINGS, WEEKENDS
DETAILS: GRADES 9-12, MULTICULTURAL
AESTHETIC VALUING, CREATIVE EXPRESSION
HISTORICAL/CULTURAL CONTEXT
TRAVEL TO SCHOOLS

Youth

PROGRAMS: PERFORMANCES, WORKSHOPS
SCHEDULE: YEAR-ROUND, WEEKDAYS, EVENINGS, WEEKENDS

Families

PROGRAMS: PERFORMANCES, WORKSHOPS
SCHEDULE: YEAR-ROUND, WEEKDAYS, EVENINGS, WEEKENDS

YALE CONNECTION, THE

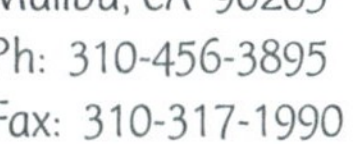

23316 Bocana Street 501(c)3 **WS**
Malibu, CA 90265
Ph: 310-456-3895
Fax: 310-317-1990

Stephen Keep Mills Officer malvu@earthlink.net
Asaad Kelada Officer/ 818-784-6882
Stephanie Nash Officer/ 818-761-0961
Mark Travis Officer/ 818-508-4600

The Yale Connection is a community of theatre professionals committed to promoting the process of new play development, engaging audiences on themes which heighten contemporary conflicts, and celebrating the elasticity, craft, and experience of live theater.

- each year a series of performance readings of new play is offered free of charge at a variety of Los Angeles locations

YARGER FINE ARTS, TIMOTHY

314 N. Rodeo Drive **WS**
Beverly Hills, CA 90210
Ph: 310-278-4400
Fax: 310-278-6771

Timothy Yarger timyarger@earthlink.net

Modern and contermporary art, master graphics.

YORUBA HOUSE

3264 Motor Avenue **WS**
Los Angeles, CA 90034
Ph: 310-838-4843
Fax: 310-842-3742
www.primenet.com/~yoruba/

Carole Adeyemi Co-Director yoruba@primenet.com

West Africa drumming, dance, song and culture. Programs for schools and at Yoruba House.

- artist in your classroom series
- assembly and single visit workshops for schools
- on-going drumming classes at Yoruba House for teachers and parents
- family fun workshops at Yoruba House
- make your own drum workshops
- children's ongoing drum classes
- the ensemble is also available for private parties

Experience the exciting culture of West Africa right in your school. The Yoruba House education programs inspire children of all ages to discover their rhythmic nature, cultural commonalities, and individual uniqueness. Programs feature African music and dance, language, traditional dress and authentic artifacts to introduce students to the treasures of African culture.

Pre/K-12

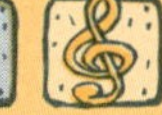

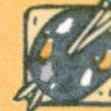

PROGRAMS: PERFORMANCES, WORKSHOPS, RESIDENCIES
SCHEDULE: YEAR-ROUND
DETAILS: GRADES PRE/K-12, VISUAL & PERFORMING ARTS
MULTICULTURAL, CREATIVE EXPRESSION
HISTORICAL/CULTURAL CONTEXT, TRAVEL TO SCHOOLS
INDIVIDUALLY TAILORED PROGRAMS

Youth

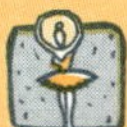
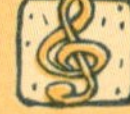
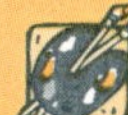

PROGRAMS: WORKSHOPS, CLASSES
SCHEDULE: YEAR-ROUND

Families

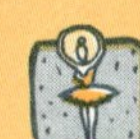
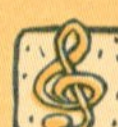
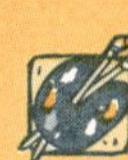

PROGRAMS: WORKSHOPS, CLASSES
SCHEDULE: YEAR-ROUND

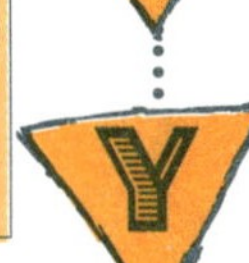

YOUNG ARTISTS INTERNATIONAL, INC.

501(c)3 **HSM**

2430 Apollo Drive
Los Angeles, CA 90046-1628
Ph: 310-281-3303
Admin: 323-969-8243
Fax: 323-969-8742
www.youngartistsintl.com

Kathryn Leitner — Secretary/ 310-476-7356
Laura Schmieder — Artistic/Executive Director — yaimusic@aol.com

Young Artists International, Inc. is a nonprofit organization formed to support, promote, and serve as transitional management for exceptionally gifted young musicians.

- presents Benefactors Concert Series throughout the year
- annual International Laureates Chamber Music Festival based in Los Angeles (also presented in NM, MA, CO, and other states)
- presents selected group of Laureates through YAT management program solo (with orchestras) and in group recitals featuring a variety of solo and chamber music

YOUNG ARTISTS PENINSULA MUSIC FESTIVAL

501(c)3 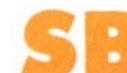

6931 Vallon Drive
Palos Verdes Peninsula, CA 90275
Ph: 310-377-8891
Fax: 310-544 6319

Erika Chary — Founder/Director

The Young Artists Peninsula Music Festival, a two-day festival in June, provides performance opportunities for gifted young musicians up to 28 years old from all over the world.

- performance opportunities for young soloists and ensembles

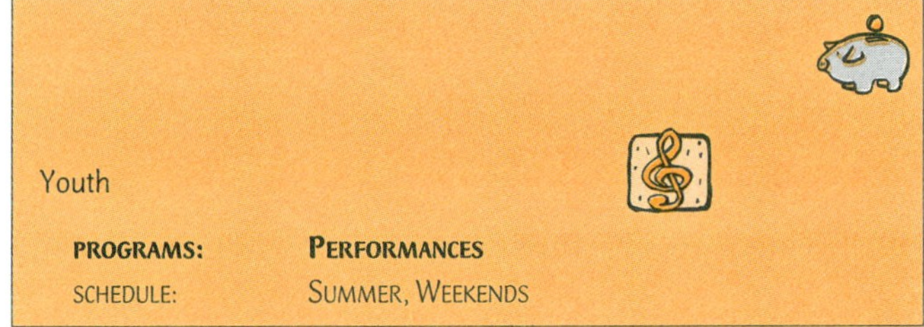

Youth

PROGRAMS: PERFORMANCES
SCHEDULE: SUMMER, WEEKENDS

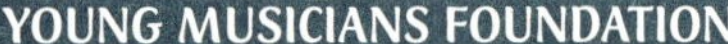

YOUNG MUSICIANS FOUNDATION

501(c)3 **WS**

195 S. Beverly Drive, Suite 414
Beverly Hills, CA 90212
Ph: 310-859-7668
Fax: 310-859-1365

Mike Duckworth — Programs Director
Bundit Ungrangsee — Music Director
Edye Rugolo — Executive Director

Young Musicians Foundation (YMF), a nonprofit organization founded in 1955, is currently celebrating its 44th anniversary of providing encouragement and recognition to gifted young musicians through financial assistance and performance opportunities.

- debut orchestra
- scholarship program
- chamber music series
- Youth Mentor Artists Program
- Instrument Loan Program
- Arts Management Training Program
- Disney's Young Musicians Symphony Orchestra
- Conductor Training Program
- outreach program
- debut competition
- volunteer opportunities
- soloists, chamber ensembles, and orchestra for hire

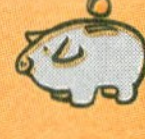

YMF's Youth Mentor Artists Program assigns instrumentalists and vocalists to underserved and minority elementary and middle schools. Mentors rehearse with orchestras and choruses, lead sectional rehearsals, provide individual tutoring, and develop music appreciation programs. The Greendale Instrument Loan Program loans instruments and provides mentors to schools that do not have an instrumental music program.

Pre/K-12 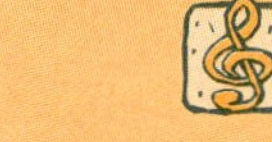

PROGRAMS: PERFORMANCES, RESIDENCIES
SCHEDULE: SPRING, FALL, WINTER, WEEKDAYS
DETAILS: GRADES PRE/K-8, VISUAL & PERFORMING ARTS
CREATIVE EXPRESSION, TRAVEL TO SCHOOLS
INDIVIDUALLY TAILORED PROGRAMS

Youth 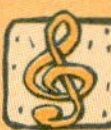

PROGRAMS: PERFORMANCES
SCHEDULE: SPRING, FALL, WINTER, WEEKDAYS

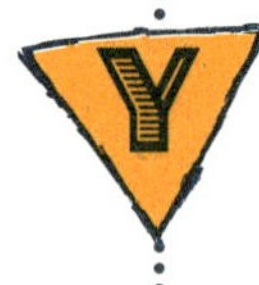

YOUNG SAINTS SCHOLARSHIP FOUNDATIONS, INC.

2000 Wellington Road
Los Angeles, CA 90016-1825
Ph: 323-734-5379
Fax: 323-735-4026

501 (c) 3 **HSM**

Evelyn Roberts — President and CEO
Lisa Roberts — Artistic Director/Chief Instructor

Young Saints Scholarship Foundation provides free professional training and experience in performing arts and telecommunications skills for youth, ages five to young adult.

- free quarterly in-house concerts
- annual festival "Celebration of the Arts"
- performances for church, community and civic organizations

Young Saints Scholarship Foundation, Inc. presents a free year-round program in Southern California for at-risk youth, ages five to twenty-one, in a supportive environment where their talents and interests are channelled constructively through training in performing arts and associated skills.

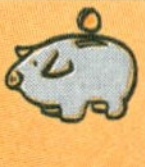

Youth

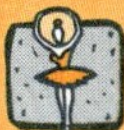 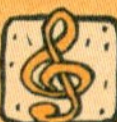 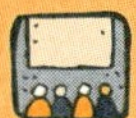

PROGRAMS: **PERFORMANCES, CLASSES**
SCHEDULE: YEAR-ROUND, WEEKDAYS

YOUR OWN SKY, A THEATRE ENSEMBLE

2700 Cahuenga Blvd. E, Ste. 3107
Los Angeles, CA 90062
Ph: 323-882-6669
Fax: 323-851-1454

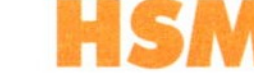

Kate Randolph — Artistic Director/ 323-851-1454

Located in Hollywood, "Your Own Sky" is a membership theater ensemble which produces 3 to 4 productions per year.

- full-length productions of previously performed works
- world premieres
- one-act play festivals
- readings
- salons
- exhibits of art/photography (in lobby during productions)
- street theater
- classes in acting: beginning, Intermediate, advanced
- classes in theater arts for the non-professional
- private coaching
- volunteer opportunities

YOUR OWN SKY, A THEATRE ENSEMBLE (CONTINUED)

Our company's approach to teaching theatre arts skills to non-professionals is unique in that it deals with centering and listening techniques that are valuable in all disciplines. Our exercises also are designed to break down barriers both within people and between people.

Pre/K-12

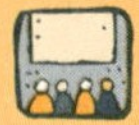

PROGRAMS: **PERFORMANCES, WORKSHOPS, STUDIO CLASSES RESIDENCIES**
SCHEDULE: YEAR-ROUND, WEEKDAYS, EVENINGS, WEEKENDS
DETAILS: GRADES PRE/K-12, VISUAL & PERFORMING ARTS
LANGUAGE ARTS, CREATIVE EXPRESSION
TEACHER TRAINING PROGRAMS, TRAVEL TO SCHOOLS
PROGRAMS ON-SITE, INDIVIDUALLY TAILORED PROGRAMS

Youth

PROGRAMS: **PERFORMANCES, WORKSHOPS, CLASSES, RESIDENCIES**
SCHEDULE: YEAR-ROUND, WEEKDAYS, EVENINGS, WEEKENDS

Service Providers: Individuals and Organizations

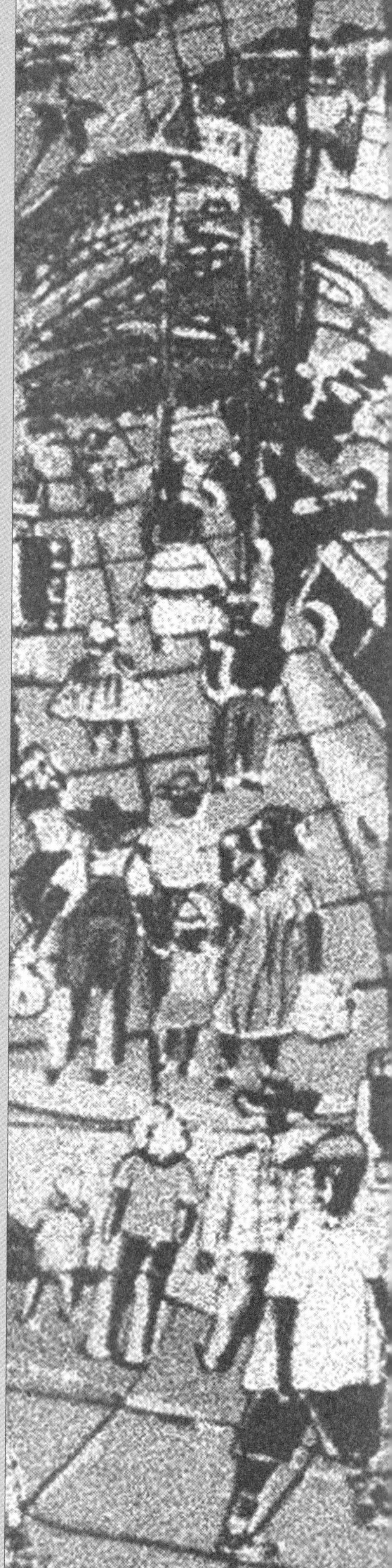

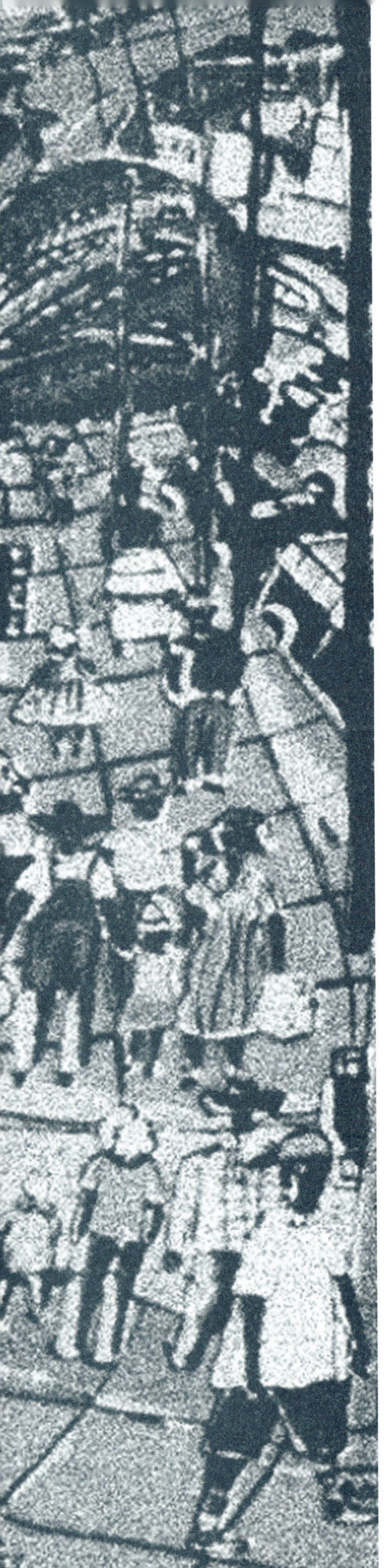

Introduction: Service Providers-Individuals and Organizations

Across greater Los Angeles, the universe of support services is tremendous, an intricate web of creative talent blended with an array of expanding creative resources. Artists and arts organizations working in a variety of contexts and across disciplines have access to a comprehensive network of local/national arts specialists and a menu of services customized to meet changing needs.

This section of the Arts Resource Directory links you to the individual consultants, service organizations, public agencies and allied service providers you may need to produce and market your work, sustain and build your operation, or advance your skills and career. You can find technical support and guidance on funding, planning, marketing, artistic and professional development—discipline-specific and the general expertise necessary to take a studio or organization from start-up to established phase. Stretching beyond the city's borders to encompass the cultural communities in Santa Monica, Pasadena, Long Beach, Whittier, Santa Clarita and everywhere in between, this guide connects you to the systems of support that shape the cultural landscape and creative force of greater L.A..

Service providers are a vital component of the cultural infrastructure in the region—working behind the scene to communicate with the general public and decision makers about the value of the arts to community vitality, as well as the role of the arts in fueling innovation and creativity in Southern California. Whether you are looking for a fresh perspective, facing challenges or responding to new opportunities, the Greater Los Angeles area offers a variety of service options geared toward helping you to achieve your goals.

The Directory provides you with a roadmap to discover the arts and culture of the metro area—a powerful testament to the vast cultural resources and the vibrant arts activity found throughout the region.

Sandra Gibson, Executive Vice-President and Chief Operating Officer
Americans for the Arts

SERVICE PROVIDERS

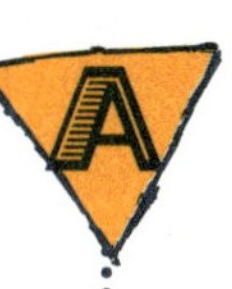

A.S.K. THEATER PROJECTS

11845 W. Olympic Boulevard, Suite 1250
West Los Angeles, CA 90064
Ph: 310-478-3200
Fax: 310-478-5300
www.askplay.org

Sydney Young — Office Manager
Kym Eisner — Executive Director

A.S.K. Theater Projects, a local and national resource for the theater and its artists, offers an energetic year-round schedule of activities. All of A.S.K.'s programs, services, and publications are free of charge.

- writer's Retreat
- rehearsed Reading Series
- community Affinity Groups
- workshop Productions
- Stage One Readings
- national Playwright Exchanges
- playwright Composer Studio
- playwright practical labs
- play Commissioning
- Common Ground Festival
- ASK Interchange Online
- playwrights-in-the-Schools
- workshop Playscripts
- ASK newsletter

ACCESS CULTURAL LIAISON SERVICES

418 S. Mansfield Avenue
Los Angeles, CA 90036
Phone: 323-938-0088
Fax: 323-938-0088

Cameron Taylor-Brown — Consultant — catbrown@ix.netcom.com

Consultant in Arts & Education.

- board development
- meeting facilitation
- workshop/seminar/symposia
- connecting community resources with schools

ACTION ARTS

215 S. Madison Avenue, Suite 207
Pasadena, CA 91101
Ph/Fax: 626-584-6368

Aloma Law — Executive Director

Located in Pasadena, Action Arts is a multi-disciplinary community-based arts services organization that offers technical support to emerging artists and arts organizations.

- production of original art work, program development, technical assistance, fiscal receiverships, grantwriting, and fundraising.
- production of dance, exhibitions, concerts, plays, readings, etc.
- program development of children's programs and activities

ACTORS' FUND OF AMERICA, THE

4727 Wilshire Boulevard, Suite 310
Los Angeles, CA 90010
Ph: 323-933-9244
Fax: 323-933-7615
www.actorsfund.org

William Jones — Development Consultant
Lyn Sherman — Director, Human Services

The Actors' Fund provides assistance to people who work in the performing arts and entertainment field, including seniors, people with HIV/AIDS, etc.

- social services
- financial assistance
- housing
- vocational counseling

ADAMS, MOIRA

230 Deer Trail
Yucca Valley, CA 92284
Ph: 760-364-1146
Fax: 760-364-3446

Moira Adams — moiraadams@aol.com

Moira Adams provides program planning, development, and evaluation consulting to nonprofit organizations and public institutions working in the arts and social services.

- grantwriting
- needs assessment
- audience studies
- program evaluation

ALLIANCE OF LOS ANGELES PLAYWRIGHTS

7510 Sunset Boulevard, Suite 1050
Los Angeles, CA 90046
Ph: 323-957-4752

Dick Dotterer — Co-Chair

The Alliance of Los Angeles Playwrights (ALAP) is a support and service organization dedicated to addressing the needs of the Los Angeles playwriting community.

- annual Playwrights Expo
- "In Our Own Voices" reading series
- symposia
- social events

AMERICAN ASSOCIATION OF MUSEUMS

1575 Eye Street NW, Suite 400
Washington, DC 20005-1105
Ph: 202-289-1818
Fax: 202-289-6578
www.aam-us.org
membership@aam-us.org

The AAM provides professional education, information, representation, access to resources and services, and publications to promote growth and stability in museums.

AMERICAN FEDERATION OF ARTS

41 E. 65th Street
New York, NY 10021-6694
Ph: 212-988-7700
Fax: 212-861-2487
www.afaweb.org

Kathleen Flynn	Program Manager	tap@afaweb.org
John Nichols	Director of Museum Services	

The AFA is a service organization dedicated to expanding the resources of art museums. The AFA does this primarily through its program of travelling exhibitions, developed to meet the needs of a broad range of museums and their communities.

- AFA Institutional Membership
- Artsure Insurance
- Vango surface transport
- Airgo flight transport

AMERICAN INDIAN RESOURCE CENTER

Huntington Park Library
6518 Miles Avenue
Huntington Park, CA 90255
Phone: 323-583-1461
Fax: 323-587-2061

Joanne Bliss	Librarian	airc@colapl.crl

The American Indian Resource Center (AIC), located in the Huntington Park Library, was established in 1979 to meet the informational and cultural needs of the large American Indian population

- core multimedia collection will document all aspects of American Indian life and culture (in development)
- bibliographies available
- referrals to other libraries with collections
- a focus for the Indian Community by providing programs and a meeting place for American Indian groups

AMERICAN SYMPHONY ORCHESTRA LEAGUE

1156 15th Street NW, Suite 800
Washington, DC 20005-1704
Ph: 202-776-0212
Fax: 202-776-0224
www.symphony.org

Grace Chang	Public Relations Manager/ x214
Charles Olton	President & CEO/ x242

The league provides leadership and service to American orchestras while communicating to the American public the value and importance of orchestras and the music they perform.

- research and information center
- variety of publications
- professional development and training programs
- award-winning magazine, Symphony
- advocacy for the arts
- annual national conference

AMERICANS FOR THE ARTS

1000 Vermont Avenue, NW, 12th Floor
Washington, DC 20005
Ph: 202-371-2830
Fax: 202-371-0424
www.artsusa.org

Millie Lee	Administrative Assistant	mlee@artsusa.org
Robert Lynch	President & CEO	rlynch@artsusa.org
Sandra Gibson	Executive Vice President & COO	sgibson@artsusa.org
Jennifer Gottlieb	Director of Communications	jgottlieb@artsusa.org

Americans for the Arts is the national organization for groups and individuals dedicated to advancing the arts and culture in communities across the country. To this end, Americans for the Arts works with cultural organizations, arts and business leaders, and patrons to provide leadership, advocacy, visibility, professional development, and research and information that will advance support for the arts and culture in our nation's communities.

AMS PLANNING & RESEARCH

915 D Street
Petaluma, CA 94952
Ph: 707-778-8445
Fax: 707-769-0329
www.ams-online.com

Bob Bailey	rbailey@ams-online.com

National marketing consultants.

- marketing
- strategic planning
- workshop/seminar/symposia

ARCHIVES OF AMERICAN ART, SMITHSONIAN INSTITUTION

1151 Oxford Road
San Marino, CA 91108
Ph: 626-583-7847
Fax: 626-583-7207
www.aaawcrc.si.edu

Barbara Bishop	Center Manager
Paul Karlstrom	Regional Director
Marian Kovinick	Archival Technician

The Archives of American Art, a bureau of the Smithsonian Institution, is the world's largest collection of primary source manuscript material relating to the visual arts in this country, from colonial times to the present.

ART DIMENSIONS, INC.

2044 Broadway, A-1
Santa Monica, CA 90404
Ph: 310-828-5532
Fax: 310-829-6843

Jill Rosenberg	Gallery Director
Whitney Rosenson	President/CEO

Art Dimensions, Inc. offers contemporary art in all media by well-known, established and emerging artists. The lease/purchase option provides a unique opportunity to acquire fine art at affordable prices.

- on-site consultation
- provides clients with an affordable way to live with art and rotate a collection
- tax deductible business expense

ART INFORMATION SERVICES

P.O. Box 69301
Los Angeles, CA 90069
Ph: 310-278-4468
Fax: 310-659-1492

Michelle Hayden	Director	etacm@aol.com

Art Information Services answers questions and provides referrals to galleries, museums, and insurance companies in reference to art storage, transportation, restoration, and appraisals.

- referrals

ART MEDIA DESIGN, PRODUCTION & NETWORK

1720 Granville Avenue, #6
Los Angeles, CA 90025
Ph: 310-826-1443
Fax: 310-826-7066
www.artmedia.net

A.C. Costa	General Manager	accosta@artmedia.net

- computer use
- customized mailing lists
- fundraising development
- internet service provider
- marketing
- media lists
- publications
- website development

ARTIST'S ALLIANCE OF CALIFORNIA

P.O. Box 2424
Nevada City, CA 95959
Ph: 530-272-7357
www.nccn.netnevadacountybusinesssect.net

Bonnie Hall	President
Jessica Chase	Assistant Director/Editor

The Artist's Alliance focuses on bringing business together with artists to create opportunity. In addition, we offer support through discounts on supplies, health care, and public exposure.

- Internet Media Festival that culminates each year in a different county community festival
- services and workshops year-round

ARTNETWORK

P.O. Box 1268
Penn Valley, CA 95946
Ph: 530-470-0862
Fax: 530-470-0256
www.artmarketing.com

Sarah Meyers	Manager	info@artmarketing.com

ArtNetwork is a publisher of books teaching fine artists how to market their work.

- ArtNetwork sells the following books: Art Marketing 101, Art Marketing Sourcebook, and the Encyclopedia of Living Artists
- ArtNetwork has two newsletters: "Art Source Quarterly" and "Art World Hotline"
- sells mailing list of artworld professionals

ARTS CONSULTING

519 N. Windsor Boulevard
Los Angeles, CA 90004
Ph: 323-463-1005
Fax: 323-463-1911
www.artsconsulting.com

Bruce Thibodeau — President — bdthibadeau@artsconsulting.com

- accounting assistance
- board development
- computer use
- corporate sponsorship solicitation
- meeting facilitation
- human resources--
  board members,
  executive recruitment,
  employment assistance
- workshops/seminars/symposia
- administrative assistance
- board/staff training
- fundraising development
- marketing
- public relations
- strategic planning

ARTS, INC.

315 W. Ninth Street, Suite 201
Los Angeles, CA 90015
Ph: 213-627-9276
Fax: 213-627-9914

Jennifer Wong — Program Coordinator
Beth Fox — Executive Director

ARTS, Inc.—greater Los Angeles' Arts & Business Council—makes connections to vital information, opportunities, and resources for local nonprofit arts organizations and artists of all disciplines.

- Los Angeles Arts Loan Fund provides interest-free loans of up to $15,000 to sustain local non-profit arts organizations, individual artists will be eligible for loans beginning year-end 1999
- Arts Resource Directory and Arts & Education Guide
- Arts Referral Service is a free clearinghouse source for arts-related information
- Downtown Cultural Facilities Brokering Service connects arts organizations and artists with available office, studio, and rehearsal space
- Board Bank matches interested individuals with leadership positions in area cultural organizations
- Issues & Opportunities monthly public forums and newsletter encourage problem-solving among those working in the arts, business, academic, and governmental sectors
- Art at ARTS, Inc. showcases local artists in a series of quarterly exhibitions at our offices co-curated with area visual arts groups

ARTS OPTIONS

214 N. Encinitas Avenue
Monrovia, CA 91016
Ph: 626-303-2058
Fax: 626-303-2058

Anne Oncken — Director — arstoptions@worldnetatt.net

Consultant

- accounting assistance
- board development
- computer use
- corporate sponsorship solicitation
- mailing list maintenance
- media lists
- public relations
- workshop/seminar/symposia
- administrative assistance
- board/staff training
- customized mailing list
- fundraising development
- marketing
- non-profit incorporation
- strategic planning

ASSOCIATION OF CALIFORNIA SYMPHONY ORCHESTRAS (ACSO)

2717 Cottage Way, Suite 5
Sacramento, CA 95825
Ph: 916-484-6744
Fax: 916-484-0503
www.acso.org

Kris Saslow — Executive Director — ksaslow@acso.org

ACSO is the state membership association of symphony orchestras.

- annual conference
- quarterly newsletter
- workshops in professional development for the young musician
- management consulting and technical assistance for symphonic organizations

ASSOCIATION OF PERFORMING ARTS PRESENTERS

1112 16th Street NW, Suite 400
Washington, DC 20036
Ph: 202-833-2787
Fax: 202-833-1543
www.artspresenters.org/artspresenters

A membership organization for presenters and programmers of the performing arts.

- annual conference
- membership directory
- continuing education courses
- significant funding opportunities
- information resources
- networking opportunities
- seminars
- Inside Arts magazine

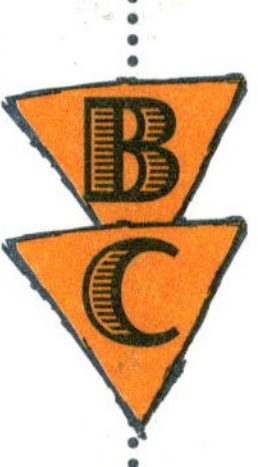

BERGLASS CONSULTING, NANCY

3411 Gardenside Lane
Los Angeles, CA 90039
Ph: 323-665-1020
Fax: 323-665-1014

Nancy Berglass Consultant nberglass@aol.com

- administrative assistance
- board development
- board/staff training
- corporate sponsorship solicitation
- human resources--board members, executive recruitment, volunteers, interns
- meeting facilitation
- referrals
- strategic planning
- fundraising development

BRAIG, SUSAN

2259 Country Club Drive
Altadena, CA 91001
Ph/Fax: 626-398-9276

Susan Braig Consultant mtcompcal@aol.com

- administrative assistance
- grants
- marketing
- graphic design

BRANFMAN & ASSOCIATES, JUDY

221 1/2 3rd Avenue
Venice, CA 90291
Ph/Fax: 310-392-2076

Judy Branfman Consultant jbranfman@loop.com

- meeting facilitation
- public relations
- strategic planning
- project development
- outreach
- education

BREAKAWAY TECHNOLOGIES

3417 W. Jefferson Boulevard
Los Angeles, CA 90018
Ph: 323-737-7677
Fax: 323-737-7710
www.breakaway.org

Joseph Loeb Founder/President jloeb@breakaway.org

Breakaway Technologies provides training in computer software and hardware at an affordable cost.

- classes in Windows, Microsoft Office, Adobe Photoshop, website design, and building your own PC

CALIFORNIA ARTS COUNCIL

1300 I Street, Suite 930
Sacramento, CA 95814
Ph: 916-322-6555
Ph: 800-201-6201
Fax: 916-322-6575

Adam Gottlieb Marketing & Communications Officer

The CAC was established in 1976 to encourage artistic awareness, participation and expression, to help independent local groups develop their own art programs; to promote employment of artists and craftspersons in both the public and private sector; to provide for exhibition of artworks in public buildings throughout California; and to enlist the help of all state agencies in the fullest expression of our potential.

CALIFORNIA ASSEMBLY OF LOCAL ARTS AGENCIES (CALAA)

693 Sutter Street, 3rd Floor
San Francisco, CA 94102
Ph: 415-441-5900
Fax: 415-441-5938

Barry Hessenius President/CEO calaa@aol.com

The California Assembly of Local Arts Agencies (CALAA) is a nonprofit membership organization whose primary purpose is to champion local arts agencies and their growth as essential for promoting the vitality of California Communities.

- professional development and leadership opportunities
- workshops, conferences
- statewide network of local arts agencies
- publications

CALIFORNIA ASSOCIATION OF MUSEUMS (CAM)

2002 N. Main Street
Santa Ana, CA 92706
Ph: 714-567-3645
Fax: 714-480-0053
www.nhm.org/~cam

Teri Knoll Executive Director cam1802@aol.com

The California Association of Museums (CAM), founded in 1979 by staff and trustees from diverse museums throughout the state, is a nonprofit service organization formed to represent the interests of California museums. CAM assists its members in fulfilling their missions as educational and research institutions that interpret and preserve art and cultural and scientific artifacts for public benefit.

- state-wide workshops with experts on a variety of topics
- annual conference held at the close of each fiscal year
- on-line presence for inter-museum networking public awareness
- legislative advocacy network

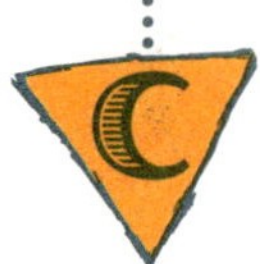

CALIFORNIA ASSOCIATION OF NONPROFITS

315 W. Ninth Street, Suite 705
Los Angeles, CA 90015
Ph: 213-347-2070
Fax: 213-347-2080
www.CAnonprofits.org

Gregg Davidson	Operations Manager	gdavidson@CAnonprofit.org
Florence Green	Executive Director	fgreen@CAnonprofit.org
Stephen Stein	Public Policy Coordinator	sstein@CAnonprofit.org

The California Association of Nonprofits is a state-wide association for all 501 (c) (3) organizations.

- newsletter
- state-wide directory of nonprofits
- discounts on office supplies and other items
- advocacy on behalf of our members.
- public policy

CALIFORNIA COUNCIL FOR THE HUMANITIES

315 W. Ninth Street, Suite 702
Los Angeles, CA 90015
Ph: 213-623-5993
Fax: 213-623-6833
www.calhum.org

Felicia Kelley	Program Officer	fkelley@calhum.org
Jim Quay	Executive Director	jquay@calhum.org

CCH is a nonprofit organization that serves as the state affiliate of the National Endowment for the Humanities. It conducts and funds public and media projects that foster lifelong learning in the humanities in California.

- small grants program ($2500 or less)
- major grants program ($10,000/project)
- council conducted programs on selected topics.

CALIFORNIA CULTURE NET

693 Sutter Street, 3rd Floor
San Francisco, CA 94102
Ph: 415-447-1354
Fax: 415-441-5938
www.californiaculture.net

Danielle Restaino	Project Manager	restainod@aol.com

California Culture.Net is an electronic gateway and online community providing a rich, interactive presence for California Culture on the internet.

- database of California's cultural resources
- high quality web environment
- increased visibility for artists and organizations
- online professional community network for the arts
- secured electronic commerce, collective merchandising, marketing and ticket sales

CALIFORNIA HUMANITIES ASSOCIATION

5854 Hillview Park Avenue
Van Nuys, CA 91401
Ph: 818-780-7387
Admin: 909-882-5641
Fax: 818-780-5254

Nita Corinblit	Secretary/ 818-780-7387	ncorinblit@aol.com
Fran Cornell	Vice-President/ 619-472-2205	
Mark Mrotek	Treasurer/ 213-462-2288	

The California Humanities Association is an association of teachers, kindergarden through college, organized to strengthen education in interdisciplinary studies, the arts and humanities statewide.

- curriculum development workshops
- lectures and demonstrations by visual artists, performing artists, art historians, authors, poets, composers, critics, etc.
- teacher professional development

CALIFORNIA LAWYERS FOR THE ARTS

1641 18th Street
Santa Monica, CA 90404
Ph: 310-998-5590
Fax: 310-998-5594
www.sirius.com/~cla

Alma Robinson	Executive Director	UserCLA@aol.com

Founded in 1974 by lawyers and artists, California Lawyers for the Arts programs and services are designed to help artists and arts organizations understand and apply legal concepts for their benefit.

- lawyer referral service
- resource library
- arts arbitration/mediation services
- publications
- volunteer/internship program
- membership
- advocacy
- arts and community development project
- educational programs: workshops, seminars, and copyright clinics

CALIFORNIA PRESENTERS

16007 Crenshaw Boulevard
Torrance, CA 90506
Phone: 310-660-3748
Fax: 310-660-3734
www.capresenters.org

Tim Van Leer	President	Tvanleer@admin.elcamino.cc.ca.us
Geof English	Membership/949 582-4763	Geofrey100@aol.com

California Presenters is a service organization for presenters of the performing arts. California Presenters sponsors an annual meeting for artist information exchange in June, produces a quarterly newsletter, and advocates the arts

- volunteer opportunities

CAMPBELL COMMUNICATIONS

8530 Holloway Drive, #226
Los Angeles, CA 90069-2477
Ph: 310-659-5427
Fax: 310-659-6427

Carolyn Campbell ccampbel@ucla.edu

Campbell Communications has provided the visual and performing arts, architecture, literary, design and entertainment communities with marketing, public relations and special events consulting services for over twenty years.

CENTER FOR NONPROFIT MANAGEMENT

315 W. Ninth Street, Suite 1100
Los Angeles, CA 90015
Ph: 213-623-7080
Fax: 213-623-7460

Pete Manzo Executive Director

The Center for Nonprofit Management provides information, education and consulting services in order to increase the effectiveness of arts and other nonprofit organizations.

- Opportunity NOCS bi-weekly job listing publication
- Nonprofit Resource Library
- Management Seminar Series
- consulting services

CHICANO RESOURCE CENTER

4801 E. Third Street
Los Angeles, CA 90022
Ph: 323-263-5807
Admin: 323-264-0155

Brigida Campos Director

Part of the County of Los Angeles public library system, the Chicano Resource Center collects, manages and promotes a public library collection of Chicano/Mexican Studies books, videos, posters, slides, compact discs and films. Materials are available free for check-out with a County Library card.

- free local history and information on Los Angeles and East Los Angeles
- free cultural programs at various times of the year include author readings, book signing individuals, families and community groups.
- friends of the library volunteer opportunities

CHISOLM, CHERYL

1307 18th Street, #1
Santa Monica, CA 90404
Ph: 310-828-5754
Fax: 310-828-5754

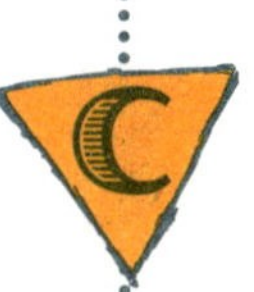

Cheryl Chisolm Consultant

- programming/curating thematic film/video programs, series, seminars, festivals.
- writing/editing/publishing catalogues, final reports, annual reports
- audience development
- technical assistance
- festivals, series, seminars on themes

CLAREMONT COMMUNITY FOUNDATION

205 Yale Avenue
Claremont, CA 91711
Ph: 909-398-1060
Fax: 909-624-6629

Beverly Speak Executive Director bspeak@claremontfoundation.org

Claremont Community Foundation accepts grant proposals twice a year for local projects in Visual and Performing Arts fields of interest. Donor-advised, donor-directed and agency endowments are managed and invested for individuals, families and community groups.

- monthly exhibitions featuring local artists
- grant funding for local arts projects (by proposal)
- donor-advised special fund management for major projects

CLEARINGHOUSE FOR VOLUNTEER ACCOUNTING SERVICES

27863 Lassen Street
Castaic, CA 91384
Ph: 805-295-8912

Tammy Lamson Program Administrator

Provides volunteer accountants and referrals to volunteers throughout the state to nonprofit 501(c)3 organizations with administrative budgets under $500,000. Also operates a board placement service to place accountants on nonprofit boards.

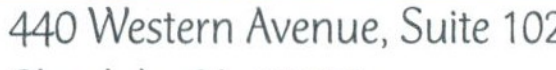

COLLAGE DIGITAL VIDEO

440 Western Avenue, Suite 102
Glendale, CA 91201
Ph: 818-240-4040
Fax: 818-240-5650
www.digital-post.com

Adam Soch	Video Artist	adamsoch@artlover.com

Collage Digital Video has served the arts community for the past fifteen years with all video needs.

- two full on-line digital video editing
- two broadcast locations
- video crews

COMMUNITY ARTS RESOURCES, INC. (CARS)

1724 N. Whitley Avenue
Hollywood, CA 90028
Ph: 323-962-1976
Fax: 323-962-6710

Lucy Lin	Operations Manager	carsemail@aol.com
Aaron Paley	President/Executive Director	
Laurel Kishi	Producer	

Community Arts Resources (CARS) produces festivals and consults in Southern California and across the country on a wide range of arts related mailing lists/labels of 57,000+ artists, arts organizations, venues, and audiences.

- two publications: "Doing it Right In LA" and "Southern California Performing Arts Venues"
- family festivals and programming around Southern California
- mailing lists/labels of 57,000+ artists, arts organizations, venues and audiences

COMMUNITY PARTNERS

3580 Wilshire Boulevard, Suite 1660
Los Angeles, CA 90010
Ph: 213-368-2362
Fax: 213-368-2371

Karen Mack	Director, Organizational management
Paul Vandeventer	President

Through our incubation, facilitation, and project management services, Community Partners supports the emergence of innovative community programs in the arts and other fields of service within the nonprofit sector.

COMMUNITY REDEVELOPMENT AGENCY OF THE CITY OF LOS ANGELES (CRA/LA)

354 S. Spring Street
Los Angeles, CA 90013
Ph: 213-977-1600
Fax: 213-687-9546

Mickey Gustin	Arts Planner/ 213-977-1763	mgustin@cra.ci.la.ca.us
John Molloy	Administrator/ 213-977-1801	jmolloy@cra.ci.la.ca.us

The CRA/LA transforms economically and aesthetically blighted geographic-specific communities into viable neighborhoods. The Art Program of the CRA is a tool which serves the mission of the Agency through public art and grants.

- public art
- grants
- support for various media as appropriate to project areas

CONSULT'HER

3181 Perlita Avenue
Los Angeles, CA 90039-2459
Ph: 323-666-2846
Fax: 323-666-2846

Terry Wolverton	Consultant	consulther@aol.com

- board development
- board/staff training
- fundraising development
- marketing
- meeting facilitation
- strategic planning

CONTEMPORARY ARTISTS SERVICES

2022 B Broadway
Santa Monica, CA 90404
Ph: 310-828-6200
Fax: 310-453-7544
www.sylviawhite.com

Sylvia White	artadvice@aol.com

Contemporary Artists Services offers career guidance to artists.

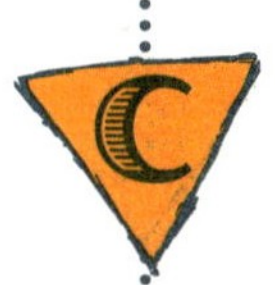

CORO SOUTHERN CALIFORNIA

811 Wilshire Boulevard, Suite 1025
Los Angeles, CA 90017
Ph: 213-623-1234
Fax: 213-680-0079
www.coro.org

Carol Baker Tharp Executive Director/ x12 ctharp@coro.org

Located in Downtown Los Angeles, CORO Southern California is a non-profit organization which provides leadership training programs to prepare individuals to become effective and ethical leaders in the public arena.

- three month Arts Leadership Program, prepares participants for careers or volunteer service in arts and culture while emphasizing the importance of business, politics, education, government and the needs of other nonprofit entities
- telephone consultations
- Literary Network access
- workshops

COUNCIL OF LITERARY MAGAZINES & PRESSES

154 Christopher Street, Suite 3C
New York, NY 10014-2839
Ph: 212-741-9110
Fax: 212-741-9112

Celia O'Donnell Executive Director clmp nyc@aol.com

America's largest service organization exclusively dedicated to supporting and promoting independent literary publishing. Benefits of membership include:

- Marketing Monograph series of publications focusing on various components of literary publishing
- technical resources
- Directory of Literary Magazines
- newsletter, CLMPages
- Ad Brokerage Program participation
- granting and regranting notifications
- telephone consultations
- Literary Network access
- workshops

CRAFT AND FOLK ART MUSEUM

5814 Wilshire Boulevard
Los Angeles, CA 90036
Ph: 323-937-4230
Fax: 323-937-5576

In December 1998, the Folk and Traditional Arts Division of the City of Los Angeles Cultural Affairs Department merged with the Los Angeles Craft and Folk Art Museum.

- exhibitions and special events
- biennial national folk arts conference "Living Roots"
- conduct field research, document and publish materials that serve the field
- sponsor regularly scheduled folk & traditional art workshops, craft and traditional design works
- clearinghouse and database resource for folk & traditional artists, craft & design makers, etc...
- biennial newsletters "Folkways" and "Craft and Design"

CULTURE-CALL

P.O. Box 5215
Santa Monica, CA 90409
Ph: 310-450-4771
Fax: 310-396-2307

Sharon Toriello CEO info@culture-call.com

CULTURE-CALL provides free audience development services for the arts via the marketing and promotion of discount tickets.

- e-mail notification of discounts
- some free tickets
- public service announcements of events that are free to the public
- reservation service
- free registration

CURATORIAL ASSISTANCE, INC.

113 E. Union Street
Pasadena, CA 91103
Ph: 323-681-2401
Fax: 626-449-9603
www.curatorial.com

Hilary Snow Projects Services Manager/ x110
Graham Howe Director/ x107

Curatorial Assistance is a museum services firm specializing in the creation, fabrication and traveling of exhibitions and related multi-media projects for museums, entertainment centers and corporations world-wide.

DANCE & FITNESS MAGAZINE

627 N. Palm Drive
Beverly Hills, CA 90210
Ph: 310-271-1966
Admin: 310-271-7766
Fax: 310-271-1288

Mary Miller	Office Manager/SubscriptionSales	ladance@ni.net
Grover Dale	Editor/Publisher	

Dance and Fitness Magazine provides real, relevant, and useful information to career-minded artists, performers, dance companies, and choreographers.

- performance calendar
- 800 dance class listings
- reports from 12 major American cities
- history of dance
- appreciation of dance
- technical advances
- affordable advertising

DANCE RESOURCE CENTER

P.O. Box 41708
Los Angeles, CA 90041
Ph: 818-769-3093
Fax: 818-769-2497

Irene Feigenheimer	Managing Director

The Dance Resource Center of Greater Los Angeles (DRC) provides access to information, resources, and services. We are dedicated to serving and promoting the growth of Los Angeles dance, choreographers, dancers, dance educators, and students.

- "Dance-Zine", a bimothly newsletter featuring selections on dance, arts advocacy, the jobmarket, auditions, new and old faces in the community, Los Angeles archives, etc.
- Horton Awards, community workshops, career day, and special events for members
- referrals, DRC Directory, fiscal receivership, and technical assistance workshops
- DRC mailing list rentals
- discounts for participating Performing Arts Events
- individual health and life insurance
- voting privileges for the Lester Horton Awards and the DRC Board of Directors

DANCE/USA

1156 15th Street NW, Suite 820
Washington, DC 20005-1704
Ph: 202-833-1717
Fax: 202-833-2686
www.danceusa.org

Martin Cohen	Executive Director/ x14
Allison O'Brien	Government Affairs/Communications Associate/ x17
Shoshana Riley	Administrative Assistant/ x13

Dance/USA is the national service organization for nonprofit professional dance.

- quarterly Dance/USA Journal
- monthly Dance/USA Member Bulletin
- biennial National Roundtable
- periodic Managers' and Artists' Council meetings
- professional development training seminars for administrators in the dance field

DIRECTOR'S GUILD OF AMERICA

7920 Sunset Boulevard
Los Angeles, CA 90046
Ph: 310-289-2000

DOYLE/LOGAN COMPANY, THE

7836 Santa Monica Boulevard
West Hollywood, CA 90046
Ph: 323-484-8492
Fax: 323-848-8494
www.doylelogan.com

Konrad Kemper	Office Manager	knrad@doylelogan.com
Clay Doyle	Gallery Director	clay@doylelogan.com

Centrally located in West Hollywood, we provide graphic design services for corporate and institutional clients, and feature quarterly exhibitions featuring emerging and unknown artists.

- graphic design services
- quarterly art exhibitions

DRAMATISTS GUILD INC., THE

7510 Sunset Boulevard, Suite 1123
Los Angeles, CA 90046
Ph: 323-960-5115

Dan Berkowitz	West Coast Representative	ICIMEDIA@aol.com

The Dramatists Guild Inc. is the professional association of playwrights, composers and lyricists.

- contracts
- symposia
- publications
- events

DRAPER CONSULTING, LEE

10811 Washington Boulevard, Suite 380
Culver City, CA 90232
Ph: 310-559-3434
Fax: 310-559-4586

Lee Draper Consultant LDConsult@aol.com

- board development
- board/staff training
- fundraising development
- workshop/seminar/symposia
- meeting facilitation
- strategic planning
- grants

EDWARDS & ASSOCIATES, PATRICE D.

P.O. Box 70604
Pasadena, CA 91117
Ph: 626-821-4023
Fax: 626-405-0016

Patrice D. Edwards Consultant

- board development
- board/staff training
- fundraising development
- workshop/seminar/symposia
- meeting facilitation
- strategic planning
- grants

ESTATE PROJECT FOR ARTISTS WITH AIDS

8581 Santa Monica Boulevard, #400
West Hollywood, CA 90069
Ph: 310-652-1282
Fax: 310-652-0769
www.artistswithaids.org

Patrick Moore Director estate@ix.netcom.com

The Estate Project, which operates in Los Angeles, New York, and Miami, provides counseling and information for artists who are planning their estates and making decisions about the long-term survival of their work.

EXECUTIVE SERVICE CORPS OF SOUTHERN CALIFORNIA

520 S. Lafayette Park Place, Suite 210
Los Angeles, CA 90057
Ph: 323-381-2891
Fax: 323-381-2893

Barrie Segall Associate Director exec@soca.com
Megan Cooper Executive Director

Since 1981, ESC has served nearly every type of nonprofit agency in Los Angeles, Orange and Ventura Counties. By providing retired business executives as volunteer consultants to work alongside agency staff and Board, ESC can help agencies survive and thrive in today's more competitive environment.

- management consulting
- sounding board sessions
- board coaching program
- board bank

EZTV

6522 Hollywood Boulevard
Los Angeles, CA 90028
Ph: 323 462-3678
Fax: 323 462-3673

Kate Johnson President

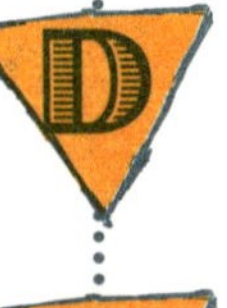

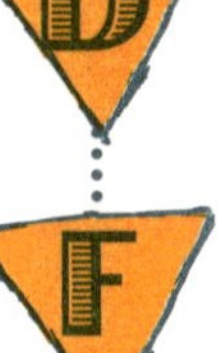

EZTV is a multifaceted organization that offers media and web services and tools to artists. It is also a center that celebrates, produces and exhibits new media works.

- video editing and production
- image manipulation
- website production
- curated video and new media screenings
- community center for digital filmmakers
- access grants
- media training & seminars
- on-line digital art gallery

FILMANTHROPIC

1722 1/2 Whitley Avenue
Los Angeles, CA 90028
Ph: 323-464-9119
Fax: 323-856-8529
www.showbizjobs.com

Nanci Rossov Creative Director

Filmanthropic provides training and opportunities in film (entertainment) production to women, people with disabilities, people over 40 and members of ethnic communities.

- on-the-job training in film production to those under-represented in the entertainment industry.
- script (features) development to same clients
- round-Table discussions on professional development in Entertainment (Film, TV, etc...)

FINNEGAN, D.B.

P.O. Box 634
Topanga, CA 90290
Ph: 310-455-1692
Fax: 310-455-0492

D.B. Finnegan Consultant dbfinn@sciarc.edu

- administrative assistance
- board development
- workshops/seminar/symposia
- strategic planning
- organizational start-up and problem-solving
- public relations
- fundraising development
- grants

FLINTRIDGE FOUNDATION, THE

1040 Lincoln Avenue, Suite 100
Pasadena, CA 91103
Ph: 626-449-0839
Fax: 626-585-0011

Pam Gregg Wolkoff Senior Program Officer
Jaylene Moseley Managing Director

The Flintridge Foundation is a private grantmaking foundation, which focuses on theater and visual arts in California, Oregon, and Washington.

- Philanthropy Resource Library
- biennial award program for individual artists who have been working in a mature phase of their art for at least 20 years, and who reside in California, Oregon, or Washington
- grants program for small-to mid-sized theaters in California, Oregon, and Washington that have a history of working as collaborative ensembles

FOLK DANCE FEDERATION OF CALIFORNIA, SOUTH

236 DeAnza Street
San Gabriel, CA 91776
Ph: 626-300-8138
Admin: 818-790-6037
Fax: 310-786-6000

Sylvia Stachura Publicity Chair/ 626-300-8138
Marilyn Pixler President/ 818-790-6037 marilynn@pacbell.com
Dorothy Daw Research/ 562-924-4922

The Federation is interested in perpetuating folk dancing of all nations. To encourage the enjoyment of international folk dancing and related arts, and the promotion of a spirit of friendship.

- weekly to daily folk dancing in communities from San Diego to Santa Maria
- groups meet everyday of the week at various hours
- most offer instruction and a dance program
- donation is requested at most groups
- frequent festivals are held in various communities
- folk dance camps are also available every year
- costume workshops

GARNETS, LINDA

3331 Ocean Park Boulevard, #201
Santa Monica, CA 90405
Ph: 310-450-1188
Fax: 310-399-0363

Linda Garnets Organizational Consultant lgarnets@ucla.edu

- administrative assistance
- board development
- workshop/seminar/symposia
- meeting facilitation
- strategic planning
- board/staff training

GETTY CENTER, THE

1200 Getty Center Drive
Los Angeles, CA 90049-1681
Ph: 310-440-7300
Admin: 310-440-7360
Educ: 310-440-7331
Fax: 310-440-7722
www.getty.edu

Lori Starr Director of Public Affairs
Barry Munitz President and CEO/310-440-7555
Deborah Marrow Director, Getty Grant Program/310 440-7320

GODBOLD, LOUISE

1621 Ewing Street
Los Angeles, CA 90026-1915
Ph: 323-953-0778
Fax: 323-665-8348

Louise Godbold Consultant lgodbold@worldnet.att.net

- board/staff training
- strategic planning
- workshops/seminars/symposia
- organizational dynamics, evaluation, and international relations

GRANTWORKS PROPOSAL WRITING SERVICES

P.O. Box 365
Santa Monica, CA 90406
Ph: 310-312-5010
Fax: 310-826-7066
www.grantworks.com

Katherine Kubarski Principal kk@grantworks.com

- collaborative proposal writing
- workshop/seminar/symposia
- fundraising development
- grants

HARBOUR ENTERTAINMENT INSURANCE

100 Corporate Pointe
Los Angeles, CA 90230
Ph: 310-348-2300
Fax: 310-348-2330
www.harbourinsurance.com

Sandra Zumbado Representative

Each year, Harnour Entertainment Insurance insures thousands of special events throughout the United States. This specialization provides the broadest special event insurance products available at very affordable prices. Coverage is arranged through nationally recognized and licensed insurance companies on a per-event or annual basis.

- "no-hassle" insurance programs for arts related companies
- event liability
- umbrella liability
- worker's compensation and accident medical coverage
- event cancellation
- property
- automotive liability
- bad weather protection
- liquor liability

HERRON, ROYCE

1714 E. Chevy Chase Drive, #F
Glendale, CA 91206
Ph: 818-502-9920
Fax: 818-550-1962

Royce Herron   Consultant   fansyflite@aol.com

- board development
- board/staff training
- corporate sponsorship solicitation
- fundraising relations
- grants
- strategic planning

HIMOT & ASSOCIATES, DONNA M.

1563 Solano Avenue, #125
Berkeley, CA 94707
Ph/Fax: 510-558-0674

Donna Himot   President

- board/staff training
- meeting facilitation
- strategic planning

HUGGINS, LINDA

2331 Echo Park Avenue
Los Angeles, CA 90026
Ph: 323-662-5420
Fax: 323-662-5420

Linda Huggins   Consultant

- fundraising development
- grants
- public relations

IMAGE ARTS FOUNDATION

P.O. Box 996
La Mirada, CA 90637-0996
Ph: 562-943-5174

Victoria Summers

The Image Arts Foundation is a very energized organization emphasizing education and practical training with focus on advertising and public relations efforts toward program development.

- Project coordination including celebrity spokesperson, corporate sponsorships, and program development
- College level internship programs in Public Relations Program Efforts, Advertising Program Efforts, and Graphic Arts Efforts

INDEPENDENT FEATURE PROJECT/WEST (IFP)

1964 Westwood Boulevard, Suite 205
Los Angeles, CA 90025
Ph: 310-475-4379
Fax: 310-441-5676
www.ifpwest.org

Jeff Brown   Membership Manager/x15
Dawn Hudson   Executive Director
Sean McManus   Director of Development/x 21

Independent Feature Project/West is a nonprofit organization dedicated to promoting quality American independent feature filmmaking. IFP/West is a primary support system for independent filmmakers in Southern California advocating diversity and innovation. Membership includes:

- monthly calender of events and announcements
- quarterly publication of "Filmmaker" an internationally distributed magazine covering independent films

INSTITUTE OF MUSEUM AND LIBRARY SERVICES

Office of Museum Services
1100 Pennsylvania Avenue NW, Room 609
Washington, DC 20506
Ph: 202-606-8539
fax: 202-606-8591
www.imls.fed.us/

Giuliana Bullard   Public Affairs Specialist   gbullard@imls.fed.us
Dianne Frankel   Executive Director

A federal agency serving the public by strengthening museums & libraries. Museum programs strengthen museum operations, improve care of collections, increase professional development opportunities, and enhance the community service role of museums.

INTERNATIONAL FEDERATION OF FESTIVAL ORGANIZATIONS (FIDOF)

4230 Stansbury Avenue, #105
Sherman Oaks, CA 91423
Ph: 818-789-7596
Fax: 818-789-9141

Armando Moreno   President   MM412@aol.com

FIDOF coordinates all information about festivals and cultural events. FIDOF is the only official organization of its kind. We have contacts with about 1,600 festivals and cultural events organized in 102 countries worldwide.

- FIDOF monthly bulletin (information about festivals and cultural events from around the world).
- Annual General Assembly at MIDEM in Cannes, France.
- Distant Accords Awards Gala Ceremony
- volunteer opportunities

KHAN MANAGEMENT

11615 Missouri Avenue, #6
Los Angeles, CA 90025
Ph: 310-477-6612
Fax: 310-477-5059
www.khanmusic.org

Zain Khan zaink@earthlink.net

Khan Management, specializing in artist management, also offers its clients a variety of other services including grants writing, audience development, and board development.

- board development
- corporate sponsorship solicitation
- fundraising development
- grants
- legal assistance
- marketing
- non-profit incorporation
- performance opportunities
- rehearsal facilities

KNUDSEN ASSOCIATES, INC.

4937 Oakwood Avenue
La Cañada, CA 91011
Ph: 818-952-1938
Fax: 818-952-1938

Larry Knudsen Consultant lketal@aol.com

- board development
- board/staff training
- fundraising development
- grants
- strategic planning

KUMAMOTO ASSOCIATES

4130 Sea View Lane
Los Angeles, CA 90065
Ph/Fax: 323-223-6473

Alan Kumamoto Consultant AKumamoto@aol.com

- administrative assistance
- board development
- board/staff training
- fundraising development
- grants
- meeting facilitation
- public relations
- strategic planning
- program evaluation

L.A. SHARES

3224 Riverside Drive
Los Angeles, CA 90027
Ph: 213-485-1097

Bert Ball Executive Director

L.A. SHARES provides equipment and supplies from corporations (new and used) at no cost to Los Angeles County schools and non-profits.

L.A. WORKS

351 S. La Brea Avenue, Suite 202
Los Angeles, CA 90036
Ph: 323-936-1340
Fax: 323-936-1454
www.la-volunteer.org

Shelby Holguin	Director of Programs	laworks@deltanet.com
Julie Rajan	Executive Director	

L.A. works is a nonprofit volunteer action center that creates hands-on volunteer service projects addressing vital community needs.

- access to volunteer opportunities
- other resources to community service organizations

LOPEZ CONSULTING, ESTELA

949 S. Hope Street, Suite 303
Los Angeles, CA 90015
Ph: 213-627-4171
Fax: 213-627-0345

Estela Lopez Consultant correoelc@aol.com

- marketing
- media lists
- public relations
- government relations
- community outreach

LOS ANGELES CONVENTION AND VISITORS BUREAU (LACVB) CULTURAL TOURISM DEPARTMENT

633 W. Fifth Street, Suite 6000
Los Angeles, CA 90071
Ph: 213-624-7300
Fax: 213-624-9746
www.californiasedge.com

Robert Barrett Vice-President, Cultural Tourism rbarrett@lacvb.com

The Cultural Tourism Department of the Los Angeles Convention & Visitors Bureau promotes the cultural destinations of Los Angeles to domestic and international markets.

- cultural promotions
- cultural publications
- cultural Calendar of Events
- website

LOS ANGELES COUNTY ARTS COMMISSION

500 W. Temple Street, #374
Los Angeles, CA 90012
Ph: 213-974-1343
Fax: 213-625-1765
www.lacountyarts.org

Andrew Campbell	Grants Manager	acampbell@bos.co.la.ca.us
Laura Zucker	Executive Director	lzucker@bos.co.la.ca.us

The Los Angeles County Arts Commission fosters excellence, accessibility, vitality, and diversity of the arts by providing cultural resources, services, and information to the community, arts organizations, and municipalities.

- grant programs for small, mid-size, and large budget organizations
- multi-disciplinary series at John Anson Ford Ampitheatre
- annual Holiday Celebration in the Dorothy Chandler Pavilion, broadcast on KCET
- free music concerts in public sites
- free county-wide arts open house first Saturday of October
- cultural tourism marketing
- technical assistance— workshops, seminars, and one-on-one consultancies

LOS ANGELES DANCE FOUNDATION

627 N. Palm Drive
Beverly Hills, CA 90210
Ph: 310-271-1288
Fax: 310-271-1966

Grover Dale	President	ladance@ni.net

- recognition program for choreographers
- referrals to video broadcasting of deuce films
- workshops and seminars
- community dialogs
- career development
- skill building
- dance video archive

LOS ANGELES JUNIOR CHAMBER OF COMMERCE

350 S. Bixel Street, Suite 100
Los Angeles, CA 90017
Ph: 213-482-1311
Fax: 213-580-1490

Kathy Lindell	Director, Riordan Volunteer Leadership Development Program

LOUD MOUTH

2306 1/2 Ocean Avenue
Venice, CA 90291
Ph: 310-823-6389
Fax: 213-895-4649

Rochelle Fabb	Partner
Michael Sakamoto	Partner

Consultants
- administrative assistance
- marketing
- public relations

MALIBU, CITY OF

23555 Civic Center Way
Malibu, CA 90265
Ph: 310-317-1364
Admin: 310-456-2489
Fax: 310-456-0539

Catherine Walter	Director of Parks & Recreation/x235

The City of Malibu Parks and Recreation Department sponsors community performing and visual arts events. We have professional and community groups.

- exhibition opportunities
- performance opportunities

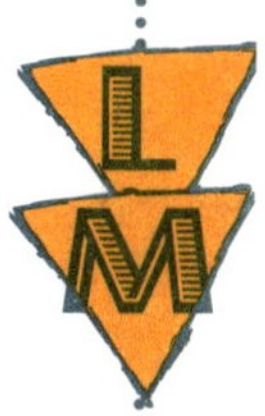

MALLORY PUBLIC RELATIONS/ SPECIAL EVENTS, BLAINE

725 N. Alfred Street
Los Angeles, CA 90069
Ph: 323-655-1834
Fax: 323-655-2142

Blaine Mallory	Consultant

- marketing
- media lists
- public relations
- workshop/seminar/symposia
- special event planning and implementation

MEET THE COMPOSER

2112 Broadway, Suite 505
New York, NY 10023
Ph: 212-787-3601
Fax: 212-787-3745
www.meetthecomposer.org

Fard Johnson Public Information Coord. fjohnson@meetthe composer.org

A national nonprofit organization, Meet the Composer aims to serve American composers at all career levels, devoting over 70% of each year's budget to composers' artistic fees. Meet the Composer helps organizations across the country develop and sustain a committment to new music, and catalyzes partnerships that bring this music into their repertories.

- grants that enable composers to participate actively in performances of their work
- commissions new works in all music genres
- composer residencies
- international and intercultural commissioning projects
- collaborations between composers and choreographers

MILLER AND ASSOCIATES, DEANNA IZEN

13700 Tahiti Way, Studio 331
Marina Del Rey, CA 90292
Ph: 310-822-3333
Fax: 310-822-7773

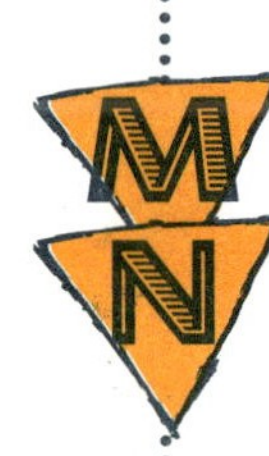

Deanna Izen Miller Art Advisor

- marketing

MILLIKAN CONSULTING, ALICIA

10824 Lindblade Street
Culver City, CA 90230
Ph: 310-837-9579
Fax: 310-845-9720

Alicia Millikan Consultant a2@gte.net

- board/staff training
- corporate sponsorship solicitation
- fundraising development
- grants
- strategic planning

MUSICARES

3402 Pico Boulevard
Santa Monica, CA 90405
Ph: 310-392-3777
Ph: 800-687-4227 (referral hotline for emergency assistance)

Kimberly Gyle Case Manager/x347
Terry Monteleone Executive Director/x344

Musicares offers a place for music people to turn to for emergency Financial Assistance & Substance Abuse Resource and Referral programs and services, and human service directories.

NATIONAL ACADEMY OF RECORDING ARTS AND SCIENCES

3402 Pico Boulevard
Santa Monica, CA 90405
Ph: 310-392-3777
Fax: 310-392-2306

Also known as the Recording Academy, awards grants to organizations and individuals to support research, preservation of music and the medical and occupational well-being of music professionals.

NATIONAL ACRYLIC PAINTERS ASSOCIATION U.S.A. CHAPTER

2525 E. 5th Street
Long Beach, CA 90814
Ph: 562-439-3276
Fax: 562-597-3750

Linda Gunn U.S.A. Director

NAPA U.S.A. is the only professional artist group that gives its members international exposure through exhibitions in the U.S. and Great Britain. Our goal is to promote the use of the acrylic medium as well as to educate the public through quality exhibitions. Catalogs are kept on file in the archives of the Tate Museum, London.

- exhibitions in the U.S.
- members receive newsletters and a prospectus from both NAPA in England and NAPA U.S.A.
- U.K. exhibitions held at the Royal Birmingham Society

NATIONAL ASSEMBLY OF STATE ARTS AGENCIES (NASAA)

1029 Vermont Avenue NW, 2nd Floor
Washington, DC 20005
Ph: 202-347-6352
Fax: 202-737-0526
www.nasaa-arts.org

NATIONAL ASSOCIATION OF ARTISTS' ORGANIZATIONS (NAAO)

918 F Street NW, Suite 611
Washington, DC 20004
Ph: 202-347-6350
Fax: 202-347-7376

Roberto Bedoya Executive Director

More than 700 artists' organizations, arts institutions, artists and professionals comprise the NAAO membership. NAAO was established to provide its constituents with a vehicle for communication in a clear and distinct national voice. For the past 15 years, it has provided services to the primary creators of new, emerging, and often experimental work. NAAO represents all disciplines.

- annual national conference
- regional meetings, forums and caucuses
- publications include a detailed membership directory and quarterly Bulletin
- reports to the field series
- public awareness, information referral and advocacy
- regranting and technical assistance programs

NATIONAL DANCE EDUCATION ASSOCIATION (NDEA)

4948 St. Elmo Avenue, Suite 207
Bethesda, MD 20814
Ph: 301-657-2880
Fax: 301-657-2882

Rima Faber	Program Director	ndea@erols.com
Jane Bonbright	Executive Director	
Elsa Posey	President/ 516-757-2700	

NDEA is a nonprofit membership service organization dedicated to the development and promotion of dance education as an art form in early childhood, K-12 schools, higher education, community programs, and studios/schools of dance.

- leadership in dance/arts education
- informational list service
- quarterly newsletter, publications, and journal
- professional development and networking
- conferences
- advocacy with national and state arts agencies
- world-class resources for dance and art education and center for research in dance education
- partnerships for collaboration
- representation for dance education at national level
- support system for the dance professional
- National Registry for Dance Education
- guidance and information about the national standards for dance education
- promotes dance education taught by qualified professionals in a sequential curriculum

NATIONAL ENDOWMENT FOR THE ARTS (NEA)

1100 Pennsylvania Avenue, NW
Washington, DC 20004
Ph: 202-682-5570
Fax: 202-682-5611
www.arts.endow.gov

Cherie Simon — Director, Public Affairs

An independent agency of the Federal government, the NEA was created by Congress in 1956 to encourage and support American art and artists. It fulfills its mission by awarding grants and through leadership and advocacy activities.

NELSON, THORA

14044 Panay Way, #236
Marina Del Rey, CA 90292
Ph: 310-823-3420
Fax: 310-823-3420

Thora Nelson — Consultant

- board development
- board/staff training
- workshop/seminar/symposia
- meeting facilitation
- strategic planning
- fundraising development

NETZEL ASSOCIATES, INC.

9696 Culver Boulevard, Suite 204
Culver City, CA 90232
Ph: 310-836-7624
Fax: 310-836-9357

Paul Netzel — Chairman & CEO — fundraising@netzelinc.com

- board development
- fundraising development
- strategic planning

NEW YORK FOUNDATION FOR THE ARTS

155 Avenue of the Americas, 14th Floor
New York, NY 10013
Ph: 212-366-6900
Fax: 212-366-1778
www.artswire.org/nyfa

Penelope Dannenberg	Director of Programs/ x214	penny@artswire.org
Theodore Berger	Executive Director/ x201	berger@artswire.org

The NYFA enables contemporary artists to create and share their works and provides the broader public with opportunities to experience and understand the arts.

- grants for schools and organizations such as Artists-in-Residence, NYC Choral Music Initiative, Community Assets, and Artists and Teachers Partnership for Excellence
- services for individual artists, schools, and organizations such as Arts Wire Internet Services, Sponsorship Program, Visual Artists Information Hotline, and a Revolving Loan Program
- FYI, a quarterly journal

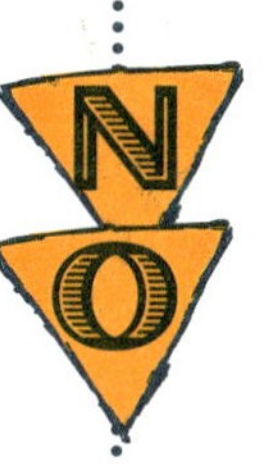

NONPROFIT INCORPORATORS

2118 Wilshire Boulevard, Suite 261
Santa Monica, CA 90403-5784
Ph: 310-828-6722
Fax: 310-315-1567

Arthur Rieman — nonprofitinc@pobox.com

- administrative assistance
- human resources--board members
- legal assistance
- nonprofit incorporation
- strategic planning

OERTEL GROUP, THE

1337 Brixton Road
Pasadena, CA 91105
Ph: 323-257-1125
Fax: 323-257-1155

Patty Oertel — Consultant — poertel@aol.com

- board development
- board/staff training
- organizational development
- meeting facilitation
- strategic planning
- fundraising development

PANKRATZ, DAVID

2022 Crestlake Avenue
South Pasadena, CA 91030
Ph: 323-259-8066

David Pankratz Consultant slswartdbpank@sprintmail.com

- fundraising development
- grants
- research
- program development

PASADENA CULTURAL PLANNING, CITY OF

175 N. Garfield Avenue
Pasadena, CA 91109
Ph: 626-744-6770
Fax: 626-793-5937
www.ci.pasadena.ca.us/arts

Rochelle Branch Public Arts Coordinator/ 626-744-6915

The City of Pasadena Cultural Planning Division serves as the administrative arm for city-sponsored arts and cultural programming and activities.

- quarterly exhibitions
- Pasadena Art Space at One Colorado
- music concerts
- performance events
- artists in the Schools
- community Arts Partnership
- public art projects
- artist and arts organization mailing list maintenance
- archive of public art in Pasadena
- website--Virtual tour of public art in Pasadena

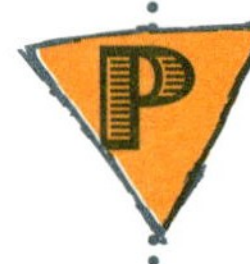

PERSONALIZED TRAVEL

5455 Sylmar Avenue, Suite 902
Sherman Oaks, CA 91401
Ph/Fax: 818-994-2402

Roberta Kritzia Owner

Personalized Travel organizes sketching/painting trips on location in Italy. This is a unique opportunity to visit and paint the hidden medieval hilltowns of Umbria, Tuscany and the Venice regions.

- painting and sketching in small groups with well known art teachers such as Corrine Hartly, Glenn Villpu and Glen Knowles
- opportunity to visit Italian artists' and craftsmen's studios in combination with the production of their own artwork while sampling the regional cuisine and wine of Italy
- daily art demos and critiques
- all services such as hotels, transportation and most meals are provided by Personalized Travel
- bilingual travel guides

POETRY SOCIETY OF AMERICA

P.O. Box 3761
Palos Verdes, CA 90274
Ph: 310-669-2369
Admin: 212-254-9628
Fax: 310-514-0302

Elena Burke Director ekduende@aol.com

We are the local chapter of the Poetry Society, the oldest national non-profit poetry organization in the United States offering a broad range of public cultural programs diverse in style and type.

- contests
- occasional library tributes
- poetry in public places
- poetry in motion™ (poetry on buses and subways)
- public readings
- bookmark, books and poster sales and free distribution available
- membership

POETS & WRITERS, INCORPORATED (CALIFORNIA OFFICE)

580 Washington Street, Suite 308
San Francisco, CA 94111
Ph: 415-986-9577
Fax: 415-986-9575
www.pw.org

Ryan Tranquilla Program Associate ryan@pw.org
Karen Clark Director of California Programs kc@pw.org

Poets & Writers (P&W) is a nonprofit national service organization dedicated to fostering the professional development of poets and fiction writers, promoting communication throughout the U.S. literary community, and helping to create an environment in which literature can be appreciated by the widest possible public.

- California Readings/Workshops Program, provides matching fees for poets and fiction writers to give readings and workshops in community settings
- Writers on Site Program, offers short-term residencies for writers in partnership with visual and literary arts organizations in California
- Techinical Assistance Services for Literary Presenters, includes publications, workshops and individual consultations
- P & W Online offers information about P & W programs, technical assistance information and online forums for writers

PRODUCTION COMPANY, THE

4848 Bonvue Avenue
Los Angeles, CA 90027
Ph/Fax: 323-664-0553

Bonnie Homsey bhomsey@earthlink.net

Arts consultancy in the area of dance.

PROFESSIONAL MUSICIANS UNION LOCAL 47

817 North Vine Street
Hollywood, CA 90038-3779
Ph: 323-462-2161
Fax: 323-461-3090
www.promusic47.org

Serena Williams — Secretary/ 323-993-3160
Hal Espinosa — President / 323-993-3181

The Professional Musicians Local 47 is a membership-based organization representing professional musicians in Los Angeles County (except that portion which is in the jurisdiction of Local 353, Long Beach), Catalina Island, San Bernardino, and Riverside counties.

- programs based on member needs

R & B DESIGN GROUP

23135 Friar Street
Woodland Hills, CA 91367
Ph: 818-340-1746

Rovane Bezerra — Owner, Creative Director

Located in the San Fernando Valley, we work directly with arts events and promoters to help with all forms of resources and art events.

- posters, banners, flyers, and other graphic services
- advertising and promotion
- t-shirts, hats, etc.
- web site design
- art creation

RADIO WEST

448 N. Kilkea Drive
Los Angeles, CA 90048
Ph: 323-655-5214
Fax: 323-651-0320

Kathy Gronau — Project Coordinator — kgronau@ix.netcom.com

Radio West serves audio producers with information and connects them with other producers, to develop community support through meetings and classes.

- hotline
- seminars
- conferences
- mailings
- nonprofit umbrella

RAE, COLEEN

P.O. Box 3006
Venice, CA 90291
Ph: 310-823-2894
Admin: 310-823-8995

Coleen Rae — Consultant, teacher for writers

RANDALL COMPANY, THE MARK

422 Mildas Drive
Malibu, CA 90265
Ph: 800-455-5543

Mark Randall — Consultant

- board development
- board/staff training
- fundraising development
- workshop/seminar/symposia
- special needs campaigns
- planning studies
- strategic planning

RIEMAN CONSULTING

2118 Wilshire Boulevard, Suite 261
Santa Monica, CA 90403-5784
Ph: 310-828-6722
Fax: 310-315-1567
www.not-for-profit.org/rc

Arthur Rieman — President — rce.pobox.com

- board development
- legal assistance
- strategic planning
- organizational effectiveness

ROSSI O'BRIEN & COMPANY LLP

One World Trade Center, Suite 2100
Long Beach, CA 90831
Ph: 562-495-3325
Fax: 562-495-3425
info@rossiobrien.com

Warren Riley — Consultant — tsmc4wbr@aol.com

- accounting assistance
- board development
- board/staff training
- corporate sponsorship solicitation
- meeting facilitation
- workshop/seminar/symposia
- fiscal receivership
- fundraising development
- grants
- marketing
- strategic planning

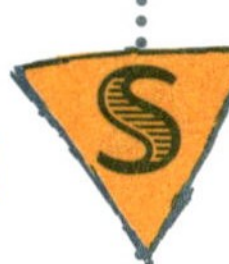

SANTA CLARITA, CITY OF

23920 Valencia Boulevard, Suite 120
Santa Clarita, CA 91355
Ph: 805-255-4910
Admin: 805-255-4945
Fax: 805-255-1996
www.santa-clarita.com

Gail Ortiz — Public Information Officer/ 805-255-4314
Rick Putnam — Director
Sean Morgan — Cultural Arts Coordinator/ 805-286-4034

The City of Santa Clarita government designs and implements cultural programs for the community and region.

SANTA MONICA ARTS FOUNDATION

1685 Main Street, Room 106
Santa Monica, CA 90401
Ph: 310-458-8350
Fax: 310-917-6641
www.pen.ci.santamonica.ca.us

Maria Luisa de Herrera Executive Director

The Santa Monica Arts Foundation is a private nonprofit agency which raises funds to finance art programs developed by the Santa Monica Arts Commission. The Foundation frequently acts as a 501 (c) (3) fiscal receiver for other Santa Monica-based arts organizations as well as for individual artists raising funds for public art projects.

- fiscal receivership for Santa Monica-based arts organizations

SANTA MONICA, CULTURAL AFFAIRS DIVISION, CITY OF

P.O. Box 2200
Santa Monica, CA 90407-2200
Ph: 310-458-8350
Fax: 310-917-6641
www.pen.ci.santa-monica.ca.us

Maria Luisa de Herrera Cultural Affairs Administrator

The Cultural Affairs Division administers Santa Monica's public art program and its annual grants programs to local arts organizations. In addition, the Cultural Affairs Division provides staff liaison to the Santa Monica Arts Commission.

- Percent for Art Program, oversees City's public art program and collection of permanent art works
- granting programs, available to Santa Monica based non-profit art organizations
- Santa Monica Festival, an annual multicultural performing arts festival held in April
- Artbank, portable collection of city-owned artworks
- technical assistance to artists, arts agencies and outside agencies wishing to produce cultural events in Santa Monica

SAVING AND PRESERVING ARTS AND CULTURAL ENVIRONMENTS (SPACES)

1804 N. Van Ness Avenue
Los Angeles, CA 90028
Ph: 323-463-1629
Fax: 323-463-1629

Seymour Rosen Director

SPACES is a nonprofit arts organization concerned with the identification, documentation, and preservation of large-scale contemporary art environments in the United States. It seeks recognition for the creators of these environments and recognition for the genre. SPACES educates and informs the public and also functions as an arts advocacy group and an information resource.

SCRIBNER & ASSOCIATES

49 Coronado Avenue
Long Beach, CA 90803
Ph: 562-433-6082
Fax: 562-439-3025

Susan Scribner Consultant Scribner@aol.com

- board development
- board/staff training
- fundraising development
- strategic planning

SIEGEL & NICHOLL

900 Wilshire Boulevard, #1000
Los Angeles, CA 90017
Ph: 213-895-4646
Fax: 213-895-4649

Michael Sakamoto Associate
Mark Siegel Partner

- administrative assistance
- board development
- board/staff training
- marketing
- public relations

SOCIETY OF SINGERS, INC.

8242 W. 3rd Street, Suite 250
Los Angeles, CA 90048
Ph: 323-651-1696
Fax: 323-651-5483
www.singers.org

Judy Varley Executive Administrator
Patrick Todd Office Administrator/Membership

The Society of Singers, Inc. is a nonprofit charitable organization that provides emergency financial aid to professional singers, world-wide, in times of crisis. Funds are derived from membership contribution and fundraising events.

- Emergency Financial Assistance Program helps professional singers of five years or more with funds for basic living expenses, medical expenses, HIV and substance abuse treatment, psychotherapy and other necessities
- case management and referral services
- vocal arts scholarships provided to select universities

SOCIETY OF STAGE DIRECTORS AND CHOREOGRAPHERS

8489 W. Third Street, Suite 1044B
Los Angeles, CA 90048
Ph: 323-653-8713

STAGE DIRECTORS AND CHOREOGRAPHERS FOUNDATION

1501 Broadway, Suite 1701
New York, NY 10036
Ph: 212-302-5359
Fax: 212-302-6195
www.ssdc.org/foundation

David Diamond Executive Director/ x242
Bob Johnson Associate Director/ x 244

The SDC Foundation is a nonprofit service organization dedicated to helping directors and choreographers both in their crafts and their careers.

- seminars
- roundtable discussions
- networking opportunities
- grants anf fellowships
- mentoring
- publications

STAMBERGER, SUSAN

18215 TophamStreet
Reseda, CA 91335
Ph: 818-342-3442
Fax: 818-342-0939

Susan Stamberger Consultant suestam@aol.com

- board development
- fundraising development
- grants

STAMBLER, MARK

3001 Maxwell Street
Los Angeles, CA 90027
Ph/Fax: 323-913-1667

Mark Stambler Consultant stambler@aol.com

- fundraising development
- grants

STANDER ENTERTAINMENT

6309 Ben Avenue
North Hollywood, CA 91606
Ph: 818-769-6365
Fax: 818-769-6365

Jacqueline Stander General Manager stander@earthlink.net

Stander Entertainment represents national recording/touring acts and is a consultant for festivals, line-ups, and artists.

TEITELMAN CONSULTING, JUDITH

1724 N. Whitley Avenue
Los Angeles, CA 90291
Ph: 323-962-6327
Fax: 323-962-6710

Judith Teitelman Principal JTConsult@aol.com

- board development
- board/staff training
- corporate sponsorship solicitation
- workshop/seminar/symposia
- meeting facilitation
- membership
- strategic planning
- fundraising development
- human resources--board members, volunteers, interns
- organizational and program assessment

THEATRE LA

644 S. Figueroa Street
Los Angeles, CA 90017
Ph: 213-614-0556
Fax: 213-614-0561
www.TheatreLA.org

Lee Lawlor Member Services Coordinator TheatreLA1@aol.com
Alisa Fishbach Executive Director
Scott Leo General Manager

Theatre LA is the nonprofit association of theaters and theatrical producers that supports theater in greater Los Angeles by uniting, representing, and promoting the theatre community.

- Theatre LA Ovation Awards
- Theatre Times Directory in the Los Angeles Times
- Times Half-Price Tix
- Kids Week at the Theatre
- Theatre LA News and Opening Night Calendar
- Job Bank
- workshops, conferences and roundtables
- discount liability insurance
- advocacy
- advice and referrals

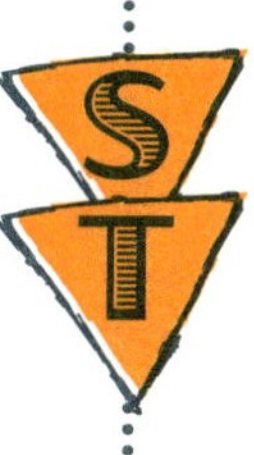

THINK JACOBSON & ROTH

339 Beloit Avenue
Los Angeles, CA 90049
Ph: 310-476-9842
Admin: 323-954-1226
Fax: 310-476-5972

Lori Jacobson Director laj@primenet.com
Carla Roth Director

- strategic planning
- workshops/seminar/symposia
- exhibit development
- media planning

TINCHER CHARITABLE MARKETING COMPANY

1377 E. Citrus Avenue, #244
Redlands, CA 92374
Ph/Fax: 909-585-6953

John Tincher President

- fundraising development
- marketing
- planned giving

TREEN ARTISTS MANAGEMENT, MARY BETH

1221 Scott Road
Burbank, CA 91504-4240
Ph: 818-846-6869
Fax: 818- 846-6863

Mary Beth Treen Talent Agent

Mary Beth Treen Artists Management provides performing artists suitable for formal and informal, indoor and outdoor settings. The artists are nationally recognizable names as well as established emerging artists performing in music, children's theatre and musical theatre. Most artists provide residencies and all provide full orchestral charts.

UCLA, AMERICAN INDIAN STUDIES CENTER

3220 Campbell Hall, Box 951548
Los Angeles, CA 90095-1548
Ph: 310-825-7315
Fax: 310-206-7060
www.sscnet.ucla.edu/indian/

Duane Champagne Director aisc@ucla.edu

Located on the Westwood Campus, the center serves the educational and cultural needs of the university's American Indian community, including faculty, staff, resident scholars, researchers, undergraduate and graduate students. The center sponsors national conferences, workshops, lectures, and symposia. As an Organized Research Unit, the Center also sponsors research and administers competitive grants.

- academic unit at the university level (minor, master, JD degrees)
- library/reference center
- academic journal
- student groups
- sponsors annual powwow
- post and predoctoral fellowships

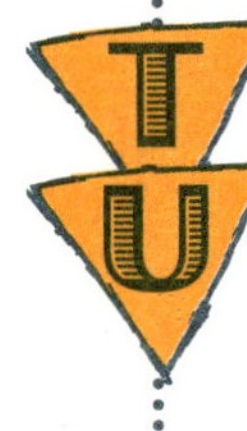

UMBRELLA LATCH-KEY ARTIST PROGRAM

15864 Rimrock Road
Apple Valley, CA 92307
Ph: 760-242-0912

Viletta Martin Artistic Consultant vmartfly@aol.com

Umbrella Latch-Key Artist Program inspires self-confidence and helps keep kids interested in school, energizes the school environment, improves student performance in other subjects and impacts hard-to-reach students in a positive way.

- arts education consultant
- arts instruction
- seminars/conferences
- professional development training
- teacher art awareness for at-risk-youth
- staff training for after school art programs
- staff workshops in team building
- design techniques and projects for team building

UNITED ARTS

3906 Sunbeam Drive
Los Angeles, CA 90065
Ph: 323-256-7828
Fax: 323-256-8396
www.uarts.com

Linda Chiavaroli President performingarts@uarts.com

- marketing
- publications
- public relations

UNIVERSITY/RESIDENT THEATRE ASSOCIATION

1560 Broadway, Suite 1307
New York, NY 10036
Ph: 212-221-1130
Fax: 212-869-2752
www.urta.com
URTA@aol.com

The U/RTA, a membership organization, was established in 1969 to work towards the highest standards in theater production and performance, and to help bring resident professional theater to the university campus and its community.

- annual membership meetings
- professional consultation and technical assistance
- national unified auditions/interviews
- the U/RTA contract management program
- the U/RTA-AEA contract and U/RTA-SSDC contract
- master audition programs
- newsletter

VALLEY CULTURAL CENTER

21550 Oxnard Street, Suite 470
Woodland Hills, CA 91367-7110
Ph: 818-704-1587
Admin: 818-704-1358
Fax: 818-704-1604
www.valleycultural.org

Suzanne Hackett — Executive Director — yetilvft@valleyculturalorg
Pamela Peterson — Office Manager

The Valley Cultural Center seeks to enlighten, educate, and enrich present and future generations by providing diverse programs through the performing and visual arts.

- "Concerts in the Park", a free 14-week performing arts series
- artist-in-residence program
- music-in-the-schools program
- children's concert series
- scholarship programs
- arts services organization offering technical assistance and informational services to the arts community in the San Fernando Valley
- volunteer opportunities

VOLUNTEER CENTER LOS ANGELES, SOUTH CENTRAL

7655 S. Central Avenue
Los Angeles, CA 90001
Ph: 323-277-8076
Fax: 323-277-4714

La Quita Howard — Coordinator

The purpose of the Volunteer Center of Los Angeles shall be to enhance the quality of life in our community, for both the receivers and the givers, through the volunteer movement.

VOLUNTEER CENTER OF LOS ANGELES

2550 Beverly Boulevard
Los Angeles, CA 90057-1019
Ph: 213-387-7201
Fax: 213-387-7507

Sandy Lopez — Director of Volunteers
Walter Kirwan — Executive Director

VOLUNTEER CENTER OF WEST LOS ANGELES

8709 La Tijera
Los Angeles, CA 90045
Ph: 310-215-1039
Fax: 310-215-1131

Angela Edwards — Director

WALCH CONSULTING, NANCY

10521 Ilona Avenue
Los Angeles, CA 90064
Ph: 310-475-6254
Fax: 310-474-5964

Nancy Walch — Principal — walchn@aol.com

- board development
- board/staff training
- organizational development
- strategic planning
- meeting facilitation
- educational programs

WALL-LAS MEMORIAS PROJECT, THE

111 N. Avenue 56
Los Angeles, CA 90042-4111
Ph: 323-257-1056
Fax: 323-257-1625
www.geocities.com/West Hollywood/Village/6543

Richard Zaldivar — Executive Director
Eddie Martinez — Community Outreach Director

Located in the Highland Park community of Northeast Los Angeles, the organization is striving to construct a memorial at Lincoln Park to remember those we have lost to AIDS and to serve as an educational forum for the Latino community concerning the issues of cultural denial and the dangers of HIV/AIDS.

- Latino Mens group
- Cultural AIDS Prevention/Education
- Mothers of the Wall
- Mothers of Latino Men
- Community Leadership Program
- Mayan Warriors Softball Club
- Noche de Las Memorias (World AIDS Day)

WEST HOLLYWOOD FINE ARTS COMMISSION

8300 Santa Monica Boulevard
West Hollywood, CA 90069
Ph: 323-848-6400

Lester Burg — Art Coordinator/ x300

The Fine Arts Commission oversees percent for art projects, public art and an annual grant program for local nonprofit cultural organizations.

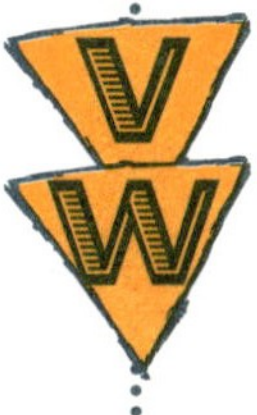

WESTERN ALLIANCE OF ARTS ADMINISTRATORS (WAAA)

44 Page Street, #604B
San Francisco, CA 94102
Ph: 415-621-4400
Fax: 415-621-2533

Robin James — Conference Manager
Tim Wilson — Executive Director

WESTERN STATES ARTS FEDERATION (WESTAF)

1543 Champa Street, Suite 220
Denver, CO 80202
Ph: 303-629-1166
Fax: 303-629-9717
www.westaf.org

Denise Montgomery — Director of Marketing
Anthony Radich — Executive Director

WESTAF is a nonprofit arts service organization dedicated to the creative advancement and preservation of the arts. By providing innovative programs and services, WESTAF focuses on strengthening the financial, organizational, and policy infrastructure of the arts in 12 western states.

- arts policy research
- information systems development
- convening of arts experts and leaders to address critical arts issues
- presenting
- literature
- visual arts
- American Indian culture
- folk arts
- please see our website for current activities

WEXLER & ASSOCIATES, GARY

315 W. 9th Street, Suite 408
Los Angeles, CA 90015
Ph: 213-624-0501
Fax: 213-624-0712

Jonathan Schreiber — Account Supervisor — wexlerjungle@earthlink.net

- board development
- fundraising development
- workshops/seminar/symposia
- marketing
- public relations
- grants

WHITE, THOMAS

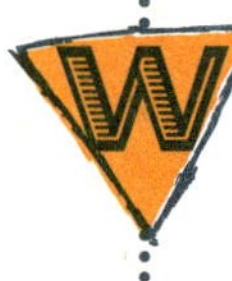

850 N. Edinburgh Avenue
Los Angeles, CA 90046
Ph: 323-653-3972
Fax: 323-653-3972 *99

Y

Thomas White — Consultant — mackwhite@aol.com

- corporate sponsorship solicitation
- fundraising development
- grants
- marketing
- strategic planning

WHITTIER CULTURAL ARTS FOUNDATION, CITY OF

7630 S. Washington Avenue
Whittier, CA 90602
Ph: 562 464-3430
Fax: 562 464-3581

Kimberly Powell Albarian — Cultural Arts Supervisor

- Arts Alive Program, provides field trips for students from the Whittier Union High School District to visit major museums in the Los Angeles area.
- Art Reach Program provides training in arts instruction and curriculum development to Whittier and East Whittier Elementary school districts.
- Music Enrichment Program for elementary school children, directed by the Rio Hondo Symphony Association, includes visits by musicians who familiarize students with instruments and the orchestral music performed by the Symphony.
- membership in the Foundation is offered.

YURIKA!

518 E. Lexington Avenue, #3
Glendale, CA 91206
Ph: 818-546-2574
Fax: 818-551-0720

Yuri Rasovsky — Consultant — audiodrama@rocketmail.com
Catherine Romero — CPA

- accounting assistance
- administrative assistance
- board/staff training
- fiscal receivership
- nonprofit incorporation

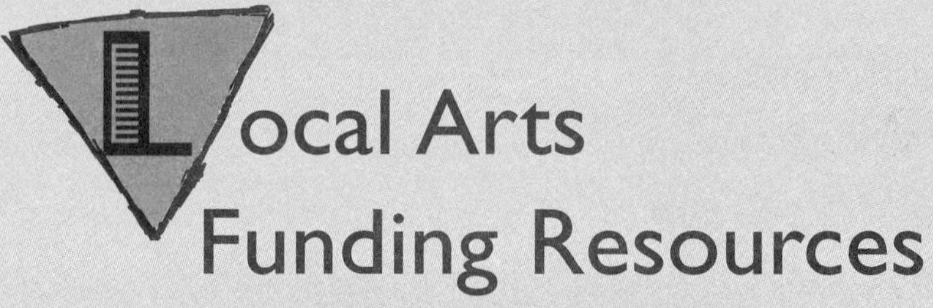

Local Arts Funding Resources

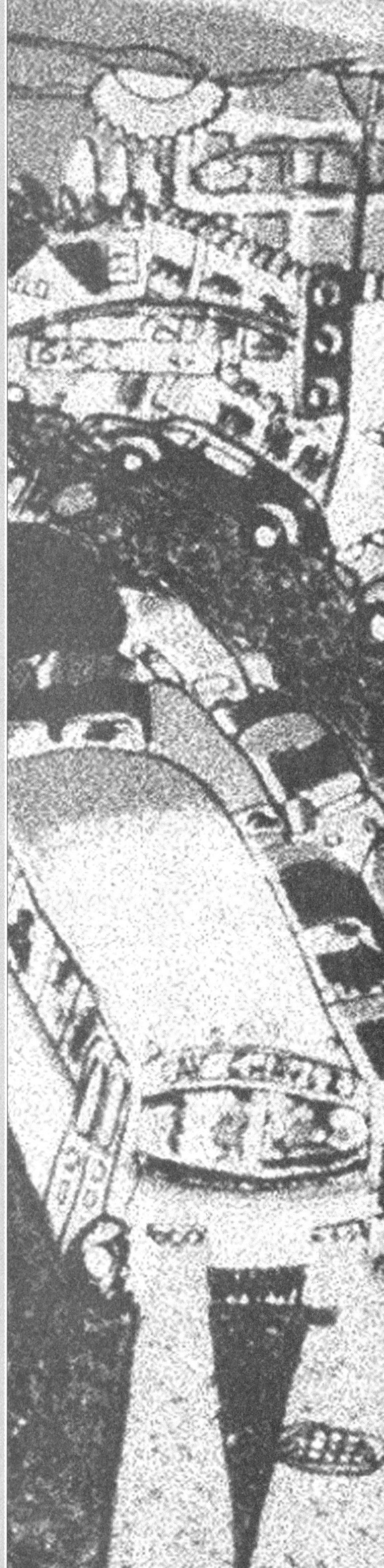

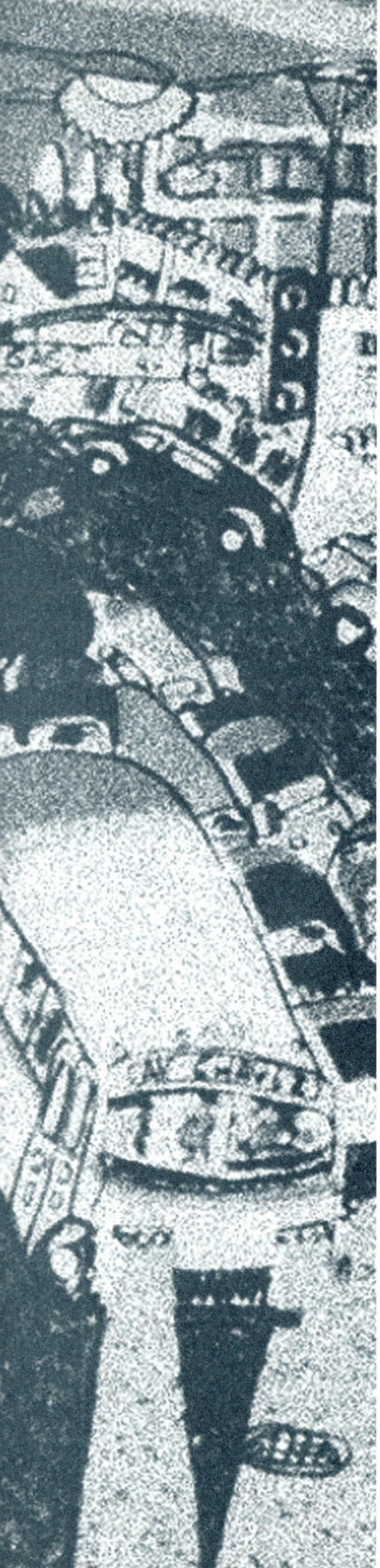

Introduction: Local Arts Funding Resources

By bringing art and culture into our daily lives, the individuals and organizations in this *Directory* draw out the dreamer in each of us. The moments when we encounter a timeless expression of art—be it a stunning photograph, an exquisite sculpture, a breathtaking dance movement—are often too far and few between in our hectic modern day lifestyles. We cherish those experiences because they enable us to transcend our limited space and touch the deepest part of our spirit.

In recent years, sustaining this life-giving endeavor has proven to be more and more of a challenge. Pressures to meet competing societal needs and the constant search for new sources of funding have been countervailing forces to the creative genius in our communities. That is why we applaud ARTS, Inc. for adding a new funding resources section to its already indispensible guide.

Ears perk up whenever people hear the word "funding." This funding resources section is meant to be a starting point. It does not contain all the answers to your fundraising needs. It does contain the most basic of reference tools, however. You will find a list of both private and public organizations that you can call for information, and to determine whether your work falls within the areas of interest to the funder. Doing this research is an essential step in the fundraising process, and an excellent source of in-depth information is the Resource Library at the Center for Nonprofit Management.

During this time of unprecedented increase in wealth, it is hoped that we will see more individuals contributing to the cultural life of our community. They will do so when they learn more about the hidden cultural treasures in the greater Los Angeles metropolitan area. The *Directory* is a superb tool that enables people to find, enjoy and support our diverse world of art activities. Join us in discovering and creating a new vibrant megalopolis!

Miyoko Oshima, President
Southern California Association for Philanthropy

LOCAL ARTS FUNDING RESOURCES

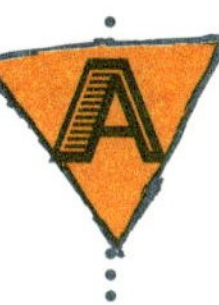

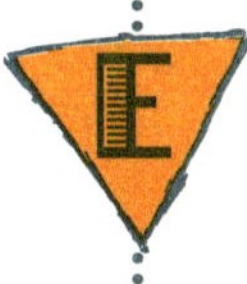

AHMANSON FOUNDATION
9215 Wilshire Boulevard
Beverly Hills, CA 90210
310-278-0770
www.cerritos.edu/cerritos/development/funders_ahmanson.html

ALLEQUASH FOUNDATION
70 S. Lake Avenue, Suite 1075
Pasadena, CA 91101

ARCO FOUNDATION, INC.
315 S. Flower Street
Los Angeles, CA 90071
213-486-3342
www.arco.com/corporate/reports/foundation/AR1998

ARMSTRONG FOUNDATION, ETHEL LOUISE
2856 Marengo Avenue
Altadena, CA 91101
626-398-8840

ASSOCIATED FOUNDATIONS, INC.
225 S. Lake Avenue, Suite 1125
Pasadena, CA 91101
626-796-3917

AT&T
611 W. 6th Street, Suite 2200
Los Angeles, CA 90017
213-239-7874
www.att.com/foundation/

B.Y. FOUNDATION
2049 Century Park East, #2500
Los Angeles, CA 90067
310-277-1900

BANKAMERICA FOUNDATION
P.O. Box 37000, Dept. 3246
San Francisco, CA 94137
415-953-3175
www.bankamerica.com/community/community.html

BANNERMAN FOUNDATION, WILLIAM C.
9255 Sunset Boulevard, Suite 400
West Hollywood, CA 90069
310-273-9933

BROTMAN FOUNDATION OF CALIFORNIA
16830 Ventura Boulevard, Suite 236
Encino, CA 91436
818-909-2012

CALIFORNIA ARTS COUNCIL
1300 I. Street, Suite 930
Sacramento, CA 95814
916-322-6555
800-201-6201
www.cac.ca.gov

CALIFORNIA COMMUNITY FOUNDATION
606 S. Olive Street, Suite 2400
Los Angeles, CA 90014-1526
213-413-4042
www.callfund.org

CALIFORNIA COUNCIL FOR THE HUMANITIES
315 W. Ninth Street, Suite 702
Los Angeles, CA 90015
213-623-5993
www.calhum.org

CANTOR FOUNDATION, IRIS AND B. GERALD
1801 Avenue of the Stars, Suite 435
Los Angeles, CA 90067
310-277-4600

CHARTWELL FOUNDATION
1999 Avenue of the Stars, #3050
Los Angeles, CA 90067
310-556-7650

CLAREMONT COMMUNITY FOUNDATION
205 Yale Avenue
Claremont, CA 91711
909-398-1060
bspeak@claremontfoundation.org

COLUMBIA CHARITABLE FOUNDATION
9465 Wilshire Boulevard, Suite 900
Beverly Hills, CA 90212-2608
310-248-2320

CULVER CITY REDEVELOPMENT AGENCY
4117 Overland Avenue
Culver City, CA 90230
310-25-6640

DURFEE FOUNDATION
1453 Third Street Promenade, Suite 312
Santa Monica, CA 90401
3108995120
www.durfee.org

ELA FOUNDATION
2858 Marengo Avenue
Altadena, CA 91001
626 398-8840
www.ela.org

EMPLOYEES COMMUNITY FUND OF BOEING, CALIFORNIA
3855 Lakewood Boulevard
Mail Code D802-0011
Long Beach, CA 90846
562-593-2612
www.boeing.com/companyoffices/aboutus/community/citizen-ship/culture/arts.html

LOCAL ARTS FUNDING RESOURCES

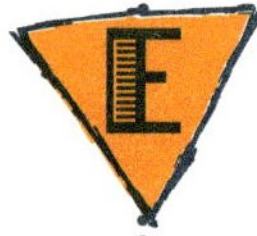

ENTERTAINMENT INDUSTRY FOUNDATION PERMANENT CHARITIES
11132 Ventura Boulevard, Suite 401
Studio City, CA 91604-3156
818-760-7722
www.eifoundation.org

FELLNER FOUNDATION, LEOPOLD & CLARA M.
555 S. Flower, Suite 4640
Los Angeles, CA 90071
213-624-7391

FIELDSTEAD & COMPANY
P.O. Box 19061
Irvine, CA 92713
949-474-0242

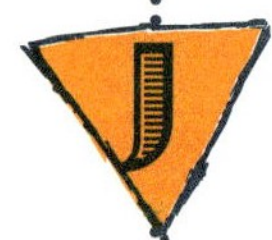

FITZGERALD CHARITABLE FOUNDATION, THE ELLA
16255 Ventura Boulevard, Suite 600
Encino, CA 91423-2311
818-784-7848

FLAGG FOUNDATION, ANGELICA & HOWARD
19528 Ventura Boulevard, Suite 322
Tarzana, CA 91356
818-704-1171

FLINTRIDGE FOUNDATION
1040 Lincoln Avenue, Suite 100
Pasadena, CA 91103
626-449-0839

FLUOR FOUNDATION
3353 Michelson Drive
Irvine, CA 92698
949-975-6797

FREEDMAN FOUNDATION, LEO
c/o Tygir Enterprises
1801 Avenue of the Stars, #442
Los Angeles, CA 90067

GEFFEN FOUNDATION, THE DAVID
3801 Barham Boulevard, 2nd Floor
Los Angeles, CA 90068
818-733-6333

GETTY GRANT PROGRAM, THE
J. Paul Getty Trust
1200 Getty Center Drive, Suite 800
Los Angeles, CA 90049-1685
310-440-7320
www.getty.edu/grant

GLUCK FOUNDATION, INC., MAX H.
10375 Wilshire Boulevard, Suite 2
Los Angeles, CA 90024

GOOD WORKS FOUNDATION
253-A 26th Street, Suite 311
Santa Monica, CA 90402
310-828-1288

GRIFFIN FOUNDATION, FRANCIS D. & IRENE D.
1101 Charm Acre Place
Pacific Palisades, CA 90272
310-459-2025

GUMBINER FOUNDATION, JOSEPHINE S.
401 E. Ocean Boulevard, Suite 905
Long Beach, CA 90802-4933
562-437-2882
www.rgfa.com/index.htm

HAFIF FAMILY FOUNDATION
265 W. Bonita Avenue
Claremont, CA 91711
909-625-7971

HAN CHARITABLE FOUNDATION, EDNA & YU-SHAN
606 S. Lucerne Boulevard
Los Angeles, CA 90005
213-277-0300

HAYNES FOUNDATION, THE JOHN RANDOLPH & DORA
888 W. 6th Street, Suite 1150
Los Angeles, CA 90017-2737
213-623-9151

HOPE CHARITABLE FOUNDATION, BOB & DOLORES
10346 Moorpark Street
North Hollywood, CA 91602

IRMAS CHARITABLE FOUNDATION, AUDREY AND SYDNEY
16027 Ventura Boulevard, Suite 601
Encino, CA 91325
818-382-3313

IRVINE FOUNDATION, THE JAMES
777 S. Figueroa Street, Suite 740
Los Angeles, CA 90017
213-236-0552
www.irvine.org/home.html

JAPAN FOUNDATION, LOS ANGELES OFFICE
2425 Olympic Boulevard, Suite 650 E
Santa Monica, CA 90404
310-449-0027
www.jflalc.org

JEWISH COMMUNITY FOUNDATION OF THE JEWISH FEDERATION COUNCIL OF GREATER L.A.
5700 Wilshire Boulevard, Suite 2000
Los Angeles, CA 90036
323-761-8700

KECK FOUNDATION, W.M.
555 South Flower Street, Suite 3230
Los Angeles, CA 90071
213-680-3833
www.cerritos.edu/cerritos/development/funders_keck.html

LABAND FOUNDATION, WALTER & FRANCINE
3311 E. Cameron Avenue
West Covina, CA 91791
626-332-2472

LANTZ FOUNDATION, WALTER
4444 Lakeside Drive
Burbank, CA 91505
818-842-1616

LITTON INDUSTRIES FOUNDATION
21240 Burbank Boulevard
Woodland Hills, CA 91367
818-598-5000

LLOYD E. RIGLER - LAWRENCE E. DEUTSCH FOUNDATION
P.O. Box 828
Burbank, CA 91503-0828
323-878-0283

L L W W FOUNDATION
1260 Huntington Drive, Suite 204
South Pasadena, CA 91030
323-259-0484

LOCKHEED MARTIN CORPORATION
310 N. Westlake Boulevard, Suite 200
Westlake Village, CA 91362
805-381-1408

LOS ANGELES COUNTY ARTS COMMISSION
500 W. Temple Street, #374
Los Angeles, CA 90012
213-974-1343
www.lacountyarts.org

LOS ANGELES CULTURAL AFFAIRS DEPARTMENT, CITY OF
433 South Spring Street, 10th Floor
Los Angeles, CA 90013
213-485-2433

LUDWICK FAMILY FOUNDATION
P.O. Box 1796
Glendora, CA 91740
626-852-0092

MANN FOUNDATION, TED
10100 Santa Monica Boulevard, Suite 900
Los Angeles, CA 90067
310-284-8528

MATTEL FOUNDATION
333 Continental Boulevard
MS/MI-M18
El Segundo, CA 90245-5012
310-252-3802
www.voiceinternational.org/fd/mattel.htm

MAYER GREENBERG FOUNDATION
6060 Sepulveda Boulevard
Van Nuys, CA 91411
818-786-2525

MCA FOUNDATION, LTD.
100 Universal City Plaza
Universal City, CA 91606
818-777-1208

MERVYN'S, CALIFORNIA
22301 Foothill Boulevard MS4790
Hayward, CA 94514
510-727-5679
www.mervyns.dhc.com/mervynswww/html/community.html

NAKAMICHI FOUNDATION E.
800 WIlshire Boulevard, #1040
Los Angeles, CA 90017
213-683-1608

NATIONAL ENDOWMENT FOR THE ARTS (NEA)
1100 Pennsylvania Avenue, NW
Washington, DC 20506
202-606-8446
www.nea.gov

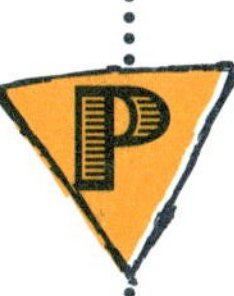

NATIONAL ENDOWMENT FOR THE HUMANITIES (NEH)
1100 PennsylvaniaAvenue, NW
Washington, DC 20004
202-606-8446
www.neh.gov

NORMAN FOUNDATION, ANDREW
10960 Wilshire Boulevard, Suite 1111
Los Angeles, CA 90024
310-478-1213

NORRIS FOUNDATION, KENNETH T. & EILEEN L.
11 Golden Shore, Suite 450
Long Beach, CA 90802
562-435-8444

NORTON FAMILY FOUNDATION, PETER
225 Arizona Avenue, 2nd Floor West
Santa Monica, CA 90401
310-576-7700

PACIFIC BELL FOUNDATION
130 Kearney Street, Room 3309
San Francisco, CA 94108
415-394-3685
www.pactel.com/community/foundation/index.html

LOCAL ARTS FUNDING RESOURCES

PACIFIC LIFE FOUNDATION
700 Newport Center Drive
Newport Beach, CA 91660
949-640-3214

PARSONS FOUNDATION, RALPH M.
1055 Wilshire Boulevard, Suite 1701
Los Angeles, CA 90017
213-482-3185

PASADENA ART ALLIANCE
145 N. Raymond Avenue
Pasadena, CA 91103
626-795-9276

PASADENA CULTURAL PLANNING, CITY OF
175 N. Garfield Avenue
Pasadena, CA 91109
626-744-6770
www.ci.pasadena.ca.us/arts

PEPPERS FOUNDATION, THE ANN
P.O. Box 50146
Pasadena, CA 91115-0146
626-449-0793

PLUM FOUNDATION
P.O. Box 1613
Studio City, CA 91604
818-766-8064

PUBLIC CORPORATION FOR THE ARTS
434 E. Broadway
Long Beach, CA 90802-4908
562-570-1930
artpca@aol.com

REID FOUNDATION, WILL J.
345 Bay Shore Avenue
Long Beach, CA 90803-1956
562-439-6933

ROTH FAMILY FOUNDATION, THE
12021 Wilshire Boulevard, Suite 505
Los Angeles, CA 90025
310-476-3323

SANTA CLARITA, CITY OF
23920 Valencia Boulevard, Suite 120
Santa Clarita, CA 91355
805-255-4910
www.santa-clarita.com

SANTA MONICA CULTURAL AFFAIRS DIVISION, CITY OF
Post Office Box 2200
Santa Monica, CA 90407-2200
310-458-8350
www.pen.ci.santa-monica.ca.us

SANWA BANK, CALIFORNIA
601 S. Figueroa Street W9-5
Los Angeles, CA 90017
213-896-7346

SCOTT FOUNDATION, VIRGINA STEELE
1151 Oxford Road
San Marino, CA 91108
626-405-2148

SEAVER INSTITUTE
555 S. Flower Street, Suite 4580
Los Angeles, CA 90071
213-673-2090

SHAPELL FOUNDATION, DAVID & FELA
8383 Wilshire Boulevard, Suite 700
Beverly Hills, CA 90211
310-655-7330

SONY PICTURES ENTERTAINMENT
10202 W. Washington Boulevard
Culver City, CA 90232-3195
310-244-8293

SOUTHERN CALIFORNIA EDISON
P.O. Box 800
Rosemead, CA 91770
626-302-9853
www.edison.com/spotlightexa/communityinv/arts/index.htm

SPRING STREET FOUNDATION
4056 Farmouth Drive
Los Angeles, CA 90027
213-668-0142

STREISAND FOUNDATION, THE
1460 4th Street, Suite 212
Santa Monica, CA 90401
310-395-3599

TAPER FOUNDATION, S. MARK
12011 San Vicente Boulevard, #400
Los Angeles, CA 90049
310-476-5413
www.cerritos.edu/cerritos/development/funders_taper.html

THORNTON FOUNDATION
523 W Sixth Street, Suite 636
Los Angeles, CA 90014
213-629-3867

TIMES MIRROR FOUNDATION
Times Mirror Square
Los Angeles, CA 90053
213-237-3898

TOYOTA MOTOR SALES U.S.A., INC.
19001 S. Western Avenue
Torrance, CA 90509
310-618-5278

TRANSAMERICA LIFE COMPANIES
1150 S. Olive Street
Los Angeles, CA 90017
213-742-2111

UNION BANK OF CALIFORNIA FOUNDATION
445 S. Figueroa Street
Los Angeles, CA 90071
213-236-6960

UNIVERSAL STUDIOS, INC.
100 Universal City Plaza, Suite LRW/3
Universal City, CA 91608
818-777-5636

UNOCAL FOUNDATION
P.O. Box 7600
Los Angeles, CA 90051
213-977-6877
www.unocal.com/pep/pepfound.htm

VAN NUYS FOUNDATION, I.N. & SUSANNA H.
444 S. Flower Street, Suite 2340
Los Angeles, CA 90071

WALLIS FOUNDATION
4100 W. Alameda Avenue, Suite 204
Burbank, CA 91505

WALT DISNEY COMPANY, THE
500 S. Buena Vista Street
Burbank, CA 91521-0987
818-560-5025

WEISZ FOUNDATION, DAVID & SYLVIA
1933 S. Broadway, Suite 244
Los Angeles, CA 90007

WELLS FARGO BANK
333 S. Grand Avenue
Los Angeles, CA 90071
213-253-7116

WEST HOLLYWOOD FINE ARTS COMMISSION
8300 Santa Monica Boulevard
West Hollywood, CA 90069
323-848-6400

WHITE FAMILY FOUNDATION, STLN
1120 E. Balboa Boulevard
Balboa, CA 92661
949-675-7102

WINDFALL FOUNDATION
c/o Manatt Phelps & Phillips
11355 W. Olympic Blvd.
Los Angeles, CA 90064
310-312-4000

WOLF FAMILY FOUNDATION
12100 Wilshire Boulevard, Suite 1030
Los Angeles, CA 90025

WRATHER FAMILY FOUNDATION
227 Broadway Street, Suite 302
Santa Monica, CA 90401

YAMAGATA FOUNDATION
c/o Dreyer Edmonds & Assoc.
355 S Grand Avenue, Suite 4150
Los Angeles, CA 90071-3103

ZANUCK CHARITABLE FOUNDATION, VIRGINIA
c/o Loeb & Loeb
10100 Santa Monica Boulevard, Suite 2200
Los Angeles, CA 90067
310-282-2000

ZAREM FOUNDATION
9640 Lomitas Avenue
Beverly Hills, CA 90210

ZOLINE FOUNDATION
624 North Canon Drive
Beverly Hills, CA 90210
310-278-8184

ALPHABETICAL & ARTISTIC DISCIPLINE INDEX

ALPHABETICAL & ARTISTIC DISCIPLINE INDEX

ALPHABETICAL & ARTISTIC DISCIPLINE INDEX

INDEX OF PRE/K-12 PROGRAMS

INDEX OF PRE/K-12 PROGRAMS

INDEX OF PRE/K-12 PROGRAMS

Thank You! **Please register your copy of the 4th edition Directory so we can send you updated listings and valuable special offers throughout the year.**

Name:

Title: Occupation:

Organization:

Address:

City: State: Zip:

Phone: Fax:

E-mail:

How do you plan to use this Directory? (check all that apply):
- ❑ general contact information
- ❑ specific arts programs
- ❑ arts funding sources
- ❑ pre/K-12, youth or family programs
- ❑ potential artistic collaborations
- ❑ potential marketing collaborations
- ❑ booking arts talent
- ❑ specific service organizations
- ❑ other

What additional information would you like to receive? (check all that apply):
- ❑ updated Directory listings
- ❑ discount offers from advertisers
- ❑ other promotions from advertisers
- ❑ direct mail/e-mail from Service Providers
- ❑ direct mail/e-mail from funders
- ❑ other

What other formats/services would you like to see available? (check all that apply):
- ❑ customized mailing labels
- ❑ information on CD-ROM
- ❑ information on-line
- ❑ other

How many others (colleagues/friends) use your Directory?

Do you want to participate in a ❑ written survey or ❑ focus group to help design the 5th Edition Directory ? Yes ______ No ______

(**YES!** **I want a copy of the single most comprehensive arts reference source for metropolitan Los Angeles!**

) order yours through the mail today. order form on back.

only $25 (19.95 + tax + shipping/handling)

Regarding corrections or updates to this or future editions.

Please call ARTS, Inc. at:
213-627-9276

or mail to:
ARTS, Inc.
Directory Corrections/Updates
315 W. Ninth Street, Suite 201
Los Angeles, CA 90015

Place
Stamp
Here

ARTS, Inc.
4th edition Greater Los Angeles Arts Resource
Directory and Arts & Education Guide
Warranty Card
315 W. Ninth Street, Suite 201
Los Angeles, CA 90015

Mail this order form with your check made payable to:

ARTS, Inc.
315 W. Ninth Street, Suite 201
Los Angeles, CA 90015

Please send __________ copy(ies) of the 4th edition Arts Resource Directory and Arts & Education Guide at $25 each.
(includes tax, shipping & handling)

Name: ______________________________

Organization: ______________________________

Address: ______________________________

City: ______________ State: ________ Zip: __________

Phone: ______________ Fax: ______________

E-mail: ______________________________